# Foundations of Public Service

## Second Edition

# Foundations of Public Service

## Second Edition

Douglas F. Morgan, Richard T. Green, Craig W. Shinn, and Kent S. Robinson

Routledge
Taylor & Francis Group

LONDON AND NEW YORK

First published 2013 by M.E. Sharpe

Published 2015 by Routledge
2 Park Square, Milton Park, Abingdon, Oxon OX14 4RN
711 Third Avenue, New York, NY 10017, USA

*Routledge is an imprint of the Taylor & Francis Group, an informa business*

**Library of Congress Cataloging-in-Publication Data**

Morgan, Douglas F., 1943–
 Foundations of public service / Douglas F. Morgan, Richard Green, Craig W. Shinn, and
Kent S. Robinson.—Second edition.
    pages. cm.
 Includes bibliographical references and index.
 ISBN 978-0-7656-3459-7 (pbk. : alk. paper)
 1. Public administration—United States. 2. Public administration—United States—Case
studies.  I. Title.

JK421.F68 2013
351.73—dc23                                                                          2012038674

ISBN 13: 9780765634597 (pbk)

# CONTENTS

Preface to the Second Edition ... vii

1. A Constitutional and Political Approach to Public Administration ... 3

**Part I. Public Organizations and Democratic Governance** ... 25

The Case of the Angry Library Patron ... 27

2. The Challenges and Opportunities of Public Service ... 33
3. Administrative Discretion: Issues and Conflicts ... 51
4. Democracy and Administration ... 72
5. The Troubled History of American Public Administration ... 89
6. Administrative Ethics and Responsibility ... 130

**Part II. Designing and Managing Organizational Systems** ... 165

Tumult in Prairie County: A Case Study ... 167

7. Organization Structure and Behavior ... 173
8. A Political History of Public Personnel Administration ... 199
9. Contemporary Human Resources Management ... 233

**Part III. Financing and Budgeting for the Public's Business** ... 263

The Case of the Medler School System ... 265

10. Public Revenue and Financial Management ... 271
11. Budget Formation and Resource Allocation ... 312

**Part IV. Strategic Management of Public Organizations** ... 345

Eagle Rock: The Case of the Peregrine Falcon ... 347

12. Public Service Leadership in a Shared-Power World ... 351
13. The Role of Public Administration in Public Policy and Analysis ... 378
14. Policy Implementation and Administrative Law ... 413

15.  The Future of American Public Administration                                452

Appendix A. Constitution of the United States                                    473
Appendix B. The Bill of Rights                                                   485
Bibliography                                                                     487
Index                                                                            517
About the Authors                                                                533

# PREFACE TO THE SECOND EDITION

This second edition of *Foundations of Public Service* builds on the lessons we have learned over the past 30 years teaching public service practitioners. Our students come from all sectors—public, private, and nonprofit—and they possess varying degrees of experience as street-level supervisors, middle managers, and strategic or top-level administrators. We have written *Foundations of Public Service* to help these present and future practitioners make sense out of the everyday public responsibilities to which they have dedicated their lives.

We construe the term *public service* broadly, so that it includes not only those who work in government but also those who work in nonprofit organizations and private firms that carry out public responsibilities through contracts, charters, or other authorizing instruments. This definition also comprises special districts, which cover a wide range of governmental, quasi-governmental, and private-sector entities that perform specialized functions for the public. Though few realize it, special districts are by far the most numerous governing entities in the United States. Together, these organizations in the public, nonprofit, for-profit, and civil society sectors coproduce the public good. Successful governance and administration depend largely on how well public service leaders understand and use their discretionary authority to develop creative synergy among these partners.

We have written this book from a governmental perspective. There are three reasons why partners in the coproduction process benefit from such a perspective. First, private and nonprofit managers who maintain contractual or other types of relationships with government need to understand the distinct values, obligations, functions, and processes that form the governmental perspective. This can help them manage their relationships with government more effectively. Second, by dint of their formal relationships with government, organizations in the private and nonprofit sectors add to, or broaden, their responsibilities to the public. Their fiduciary responsibilities increase in ways that often entail changes in both their practices and their business methods. Third, most public employees need to understand the governance complexity that provides the distinctive context for carrying out their public duties. Surprisingly, even public servants with extensive experience may know little about how the larger governing context shapes and influences their obligations and practices. In the absence of such knowledge, many feel buffeted by forces they do not understand—forces that transform them from leaders of change into victims of circumstance. Our challenge in this book is to help these professionals become more aware of the connections between their daily work and the broader context of governance and, in so doing, empower them to become leaders in responsible governance rather than pawns of political and administrative games or corks floating in a sea beyond their control.

The central theme of this second edition, like the first, is *democratic constitutionalism.* Under democratic constitutionalism, sovereignty resides in the people of the United States through their constitutions and charters. Thus, American systems of governance are called *rule-by-law* systems:

The people govern through these deliberately created structures of authority. And the people can adopt new principles and change how our various governance systems operate. The administrative implication of this approach is that public servants must acquire the competencies needed to *govern* in addition to the competencies needed to *manage*. The second edition of *Foundations of Public Service* expands and develops this central theme in several important ways.

## ELABORATION OF OUR CONSTITUTIONAL APPROACH TO PUBLIC ADMINISTRATION THEORY AND PRACTICE

The major modification to this second edition is the addition of a new introductory chapter that makes explicit the constitutional foundation for public administration theory and practice. In the first edition, our legal approach was more implicit than explicit. In the first chapter of this edition, however, we make our approach—one of democratic constitutionalism—explicit, contrasting it with the traditional approach that grounds public administration in the management sciences.

## EXPANDED DISCUSSION OF CIVIL SOCIETY AND NONPROFIT ORGANIZATIONS

We have expanded our discussion of the role of civil society in producing the common good. This is in keeping with our thesis that the nonprofit sector and civic organizations, both formal and informal, are critical partners of government in producing the common good. In particular, we have extended our coverage of nonprofit organizations because of the increasing reliance by government on these formal civic organizations to provide a variety of contracted social services. In the near future, demands for balanced budgets and reduced government spending will shrink resources for social services. Private charitable donations and foundation grants will not be able to make up for the broad loss in government support, and many nonprofit contract providers will face growing stress, consolidation, and closure. In the face of shrinking resources, community civic organizations and other informal responses will grow in importance. Without more mindful attention by government leaders to the role that formal and informal civic organizations play in creating the common good, public service as a whole will be adversely affected.

## POLITY LEADERSHIP

In making explicit another theme that was largely implicit in our first edition, we argue that public administrators, especially at the local level, have responsibility for what we call *polity leadership*. This term refers to the intentional identification and coordination of resources across organizations in all sectors of the political economy—formal and informal—to promote the larger common good. The notion of polity leadership includes the traditional coordination among governing jurisdictions as well as coordination of the delivery of public goods by organizations in civil society. A variety of factors have undermined the traditional assumption that these formal and informal civic organizations will self-organize to meet the needs of the community (Sirianni 2009; Skocpol and Fiorina 1999). In some cases, the formalization, commercial self-interest, and donor and grantor pressures of nonprofit organizations have reduced the space for the development of civic organizations; in other instances, reliance on technology has encouraged a less communitarian focus, as individuals organize around subcommunities of special interest. At the same time, the globalization of the economy has weakened the attachments of citizens to their local communities.

These developments have increased the need for administrators from all sectors to spark and nurture informal relationships among civic organizations as critical elements of the polity network. But this polity leadership role will vary widely from one community setting to another. In large metropolitan regions, the polity may be composed of a rich network of nonprofit, for-profit, civic organizations, and government members with recognized leaders and substantial public resources contributing to the common good. In medium-sized communities, the polity network may be developed only partially or inconsistently. Here, a few established or major nonprofit providers may serve as the only procurement options, and the local government is likely to remain the dominant source for leadership, resources, and coordination in public service. Finally, in small, isolated, largely rural communities, the main polity resources are typically local churches, a few voluntary associations, and area families. In such cases, the local government (with state government support) may need to take a more active role in enabling leadership for coordination, provision of resources, and service delivery.

## THE EMERGENCE OF NEW PUBLIC GOVERNANCE

We recognize the emergence of a "new" focus in public administration research and practice called *New Public Governance* (NPG). At the end of chapter 4 of this second edition, we have added a section that explains the development, meaning, and implications of NPG as a response to both *New Public Management* (NPM) and to the reinvention of government that first became popular in the 1990s. Our ideas differ from those of some of our colleagues who view NPG as something new: We see NPG's emphasis on public values, networks, collaboration, and negotiated agreements as a return to a very old notion of public administration that was in play during the early phases of the formation of numerous nation-states. During these "founding periods," the focus of public administration generally is on building trust and legitimacy in governing institutions, especially by relying on existing social institutions to complement governmental power. Rather than treat public administration as a science of means, NPG returns public administration to a political role—that of an active agent, in partnership with other governing institutions, helping to define and give expression to substantive political ends.

Over the past several decades, numerous factors have combined to make public service and public administration increasingly challenging. A long-term downturn in the American economy, taxpayer initiatives to limit government spending, a renewed debate over the role of government in democratic society, demographic shifts in the population, technological innovations, and the globalization of the economy have combined to weaken citizen confidence in our governing institutions at every level of government. We hope that this second edition of *Foundations of Public Service* delivers on its promise of helping administrators in all sectors to navigate the contentious waters that dominate their field. Armed with an understanding of administrative work that is grounded in constitutional values and historically evolving practices, present and future administrators will be well equipped to participate in the ongoing debate over the role of government—along with civic, nonprofit, and for-profit organizations—in preserving our democratic system of ordered liberty

## ACKNOWLEDGMENTS

Our approach builds on many fine contributions by scholars and distinguished practitioners who have helped us test and refine our thinking over the past several decades. We owe a deep debt of gratitude to a small core of public administration colleagues—among them Herbert Storing (1981a, 1981b; see especially Morgan et al. 2010), John Rohr (1989, 1986), David Rosenbloom

(2000, 1983, 1977, 1971), Phillip Cooper (2009, 2003, 2002), Brian Cook (1996), and Larry Terry (1995)—all of whom have placed the U.S. Constitution at the center of public service education and training.

We have drawn heavily from other scholars such as Stephen Elkin and Karol Soltan (1993), Camilla Stivers (2002a, 2002b), Paul Van Riper (1983, 1958), Leonard White (1958, 1954, 1951, 1948, 1926), Dwight Waldo (1948), Philip Selznick (1992, 1957, 1949), Richard Scott (1995); William Scott and David Hart, 1989); Richard Stillman (1984), Terry Cooper (1991), Michael Spicer (1995), Daniel Kemmis (1990), Walter Powell and Paul DiMaggio (1991), and Carmen Sirianni (2009), who have sharpened our thinking about the historical and institutional forces that shape administrative roles.

Perhaps most important, our work has been influenced by exemplary practitioners who have helped to test and shape our ideas. We are grateful for the role models of reflective practice that have been provided to us by such exemplars as Charles Cameron (retired county administrator), Deb Whitall (U.S. Forest Service), Davis Moriuchi (Army Corps of Engineers), Don Bohn (active county administrator), Elaine Zielinski (Bureau of Land Management), Dan Vizzini (retired city administrator), Jean Thorne (state administrator), Gary Larson (retired U.S. Forest Service), Rick Mogren (retired Army Corps of Engineers), Scott Lazenby (city manager), James Lindsay (retired police chief), Ken Kamis (former health department director), and numerous others who have been splendid teachers. This book is intended to cultivate all of the public service qualities their careers embody.

Finally, we wish to acknowledge the significant editing and formatting work that has gone into this text. Our gratitude goes out to Jordan Robertson and Tricia Jack, who gave many hours of valuable assistance in the preparation of the first edition. We thank David Jarvis, a Ph.D. candidate in Portland State University's Public Administration and Policy Program, for his fine work on the bibliography, and Caitlin Shinn Alcorn for her work in formatting many of our tables. We also want to thank the exceptional work of our M.E. Sharpe team, especially our superb copyeditor Barbara Bigelow, Stacey Victor, our production editor, associate editor Elizabeth Granda Parker, and executive editor Harry Briggs for his patience and always sage advice. We couldn't have asked for a better team!

# Foundations of Public Service

Second Edition

# A CONSTITUTIONAL AND POLITICAL APPROACH TO PUBLIC ADMINISTRATION

> [A] government must be fitted to a nation, as much as a coat to the individual; and consequently, that what may be good at Philadelphia may be bad at Paris, and ridiculous at Petersburgh.
>
> *(Alexander Hamilton 1799/1975, 22:404)*

This book takes Alexander Hamilton's claim seriously. The proper forms and operations of a nation's governments depend on the values and character of its people as they evolve over time. Learning how to govern properly requires that, at minimum, public servants in all levels of government and in all sectors cultivate their understanding of this evolutionary history—and use it to inform their governing practices. This book is committed to that end. In the chapters that follow we explore the enduring values that shape the nature, dynamics, and evolution of public service in the United States. Our approach immerses the reader in the historical development of our governing institutions; it provides an essential context for understanding proper administrative practice and explains the origins of ideas about what constitutes "good government." Moreover, this approach helps us identify administrative traditions that have evolved from the founding era to the current day, and it aids in our understanding of why these traditions both confer and challenge the legitimacy of government decisions. We will illustrate why and how these traditions remain relevant to today's public service at all levels.

In keeping with our goal of grounding public servants in the historical and institutional foundations of their practice, this book is written as an extended narrative text rather than an encyclopedia of substantive information. Furthermore, in keeping with the spirit of a narrative text, we weave common themes throughout the chapters, emphasizing that governance is more about balancing tensions than resolving them. As such, a thorough knowledge of how these tensions have played out historically is crucial to acquiring the competency needed for governing. Our concentration on the governing role of administrators provides a focal point for our narrative history of public administration, as is illustrated more fully in the following sections of this chapter.

## FOCUS ON THE CAREER PUBLIC SERVANT

In this text, we focus primarily on the role of *career* public servants rather than on *elected* officials. We do this for four reasons: First, government and special district civil servants are subordinates

in our governing systems, and confusion often abounds concerning their relative position in the hierarchy. In an organization of divided and checked powers, public servants have many bosses. Ultimately, in a regime based upon popular sovereignty, these bosses are the people, not just politicians and judges. Ironically, this situation places career officials at the center of politics and policymaking and holds them responsible for translating an often conflicting mix of policy intentions into agency action at all levels. They share in a big way with their political superiors the task of "creating public value," maintaining "operative capacity," and building legitimacy for government policy and action (Moore 1995, 5–12 passim). Though often preoccupied with internal organization issues and fundraising, nonprofit administrators share responsibility as well for creating public value, building governance capacity within the community, and increasing the legitimacy of public institutions. Whenever nonprofit administrators enter into the community polity to develop and provide public services or to coordinate with other providers, they act as governing agents who face public concerns over their legitimacy to act for the community and over uncontrolled concentrated power.

Second, career tenure gives public administrators some advantages over elected officials, who often do not or cannot make public service a lifetime calling. Term limits, low pay, staff limitations, and broad ambitions mean that most elected politicians stay in a particular office for a relatively short period of time. This tendency, in turn, bolsters the power of career public officials in determining how our systems of democratic governance work. They exercise powerful discretionary judgments that affect the health (good or bad) of democratic governance. Career public officials help design, organize, implement, and maintain our public safety and defense systems, our transportation infrastructure, our sewer and water systems, our social service programs, our school systems, our land use planning patterns, and our public health and environmental programs. In the process, they contribute to, and may also detract from, the engagement of citizens in democratic life. The initiatory influence of career public officials in shaping the meaning and practice of democratic government is especially significant at local levels of government, which are frequently governed by elected bodies of part-time officials who have no staff.

Third, career public officials greatly outnumber elected officials and their political appointees. In all of the United States, there are only several thousand elected and appointed officials compared with several million career officials. The breadth and diversity of practices among career officials can easily overwhelm the capacity of superintending officials to adequately monitor and control them. This situation tends to reinforce a common image of a massive, monolithic, and unresponsive bureaucracy, but as we shall see, the reality is neither that simple nor that ominous.

Finally, career administrators play a pivotal role in creating and maintaining an appropriate balance among the general government, special district government, and the for-profit, private, and nonprofit sectors within American communities. Career administrators manage these boundaries on a daily basis; those in charge of making any alterations to these boundaries must work to meet the expectations of participants. In doing so, it is incumbent upon public officials to understand the rationale underlying each sector and how the work in those sectors can be harnessed to serve the greater good of the community.

## THE ROLE OF PUBLIC SERVICE IN A DEMOCRATIC REPUBLIC

For the reasons outlined above, the work of public servants plays an integral part in the governing process. Public servants are not merely subservient clerks who carry out the wishes of one superior or another; this "instrumental" view, misleading as it is, was popularized by the academic field of public administration in the late nineteenth and early twentieth centuries. Scholars and

fellow reformers articulated the instrumental approach as a politically expedient solution to a vexing problem: how to reduce partisan meddling and influence that tended to corrupt and distort governmental operations, while simultaneously preserving democratic principles of governance. The solution offered by early reformers was to create a public service that possessed technical and scientific expertise for carrying out the wishes of the people as expressed through elected policymakers. They thereby redefined public service as a politically neutral and responsive field of administration—a field largely confined to the executive branch. Administration involved questions of *how* to get things done, while the politicians determined *what* things needed to be done in the first place.

This simple formula enabled administrative theorists to conceive of administrative practice as a neutral, independent field of scientific study that could be applied universally to organizations, whether private or public, and regardless of culture or context. The instrumental, executive-based theory of administration has undergone a variety of permutations of varying sophistication over succeeding generations, and even today it remains influential among many scholars, politicians, and career public servants. We view this approach not only as an inadequate explanation of the role of public service in American government but also as a distortion of what really happens in the governing process.

The approach we take in this book treats public service and administration as a *sublimated* political process. An insightful scholar of the field, Herbert Storing, once observed, "Age-old political and constitutional problems now present themselves as problems of (or in) public administration" (1965, 48). By this Storing meant that the founding fathers designed a constitutional system that would hold conflicting principles in irresolvable tensions, thus forcing public servants at all levels (even street level) to cope with them in the ongoing administration of government. In the design process, the founders left many broad political and constitutional questions unanswered, in part because they could not agree among themselves about the "right" answers. For example, though all of them "believed in the importance of attracting the best individuals to public office, they failed to establish any mechanisms ensuring that this would happen on a consistent basis" (Morgan et al. 2010, 631, paraphrasing Storing 1981b, 1:73). They also differed in their views of fundamental issues about governance, such as (1) what constitutes proper representation of the people by public officials, (2) whether and to what extent the people themselves should play a role in public policy and administration, (3) which powers should be invested in the states versus the national government, and (4) how much power should be held by any single branch of government. The architects of the U.S. Constitution left these and other important disagreements (to be discussed in subsequent chapters) unresolved for future generations to cope with as they saw fit for their times.

The founders shared a healthy respect for diverse opinions about democracy in general and the elements most crucial to securing the blessings of liberty in particular. Toward that end, they stressed a common belief in the need for balancing contending principles and interests. They subscribed to the Aristotelian view that regimes tend to fail from an excess of their virtues or dominant principles. Hamilton, for example, often advised that no matter how well-crafted and executed a given policy seemed to be, it inevitably contained the seeds of its own excess and demise. Consequently, wise leaders need to anticipate this tendency and build in precautions against abuse and excess whenever possible. The designers of our Constitution integrated such precautions through checks and balances that would force separate, superintending branches and levels of government to negotiate for control over the administrative machinery of government. Thus, they did not confine administration exclusively to the executive branch of government. Even Hamilton, one of the most ardent supporters of broad executive powers, acknowledged this idea in his definition of public administration from

the 72nd essay of *The Federalist Papers:* "The administration of government, in its largest sense, comprehends all of the operations of the body politic, whether legislative, executive, or judiciary" (Hamilton 1788, Federalist No. 72, quoted in Rossiter 1961). As we shall see, the founders instilled irresolvable tensions in the Constitution in three ways: by blending powers horizontally between the branches of government, vertically between levels of government, and by using the extended sphere of a large republic to encourage proliferation of factions or special interests that would help prevent any one group from dominating the political system.

Our approach to the teaching of public service and administration treats the governing principles embraced by the founding fathers as meaningful, obligating, and enduring, but also as ambiguous, unsettled, and conflicting. The Constitution they designed embodies these principles and their inherent tensions, and the public service must inevitably reflect the resulting controversies. Public service is thus mired in politics at all levels. It is, however, a coherent and structured politics, not simply a chaotic melee among egos and interests. By this we mean that there are different types and spheres of politics. Partisan politics is what most people think of when talking about politics in general, but there are other arenas of politics where we seek to reduce or even eliminate partisan influence, such as in our court systems and in some local elections where candidates are required to run for office on a nonpartisan basis. The career administrative sphere of public service is another arena where, because of hard lessons involving unchecked partisan abuse, we have restrained partisan influence in favor of preserving independent professional judgment and technical competence. This is the sphere of bureaucratic politics, where civil servants vie for power among themselves as well as with political parties, judges, professions, interest groups, and even persistent individuals who have axes to grind.

In all of these arenas, politics is channeled through legal, organizational, and institutional processes that tend to slow down decision making and provide a forum for varying degrees of public input and scrutiny. Public input, deliberation, and accountability are high principles of democratic governance, but they are also the source of delay, red tape, and occasional gridlock. This double-helical set of relationships results in an aggravating trade-off with efficiency and effectiveness—values often associated with business and touted by many as preeminent in public administration. We commonly hear politicians claiming they want government run more like a business, but of course they cannot abandon deliberation, accountability, and a concern for substantive fairness. As a consequence, their intentions are continually frustrated. They run straight into a central dilemma faced by the founders—how to confer enough power to govern effectively without it becoming excessive and tyrannical. The founders had no desire to resolve this dilemma because unchecked power would subvert their ultimate purpose—to sustain a democratic republic dedicated to the principle of ordered liberty.

## THE CENTRALITY OF ORDERED LIBERTY

This book treats *ordered liberty* as the guiding purpose of American public service—a contrast to instrumental conceptions of administration that focus on efficiency and effectiveness for the sake of democratic responsiveness. Though democracy is vital to our culture and modes of governance, it remains problematic in a regime that is also dedicated to protecting individual rights. The founders shared a common concern for the excesses of both entrenched elites and unrestrained democracy. Accordingly, they subjected both the influence of elites and popular rule at the national and state levels to a system of elections and appointments that became progressively removed from direct electoral accountability, yet managed to retain degrees of representativeness and accountability through other means.

Over time we have modified our national and state constitutions to increase direct democratic rule and accountability, and increased our expectations that political leaders should avidly embrace

majority will rather than temper and resist its influence. While this is certainly appropriate given the strong democratic spirit of the American people, it also heightens the tensions with our rights-based traditions. In the current era, for example, we struggle with the balance between adequate security and protection against terrorism and the rights of detainees who are suspected of terrorist activity. Likewise, we struggle with the issue of legal and illegal immigration and which rights we should extend to immigrants as persons under our Constitution. We struggle over whether fetuses should have rights, and what meaningful rights we as individuals have to bear arms in modern society. We struggle over the condition of our prisons as a manifestation of our concern, or lack thereof, for inmate rights. We often fight over these issues even when majority opinion is strongly canted to one side. Democracy thus remains problematic for securing a regime of ordered liberty (Morgan et al. 2010, 624–625; Nishishiba, Banyan, and Morgan 2012, 21–52).

Ordered liberty is an end fraught with conundrums and tensions that we will explore at length in this book. It will be helpful here to consider the nature of the relationship between order and liberty. Americans are passionately committed to individual liberty, yet divided over how best to achieve it. Should we minimize the role and presence of government in order to maximize free-dom from governmental restraint, or should we increase the power of our governments in order to protect and enhance our liberties within various spheres of life? The implications for public policy and administration change significantly the more we favor one approach versus the other, and both have merit. In the twenty-first century, these two approaches inform the basic ideological differences between our two major political parties, and implicit in each approach is a differing sense of how we should order our lives together.

The important point is that each approach embraces a type of order that adherents believe enhances liberty while restraining those powers and interests that they believe will compromise liberty. For example, those who advocate for free, unregulated markets believe our liberties are enhanced through a resulting competitive economy—an economy structured primarily through institutions such as courts that protect property rights, and through legislative bodies that restrict the power of government, labor, or any other group that attempts to interfere with private economic development. On the other side are those who want to regulate markets against abuses to society as a whole and to individual rights that result from inordinate combinations of wealth and power, and from harmful externalities such as pollution, depletion, or the destruction of things we hold in common. Each side seeks varying types and degrees of order that both enhance and restrain our liberties in meaningful ways. Thus, order and liberty exist in a paradoxical relationship that requires shifting negotiations and compromises over their meaning as well as their application through time. Together, order and liberty form a moving target that is never fully captured by one or another agenda or institutional arrangement. In the early chapters of this book, we will lead readers to a "Balancewheel" (see chapter 6) model of public service that reflects the paradoxical nature of ordered liberty and its effects on the character of American public service. The Balance-wheel is grounded in the multiple purposes that have to be successfully accomplished to ensure the preservation of liberty: protecting minority rights, being responsive to majority will, efficient and effective delivery of services, and honoring the unique institutional differences across America's diverse geographic landscape.

## ORDERED LIBERTY AND THE QUEST FOR EQUALITY

The Declaration of Independence asserts that "all men are created equal, that they are endowed by their Creator with certain unalienable Rights, that among these are Life, Liberty and the pursuit of Happiness." The Declaration has served as a standard by which we measure our democratic suc-

cess. It was the cornerstone of President Abraham Lincoln's early campaign against slavery (see Lincoln, "Speech at Springfield, Illinois," June 26, 1857, II, 398–409) and Martin Luther King, Jr.'s civil rights campaign (see King's "Letter from Birmingham Jail," 1963, available online and in Storing, 117). It also inspired many of those spearheading the Occupy Wall Street Movement of 2012. While the American Revolution was fought in the name of liberty rather than equality, the equality principle has remained a core national value to which administrators hold a fiduciary responsibility (Rohr 1989, chap. 3).

There are three dimensions of the "equality problem" that have implications for career public administrators. First, equality is often thought of as "equality of social condition" or a measure of income disparity and all of the consequences that follow from being poor (i.e., issues related to employment, housing, food, clothing, and medical care). The American Revolution, unlike the French, Russian, and most Latin American revolutions, was not fought to redistribute wealth, or to produce more bread, housing, and jobs (Arendt 1963, especially chap. 4). Rather, it was fought to secure liberty on the assumption that this liberty would be used by individuals to better their own lot in life. In his travels across the United States in the early 1830s, Alexis de Tocqueville was struck by the American drive for advancing one's economic well-being. He referred to it as "a tenacious, exclusive, universal but contained passion" that makes it difficult "to draw a man out of himself to interest him in the destiny of the whole state, because he understands poorly the influence that the destiny of the state can exert on his lot" (Tocqueville, 1835–1840/2000, 508–509, 487). Our preoccupation with material well-being poses a daily practical challenge for administrators as they seek to elicit ownership by citizens in the affairs of more than 85,000 local democratic communities throughout the United States (Putnam 2000). This is a theme we address throughout the book, especially in chapter 12, where we argue that administrators across all sectors need to view their role as polity leaders in addition to serving as managers of their organizations.

A second way the equality issue arises for administrators is through their leadership role in addressing income disparity and equality of economic opportunity. The American founders assumed that liberty was a sure ticket to enhanced economic well-being. In making this assumption, they were not unmindful of the great disparities in the socioeconomic setting. However, they believed that there was sufficient abundance of resources and open access to assure that the advancing tide of economic prosperity would raise the boats of all, thus making the "pursuit of happiness" universally attainable. Clearly, this is no longer the case because of human, political, and natural limits on the growth of the gross national product (GNP) and gross domestic product (GDP). Still, career public administrators do influence the framing of these debates and play a key role in the development and implementation of policies that aspire to improve the economic well-being of *all* Americans. Nonprofit administrators may have enhanced responsibilities advocating for equality and social justice. Nonprofit organization missions and goals, along with the personal convictions of its leaders and supporters, may require nonprofit administrators to engage in active political and policy advocacy or in service activities to those in need.

A third way in which the equality issue arises for administrators across all sectors is through their leadership role in embracing and promoting various kinds of social, racial, gender, ethnic, and religious diversity in their communities. As will become evident, there are no clear answers to these issues, at least from the standpoint of the meaning and purpose of the American constitutional order. On the one hand, the constitutional commitment to liberty allows individuals to decide who is special and who is not, and to make decisions about friends, family, and associational relationships on the basis of their personal preferences. In fact, love and friendship require us to give preferential treatment to some of our fellow citizens over others (Schaar 1964, 885–886). But at what point is it appropriate to place limitations on the rights of individuals to use their liberty to make life

choices? As it turns out, equality of treatment inevitably comes at the expense of someone else's "right to choose." These kinds of tensions are manifest in the Fourteenth Amendment provision for "equal protection of the laws," a provision that gives practical meaning to the Declaration's assertion that "all men are created equal." Throughout this book, we will remind readers that the tensions faced by the American founders persist to this day and require a continual process of reexamining the balance among competing values important for securing the blessings of liberty. Career administrators play a vital role in shaping both the process and substance of these rebalancing efforts through their role in shaping and implementing the rule of law.

## ORDERED LIBERTY AND RULE BY LAW

In American public life, the first method by which we provide for ordered liberty and the protection of equality is through the principle of *rule by law*. This is distinguished from rule by divine revelation or by human fiat or will. Our rights are enshrined in law, and we bind all who engage in public decisions and actions to established legal procedures that help preserve those rights. This principle, more than any other, is what distinguishes government administration from for-profit business and nonprofit management—and from the traditional instrumental approach that has dominated administrative thought since the Progressive Era. Early textbooks on public administration asserted that public "management" was separate from law and had more in common with business management (cf. White 1926).

We will, to the contrary, illustrate how law provides the defining element of public administration. Law integrates ends with means and in many cases provides vague and/or ambiguous language subject to nuance and arguable interpretations. It establishes a minimum standard of reasonability to which all administrative decisions are subject. Public servants must give reasons for their decisions, and these reasons are subject to scrutiny on both substantive and procedural grounds. Law is therefore integral to public decision making and the administrative process. In fact, under the American legal system, no administrator can take official action without clearly identifying a source of legal authority that permits such action. This gives real meaning to the principle of "limited government." The powers granted to all officials, and the ends prescribed for them, are defined and circumscribed by law.

The legal foundation for public administration in the United States means that legal knowledge and analysis cannot be left exclusively to lawyers. Public servants of all stripes must cultivate an understanding of the Constitution and laws that guide their work; they must use law and comply with it. Those officials who do not give it due regard endanger their fiduciary role (a public trust) as agents of democratic governance.

## THE RULE OF LAW GROUNDS PUBLIC INSTITUTIONS

Beyond shaping administrative decisions and processes, the law also grounds public institutions. In his book *The Moral Commonwealth*, Philip Selznick gives an apt description of how institutions emerge in the context of law. They exist as an intermediate stage between organizations and community, achieving institutional status over time:

> Orderly, stable, socially integrated patterns [emerge] out of unstable, loosely organized, or narrowly technical activities. . . . Institutions, it is said, "fix processes that are essentially dynamic." This fixing legitimizes and thereby establishes social groupings. The starting mechanism is often a formal act, such as the adoption of a rule or statute. To be effective,

however, the enactment must build upon preexisting resources of regularity and legitimacy and must lead to a new history of consistent conduct and supportive belief. Institutions are established, not by decree alone, but as a result of being bound into the fabric of social life. Even so weighty an enactment as the United States Constitution cannot be understood apart from the legal and political history that preceded it, the interpretive gloss given it by the courts, and the role it has played in American history and consciousness. The formal acts of adoption and ratification were only part of a more complex, more open-ended process of institution-building. (Selznick, 1992, 232)

The law is used, then, to formally establish or recognize public institutions and to codify the relationships, processes, and practices that comprise them. By *codify*, we mean more than merely writing these things into rulebooks and standard operating procedures. The administrative processes and practices developed in these institutions are used by public servants to relate the often ambiguous content of law to daily life in distinct and meaningful ways. Without this, the law is a dead letter. The open-ended character of our constitutional legacy places administrators in an especially critical interpretive role for shaping these public institutions and the lives of people who interact with them. One goal of this book is to help public officials see how the legal dimensions of their work can be used to build trust and legitimacy in democratic institutions. As a starting point, it will be helpful to review the basic types and functions of law that are germane to administrative practice.

## TYPES OF LAW IN PUBLIC LIFE

Public servants in government service encounter and apply four basic types of law in their work: *constitutional law, statutory law, administrative law,* and *common law.* Our constitutions are the foundational law of the country. The Federal Constitution is provided in Appendix 1 of this book for handy reference. Students are strongly encouraged to read it. State and local officials are strongly encouraged to read their state constitutions. All other written laws derive or proceed from these foundational documents. Constitutions are generally written in broad language and meant to be adapted to future circumstances. The U.S. Constitution begins with the following preamble, which expresses the basic purposes and aspirations of the people and their government.

> We the people of the United States, in Order to form a more perfect Union, establish Justice, insure domestic Tranquility, provide for the common defence, promote the general Welfare, and secure the Blessings of Liberty to ourselves and our Posterity, do ordain and establish this Constitution for the United States of America.

### The U.S. Constitution

The Constitution is not simply another legal document. It is also a political and economic document of the first order, establishing a complex commercial republic, a robust civil society, and a superintending organizational structure for the national government. It is a moral document as well, in the sense that it expresses our common ideals and obligates all public servants who operate under its auspices. In short, it has become a consummate example of what Selznick describes as an "institution." Federal employees and most state and local employees swear oaths to uphold the Constitution and laws of the country. Most Americans also revere the Constitution, even if they have not read it, and this gives it a heightened legitimacy. It is an authoritative text for American

public life that we should try hard to understand and apply in our work. This is a challenging responsibility, however; as we mentioned earlier, many of its clauses are broad, vague, or ambiguous and therefore subject to arguable interpretations. Although the U.S. Supreme Court is the ultimate arbiter of the meaning of these clauses, it is important to understand that many public servants at all levels of government must interpret and apply provisions of the Constitution in their daily responsibilities, and the vast majority of their decisions never reach a court.

Some of the more notable provisions of the Constitution important for administrative work include the following.

*Structure and Processes of Government*

Articles I, II, and III together define the governance structure and processes of the national government, and they include the guarantee of a republican form of government for each state.

*Powers of Government*

Articles I, II, and III respectively define the powers of the legislative, executive, and judicial branches of government. The subordinate public administration receives its budget and the statutory authority to implement legislation from the powers enumerated for Congress in Article I, and operates mainly, but not exclusively, under the supervening authority of the executive branch as specified in Article II. All three branches exercise limited supervening power over the public administration.

*Some Notable Differences*

Article I, establishing the legislative branch, is the longest of the first three articles. Importantly, Article I begins by stating: "All legislative Powers herein granted shall be vested in a Congress of the United States, which shall consist of a Senate and House of Representatives." It then proceeds in Section 8 to specify 18 important legislative powers. By contrast, Article II simply notes, "The executive Power shall be vested in a President of the United States"; it does not specifically enumerate executive powers in the kind of detailed manner found for Congress in Article I. This difference has spawned a debate over the limits of presidential appointment and removal power, and more generally regarding whether the executive branch enjoys "inherent powers." This is an issue we address more fully in chapter 8.

*Judicial Review*

Readers should note that Article III does not explicitly confer the power of judicial review upon the courts. That is an inherent power established by interpretation in the famous case of *Marbury v. Madison* (1803).

*Supremacy Clause*

Article VI contains the *supremacy clause,* which establishes federal law as the supreme law of the land, requires an oath of office from all federal public servants, and bars religious tests as a qualification for any office under the United States. This clause provides the basis for a preemptive claim by federal administrators over state-level interpretations of federal law when the two

may be in conflict or when a state law conflicts with a federal law (as illustrated in the matter of criminalizing medical marijuana, or in state efforts to control illegal immigration).

*Bill of Rights*

The first 10 (of 26) amendments constitute the Bill of Rights; they were passed by the first Congress shortly after ratification of the Constitution. The Fourteenth Amendment contains *due process* and *equal protection* clauses that apply to the states as well as to the federal government, and it gives Congress the power to pass laws enforcing its provisions. The Fourteenth Amendment was passed shortly after the Civil War to ensure the protection of the civil rights of newly freed slaves from abuses by southern states. While originally intended to check the abuse of state power in discriminating against newly freed slaves, the due process and the equal protection clauses of the Fourteenth Amendment have been interpreted by courts to apply most of the Bill of Rights restrictions to states as well as the U.S. government. For example, the due process clause has been interpreted by the U.S. Supreme Court to require both the U.S. and state governments on an equal basis to protect freedom of speech, assembly, religion; desegregate schools; provide indigent defendants with lawyers; protect the rights of privacy; and discontinue practices deemed to be "cruel and unusual punishment." In making the Bill of Rights provisions equally applicable to both the U.S. and state/local governing bodies, the courts have broadened the responsibility for administrators at all levels of government.

The Seventeenth Amendment changes the way senators are elected—from election by their state legislatures to direct election by the people—and the Twenty-second Amendment limits persons to two terms as the nation's president. Together, these changes provide the basis for an argument that career public servants now fulfill more of the role that was originally intended to be performed by the U.S. Senate (Rohr 1986). This is an issue we will discuss in greater depth in chapter 6.

**Statutes**

*Statutes* are laws passed by Congress and state legislatures with the concurrence of the chief executive. In most cases, statutes are intended to have general and future effect; that is, they apply to broad classes of people and activities beginning at a future designated point in time, and are in force in perpetuity except when expiration dates (sunset provisions) are included, or when repealed, or when determined by a court to be unconstitutional. Many statutes also contain preambles stating their intended purposes up front. At the local level, bills passed by councils are often called ordinances, but they have the same status as laws, though are subordinate to state and federal statutes.

**Administrative Law**

*Administrative law* is made by government agencies under a set of legislative guidelines and standards that are usually codified in administrative procedures acts. Agencies make both procedural and substantive rules, and they issue orders with the force and effect of law. Through these procedures, agencies create many regulations that impose substantive standards, set rates, and issue orders and licenses covering a variety of professional, social, and economic activities. In this book, we treat all of these activities as aspects of administrative law. Federal and state agencies are, at a bare minimum, subject to rulemaking and adjudicative standards by their respective administrative procedure acts, and many agencies must meet much higher standards as prescribed in their enabling acts. Local governments and special districts often do not have a formal administrative

procedure act but nevertheless are subject to constitutional and statutory standards that impose some procedural and substantive requirements on them. Most local governments have detailed administrative procedures in place for dealing with land use issues.

## Common Law

*Common law* is case law established in the judicial courts of the country. Judges resolve civil cases brought by complainants concerning myriad problems—disputes over property, contracts, estates, divorce, and torts (civil wrongs such as trespass, negligence, and the like). In the course of adjudicating these cases, courts establish standards and principles that take on the force of legal precedents. This accumulation of standards and legal precedents is also known informally as *case law.* A good example of common law are the changing standards that have occurred over time in deciding who is liable for a "faulty" product that is sold in the marketplace (Levy 1964). The changing standards that have moved from "strict" to "limited liability" are an example of "common law" in the making. Both public officials and private persons may find themselves involved in civil suits that are subject to common law

## FUNCTIONS OF LAW IN PUBLIC LIFE

Many people think of law as commands backed by the force of government. This is certainly correct, but is also grossly insufficient for understanding other vital functions of law. Beyond command, the law establishes institutions and both confers and limits power; it maintains boundaries among the sectors; it partitions sovereignty; it provides purposes, goals, and standards for appropriate action; it educates and persuades; and, finally, it authorizes the collection of taxes and the expenditure of funds.

### Law Creates and Limits Organizations and Institutions

We use law to give legal status to a complex array of organizational entities, from the basic government agency to local governments, special districts and authorities, corporations, and government-sponsored and government-owned enterprises. The legal system also prescribes widely varying governing structures such as boards and commissions, centralized hierarchies, adversarial and dispute resolution structures, and collegial bodies, just to name some of the most common. As part of the role of law in creating governance processes and structures, the law also confers power on legally established entities (officers, associations, and organizations), usually taking great care to specify the limits of that power along with various methods of holding it accountable through various checks and balances. Public officials often perceive this as a case of handing power over with one hand, and then compromising its use with the other. Power, like money, always comes with strings attached.

### Law Creates and Maintains Boundaries Among the Sectors

The very definition of limited government we have already outlined means that government authority is carved out of preexisting authority held by the states, by individual citizens, and by organizations. This foundational "right to organize" is specifically recognized in constitutional, statutory, regulatory, and common law, and it has produced a dizzying array of religious, commercial, and most every kind of civic association imaginable. The body of law governing the

relationship among the sectors has undergone review, debate, and changes over time, producing more clearly separated boundaries around nonprofit organizations (i.e., religious, nonreligious, and eleemosynary or charitable), government, and for-profit private-sector organizations.

In the colonial era, government and church were closely connected through colonial charters, shared tax revenues, and government land grants. This relationship extended government control into the community and reinforced the position of the dominant church. The Anglican Church of England took this role in many of the colonies, but the Congregationalist Church held preference in the New England colonies, as did the Roman Catholic Church in Maryland. As an expression of charity, churches provided the primary source of social and educational services to the community.

The adoption of the U.S. Constitution and the Bill of Rights altered the boundaries between the church and the state. It strongly restrained national government power and severed the formal tie between church and state at the federal and state levels. To ensure the protection of individual liberties, the First Amendment provides that the national government adopt no law establishing a religion or prohibiting the exercise of a religion (Gaustad and Schmidt 2002). Disestablishment, or the severing of ties between governments and their state religions, was a fearful moment for the favored denominations in a particular state, as it put all religions and denominations on the same footing. On reflection, however, the denominational leaders of the dominant majority found that direct citizen support brought clarity of purpose and freedom from political influence over church messages (Gaustad and Schmidt 2002, 132 and 139; Hammack 1998, 118). Churches of all denominations actively continued to provide social, medical, and educational services, but facing a vacuum of governmental leadership and resources, citizens responded by establishing numerous independent schools and charitable associations (Hammack 1998, 116). During his tour of America in 1831, Tocqueville marveled at the strength and activism of the country's civic associations, commenting, "Everywhere . . . at the head of a new undertaking . . . count on it that you will perceive an association in the United States" (Tocqueville 1835–1840/2000, 489).

While constitutional law broke the link between the federal government and churches, the right to form a corporation independent of government followed a different process. But, as was the case for the relationship between the church and state, the outcome of this process again restrained government. The Supreme Court decision in the case of *Dartmouth College v. Woodward* (1819) allowed state governments the authority to enter into a contract to establish a corporation, but not to unilaterally modify or impair the contract after the fact. This quashed New Hampshire's efforts to reassert control over Dartmouth College against the will of its Congregationalist trustees. By implication, the ruling provided independence for both commercial and nonprofit corporations. Even with this ruling, New York and many southern and western states made it difficult to establish corporations and tried to require state supervision of them (Hammack 1998, 124).

Since the 1980s and the Reagan Revolution (see chapter 5), over the past several decades, the relationship among the sectors has been undergoing a major transformation spawned by a *limited government* movement as well as by changes in the law. At a philosophical level, the private and nonprofit sectors have grown in importance as government has been encouraged to "steer, rather than row" (Osborne and Gabler, 1992), leading to greater contracting of functions with private firms and nonprofit organizations. The United States is notable for the extent to which it delegates and devolves so many governmental functions to the business and nonprofit sectors. Whenever government relies on other sectors for the provision of goods and services, the law also confers authority on people in these sectors to make decisions on behalf of the government. No public official or private person may act in an official capacity for government without some kind of formal, affirmative authorization.

In addition to changes spawned by a philosophical desire to limit the scope and power of government, there has been a concomitant shift in the legal decisions by courts, which have greatly expanded the rights of corporations and private property owners. Private organizations now have the First Amendment right to be free from campaign spending limitations (see especially *Citizens United v. Federal Elections Commission* [2010] and *American Tradition Partnership, Inc. v. Steve Bullock* [2012]), and landowners can't have their property taken for a public purpose without a strong showing by government that it is proportionately contributing to a clearly articulated public good (see especially *Dolan v. Tigard* [1994]). As a result of simultaneous growth in government reliance on the nonprofit and for-profit sectors and increased constraints on government regulations, career administrators at all levels of government in the decades ahead will have an opportunity to forge a new set of relationships among and across the public, private, and nonprofit sectors. We give further attention to the development of these issues in chapter 5.

## Law Partitions Sovereignty

One of the increasingly important functions of law is that it partitions sovereignty. This partitioning is reflected in the American system of *federalism,* without which the compromise to establish the U.S. Constitution in 1787 would not have been achieved. Federalism ensures that states have independent authority to maintain the public health and safety of their communities. States determine how they will organize and distribute this responsibility among various subunits (i.e., counties, cities, township, boroughs, regional governments, etc.) and what kinds of powers these subunits can exercise.

For several decades, states and Native American tribes have been the beneficiaries of court decisions that have placed greater importance on their sovereign rights than at any point in the past. For example, courts have invoked the principle of tribal sovereignty to place limitations on the ability of states and the federal government to regulate people and resources on tribal lands (see Wilkinson 2005). The courts have held that federal law and regulation does not preempt states from suing manufacturers of defective products (see *Wyeth v. Levine* [2009]). States can afford their citizens greater legal protections than those provided by the U.S. Constitution (Crusto 2000). And with the Supreme Court's 2012 decision on President Barack Obama's national health care initiative, it is no longer a foregone conclusion that the federal government can rely on its right to regulate commerce as the means for adopting nationwide programs that may impose penalties on states for their failure to participate (see *National Federation of Independent Businesses, et al. v. Sebelius, Secretary of Health and Human Services, et al.* [2012]; Stewart [2012]). The reinvigoration of the principles of state and tribal sovereignty require administrators at all levels of government to have a firm grounding in why sovereignty is important and why its importance has waxed and waned over the course of American history.

## Law Provides Purposes, Goals, and Standards for Appropriate Action

Law is used (1) to create new organizational entities with clearly defined authority, (2) to define the boundaries among the sectors and partition sovereign boundaries rights, and (3) to promote values and establish standards for appropriate action. The more significant laws of the states and nation often include statements of goals and values that contain lofty language intended to inspire and obligate citizens and officials alike. They express hopes and aspirations toward which public servants should strive yet may never fully attain. In this sense, laws can provide or exhort moral tone but fall short in achieving it. This leads to some degree of skepticism about the relationship

between law and morality in general. It is, nevertheless, an essential relationship that we will explore in terms of a *public morality* (chapter 6) that obligates public servants in distinctive ways.

### Law Promotes Values, Edifies, and Teaches

While most people associate law with power and coercion, many legal requirements are intended to edify and teach. For example, our governments provide a wealth of information for the public—as a public service as well as a means to empower and engage the citizenry in their social, economic, legal, and political spheres of life. Second, the law prescribes standards or expectations of proper behavior in a variety of settings, and the sponsoring agencies often work very hard to educate the populace accordingly. Third, the law is often subject to argument over meaning, intent, and outcome, and judges are not the only officials charged with educating the public about these arguments. Most public servants find themselves educating people about what the law says, how it is applied, and why it should or should not apply to them. This can result in discussion and argument that includes both an educational and a persuasive component.

### Law Authorizes Revenue Collection and Expenditure

The popular prerevolutionary slogan of the 1750s and 1760s, "No taxation without representation," has been an important legal benchmark for measuring the legitimacy of government. Nearly 50 years after this saying became the rallying cry for the American Revolution, Chief Justice John Marshall echoed these earlier sentiments in a slightly different form in the famous case of *McCulloch v. Maryland* (1819), when he observed that the "power to tax is the power to destroy." At particular issue was the power of states to impose a tax on bank notes, including those issued by a separate bank chartered under law by U.S. Congress. When confronted for the first time with the question of whether states could tax a federal entity, Marshall advanced his famous axiom as a reason for denying states the legal power to tax federal organizations.

Throughout America's young history, the power to collect and spend public tax dollars has been regarded as a dangerous one—a power that needs to be guarded by clear legal parameters. As a result, a government cannot collect taxes or spend revenue without clear affirmative legal authority. It is not unheard of for a legislative body to establish a new governmental entity and then, in a fit of controversy about the entity, decline to fund it with an appropriation. As we shall see in chapters 10 and 11 the financial and budgetary systems of our governments are subject to legal procedures and authorizations that reflect the jealous interplay of the legislative and executive branches of government over extracting and then spending taxpayer's money.

### THE MEANING OF A CONSTITUTIONAL APPROACH TO PUBLIC SERVICE

In taking a constitutional approach to public service, we narrow the focus to regime-based characteristics without creating orthodoxy around any single point of view. In Exhibit 1.1, we summarize eight different but, in our opinion, complementary aspects of constitutionalism. All of the approaches share the belief that the foundations of public administration theory and practice are grounded in regime principles, structures, processes, functions, history, and values of a given political system. The unifying principles of public administration are not likely to be found in some kind of neutral science that transcends historical and political boundaries. Good administration facilitates the realization of the values of a particular regime. If those values are evil, corrupt, or

have no redeeming value, then we resort to a more transcendent set of universal values to serve as a critique and goad for improvement (Adams and Balfour 2009; Arendt 2006). Frequently, organizations in civil society perform this role, as has been the case throughout American history with respect to campaigns for the rights for African Americans, women, and other groups that have been subjected to less-than-equal treatment. As these countervailing values become incorporated into and legitimated by American legal institutions, they provide a diverse and robust moral text to serve as a guardian of the larger public interest. But that will not be the case unless public administrators are well schooled and educated in the diverse moral traditions that are an integral part of our public service history. We agree with the noted German American political philosopher Hannah Arendt, who argued that the banality of evil is best checked by the cultivation of imaginative capacities that make the moral dimensions of our activities tangible through a constant internal dialogue with ourselves (Arendt 2006). This dialogue facilitates self-awareness, but it needs some kind of script or narrative that provides a moral benchmark. Our constitutional approach to the study and practice of public administration, summarized in Exhibit 1.1, serves as that narrative.

Whether public, private, or nonprofit, the framework summarized in Exhibit 1.1 provides a moral context against which organizational leaders and their governing boards can test and align their mission with a larger public good. Organizational dialogue that sharpens the moral purpose of the organization helps to check the undue influence of vested interest groups, major donors, primary partners, and contracting organizations. In addition, as the bright-line distinction among the sectors continues to blur, the American legal and moral framework in Exhibit 1.1 provides a common anchor for an array of public, private, and nonprofit partner organizations as they engage in policymaking, resource allocation, and service delivery for a diverse community polity.

The typology in Exhibit 1.1 describes a wide variety of constitutional approaches to the study and practice of public administration—approaches based on legal and constitutional foundations. Those who take a regime-centered approach emphasize foundational legal values and principles; these values and principles are embedded in governing institutions that undergo change over time. Those who embrace a value-centered approach are inclined to place less emphasis on institutions and more emphasis on the core values memorialized either implicitly or explicitly in the U.S. Constitution and the Declaration of Independence. Core regime values can be used to critique and reform institutions that are discriminatory, ossified, and give privileged access to the few. Legal structuralists place priority on mechanisms like checks and balances, separation of powers, federalism, and the Bill of Rights as the anchoring pillars for the American rule-of-law system. Legal functionalists emphasize the role that administrators play in carrying out their human resource, budgeting, management information, citizen engagement, policy evaluation, and implementation functions. Process-centered legal approaches emphasize the role administrators play in a variety of legal processes, including administrative rulemaking, hybrid rulemaking, negotiated rulemaking, contracting, purchasing, and all of the related legal processes that require administrators to make use of their knowledge and skills in legal interpretation.

Legal approaches to public administration share the same kind of divisions found among judges on our appeals and state and federal supreme courts. At one end are the loose constructionists, who emphasize the values, purposes, and history more than the strict letter of the law to guide their understanding and meaning of legal principles. At the other end are those who are more "positive law" in their approach, emphasizing the legal doctrines and literal language of statutes, rules, and court opinions to guide their understanding of the limits and scope of administrative discretion. This approach is captured in Exhibit 1.1 under the heading Doctrinal and Formalistic Approaches.

Exhibit 1.1 **Typology of Constitutional Approaches to Public Administration**

| Type of Approach | Characteristics | Exemplars |
|---|---|---|
| Regime-centered | • Emphasis on the character-forming and value-generating nature of governance and the roles public administrators play<br>• Focus on the underlying philosophic principles unique to each political system and subsystem<br>• Emphasis on the emergence of political legacies that create and inform administrative traditions<br>• Emphasis on the foundational tensions upon which the political systems rests<br>• Constitutionalist school of PA<br>• Regime vs. science-centered PA | Cooper, P. 2003. *Governing by Contract*<br>Cooper, T. 1991. *An Ethic of Citizenship . . .*<br>Elkin 2006. *Reconstructing the Commercial Republic*<br>Elkin and Soltan 1993. *A New Constitutionalism*<br>Morgan, Green, Shinn, Robinson 2008. *Foundations of Public Service*<br>Morgan et al. 2010. "Recovering, Restoring, and Renewing the Foundations of American PA"<br>Newbold 2010. "Toward a Constitutional School for American PA"<br>Richardson 1997. *Democracy, Bureaucracy and Character*<br>Rohr 1986. *To Run a Constitution*<br>Rohr 1978. *Ethics for Bureaucrats*<br>Rosenbloom 1971. *Federal Service and the Constitution*<br>Spicer 1995. *The Founders, the Constitution and PA*<br>Storing 1981a. *The Complete Anti-Federalist*<br>Storing 1981b. *What the Anti-Federalists Were For*<br>Van Riper 1983. *History of the U.S. Civil Service*<br>White, L.D. See administrative history series: 1958, 1954, 1951, and 1948. |
| Value-centered | • Emphasis on central constitutional values<br>• Use of cases to illustrate development of values over time<br>• Focus more on the goals and purposes of the Constitution than doctrinal case law as the source of guiding values<br>• Emphasis is normative and institutional<br>• Value pluralism in constitutional tradition | Cooper, P. 2003. *Governing by Contract*<br>Cooper and Vargas 2008. *Sustainable Development in Crisis Conditions*<br>Cooper and Vargas 2004. *Implementing Sustainable Development*<br>Cooper, T. 1991. *The Responsible Administrator*<br>Frederickson 1996. *The Spirit of PA*<br>Frederickson 1982. "The Recovery of Civism"<br>Jeavons 2001. "Ethics in Nonprofit Management"<br>Marini 1971. *Toward a New PA*<br>Rohr 1989, 1978. *Ethics for Bureaucrats*<br>Stivers 2002a. *Gender Images in PA*<br>Stivers 2002b. *Bureau Men, Settlement Women*<br>Spicer 2010. *In Defense of Politics in PA*<br>Terry, L. 1995. *Leadership of Public Bureaucracies* |

| | | |
|---|---|---|
| Structuralist | • Emphasis on the structure of the Constitution<br>• Cases used to illustrate the changing relationship of the government to the nonprofit, private and public sector, the changing nature of federalism, and the changing nature of the relationship among the legislative, executive, and judicial branches of government<br>• Emphasis on the "problematic" of balancing competing democratic goals/values<br>• Focus on the balancing role administrators play in structural arrangements that institutionalize competing constitutional values<br>• Organization theory and the Constitution | Box 1998. *Citizen Governance*<br>Burke 1988. *Bureaucratic Responsibility*<br>Cook 1996. *Bureaucracy and Self-Government*<br>Cooper, P. 2009, 2005, 2003, 1988<br>Morgan, Green, Shinn, Robinson. 2008. *Foundation of Public Service*<br>Morgan et al. 1996. "What Middle Managers Do in Local Government"<br>Newbold 2008. "Teaching Organization Theory from a Constitutional Perspective"<br>Rohr 1986. *To Run a Constitution*<br>Rosenbloom 2000. *Building a Legislative-Centered PA*<br>Wamsley et al. 1990. *Refounding PA* |
| Process-centered | • Emphasis on legal reasoning in relationship to the reasoning characteristic of administrative work<br>• Emphasis on the unique constitutional role administrators play in the process of policy development and implementation<br>• Emphasis on the role relationship of administrators and elected officials in local governments which rely on "fused power" models of governance | Carver 2001. "Setting Limits"<br>Cooper, P. 2003. *Governing by Contract*<br>Green 2002b. "Common Law, Equity, and American PA"<br>Morgan, D. 1990. "Administrative Phronesis"<br>Spicer and Terry 1996. "Administrative Interpretation of Statutes" |
| Functionalist | • Emphasis on administrative functions, such as personnel policy, budgeting, policy development and implementation<br>• Use of cases to illustrate development of functional policies over time<br>• Emphasis on legal principles and doctrines to inform and guide administrative functions | Cooper, P. 2005a. *Cases on Public Law and PA*<br>Ott 2001. *Understanding Nonprofit Organizations*<br>Rosenbloom 2003. *Administrative Law for Public Managers* |
| Doctrinal and formalistic approaches | • Emphasis on the development of constitutional doctrines in relationship to public administration<br>• Emphasis on the importance of doctrinal legal principles to guide administrative practice and educate administrators | Cooper, P. 2007. *Public Law and PA*<br>Cooper, P. 2002. *By Order of the President*<br>Hammack 1998. *Making the Nonprofit Sector in the U.S.*<br>Rosenbloom 1985. *Public Personnel Policy*<br>Rosenbloom 1971. *Federal Service and the Constitution* |

*(continued)*

Exhibit 1.1 *(continued)*

| | | |
|---|---|---|
| Methodological | • Normative—reasoning about principles and ends as much as means<br>• Interpretive—emphasis on derivation and construction of meaning, entails imagination and judgment as well as analysis. Oriented to tacit knowledge<br>• Historical—contextual, evolutionary, synthesizing, pragmatic and critical<br>• Casuistic—reasoning by analogy from cases. Structured around doctrines, conventions, principles<br>• Institutional—focus on roles, integrity of processes and practices<br>• Comparative—contextual, critical, and perspectival | In addition to all of the previously cited works, see:<br>Green and Zinke 1993. "The Rhetorical Way of Knowing and PA"<br>Rohr 2002. *Civil Servants and Their Constitutions*<br>Rohr 1995. *Founding Republics in France and America*<br>Spicer 2010. *In Defense of Politics in PA*<br>Spicer 1995. *The Founders, the Constitution, and PA* |
| Historical | • Emphasis on tying PA practices and institutions to a regime's history and culture<br>• Emphasis on history as the source of administrative values and the meaning of practice<br>• Emphasis on political rationality over scientific rationality<br>• Emphasis on civil association vs. purposive state | Cook, B. 1996. *Bureaucracy and Self-Government*<br>Hammack 1998. *Making the Nonprofit Sector in the U.S.*<br>Morgan et al. 2008. *Foundations of Public Service*<br>Spicer 2010. *In Defense of Politics in PA*<br>Spicer 1995. *The Founders, the Constitution, and PA*<br>Storing. 1981a. *The Complete Anti-Federalist*<br>Storing. 1981b. *What the Anti-Federalists Were For*<br>Van Riper. 1983. *History of the U.S. Civil Service*<br>White, L. See administrative history series: 1958, 1954, 1951, 1948 |

*Source:* This is an expanded version of a paper originally presented by Douglas Morgan and Rick Green at the Southern Political Science Association meeting in New Orleans, March 2008.

To summarize, the debate among the scholars in Exhibit 1.1 is over where one looks to find and give legal meaning to public administration values. Some legal scholars look to concrete statutes, court opinions, administrative rules, and other variations on the "black letter of the law." Others look more broadly to the federal and state constitutions as whole, or to the purposes and intent of the American founders. Still others look to history and the embeddedness of values in social and political institutions. But regardless of their source of inspiration, all scholars in Exhibit 1.1 share the assumption that politics—not substantive and methodological expertise in the science of administration—is the starting and ending point of public administration. This is also the starting and ending point for the second edition of this book.

In restoring the unique political role that administrators play in the democratic governance process, we hope this book will assist career public servants at all levels and in all sectors to better understand the formative role they can play in making our multiple democratic systems of government work. For example, they are obligated to serve as Balancewheels that help protect our regime of ordered liberty from its own inherent weaknesses or extremes. They must sustain administrative practices and make astute discretionary choices toward that end. They also contribute to, or obstruct, the infusion of democratic principles and practices in our governing institutions, thus affecting their impact on other sectors of civil society.

Playing these roles successfully requires legal, political, and ethical competencies as much as, or perhaps more than, technical expertise. Public administrators need to know how to build as well as reform public institutions—how to develop and sustain practices that integrate contending interests and values, and then adapt them to changing circumstances. Governance in this sense is a form of institutional politics marked by complicated relationships between public administrators, their political and judicial superiors, and the public at large. We explore these relationships in an effort to promote a better understanding of the nature of administrative responsibility in the American governing system. This is not an easy task because administrative responsibility in the United States is not a settled matter. It remains a rather complicated and controversial topic, which means that public administrators face serious difficulty in articulating a legitimate basis for the exercise of their discretionary powers. Nevertheless, a variety of theories have been developed that offer varying degrees of insight. We attempt to weave aspects of these theories into a workable synthesis that will help administrators engage in responsible democratic governance.

## THE PLAN OF THIS BOOK

As the table of contents indicates, this book is divided into four parts. At the beginning of each part, we provide a case study that underpins the discussion in subsequent chapters. Students are strongly encouraged to read each introductory case first and then look for ways in which the theories and insights provided in the following chapters can help one deal with the issues presented in that case. In addition, we employ many shorter cases, vignettes, and examples within each chapter to help demonstrate the practical significance of the historical traditions, theories, and general ideas described in the text.

Chapter 2 (the initial chapter in Part I) reviews the common challenges and opportunities of public service, and chapter 3 illustrates the centrality of various types of administrative discretion as a source of power and responsibility. This sets the stage for the remaining chapters of Part I, which present our historically informed and institutionally grounded constitutional approach to the theory and practice of public service. Chapter 4 begins with the relationship between democracy and administration as it evolved during the founding era. This entails a brief review of the political theories that informed the founders' thinking and the ways in which they wove contending notions

of ideal republics and good citizenship into the design of our Constitution. Here we introduce readers to the basic tensions the founders experienced in trying to integrate their personal experiences and formal knowledge into a practical model of democratic governance that could survive over time. We focus this analysis on the four vexing problems they faced in balancing liberty with democratic governance. In chapter 5, we describe four early models of public service and administration that are identified with prominent founding fathers. Each of these models emerged in response to a different set of threats to democratic governance. We then describe the troubled evolution of these models through watershed historical eras to the current day, illustrating in the process how that history still matters. Each era leaves a legacy that informs our practices today. Chapter 6 culminates with a presentation of our approach to administrative ethics and responsibility that draws from the previous chapters and integrates four evolving administrative traditions into a Balancewheel model of the public interest. The model is then applied in the succeeding parts of the book that address the traditionally understood functions and roles of public servants, demonstrating along the way the model's relevance to each.

Part II begins with chapter 7, an examination of the evolving theories of organization structure and behavior. We use our Democratic Balancewheel model to assess the strengths and weaknesses of these theories. Most of the models of structure and behavior in organizations have been developed from managerial, economic, sociological, psychological, and political science disciplines, all of which add important perspectives for understanding what counts for successful organizational structure and management. What is frequently missing, however, is the role played by the normative values and practices that are unique to public service in the United States. The remaining chapters in Part II focus on the basic question of who should rule in a democratic republic that is committed to individual liberty. In chapter 8, we review the political history of public personnel administration in terms of four broad qualifications for office and examine how the meaning of each qualification changed in the different political eras from the founding period to the current day. Each era's dominant view of appropriate qualifications for office posed conundrums relative to the abiding tensions in our governing system, and again leaves a legacy that informs our current practices. Chapter 9 addresses contemporary issues faced by human resource managers, reviews the field's basic functions in light of those issues, and relates this analysis to our administrative traditions and model of administrative responsibility.

The chapters in Part III (10 and 11) relate the issues and practices of modern public finance and budgeting to the Balancewheel model, again exposing the enduring tensions that dramatically affect the types and means of public finance as well as the various budgeting systems that public servants try to put into practice. The subject of raising, managing, and allocating revenue according to public priorities is consistently one of the most contested matters of public life, requiring far more in the way of political art than any kind of science. As with human resources management, understanding how the Balancewheel applies to public finance and budgeting can help greatly in coping with the ongoing controversies, but there is no magical formula for making these controversies disappear. That is because they emanate from contested views as to what democratic governance requires for the sake of both legitimacy and effectiveness.

The four chapters in Part IV address management issues in public organizations. In chapter 12, we emphasize leadership roles in the context of shared power—an idea that is integral to the U.S. system of governance but is also increasingly relevant to the rapidly emerging global contexts where power is shared among nations, corporations, and NGOs. Networks of leadership and influence have in many cases overtaken and transformed older bureaucratic systems that are less adaptive in a globalized world. A growing array of administrative tools have been created and adapted for use in these networks as well as in host countries. There are limits, however, to this adaptability,

and it is up to leaders at all levels to sense when adaptations threaten the integrity of governing systems at home and abroad. Recalling the words of Alexander Hamilton, we must still fit the administrative "coat to the individual." Chapter 13 tackles the role of subordinate public servants in policymaking and analysis—a topic that merits further explanation. (It is often treated as an unacceptable perversion in instrumental conceptions of public service.) We review the standard models of policymaking and analysis in the context of our Balancewheel model, exposing their shortcomings as well as their insights relative to the model. In Chapter 14, we review the types of external accountability that are present in the policymaking and implementation process, illustrating just how much of that process is managed through administrative law. In effect, we circle back to our chapter on administrative ethics and responsibility and to the centrality of rule by law to public governance in the United States. In the final chapter (15), we discuss the significant drivers of change that we believe will challenge our ability to govern effectively according to the values central to public service roles within the American political system. We end with a case study that illustrates a successful response to some of these drivers on the coordinative machinery of a local county's criminal justice and social services systems. The case shows how administrative leaders use their discretion to change the way basic government business gets done. This redefining role represents the highest aspiration for public service leaders, especially when it leaves a legacy that preserves the core constitutional values of the American democratic system of government.

# PART I

## PUBLIC ORGANIZATIONS AND DEMOCRATIC GOVERNANCE

# THE CASE OF THE ANGRY LIBRARY PATRON

## CASE DESCRIPTION

Cheryl Miller was working quietly on her monthly administrative report to her supervisor and doing double duty at the library circulation desk when an angry father dragging a six-year-old child by the hand confronted her unexpectedly.

"Why is this kind of book on the children's bookshelves? It clearly is unfit reading and should be removed immediately to another section of the library."

This is not what you, the children's librarian at a local branch library, need to hear on this particular day. Two of your clerks failed to appear for work today because of icy road conditions; however, that did not seem to stop the hordes of school kids who flocked to the library to pass the time of day. Having worked without a break checking out books all day at the circulation desk, you will have to spend the evening completing your budget request for the next fiscal year in order to meet the 8:00 A.M. deadline set by your library director.

As a professional children's librarian, you resent the endless hours of administrative tasks that take you away from what you most enjoy and have been best prepared to carry out: selecting and recommending good literature to children and their parents. You've been having second thoughts about whether you really are cut out for your current position. There is just too much time spent on keeping track of employee hours, preparing budgets, undertaking personnel evaluations, and responding to patrons' complaints. You find yourself thinking about what it might be like to work in a larger library system—one that would allow you to make better use of the knowledge and skills you've gained through years of rigorous study. Then, you are suddenly jolted into the reality of this training by a distraught parent who insists that he, not you, should make the choices about the suitability of children's library selections.

You notice that the book in question is a copy of Maurice Sendak's *In the Night Kitchen*, one of the most popular children's stories of the past four decades and a 1971 Caldecott Honor Book. You've dealt with this kind of situation before, so you politely give your standardized response: "We encourage parents to help their children select material that is appropriate to their interests and level of reading skill. Could I help you find a more suitable book?"

"That's not the point. Both the nudity and bizarre images in this book make it unsuitable reading for any kids under the age of ten. I want it removed from the children's section of the collection to the juvenile section."

As the line of patrons waiting to check out books begins to build, you see that your efforts are not going to prevail. So you resort to another technique that has usually worked in the past. You give the angry patron a form to put his objections in writing, which usually ends the matter.

That did not happen in this case. The following week, the director of the library hands you the following letter from the angry patron, Charles Jones, with a request to draft a response that can be sent out under the library director's signature. She gives you a sample letter that was mailed last week to another library patron who had a complaint about the appropriateness of having *The Joy of Gay Sex* in the library collection.

## CASE SUPPORTING MATERIALS

### Patron's Complaint Form for Library Materials

Your Name:      Charles Jones
Your Address:   2004 SW Happy Lane
Title:          *In the Night Kitchen*
Author:         Maurice Sendak

1. *What do you find objectionable about the material?* (Please be specific and cite pages, etc.)
   Specifically, the nudity of male genitals and the fanciful and unrealistic images.

2. *Why do you object to the material?*
   The nudity is not suitable for young children who will have access to this material in the library, especially when reading books unsupervised after school or on weekends. Many of the images frighten young children and encourage an unhealthy attitude toward the unreal and supernatural.

3. *Did you read the material in its entirety?*
   Yes.

4. *What do you believe is the theme of the material?*
   Magic is responsible for producing the things we most like in life, i.e., cake.

5. *Do you think that people who want to read this material should be able to find it in the library?*
   Not paid for by public tax dollars.

6. *Do you think groups or other members of the community should have the right to keep you from having access to materials you want if they disapprove of your viewpoint?*
   Yes, especially when books like this are harmful to others.

7. *Do you believe that parents have the right and responsibility for guiding their own children's reading and deciding what limits, if any, they place upon it?*
   Yes, of course, but they need the help of professionals and adults—especially when they cannot be supervised by their parents.

8. *Do you think other people should be able to tell you what you or your children should or should not read?*

Yes. This happens all the time. Schools and libraries don't have money to buy everything. They have to make choices. This is what we pay our professional librarians and teachers to do. Some parents either do not pay attention to what their children are reading or do not understand the kind of harm that some books can have on the development of their children. That is why we trust professionals like you to assist us.

9. *Are you usually able to find what you want in the library? If not, what materials would you like to be able to find in the library collection?*
   Yes.

Date:          June 26, 2012
Signature:     Charles Jones

<div align="center">

Happy Valley Regional Library
2404 Happy Valley Road
Happy Valley

LIBRARIES to be proud of!

</div>

**Draft Letter to Library Patron**

July 8, 2012

Dear _____:

Thank you for expressing your opinion of the book *The Joy of Gay Sex* by Dr. Charles Silverstein and Edmund White. The library's Selection Review Committee has reviewed the material and the issues you have raised.

As you have noted, the book is an illustrated manual on adult male homosexual practices. You have asked that the book be removed from the collection because it provides information on sexual practices that may result in the transmission of the AIDS virus.

*The Joy of Gay Sex* was first published in 1977, prior to the identification of the AIDS virus, and therefore does not mention it specifically. However, it does include a section on the dangers of sexually transmitted diseases and the importance of practicing "safe sex." It also recommends frequent medical examinations. Finally, when discussing potentially dangerous sexual practices, the authors provide explicit information on possible harm.

*The Joy of Gay Sex* has been in the library's collection for more than 10 years. It has been useful to a variety of people in our community. It continues to be an important book for male homosexuals. They recommend that it be read along with more recently published materials on the prevention of AIDS.

In addition, this book is used frequently by people seeking information on male homosexual lifestyles. An article by Gary Bullert published in both the *Conservative Review* (February 1990) and the *Journal of the American Family Association* (April 1990) offers an example of how this book has been used by

people who are not homosexuals. While opposing the gay rights movement, Bullert, highly recommends *The Joy of Gay Sex* as one of the two best sources of information on homosexual lifestyles.

American democracy is dependent upon a free flow of ideas, many of which conflict with each other. The library's responsibility is to provide information on as many points of view as possible. For example, we believe that readers on both sides of the spectrum—from those groups strongly opposed to homosexuality, like the American Family Association, to practicing male homosexuals and other people who wish to inform themselves about gay issues—should have unencumbered library access to information about homosexual lifestyles and practices. *The Joy of Gay Sex* continues to fill this need. Therefore, we have decided to retain it in the collection.

The Happy Valley Regional Library, which serves three counties and 13 cities, has a number of books on AIDS and we will continue to add new titles as they become available. If there are titles you would like to recommend, we will be happy to consider them for inclusion in the collection.

We appreciate the concern that prompted you to express your opinion. The issues you raised are serious.

We are pleased that you usually find the reading and reference materials you seek in your local public library.

Sincerely,

Constance Harmony
Library Director

Happy Valley Regional Library
2404 Happy Valley Road
Happy Valley

LIBRARIES to be proud of!

## CASE ANALYSIS

What should Cheryl Miller do under the circumstances described above? This case raises at least four different levels of conflict that cannot be resolved successfully without taking into account one's responsibilities as a steward of our constitutional system of government. There is, first of all, one's responsibility to ensure the efficient and effective delivery of the services outlined in the Happy Valley Regional Library's organizational mission. Second, there are one's own personal values, which may be more or less consistent with the mission of the organization and/or the application of that mission to the circumstances at hand. Third, as a children's librarian, one is trained as a professional to make use of a specialized body of knowledge and skills. Additionally, in this case, there is a fourth responsibility: to act in a manner that is consistent with the larger structure of constitutional procedures and values within which one works.

As a member of a hierarchical organization, Cheryl must necessarily consider the impact of her response on other standard operating procedures and on the efficiency of the organization as

a whole. How should she phrase a response that can be used in other similar circumstances? How might her response encourage or discourage other similar communications from angry parents? How much time and energy should be spent on this assignment at the expense of other activities that will improve the quality and amount of service to patrons in the local community? Is Mr. Jones's letter part of an organized campaign by a local organization to obtain greater community control over the purchase of and access to library materials? The kinds of questions that Cheryl raises, and how such questions are answered, are influenced first by what will best contribute to the efficient and effective running of the organization, and second by the understanding she has of her personal, professional, and larger stewardship roles.

Previously, Cheryl found herself in an uncomfortable position responding to teenage requests for appropriate reading material on birth control. Her personal religious views are very much opposed to making this material available, especially when the parents are not involved in the process. However, since the library has a policy of allowing children and teenagers to check out materials without the consent of their parents, her personal views have not had an opportunity to influence the administration of policy. In the case at hand, her personal views could very well shape the tone and structure of her response to Mr. Jones, the angry parent.

In some ways, this may be the perfect opportunity for Cheryl to use her discretionary authority to encourage the library staff and governing board to revisit the library's existing policy. While not necessarily supportive of the patron's complaint regarding *In the Knight Kitchen*, she strongly believes the library needs to take a stronger *in loco parentis* role with respect to materials made available to children. And there has been growing pressure from some members of the community that the library require filters on all computers. However, Cheryl questions using the parent's complaint as the occasion to foster a likely contentious community debate on the role of the library in serving under-age adults. There is first of all her duty to the library profession: The code of ethics for librarians commits its members to "resist all efforts to censor library resources," to "distinguish between our personal convictions and professional duties and . . . not allow our personal beliefs to interfere with fair representation of the aims of our institutions or the provision of access to their information resources." In addition, she is confident that the larger issue about which there is considerable disagreement in the community and among members of the library staff is mandatory filtering of all computer terminals available to patrons for their Internet searches. Finally, she has been considering the need to advance her career elsewhere within a larger library system where she would have more program management responsibility and less responsibility for direct service delivery.

In the final analysis, this case also implicates larger values of our constitutional system of government. There is, of course, a foundational requirement to be responsive to the needs of the people you serve. But what does responsiveness require in this case? What are the terms upon which discourse between Cheryl Miller and Charles Jones should take place? The complaint provides a unique educational opportunity for members of the library staff to engage citizens on issues that go to the very heart of our democratic system of government. Where should we draw the line between parental authority and public organizational responsibility? Yes, parents need the help of public organizations in carrying out their parental roles, but how far should this help go? Should it stop with the advice from professional librarians about the contents of a given book and the appropriateness of that content to the intellectual and social maturity of the potential reader? Even to be this minimally responsive requires an intimate knowledge of each individual client, which is unlikely. In this respect, librarians must function as teachers, psychologists, members of the clergy, therapists, and others who administer to the needs of the public. But this kind of intimate familiarity with those being served is neither necessary nor possible.

It is not possible because organizations are constructed around abstractions. Cheryl Miller functions in an organizational environment that has some notion of the average child, the typical parent, the presumed standards of acceptability within the local community, and so on. Books are purchased, collections are developed, and levels of service are defined based on considerations drawn from the needs of this or that particular patron or client. This necessity for abstraction is made into a virtue, especially in the public sector, where organizations like libraries are purposely created to meet the needs of citizens, not simply individuals. Thus, the notion that a librarian needs to be responsive to readers opens up larger questions about the nature of the community and the relationship of the library to its citizens.

These larger questions are troublesome for Cheryl Miller. She has thought about the possibility of other groups and individuals objecting to the choices the library has made about its collection and the access to it. She has wondered what might happen if the appointed library board is pulled into the debate by Mr. Jones. Given the existing membership on the board, Cheryl believes this would likely lead to a change in the existing library policy, making access more restrictive than it has been in the past. While this might bring the world more into conformance with her personal views, she questions whether it would be a good thing for the library and for the community at large. Since the members of the Regional Library Board are appointed by the County Board of Commissioners in three separate counties, how adequately do the appointed board members reflect the sentiment of the community? And even if they did, to what extent should minority views be held subservient to a dominant local majority that restricts the freedom to read, either by placing limits on what is purchased and/or on who can obtain access to it? These questions trouble Cheryl as she ponders her assigned task to respond to Mr. Jones's letter.

In the chapters that follow, we will explore these issues in much greater detail. Chapter 2 examines the central role that career officials play in preserving the legitimacy of American constitutional governance through the exercise of their administrative discretion. Chapter 3 explores the distinct discretionary role that career administrators play at each level of organizational responsibility: first-line supervisors, middle managers, and executive leaders. Chapter 4 continues the discussion of administrative discretion by shifting the focus to an institutional perspective and the long-debated relationship between democracy and bureaucracy. At the state and federal levels of government, our systems are characterized by separation of powers and checks and balances, which create executive, legislative, and judicial masters for career administrators. The issues are not so clear in local levels of government, where authority may be divided across jurisdictional boundaries and where official policymaking is in the hands of part-time appointed officials who are not directly accountable to the voters through the electoral process. This is the situation with Cheryl Miller, who works in a regional library system that is controlled by three counties but serves 13 separate cities. Whom does Cheryl Miller serve? What is the best approach for gauging accountability in the exercise of her discretion? Chapter 5 revisits the issue of administrative role responsibility from a historical perspective, examining the evolutionary changes in the role of the career public service in the United States over the past 236 years. We complete our discussion of the role responsibility of career public administrators in chapter 6, where we review the multiple ethical responsibilities that compete for the loyalty of our career public servants. By the end of chapter 6, each of us should be in a better position to assess what Cheryl Miller should do, and to justify our choice in terms of the core democratic values that guide our administrative work as stewards of our many and varied American systems of democratic governance.

CHAPTER 2

# THE CHALLENGES AND OPPORTUNITIES OF PUBLIC SERVICE

The image of public administration presented in eighteen introductory college texts in American government . . . overwhelmingly stressed what was regarded as bureaucracy's size and permanence, its unintelligible language and political power, and its uncontrollability. . . . Not one of them made any reference at all to the profession of public administration or the call to public service.

*(Charles Goodsell 2004, 3)*

There is now no ideology with pretensions to universality that is in a position to challenge liberal democracy, and no universal principle of legitimacy other than the sovereignty of the people.

*(Francis Fukuyama 1992, 45)*

Consider the following brief scenarios:

1. A city council and its city manager debate whether to allow more apartment complexes to be built in the city to accommodate lower-paid workers who serve a predominantly affluent population. The police chief and some influential home and business owners provide a wealth of data that demonstrates a high correlation between such complexes and rapidly rising crime rates, declining real estate values in adjacent neighborhoods, and a tarnished sense of "quality of life."
2. Administrators and doctors in a local private hospital heatedly debate whether people on Medicaid should be denied care because reimbursement rates from federal and state governments are so low that the hospital cannot cover its costs.
3. Local housing authority officials try to take advantage of some new property acquisitions in a declining industrial district of their city. They develop an economical plan for housing the chronically homeless population there but face stiff resistance from social service providers who insist that both the design and location are inappropriate given the characteristics and treatment regimens of their clients.
4. Building-inspection officers in a southwestern city deliberate over how, if at all, they should adapt their uniform building codes to economical building designs that employ

innovations such as straw-bale construction. An increasing number of permit requests from property owners include such designs.

5.  A U.S. Bureau of Land Management (BLM) permit officer in a western regional office is inundated with requests for expedited natural gas drilling permits. Given sharply higher market prices, oil and natural gas firms are very impatient. They offer a proposal to assist the BLM in processing permits through a contract-for-services agreement. Congressional representatives from western states have spoken favorably of the idea.

These short vignettes describe typical problems faced by professional administrators who operate through governmental, nonprofit, and for-profit organizations to serve the public. Their work is challenging and at times very frustrating, but it is also interesting and motivating. The complications of their work present opportunities to make a real difference in the daily lives of citizens. In short, their work matters, and that is a major reason why so many people choose public service careers.

As Charles Goodsell notes in the opening quotation of this chapter, the textbooks on American government ignore this reality in favor of characterizations that are generally negative and suspicious about career public servants and their agencies. These texts help socialize high school and college students to an abiding distrust of "bureaucrats" and "bureaucracy"—terms laden with pejorative meaning. As we shall see, there is nothing new about the distrust of Americans for those who hold governing power. It is an abiding disposition in American culture that is also profoundly dedicated to democratic principles. Americans fully embrace Francis Fukuyama's testament to popular sovereignty.

This book explores these contradictions between America's devotion to democracy, its distrust of administrative institutions that give effect to people's demands, and the obscured reality that most public servants find their work inherently satisfying. We do not intend to resolve these contradictions. That is not possible and may not even be desirable. However, we do hope to shed light on them and in the process of doing so reinforce the commitment that many have made to public service careers. Goodsell's statement reflects his concern that distrust of governing institutions may overwhelm an equally long-held conviction among Americans that public service involves an important and noble calling. We share his concern. Sobering studies of the public service indicate that it is a field in crisis (cf. Light 2010, 1999a, 1999b; Volcker 2003). It no longer attracts the kind of talent it once took for granted, and it is rapidly losing the talent it has. Many public service organizations are expected to lose through retirements up to 50 percent of its middle- and upper-level leadership before the end of the decade (Young 2005, 2003; Lazenby 2009).

In drawing attention to the high calling of public service, we will not sugarcoat the nature of the work. It is often stressful and complicated, but it is also rewarding. We offer a full and balanced exploration of the character of public work not only to build more appreciation for it but also to help those working or seeking work in public service to better understand its context of competing purposes and institutional dynamics. Our aim is to enhance public service competency.

## THE IRONY OF AMERICAN DEMOCRATIC GOVERNANCE

There is great irony in the fact that America is widely heralded as the most successful liberal democracy in the world, while those who are its caretakers are generally held in very low esteem. This irony plays out on a daily basis as we witness constant efforts to place ever more popular checks on our public servants while simultaneously urging them to conduct government "more like a business." In fact, our affection for democracy seems inversely related to affection for those who are responsible on a daily basis for making the system work on our behalf. Why is this?

In large part, this incongruity stems from our long tradition of distrust of governing power—a sense of distrust so strong that it fueled colonial unrest, a revolution, and a civil war that nearly tore apart a newly formed American nation. Beginning in the seventeenth century, many immigrants fled oppressive regimes and arrived on the shores of the New World determined to establish governments that would closely represent their interests. Limited electoral terms at top levels, jealous oversight of administration, and vigorous scrutiny through a free press would provide the means to ensure a government strictly accountable to citizen interests. In short, suspicion of power and authority has become high political doctrine among Americans, sewn as deeply in our breasts as our devotion to democracy and individual rights.

Our current era displays many of the familiar political conflicts that sustain the historic distrust of government. Contentious issues over states' rights versus a powerful national government have reemerged in the twenty-first century, as have debates over the role of our governments in the economy. The regulated economy has been challenged in favor of laissez-faire policies that promote a more freely operating business environment, but this has also prompted bitter reaction by consumer, labor, and environmental advocates. Taxpayers have reasserted their disdain for taxes, while taking for granted a plethora of public goods and services. Some advocate for government spending to stimulate the economy, care for vulnerable citizens, and build infrastructure; others are increasingly alarmed at the growing government debt, especially unfunded liabilities of state and local governments for pensions and other postemployment benefits. Collins and Rettenmaier (2010) analyzed 153 state and local pension plans, representing more than 85 percent of liabilities for state and local pensions and other benefits, and recalculated their liabilities using a lower discount rate. Their calculations show:

Unfunded pension liabilities are approximately $2.5 trillion, compared to the reported amount of $493 billion.

Unfunded liabilities for health and other benefits are $558 billion, compared to the reported $537 billion.

Thus, total unfunded liabilities for all benefit plans are an estimated $3.1 trillion—nearly three times higher than the plans report.

In the face of these economic challenges, many government functions and services are again subject to privatization in the effort to make governments smaller, which then breeds more suspicion of improper influence and corruption by contractors and lobbyists. Mistrust is compounded, in turn, by a deepening cultural rift between those seeking to preserve or restore aspects of a traditional social life and those seeking liberation from the moral and legal restrictions imposed by such bonds. In all of these conflicts, government is simultaneously demonized as a contributing cause of affliction and beseeched to intervene with solutions.

Public servants find themselves pitted squarely in the middle of these dilemmas. Many of them enjoy the challenges, seeing in them opportunities to achieve worthwhile agendas for their neighborhood, community, state, or nation. Others enjoy mediating the conflicts, helping people find livable compromises, and drawing people together around some common ground for sustained action. Still others seek to bring the benefits of technical and professional training to the public, hoping to transcend or bypass conflict by devising expert solutions. But some public servants gradually become dispirited or even jaded by the perennial attacks on their roles, their legitimacy, and their efficacy. Some burn out and leave the public service for more peaceful and prosperous work in other sectors. The challenges are daunting and often confusing, and while the conflict over specific issues ebbs and flows, there is no cure for the underlying tensions that give rise to them. These tensions are deeply rooted in the American constitutional tradition.

This text explores the ideas that undergird these tensions and traces the effects of their interaction on the many practices that comprise American public administration. We believe that improved understanding of the relationship between bureaucracy and democracy will help new students as well as experienced public servants gain a greater appreciation for the significance of public service, while providing some important bearings and context to guide them in the proper exercise of their discretionary powers.

We focus on American systems of democratic governance, rather than just the American national system, in order to highlight the incredible scope of administrative practices and the plurality of jurisdictions and organizations—the vast majority of which are small and local in character. The immense variety of administrative practices suggests that neither "management" nor "administration" should be conceived of as a uniform endeavor.

For example, water bureau administrators go about their work quite differently if they (1) operate as a single-purpose taxing district, (2) exist as a department within a general-purpose government (city/county/borough), or (3) function within a regional governmental consortium. Even officials working in general-purpose jurisdictions must account for the differences among county, borough, and township governments that have full-time chief administrators and those that do not. Many jurisdictions have separately elected officers such as auditor, clerk, prosecutor, and sheriff, which further shapes the way in which administrative discretion is exercised. In addition, administrators must work differently if services are provided with in-house government staff, or with some mix of in-house staff and contracted services. Similarly, some jurisdictions rely heavily, if not exclusively, on nonprofit organizations to provide a variety of social services that often involve volunteers in service delivery activities. Moreover, within any complex organization, administrative practices vary by level of responsibility and by function or purpose. For example, the work of task-focused, street-level supervisors differs dramatically from the coordination roles of middle managers. Regulating clean water requires different skills than building sewer systems, administering a social service program, or engaging in community policing. Public administrators practice under an amazingly wide variety of organizations, political and community contexts, and tasks.

Our hope throughout the book is that readers will gain greater appreciation for public service writ large, which includes service in the general government, special district, nonprofit and for-profit sectors of the economy. We also hope that career administrators from all sectors will gain an understanding of the central role they play as active agents of our systems of democratic governance. In their role as democratic stewards, career public servants help maintain the legitimacy of our democratic institutions, including those in the for-profit and nonprofit sectors as well as institutions that sit somewhere in between. Through their constant contact with citizens and the communities tied to the different sectors, career officials give daily witness to what democratic governance means. Each governmental encounter, however small and seemingly insignificant, provides an opportunity to learn more about the problems, prospects, and responsibilities of democratic governance. Helping students understand the importance of maintaining the legitimacy of democratic government is the first major theme of this book.

We also emphasize that the knowledge and responsibilities of career public servants as applied to administrative processes and structures constitute a *practice*. Like other practices, public administration requires standards and skills that must be cultivated and tempered by working in the field and in concert with others, not just studying it as a detached observer. Public servants must gain a feel for their work and understand the context and pressures of their practice.

## LEGITIMACY: THE INSTRUMENTAL AND CONSTITUTIVE ROLE OF ADMINISTRATIVE PRACTICE

As observed earlier, our governments operate under a constant cloud of suspicion. One consequence is that public servants are frequently required to justify the exercise of their authority and power. This ongoing process of justification and legitimation is not simply a matter of finding a rule or a law that authorizes a given course of action. The case of the angry library patron illustrates how the lawful and legitimate exercise of public authority requires a combination of professional training, experience, consultation, engagement, attention to organizational practices, and personal judgment. The case reveals that legitimacy and authority have as much to do with building and maintaining relationships and dialogue with all the players as they do with coming to any particular decision or claiming a legal prerogative.

Consider another example—developing and operating a community policing program. To get such a program started requires countless organizational "get-togethers" involving community groups, police professionals and consultants, and elected policymakers and their staffs. New relationships must be forged, which takes considerable time and significant resources. Leaders in the neighborhoods must be identified and cultivated to help bring others into cooperative policing activities. The program requires new training for officers on how to interact with the public to meet program goals. They must be deployed in new ways, and they too must be convinced that the program is worth the effort. Career administrators are the ones who "keep the ball rolling," prioritize decision making, cultivate trust internally and externally, and sequence the flow of multiple streams of resources. Once a community policing program has been created, think of the wide variety of activities that police officers undertake and coordinate. For example, to remove abandoned vehicles from the streets or to take action against a local drug house, they need to enlist the support of other departments, jurisdictions, local citizens, and community organizations.

In the course of carrying out all of these activities, administrators affect the legitimacy of democratic governance in at least three ways: (1) the processes administrators use to carry out their work helps to shape citizen attitudes about the basic "fairness" of democratic governance; (2) the substantive outcomes of administrative work affect citizen attitudes about whether government is effectively "delivering the goods"; and (3) the constant interplay between public officials and citizens from one activity to another over an extended period of time develops or constitutes the democratic relationships between citizens and officials (Cook 1996). This constitutive work is essential if a rule-of-law system is to maintain popular support and successfully adapt to changing social, political, and economic conditions.

### Process Legitimacy

Even when citizens do not agree with the substantive outcomes of public decisions, they want to know if everyone has played by the same rules of the game, has had an opportunity to be heard, and has been provided with a fair chance of influencing the outcome. Like the outcome of elections, citizens can accept the outcome of administrative initiatives more easily if they believe the process has been conducted fairly.

Public servants in government have a unique set of process expectations that set them apart from their for-profit and nonprofit sector counterparts. While not strictly bound by these procedural steps, nonprofit administrators may need to take similar actions for process legitimacy. Consider for a moment the set of expectations that citizens have of their public servants (see chapter 6 on ethics for a fuller elaboration of these expectations).

*Responsiveness*

Public agencies cannot place a sign above the door that proclaims: "We have the right to refuse service to anyone." Unlike the private sector, public servants deal with people who may not be able to find alternative service providers when they are dissatisfied. As a result, citizens interact with government agencies with heightened expectations regarding responsiveness and respect.

*Legal Correctness*

Public servants must always act in a legally correct fashion, even when doing so does not serve the perceived interests of the citizens. Unlike the private sector, public servants cannot simply give a dissatisfied citizen a replacement item. Driver's licenses and other public privileges have to be administered as legally prescribed, not simply to please one customer or another. This helps avoid favoritism or other undue biases in public decisions.

*Appearance of Fairness*

Even when the law does not require equal treatment and "procedural fairness," citizens expect government and its agents to maintain the appearance of fairness. This often results in more elaborate public notice, access, and time taken to make decisions about even seemingly minor affairs.

*Respect for All Persons*

Whatever else the words "we the people" may mean in the U.S. Constitution, it includes being treated with dignity and respect, regardless of gender, age, sexual orientation, ethnic background, education level, economic status, religion, or emotional or physical capability. The private sector can develop niche markets that cultivate exclusive populations. Public servants are expected to demonstrate equal respect for all, regardless of whom they serve.

## Result-Oriented Legitimacy

Public servants are also judged by their ability "to deliver the goods." Citizens, customers, and nonprofit donors want results, especially in matters that affect them directly. It may be about getting their building permit processed as quickly as possible, or obtaining access to municipal utilities without much hassle or interruption, or keeping their neighborhoods safe and quiet, or seeing the results of their charitable gifts in meals and beds for the homeless. Most public services are delivered unobtrusively, with hardly any thought on the part of citizens about what is required to make the service work. This quiet and trouble-free delivery is usually taken for granted and thereby indicates a significant degree of legitimacy accompanied by a sense of entitlement.

There are also some less obvious ways that public servants foster results-oriented legitimacy through the exercise of their administrative discretion. First, many studies of administrative and organizational behavior have revealed a variety of organizational problems or pathologies that harm employees, erode public accountability, and compromise effectiveness. These findings have prompted continual efforts to make bureaucracies more humane in the sense of providing more personable and enriching working environments, less rigid organizational structures, and less stultifying procedures, and making agencies more representative of the people they serve.

When taken seriously, these administrative reforms alter bureaucratic outcomes and thereby affect administrative legitimacy among employees and the citizens who receive services. These matters are elaborated upon in chapters 4 and 7.

Second, since government mostly produces services with nuanced qualities and value-laden connotations, it ends up having to define what "good service" means. It has to do this at various levels within the organization as well as outwardly to clients and other interested parties (Morgan et al. 1996). Good service standards are difficult to measure in the public sector, which has to reconcile competing public values of satisfaction, need, efficiency, effectiveness, equity, and available resources. This places a burden on public servants to negotiate and mediate conflicting views of what counts for good service. Private for-profit organizations generally have an easier time than public agencies in addressing "good service" problems. In the commercial market, dissatisfied customers can find more accessible, relatively standardized alternatives and simply purchase them from other vendors. In special district governments, the quality of service is often measured by the satisfaction of the target population. But special district governments also face questions about what constitutes good service. For example, parks and recreation districts may need to justify their land use and development decisions, while renewal and development districts may face challenges on just how to welcome and support businesses.

Nonprofit organizations face a mix of market controls and ambiguous standards of service success. Well-developed provider markets in large metropolitan areas offer dissatisfied clients alternate choices of nonprofit, for-profit, and government service providers. Similarly, charitable and philanthropic donors typically have many choices of where and how to donate funds to support community services and organizations. But like governments, nonprofits often provide difficult-to-define services. Human services, health services, and education all depend to a large extent on interpersonal relationships and a number of intangible qualities that stimulate success or failure. The success of museums, theaters, and other art projects rests with personal and community taste and acceptance. The personalized nature of these services may leave clients with a limited number of acceptable alternate providers. Organization-level objections may limit choices even further. Nonprofit providers may be linked to governments or have religious affiliations that limit certain services or require client responsiveness as a condition of service delivery. Clients in rural areas may find themselves with few providers from which to choose. In the end, consumers of a given public service may need to move to another jurisdiction or community to have their needs satisfied.

An additional factor that compounds the problem of defining good service is that it is continually being redefined at all levels of the organization under the constraints of politically established budgets. This redefinition frequently results in nonprofit contractors and partners receiving limited government funding. Street-level bureaucrats and front-line supervisors routinely make trade-offs in the amount of time and effort they devote to competing demands; furthermore, they are obliged to make judgments about how workable any given policy may be in light of the individual cases they encounter. The attention they confer on any given client and to various priorities over a given span of time redefines much of the meaning, as well as effectiveness, of public policy (Lipsky 1980; Vinzant and Crothers 1998). As the question of good service moves upward in the organization, public servants play a central role in negotiating the tension between those at the street level who are concerned about the ability to meet the needs of each individual served, and those above who have to stretch public tax dollars as far as possible. This impulse to stretch dollars predisposes upper levels of administration to base their decisions on more general and formulaic standards, such as average number of clients served, the greatest cost/benefit ratio, the total number of tasks performed, and so on.

As questions of good service reach the top of public organizations, administrators must deal with the ambiguity of what good service means externally to various clientele groups and interested parties. These groups may tend to define good service differently than the individual client being served. Taken together from the very bottom to the very top of public organizations, career public servants invariably play the decisive role in determining the meaning of good service. In so doing, they greatly influence the legitimacy of democratic governance.

## Constitutive Legitimacy

Career administrators also play an important role in redefining what democratic governance means. They do this in a variety of subtle ways, most often driven by changing public values that alter the relationship between the government and civil society (the world of nonprofits and voluntary associations), or the relationship between government and the business sector. The following example illustrates what we mean by *constitutive legitimacy.*

A parks manager is responsible for a large county park and another small neighborhood park. Her span of control is rather small during the winter but grows during the peak summer season with temporary help. A new "County 2012 Plan" mandates that the county will not be in the park expansion and development business. Pressures against this hold-the-line strategy include a large influx of population, a park advisory board, and an enthusiastic group of fans who actively maintain the pressure for park expansion and improvements.

What does the parks manager tell her rangers, her overworked seasonal workers, and the parks advisory board? How does the new plan affect day-to-day service to the park areas? Is "County 2012" a vote of nonsupport for parks? If so, does the staff have license to give the citizens of the county what they pay for—that is, inadequate services? Or should the parks manager take the initiative to privatize the park, create a special district, or mobilize the community to create a nonprofit organization to provide supplemental support to run the park?

The parks manager decided to use the "County 2012 Plan" to communicate to employees and other stakeholders that the county is not in the park expansion business. She took the lead in explaining the reasons behind this position; at the same time, though, she did not allow the policy to become an excuse for *declining* public service. Instead, the parks manager sought to identify alternative sources of revenue and ways of meeting the service expectations of her growing clientele. She collaborated on a timber-thinning project on county land and used the revenue to acquire federal matching funds. She was then able to make park improvements and sustain high-quality park services to more people without affecting the county general fund.

The parks manager is expected to run an effective and efficient operation using practices that stand the test of public scrutiny. She is also expected to ensure that county residents enjoy the use of the park and are treated with respect by county staff. All of this must be accomplished within a set of severe budgetary constraints. Translating these multiple directives and constraints into some meaningful unit of service to the citizens—an enjoyable day at the park—is what public servants do. This role is replicated throughout public organizations on a daily basis.

Through this complicated process of translating guidelines, juggling multiple expectations of advocacy groups, and turning organizational constraints into acceptable services, public servants play a central role in constituting what government itself means in the hearts and minds of the citizens it serves. The parks manager accomplished this by rethinking the relationship with other levels of government and with the private sector to craft a new arrangement. This, in turn, redefined public expectations while maintaining park services for a growing population. We will explore this constitutive role in greater detail in chapter 4.

## UNDERSTANDING ADMINISTRATIVE PRACTICE AND THE VARIETIES OF KNOWLEDGE IT REQUIRES

Another major theme of this book is that public administration is a special kind of "clinical practice" that requires the appropriate knowledge and skills to be successful. There are several ways of illustrating this point. First, an administrator cannot become accomplished without knowing what constitutes the standards of good practice. In matters of governance, few standards are settled in the sense that they are clear and accepted by everyone. Most are ambiguous and therefore subject to rival definitions and uncertainty in proper application. Nevertheless, accepted standards do exist in the practice of American governance—standards that have a long history and continue to guide administrative work. Understanding their development is vitally important. As a result, we pay close attention in this text (especially in chapters 4, 5, and 8) to the history of public service. This history improves our understanding of who we are and how our standards of governance have cycled and evolved in their meaning.

A second factor that makes public administration a clinical practice is that career officials derive knowledge from systematic experimentation and study that meets the tests of scientific validity and reliability. Many public decisions are assisted today through the use of data-based techniques in which facts are gathered and sifted analytically. Agencies employ analysts to use techniques ranging from survey feedback instruments to various kinds of programmatic experimentation. Programs with highly technical and scientific missions are often dominated by professions with specialized methods for deriving knowledge. Military weapons programs, environmental monitoring efforts, and crime labs are examples of public programs that rely heavily on scientific knowledge. Most professions have acquired substantial power and status because they have developed a coherent and esoteric body of theoretical knowledge to which others must largely defer. But scientific knowledge is hardly the end of the matter, at least as it concerns the practice of managing organizations. There is a third kind of knowledge that pervades administrative practice and therefore receives sustained attention in this text.

## TACIT KNOWLEDGE IN ADMINISTRATIVE PRACTICE

Over the last several decades, the theoretical knowledge of the social sciences has undergone serious challenge from critical theorists (Habermas 1985), humanists (Hummel 2007), feminists (Gilligan 1993), and organizational theorists (Argyris and Schon 1974; Lipsky 1980). As part of their critique, these theorists have recognized at least three forms of tacit knowledge that can be derived only through action, not through formal scientific analysis. These implicit forms stand on a separate, if not equal, footing with theoretical knowledge (Jonsen and Toulmin 1988; Vickers 1965; Weick 1979). More important, in the world of administrative practice, these forms of experiential knowledge overshadow scientific knowledge as the most common bases for making judgments about the what, where, when, and why of public policy decision making and especially implementation.

There is, first, the prudential understanding that is acquired by undertaking an activity over a prolonged period. The subtle nuances and complex interactions among materials, people, and settings acquired by master artisans and crafters through a long period of hands-on experience exemplify this kind of tacit knowledge. Police officers, case managers, and city planners rely on it routinely to make decisions under conditions of limited resources, short time frames, significant uncertainty, and political conflicts that often make systematic analysis impossible.

A second kind of tacit knowledge can be described as a "feel for the whole," and it is critically important to successful administrative practice. For public servants, knowledge of the whole tends to accrue through experience in a variety of positions, and by moving to higher-level administrative roles that require an increasingly broad or strategic sense of their institution. As they do so, they become more aware that their work forms part of the larger process of democratic governance. They develop a sense of proportion among priorities and become skilled in balancing competing demands. They learn how to weave together people and programs and how to mobilize interests into new missions and institutional arrangements. From this point of view, knowledge of the whole is transitory in nature (Schmidt 1993, 527)—about managing change for the common good—and is thus inseparable from democratic statesmanship (Green 1998). We will develop this point more fully throughout Part I of this book.

Third, there is critical knowledge that gives skilled practitioners a sense of when things are not quite right, or when things do not add up. In such situations, their judgments often run against perceived facts and guiding principles. They also tend to run against the tide of opinion among colleagues, or in the general public, which then invites conflict. The capacity to preserve and protect critical knowledge for the public benefit requires institutional safeguards such as secure tenure for key positions and careful staffing of critical workgroups to avoid problems with *groupthink* and related organizational pathologies. Critical knowledge comprises a sixth sense for public servants who know that good administrative work cannot always follow prescribed formulas or seemingly convincing data.

These three types of tacit knowledge contribute to the vital capacity for making judgments where other types of rational or systematic decision making fail because they lack conditions sufficient for their application. Our goal in elevating the status of tacit knowledge is not to denigrate theoretical or scientific knowledge. Instead, we want readers (1) to recognize that tacit knowledge is central to successfully managing public affairs, and (2) to connect it to the larger purposes that administrative work is intended to serve. While it is important to capture what our public servants know, it is equally important to assist them in better understanding how their work fits into the enterprise as a whole. Like many of our colleagues in the profession, we believe that public servants share responsibility for the "practice of democratic politics and the cause of effective public policy" (Burke 1988). This includes responsibility for more than just one's own job. That job is conditioned by an "encompassing web of offices, processes and institutions" that require implicit obligations which transcend the boundaries of any given position (Burke 1988, 42; also see Cook 1996; Elkin and Soltan 1993; Schaefer et al. 1998; Richardson 1997; Rohr 1986; Spicer 1995; Terry 1995; Wamsley et al. 1990).

Holding career government public servants responsible for making our systems of democratic governance work raises a serious question about their status in our governing system. What distinguishes them from other public officials, such as judges and elected officeholders? This is a question we explore throughout this book, but special emphasis is given in chapter 6 on administrative responsibility, and in Parts II and III, where we focus on the specific domains of activity public servants must master, such as budgeting, human resources management, planning, analysis, and evaluation.

## THE IMPORTANCE OF AN INSTITUTIONAL PERSPECTIVE

A third theme of this book is the treatment of public administration from an institutional perspective. Public service involves the management of a complex stream of interrelated activities and organization structures that accumulate significance and meaning over time. (See discussion of

Philip Selznick's quotation on institution building [1992] in chapter 1.) American public administration is more than a set of administrative functions, more than a mere instrument of someone's will. Many of its practices form traditions that gradually acquire institutional status.

This process of institutionalization establishes cultural identity that makes the whole greater than the sum of an organization's parts. The entity is valued not only for what it can do, but for what it is as an organ of civil society. The Green Bay Packers, for example, mean far more to their fan base and their community than their game-winning, money-making stature suggests. The team engenders ways of dressing, conversing, and living in anticipation of, and during, the football season. It is literally and figuratively "owned" by the community. It is the pride of the community. Likewise, the transformation of a set of religious beliefs, practices, and policy decisions into something like the Catholic Church; the development of the market economy in the United States; and the role of the U.S. Forest Service in public land management exemplify institutions built through such processes. And they illustrate why government, philanthropic, and nonprofit institutions have to be understood historically in order to fully grasp their significance.

There are at least three major advantages to taking an institutional approach to the practice of public service: (1) it greatly influences our understanding of how change occurs; (2) it significantly improves our understanding of the interface between public- and private-sector activities; and (3) it enriches our understanding of the processes for generating legitimacy.

**Understanding Administrative Change**

Change in public-sector organizations comes about through markedly different processes than those seen in the private sector. Change processes in public institutions are governed by different norms and expectations, cemented by public sentiments that grow out of our constitutional traditions. Legislative bodies often give vague or ambiguous policy directions in order to please disparate factions. Constituency groups seldom agree about policy directions, and some have greater status and influence than others in legislative and agency processes. Governing powers are diffused through multiple structures of authority, and revenue streams operate through varied and independent processes of taxation, fee assessments, bonded debt, and sale of lands, goods, and services. These are all institutional factors that mix in unique ways to condition changes in public policy and administrative process.

Public entities in metropolitan regions illustrate the importance of adopting an institutional perspective about change in the public sector. These entities engage in an almost continuous dialogue with one another on a wide range of issues, including regional transportation, metropolitan-area land use planning, open space acquisition, law enforcement, sewer and water service coordination, education policy, and taxation issues. This cooperation and information sharing is essential to the success of local governments and their elected officials, and it differs substantially from the private sector, where such cooperation among firms in an industry would normally be considered competitively unwise and could also constitute illegal collusion. The dynamics of cooperation and competition in each sector differ dramatically. Public servants who understand the institutional dynamics at work in this milieu are the ones who will succeed in achieving general cooperative agreements and translating them into workable plans of action that meet the test of public accountability.

One of the most important criticisms of the institutional perspective is that it provides excuses for racism, sexism, ethnocentrism, and other discriminatory practices that marginalize the weak and powerless. We recognize the validity of this concern, which is why we place so much importance on the exercise of administrative discretion and a flexible array of practices and principles

upon which administrators can draw to serve as a counterbalancing force to these defects. In doing so, we recognize that administrators alone cannot correct deeply embedded discriminatory or pathological institutional practices. We do believe, however, that administrators must play an important leadership role in calling attention to the existence of such practices and the need for them to be addressed by the community.

### The Polity-Making Role of Public Administration: The Relationship Between the Public, Private, Nonprofit, and Special District Sectors

An institutional approach to public service blurs any bright-line distinction among the public general government, special district government, for-profit private, and nonprofit sectors. Exhibit 2.1 summarizes the essential differences among the sectors based on how they arbitrate value differences and the breadth of interests they serve. The for-profit private sector negotiates value differences through the market, and its interests are parochial. The interests of the nonprofit sector, on the other hand, are usually regarded as part of the larger common good. Special districts and general-purpose public bodies arbitrate value differences through the political process, but they differ in the scope of interests they embrace. Special districts are established to pursue parochial interests in contrast to the broader common interests of general-purpose governmental units. The distinctive characteristics summarized in Exhibit 2.1 are not meant to be exhaustive; they simply illustrate that each of the sectors has its own logic and that there is complex interplay among these sectors, marked by mutual dependence.

The general government sector plays a pivotal role for for-profit private, nonprofit, and special district organizations. Markets cannot sustain themselves without a stable infrastructure of roads, communication systems, defense systems that protect and maintain international lanes of commerce, banking systems that provide security for loans, a legal system that enforces contracts, and a regulatory system that stabilizes the rate and complexity of change in markets as well as their relations with consumers and communities. The nonprofit sector relies on this infrastructure, depending heavily upon the grants, contracts, and other forms of sponsorship by governments at all levels, not to mention its privileged tax-exempt status. The elaborate legal and procedural environment of many governments helps provide stability for the other sectors, but it also presents impediments to highly efficient operations. Private-sector firms and nonprofit organizations enjoy substantial advantages over the public sector in this regard.

Government special districts offer an alternative way of providing public services. Unlike general-purpose governments that administer a broad range of services, special districts are established to administer one specialized activity on a "cost of service" basis. Special district governments face the same institutional and procedural checks as faced by general-purpose governments. Fire and emergency response, hospital, police, water, sewer, library, and other services can be provided by creating a unit of government whose sole purpose is to administer that service at a specified cost to each member of the district. Local school districts present a well-known example of this type of special district government. The advantage of the special district approach is twofold: it allows citizens to purchase additional levels of service that government may not be able to provide, and it controls the price the public is willing to pay. One of the disadvantages of special districts is that they further balkanize public service delivery and allow those with more financial resources to obtain more and better service than the poor. Under such circumstances, it becomes more difficult to build a shared sense of the common public or community interest (Burns 1994). Communities utilizing multiple special districts struggle to ensure that citizen voices reach the correct officials before a district takes formal action. Special district governments can enter into agreements with

Exhibit 2.1    **Institutional Forms**

| | | Scope of interests | |
|---|---|---|---|
| | | Parochial | Common |
| **How values are arbitrated** | Political | Special district governments | General governments |
| | Market | For-profit private agencies and firms | Nonprofit organizations |

nonprofits organizations, but they more often enter into intergovernmental agreements (IGAs) with other governments. For example, a small city might enter into an intergovernmental agreement with an adjacent fire district for emergency services. Likewise, the county sheriff might provide law enforcement services to the small city under a different by similar agreement.

The for-profit private sector's concern for innovation, creativity, and customer satisfaction is assumed to be the best mechanism for efficiently maximizing the allocation of society's resources. This may be the case, as long as the goals of society are compatible with those of individuals, and the demands of customers can be arranged to induce a market response. But there are numerous instances when these private marketplace conditions do not exist. The following are the most common examples of market failures or exceptions that have provided justification for public-sector intervention: (1) the provision of *public goods,* such as national defense; (2) the amelioration of some of the *diseconomies* or *externalities* of collective action—pollution of the environment and drug abuse among them; (3) the avoidance of *tragedy of the commons* problems, such as natural resource depletion; (4) reaping the collective benefits of *public economies,* such as education and early childhood development programs; and (5) taking advantage of *natural monopolies,* including water, sewer, and other public utilities. In these and other instances, the public sector is encouraged to intervene in the private marketplace in the interest of promoting greater equity (Okun 1975; Wanat 1978, chap. 2), which we will explore in more detail in chapter 6.

The interdependence of the multiple sectors of the American political economy also has some important leadership and budgeting implications for public administrators, particularly at the local levels of government. We believe that local governments will increasingly play a *polity-making* role as demands grow on shrinking public resources. By definition, a polity-making role involves the formation of a politically organized unit; our use of the term polity-making refers to a concern for how the community's assets across the nonprofit, government and for-profit sectors can be identified and mobilized to make the highest and best contribution to the community's common good. This goes beyond the traditional jurisdiction's concern for using its own resources to preserve the delivery of high-quality government services, even in the face of diminishing resources. Furthermore, it suggests additional measures of success for public action related to the health and well-being of communities and the capacity of communities to function well politically (Sirianni 2009).

Debate over the proper role that public administrators should play with respect to nonprofit organizations is often subsumed in discussions of civil society. Three different approaches to the idea of civil society (Edwards 2009; O'Connell 1999; Seligman 1992) have implications for public service leaders and government performance. For Aristotle, a classic approach, "civil" society resulted from the functions performed by the state, whose collective activities cultivated the civility necessary for successful citizenship and thereby governance. Here, civil society is a coproduced outcome of good governance and a precondition for good governance. The classic model treats civil society as an organic part of a larger set of regime values. This view contrasts with the Enlightenment thinkers who laid the intellectual foundations for the American experiment in democratic governance. Enlightenment scholars argued that civil society was a safe harbor outside the influence of the state and economy. It is the harbor of "limited government" and a reserve against the market economy. As Tocqueville (1835–1840/2000) noted in his travels through America in the early 1830s, a robust civil society gives rise to the impulse to associate with others, which facilitates citizen and neighborhood-centered problem solving and provides the glue for larger scale representative democracy. In recent literature, Putnam and his followers (2000) underscore the increased importance of this view as the robustness of civic organizations have withered over the past several decades. A third view of civil society emphasizes its importance in laying the groundwork for serious, but civil, political discourse. These scholars (Arendt [1958], Boyte [1989], Dewey [1927], and Kemmis [1990]) suggest that civil society is the "public space" in which people—through everyday interaction—create meaning and understanding about public values, and through this practice civil society becomes a reservoir of the habits of good citizenship. A healthy civil society within and among states and civic capacity within communities fosters good governance in an increasingly power-shared world.

Public administration has recognized the growing importance of the nonprofit sector as the formal expression of civil society. The nonprofit sector provides citizens and corporations with a way to express their personal values and voices through civil society. Routine small-scale charitable giving and larger-scale planned philanthropy provides donors with the means to take action in close conformance with their values and preferences, and to make a difference in their communities and in people's lives. Nonprofit organizations present an independent alternative to both the governmental sector and the private-market sector. Independence from government reflects a separation from government institutional values, detailed procedures and processes, and majority-centered balanced decision making. Nonprofit charitable giving can directly aid an underheard minority group or support a one-sided advocacy position on a community issue. Independence from government allows religious organizations and other nonprofits the space to express and live their institutional values. Similarly, independence from the for-profit commercial market removes the profit motive from nonprofit decisions and activities. Freedom from the profit motive is an important value for many nonprofit donors and volunteers. Nonprofit organizations can capture the pure motives of voluntary labor and personal commitment to a cause. In addition to citizen initiative and expression, nonprofits respond to a variety of impulses, including government failure to provide sufficient public goods (for example, United Way), the American tradition of self-help (for example, Alcoholics Anonymous), or a commitment to helping others (for example, Catholic Charities).

At the community level, the many different voices in a well-developed nonprofit sector combine into a civil society that provides some societal balance to the government and for-profit sectors. The check appears both as voices in the polity and as the providers of substantial resources that can meet public needs. Nonprofit philanthropic trusts and foundations; federated intermediary organizations including United Way, Catholic Charities, and other mid-level organizations; and

many larger nonprofit service providers exert their legitimacy through their success in developing independent financial resources. With independent funding, nonprofits can operate their arts, social service, and youth programs without government intervention. Nonprofit organization independence also provides space for advocacy on behalf of issues and clients. Such advocacy may be strongly critical of governments and public programs in the community, and nonprofits may be able to present clear messages that government institutions are reluctant to present.

Nonprofit financial resources provide an important complement to government resources. Strategic joint plans and interorganizational agreements may lay out the framework for coordinated action by many actors in a community. We describe such a coordinated effort in chapter 15. On an operational working level, nonprofits and governments coordinate their activities through formal agreements. These agreements are a form of contract that prescribes the amount, form, and timing of resources contributed by the parties, as well as the commitment of staff and organizational support for the project. Agreement provisions may bind government to certain commitments, and government needs may bind nonprofits and foundations to certain actions.

Finally, neither the public nor the private sectors are as capable as the nonprofit sector in meeting individual clientele needs with minimal rules and costs to the client. Access to soup kitchens and shelters for the homeless, safe houses for runaway youth, and refuge and protection for domestic violence victims rarely require clients to meet some extensive eligibility requirements. Nonprofit organizations serve virtually all in need. Those who provide these kinds of services to target populations are passionate about what they do, and this passion—combined with flexible, adaptive approaches to care—is clearly reflected in the quality of treatment that is extended to each person in need. Because of these factors, higher levels of service can usually be provided for fewer dollars than is the case with either the public sector or the private marketplace. To gain the advantage of nonprofit efficiencies in service delivery, governments contract extensively with nonprofit service providers. These relationships may take the form of specific short-term service contracts, grants for professional services, and long-term, contracted program-level partnerships. Nonprofits entering into contracts to provide services must understand how that contract and partner could affect the nonprofit mission and capacity. These are major issues for a nonprofit board to consider.

In short, the general government, special district, for-profit, and private nonprofit sectors are each suited to perform distinctive tasks. It is important for public administrators to know what each sector can do particularly well and why, as they are occasionally called upon to use their discretionary authority to help restructure the relationship among the four. The distinct characteristics of each sector are summarized in Exhibit 2.2 and hold important implications for shaping the nature of ethical obligations for public servants. In the future, we believe local governments will increasingly use their *soft power* of influence rather than relying on their smaller sphere of constrained *hard power* and formal legal authority to leverage all of the community's assets to promote the public good. This is an argument we will develop further in chapters 11 and 12 on budgeting and leadership respectively.

### Administrative Legitimacy: Political Community, Civil Society, and Community Capacity

A final advantage of taking an institutional approach to understanding administrative practice is that it sheds light on an important set of conditions necessary for creating and maintaining the legitimacy of governance and governmental work. Public organizations have to conduct their functions in a public fishbowl, where all of the decisions they make and almost every document

Exhibit 2.2  **Comparative Characteristics of Sectors**

| Private Sector | Nonprofit Sector | Public Sector | Special Districts |
| --- | --- | --- | --- |
| Mission driven | Clientele driven | Legal/rule driven | Purpose driven |
| Results oriented | Needs oriented | Process oriented | Service oriented |
| Entrepreneurial | Meeting needs with few rules and questions asked | Bureaucratic | Technical expertise |
| Motivating others for high performance | "Doing the right thing" | Constitutional agent of a sovereign power | Bounded legal authority |
| Customers | Target populations | Citizens | Target population |
| Flexibility | Service | Control | Service |
| Innovation | Flexibility for target population | Following rules | Service within narrow legal authority |
| Customer satisfaction | Clientele needs | Citizen rights and responsibilities | Client satisfaction |
| Incentives | "Doing good" | Regulations | Service |
| Employee empowerment | Voluntary commitment | Hierarchy | Functional competence |
| Delegation of authority | Informal coordination | Centralization of authority | Parochially governed |
| Self-interest | Responsibility | Accountability | Efficiency |
| Interests | Values | Rights | Service |
| Preferences | Needs | Equity | Effectiveness |
| Profit | Moral duty | Duty to the law | Duty to clients |

they produce can be scrutinized and second-guessed by any citizen within the jurisdiction. Public organizations must also cope with political pressures. They must adhere to governing board policies, detailed strategic plans, purchasing rules, civil service guidelines, public hearings, and organized citizens' groups that may have conflicting or partially informed opinions.

But there is an even more fundamental set of considerations that shape the legitimacy of administrative work. An institutional perspective calls public service leaders to consider the fabric of the society in which they serve. Political culture, institutions, and regime values are all rooted in community. These attributes of a society vary geographically, creating the need for administrators to be mindful not only of the differences and similarities among citizens regarding policy and governance processes but also of the way these differences and similarities are rooted in the community. The American founders understood this important reality and kept it in mind as they negotiated agreements that preserved the sovereignty of the states and recognized differences in the political sociology of communities in New England, the Mid-Atlantic, and the South. We know today that urban settings differ in political sociology from rural settings. We know that Cascadia (a bioregion of the Pacific Northwest) differs from the interior West. Towns in Vermont vary from southern cities. Communities seen this way are artifacts of history (see McCrone 2007), but despite being anchored in history, they are not entirely captured by it.

The American experiment in democratic governance is a testimony to change, and the capacity for change is also a function of communities. We know that some communities have greater resilience in facing change and vary in their ability to be self-authoring. We describe this as *civic capacity* (Shinn 1999) and *community resilience* (Magis 2010; Magis and Shinn 2009). This

mixture of social capital or trust, civic competency, and civic enterprise rooted in communities is what allows communities to have a sense that they can solve public problems and influence the impact of changes within their realm. The ability of public administrators to be successful in their work depends to a large extent on the social capital, civic competency, and civic enterprise in the communities they serve. These resources cannot always be taken for granted.

In fact, the need to intentionally foster a robust civil society in order to build viable systems of governance has been increasingly recognized in international development, where the United Nations Department of Economic and Social Affairs, the International Monetary Fund, and the World Bank have all established *civil society organization* initiatives as a part of development planning. Most of these initiatives focus on the enhancement of a "third way" that relies on locally based rather than state- or market-based organizations. This strategy in part reflects the long-standing importance of nongovernmental organizations (NGOs) in international development as primary implementing agents for policy. However, it also reflects more recent political efforts and scholarship regarding the importance of creating community capacity to "own" change initiatives related to both self-governance and economic development (Sirianni 2009; Smith and Smyth 2010).

The growing recognition of civil society in successful governance has several important implications for public administration. First, many small community-based organizations are, in fact, not formal. In the United States, this typically means that they have not established a tax status for their organization. For example, service learning initiatives in schools at all levels of education have been established to build civic virtues and practices related to citizenship and compassion for others. In fact, a growing number of schools are engaging in community partnership projects, voluntary service, and "community good" activities. Churches, service groups (e.g., Kiwanis), and mutual benefit organizations (e.g., Elks, Girl Scouts, softball clubs) often include direct service components ranging from running soup kitchens to beach cleanups. Some of these activities become the basis for formal organizations, but many remain part of the informal fabric of a community. It is important for public administrators to recognize this formal and informal mix of organized civic activity if they are to be successful in building community trust and legitimacy.

There may be an even more fundamental and far-reaching implication for administrators regarding the importance of civil society to successful governance. If scholars are correct in their finding that we can no longer take for granted the state and condition of civil society (Putnam 2000; Sirianni 2009; Skocpol 1997; Skocpol and Fiorina 1999), then public administrators will increasingly need to tend to the condition of civil society as an outcome of public (not just governmental) actions. This perspective significantly changes the role relationship between nonprofits and the government. Instead of being an instrumental, low-cost alternative to service delivery, they (along with all of the informal civic organizations in the community) may serve as valuable partners in building trust, civic competency, and civic enterprise. This will require future administrators to become expert in what Tocqueville called the "science of association" (1835–1840/2000, 492).

## REFLECTIVE PRACTICE AND CONTINUITIES IN CONFLICT

A fourth theme woven throughout this book is the importance of *reflective practice,* a phrase first popularized by Argyris and Schon (1996). Their research emphasizes the importance of distinguishing two kinds of theory: *espoused theory* and *theory in action.* Experienced practitioners develop a theory in action that embodies the subtle understanding of what it takes, for example, for architects to design the right building for a given setting, for experienced social workers to understand just what to do when they are being "shined on" by one of their clients, or for surgeons to apply their techniques to perfectly fit a new situation they have never before encountered. This

capacity entails more than just good judgment: according to Argyris and Schon, it is based on a "theory in action." One of the goals of helping practitioners to become better at what they do is to elicit this theory in action and make it self-consciously accessible to oneself and others for examination and criticism—an objective that requires getting access to the various kinds of tacit knowledge discussed above. Once this is done, it becomes possible for the practitioner to become reflective-in-practice and thus an agent of continuous self-improvement.

Reflective practice is not easy, especially since it requires officials to step back from the daily grind of administrative work to ask a variety of questions such as: Where are we headed? What are we to do? What ends should we be serving? How are they defined? What means were used in the past? Who should be involved? What failures as well as successes have occurred? How can we improve upon what the organization is doing? This habit of reflective practice is especially important in large, complex organizations, the type of organizations that can create pathological cultures and propensities for groupthink.

The most important consequence of the habit of reflective practice is that it reminds public servants that they are ultimately stewards of our system of democratic governance. Being a good steward requires that a public servant understand the defects that can cause our system of democratic governance to lose its particular virtues. We argue that there are four major defects to which our democratic polity can succumb: (1) it can become incompetent and ineffective in its performance; (2) it can become indifferent to civic engagement and the unique history and values that give a community its distinct character; (3) it can fail to protect minority rights; and (4) it can be compromised by public officials who have become tyrannical. We explain these defects more fully in chapter 4, showing how the framers of the American Constitution intentionally created a legal structure and set of processes to address each possible defect. The framers well understood, however, that solutions to any one of these challenges tend to exacerbate the others. The spirit of these difficulties is captured in a useful aphorism illustrated throughout this book.

### The Founding Beatitudes

Too much power begets usurpation, to which majority rule is a corrective;

Too much majority rule begets majority tyranny, to which separation of powers and checks and balances is a corrective;

Too much separation of powers and checks and balances begets incompetent government, to which unity at the center is a corrective;

Too much unity at the center begets usurpation, to which civic engagement is a corrective. (Morgan 2001, 156)

We believe career public servants perform a critical role in maintaining a balance among these competing concerns. In balancing competent delivery of services with responsiveness and protection of minority rights, our public servants play a decisive role in maintaining "continuities in conflict" (MacIntyre 1984). This will serve as the overarching theme of this text and will be developed more fully in the chapters that follow.

# ADMINISTRATIVE DISCRETION

## Issues and Conflicts

> Discretion is a tool only when properly used; like an axe, it can be a weapon
> for mayhem or murder. In a government of men and of laws, the portion that is
> a government of men, like a malignant cancer, often tends to stifle the portion
> that is a government of laws. Perhaps nine-tenths of injustice in our legal
> system flows from discretion and perhaps only one-tenth from rules.

*(Kenneth Culp Davis 1971, 25)*

Kenneth Culp Davis reminds us that a distrust of *administrative discretion* is deeply embedded
in the founding principles of the American republic (see chapter 4). Our Anti-Federalist found-
ers viewed bureaucrats as unreachable, faceless, and self-serving. They believed a large national
government administered from afar would develop a self-serving life of its own and, over time,
would produce staff and administrators with little sympathy for the needs of local communities.

The concerns of the Anti-Federalists are still very much on the minds of American citizens. Do
career administrators have too much or too little discretion? Do we need more rules or fewer of
them in order to make government organizations serve their intended purposes? Even the critics of
bureaucracy cannot agree on an answer to these questions. For example, the proponents of "making
government run like a business" want more discretionary authority in order to reap the entrepreneurial
benefits that accompany high levels of autonomy and personal responsibility. On the other hand, many
critics want more oversight and control in order to limit arbitrary judgment by individual bureaucrats
and to prevent bureaucracies as a whole from being captured by their chief clientele interests.[1]

For administrators working in the nonprofit sector, issues of discretion take on different forms.
Administrators in all types of nonprofits struggle to reconcile well-intentioned direction and vi-
sion from their boards of directors with the reality of limited resources. Administrators working
with foundations and larger nonprofits are preoccupied with the question of how well their fund-
ing criteria align with community needs and how well a given organization can be entrusted as
a good fiduciary partner in meeting these needs. Government grants and contracts add a layer
of complexity to the exercise of administrative discretion, as government has added a variety of
performance and accountability requirements that arguably take money away from providing direct
service to clients. Nonprofit administrators who rely on these grants and contracts have to match
contract and grant requirements with professional expectations, their organizational mission, and

direction from their governing board of directors. Frequently, these requirements may conflict with community needs, with their organizational mission, or with local agreements. Nonprofit administrators and boards of directors are left to sort out the tension between these requirements and their organization's values. (These conflicts are discussed in much greater detail in chapter 5 as part of our discussion of the rise of the administrative state and its increasing reliance on non-profits to provide a wide array of public services.) Much is at stake for nonprofits as they decide how to use their discretion to manage these tensions. The exercise of administrative discretion is driven by a desire to ensure continued funding, nonprofit survival, and the effective delivery of needed services to the community.

For most of us in the field of public administration, the question of whether we have too little or too much discretion is difficult to answer in the abstract. Some would argue that administrative discretion per se is dangerous, because it allows government to be run by unelected and uncontrolled officials. But for most of us, the question of too little or too much discretion requires some understanding of the contextual setting, including who is exercising the discretion, what kind of discretion is being exercised, and the potential dangers for abuse. These are the questions that will guide our discussion in this chapter.

The case of the angry library patron at the beginning of this section is typical of how the problem of discretion arises for most of our public servants. Discretion is usually not the result of some failure in the design and management of our public organizations. Nor is it the result of over-reaching employees seeking to preserve their turf and decision-making prerogatives. It is simply an incidental and necessary element of doing one's job as a public servant. Despite the multitude of accountability requirements placed on public employees, discretion is probably as ubiquitous in public and nonprofit organizations as it is in the private sector.

## THE UBIQUITY OF ADMINISTRATIVE DISCRETION

Discretion necessarily pervades all levels of our public organizations. It starts with our street-level bureaucrats and frontline service providers who deal directly with the citizenry. It includes supervisors and middle managers who have the responsibility for translating vague and sometimes competing policy directives and contract requirements into clear operating procedures. And it ends with the senior administrators at the apex of public and nonprofit agencies who establish policy directions in partnership with elected public officials.

### Street-Level Bureaucrats and Frontline Service Providers

As we suggested in chapters 1 and 2, street-level bureaucrats form a great part of the public face of democratic governance. Their discretionary authority plays a key role in maintaining the legitimacy of our governing systems. Studies document a remarkable devotion to duty among these officials under conditions of high stress and scant recognition (Goodsell 2004; Lipsky 1980; Vinzant and Crothers 1998). Numerous studies indicate that most Americans are pleased with their direct interactions with street-level bureaucrats, despite the general decline in the legitimacy of government. Exhibit 3.1 provides a summary undertaken more than 40 years ago of the overall level of citizen satisfaction with bureaucratic encounters.

Interestingly, this level of satisfaction may have increased, rather than decreased, in recent decades, despite a general decline in the level of governmental trust among citizens. After reviewing more than 50 years of surveys regarding our attitudes toward government, Charles Goodsell (2004) concluded: "One finding that comes through loud and clear is that citizen assessments of

Exhibit 3.1    **Evaluation of Bureaucratic Encounters Compared to General Evaluation of Bureaucracy**

☐ Positive evaluation of service agency performance in general    ☐ Positive evaluation of police/regulatory encounters
■ Positive evaluation of encounters

*Source:* Katz (1975, 121–25).

specific, personal experiences with administrative agencies tend to be positive." The levels of satisfaction generally range from a low of 70 percent to a high of over 90 percent. In addition to confirming high levels of satisfaction, the surveys demonstrate that "performance in the private sector is not necessarily superior to that in government" (Goodsell 2004, 31, 33).

However, as Exhibit 3.1 indicates, Americans do not rate government in the abstract nearly as well as they rate their actual personal experience with agencies. It is also no surprise that our evaluation of agencies that constrain or regulate us ranks lower than our personal experience with agencies that provide us with services. However, many of our agencies have to do both. This is one of the reasons why agencies responsible for revenue collection, immigration, and policing operate under considerable pressure, and why many of them have redesigned their organizations to separate the service function from the policing and enforcement functions. The goal of these redesigns is to forestall the cycle of criticisms by citizens and oversight bodies for being too enforcement oriented at the expense of customer service in one period, and vice versa in the next.

The overall high level of satisfaction with street-level bureaucracy is often the result of exercising the kind of discretion necessary to get the job done. For example, consider the following:

- A patrol officer is asked by a community group to shut down a neighborhood drug house.
- A social worker has been alerted by a concerned citizen about suspected child abuse related to a case she is managing.

- An electrical inspector notices some incidental violations from a previous owner while inspecting a rewiring project by the new owner.
- A solid waste employee notices that the elderly occupant of a home never sorts the recycling according to instructions.
- A wildlife bird biologist is uncertain whether to oppose recreational climbing on a rock 500 feet from a nesting peregrine falcon.

These examples of street-level discretion are replicated on a daily basis in every governmental and nonprofit organization across the land. Such discretion frequently requires balancing complicated and conflicting claims that defy resolution through the application of some formulaic response. Certainly, that is the case with Cheryl Miller, who is struggling with how best to respond to the angry library patron in the case presented at the beginning of this section. But this discretion is not limited to street-level bureaucrats; it occurs at the middle-management levels of all of our public organizations as well.

### The Discretion of Middle Managers

Middle managers play a decisive role in creating the necessary legitimacy to implement policy initiatives of the larger organization. For example, they make it possible to get necessary work done within the constraints of limited resources and multiple sources of oversight. Middle managers are clearly identifiable in larger organizations. In smaller organizations, the tasks typically assumed by middle managers may be split between executives and senior service providers. In a study of the consequences of flattening local government organizations, the following four tasks were identified as critical to the work of middle managers (Morgan et al. 1996).

1. They interpret and represent the interests of their organizational unit.
2. They lend and secure the cooperative assistance of other work units.
3. They develop organizational relationships across legal and budgetary boundaries.
4. They leverage other people's time.

*Interpreting and Representing the Interests of the Organizational Unit*

One of the most important and frequent tasks of middle managers in organizations is working out agreements with other middle managers on how best to allocate scarce resources and coordinate work across organizational units. Any time budgets, grants, and other financial resources are at stake, one will find representatives from various groups and organizations meeting to plan, organize, debate, and think about the appropriate use and allocation of these resources. Such meetings reflect a requirement for the effective use of resources, whether they involve public taxpayer dollars or grants from private foundations. These kinds of meetings are part of the daily routine in the life of a middle manager.

Middle managers also develop public policy responses to issues of the day. They field questions regarding their work units' capacities, weaknesses, and interests. Their influence with the interests of the parent organization will likely affect the distribution of duties, responsibilities, or tasks. New community or neighborhood projects, task forces, attempts at defining performance standards, and bids to change or alter the manner in which tasks are performed and delivered draw immediate interest from middle managers. Recall, for instance, the earlier example of the introduction and evolution of community policing within police departments: A project like this

requires countless organizational gatherings involving community groups, police professionals, elected policymakers, and those with related kinds of expertise. The efforts in these gatherings are directed at moderating, changing, and influencing the manner in which police work and social services are delivered. The same kind of deliberative interaction attends the creation of new customer/client service units within private, public, and nonprofit organizations.

*Lending or Securing Cooperative Assistance from Other Work Units*

Another major task of middle managers is marketing and delivering the workgroup's expertise to others. Prosecutors meeting with police officials and members of the Federal Bureau of Investigation (FBI), the U.S. Immigration and Customs Enforcement (ICE), and local community groups to plan antidrug strategies are entrusted by the prosecutor's office to represent and project the interests of the organization beyond its own walls. Much of what they are doing is finding areas in which the organization can be helpful without compromising the resources necessary to achieve its organizational mission.

Other examples might involve a fire battalion captain's efforts in working on an enhanced 911 system, or a precinct captain's development of a policy that would allow business owners to directly and legally prepare police reports on shoplifters. Similar responsibilities exist in the private sector, when, for example, private utilities are called upon by the public sector to work out joint billing arrangements, electronic meter reading, coordinated conservation programs, and special relief for the needy.

*Developing Organizational Relationships*

When faced with tasks that a work unit cannot undertake on its own, the middle manager develops and relies upon organizational relationships with others outside of the unit in order to get things accomplished. A successful and seasoned middle manager, new to an organization, will quickly take steps to identify and associate with contemporaries in allied organizations, knowing that familiarity and personal relationships go far in getting things done. In this fashion, middle managers serve a vital "boundary spanning" function that links their work unit with the outside world (Thompson 1967).

*Leveraging Others' Time*

Middle managers often are called upon to attend meetings and perform tasks that have a vague, ill-defined, or even ill-conceived purpose. In such settings, middle managers are expected to ably represent a collection of interests and be incisive enough to determine whether the issues discussed have a bearing on and a relationship to the abilities, concerns, and interests of their own organizational unit. Sometimes it is simply a "flag-flying exercise" to maintain visibility and recognition that the organization or the unit has a sphere of interest and a stake in the topic under discussion. More often, though, their work requires reading between the lines, attending to what others are *not* saying, assessing the interests at stake in the room, and determining what actions and resources their own work units must commit as a result of such meetings. Middle managers' judgments in this regard are vital to protecting time as a most precious resource for their units. Many proposals made in cross-unit meetings are problematic in terms of resource and time demands, and an astute mid-level manager can avert premature commitments or sidestep such proposals altogether. Developing such acuity requires great knowledge about other players, their

histories, their capacities, their powers, their character, and their interests. Middle-management work requires well-developed skills in diplomacy and interpersonal relations more than it requires deep technical knowledge. This work, though vital, is often indirect and seldom acknowledged by street-level and strategic-level officials.

All complex organizations need middle managers to represent a work unit's interests, to secure or lend assistance, to develop professional relationships, and to leverage other people's time (especially that of their superiors). These four functions are common to middle managers in the public, private, and nonprofit sectors. However, middle managers in the public sector carry out these functions quite differently than their counterparts in the private sector and, to a lesser extent, in the nonprofit sector. These differences result from two characteristics that distinguish the public and private sectors: one is the lack of a common dollar denominator for measuring successful service in the public sector; the other is the impact of free market barriers to collaborative activity in the private sector. For example, Microsoft Corporation's financial interests are not well served by developing its Windows[2] operating system so that it is compatible with all of the operating systems of its competitor software providers. Because of these differences in financial benchmarks, middle managers in the public sector encounter service and accountability responsibilities that their counterparts in the private sector do not face.

Consider the dilemma of a middle manager in a planning department dealing with a request from a low-income family to allow a camper trailer to be located on a property until a new structure is built where their house had stood prior to a fire. Or reflect on the choices open to a code enforcement officer who discovers 156 people occupying disabled recreational vehicles, old buses, and campers in mobile home parks located within the city limits. The decision to strictly enforce the letter of the law and enlarge the homeless population on the one hand, or to allow continued occupancy by seeking amendments to the city code on the other, is primarily the role of the middle manager. The middle manager must exercise the initial leadership to persuade key decision makers within the jurisdiction to set aside the efficiency of code enforcement for the sake of a larger community good.

In the previous chapter, we made the point that defining "good service" and maintaining multiple kinds of accountability are distinctively unique to public-sector work. Middle managers have the chief responsibility for successfully carrying out these two tasks (Morgan et al. 1996). What "good service" means in the public sector must be negotiated among competing claimants, all of whom potentially have an equal voice at the ballot box. The perspective of the taxpayers who fund public programs has to be balanced with the needs of clients. Similarly, the perspective of foundation donors may not square with client needs or the expectations of co-contributing donors. The middle manager provides the key information, and at times the persuasion, that is needed to strike the balance between these competing claims.

### Discretion and Senior Managers

Senior-level administrators face some of the most difficult challenges in our system of democratic governance. They are expected to be "on tap, not on top." Yet, in most small local jurisdictions and special districts, part-time elected officials do not have the time or the expertise to take full responsibility for most public policy decision making. An elected official may have an initial idea or want to take a policy initiative, but it is the senior administrative staff that is responsible for transforming initiatives and ideas of elected officials into practical, legal, and politically acceptable courses of action. To get this work done, senior managers need to work as a team to assist elected officials with the following "sense-making" activities:

1.  interpreting and reconciling multiple sources of authority;
2.  building public support and authority for government activities;
3.  facilitating interorganizational cooperation;
4.  initiating interjurisdictional collaboration;
5.  negotiating interorganizational service standards; and
6.  interpreting the needs and culture of the community.

*Interpreting and Reconciling Multiple Sources of Authority*

Senior managers play a critical role in ensuring a constancy of purpose in public organizations in the face of multiple sources of authority. These sources reside in multiple agencies and special jurisdictions, in multiple levels of government, in quasi-governmental agencies, in contracted organizations, in funding organizations, and among members of the general public. Together, these multiple sources of authority present real challenges of coordination, conflict, and compromise as officials reconcile and translate their missions into plans for action. For example, a seemingly simple process of establishing a minimum level of police service in a county bedroom community may require coordination with several surrounding cities and adjacent counties. If a decision is made to increase the level of police service in response to citizen concerns, additional meetings have to be held by senior managers to explore the implications for other justice system managers, including the courts, corrections, parole, and probation. Each of these units may have its own separate source of legal authority, budget support, and political constituency. In working out the operating policy implications of these overlapping bodies, senior managers have to comply with a variety of state and federal laws, multitudinous board governance policies, and department-level guidelines. How can this jumble of complexity be translated into meaningful organizational policies? How can it be assembled so that there is sufficient coherence and integrity to obtain the support of elected officials, the citizens at large, and the employees on the frontline? Senior management plays a key role in answering these critical questions.

*Building Public Support and Authority for Government Activities*

Senior leaders in public organizations have a much more complex task than their private- and nonprofit-sector counterparts in building legitimacy for their work: When drawing on multiple sources of authority that are sometimes in conflict, public organization leaders must operate in a "glass house," constantly satisfying elected officials and complying with governing board policies and the organization's strategic plans. Public agency and special district administrators must further adhere to purchasing rules, civil service guidelines, and public hearing requirements, the last of which entails listening to organized citizen groups who may have conflicting or uninformed opinions.

The success of an organization in balancing these multiple sources of authority is critical to acquiring legitimacy for subsequent action. Consider the steps necessary to complete a neighborhood revitalization project. Senior planners have the primary responsibility for responding to multiple concerns residents have about impacts on parking, safety, noise, and so forth; furthermore, they must coordinate with other bureau managers to create satisfied citizens while also completing the project on time and on budget. They must maintain political as well as fiscal support for the project and ensure proper conditions for effective execution of its many stages to completion. If they do this work well, the elected officials can take credit for the project. If the process does not go well, senior managers are summoned to give an account of what has gone wrong and what

they are going to do to fix it. In short, senior managers are held responsible for making sure that things work and, when they do, give credit to their elected superiors.

*Facilitating Interorganizational Cooperation*

Senior managers in the public sector spend considerable time and energy laying the groundwork for solutions to problems that cut across organizational boundaries within their own jurisdictions. An example of this complex process of defining interorganizational accountability is found in one local county's quest to preserve affordable housing in a high-growth housing market. As the county expanded its major arterial street system, it aggressively acquired privately held parcels needed for widening and realignment projects. During and after construction, the county was left with parcels of land and houses that needed to be sold, moved, or demolished. Traditionally, these surplus properties had been offered to the highest bidder in a public auction. This process ensured the taxpaying public the highest rate of return and provided the street fund with the greatest amount of revenue. However, faced with a growing demand for low-cost housing, the new housing director approached other county managers to generate some organization-wide support in helping the jurisdiction solve its problem. The transportation director arrived at an obvious conclusion: move surplus houses to surplus land and turn the units over to the housing authority.

This simple solution was difficult to implement, however. The transportation staff was known throughout the jurisdiction for its commitment to excellence, for its desire to preserve the integrity of transportation programs, and for its ability to stretch scarce transportation dollars to meet the county's growth needs. To succeed, the director was required to broaden the source of staff accountability away from traditional transportation-centered departmental loyalties to encompass a larger accountability for the overall socioeconomic well-being of the community. After several months of discussion led by senior managers, this reframing of perspective persuaded the support staff to go along with the project.

Senior managers in nonprofit organizations perform an analogous role to their public-sector counterparts. They frequently take on a coordination and policy-envisioning role for the sector and for the community. For example, United Way chapters and local philanthropic foundations frequently use their control of resources to guide policy, set community goals, and define collaboration practices among participating United Way organizations.

*Initiating Interjurisdictional Collaboration*

Senior managers in most fragmented or loosely coupled metropolitan regions are engaged in an almost continuous dialogue with other governmental entities. The objective of this dialogue is to facilitate more efficient coordination of operations (Crumpton 2008). The following example illustrates that within a typical metropolitan region, extensive cooperation and information sharing are essential to maintaining regional transportation systems, land use planning efforts, open space acquisition, effective law enforcement, sewer and water service coordination, and revenue generation.

This coordinating role is illustrated by the work of the board of commissioners in a local jurisdiction, where the board also serves as the governing body for a special sewer district. The special district is treated under state law as an entirely separate local government. A recent performance audit of the sewer district's operations recommended that consolidating with the county's operation would result in cheaper fleet management and maintenance. However, the recommendation presented a challenge for both the county and the sewer district. First, serious customer service

problems could arise if the consolidation occurred with the grudging reluctance of the separate staffs. Second, the audit indicated that the savings from the consolidation would accrue exclusively to the special district, with little savings to the county. In short, the residents of the county as a whole would benefit from reduced sewer rates, but no reduction in their property tax rates. This meant that the county staff had little to gain and possibly much to lose as a result of the consolidation. Without strong leadership support on both sides, the consolidation was unlikely to occur.

Senior managers in both organizations played a critical role in laying the groundwork for a successful consolidation. As with the housing and transportation example discussed above, the senior managers of the two entities took the leadership initiative to redefine the issues governing consolidation away from narrow questions of organizational efficiency and effectiveness in fleet operation to those of greater accountability in both jurisdictions to the taxpayers as a whole. The senior leaders realized that most citizens do not make distinctions about what governmental entity is providing what service at a given cost. They took advantage of this condition to educate the citizens, and in the process made the proposed changes seem more compelling to many of the internal staff of each agency.

*Negotiating Interorganizational Service Standards*

Senior managers are the chief agents in facilitating interorganizational standards of service. For instance, the police department within the local jurisdiction may have a radically different service standard than its sibling planning department. Because of budget and legal constraints, the planning bureau may take three weeks to process a building permit, while the police department responds to every "prowler" call within 10 minutes. The jurisdiction next door may have a policy of never responding to prowler calls unless someone's personal safety is threatened. These differences do not go unnoticed by citizens and elected officials.

Senior managers in the federal and state governments may not have to worry quite as much about these differences in service standards. Within larger and more complex bureaucracies, service delivery is frequently organized around target populations with specialized needs. Whenever this occurs, these target populations have easier access to the decision makers and can make their concerns known through the newspapers, neighborhood associations, and advocacy groups. As a result, senior managers are under unflagging pressure to work in cooperation with one another to meet the service expectations of the citizenry at large as well as across multiple target populations.

Federal managers and state managers face the problem of providing consistent and uniform service across regions and states. For example, a district ranger office in one part of the country may have a permit system process for the use of the backcountry that is completely different from the permit system in another part of the country or even within the same state. When you add the other natural resource agencies such as the National Park Service, the Bureau of Land Management, and all state-level offices into the mix, you have a recipe for confusion and frustration on the part of citizens who are trying to obtain access to their public domain. Senior managers among the agencies must initiate the efforts to fix these kinds of service problems.

*Interpreting the Needs and Culture of the Community*

The definition of "good service" depends heavily on the culture of the community that the agency serves. Senior managers must understand and honor the values that emanate from this culture. Ethnic and racial group experiences may deeply affect citizen expectations of government agencies and nonprofit service providers. Communities with large minority populations may have ingrained

fears of racial profiling by law enforcement agencies. Minority citizens may believe in the existence of institutional racism based on past treatment and community expectations. Additionally, recent immigrants may harbor a deep suspicion of law enforcement based on experiences from their home countries.

In more subtle examples, some communities with large concentrations of high-tech firms may favor supporting the infrastructure for economic growth at the expense of meeting the changing social service needs of the community. Some jurisdictions do not expect robust and widespread participation processes prior to reaching a decision, while others may expect extensive public consultation. Elected and career officials need to know the community expectations and culture, and then translate these to middle managers and street-level bureaucrats, who, in turn, are responsible for transforming community expectations into effective delivery of services and management of the public's business. The key to keeping in touch with this knowledge is the existence of information exchange and community engagement processes.

Consider, for example, the difficulty faced by state transportation planners who are challenged by local residents who oppose projects because they conflict with "quality of life" considerations. Senior managers set the tone for how responsive the organization will be to these community concerns. Responding to these concerns is not an easy decision, mainly because they require a willingness to delegate considerable amounts of discretion to the middle managers who play a key role with local communities in negotiating how much transportation efficiency will be compromised to serve local community values. Any concessions to cities to alter state highway interchanges, or concessions to a local neighborhood to close streets or install speed bumps and similar devices to slow or divert traffic, compromise the overall integrity of transportation plans and may inhibit emergency access. Haphazard accommodations to these local pressures can lead to equity problems, especially for communities that are not well organized.

Local land use planners frequently find themselves in a similar negotiating role with local residents. For example, the market forces in many wealthy communities have resulted in housing densities considerably lower than what is required under state-mandated land use goals and the professional norms of planners who have been schooled in certain notions of adequate housing choices for those with moderate incomes. Faced with this conflict between community standards and those of the state and the planning profession, senior managers have to craft a course of action that develops consensus and produces legally acceptable solutions through neighborhood planning processes. In short, the standard of "good service" must be informed and guided by the deeply held beliefs of residents across the community. Once identified, this "sense of the community" standard allows administrators to temper the enthusiasm of elected officials and to package initiatives that will meet varying criteria of legitimacy among the neighborhoods and governing units.

## TYPES OF DISCRETION AND THE "LOGIC OF PUBLIC POLICY"

The ubiquity of administrative discretion throughout all levels of government does not mean that all discretion can be treated equally. In fact, as we have already seen, the discretion exercised by street-level administrators is different from the discretion exercised by middle and senior managers.

In addition to organizational structure, another factor that greatly influences the exercise of administrative discretion is the type of public policy that administrators are charged with administering. For example, Exhibit 3.2 demonstrates the importance of distinguishing between those who have responsibility for administering services and those who bear regulatory responsibilities. Most of us respond more favorably to our mail carrier than to an Internal Revenue Service agent. These differences in the types of policy being implemented are important for administrators at all

levels to understand, since they have implications for how to structure and design organizations and to determine what is needed to build support and legitimacy among those affected by the work of the organization.

One way to understand the significance of different types of policy on the exercise of administrative discretion is to review the mix of motivations that create public policy in the first place. Although legislative intent is not always clear and unambiguous, there exists a basic logic in the legislative process that is fairly obvious and holds important implications for the exercise of administrative discretion. Some of the most useful work in clarifying this logic has been done by a group of political scientists, including Theodore Lowi, Robert Salisbury, and John Heinz. In general, they argue that there are different kinds of political structures and processes that have developed over time to accommodate distinctively identifiable kinds of public policy. According to Lowi (1979, 1967), policy outcomes are less the result of the mobilization of political forces and more the result of institutional patterns of relationships that have developed gradually.

For example, most *pork barrel* projects targeted for the benefit of a given constituency district are simply the result of long-standing working relationships among specialized subcommittees of U.S. Congress, interest groups, and agency experts who have to implement the policy. Likewise, regulatory policy can best be understood as the product of an affinity of interests consisting of the regulated industry, an oversight committee of Congress, and a regulatory agency. This institutional set of relationships is more important for understanding policy outcomes than any specific set of policy goals. We will explore these institutional patterns in greater detail in chapters 13 and 14. For present purposes, we wish to focus on some of the implications of these relationships for the exercise of administrative discretion.

The administrative implications of various types of public policy become quite clear once we put ourselves in the shoes of the legislators who are officially responsible for making public policy. Political scientists remind us that legislators at the national and state levels are primarily concerned with two questions about a policy before deciding how they will act (Salisbury and Heinz 1970): (1) What political interest will be served by getting involved, and (2) what opportunity does the policy problem provide for successful involvement? The combination of the political interest (motivation) to get involved and the opportunity to produce a successful solution (desired outcome) result in four basic institutional patterns of *policy logic*—redistributive, distributive, self-regulatory, and regulatory—summarized in Exhibit 3.2.

The political interest a legislator takes in a given issue is determined by the number of interested clientele groups in the legislator's district and the extent to which those groups are fragmented. The larger the number of groups and the more divided they are, the easier it is for the legislator to take stands that are of benefit to local stakeholders without offending other important constituent interests. In short, the more local and invisible the issue, the greater the opportunity a legislator has to take a firm and clear stand. For example, a member of Congress can gain support for a local port improvement project or a farm subsidy by trading or *logrolling* votes for subsidies important to other legislators. Collectively, there is no overarching group of voters who have organized to make the elected official pay a high price for her vote of support on behalf of local constituents. These structural conditions produce what is now popularly characterized as pork barrel politics. Under such conditions, the legislative body need not delegate large amounts of undefined discretion to administrators. The purpose of the legislation is clear, and the interests are well defined and localized.

The opportunity for a legislator to take on an issue is determined largely by the investment of time, energy, and knowledge required to pass a piece of legislation. The more time and technical competence it takes to understand the complexities underlying a legislative initiative, the greater incentive there is for representatives to delegate away large amounts of discretion. The costs of

Exhibit 3.2  **Types of Public Policy**

|  |  | Redistributive Policy | Self-Regulatory Policy |
|---|---|---|---|
|  | Integrated | (i.e., tax, race, ethnicity, and gender policies) | (i.e., licensing of lawyers, doctors, teachers, etc.) |
| Degree of Integration by Stakeholders | Fragmented | Distributive Policy | Regulatory Policy |
|  |  | (i.e., "pork barrel" projects, such as port improvement, research, subsidies, earmarked projects, etc.) | (i.e., EPA—regulation of clean air and water; FTC—determination of fair competition) |

Low                                    High

Opportunity Costs of Reaching a Decision

reaching a decision by themselves may be too high in terms of time and energy. When this occurs, legislative bodies create policies that have been characterized as *regulatory* or *self-regulatory*, depending on the size and the degree of organization of the clientele groups. The larger and better organized the clientele, the more incentive there is for a legislator to delegate considerable policy discretion to the affected group to be responsible for its own self-regulation. This is the case with lawyers and doctors who have been delegated the authority, through the auspices of the American Bar Association (ABA) and American Medical Association (AMA), respectively, to determine who is fit to practice law and medicine.

What is most significant about the policy framework represented in Exhibits 3.1 and 3.2 is that they generate a characteristic pattern of administrative discretion, as summarized in Exhibit 3.3. Recognizing these patterns and knowing why they exist is an important part of the "street smarts" administrators need to acquire if they are to exercise their administrative discretion successfully. This is particularly true of senior managers, who have responsibility for the strategic leadership of their organizations. In this role, they need a thorough understanding of the way in which external socioeconomic and political conditions create both opportunities and constraints on organizational strategic alternatives.

### Distributive Public Policy and Technical Discretion

*Distributive* or pork barrel policies put administrators in the position of using their technical discretion and professional competence to build a dam, construct an aircraft bomber, or improve a waterway. Since the ends of a distributive policy are usually uncontested, and the means are assumed to require the application of commonly accepted technical knowledge, discretion tends to be narrower and less controversial than is the case with the other three policy arenas (redistributive, self-regulatory, or regulatory). At least at the political level, elected officials do not assume they need to worry much about what administrators do to carry out their will. For example, once a decision has been made to authorize an infrastructure project, administrators are generally trusted to use their technical competence to get the job done. Technical requirements and competence act to limit and constrain administrative discretion.

### Regulatory Policy and Social Planning Discretion

Elected officials do not generally entrust administrators with the same kind of discretion that is characteristic of distributive public policy. This is because the ends that *regulatory* agencies are

Exhibit 3.3  **Policy Domains and Corresponding Types of Administrative Discretion**

| Degree of Integration by Stakeholders | | Redistributive Policy Produces Administrative Political Discretion | Self-Regulatory Policy Produces Administrative Professional Discretion |
|---|---|---|---|
| | Integrated | Redistributive Policy Produces Administrative Political Discretion | Self-Regulatory Policy Produces Administrative Professional Discretion |
| | Fragmented | Distributive Policy Produces Administrative Technical Discretion | Regulatory Policy Produces Administrative Planning Discretion |
| | | Low | High |

Administrative and Political Costs of Reaching a Decision

supposed to achieve are a matter of disagreement among legislators. While there may be a common desire to create safe working environments, clean air and water, and safe foods, the uncertain state of our knowledge leads inevitably to some disagreement over exactly what is harmful and how the harm should be addressed. Even when there is agreement that a certain substance is toxic, the level of risk we are willing to assume varies from one person to the next. Legislatures generally saddle administrators with handling these unresolved questions, which at a practical level places regulatory administrators in the position of answering two questions: (1) What is the problem, and (2) do we have a solution that will fix it? Taken together, the dual task of deciding what constitutes a problem and what an acceptable solution looks like puts regulatory bodies in the position of engaging in social planning. The following water treatment debate in a local community illustrates this point.

Since the early 2000s, local water bureaus across the United States have been faced with increasingly stringent federal requirements for water treatment from the Environmental Protection Agency (EPA), especially for waterborne pathogens like *Giardia* and *Cryptosporidium*. To obtain assistance in meeting these requirements, a local water bureau developed a planning process consisting of two panels, one technical and one composed of lay citizens. The panel of high-level lay citizens was charged with making a recommendation based on options prepared by the technical support committee, which consisted of scientists and experts on best practices. The citizens' committee assessed the risks and costs of a combination of different options, including building a filtration plant, covering several reservoirs within the city, and using ultraviolet treatment to destroy the pathogens. The water bureau administrators accepted the citizen panel's final recommendation to build a filtration plant and cover all of the city's reservoirs. But local neighborhood groups surrounding the reservoirs organized against the recommendations, arguing that the risks were low, the costs high, the evidence weak, and that existing reservoirs added important quality-of-life benefits that would be lost if they were covered. In short, the technical concerns over water quality paled in comparison to the social effects of the chosen policy option. As a result, elected officials chose to put the matter on hold indefinitely. This example illustrates the difficulty administrators face in using their discretion to carry out regulatory policies. Whether administrators should or can successfully carry this burden of responsibility is a matter of considerable debate, as we will see in chapters 4–6 and 11–14.

## Redistributive Policy and Political Discretion

The kind of discretion inherent in social planning needs to be distinguished from the kind of political discretion exercised by administrators in implementing *redistributive policy*. When deciding redistributive policy questions involving such matters as taxation, poverty, gender, and

race, politicians create conditions of discretionary administrative authority not because they are uncertain of what the problem is or what kind of solution is best, but because a proposed solution may well create enemies politicians cannot afford to make. Administrators under these conditions are presented with ambiguous rather than vague laws (Jowell 1975; Leys 1943). An *ambiguous law* is one in which the legislature refuses to resolve competing political criteria and, instead, enacts a law that passes the difficulties on to administrators. One of the best examples is the Community Action Program passed by U.S. Congress in the 1960s. The law required the establishment of local citizen advisory committees for each community action program. These oversight committees were required to provide "maximum feasible participation"—a phrase deliberately left ambiguous by the authors of the legislation, since making it specific would have necessitated deciding between those who believed the solution to poverty required a dominant leadership role for professionals in the field, and those who believed that the poor themselves were the best judges of how poverty could be solved. The ambiguity of the law was passed on to administrators who could not sidestep the quarrel as they set up and administered community action programs in the major cities of the United States (Blumenthal 1969). As a result, administrators were caught up in a maelstrom of controversy as they tried to work their way through the debate; frequently, this led to lawsuits in which courts ultimately decided the issue (Horowitz 1977).

### Self-Regulatory Policy and Professional Discretion

The final category of discretion is associated with the kind exercised by doctors, nurses, dentists, lawyers, and other professionals. Professionals are supposed to possess the judgment necessary to determine what competence is required to perform their job; furthermore, they are assumed to be in agreement on what their job is—for example, preserving life in the case of doctors. When these conditions occur, legislative bodies delegate large amounts of unfettered discretion to professionals to *self-regulate* who is entitled to practice in a given field.

There are numerous instances of administrators invoking this kind of functional autonomy to justify their interpretation of what is legally appropriate. This has occasionally resulted in spectacular public controversies. For example, in 1969, President Richard Nixon ordered the U.S. Justice Department to petition the courts on behalf of southern school districts to delay court-ordered busing. President Nixon invoked his policy of New Federalism to argue for control of desegregation policy by citizen committees at the local level. This precipitated a civil disobedience letter from more than 15 U.S. Justice Department lawyers who asserted they had a constitutional duty to press forward on the court desegregation order (Greenburg 1984, 80). Similarly, implementation of environmental laws involving spotted owls and other endangered species have put natural resource administrators at odds with elected officials in both branches of government (Yaffee 1994).

There are several reasons why it is important for administrators to know the policy logic behind the programs they are charged with administering. First, as with the case of public land agents charged with managing our resources for multiple use, they need to know what they are getting into as they translate legal provisions into meaningful operating policy. Who is going to show up at the door? What is their agenda? What is their modus operandi? Anticipating answers to these kinds of questions will greatly increase the chances for successful policy implementation.

A second reason for paying close attention to the characteristics of a particular kind of public policy is to better understand what kinds of solutions are most likely to provide checks against the excesses of administrative discretion. In the United States, reformers have been divided over whether there is too little or too much administrative discretion in government. The *reinvention of government* movement of the 1990s emphasized the need to free bureaucracy from unnecessary

red tape and cumbersome accountability requirements in order to promote efficiency and effectiveness (Osborne and Gaebler 1992). Two decades earlier, Kenneth Culp Davis (1971) argued that administrators should aggressively engage in rulemaking in order to first eliminate unnecessary discretion, and then to confine, structure, and control necessary discretion.

These contradictory approaches to administrative discretion need to be informed and guided by the practical realities of discretion in different policy arenas. What may be appropriate for engineers working in the Army Corps of Engineers may not be appropriate for public servants working in a state department of environmental quality, or for those working in the mayor's neighborhood community action program. The engineers working for the Army Corps will tend to see discretion as relatively safe, because decisions are governed by commonly accepted technical criteria and practice. Those working for the mayor will see discretion as safe only when it is in the hands of those whose programs they favor. What counts for them is not technical competence, but political attitudes and values. For those working in the field where conditions vary from one geographic setting to another, flexibility and discretion is needed to make the technical adjustments necessary to accomplish the goals of a given project. Discretion at the field level typically requires more flexibility, while central office officials seek policy consistency. Middle managers generally have to balance these competing objectives. The different kinds of programs they are required to implement derive from differing moral and legal foundations for administrative authority. This complex variation in types of responsibility means that administrators cannot respond easily to demands for formulaic reform. They must take into account the types of policy issues they are responsible for implementing and the implications these issues have for the amount and kind of discretion required for success.

## LEADERSHIP DISCRETION IN NONPROFIT ORGANIZATIONS

Issues of discretion take on different forms for administrators working in nonprofit organizations than they do for public-sector managers. The primary responsibility of nonprofit administrators is to serve as agents of their organization's board of directors. The organization's senior executive receives both explicit and undefined authority from the governing board. Undefined authority includes the board's values and the organization's institutional values. This delegation of authority typically provides wide discretionary latitude for the director to work with managers and staff members to decide how best to position the role of the organization with donors, community partners, and clients. It empowers the director to assume leadership responsibility for the organization, staffing, and budgeting activities needed to accomplish the organization's mission and goals (Carver 2001).

How executives blend and use their broad delegation of authority is far less legally constrained than is usually the case for public-sector administrators, who may be bound by rulemaking requirements, open meeting and freedom of information laws, rights of privacy, union contracts, and other legal provisions governing purchasing, contracting, and management information systems. Nonprofit administrators with weak or indifferent boards gain even broader discretion. Without clarity in mission, values, and strategic direction, administrators have the primary responsibility for blending explicit delegated authority, board and organizational values, standing board policies, institutional values, and situational context into a defined package of policy or actions.

In addition to the primary guidance provided by the board of directors, other institutional values and principles guide the discretion exercised by the chief executive and nonprofit staff. The legal charter of the organization may define guiding values that shape the mission and how it should

be executed. For many schools, colleges, and hospitals, these guiding provisions trace back with varying degrees of attachment to the religious purposes and values that first established the organization and formed its institution. For example, many of America's most famous universities began with religious sponsorship, and many nonprofit hospitals—now major health systems—began as religious missions. The institutional values of educational excellence and care for those in need still guide these major institutions.

Society and government regulations also have expectations that influence nonprofit purpose, programs, and professional behavior. These include the values of integrity, openness, accountability, service, and the charity of putting the needs of the client before the needs of the organization and self (Jeavons 2001). Recently, with a rise in governmental contracting and partnering and increasing rigor in the application process for foundation grants, expectations for performance-based management have elevated the importance of managerial efficiency, outcome effectiveness, and detailed accountability. These managerial values often conflict with, and must be given priority over, traditional nonprofit charity and civil society values (Alexander, Nank, and Stivers 2001). A prime example of this has come to light in the last several decades, as nonprofits have increased their percentage of *credentialed staff* (i.e., development officers, human resource managers, and financial experts) in order to increase their competitiveness for grants and contracts. This change has come at the expense of direct service delivery and a close and broad working relationship with volunteers (Light 2004; see chapter 5 for a fuller discussion of this issue).

An important part of the discretionary challenge for nonprofit administrators in creating the right balance of values in their organizations is the almost constant preoccupation with fundraising and donor development. The very competitive market for donor funds demands professionalism on the part of fundraisers and organizations (Gelles 2001). Donors require assurance that their funds will be used for a clear and designated purpose and in the intended manner. Donors also require transparency in the financial processing and management of donations. Nonprofits must demonstrate compliance with state laws and regulations regarding corporate registration and fundraising activities. Nonprofits must be ready to prove to regulators and third-party certifiers that administrative expenses are limited to a small percent relative to program delivery expenses. Compliance with these values and practices takes resources that otherwise might have been used to support program and administrative expenses; board direction and executive discretion is required to balance these competing needs.

Finally, as executive and middle-level nonprofit administrators represent their organizations in the larger community, issues of discretion in community governance become important. Nonprofit administrators must strongly advocate for their institutions and their institutional values in the community discussions on policy and programs. However, once a nonprofit agrees to join into multi-organization agreements, its values and culture must accommodate the values of its partner organizations and of the community. For example, public statements and actions that may be very acceptable to a nonprofit acting on its own may violate the ethical standards of another nonprofit or local government when acting in partnership (cf. Ghere 1996). Speaking with a sense of unified purpose becomes additionally important to the credibility of a multi-organizational initiative in the eyes of the community. Citizens have limited ability to separate out the partners in a community network: They simply see an ambiguous service entity tied to a major nonprofit or to government and have no ability to parse out the organization partner responsible for particular policies and services. Thus, when nonprofits enter into polity level discussions and partnerships affecting the broad interests of the community, the larger context of constitutional expectations for government agencies (i.e., liberty, equality, the protection of property, the restraint of government) become increasingly relevant considerations for nonprofit organizations.

## ABUSES OF DISCRETION: A PROBLEM OF PERSPECTIVE

Though discretion is ubiquitous, it is also tailored and channeled to serve multiple ends. As a result, it is difficult to craft a suitable set of solutions to discretionary abuses. Solving one set of problems frequently makes others worse. For instance, there is general agreement that discretion increases flexibility to meet the needs of individuals, that it increases employee motivation, and that it allows departures from routines in the interests of organizational efficiency and effectiveness. At the same time, however, flexible discretion can threaten control, consistency, and coordination. It can undermine the integrity and consistency of public programs and policies. It can prevent the efficient planning and deployment of existing resources. It can foster favoritism and undermine public confidence in the fairness and trustworthiness of public actions. These reservations about increasing discretion clearly reflect an institutional, managerial, and organizational perspective.

Such concerns contrast with the perspective of clients who insist that discretion be used to help and not to hurt their interests. While clients want discretion to be tailored for their personal benefit, they do not want the discretion to result in arbitrariness and the use of idiosyncratic standards. For this reason, there is a general governmental and citizen interest in equal treatment, protection of rights, and uniformity in service delivery.

Standing between the top-down perspective of the management "insider" and the bottom-up "outsider" view of clients are the staff professionals. They frequently prefer discretion for themselves in order to have maximum flexibility in program development and service delivery. Staff professionals tend to see the exercise of discretion by nonprofessionals as problematic—even meddlesome. As we will see in chapters 5 and 8, the rise of the profession of public administration in the early decades of the twentieth century stressed professional performance by trained experts, which often replaces reliance on the self-help of citizens. This increasing reliance on professional standards of performance can come at the expense of citizen engagement in the governance process.

To summarize, the exercise of discretion is frequently a matter of reconciling at least the following five perspectives:

1. the *organizational perspective*, which emphasizes consistency in bureaucratic processes and maximizing of organizational resources;
2. the *professional perspective*, which places a premium on the autonomy of expert judgment;
3. the *client perspective*, which places a priority on individualized and nonformulaic problem solving;
4. the *community perspective*, which emphasizes the preservation of values that are embedded in the unique history, culture, and institutions of local communities; and
5. the *constitutional/legal perspective*, which emphasizes the protection of citizen rights, due process, public accountability, and avoidance of arbitrariness.

To further illustrate these conflicting perspectives, let us take the example of the discretion exercised by U.S. Customs and Border Protection (CBP) agents in enforcing the prohibition against the entry of undocumented immigrants from Mexico into the United States.

If the CBP allowed each officer to decide whom to stop for questioning, and we discovered that Officer A stopped only those who looked poor, or who had dark skin, we might charge the officer with arbitrariness. The arbitrariness would arise from the completely idiosyncratic criteria that the officer invoked. If Officer B followed agency policy to stop every thirtieth car during his shift, whether it was carrying passengers who appeared to be of Hispanic origin or not, we might judge the officer and the policy as being irrational. The means chosen, while not arbitrary, are not well suited to accomplishing

the goals of the policy. If Officer C were ordered as a matter of policy to stop all cars carrying passengers who appeared to be from Mexico within 50 miles of the border with the United States, we could not accuse the border patrol or the officer of being arbitrary or irrational. But we can certainly count on the American Civil Liberties Union (ACLU) appearing in court to argue that the criteria chosen were constitutionally improper because of racial discrimination. Given these difficulties, the CBP might then decide to accept the argument of Officer D, that each agent exercises the professional judgment to stop and arrest suspected illegal aliens without any bureaucratic guidelines. While we might imagine such a policy resulting in practices that are rational, proper, and nonarbitrary, we could not imagine such a policy being acceptable to Officer E, who is in charge of planning the effective and efficient allocation of resources to achieve maximum deployment of personnel. Some standards and measures of efficiency and effectiveness would no doubt be insisted upon. Finally, the values of different communities influence what is an acceptable practice and what is not, as is reflected in local reaction throughout the United States to the 2012 Supreme Court decision upholding the right of Arizona police officers to request legal documentation for residency when stopping anyone for a suspected legal violation (*Arizona v. United States*, No. 11–182, 2012; PR Newswire 2012).

Exhibit 3.4 summarizes these various perspectives on discretion and the typical abuses characteristic of each. When we suggest that a particular abuse is secondary to a given perspective, we do not mean to suggest that it is unimportant. For example, those responsible for managing the daily operations of an agency are not likely to place the same value on the needs and rights of individual citizens as they are on issues that affect the operational efficiency and effectiveness of the organization as a whole. But with education and training, what is secondary may become primary. The summary in Exhibit 3.4 points to the irreconcilable claims that are likely to arise between those on the giving end and those on the receiving end of discretion, as well as the differences that are likely to arise within each perspective. Because discretion does not produce the same kinds of abuses, and because some are of greater concern to us at certain times than at others, disagreements are bound to occur. In devising solutions to the abuses of discretion, we therefore need to recognize that such disagreements may frequently arise from differing moral claims rather than from defects of character or imperfections in our knowledge. We will revisit this issue in chapter 6 on administrative ethics and in chapter 14 on administrative accountability.

## CONCLUSION: DISCRETION, ORGANIZATIONAL CULTURE, AND THE VARIETIES OF BUREAUCRATIC SENSIBILITY

In this chapter, we have examined the ways in which the following three sets of factors affect the exercise of administrative discretion: (1) the conflicting needs of the various levels of authority within public organizations; (2) the multiple purposes of public policy, which create quite different discretionary "logics" for successful policy implementation; and (3) the multiple purposes that are served by discretionary authority and the kinds of abuse that each purpose might generate. In this concluding section, we consider how the actual practice of discretion plays out within the bureaucratic cultures of most public-sector work settings.

Despite the loose talk one hears about the homogenizing effect produced by large and complex bureaucracies, it is still difficult to talk meaningfully about a common bureaucratic experience. Based on what we know of the work settings in complex organizations, there are a variety of occupational sensibilities that take on the force of separate professional and social cultures. For example, Donald Horowitz, in a study of the litigation and counseling functions of federal lawyers, discovered that agency lawyers tend to have a programmatic focus with more of a bureaucratic interest in not pressing for "quick fixes" (Horowitz 1977). They express a greater desire to negotiate

Exhibit 3.4    **Dominant Perspectives and Abuses of Discretion**

| Types of Discretionary Abuse | Insider's or Managerial Perspective | Professional Perspective | Outsider's or Client's/ Citizen's/Community's Perspective |
|---|---|---|---|
| Arbitrariness, i.e., inconsistent treatment of individuals | Primary | Secondary | Primary |
| Irrationality; mismatch between administrative practices and policy goals | Primary | Secondary | Secondary |
| Improper standards, i.e., socially/legally unacceptable | Secondary | Primary | Primary |
| Lack of control and inability to plan, i.e., uneven performance by employees | Primary | Secondary | Secondary |
| Harm to client, i.e., not meeting each person's unique needs | Secondary | Primary | Primary |
| Contrary to community values | Variable | Secondary | Primary |
| Violation of citizen rights, i.e., civil rights, due process, public accountability | Secondary | Secondary | Primary |

differences among competing interests than is usually displayed by litigation lawyers working for the U.S. Justice Department, who work in a strictly adversarial system. Horowitz argues that these differences result from the attitudes engendered by their work. Agency lawyers have tempered their legal aspirations by acquiring a much greater concern for the integrity of their agency's programs; Justice Department lawyers typically emphasize closing or settling cases.

Another study lends further support to the importance of considering the contextual nature of the work setting when trying to construct appropriate standards for the exercise of administrative discretion. In an examination of the administration of disability benefits by the Social Security Administration (SSA), Jerry Mashaw (1981) was struck by the variability and irreconcilability of criticisms made against the disability program. Some accused the SSA of not providing the kinds of adequate service that trained professionals are capable of delivering. Others accused it of not providing adequate due process protections to claimants. A third group was concerned that the program did not produce predictable and consistent results.

Mashaw concludes that these criticisms ultimately arise from different models of justice—models that are built into the work setting itself and are not easily reconcilable. Those who accuse the program of not producing predictable and consistent results are using a *bureaucratic model* of rationality, where efficient processing of information is critical. Those who accuse the program of being arbitrary and unfair to clients are using what Mashaw calls the *moral judgment model* of justice. It is the model upon which our adversarial legal system is built, and it sees justice in terms of giving each individual what he deserves. "Whereas the bureaucratic rationality model views decision making as the implementation of previously determined values, the moral judgment model sees decision making as value defining" (Mashaw 1981, 188).

Finally, those who are concerned about the service deficiencies of the disability program are using a *professional treatment model* of justice, which "recognizes . . . the incompleteness of facts, the distinctiveness of clients' problems and the ultimately intuitive nature of judgment" (Mashaw 1981, 186). Exhibit 3.5 summarizes the distinguishing features of Mashaw's three models of jus-

Exhibit 3.5   **Mashaw's Three Models of Justice**

| Justice Paradigm | Dominant Value | Decision Structure | Primary Goals | Cognitive Approach |
|---|---|---|---|---|
| Bureaucratic | Instrumental rationality | Hierarchical with predetermined value criteria | Programmatic: efficient and effective program implementation | Information and rule-centered |
| Moral judgment | Rights-centered | Fairness and "due process" | Justice for the individual | Litigious/ adversarial |
| Professional Treatment | Service | Professional judgment | Client treatment | Clinical assessment |

*Source:* Adapted from Mashaw 1981.

tice. In the chapters that follow, we will explore some of the consequences of the heterogeneity of administrative discretion and the complexity of the bureaucratic experience in public organizations. As we will see in the next chapter, much of this complexity results from the deliberate decision to construct a public life that achieves multiple and conflicting political ends.

## STUDY QUESTIONS

1. If you have experience working in a government agency, in a service district, or for a nonprofit service provider, how much discretion do you have in your administrative role? From your viewpoint, is/was this discretion sufficient or excessive?
2. Imagine yourself as a homeowner. You face a property tax bill on an annual basis. How much discretion should the representative from the county assessor's office have as she evaluates the value of your home or property?
3. As a homeowner, if you disagree with the assessed value of your home and property, you may appeal to an administrative reviewing officer. How much and what forms of discretion should this administrator apply in reviewing property values appeals?
4. Imagine yourself as a small business owner. You are subject to numerous personnel and worker safety regulations. How much discretion should government representatives possess in dealing with you and your business? Explain how the application of government regulations could affect the profitability of your business.
5. Upon your return to your university after the summer break, you find that the business and finance office requires every student to obtain a debit card account, which will serve as your new Student I.D. The decision for this requirement was made by the university's director of finance in order to find an economical replacement for reliance on Social Security numbers. What type of discretion has this official exercised? Has the official exercised excessive discretion in requiring the new card?
6. Imagine that you are director of student services for your university. How do the kinds of discretion you exercise compare to the three forms described by Mashaw? How do these different perspectives conflict?
7. How would your answers to question 6 differ if you were director of finance instead of director of student services?

8. How does the kind of policy implementation discretion affect the kinds of challenges faced by administrators? For example, how does regulatory discretion differ from service delivery discretion? How does service delivery discretion differ from technical discretion?

9. A local government administers services to the elderly using a combination of in-house staff and staff from a nonprofit contract partner. Consider how regulations to staff and contract provisions would limit service delivery discretion. For the same services, how might the quality and nuance of service delivery from the contract partner differ from the in-house delivery?

10. Consider Mashaw's three models of professional practice for administering Social Security disability benefits. How would a professional treatment model contrast with the bureaucratic model and the moral judgment model?

## NOTES

1. For those who favor more discretionary authority for the sake of achieving greater entrepreneurial freedom, innovation, efficiency, effectiveness, and performance accountability, see Hatry (2010, 2002); Moynihan and Pandey (2005); Wholey and Hatry (1992); Barzelay and Babak (1992); Johnston (1993); Gore (1993); Osborne and Gaebler (1992). For old-line critics who worry more about the abuses of discretion than about its creative benefits, see P. Cooper (2005b, 2003); Moe (1994); Moe and Gilmour (1995); Davis (1971); Lowi (1979).

2. Windows is a registered trademark of Microsoft Corporation in the United States and other countries.

CHAPTER 4

# DEMOCRACY AND ADMINISTRATION

> The American Constitution rests on an entirely new theory that
> will be marked as a great discovery in the political science of our day.
>
> *(Alexis de Tocqueville 1835–1840/2000, 147)*

> Ambition must be made to counteract ambition. The interest of the man must be
> connected with the constitutional rights of the place. It may be a reflection on human
> nature that such devices should be necessary to control the abuses of government. But
> what is government itself but the greatest of all reflections on human nature? If men
> were angels, no government would be necessary. If angels were to govern men, neither
> external nor internal controls on government would be necessary.
>
> *(Madison 1788, Federalist No. 51, quoted in Rossiter 1961)*

> In the United States, the dogma of the sovereignty of the people is . . . the last link in a
> chain of opinions that envelops the Anglo-American world as a whole. Providence has
> given to each individual, whoever he may be, the degree of reason necessary for him to be
> able to direct himself in things that interest him exclusively. Such is the great maxim on
> which civil and political society in the United States rests: The father of a family applies it
> to his children, the master to his servants, the township to those under its administration, the
> province to the townships, the state to the provinces, the Union to the states. Extended to
> the entirety of the nation, it becomes the dogma of the sovereignty of the people.
>
> *(Alexis de Tocqueville 1835–1840/2000, 381)*

Public organizations reflect the character of the larger organic whole of which they are a part. Public bureaucracies in the United States, unlike most other countries in the world, have been deliberately created to serve fairly explicit purposes, which are legally defined within a larger structure of constitutional authority. The constitutional foundations of American public administration have the following three implications for understanding the role of American public organizations: (1) The Constitution plays a central but indeterminate role in shaping both public policy development and implementation; (2) the Constitution creates a system of divided and separated powers with checks and balances; and (3) the meaning of the Constitution is subject to ongoing change and

interpretation. The implications of these characteristics for public administration will be discussed more fully in the following pages.

The U.S. Constitution is a written document that enshrines competing values which have played a decisive role in shaping the American regime as a whole. This differs dramatically from regimes like Great Britain, which has a long history of evolving institutions and social classes that "constitute" British society without the existence of a written document. Britain's institutions are well understood and respected for their historical as well as contemporary meaning. Such is not the case with the U.S. Constitution. Consequently, the written document itself sometimes becomes the focal point for public policy debates. For example, the ongoing debate over whether the United States should adopt some kind of universal health care becomes a debate over whether such action is constitutionally permissible. The Constitution is so central to U.S. governance that "citizens in America usually ask two questions about public policy, while those of many other countries ask only one: Others simply ask '*should* their national government do this or that'; we must also ask '*may* ours do it under the constitution'" (Diamond, Fisk, and Garfinkel 1966, 101). It is common practice for citizens to assert arguments about the constitutionality of a proposed policy as a reason to favor or oppose its passage. This propensity to *constitutionalize* policy differences gets carried over into debates over the role responsibilities of career administrators. Americans want to know if their administrators are exercising their discretion in a constitutionally correct fashion.

A second important characteristic of the American Constitution is the flexibility of the document. This is reflected in debates that invariably surround the appointment of U.S. Supreme Court justices. Everyone wants to know how the future appointee is going to interpret various provisions of the Constitution. In his travels across the United States in the early 1830s, Alexis de Tocqueville was especially struck by the nature of this flexibility in comparison to the constitutions of France and England. He observed that in England, Parliament has the right to modify the constitution so easily that, in practice, the constitution "does not exist at all." In France, the constitution is supposed to be an immutable embodiment of the general will of the people. By contrast, the "American constitution is not supposed to be immutable as in France; [and] it cannot be modified by the ordinary powers of society as in England. It forms a separate work that, representing the will of the whole people, obliges legislators as well as plain citizens, but that can be changed by the will of the people" following preestablished processes (Tocqueville 1835–1840/2000, 95).[1]

Over the years, the U.S. Constitution has been changed quite dramatically, through both formal amendments and case law interpretations by the U.S. Supreme Court. Some of these changes have significantly modified the role responsibilities of career administrators. Since the mid-1990s, we have witnessed American courts interpreting the U.S. Constitution to require that administrators hold the rights of private property in higher regard, give greater respect to the role of states in the U.S. federal system, and pay closer attention to the will of the legislative branch when implementing public policy.[2] All of these decisions have resulted in restricting administrative discretion in the name of the higher constitutional principles of separation of powers, federalism, and protecting individual rights.

A final and perhaps most important distinguishing feature of the U.S. Constitution is the way in which it divides and allocates authority among three branches of government (ensuring the aforementioned separation of powers and checks and balances). In England, career administrators operate under a doctrine of "ministerial responsibility," which attaches their stewardship responsibility to the government ministers of the day. In France, however, where the principle of the "general will" is embodied in the doctrine of parliamentary supremacy, career administrators hold stewardship allegiance to Parliament rather than to the individual government ministers. At a practical level, this creates the possibility for French career administrators to invoke their

stewardship responsibility to Parliament as a whole in opposition to the policies or practices of a given minister (Rohr 1995). In the United States, it is not so clear where the primary allegiance of administrators should reside: They receive their legal and budgetary authority to act from Congress, but they operate under the supervening authority of the executive branch of government. Taken together, these distinguishing features of the American Constitution shape the role responsibilities of career administrators. Because of the American constitutional tradition of separation of powers, the centrality of the written document, and the evolving meaning of its various provisions, the locus of stewardship responsibility for career administrators is much more ambiguous than is the case for administrators in France and England. To whom do American administrators owe allegiance? Is it to the legislative body, which makes the laws? Is it to the chief executive, who executes the laws? Is it to the courts, which interpret the laws? Or is it to the U.S. Constitution as a whole and its encompassing web of offices, processes, and institutions? We will explore these questions in greater detail in the following chapters. Before doing so, however, we must consider the roots of our Constitution and the ideas that informed the founding debates.

## ENGLISH ROOTS OF AMERICAN DEMOCRATIC GOVERNANCE[3]

Publius's famous observations in the Federalist No. 51 (Madison 1788), quoted at the beginning of this chapter, reflect the victory of a new universe of political discourse that, by the end of the seventeenth century, had stood 1,500 years of tradition on its head. (Alexander Hamilton, John Jay, and James Madison used the pseudonym "Publius" in the 85 essays that make up *The Federalist Papers.*) This new discourse begins with the private interests of individuals rather than with some teleological summum bonum[4] (Latin for "ultimate good") as the basic building block upon which to construct a stable and prosperous political order. Up until the sixteenth century, there was a widely shared assumption that individual interests ought to be subordinated to a larger set of communal values. Sometimes these values were religious in nature, such as doing God's will or living a morally virtuous life. Other times these public values were more secular in nature, such as ensuring domestic tranquility or doing one's patriotic duty against foreign enemies to ensure the safety of the nation (Gunn 1969, 36–44; Hirschman 1977, 3–66).

In the sixteenth and seventeenth centuries, these long-held assumptions underwent dramatic changes as various parties challenged the dominant religious, economic, and political orthodoxies of the day in the name of promoting and even liberating the private interests of people. The majority of these critics rejected the traditional view that the common good could be defined apart from the interests of the individual members of the community. Instead of seeing the common good as a check on private interests and a moral guide for the cultivation of human virtue, they argued that the common good *resulted* from forming private interests. This turnabout in thinking occurred as partisans of this new orthodoxy saw the important role that private interests could play in constructing a stable political order. While "interest still remained a term of abuse to describe the motivations of wicked governors," by the end of the seventeenth century the language of interest had become such a dominant centerpiece of public discourse that the "public interest" supplanted "the common good" as the characteristic way of talking about the good of the polity (Gunn 1969, 36, 44).

As with the previous use of terms like "common good" and "public weal," the "public interest" lacked considerable precision. In seventeenth-century England, however, it is possible to identify at least two major characteristics of the public interest. One emphasizes the importance of balancing competing interests, and the other emphasizes the protection of private interests and rights. Each of these characteristics has its counterpart in both the tradition and practice of American public administration (Hirschman 1977, 20–47).

## Public Interest as Balancing

The debate over religious toleration during and after the English Restoration (1677)[5] spawned a variety of political tracts advocating a multiplicity of religious sects as the best way to secure the public peace. Dr. Jeremy Taylor, chaplain to King Charles I, observed that "if you persecute heretics or discrepants, they unite themselves as to a common defence. If you permit them, they divide themselves upon private interest" (Gunn 1969, 156). When applied to the traditional estates of the monarchy, clergy, and nobility, this approach reduced them to critical, but not necessarily exclusive, interests that needed to be balanced in order to secure the public peace.

## Public Interest as the Promotion and Protection of Private Interests

As political thinkers and politicians came to recognize the importance that self-interest could play in balancing religious and political differences, they similarly came to see the importance of self-interest in promoting the economic prosperity of the nation-state. Appeals to charity, to altruism, or a summum bonum were abandoned in favor of the more secure ground of appealing to individuals' interests to do the right thing. By the end of the seventeenth century, the English debate over free trade, mercantilism, and enclosure had produced a widespread belief that economic interest consisted of, and resulted from, the individual pursuit of private economic gain (Gunn 1969, 205–265). This belief, coupled with the religious and political utility of balancing private interests, set the stage for arguing that the public interest requires protection of private interests.

From this period of English history we have inherited a legacy that embodies four important assumptions which greatly influence the role of administration in democratic governance. First, the public interest cannot be defined without taking into account the private interests of citizens. Second, the existence of the public interest is a matter of artificial creation, an instrumental contrivance, rather than something that is "laid up in the heavens" or has universal moral status. Third, the main goal of government is to secure a proper balance of interests between rulers and the ruled rather than actively and aggressively cultivating the intellectual and moral virtue of citizens. Finally, interest is not seen as the ideal foundation of government, just the best possible. William Penn, the Quaker founder of Pennsylvania, observed: "Interest has the security though not the virtue of a principle. As the world goes, it is the secure side" (Gunn 1969, 187).

The legacy of these assumptions about the public interest creates a central dilemma for our present-day system of democratic governance. How can we appeal to a higher and commonly shared sense of ethical duty within a society almost exclusively devoted to the protection and promotion of the pursuit of individual interests? The dilemma has increased in severity as a result of *hyperpluralism*, where the proliferation of single-issue interest groups further undermines the capacity of citizens to think and act in the name of a larger community of shared values and interests.[6] This situation poses real problems for public administrators who share responsibility in building support for a common vision of the community good as well as for protecting individual liberty.

In the remaining sections of this chapter, we will explore how the framers of the U.S. Constitution dealt with this individual liberty versus community good problem. Their solutions have dramatically affected the roles of career administrators in the American democratic system.

## THE FOUNDING DEBATES

The founding of the American political system was an extraordinary and fortuitous achievement. Nowhere in the history of the world had a democratic republic been established and maintained

over such a large and diverse territory as the United States. The framers of the republic were acutely aware of the unique moment in history when they gathered in Philadelphia in 1787 to reconsider ways of correcting defects in the Articles of Confederation. The Articles had proven extraordinarily weak during the Revolutionary War. The authority to raise taxes, the capacity to organize and supply armies, and the ability to respond quickly to external threats proved frighteningly difficult. As with the United Nations, the North Atlantic Treaty Organization (NATO), and other loosely coupled confederations, it is difficult to act decisively when consent from nearly all, or at least the major members, is required.

After the war, problems continued as states developed their own taxes on goods from other states and disagreed on the proper way to secure their borders from European encroachment. Despite dissatisfaction with the Articles of Confederation, participants in the Constitutional Convention knew that any attempt to correct the defects was an iffy undertaking at best. James Madison's *Notes of Debates in the Federal Convention of 1787* (Madison 1787/1987) document the attendees' concerns. Never in the history of humankind had a nation been able to protect the liberty of its citizens over such a large and diverse geographic base. In the convention hall, Benjamin Franklin remarked that he was uncertain whether the sun that appeared on the horizon in a large tapestry hanging on one wall was rising or setting; he happily announced at the end of the convention that it was, indeed, rising.

The rising sun celebrated by the framers at the end of their work was a new government devoted to the preservation of individual liberty. The American system of government was founded on the principle that public life is secondary to the pursuit of one's personal choices in the private and social spheres. Most Americans live out this commitment by placing family, friendship, and economic well-being above civic responsibility. This *libertarian* interpretation of the Constitution emphasizes negative over positive freedom (Berlin 1969). "'Negative freedom' means freedom from interference, from being pushed around, restricted, locked up" (Held 1984, 124). The American system of government, according to this view, was not established to cultivate human excellence (either moral or intellectual) or to advance the interests of the rich and wellborn. But such a view does not necessarily mean that those who are aristocratic or oligarchic in spirit are not able to cultivate their respective excellences: They are permitted to do so, but only because liberty is defined *negatively,* as the pursuit of individual interests (Diamond 1979, 45–49). As one commentator on the Constitution has observed, the founders solved the problem of establishing a working uniformity out of diversity by creating a "constitutional everyman"—a new kind of citizen—that served as the building block of the new political order.

> Citizenship is not a moral adventure or an educational experience. It is merely a legally defined bundle of rights and powers which the individual may use to defend and advance his interests. . . . The citizen is expected to disclose but a fraction of himself to the public gaze. . . . The construct of public equality serves as a mask behind which one's inner self can hide from the probing, judging eyes of anonymous others. . . . The [public] space is kept as small as possible. Liberty, which expresses men's inequalities and diversities, resides within the zone of privacy. The fundamental convention, then, is that all men shall be treated as equals in the public realm, in order that they will be able to express their inequalities in the private realm. By assigning the principle of equality to one territory and the principle of inequality to another, the constitutionalists thought that both could be preserved without conflict. (Schaar 1964, 887–888)

The libertarian focus of American government deflects attention away from the ends of governance to the means necessary to preserve private liberties. The consequence of a libertarian

bias is that career public administrators frequently encounter difficulty engaging citizens in the business of government. The dominance of private over public life is what distinguishes American democracy from the democracy of classical Greece. As Tocqueville observed in his travels in the early 1830s, Americans are so preoccupied with the activities affecting their economic well-being that it is difficult to get them involved in the larger good of the community.

> Only with difficulty does one draw a man out of himself to interest him in the destiny of the whole state, because he understands poorly the influence that the destiny of the state can exert on his lot. But should it be necessary to pass a road through his property, he will see at first glance that he has come across a relation between this small public affair and his greatest private affairs, and he will discover, without anyone's showing it to him, the tight bond that here unites a particular interest to the general interest. (Tocqueville 1835–1840/2000, 487)

Tocqueville did not view this preoccupation with economic and private well-being as particularly problematic. In fact, it could be used as a mighty engine to cultivate a deep and abiding concern for public affairs. The trick was in learning how to connect the self-interest of each individual to the larger good of the whole, what he termed the "science of association" (Tocqueville 1835–1840/2000, 492). Nor did Tocqueville believe that preoccupation with one's economic well-being was peculiarly unique to American democracy. It was, he maintained, inherent in the very nature of democracy itself, simply the logical consequence of democracy's deep commitment to liberty. If left free to pursue their own interests, the vast majority of human beings would naturally engage in commercial activities to enhance their economic well-being.

The framers of the American state and federal constitutions anticipated this inherent tendency of the citizenry to give greater primacy to their private affairs than to the public affairs of their community. By *framers,* we mean two groups of adversaries, the Federalists, who took the initiative in arguing for replacement of the Articles of Confederation, and the Anti-Federalists, who opposed the creation of a more consolidated national union. Both parties agreed that liberty was the prize, but they disagreed fundamentally about the conditions necessary for its long-term survival.

The Federalists believed that the self-interest of human beings could be structured and channeled through carefully designed systems of representation, separation of powers, checks and balances, and federalism to secure the blessings of liberty. The Anti-Federalists, on the other hand, favored a face-to-face approach to politics—one of active and constant personal engagement supported by a life that cultivated what has come to be called "republican virtue" (Storing 1981b, 15–23). They believed a certain kind of democratic virtue was necessary for the healthy functioning of a liberty-serving democratic order and that this virtue could not be taken for granted: *It required systematic cultivation.* While the Federalists certainly were not indifferent to the impact that the formation of character had on public life, they did not believe the U.S. Constitution could—or for that matter should—make government dependent on the continued existence and cultivation of personal virtue among either the rulers or the ruled. The Anti-Federalists offered an important counterpoint to the dominant Federalist tradition of our constitutional system.

As a consequence of this founding debate, career public administrators are blessed with two rich strands of discourse, each of which shapes how we talk about their role and the role of the citizenry in American systems of government. The Federalists have provided us with the *procedural republic model*, emphasizing the importance of structures, processes, and formal rights to protect liberty. The Anti-Federalists have provided us with a *civic republic model,* emphasizing the importance of small face-to-face government (Kemmis 1990, chap. 2). Understanding both

of these strands is essential for effective administration of the public's business, since together, they provide a foundation for understanding the unique roles career officials play in sustaining the American constitutional order (Tocqueville 1835–1840/2000, 90).

## The Federalists and the Procedural Republic

The Federalists argued that, to ensure the preservation of liberty, mechanisms had to be put into place to control the excesses of self-interest. They argued that a healthy and long-lived democratic polity could be created by (1) mitigating the adverse effects of undesirable popular passions at the base of the system, and (2) manipulating the structures and duties of public office at the top of the system. At the base of the system, new mechanisms of indirect democracy needed to be created; at the top, new devices had to be invented that would encourage ambitious and qualified leaders to ensure high regard for the interest of the larger public good without expecting them to be primarily motivated by "other regarding" values. Fortunately for the friends of liberty, argued Publius, "the new science of politics," like most other sciences of the day, had improved sufficiently to make this difficult task possible (Hamilton 1787, Federalist No. 9, quoted in Rossiter 1961). There were two key elements in this new science of politics: controlling majority tyranny and checking the abusive exercise of power by officialdom.

*Controlling the Adverse Effects of Popular Passions*

One of the vital discoveries of the "new science of politics" was how to establish liberty over a vast expanse of territory while simultaneously guarding against majority tyranny. Before 1787, all democratic regimes throughout the world had fallen prey either to the mob or to the precipitous centralizing tyranny of a large standing army. Both fates, argued Hamilton in Federalist No. 9 (1787), could be avoided by the "enlargement of the orbit," or incorporating a multiplicity of interests within a larger territorial whole. Consolidating the 13 colonies in a common geographic area would have a threefold advantage. Following the insights of the Scottish philosopher David Hume, Hamilton asserted first that the larger orbit (assuming open access to commercial diversity) would (1) increase the multiplicity of interests; (2) make it more difficult for any single interest to see what it had in common with others, thus making the formation of a tyrannical majority difficult; and (3) make it harder for a tyrannical majority to take common action that would threaten the rights of the minority. In short, a large and commercially diverse territory with open access to development would fragment opinion, multiply sectarian organizations, and balkanize the formation of interest groups. For the first time in history, democratic government could be protected from the tyranny of one or the many (see The Federalist Nos. 9 and 51, quoted in Rossiter 1961).

*Structuring the Duties of Public Office: Appealing to Personal Interests to Maximize Public Benefits*

One of the key discoveries of the sixteenth and seventeenth centuries was that the public interest could be achieved by preserving and protecting the private interests of individuals. This principle came into play in thinking about how to structure the offices of government. Madison (Federalist No. 51. 1788) observed that the "new science of politics" must keep government safe from the usurpation of authority without discouraging the best and the brightest from offering themselves up as candidates. The secret to achieving these dual objectives was to structure the duties of public office so that "the interest of the man" is "connected with the constitutional rights of the

place." The application of this principle is nicely illustrated in the argument Publius makes in the Federalist No. 72 (attributed to Hamilton) against limitations on the terms of office for elected officials, especially the president.

> There are few men who would not feel much less zeal in the discharge of a duty when they were conscious that the advantage of the station with which it was connected must be relinquished at a determinate period, than when they were permitted to entertain a hope of obtaining, by meriting, a continuance of them. . . . The desire of reward is one of the strongest incentives of human conduct; or that the best security for the fidelity of mankind is to make their interests coincide with their duty. . . . Another ill effect of the exclusion would be the temptation to sordid views, to peculation, and, in some instances, to usurpation. An avaricious man, who might happen to fill the office, looking forward to a time when he must at all events yield up the advantages he enjoyed, would feel a propensity, not easy to be resisted by such a man, to make the best use of his opportunities while they lasted, and might not scruple to have recourse to the most corrupt expedients to make the harvest as abundant as it was transitory; though the same man, probably, with a different prospect before him, might content himself with the regular perquisites of his situation, and might even be unwilling to risk the consequences of an abuse of his opportunities. His avarice might be a guard upon his avarice. Add to this that the same man might be vain or ambitious, as well as avaricious. And if he could expect to prolong his honors by his good conduct, he might hesitate to sacrifice his appetite for them to his appetite for gain. (Hamilton 1788, Federalist No. 72, quoted in Rossiter 1961)

The Federalists believed the most to be hoped for under a properly constructed system of government lay in displacement of the lower passions of avarice and vanity by the higher motivations of ambition and honor. If the duties and terms of office could be structured to appeal to the ambitious, then individuals would be encouraged to launch long-term projects that would advance the public good. Projects like the New Deal, the Fair Deal, the Great Society, and the New Frontier give one a place of honor in history. This desire for honor or fame in the eyes of posterity (as distinguished from a desire for immediate popularity) could thus be turned into a powerful engine to promote the larger public good (Adair 1974).

## The Anti-Federalists: The Civic Republic Tradition

The Anti-Federalists entered the Constitutional Convention with the idea that liberty could not be maintained over a large and extended territory like the United States. And the lessons of history were clearly on their side. An obvious danger arose from the large standing army needed to protect the frontiers from invasion by greedy and envious foreign powers. A standing army would be costly to maintain, requiring a heavy tax burden, and would inevitably develop a will of its own that would endanger the liberty of the people. But more important, a large territory could not provide the conditions that would cultivate the right kind of citizen virtue.

The Anti-Federalists worried that the energies of the people in a large commercial republic would be mobilized to increase trade and commerce in the service of what Patrick Henry in the Virginia ratifying convention characterized as "grandeur, power and splendor," rather than in guarding their liberties. "Those nations who have gone in search of grandeur, power and splendor have also fallen a sacrifice, and been the victims of their own folly. While they acquired those visionary blessings, they lost their freedom" (Henry quoted in Storing 1981a, V:214). The quality

most vital to the public interest, then, was a vigilant temperament, and this was thought to exist especially among those in "middling circumstances," who "are inclined by habit, and the company with whom they associate, to set bounds to their passions and appetites." The substantial yeomanry of the country was thought to be "more temperate, of better morals, and less ambition, than the great" (Storing 1981a, VI: 158).

In short, for the Anti-Federalists, the public interest was inseparable from right living: The habit of virtue cultivated by living as a yeoman farmer fostered the essential virtues of moderation, vigilance, industry, and thrift. These "republican virtues" were believed by the Anti-Federalists to be essential elements in protecting citizens from the overreaching power of government (Storing 1981b, chapter 4). This Anti-Federalist view of what has come to be called the "civic republic tradition" contrasts in important ways with the version that most captivated Tocqueville's attention during his travels across the United States during the early decades of the new republic. Tocqueville's travels throughout the United States coincided with the very first years of the Jacksonian era (1828–1860), and he was struck by the infinite art with which the inhabitants of the United States managed to fix a common goal to the efforts of many men and to then to advance to it freely through the formation of associations. He observed that instead of relying on government, Americans use associations "to found seminaries, to build inns, to raise churches, to distribute books, to send missionaries to the antipodes . . . to create hospitals, prisons, schools" (Tocqueville 1835–1840/2000, 182, 489 passim. He was so impressed by the vibrancy of voluntary associations, religious sects, and organized acts of self-help that he was moved to conclude that the "in democratic countries the science of association is the mother science; the progress of all the others depends on the progress if that one. . . . In order that men remain civilized or become so, the art of associating must be developed and perfected among them in the same ratio as equality of conditions increases" (1835–1840/2000, 492). Tocqueville viewed the formation of associations as a necessary antidote to the balkanizing forces of the pursuit of economic well-being. Although done for reasons of self-interest, the formation of associations created a habit of "civic-mindedness" and introduced the importance of a communitarian perspective. Because this communitarian impulse emanated from the enlightened pursuit of one's own self-interest, Tocqueville dubbed this republican virtue "self-interest rightly understood," to distinguish it from the older aristocratic tradition that considered the virtue of public service an end in itself. Republican virtue based on "self-interest rightly understood" also differs from the Anti-Federalist version of civic republicanism, which emanated from the habits produced by living the life of the yeoman farmer. Whether grounded in virtue or enlightened self-interest, Americans are beholden to the Anti-Federalists for their communitarian-centered view of democratic governance. Today, in the Anti-Federalist tradition, many citizens pursue active public service in their local communities but find frustration with organized politics and national government.

### The Administrative Implications of the Federalist and Anti-Federalist Visions

The Federalists and Anti-Federalists leave us with two quite different visions of public service, both of which have affected American public administration. The Federalist vision is reminiscent of the classical Roman tradition, where honor and devotion to the common good are high callings, where grand and ambitious public ventures are encouraged, and where the doers of such grand deeds are held in high esteem (Green 1993). There is a decisive difference, however, separating the Federalist vision from its classical forebears. The Federalists held a truncated view of public life in which the state becomes an instrument of negative rather than positive freedom. They saw government as a regulatory agent for promoting peace and prosperity without assuming any

responsibility for cultivating virtue or even the minimum qualities of character that they believed were needed for good government. The Federalists took for granted that the full range of higher virtues would have suitable opportunity to flourish in private life. They presumed that human nature included a weak but nonetheless natural inclination to certain virtues. They believed that these higher virtues would develop from religion, education, family upbringing, and simply out of the natural yearnings of human nature. Indeed, they even accorded to these higher excellences a quasi-public status in the expectation that "American democracy would seek out and reward the 'natural aristocracy' with public trust" (Diamond 1979, 71–72).

Whether or not the Federalists were correct in assuming that virtuous individuals would be favored in the electoral process, they developed a political system that did not depend on these higher human virtues for its well-being. In terms of public service, they planned for the worst in human behavior by designing a government based on checks and balances, one that would at least deter egregious abuse of office. This is why, to this day, government jobs are hedged about with so much oversight and elaborate rules of procedure.

The Federalists, however, exemplified the natural aristocracy they hoped would be attracted to public service. This was reflected in the way George Washington staffed his first administration. He appointed public servants who could successfully pass a "fitness of character test." This test required that individuals possess impeccable personal integrity (cultivated in private life), high levels of competence, and high standing in their local communities. Through this fitness of character test, Washington sought to appoint public servants who "would give dignity and luster to our national character" (White 1948, 259).

The Anti-Federalists also left us with a legacy of public service that has served as a precedent for some important features of our modern-day career civil service. First, they insisted that agents of the republic be comprised of those with modest means, neither rich nor poor. This feature is preserved in the open access of our competitive merit system, which sets minimal technical qualifications that are job specific. Second, they argued that public agents were to be drawn from the local community and have knowledge of local circumstances. The federal civil service system follows this practice by hiring local employees to administer national programs, or by having such programs administered by state and local public officials rather than by federal employees. Finally, career public servants display those qualities of prudent judgment and modest expectations of the general citizenry that Anti-Federalists believed were essential for moderating unreflective, overly bold, and self-serving initiatives undertaken by elected public officials.

Citing studies that compared the attitudes and values of career administrators with the citizenry, Charles Goodsell (2004, 84–111) found that the public service mirrors the public at large to a surprising degree. Although government bureaucrats are sometimes negatively portrayed as "poor performers as well as budget maximizers; ants and megalops as well as empire builders; and merciless oppressors of their own kind as well as their clients" (Goodsell 1983, 19), Gregory Lewis found in his wide-ranging attitudinal study that "bureaucrats in general seem to be quite ordinary in their politics, values and personal lives. . . . Top officials are as likely as ordinary people to favor cutting government spending and no more likely to place confidence in the people running the executive branch or the military" (Lewis 1990, 227).

The civic republic tradition of the Anti-Federalists—with its emphasis on active citizenship, face-to-face communication, and the intelligence of ordinary people—provides significant norms for the exercise of administrative discretion. First, it means that career administrators may need to relegate technical expertise to a lower priority in favor of listening and honoring the opinions of the uninformed, even when it does not result in efficient public policy outcomes. Transportation planners, for example, frequently find themselves facing this kind of dilemma when concerned

citizens in a neighborhood insist on speed bumps, roundabouts, and other traffic-calming devices that interfere with the efficient flow of traffic and access by emergency vehicles.

Second, the civic republic tradition requires more than simply listening and being responsive. It means engaging in collaborative decision making, where neither the problem nor the solution is presupposed at the outset of a process. There are numerous examples of this at the local levels of government, where planners, educators, environmental experts, and neighborhood officials work with citizens to create shared solutions that do not necessarily fit a predetermined mold. Parent-led site councils in public schools and neighborhood community councils perhaps best exemplify this civic republic tradition at work.

Finally, the civic republic tradition emphasizes coproduction and delivery of public services (Levine 1984). Community policing is a classic example of putting the principle of coproduction to work. The process enlists citizens in a joint effort by a public agency to define a given level and quality of service, and then the citizens participate in the delivery of that service. In the case of community policing, this may take the form of neighborhood watch groups or community courts where citizens participate in adjudicating neighborhood-level disputes.

Watershed restoration projects represent another increasingly popular example of coproduction. Citizens within a common geographic watershed identify ways in which multiple stakeholder groups can preserve and protect the watershed from degradation. Joint actions by interest groups and individual citizens might include governing the use of pesticide runoff, erosion control, grazing practices, irrigation use, and reforestation practices. To the extent these common actions are successful, citizens collectively join with career administrators to produce a public good that may reduce the need for harsh regulatory intervention by government agencies. The goal of coproduction is not to replace administrators with volunteers; rather, it is to link the professional expertise and accountability of career administrators with the local knowledge and attachment of citizens to produce a public good.

Together, the Federalists and Anti-Federalists leave us with two different traditions by which Americans judge the appropriate relationship between career officials and citizens. The *civic republic tradition* of the Anti-Federalists assesses citizenship in terms of substantive traits—traits that emphasize the deliberative and participatory role of each individual in constituting a commonly shared sense of purpose and action. The *procedural republic tradition* of the Federalists assesses citizenship in terms of the formal rules, processes, and structures that create opportunities for access, a fair hearing, rule-bound decision-making processes, and the right to vote either directly or indirectly for those who make the decisions. The civic republic tradition emphasizes face-to-face communication, the building of interpersonal trust, and the importance of local knowledge, while the procedural republic tradition emphasizes the indirect representation of interests, the crucial role of expertise, and the value of mediating processes and structures in achieving the public interest.[7]

Exhibit 4.1 summarizes the chief characteristics of these two "good citizenship" traditions. For the civic republic tradition, good citizenship is measured by the extent to which each citizen in the community is willing and able to sit at a metaphorical public table and deliberate with others about what constitutes the public interest. This tradition assumes that individual citizens possess, or are willing to develop, crucial self-governing skills. For the procedural republic tradition, good citizenship is measured both by the extent to which interest groups, associations, and the formal processes of government are able to reflect the interests of the citizenry and by the extent to which the citizenry at large accepts the results of these efforts as legitimate. The requirements of good citizenship under the procedural republic tradition are far less demanding. It is enough that citizens vote; care enough to pay attention to general, but not specific, issues; are tolerant of diversity and

Exhibit 4.1 **Good Citizenship Traditions**

|  | Civic Republic Tradition | Procedural Republic Tradition |
|---|---|---|
| Origins | • Anti-Federalists<br>• small republic agrarian tradition | • Federalists<br>• interest group pluralism |
| Characteristics | • face-to-face communication<br>• emphasis on substantive equality<br>• emphasis on substantive agreement and consensus<br>• community is socially constructed<br>• emphasis on importance of place<br>• emphasis on action, i.e., doing things together, rather than getting formal agreement<br>• emphasis on duties as well as rights | • reliance on indirect representation<br>• reliance on procedural equality<br>• emphasis on voting and majority rule principle<br>• community is a legal agreement<br>• emphasis on procedural fairness with open access and right to participate<br>• rule-of-law orientation<br>• emphasis on rights over duties |
| Citizenship requirements | • high level of deliberative skills<br>• development of relevant knowledge and expertise<br>• personal participation<br>• citizen ownership and control of decision | • voting<br>• heavy reliance on interest group participation<br>• opportunity for individuals to advise and counsel<br>• heavy reliance on elected officials and career administrators |
| Legitimating criteria | • degree of participation<br>• degree of citizen control<br>• sense of ownership of both process and outcome | • due notice of important decisions and open access to decision making<br>• opportunity for a "hearing" and right to be heard<br>• procedural fairness in gathering and assessing information |

differences of opinion; and defend the principles of procedural fairness. The burden of democratic governance in the procedural republic model is born by formal institutions and knowledgeable, interested, expert citizens rather than by the citizenry at large.

These two traditions of governance give rise to a wide range of motivations and purposes for participating in public affairs. It is important for career administrators to understand them, especially as they seek to develop and implement various kinds of public programs that depend on citizen support.

## LIBERTY AND DEMOCRATIC GOVERNMENT: A PROBLEMATIC TENSION

The content of the procedural republic and civic republic traditions turned on a central question for the founding generation: *What most endangers liberty?* The founding debates and the structure of the Constitution itself do not give clear guidance as to how this question should be answered. Instead, we are introduced to a problematic tension among four different answers that are to this day passionately embraced by the American people. These include arguments that we have: (1) too much government, (2) too little government, (3) government that fails to protect the minority from the tyranny of the majority, and (4) government that provides too little opportunity for civic engagement. These answers reflect quite distinct and very real problems that are deeply rooted in American political life. We describe these problems in terms relating to the American found-

ing, while emphasizing that the problems persist as a seemingly permanent feature of American public life.

## The King George Problem

The excesses of King George and an overbearing monarchy sparked the American Revolution. Famous events such as the Boston Tea Party and the ride of Paul Revere represented a call to check the abusive exercise of tyrannical governing power, especially executive power. In response, each newly adopted state constitution (except New York's) concentrated governmental power in the popularly elected legislative branch, providing for only a very weak executive branch (Thach 1969, chap. 2). And under the Articles of Confederation, the national government remained totally dependent upon the good will of the states for its resources and exercise of meager powers. At all levels of government, the prevailing attitude was, "We do not want too much government!" The excitement resulting from giving "all power to the people" soon foundered, however, on the dual shoals of incompetent government and majority tyranny.

## The George Washington Problem

The inability of General Washington to acquire the necessary troops, arms, and supplies during the Revolutionary War demonstrated the need for unity of command operating within a stable and more robust system of funding. It was nearly impossible to conduct coordinated and sustained military campaigns under the authority of the Articles of Confederation, which gave this responsibility to a committee. Severe war losses and economic depredations taught painful lessons about the need for unity of command, coordinated planning, functional specialization, expertise, adequate powers to implement legislative will, and the ability to respond quickly to emergencies. The lesson learned, at least by some of the founding generation, was that too little government was as bad as too much.

## The Shays' Rebellion Problem

In 1786 and 1787, the fear of tyrannical majorities surfaced when debt-ridden farmers in western Massachusetts took up arms to prevent the courts from foreclosing on their mortgages. Since debtors always outnumber creditors in a large commercial republic, many of the framers realized that the success of Shays' Rebellion would undermine fundamental rights and threaten the kind of long-term stability necessary for the new nation's economic growth and development. By the time of the call for a Constitutional Convention to revise the Articles of Confederation, considerable sentiment existed in favor of checks on unrestrained legislative power. Unchecked legislative majorities seemed as threatening as a tyrannical executive to the protection of basic political rights.

## The Bowling Alone (Engaged Citizen) Problem

The debates over the adoption of the U.S. Constitution highlighted the importance of an older vision of self-government that could not be satisfied by simply protecting citizens from the abuses of rulers like King George. Small democratic communities were important not only because they played a key role in maintaining eternal vigilance over suspicious rulers but also because they produced policies and practices that were informed by local knowledge, and they provided processes that enabled citizens to acquire the knowledge, skills, and competencies to be civically

engaged in meaningful ways. To be so engaged enhances one's liberties and heightens the sense of self-interest rightly understood. A constitution that provides for a strong, professionalized central government and encourages private pursuit of material gain tends to discourage civic engagement. Ultimately, this distracts the public from a proper vigilance over each other's liberties as well as from civic-mindedness more generally. The "bowling above" reference comes from the work of Robert Putnam (2000) who documents the decline of civil engagement and the adverse impact this has on political life. He argues that people prefer to bowl alone, rather than bowl with others, which serves as a metaphor for the engaged citizen problem.

To summarize, for the founding generation, satisfying the public interest was a problematic balancing act. An irreconcilable tension existed in the need for (1) competent government, (2) popular sovereignty, (3) preservation of minority rights, and (4) civic engagement. Attempts to address any one of these four major dangers to liberty seemed only to exacerbate the other three. For example, creating a more consolidated government at the center, with greater executive power to protect against external threats and tyranny of the majority, potentially endangers the liberty of citizens from internal abuses of power by governing officials. The corresponding lack of civic engagement dulls the instinct for vigilance and suspicion among the populace for the abuse of governmental power. For the Federalists, too little governmental power at the center and majority tyranny were far more deleterious to the public interest than the Anti-Federalists' fear of too much power at the center and the desire for a civic republic. Accordingly, under the aegis of President George Washington, the Federalists established a range of administrative institutions and practices as correctives to the dangers they feared most. And this, of course, provoked heated responses from Anti-Federalists who insisted on preserving administrative practices designed to protect against abuses of increased power at the center and to maintain a robust tradition of local civic governance. Thus, from each of the four threats to liberty there emerged corresponding and rival correctives. As mentioned first in chapter 2, the problems and their correctives are neatly summarized in the following beatitudes:

### The Founding Beatitudes

Too much power begets usurpation, to which majority rule is a corrective;

Too much majority rule begets majority tyranny, to which separation of powers and checks and balances is a corrective;

Too much separation of powers and checks and balances begets incompetent government, to which unity at the center is a corrective;

Too much unity at the center begets usurpation, to which civic engagement is a corrective. (Adapted from Morgan 2001, 156)

The tensions captured in these beatitudes remain as permanent features of American politics and governance. As we shall see in the chapters that follow, their dynamics are apparent in the turbulent history of the American republic and have contributed to the development of distinct traditions of American administrative practice.

## CONCLUSION

The American founders gave us a constitutional system that embraces contending principles of good republican governance. These contending principles reflect basic disagreement as to what is required to preserve a regime of ordered liberty. In Exhibit 4.2, we summarize these tensions.

Exhibit 4.2 **How to Address the Multiple Threats to Individual Liberty**

| Sources Of Danger to Liberty | Solutions | Citizenship and Expertise Implications |
|---|---|---|
| **Arbitrary abuse of power by government officials:** "The King George Problem" (A shared Federalist/Anti-Federalist priority) | • "Rule of Law" prophylactics such as the Bill of Rights<br>• Separation of powers<br>• Checks and balances<br>• Federalism<br>• Strong representative government and frequent elections<br>• Limited and enumerated government powers | • Reliance on representational institutions by which citizens exercise control through periodic elections<br>• Reliance on the "auxiliary precautions" of formal legal structures and processes, which reduce citizenship demands |
| **Weak, incompetent and fickle government:** "The George Washington Problem" (Federalist priority) | • Strong executive branch<br>• Reliance on experience and expertise<br>• Separation of powers<br>• Checks and balances<br>• Structural incentives to encourage continuity in office and independent and informed judgment | • Creation of mediating structures that reduce dependence on highly active and knowledgeable citizenry (i.e., Senate chosen by the states, court with life tenure, president elected by an electoral college with no term limits) |
| **Majority tyranny:** "The Shays' Rebellion Problem" (Federalist priority) | • Structural checks and balances, both internally in the government and externally in the socioeconomic setting<br>• Foster a large commercial republic that would create a multiplicity of interests<br>• Bill of Rights | • Reliance on a procedural democracy which places few demands on citizens except to pursue their own interests within a limited legal framework that protects rights |
| **Disengaged citizens and loss of republican virtue:** "The Bowling Alone Problem" (Anti-Federalist priority) | • Small, simple and limited government<br>• Large representative body composed of the "those in middling circumstances"<br>• Constraints on the "emergence of a large commercial republic" | • Reliance on a civic republic where small, local and direct democracy is sufficient to address the major problems faced by citizens |

Column 1 enumerates the dangers to liberty that the founders sought to avoid. Column 2 summarizes the solutions they crafted to address these dangers. Column 3 lists the implications of these solutions on democratic citizenship. The Constitution divides and checks governing power in part to keep the arguments perpetually in play. The founders joined the argument in their own administrations, pitting Federalist measures favoring a procedural republic against the Anti-Federalist measures in favor of a civic republic. These competing visions spawned quite different traditions of administrative practice. The history of American administrative development begins here, but it must be reviewed in the broader context of a history that adds layers and permutations to American administrative theory and practice. As we shall see in the next chapter, it remains a troubled history with profound ambivalence about the proper roles of public administration in a democratic republic.

## STUDY QUESTIONS

1. What are the multiple problems of democratic governance the Federalists wished to solve in establishing the American system of governance? How did they resolve the complex trade-offs implied?
2. To what extent do you think there is a need for modern-day communities to remain as concerned with the problem of "majority tyranny" as the Federalists were in the late 1700s? How, if at all, does this problem express itself administratively within an organization with which you are familiar?
3. Use a case study or situation from your administrative experience to assess the adequacy of the Federalist assumptions and principles underlying our system of democratic governance.
4. What does Publius mean in Federalist No. 51, when he claims that the American system of separation of powers and checks and balances relies on a "policy of supplying, by opposite and rival interests, the defect of better motives"? Give some examples of how this principle might be applied at the administrative level to achieve successful administrative outcomes.
5. What dangers did the Anti-Federalists fear most about government? What correctives did they recommend for overcoming such dangers?
6. What are the consequences of the Anti-Federalist view for the administrative function of government? How do these consequences compare with those of the Federalists?
7. Use a case study or situation from your administrative experience to assess the adequacy of the Anti-Federalist assumptions and principles underlying our system of democratic governance.

## NOTES

1. We rely heavily throughout this book on the insightful observations of Alexis de Tocqueville, who traveled to the United States from France to study American prison reform. Over the course of his stay from 1831 to 1832, he became so infatuated with the workings of American democracy that he put his writing project aside and focused on capturing the logic of the newly emerging democratic impulse—an impulse he believed would forever change the world. Tocqueville recorded his observations and insights in a two-volume work, *Democracy in America* (originally in French; the first volume was published in 1835, the second in 1840). It has come to be regarded by many as one of America's founding documents, along with the constitutional and state ratifying convention debates and the Federalist and Anti-Federalist papers.

2. For property rights cases, see *Dolan v. Tigard*, 512 U.S. 374 (1994) and *Babbit v. Sweet Home*, 515 U.S. 687 (1995). For important cases reaffirming states' rights, see *University of Alabama v. Garrett* (99–1240), decided February 21, 2001; *Alden v. Maine*, 527 U.S. 706 (1999); and *Florida Prepaid Post-Secondary Education Expense Board et al. v. College Savings Bank,* 527 U.S. 666 (1999). For discussion of general trends

regarding federalism, see Peterson (1995) and Walker (1999). For important cases reaffirming the nondelegation of legislative authority, see *FDA v. Brown and Williamson Tobacco Corp.*, 529 U.S. 120 (2000) and *American Trucking Association v. EPA,* 175 f.3d 1027 (DC cir. 1999). For excellent reviews of this debate, see Wood (1973, vii–xv); Levy (1969); and Goldwin and Schambra (1980).

3. The material for this section has been adopted from previous work published in Morgan (2001, 151–175).

4. Summmum bonum is a Latin term that means "highest or greatest good." The Greek, Roman, and Christian traditions believed that governing agents were to be judged in the light of some higher and greater good that stood apart from the ends of a particular political regime. For Christianity, it is God; for Plato, it was the "idea of the Good"; and for Romans, it was natural law.

5. The English Restoration began in 1677, when monarchy returned to England under King Charles II. The monarchy had ended in 1649 with the execution of King Charles I and the installation of Oliver Cromwell, who ruled under the doctrine of parliamentary sovereignty. In 1653, Cromwell dissolved Parliament and had himself installed as Lord Protector of the Commonwealth of England, Scotland, and Ireland under the authority of a constitution.

6. For further discussion of the problem of hyperpluralism and its connection to America's emphasis on individual freedom, see Roelofs (1991), Bellah et al. (1985), and Bell (1973).

7. For a more extended case-based discussion of the practical significance of a variety of citizenship models for administrative practice, see Morgan and Vizinni (1999) and Robinson (2004).

# THE TROUBLED HISTORY OF AMERICAN PUBLIC ADMINISTRATION

> What I admire most in America are not the *administrative* effects of decentralization, but the *political* effects. . . . Often the European sees in the public official only force; the American sees in him right. . . . As administrative authority is placed at the side of those whom it administers, and in some way represents them, it excites neither jealously nor hatred. . . . Administrative power . . . does not find itself abandoned to itself as in Europe. One does not believe that the duties of particular persons have ceased because the representative of the public comes to act.
>
> *(Alexis de Tocqueville 1835–1840/2000, 90)*

The history of American public administration has been characterized as a "History of Sheep in Wolves' Clothing" (Karl 1987, 26). It is the story of a love/fear relationship between bureaucracy and democracy that reflects a troubled conscience about the practice of American democratic governance. While Americans expect their government administrators to be ever responsive to the will of the people, they do not want this responsiveness to erode the capacity of government to manage complex problems. And even though Americans may value efficient problem solving, they do not want solutions to come at the expense of protecting individual rights and preserving community identity and culture. Balancing these conflicting values in ways that enable things to work out in the end is what makes American public administration so difficult. Moreover, career officials are expected to share the sensibilities of their fellow citizens in the process. This is why Americans simultaneously view public servants as both wolves and sheep. As sheep, they are expected to be familiar and trusting creatures, faithfully representing and docilely following the will of the people. But they also live under constant suspicion that they will abuse their powers and take advantage of the citizens they are expected to serve. As noted at the end of chapter 4, this ambivalence emanates from four contending principles of good republican governance that the founders sought to balance as they designed and implemented a new Constitution. The central challenge for all sides in the founding debate lay in designing a government that would effectively balance the principles of responsiveness, effectiveness, protection of rights, and engaged citizens, all of which were viewed as necessary for the preservation of individual liberty.

In this chapter, we identify four contending models of administration drawn from the founding debates and illustrate their continued relevance as well as their strengths and weaknesses. We then

review successive generations of political change and reform, illustrating the dynamics of these models in the context of intersectoral development and evolving relationships among levels of government (referred to as *federalism*). Each era adds modifications that influence administrative thought and practice, and affect the balance among the contending models of "good administration."

## THE FOUNDING LEGACY: CONTENDING MODELS OF ADMINISTRATION

The founding era experienced robust debate over two fundamental questions: (1) Who should govern, and (2) what role should government play in a liberal democratic society? These two questions remain at the center of debate for each generation of public servants. As we saw in chapter 4, the American Revolution celebrated the principle that government should be based on "we the people," which is memorialized in both the Declaration of Independence and the Preamble to the American Constitution. But this "ode to the people" was tempered by a lack of success in repeated attempts to levy and collect taxes, raise and supply an army, and negotiate complicated relations with foreign nations without an experienced and empowered cadre of governing agents who could devote full time to their work. The issue of citizen versus expert-centered governance came into sharp focus in the Constitutional Convention as delegates debated the kind of government that was most needed to preserve liberty.

Their solutions reflected a bundle of compromises and yielded the design of two sovereign levels of government with three superintending branches that would share checked and balanced powers over the subordinate public administration. None of the founders considered the new Constitution perfect by any means, and 16 of the 55 delegates refused to sign it, feeling it was unworthy of ratification. Nevertheless, the remaining delegates found the design acceptable despite their own reservations, many of them seeing sufficient breadth of meaning in its provisions to accommodate contending views. They were quite right about that, and many of them immediately sought political and administrative offices under the new Constitution in order to institutionalize their particular views on the proper staffing and roles of the new governments.

Out of their efforts emerged four nascent and competing models of "proper" administration, versions of which have been addressed to a varying extent in administrative histories (cf. Caldwell 1964; Green 1987, Newbold 2006; Stillman 1983; White 1951, 1948). Each model boasts certain strengths that one group or another of the founders thought desirable in a democratic republic, and yet each possesses inherent limitations or weaknesses that contribute to the problematic tensions described in the Founding Beatitudes addressed at the end of chapter 4. The models are labeled here as:

1. The *Madisonian interest-group balancing model*,
2. The *Washingtonian systematic planning model*,
3. The *Hamiltonian entrepreneurial model*, and
4. The *Jeffersonian community preserving model*.

### The Madisonian Model: Administration as Interest-Group Balancing

The legacy of political *pluralism* derives from James Madison's view that a multiplicity of interests in the economic and social spheres is the best check against the tyranny of an overpowering majority. As the founders observed in *The Federalist Papers:* "The regulation of these various and interfering interests forms the principal task of modern legislation and involves the spirit of party

and faction in the necessary and ordinary operations of government" (Madison 1787, Federalist No. 10, quoted in Rossiter 1961; see also Hamilton 1788, Federalist No. 79). The public manager shares responsibility for balancing these interests in the daily operations of the administration.

In addition to relying on the informal checks from a contending multiplicity of interest groups, Madison's model relied on an "auxiliary system" of formal checks and balances between and within each of the branches of government. This formal approach to interest balancing also shapes public administration. For example, from the beginning, accountability principles have been incorporated into administrative practice in the form of independent audits, evaluations, elaborate rules of procedure, and multiple avenues of redress when agency actions threaten basic rights or vested interests.

The pluralist legacy is alive and well in the modern administrative state. Everywhere we turn, organized interests are at the administrative doorstep, sometimes seeming to co-opt or even paralyze decision-making processes. Pluralism assumes that political interests affect all aspects of policymaking and implementation. We use the term *pluralism* to describe theories of governance that affirm the dominant role that interest groups play in the operation of the American systems of government, as well as the legitimacy of these interests in making the systems work effectively. Good administration under the legacy of pluralism creates an atmosphere of openness on an issue and then supports discourse until common agreement and action is possible. Compromise and trade-offs are assumed to be central and morally necessary.

The pluralist model works best when interests are well developed, when these interests are securely attached to stable groups in the larger society, and when the issues under discussion are well understood. This model is particularly effective in reconciling pragmatic differences; however, it is not especially useful when dealing with strong ideological differences, attempting to optimize the use of limited resources, working to achieve a planned set of objectives, or trying to resolve problems that are fundamentally technical. Moreover, since the model starts with the status quo, it neglects interests that are not well organized and funded; it is not always appropriate when planning for long-term needs; and it frequently results in inefficiencies through overlap and duplication of efforts and programs. At its worst, it stymies effectiveness and favors private interests over the public good.

### The Washingtonian Model: Administration as Systematic Planning

The story of George Washington at Valley Forge is the story of the failure of government to carry out its assigned work efficiently, effectively, and energetically. In short, it is a story of incompetent government—one not up to the task of achieving the goals it was assigned. Over time, the continued failure to deliver the goods is a recipe for the erosion of popular confidence and support. This is a message that has been repeated throughout history, including the more recent call (1990s) to "reinvent government" in order to improve its performance. At its base, the Washingtonian model embraces the argument that a powerful government is needed to both protect and enhance our liberties.

The Washingtonian model emphasizes the importance of systematic planning, coordinated implementation with adequate resources, and the ability to act quickly and decisively. Alexander Hamilton's principle of "energy in the executive" required adequate unity of command, duration in office, competent powers, sufficient resources, and a core group of experienced, knowledgeable officials, all of which characterized President Washington's administration. Washington's presiding leadership and sound judgment enabled subordinate colleagues such as Hamilton to develop sophisticated plans and proposals, and to help establish new institutions and practices that would

help stabilize the new nation and set it on course for commercial and agricultural prosperity. The Washington administration either bolstered or put in place the basic elements of a stable commercial economy, a sound defense, a basic communications system, and a revenue system, all of which instilled broad public confidence in the viability of the new nation.

This model works best when problems require systematic solutions, where there is general disenchantment with the current state of affairs, and when experienced and knowledgeable people needed to address the problems are available and seen as legitimate. It works less well in solving problems that are fundamentally political in nature, or when the nature of the expertise needed to solve the problems is in dispute. For example, it works much better when applied to fighting wars or dampening economic cycles than it does in ameliorating problems of racism, poverty, and economic inequality. Moreover, as early critics passionately argued, the competent powers required for the model to work are double edged. They can also be used in an oppressive manner—to abuse rights as well as to protect them, and to overwhelm smaller, weaker, but no less vital governments in the federal system.

### The Hamiltonian Model: Administration as Entrepreneurialism

Americans have a long-standing belief, dating back to the days of Alexander Hamilton's "Report on Manufacturers" (1791) that public service work can and should be run more like business. That is, agencies and organizations have purposes that can be expressed as goals toward which efficient and specific means may be prescribed. Furthermore, the entrepreneurial model assumes that public goals are well represented by individual interests. To the extent that this is true, the achievement of these goals is a matter of adhering to best management practices. Hamilton, for example, borrowed and improved upon best practices from Europe in fashioning the American financial system. His system of public credit and debt management helped stabilize the young American economy and set the stage for its prosperous commercial and agricultural development. The regulation of the economy through the Federal Reserve Board's use of refined monetary policies to manipulate interest rates exemplifies this model at work today.

Competition, choice, and measuring effectiveness by client satisfaction are the core values of the entrepreneurial model, and sometimes the best way for the public sector to achieve them is by partnering with quasi-public/quasi-private institutions, contracting out, or delivering services through nonprofits. Good administration under the entrepreneurial model is the work of the strategic apex of the organization: determining the goals, values, and principles that will guide organizational work, and then controlling the work based on market responses. The recent *reinvention of government* initiatives and the *New Public Management* (NPM) movement embody these private market principles, as we will describe more fully in subsequent sections of this chapter.

The Hamiltonian model, however, does not embrace a free-market philosophy that emphasizes a strictly hands-off approach to either administration or the economy. Rather, Hamilton argued that a robust economy required robust governments with firm regulatory powers as well as economic stimulants to provide stable infrastructure and moderated business cycles. Under this model, the government must aggressively regulate those markets deemed essential to our national interests, and it must counteract the self-destructive aspects of market behavior (Green 1993). We are reminded of these problems when contemplating abuses such as those that occurred in the savings and loan industry in the 1980s—for instance, the industry-breaking actions of Enron, MCI WorldCom Inc., and other Wall Street insider trading scandals of the 1990s—along with the rampant speculation, fraud, and abuse in the financial industry that led to the financial crash of 2008 and subsequent Great Recession. All of these severely damaging events occurred in large part due to extensive

deregulation and refusal by key public officials to use the regulatory powers still assigned to them by law (cf. Green 2012). Hamilton would have been appalled!

The entrepreneurial model works best when goals are clear and stable, when societal goals are amenable to individual choice, and where institutions are well arranged to elicit market responses. The model is not well suited when society is required to act against entrenched cultural practices, as under conditions of racism, pornography, and violence. Nor does it work well when problems need attention long before self-interest will motivate any individual to action, as in the case of pollution, or when there are public benefits that no person can afford alone (such as those provided through public defense and public education). Furthermore, the model is not effective when the knowledge and institutional capacity of government is lacking or cannot be put in place fast enough to keep pace with the rapidly changing problem that the government is seeking to control (such as with drug trafficking and computer hacking).

While this model can enhance administrative efficiency and effectiveness, it also entails an inherent bias toward powerful, vested interests (combinations of private and public power) that can easily overwhelm other vital interests and threaten the viability of local communities and nonprofits. Thus, it can exacerbate the "engaged citizen problem" and, in the process, weaken the capacity for civic governance. This was glaringly evident in the relationship between the financial industry and the public institutions tasked with monitoring and regulating it during the run-up to the 2008 economic crash. The entrepreneurial model is a policy subsystem that remains thoroughly dominated by elites and professionals and almost completely devoid of civic oversight and engagement (Green 2012).

### The Jeffersonian Model: Administration as Community Preservation and Capacity-Building

The Jeffersonian Community Building Model embraces practices that support the civic republic tradition espoused by the Anti-Federalists. It places high value on living shared lives in a common place—usually "within the fabric of a relatively small and homogenous community" (Brinkley et al. 1997, 93). It requires direct communication and assumes that differences among individuals and groups can be bridged through a web of long-standing relationships and mutual obligations. This assumption places considerable weight on facilitation, conflict resolution, and civic dialogue. For Jefferson, the ideal conditions supporting the model were found in the republican simplicity of rural, agrarian communities, where government remained close and familiar to the people. Civic governance is face-to-face governance. It is frugal and carefully limited in its scope of activity by a vigilant and engaged citizenry. Volunteerism pervades public life, and much of the community's administration is coproduced. Tenure in office is short, part-time, and generally low paid. The role of administration under this model is to gather people together to transform sharp differences of opinion into a common agenda, to give voice to this agenda, and to develop the necessary support over time to realize it. Much of the communitarian agenda is about preserving individual liberty, agrarian and nonurban values, and the traditions that underlie them.

The communitarian model works best when the groups and individuals involved have a history of working together over time on tough issues. This model focuses on a stream of engagement with concern for implications of past engagements on future work together. Individuals must be rooted in the community in such a way that they can be held accountable for what they say and do (McCullough 1991; Skocpol and Fiorina 1999). Accordingly, this model is poorly suited to settings where the participants are transitory, where there is no sense of shared past or future, and where an issue is easily shifted to another venue or external authority. Thus, the conditions for the success of the communitarian model, with its emphasis on dialogue, stand in opposition to

those found in the pluralist, interest-group balancing model and the energetic and entrepreneurial models. The communitarian model's inherent dangers lie in oppressive community majorities and weak institutions that can do little to resist them.

The administrative practices engendered in these four models exist today throughout American government, continuing to serve as correctives that stand in unresolved tension. The characteristics of each model are summarized briefly in Exhibit 5.1. The unfolding and interplay of these models over time provides insight about specific roles of public administrators, as well as about the changing relationship of politics and administration more generally—particularly as it is manifested in the enduring conflicts between sectors of society (public, private-economic, and nonprofit) and between levels of government. We track these models and their tensions through six eras, beginning briefly with the founding era and then proceeding through the Jacksonian, Populist, Progressive, and New Deal eras, and then concluding with the current entrepreneurial era.[1]

## THE FOUNDING ERA (1789–1828)

The founders' constitutional design reflected enduring arguments about the role of government in society—arguments that give American public administration its distinctive character. First, their devotion to the principle of limited government raised unresolved questions about the proper balance among the public, private market, and nonprofit sectors. To this day, administrators remain saddled with this issue as they are called on to help reshape the regulatory and service delivery relationships among governments and entities in the nonprofit and private-economic sectors.

Second, their commitment to preserving a measure of sovereignty in both the national and state governments provoked ongoing disputes over the powers of each, and left wide open the question of what roles and powers local governments should enjoy. The Constitution is silent on the place of local jurisdictions and communities in American governance, despite the fact that most of the decisions made at federal and state levels fall inevitably on the heads of local officials to implement. In recent years, this has been illustrated in reactions against unfunded mandates and growing regulatory requirements from the federal and state governments, spawning a renewed interest in devolution and local control.

The third continuing conflict centers on the debate over the proper role of career public servants in democratic governance. As subordinates, they have been viewed as instrumental agents of policymakers, but also as constitutional officers with their own measure of autonomy in serving and engaging the American people. The founders preserved this ambivalence as they wrestled with multiple perceived threats to liberty and as they prescribed the necessary correctives. In the sections that follow we will use these founding era problems (balance among the sectors, relationship between federal and state/local governments, and the role of administrators) as the organizing framework for discussing the historical development of public administration in each of the six eras we review.

### The Balance Between Public, Nonprofit, Special District, and Private Market Sectors

The founding period was marked by a strong belief in the importance of the federal government's role as a leader in building the financial and physical infrastructure necessary for the development of a strong market economy. Alexander Hamilton's "Report on a National Bank" (1790/1963) and his "Report on Manufacturers" (1791/1966) set forth the conditions for making this possible. Hamilton urged the use of national power to create a quasi-public central bank that would give

Figure 5.1  **Founding Era Administrative Models**

|  | Sources of danger to liberty | Central values | Inherent weaknesses |
|---|---|---|---|
| Systematic Planning | Incompetent and ineffective government | Competence:<br>• order<br>• stability<br>• effectiveness<br>• energetic execution | Abusive centralization, degradation of weaker local communities |
| Entrepreneurial | Inability to adapt creatively to changing needs | Energy and vitality:<br>• competition<br>• creativity<br>• innovation<br>• efficiency | Abusive combinations of private and public power |
| Community Preserving | Lack of responsiveness and usurpation of authority | Majority rule:<br>• popular control<br>• access<br>• responsiveness<br>• frugality and simplicity | Oppressive majorities, weak governing institutions |
| Interest Balancing | Majority tyranny | Minority rights:<br>• protection of property<br>• freedom of speech, press, and assembly<br>• equal protection | Ascendance of private interests over the public good |

creditors the confidence to invest their capital, protect the manufacturing sector from unfair competition abroad, and fund a public debt in order to build needed economic infrastructure. Even the U.S. Navy was conceived as much in terms of economic development (protecting sea lanes of commerce) as of common defense.

Thomas Jefferson was eager to use the power of the national government to promote science, education, and exploration, as was evidenced by his funding of the Lewis and Clark expedition and by his call for the establishment of a national university. The importance of using the power of the central government to build a nation-state that could hold its own on the international front was widely accepted. The need for a strong national government rested on the assumption that national power would strengthen the private market sector, not weaken or replace it. The policies adopted by the Washington administration quickly stabilized a weak economy and instilled sufficient confidence among commercial interests to spur private-sector investment.

Perhaps the most important steps in making a strong national government and a robust national economy a reality occurred in the case of *Marbury v. Madison* (1803). The U.S. Supreme Court declared that it had the final say in determining the constitutionality of a law passed by Congress. The U.S. Constitution was authoritative, and there was one national governing institution uniquely suited to interpret its meaning. This case helped secure the role of the federal government in relation to state and local governments and served as a spur to the private economy.

Finally, in the famous *Dartmouth College* case (1819), the U.S. Supreme Court made a key decision that foreshadowed a significant role for the nonprofit sector. The Court overturned a

decision by the state of New Hampshire to alter Dartmouth College's charter. In declaring that a private association (in this case, the college) could assert a constitutionally protected right of contract to maintain its independence from state control, the Court initiated a vital first step in giving the nonprofit sector the independence it needed to play a developmental role in America's systems of democratic governance (Hall 1992, 28–31). Civic associations and other service-oriented nonprofits would flourish in the wake of such decisions, and prepare everyday citizens for civic engagement and deliberative governance.

### Balance Between the States and the Federal Government

What was not so clear in these early years was the role that *states* could and should play in building a new nation. In the debates on the adoption of the U.S. Constitution, Hamilton argued in *The Federalist Papers* that "it will always be far easier for the State governments to encroach upon the national government than for the national government to encroach upon State authorities." After providing proofs of this proposition, he concluded that citizens would always "feel a stronger bias towards their local governments than towards the government of the Union: *unless the force of that principle should be destroyed by a much better administration of the latter*" (Hamilton 1787, Federalist No. 17, quoted in Rossiter 119, emphasis added). Elsewhere in *The Federalist Papers*, Hamilton makes clear that he believes the improved competence of the newly founded government will be extremely successful in touching the "most sensitive chords" and putting "in motion the most active springs of the human heart" (Hamilton 1787, Federalist No. 27, quoted in Rossiter 176). Although not explicit, Hamilton believed that the attachment of citizens to their states would wither as the national government played a growing role in their lives.

Hamilton's views were reinforced in the early years of the new republic by important decisions of the U.S. Supreme Court. In *Ware v. Hylton* (1796), the Court held that the treaty of peace with Britain overrode a Virginia law on the sensitive issue of debts owed by Americans to British subjects. The decision in *Chisholm v. Georgia* (1793) asserted that states could be sued in federal courts by citizens of other states, a holding so bitterly resented by the states that it precipitated the adoption of the Eleventh Amendment, which forever barred such suits. In *McCulloch v. Maryland* (1819), Chief Justice John Marshall continued the pattern of restrictions on state authority by declaring state taxation of the national bank to be unconstitutional. In rendering his opinion, Marshall boldly proclaimed that no state had any power "to retard, impede, burden, or in any manner control the operations of the constitutional laws enacted by Congress." In *Gibbons v. Ogden* (1824), Marshall struck down the right of states to interfere with Congress's constitutional power to regulate commerce. John Marshall's 34-year tenure on the U.S. Supreme Court helped secure the argument for a competent and energetic national government and for a vibrant national economy populated by powerful commercial interests—all secured institutionally through the rule of law.

On the other hand, despite these assertions of national supremacy, the U.S. Congress displayed great reticence in exercising its legally conferred powers, especially in funding national improvements. For example, it wasn't until 1820 that Congress authorized and appropriated funds for the U.S. Army Corps of Engineers to survey parts of the Ohio and Mississippi rivers to improve river navigation. While the groundwork was being laid in law and public policy for the development of a national infrastructure to support private markets, many congressmen invoked the principle of states' rights to either slow down the support or prevent it from occurring unless justified by "national security" (Smith 1966). Their devotion to states' rights doctrine foreshadowed the dominance of the states over public policy and administration during most of the nineteenth century. The rhetoric of states' rights reflects the fear of an overbearing, distant, and powerful government while embracing small,

familiar, face-to-face governments associated with local communities. These sentiments prevailed in most state governments as well as at the local level. Though these governments often lacked efficiency and effectiveness, they were frugal, deliberative, and easily controlled. The predominant administrative practices among these spheres (national and state/local) differed accordingly.

## JACKSONIAN DEMOCRACY (1829–1869): REPRESENTATIVE BUREAUCRACY, ORDINARY VIRTUE, AND THE VOLUNTARY STATE

The election of Andrew Jackson in 1828 brought an end to the dominating influence of the founding generation and reshaped the political order. The Jacksonian partisans were the first to introduce two administrative practices that have had an enduring influence on American public life. One emphasizes the importance of institutionalizing a thoroughly democratic public service, and the other emphasizes the importance of relying on the voluntary and entrepreneurial efforts of citizens and organizations to achieve the larger public good. Both of these legacies have tempered some of the elitist aspects of the Constitution.

The administrative practice that made the Jacksonian period famous was its system of rotation in office, or what came to be known later as the *spoils system*. Critics emphasize the adverse consequences of this system rather than the important principle of democratic accountability upon which it rested. For the Jacksonians, accountability meant verification by public records and constant subjection of one's performance to public judgment (Karl 1987, 26). This notion of accountability seized upon the majoritarian impulse of the Anti-Federalist and Jeffersonian traditions, identifying the voice of the people with government itself. Direct accountability to the people replaced accountability to the law—to the Constitution and its institutions of governance. By introducing mass democratic politics, President Jackson

> formalized the establishment of a two-tiered system of political management. One tier used party organization and the distribution of offices as its base, while the other depended on elite figures chosen from traditional elite families, as well as the newer elites of business, banking, the law, and the emerging professions. . . . The embedding of the conflict between mass democracy and elite professionalism in the American political structure is what really shapes the American meaning of bureaucracy and American attitudes toward it. (Karl 1987, 27)

At its worst, the Jacksonian system of accountability collapsed into the corruption of the spoils system, which awarded jobs to party loyalists without significant attention to competence. But at its best, the notion of a thoroughly democratic public service has continued in the form of a representative bureaucracy, an idea that assumes administrative agencies should be composed of a socially representative workforce (Dolan and Rosenbloom 2003). Proponents of this principle argue that when an agency is socially representative, administrative discretion is more likely to be used in ways that recognize the voices and interests of those lacking political power.

A second administrative practice introduced by Jacksonian democracy is reliance on the voluntary service of civic organizations to undertake the common work of the community. In his travels across America in 1831 and 1832, the large number and vigorous activity of voluntary associations in the United States amazed the French historian Alexis de Tocqueville.

> In America I encountered sorts of associations of which, I confess, I had no idea. Not only do they have commercial and industrial associations . . . but they have a thousand other kinds. . . . Everywhere that, at the head of a new undertaking, you see the government in

France and a great lord in England, count on it that you will perceive an association in the United States. . . . The free institutions that the inhabitants of the United States possess recall to each citizen constantly and in a thousand ways that he lives in society. At every moment they bring his mind back to [the] idea that the duty as well as the interest of men is to render themselves useful to those like them. . . . Sentiments and ideas renew themselves, the heart is enlarged and the human is developed . . . [through participation in these associations]. (Tocqueville 1835–1840/2000, 489, 488, 491 passim)

Partisans of the Jacksonian vision established a democratic literary magazine in 1837. The magazine's goal was to serve as an intellectual voice for revival of Jefferson's doctrine of self-reliance. In their first issue, the editorial board of the newly launched *United States Magazine and Democratic Review* set forth the basic assumptions of what they called "the Voluntary Principle" at the center of the Jacksonian revolution (Rozwenc 1963, 19–25).

- "The best government is that which governs least. . . . Government should have as little as possible to do with the general business and interests of the people" (22, 23).
- "We have an abiding confidence in the virtue, intelligence, and full capacity for self-government, of the great mass of our people—our industrious, honest, manly, intelligent millions of freemen" (19).
- "The floating atoms will distribute and combine themselves, as we see in the beautiful natural process of crystallization, in a far more perfect and harmonious result than if government[s] undertake . . . to disturb . . . the process" (23).

These assumptions at the core of Jacksonian democracy were translated into four governing principles that have had a lasting impact on the tension between democracy and bureaucracy in the United States: (1) energetic use of presidential power (derived from the Hamiltonian model), (2) *plebiscitarian* executive leadership (involving a direct vote), (3) direct democracy, and (4) a strong belief in limited government (especially as voiced in the Jeffersonian model).

**An Energetic Executive**

President Jackson went well beyond both his Federalist and Republican predecessors to strengthen the executive function of governance. He broadened the use of the veto power "to include mere differences of opinion concerning the expediency of legislation" (White 1954, 22). He exercised unrestrained use of his removal power, even for appointees who had been subjected to the constitutional requirement of advice and consent by the U.S. Senate. And he exercised popular leadership over a mass political party movement. Perhaps Jackson's most unique contribution in strengthening the executive branch was the belief that energetic use of presidential authority should be exercised in the name of the people themselves. He believed the people were best served by a president who vigilantly used the power of the office to limit government. This foreshadows the modern-day presidencies of Ronald Reagan and George W. Bush.

**Plebiscitarian Executive Leadership**

Jackson was the first president to articulate the novel theory that the president was a direct representative of the people, rather than an agent of a larger constitutional order. Article II, Section 1, of the U.S. Constitution establishes an electoral college to indirectly elect the president by electors

chosen from each of the several states. Jackson turned this notion on its head and recommended the direct election of the president. In his first annual message to Congress, he argued that "as few impediments as possible should exist to the free operation of the public will" (Richardson 1899, II:448). He returned to this view in his famous protest message to the Senate, justifying his right to dismiss William Duane, secretary of the treasury, for his refusal to remove deposits from the U.S. Bank.[2] In electing him president, Jackson claimed that the people of the United States had conferred upon him "the entire executive power" of government (85). Carried to its logical conclusion, this view would turn executive subordinates into mere ministerial agents of the chief executive's interpretive authority. It would save subordinate administrative officers from having to exercise independent responsibility to the Constitution, or to be independently accountable to the legislative or judicial branches of government. This principle resurfaced in the presidency of George W. Bush, who developed a unitary theory of the chief executive. According to this theory, the president enjoys exclusive authority over administrative agencies, even when it is contrary to the expressed will of the legislative branch (Cooper 2005b, 2002). This significantly expands the purpose of an energetic executive beyond the original goals of ensuring more competent governance, and obviously exacerbates existing tensions among administrative agencies that are beholden to Congress for oversight and funding.

## Representation Through Rotation in Office

President Jackson converted Anti-Federalist and Jeffersonian suspicions about long-term government service into an operating principle called *rotation in office*. The rule of frequent rotation of government officials grew out of a two-pronged belief that, over time, power tends to corrupt, and that everyone possesses the necessary qualities to rule Jackson argued that public employees needed a constant reminder that office is not a species of property, but "an instrument created solely for the service of the people." He believed that too much time in office allows individuals to "divert government from its legitimate ends and make it an engine for the support of the few at the expense of the many." We need not worry about frequent personnel changes, since "the duties of all public offices are, or at least admit to being made, so plain and simple that men of intelligence may readily qualify themselves for their performance" (Richardson 1899, II: 448–449). Jackson wished to apply the principle of representation throughout all levels of the career public service, from the very top to the very bottom.

## Limited Government

Jackson used the vigorous exercise of his administrative leadership to check "bigness" in all its forms, both within government as well as in the private sector. During his second term in office, Jackson took on "bigness" at the national level by vetoing the renewal of the charter of the National Bank, first established in 1816 to bring safer, uniform standards and predictability to banking throughout the nation. To the contrary, he viewed the National Bank as a threat to the viability and practices of state and local banks. He extended his attack on "bigness" to the private sector by issuing the Specie Circular (money in coin) in July 1836, requiring payment in gold or silver for the purchase of all public lands. This measure contributed to a run on banks by depositors who wished to convert their paper bank notes into gold or silver. Bank failures began in the West and spread quickly to the East. By the spring of 1837, the entire country was gripped by a financial panic (Temin 1969). Jackson, nevertheless, remained steadfast in his belief that unshackled business competition was "the best guaranty of the prosperity of the country. . . . If the door is thrown open to every competent man, the public wants will be attended to" (quoted in White 1958, 448).

**Consequences of the Jacksonian Democracy for Administrative Service**

*Balance Between Public, Voluntary, and Private Market Sectors*

Jacksonian democracy established a new and clearer standard regarding the separation between the public sector, the private market economy, and the voluntary sector. For Jackson, the private market economy constituted the engine of progress, with government playing the limited role of removing barriers to competition. This meant using the power of government to remove the monopolistic advantages of inherited wealth and corporate concentrations of power. In addition to this constraining role, Jackson believed government should encourage the disposal and settlement of public lands, much of which were taken from Native Americans and mixed-blood Hispanics. Securing the frontier for expansion and development formed part of Jackson's vision of making America a land of opportunity for the hard-working, ordinary citizens who could be trusted to "do the right thing." The rapid growth of voluntary associations between 1820 and 1840 added fuel to the entrepreneurial spirit of the ordinary man and gave real meaning to the voluntary sector as a vital political force.

*Balance Between States and Federal Government*

The mantra of "states' rights" also gained new life during the Jacksonian era in two important ways. First, the cotton boom revived the plantation slave economy in the South and created a vested interest against tariffs which might trigger retaliation by cotton-purchasing countries. In the Northeast and Old Northwest (Ohio River Valley), transportation improvements and increased immigration hastened the collapse of an older yeoman and artisan economy and its replacement by cash-crop agriculture and capitalist manufacturing. These new industries favored tariffs to protect them from competition during their infant stages of development. Second, the emerging defense of the institution of slavery as a positive good, rather than a necessary evil, gave further reinforcement to the states' rights advocates. Together, the controversy over slavery and tariffs set the stage for the Civil War, which ended by force the right of states to secede from the Union and set a trajectory for real dominance by the federal government over many fields of public policy.

*Implications for the Role of Public Administrators*

The founding era highlighted a separation between public service and the people. The Jacksonian period brought down this wall of separation, but in doing so, it left the administrative function of government with two countervailing propensities: One emphasized the subordination of administrative agents to a popularly elected chief executive who embodied the will of the people. The other emphasized a representative bureaucracy that directly reflected the will and energy of the people throughout all levels of the administrative process. This tension between bureaucracy as neutral minion and bureaucracy as active, constitutive agent came fully into conflict during the Populist and Progressive periods (Cook 1996).

## POPULIST REFORM (1869–1910): NEUTRAL COMPETENCE AND THE RISE OF THE REGULATORY STATE

The Civil War ended the debate over slavery and the right of states to independent sovereign authority. Equally important, out of the war emerged a unifying transformation of Hamilton's vision

of a large and feverish commercial republic. Rather than being organized around the centralized power of a national government, though, the unifying transformation was organized around private wealth and power. The success of the Civil War resulted less from newfound administrative competence at the center and more from the military, logistical, and financial support offered by private organizations like the U.S. Sanitary Commission, which took responsibility for providing medical care to the Union Army. This private organization in the 1860s was explicitly created to provide a public good—a role that, in the twenty-first century, would likely be undertaken by nonprofit organizations.

> Institutionally, evangelical enterprises of the antebellum period provided the bureaucratic organizational models for the mobilization as well as the expertise and personality types necessary for the effective operation of these administrative hierarchies. The victory of the Union was seen both by its organizers and by the significant elements of the general public as a legitimation of the claims of the organized private sector. . . . The Jacksonian persuasion, with its prejudices against private power and the institutions and elites associated with it, was on the defensive in the face of a triumphant assertion of political nationality that identified itself with private wealth and power. (Hall 1992, 36)

The unifying national vision created in the aftermath of the Civil War grew rapidly in the following decades as a result of economic development, which created an increasingly integrated and interdependent national economy. Manufacturing investment ballooned from $2.7 billion in 1879 to $8.2 billion in 1899. The value of manufactured products rose from $3.8 billion to $11 billion in constant dollars. The nation had just 23 miles of railroad track in 1830; by 1890, it had 208,152 miles. The age of high-volume production drew workers to the cities. In 1870, less than 8 percent of America's workers were engaged in manufacturing, while only one out of five Americans lived in cities with populations larger than 8,000 people. By 1910, almost a third of the population worked in manufacturing, and half the population lived in cities. Immigration skyrocketed during this period. Almost half the population of Ireland headed for the United States. By the 1870s, 280,000 immigrants arrived annually, and this number rose to more than a million by the turn of the century (Reich 1992, 26, 27, 31–32; Swindler 1969, 61).

The migration to major cities resulted in the development of large political machines and rampant corruption. It is often said that New York's Tammany Hall, under its notorious boss, William Marcy Tweed, provided more services to the poor than any city government before it, although a large share of the money went into Tweed's own pockets. One of Tammany Hall's loyal lieutenants, George Washington Plunkitt, made famous the distinction between honest and dishonest graft: The distinction rested on serving one's parochial interests versus serving the good of the larger community.

> Everybody is talkin' these days about Tammany men growin' rich on graft, but nobody thinks of drawin' the distinction between honest graft and dishonest graft. . . . I'm getting' richer every day, but I've not gone in for dishonest graft—blackmailin' gamblers, saloon keepers, disorderly people, etc.—and neither has any of the men who have made big fortunes in politics. . . . I might sum up the whole thing up by sayin': "I seen my opportunities and I took 'em."
>
> Just let me explain by examples. My party's in power in the city, and it's goin' to undertake a lot of public improvements. Well, I'm tipped off, say, that they're going to lay out a new park at a certain place. . . . I go to that place and I buy up all the land I can in the

neighborhood. Then the board of this or that makes its plan public and there is a rush to get my land, which nobody cared particular for before. Ain't it perfectly honest to charge a good price and make a profit on my investment and foresight? Of course it is. Well that's honest graft. . . . I made my pile in politics, but, I served the organization and got more big improvements for New York City than any other livin' man. And I never monkeyed with the penal code. (Quoted in Riordon 1963, 3, 29)

Plunkitt's distinction raised basic questions about the nature of enlightened self-interest and about what kinds of correctives one should apply to the public service to remove the abuses and excesses of the system. Does one remove the temptations to the passions and interests of those who serve? Does one turn temptation and self-serving interests to more public-serving ends? Or do we recruit individuals to public service who have the "fitness of character" (see George Washington's standard in White 1948, 259) to resist whatever temptations may come their way? As corruption began to infiltrate the highest levels of government, reformers needed a way to stem the tide. During Ulysses S. Grant's administration (1869–1877), the president and his cabinet were implicated in a half-dozen major scandals that included Crédit Mobilier, the Gold Conspiracy, the Whiskey Ring, the Indian Ring, and the Salary Grab.[3] This animated public ire and attention. Then, when a disaffected office seeker assassinated President James Garfield in 1881, the reformers pushed for action against the spoils system.

### The Role of Public Servants and the Principle of Neutral Competence

After winning the moral battle over slavery, reformers turned their attention to the abuses of the Jacksonian spoils system and the industrial excesses of the Gilded Age (roughly 1870–1900). They sought, in the words of James Stever, to throw the rascals out "by muckraking and otherwise arousing the public to vote." Then they would fill offices with honest, diligent, and educated "moral men." They assumed that these "good candidates would implement good policies" (Stever 1988, 30).

The passage of the Pendleton Act of 1883 and the creation of a civil service merit system institutionalized the best thinking of the day on how to correct the abuses of the spoils system. The goal was to temper greed and to restore moral integrity to public service by isolating it from undue political influence. Career administrators would be appointed and promoted on the basis of written qualifications to perform the job, not on the basis of friendship or partisan political loyalty. The Pendleton Act established the modern civil service system for the federal government and influenced the system's subsequent establishment in all 50 states and most local jurisdictions.

The standard of neutral competence became a lasting legacy of Populist reform for public administration. The commitment to protect the neutral competence of public servants takes a variety of modern forms, including conflict of interest legislation, financial disclosure laws, open government requirements, and various Hatch Act regulations (prohibiting public employees from engaging in partisan political activity) at the state and local levels of government (Morgan and Rohr 1986; Rohr 1981).

### The Beginnings of the Regulatory State: Rethinking the Balance Between the Public, Nonprofit, Special District, and Private Sectors

The post–Civil War period is commonly known as the Gilded Age, a period of wealth accumulation by some of America's great families, many of whom became famous for their philanthropy

and public service—among them Andrew Carnegie, who made his money in steel production; Edward H. Harriman, who made a fortune building railroads; John D. Rockefeller, who became rich by drilling for oil; and J.P. Morgan, who accumulated vast wealth through banking. The discovery of gold, silver, and oil; the rapid expansion of transportation; the large influx of immigrants for cheap labor; the increased demand for goods and services—all of these factors created large concentrations of wealth. This accumulation of money, power, and influence was justified by the doctrine of "survival of the fittest." Similar to Charles Darwin's argument in *The Origin of the Species* (1859), Herbert Spencer advanced the notion that the freedom of individuals in the social sphere to pursue their own interests, like the natural selection of the species in the physical world, resulted in the development of superior talents. According to Spencer, competition, not cooperation, produced these superior talents, and they became the engines for innovation, creativity, and social progress. It follows, then, that government intervention should be kept to a minimum in social and political life in order to reap the full advantages of "social Darwinism" or survival of the fittest (Spencer 1994).

There were two countervailing influences on the raw application of the "survival of the fittest" argument, both of which tempered its potential for excess. First, people of wealth were assumed to have a moral obligation to the poor and less fortunate. Second, Spencer's argument assumed that government had an important role to play in ensuring that the rules of market competition were fair and did not unduly corrupt the operations of government.

In *The Gospel of Wealth and Other Timely Essays* (1889/1962), Andrew Carnegie argued that all personal wealth beyond that required to supply the needs of one's family should be regarded as a trust fund to be administered for the benefit of the community. It must be administered wisely to deal with the causes of misfortune, rather than simply its effects. Carnegie argued:

> One of the serious obstacles to the improvement of our race is indiscriminate charity. It were better for mankind that the millions of rich were thrown into the sea than so spent as to encourage the slothful, the drunken, the unworthy. Of every thousand dollars spent in so-called charity today, it is probable that nine hundred and fifty dollars is unwisely spent— so spent, indeed, as to produce the very evils which it hopes to mitigate or cure. . . . The best means of benefiting the community is to place within its reach the ladders upon which the aspiring can rise—libraries, parks, and means of recreation, by which men are helped in body and mind; works of art, certain to give pleasure and improve the public taste; and public institutions of various kinds, which will improve the general condition of the people; in this manner returning their surplus wealth to the mass of their fellows in the forms best calculated to do them lasting good. (Carnegie 1889/1962, 26–27)

Carnegie followed his own advice and became both the wealthiest and most generous philanthropist of his day. His doctrine was radical, primarily because he called for the use of private wealth to attack the conditions of misfortune and dependency, rather than to provide charity for individuals directly. The use of private wealth for public purposes was based on Carnegie's view that individuals were part of a larger community—a joint venture, much like a private corporation. While the doctrine of "survival of the fittest" meant hierarchy and unequal distribution of talents, it was a hierarchy of mutual interdependence, whether in a private corporation or in a community of fellow citizens. This principle of mutual interdependence was reflected in the growing role that the nonprofit sector played in promoting the public good, and its importance to government was officially codified in the Tariff Act of 1894, when Congress granted tax exemption to nonprofit charitable, religious, educational, and fraternal associations.

The close symbiotic relationship between private wealth and public power was reflected throughout all dimensions of the American political economy during the latter half of the nineteenth century. For example, railroads became vital to the nation's economy. In many regions of the United States, a single company enjoyed a monopoly of rail transportation, which enabled the railroads to adopt policies that large numbers of customers believed unfair and discriminatory. The states adopted measures to cope with these abuses. Various state laws were passed to prevent the railroads from engaging in freight pricing and rebate abuses.[4] When these were declared unconstitutional in a series of decisions by the U.S. Supreme Court, pressure groups turned to the federal government for relief. Influential eastern businessmen, who believed that they too were the victims of discrimination by the railroads, joined western farm organizations. This populist political alliance persuaded both major political parties to include regulation of the railroads in their national platforms in 1884; it also induced Congress to establish the Interstate Commerce Commission (ICC) in 1887 and enact the Sherman Antitrust Act three years later.

The ICC was empowered to eliminate many of the monopolistic practices that spawned a farmers' revolt in the West and the Populist movement as a whole. The Interstate Commerce Commission Act prevented unjust discrimination by the railroads; prohibited the pooling of traffic and profits; made it illegal for a railroad to charge more for a short haul than it did for a longer one; required that the railroads publicize their rates; and established the ICC to supervise the enforcement of the law. The rulings of the commission were subject to review by the federal courts, and their decisions tended to narrow the scope of the act. The commission became less effective than the sponsors of the act had hoped, but the act in itself reflected a growing realization that only the federal government could cope with many of the new economic problems of the day. One such problem was the growing monopolistic practices of big businesses.

The 1890 Sherman Antitrust Act declared illegal all business combinations that restrained trade between states or with foreign nations. Although it was aimed at eliminating the monopolistic practices of the railroads, more than 10 years passed before the Sherman Act was used to break up any industrial monopoly. Contrary to the hopes of those who pushed for its passage, it was initially used to obtain an injunction against a striking railroad union accused of restraining interstate commerce. Such results aggravated reformers. The growing extremes between the power of wealth and the powerlessness of poverty became politically violent with the Homestead strike at a steel plant in Pennsylvania in 1892 and the Pullman strike by railroad workers in Illinois in 1894. There were growing fears of a new civil war fought on the economic front. These fears are reflected in the tenets of the Populists' successors, the Progressives, who placed a much higher emphasis on the role of administrators in promoting social justice than had been the case with their reform-oriented predecessors.

The Sherman Antitrust Act and the ICC represented the best thinking of the day about how to correct the abuses of industrial capitalism. They constitute the beginnings of what is now called the *modern administrative state*, and they acknowledge the critical role of federal administrative mechanisms in coping with the complex industrial and economic problems created by an increasingly complex economic system. This was a point argued by Alexander Hamilton a hundred years earlier; however, the move in this direction was hard fought and very gradual, largely due to U.S. Supreme Court decisions that to this day treat private corporations as "persons" under the due process clause of the Fourteenth Amendment (*Slaughter-House Cases,* 1873). By treating corporations as persons, the courts opened the door to arguments by private business that the states and the federal government could not regulate them because it constituted a deprivation of property "without due process of law." Such arguments were invoked to prevent various kinds of legislation (i.e., wages, hours, working conditions) until the U.S. Supreme Court begin to soften its stance in 1935 during the presidency of Franklin D. Roosevelt (Swindler 1969).

## Restriking the Federal Balance by Returning to Direct Democracy

The relationship between the states and the federal government during the latter decades of the nineteenth century began to change in response to political pressures to control the abuses of the Gilded Age. But the increased role for career public servants at the federal level did not come at the expense of the continuing role that states played in controlling the affairs that mattered most in the lives of average citizens. The restructuring of the relationship between citizens and their governments had more to do with the invention of new forms of direct democracy during the Populist period. The Populists raised the principle of responsiveness to the people to a whole new level.

Frustrated by the unwillingness of legislative bodies to control the growing abuses by private business, and by the unresponsiveness of elected officials to the electorate, Populist reformers introduced a variety of new accountability mechanisms that included *recall, the initiative,* and *the referendum.* While some scholars include these reforms as part of the Progressive movement in the early decades of the twentieth century, they were Populist in origin and were included in the national Populist Party platforms of 1892 and 1896 (Johnson and Porter 1973, 110). In fact, most of the electoral reforms advocated by the Populist movement became reality decades later under the banner of the Progressive movement. One of these structural changes included a provision enabling voters to recall elected public officials prior to completing their term of office. This was illustrated in 2012 in Wisconsin, where activists attempted to recall Republican Governor Scott Walker for his efforts at curtailing the power and influence of public unions in the state. Walker defeated the recall.

Another instrument of direct democracy included the initiative, which enables voters to place measures directly on the ballot without having to go through the legislative process. Such measures can include changes in statutes as well as alterations to the state constitution. The initiative process has been aggressively used to create various kinds of restrictions on government taxation (see chapter 10). A third reform, the referendum, allows the legislative body to refer a controversial piece of legislation directly to the voters for final approval. These instruments were first introduced in the West. Oregon became the first state to establish the statewide initiative and popular referendum. In the early days of the twentieth century, these institutions became widely known as the Oregon System. They fell into disuse in the middle decades of the twentieth century before being revived in 1970s and 1980s as a way of dealing with citizen dissatisfaction and loss of confidence in government policies—especially with taxation and spending. A final pillar of Populist accountability was put in place with the successful campaign to broaden the use of direct popular election for officials such as secretaries of state, education commissioners, treasurers, district attorneys, clerks, auditors, and sheriffs.

While these reforms are defended in the name of popular accountability and responsiveness, many argue that they result in greater control by special interests and reduced electoral accountability on the part of elected representatives. This is not surprising, since the primary purpose of the Populist reform agenda was to protect against moral corruption rather than to promote greater government efficiency. The efficient or "good government" agenda was carried by the rising tide of Progressive reform that eclipsed the Populist initiative at the turn of the twentieth century.

## PROGRESSIVE REFORM (1910–1921): SCIENTIFIC MANAGEMENT OR MORAL UPLIFT?

The Populist Era reaffirmed the long-standing rule-of-law principle that public office is never to be used to promote or acquire personal gain. But if discretionary choices by career admin-

istrators are not to be governed by personal relationships, political favoritism, and personal visions of the public good, what ought to fill the discretionary vacuum? If politics is taken out of administration, what should replace it? In short, what precisely is meant by *neutral competence*? What values should guide, inform, and check this competence? The Progressives gave two kinds of answers to this question, one drawing on the scientific impulse within Progressivism and the other drawing on the pragmatic and moral side of the movement. James Stever has respectively labeled these two strains as *pragmatism* and *organic idealism* (Stever 1990). The pragmatic strain is reflected in the Progressive Movement's reliance on data and professional expertise to drive reform while at the same time using government as a moral exemplar (*organic idealism*). Both of these approaches are evident in the Progressive legacy discussed more fully in the sections that follow.

### The Growing Dominance and Abuses of the Market Economy

The turn of the twentieth century was marked by an accelerating pace of economic development in the hands of increasingly more concentrated centers of power and wealth. Manufacturers organized to control prices, production, and shipping (Linseed Oil Trust, Cotton Seed Oil Trust, Lead Trust, Sugar Refiners' Company, Standard Oil Trust, and trusts in mining, railroads, meat packing, gas, hemp, and so on). What started as informal associations grew into tightly integrated systems of control and domination of the marketplace. These concentrations of wealth and power came at the expense of the growing ranks of poor people concentrated in urban areas.

> Approximately one third of the nation's manufacturing assets were consolidated into 318 giant companies with capitalization of $7.3 billion. The high tariffs that America imposed on raw materials and supplies from abroad encouraged further consolidation: the new giants preferred to buy up domestic suppliers rather than pay them high, protected prices. Thus, when tariffs prevented U.S. Steel from obtaining cheap pig iron and coking coal from Canada, the firm simply purchased Pennsylvania iron and coal producers outright rather than let them enjoy the extra profits of the protected market.
>
> Thus arose the modern corporation in America. Some of the mammoths that emerged bore names that would become synonymous with American industry—names that reflect the unambiguously national identities to which they aspired: U.S. Steel, American Sugar Refining, American Telephone and Telegraph, American Rubber, United States Rubber, American Woolen, National Biscuit, American Can, American Tobacco, Aluminum Company of America, General Electric, General Motors, Standard Oil, and, even more grandiosely, International Harvester. (Reich 1992, 36)

The abuses of the industry magnates were exposed through a variety of writings, starting in the 1890s and continuing through the first decade of the 1900s. Jacob Riis exposed the poor living conditions of the tenement slums in *How the Other Half Lives* (1890). In *The Shame of Cities* (1904), Lincoln Steffens exposed the rampant political corruption in the party machines of Chicago and New York, arguing that they served the interests of businesspeople who sought government contracts, franchises, charters, and special privileges. *The Jungle*, written by Upton Sinclair and published in 1906, traced an immigrant family's exploitation and the dangerously unsanitary practices prevalent in Chicago's meat packing industry. The collective outcome of these efforts resulted in increased federal and state oversight of the private business sector.

## Expanding Role of Both the Federal Government and the Nonprofit Sectors

In the early decades of the twentieth century, the federal government expanded its responsibility on a variety of fronts. It continued to increase its oversight of big business with the passage of the Clayton Act (1914), the Federal Trade Commission Act (1914), and the Federal Tariff Commission Act (1916). During Teddy Roosevelt's administration (1901–1909), nearly 40 companies were sued for price fixing and other antitrust violations. The exposure of abuses in meat packing, tenements, and public health by muckraking journalists produced results: Significant new legislation was passed, including the Pure Food and Drug Act and the Meat Inspection Act (both in 1906), along with laws that established minimum safety and housing standards in tenements. Finally, a third area of expansion of federal oversight and regulation occurred on the natural resource front with the formation of the National Forest Service in the Department of Agriculture (1905), the Bureau of Reclamation (1902), the National Park Service (1916), and a much-expanded role for the Army Corps of Engineers in managing harbors and rivers.

Ironically, the excesses of the private marketplace also spurred the expansion of nonprofit organizations far more than it increased the role of the federal and state governments. The increasing gap between the rich and poor spawned the expansion of private philanthropic organizations in the nation's growing cities (Hall 1992, 47–51; Stivers 2002b). Women stimulated social reform legislation, seeking to secure their own right to vote while also advocating for a wide range of progressive social issues. This included the establishment of settlement houses that provided immigrant families with various services. The Women's Christian Temperance Union attacked alcohol abuse and succeeded in lobbying for passage of the Eighteenth Amendment (1919), better known as Prohibition. Women won the right to vote with the Nineteenth Amendment in 1920. Women activists were prominent in many associations, including the Women's Trade Union League and the National Consumers' League (NCL), which worked to educate the public on issues of wages, hours, and working conditions. The NCL developed a "white label" program, an award to employers whose labor practices met with the NCL's approval for fairness and safety. It made the issue of fair wages and working conditions a front-page concern.

Reform of corporate practices came slowly, not simply because of the power and wealth of industry giants but also because of Americans' ambivalence about the role of large corporations in their lives. On the one hand, large corporations were defended in the name of efficiency, effectiveness, and economies of scale achieved through mass production. On the other hand, they were said to be guilty of greed and massive accumulation of wealth at the expense of a rapidly growing class of urban, working poor. Progressive reformers reflected this ambivalence by promoting efficiency as the polestar of the public interest, while also advocating for the moral and physical improvement of all citizens. They believed that corporations, like governments, should embody a moral commitment to efficiency while providing for the material welfare of workers and customers.

For those entering public service, the big question for Progressive reformers centered on the kind of professional expertise most needed to efficiently promote the public interest. How should we prepare this new generation of public servants? Two schools of thought emerged, one emphasizing the importance of scientific analysis and the other emphasizing the importance of the values and traditions at the contextual center of administrative practice.

## Public Service as Scientific Management and Administrative Efficiency

Woodrow Wilson has become famous in public administration for articulating the claim that science should be at the center of preparing the next generation of career administrators. In his

now-famous 1887 essay "The Study of Public Administration," written long before he became president of the United States (in office 1913–1921), Wilson called for making public administration a separate field of study in order to deal successfully with the growing complexity of managing the business of government.

> The object of administrative study is to rescue executive methods from the confusion and costliness of empirical experiment and set them upon foundations laid deep in stable principle. . . . There should be a science of administration which shall seek to straighten the paths of government, to make its business less unbusinesslike, to strengthen and purify its organization, and to crown its dutifulness. (Wilson 1887/1996, 10, 5)

While Wilson's essay went unnoticed in his day, it captured the effusive confidence that Progressives shared about the ability of science to improve the efficiency and effectiveness of any organization, be it public or private. Reformers such as Frederick Taylor answered Wilson's call for a more systematic approach to administrative practice. Taylor introduced principles of scientific management that emphasized empirically grounded research on work processes in order to identify the "one best way" of doing business (Taylor 1911/2006).

The scientific methods of the era spawned a variety of new innovations that are now taken for granted as an integral part of public service (Stever 1988). For example, the movement spawned research bureaus that for the first time emphasized data-based policy recommendations and evaluation of results. These bureaus laid the groundwork for performance measurement of managerial operations, which could then be fed into the budget allocation process. Institutionally, the Progressives established the council-manager form of government, which remains common today and is responsible for the professionalization of local administration. The council-manager model embodies the Progressives' reliance on professionals to meet the needs of citizens, whether through social work, public health, public works, law enforcement, or the management of the general affairs of the community (Stever 1988; Stivers 2002b).

### Public Service as Moral Leadership

Alongside the vision of public administration as scientific management stood a vision of professional career administrators as moral leaders (Stever 1988, chap. 3). This vision rested on the belief that human nature can reach its full potential only if the agents of government serve as exemplars, as tutors, as goads to moral and intellectual excellence. Herbert Croly, one of the intellectual leaders of the Progressive movement, observed:

> The common citizen can become something of a saint and something of a hero, not by growing to heroic proportions in his own person, but by the sincere and enthusiastic imitation of heroes and saints, and whether or not he will come to such imitation will depend upon the ability of his exceptional fellow-countrymen to offer him acceptable examples of heroism and saintliness. (Croly 1964, 454)

This larger moral vision of the Progressive movement transforms the practice of public administration from a merely scientific and technical enterprise into what Stever calls a "polity profession." By "polity" Stever means a profession that is composed of the most knowledgeable members of society (in contrast to the rich and powerful) who have regular, institutionalized control over policy and who exercise this control for the larger public good (Stever 1988, 31). In

short, the task of "speaking truth to power" was more than a matter of making things work, or making them work efficiently, or being technically proficient (Wildavsky 1979). It was a matter of keeping the democratic system on a moral course by at least modeling the appearance of civic virtue, if not cultivating its actual practice. This is strikingly similar to the founders' conception of a natural aristocracy, wherein those who seek fame before the eyes of posterity will at least mimic civic virtue.

In retrospect, the Progressive Era left career public administrators with two seemingly different roles to play in the American system of democratic governance. One emphasizes the purely instrumental role of scientifically managing public organizations and using state-of-the-art techniques in policy development and implementation. The other emphasizes moral leadership that career administrators should exercise in elevating public discourse and in fostering human development. The purely instrumental role harks back to the earlier Anti-Federalist and Jacksonian visions of an administrative process that simply facilitates the implementation of the community's will. The moral leadership role is reminiscent of the Federalist vision of an administrative elite that protects the democratic system from unenlightened impulses of the masses. But the moral goal of both the Federalists and Progressives was primarily instrumental and utilitarian, falling far short of the Anti-Federalist concern for the cultivation of civic virtue and community.

The moral and instrumental strands of the Progressive period remain important institutional legacies that are very much in evidence throughout every level of American government. The council-manager form of government, systematic budgeting and accounting practices, research bureaus, and the transformation of public service into a modern-day profession are all integral parts of the Progressive legacy.

## THE NEW DEAL (1933–1976) AND THE RISE OF THE ADMINISTRATIVE STATE

The Progressive movement's reliance on professional expertise, combined with the moral urgency of meeting the needs of the less fortunate, set the stage for the emergence of a new era of positive government, staffed by an elite corps of technically trained career administrators committed to using government to solve problems and deliver services. This legacy came to fruition during the New Deal period. Between the start of the Great Depression, precipitated by the stock market crash in 1929, and President Lyndon B. Johnson's Great Society initiatives through the 1960s, this elite corps of "good government" professionals created and implemented entirely new programs and organizational structures. Taken together, these programs and structures comprise what has come to be called the *American administrative state*.

### The Expansion of Government Through Regulation and Entitlement Programs

At the programmatic level, the administrative state consists of a variety of social services and subsidies known as *entitlement programs*. These include such benefits as social security, unemployment payments, public housing assistance, aid to dependent children, agricultural supports, loan and aid programs, and other types of social welfare assistance. Franklin D. Roosevelt succeeded, like President Jackson, in winning the affection of the poor and the working class, and thereby made the presidency an instrument of popular will and individual rights.

> FDR and his supporters sought and achieved a transformation in the *conception of rights* and integrated it into a social services or welfare conception of the positive state. In other words,

insuring the delivery of basic social services, now often referred to as the social "safety net," was the same as protecting and advancing individual rights. "With the advent of the New Deal political order, an understanding of rights dedicated to limited government gradually gave way to a more expansive understanding of rights, requiring relentless government identification of problems and the search for methods by which these problems might be solved" (Milkis 1993, 131). This identification of problems began with FDR's articulation of a "Second Bill of Rights," addressing economic security; but by the 1960s and 1970s it had expanded much farther, to encompass broad health, welfare, and "quality-of-life" problems that reformers argued required delineation of additional basic rights as part of their resolution. (Cook 1996, 110)

The expansion of new social service programs reached its zenith during President Johnson's Great Society initiatives in the mid-1960s. His administration tried to tackle the intractable problems of poverty, racism, unemployment, and inadequate education. During the Johnson presidency, Congress enacted two major civil rights acts (1964 and 1965), the Economic Opportunity Act (1964), and two education acts (1965). In addition, legislation was passed that created the Job Corps, Operation Head Start, Volunteers in Service to America (VISTA), Medicaid, and Medicare and increased Social Security benefits. During the 15-year period beginning in 1962, government spending on social welfare (Medicare, Social Security and Medicaid) grew by from 19.6 percent of the federal budget to 38.1 percent of the budget in 1985. By 2011, these programs constituted 55.6 percent of the budget. Contrary to popular opinion the major cause for the increase in the federal budget since 1962 has been Medicare, Medicaid and Social Security, which together have grown from 13.8 percent of the budget in 1962 to 43.0 percent in 2011. Safety net programs have been responsible for 6.8 percent of the increase in the federal budget from 1962–2011 (Vo 2012). As a percentage of gross national product, social welfare spending expanded from 11.5 percent to 19.5 percent in 1976 and then leveled off at 18 percent (Salamon 1999, 61). By 1999, the United States was spending 21 percent of its gross domestic product on government-funded social welfare services, compared to 30 percent or more for West European countries (53).

Although the Great Society made significant contributions to the protection of civil rights and the expansion of social programs, critics increasingly complained that the antipoverty programs were ineffective and wasteful. Their costs, combined with the staggering expense of the Vietnam War, soon overtook Johnson's domestic initiatives.

In addition to the growing concerns for economic and social security, the federal government throughout the 1950s and 1960s continued the trend established during the Populist and Progressive periods of creating agencies to regulate the economy and to control the adverse "spillover" effects of private marketplace competition. The New Deal administration established numerous new regulatory agencies, including the Federal Trade Commission, the Federal Communications Commission, the Federal Power Commission, and the Securities and Exchange Commission, just to mention a few. This trend resurged in the 1960s and 1970s with the creation of nine new regulatory agencies. Exhibit 5.2 provides a summary of these new agencies, including a comparison between the first wave created during the New Deal period and a second wave created in the 1960s and 1970s.

### The Triumph of Executive-Centered Administration

The New Deal also institutionalized a vision of good administration that is perhaps even more significant than all the agencies it established. The vision was clearly articulated in a famous re-

Exhibit 5.2    **The Rise of the Administrative State: Major Periods of Expansion**

**New Deal Period**
Food and Drug Administration (expanded in 1938)
Federal Trade Commission (expanded in 1938)
Soil Conservation Service (1938)
Federal Communications Commission (1936)
Social Security Administration (1935)
Federal Power Commission (1935)
Securities and Exchange Commission (1934)
National Labor Relations Board (1934)
Federal Housing Administration (1934)
Public Works Administration (1933)
Tennessee Valley Authority (1933)
Civil Works Administration (1933)
Rural Electrification Administration (1933)
Civilian Conservation Corps (1933)
Federal Deposit Insurance Corporation (1933)
Federal Home Loan Bank Board (1932)

**1960s and 1970s**
Department of Energy (1977)
Office of Surface Mining (1977)
Nuclear Regulatory Commission (1975)
Materials Transportation Board (1975)
Mine Safety and Health Administration (1973)
Occupational Safety and Health Administration (1973)
Consumer Product Safety Commission (1972)
National Highway Traffic Safety Administration (1970)
Environmental Protection Agency (1970)
Equal Employment Opportunity Commission (1964)
United States Commission on Civil Rights (originally created in 1957; expanded in 1960)

port by one of the intellectual leaders of the New Deal, Louis Brownlow. The Brownlow Report (officially called the President's Committee on Administrative Management, *Report with Special Studies,* 1937) provides the underlying rationale for more than 100 executive-level reorganization plans submitted to Congress since 1939.[5] It places priority on the dual principles of centralized political accountability and administrative efficiency.

*Political Accountability to the President*

The Brownlow Report's chief premise is that "the President is a political leader—leader of the party, leader of the Congress, leader of a people" (Shafritz and Hyde 1992, 90). This view, a direct descendent of Andrew Jackson's view of the presidency, collapses what had previously constituted multiple, independent streams of accountability into a single person and office. Three developments during the New Deal contributed to this unitary view, making the public administration much more subordinate to the elected chief executive than had been the case at any other time in American history. First, the presidency became the symbolic embodiment of the nation and the destiny of its people. Second, the nondelegation doctrine in the courts came to an end. Third, a successful executive initiative was launched to deal with the growth in the number and size of federal agencies during the early decades of the twentieth century.

The stock market crash of 1929 plunged the nation into a chaotic economic state. By declaring in his first inaugural address that there was "nothing to fear but fear itself," and by submitting a

flurry of bills in his famous first hundred days, President Roosevelt instilled hope and courage in the people of the United States. He galvanized the nation's focus on the president as the source of energy, power, and solutions to reverse the nation's misfortunes. This view of the president as the focal point of leadership and accountability persists to this day.

At a legal level, administrative agencies had been governed for more than a century by the doctrine of separation of powers. According to this doctrine, it is a violation of the U.S. Constitution for Congress to delegate its legislative authority to the executive branch of government unless there are clear standards to guide the exercise of administrative discretion. Justice George Sutherland succinctly summarized a version of this doctrine in the early years of the New Deal: "Congress cannot delegate any part of its legislative power except under the limitation of a prescribed standard."[6] In the mid-1930s, the U.S. Supreme Court applied this doctrine to strike down significant pieces of New Deal legislation. President Roosevelt responded in frustration by rolling out a plan that would nominate six new justices to the Court—one new justice for every justice over the age of 70. He argued that the Court was composed of nine old men who needed help to carry out their increasing workload in a responsible manner. While the plan was rejected, the Supreme Court ended up softening its view of the nondelegation doctrine.[7] By 1940 the Court declared that "delegation by Congress has long been recognized as necessary in order that the exertion of legislative power does not become a futility."[8] No longer was nondelegation necessary to preserve the power of the legislative body. Indeed, the opposite was true—delegation was the only way of preventing the legislative power from becoming futile.

The doctrine of greater political accountability to the president formed the cornerstone of the Brownlow Report. Members of the Brownlow Committee reported on the fragmentation of political responsibility as the federal government had succumbed to a lack of foresight and good planning since the latter decades of the nineteenth century. The solution required greater unity of political command by the president. The report argued that proliferation of administrative agencies by Congress, combined with overlapping bureaucratic responsibilities, necessitated more centralized coordination and control by the president. Without this centralization, political accountability and control of the federal bureaucracy would continue to be compromised. Though Congress statutorily creates the mission of federal agencies and provides these agencies with their budget authority, effective administrative accountability must channel through the executive. Nearly all of the 100 reorganization plans proposed since the mid-1930s have accepted this Jacksonian principle—that the executive branch, not the legislative branch, is the superintending agent for administrative agencies. It has resulted in the creation of a separate and ever-larger White House staff and more control over agencies on behalf of the president by an Office of Management and Budget (OMB). This executive-centered approach has been replicated in most of the 50 states, as well as in many local government jurisdictions.

*Administrative Efficiency*

The second principle of the Brownlow Report advocated greater efficiency through the elimination of overlap and duplication of administrative functions. In addition to the political agenda served by consolidation, there has always been a consistent administrative agenda driven largely by the private-sector managerial principles of control, coordination, and efficiency. In chapter 9, we will revisit the influence of these private-sector organizational models on our thinking about the design and operation of public agencies. These models stand in sharp contrast to public-sector structures that emphasize the importance of divided sources of accountability within a constitutional system of checks and balances.

The New Deal represents the triumph of an instrumental view of administrative agencies, subordinate to the popular will embodied in the president. One scholar of this period has noted "the stunning absence of any attempt," during the debates on the Brownlow Report, "to articulate alternative ideas about public administration and its place in the regime. . . . In the end, then, the representatives and senators of the seventy-fifth Congress never actually confronted the challenge of trying to define for themselves what constituted an executive officer" (Cook 1996, 120). Do career public servants qualify as executive officers under the definition of the Brownlow Report, or do they deserve some other kind of designation within the American constitutional system of government? If some other designation, what might that be, especially given the fact that the Constitution speaks only of three branches of government? The New Deal represents the triumph of the view that public administration is the ward of the executive. Though it is the dominant view, it has not gone unchallenged (Cook 177; Elkin 2006).

## The Rise and Transformation of the Nonprofit Sector

One of the less noticed consequences of the growth of the administrative state since the New Deal has been its impact on nonprofit organizations and private-sector service organizations. Government spending on social services increased by 259 percent in inflation-adjusted dollars between 1965 and 1980 (Salamon 1999, 61). But, beginning in the 1980s, government spending began a sharp reversal, experiencing a 15 percent decline in inflation-adjusted dollars between 1977 and 1994 (116).

Despite the decline in government, support for the social service sector continued to grow as a result of the increased role played by the nonprofit and for-profit sectors. For example, between 1977 and 1992:

- Private social service agencies grew by 130 percent.
- The number of employees working for these agencies grew by 140 percent.
- The revenues of these agencies rose nearly 240 percent above what they had been in 1977, even after adjusting for inflation. (Salamon 1999, 116)

Exhibit 5.3 summarizes the key trends in social service delivery between 1977 and 1996. The paradox of declining government support and expansion of spending is explained by the shift of service provision to nonprofits and the private sector, which relied increasingly on fee income and greater support from private giving. By 1996, "fees came to outdistance both government and private giving as a source of nonprofit human service agency income" (Salamon 1999, 117). As of 1980, "approximately 25 percent of all government spending in the fields where nonprofit organizers were active flowed to such organizations" (63). In Massachusetts, the dollar amount of purchase-of-service contracts with private nonprofit service agencies more than doubled between 1977 and 1981, increasing from $36 million with 380 contracts to $84 million and over 1,000 contracts (Smith and Lipsky 1993, 56). In addition to these service contracts, federal block grants and federal programs providing funding for Head Start, runaway shelters, and an extensive array of other social services have been funneled to nonprofit organizations.

What are the consequences of this enlarged role for nonprofit organizations in becoming major providers of public goods and services? From one point of view, it represents the triumph of America's reliance on associations to achieve the common good of the community. Huge numbers of volunteers become enlisted in this effort and, in the process, to quote Alexis de Tocqueville, "sentiments and ideas renew themselves, the heart is enlarged and the human is developed" (1835–1840/2000, 491). But from another perspective,

Exhibit 5.3    **Trends in Social Service Delivery, 1977–1996**

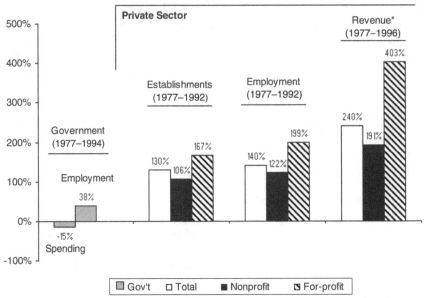

*Source:* Salamon (1999, 116).
*In constant 1996 dollars based on price deflator for services component of personal consumption expenditures.

> the mutual dependence of government and nonprofit organizations raises significant questions for the welfare state. If the state no longer directly delivers services, but authorizes private parties to conduct its business, where shall we locate the boundaries of the state? Massive contracting for services should also have significant implications for the limits of government and the autonomy of nongovernmental community affairs. . . . More dependence on nonprofit organizations means not less but more government involvement in the affairs of voluntary and community agencies. (Smith and Lipsky 1993, 5)

Why is it the case that more contracting out is likely to undermine rather than strengthen the nonprofit sector? To answer this question, we need to return to the distinctions made in chapter 2 between the public, private, and nonprofit sectors. The public sector's emphasis on providing maximum service to as many citizens as possible conflicts with the nonprofit sector's emphasis on providing as much service as possible to its chosen clientele population (see Exhibit 2.2 in chapter 2). In addition, the public sector is held to a different standard of accountability than the nonprofit sector. The dual principles of equity and accountability for public-sector officials create an incentive to write contracts that require nonprofit organizations to deliver specified levels of service to given numbers of clientele with the dollars available. To accomplish this goal, nonprofits may have to alter their mission to accomplish the specifications of the contract. For example, instead of providing homeless shelter services to a given client for as long as they are needed, the nonprofit may be required to restrict the service to a client in order to meet its contract goals with respect to target numbers. It may even be subject to direct control by government "over admission, treatment and discharge decisions" (Smith and Lipsky 1993, 229, 122–32).

In addition to the need for a nonprofit to rearrange its service mission to accommodate the specifications of a contract, the accountability requirements of the contract may require the agency to hire professionals in accounting, financial management, personnel, and fundraising in order to meet its elevated eligibility standards and reporting procedures. This pressure to professionalize the management of nonprofit organizations can displace volunteers, thereby diminishing much of the passion, flexibility, empathy, and singleness of focus that they bring to such organizations (Smith and Lipsky 1993, 83–87, 100–108).

There is a final, unintended consequence of the welfare state's reliance on the contracting process as a substitute for providing direct service. As public dollars have shrunk, there is pressure on the contracting process to squeeze greater results from the contactors. As a result, nonprofit service providers are being asked to deliver more for less, as are government agencies in general. When this occurs in the private business sector, the results are quite predictable, and so it is with nonprofit organizations. To meet the demand for greater economies and efficiencies, nonprofit organizations have consolidated and merged their operations, leaving many fewer providers in the community than in the past (Smith and Lipsky 1993, 177–82). Smith and Lipsky conclude that the nonprofit sector now reflects "a shift . . . from the informal to the formal care systems, greater homogeneity of service within particular service categories, a diminished role of the board of directors in agency governance, and destabilization among nonprofit agencies" (215). In short, many service-providing nonprofits have become more instrumental than constitutive in their mission and culture, and are thereby weakened in their ability to promote citizen engagement in governance. The next generation of public servants faces the challenge of determining how to reverse this trend.

## The Rise of Local Government

In his travels across the United States, Tocqueville was struck by the extent to which local governments constituted the heart of American democracy. He noted that the federal government appeared last upon the scene: "The great political principles that govern American society today were born and developed in the state" (Tocqueville 1835–1840/2000, 56), but the townships served as vital laboratories of street-level application.

> The institutions of a township are to freedom what primary schools are to science; they put it within reach of the people; they make them taste its peaceful employ and habituate them to making use of it. Without the institutions of a township, a nation can give itself a free government, but it does not have the spirit of freedom. . . . It is in the township, at the center of the ordinary relations of life, that desire for esteem, the need of real interests, the tastes for power and attention, come to be concentrated; these passions, which so often trouble society, change character when they can be expressed so near the domestic hearth and in a way in the bosom of the family. . . . The American system, at the same time that it partitions municipal power among a great number of citizens, does not fear to multiply the duties of the township either. (Tocqueville 2000, 57, 58, 64)

Local governments have always held a cherished place in the governance of America, but their role changed dramatically during the rise of the administrative state, both in scale and function. As the role of the central government has grown and expanded, so has the role of local government. Census reports from 2012 indicate that there are more than 89,000 local governments in the United States. These include cities, counties, townships, and special districts. In addition, as of December

2012 there were 564 recognized Native American Indian tribes, which have grown significantly in number and importance over the last 30 years (see chapter 15). While the U.S. Census Bureau does not track the number of tribes, Native American tribes are recognized in the Constitution through treaty making, giving rise to judicial recognition of tribes in the 1830s as domestic, dependent sovereign nations in possession of those aspects of sovereignty not explicitly withdrawn by treaty or statute, or by their dependent status. Exhibit 5.4 summarizes the changes that have occurred in the growth of governmental units since the middle of the twentieth century.

School districts have declined by 80 percent, while special districts have grown by nearly 300 percent. While school districts have undergone major consolidation, special districts have proliferated to provide an ever larger array of specialized services for airports, cemeteries, community services, drainage, education, flood control, water conservation, fire, health care, hospitals, harbors/ports, neighborhood improvements, irrigation, mosquito abatement/vector control, police, reclamation, recreation, parks, resource/habitat conservation, sewer, transit, utility, water, and waste management.

Similar to the growing role of nonprofit organizations, these changes in local government have created governance challenges for local administrators. At a formal legal level, cities, counties, and special districts are presumably the creatures of the state, little more than administrative subdivisions. But over the decades, the granting of home rule charters and the growth of legislation that allows differential treatment of jurisdictions has given cities, counties, and special districts considerable autonomy. It is common now for larger jurisdictions to hire their own lobbyists to fight state legislation that may have adverse consequences for local autonomy. The cities, counties, and special districts in most states have organized into their respective separate associations, which spend much of their time lobbying the state legislature for the interests of their member jurisdictions. The growing independence of local governments, combined with their increase in numbers, has added to the complexity of local communities. Instead of having one unit of government provide an integrated array of services, many citizens in local jurisdictions find themselves increasingly served by separate fire, water, police, library, and other special districts. When added to an already complex array of cities, counties, and townships, administrators face important challenges as they seek to manage significant differences of opinion over annexation, growth, taxation, public safety, transportation, and any number of other major interjurisdictional issues.

Since the New Deal, five factors have greatly influenced the growth and autonomy of cities and special districts. First, President Franklin Roosevelt began the process of expanding local jurisdictions by encouraging the creation of public corporations to float revenue bonds as a way of avoiding municipal defaults. He urged the creation of water, sewer, and electric power districts, arguing "that these governments should be used to circumvent debt limits and referendum requirements for issue of bonds" (Burns 1994, 53). Roosevelt provided model legislation for enabling citizens to form housing authorities and soil conservation districts, and he tied federal funding exclusively to the creation of these jurisdictions. Their numbers exploded as a result.

Second, the impetus for expansion of cities and special districts occurred under the pressure for economic development in the post–World War II period. The expansion of industry and housing, for example, caused the real estate industry to reorganize and apply political pressure to establish new cities and special districts. Race played heavily as a third factor in the expansion of local jurisdictions. It was common practice prior to the 1950s for neighborhood improvement associations to create restrictive covenants that excluded individuals on the basis of race. The U.S. Supreme Court declared in 1948 that race-based restrictive covenants were unconstitutional, and this encouraged cities to try to bypass the ruling by using their zoning authority in new and creative ways (Burns 1994, 60, 54–55).

Exhibit 5.4  **Number of Governmental Units by Type, 1952–2007**

| Type of Government | 1952[1] | 1962 | 1967 | 1972 | 1977 | 1982 | 1987 | 1992 | 1997 | 2007 | Change 1962–2007 |
|---|---|---|---|---|---|---|---|---|---|---|---|
| Total units | 116,807 | 91,237 | 81,299 | 78,269 | 79,913 | 81,831 | 83,237 | 85,006 | 87,504 | 89,527 | –23% |
| U.S. government | 1 | 1 | 1 | 1 | 1 | 1 | 1 | 1 | 1 | 1 | 0% |
| Native American tribes[2] | NA | NA | NA | NA | NA | NA | NA | NA | NA | 564 | NA |
| State governments | 50 | 50 | 50 | 50 | 50 | 50 | 50 | 50 | 50 | 50 | 0% |
| Local governments | 116,756 | 91,186 | 81,248 | 78,218 | 79,862 | 81,780 | 83,186 | 84,955 | 87,453 | 89,476 | –23% |
| Counties | 3,052 | 3,043 | 3,049 | 3,044 | 3,042 | 3,041 | 3,042 | 3,043 | 3,043 | 3,033 | –.6% |
| Municipal | 16,807 | 18,000 | 18,048 | 18,517 | 18,862 | 19,076 | 19,200 | 19,279 | 19,372 | 19,492 | 16% |
| Townships and towns | 17,202 | 17,142 | 17,105 | 16,991 | 16,822 | 16,734 | 16,691 | 16,656 | 16,629 | 16,519 | –4% |
| School districts[3] | 67,355 | 34,678 | 21,782 | 15,781 | 15,174 | 14,851 | 14,721 | 14,422 | 13,726 | 14,561 | –78% |
| Special districts | 12,340 | 18,323 | 21,264 | 23,885 | 25,962 | 28,078 | 29,532 | 31,555 | 34,683 | 35,052 | 84% |

*Source:* U.S. Census Bureau, *2002 Census of Governments*, vol. 1, no. 1, Government Operations, Series GC02(1)-1 and U.S. Census Bureau, *2007 Census of Governments*.

[1] 1952 adjusted to include units in Alaska and Hawaii, which adopted statehood in 1959.

[2] The U.S. Census Bureau does not track the number of tribes. As of October 2010 the Bureau of Indian Affairs (BIA) listed 564 tribal entities as eligible for funding and services from the BIA by virtue of their status as Indian tribes. The basic legal framework for tribal sovereignty was established by Chief Justice John Marshal in a trilogy of cases adjudicated in the 1830s and affirmed by more recent courts. See *Johnson v. McIntosh*, 21 U.S. (8 Wheat.) 543, 5 L. Ed. 681 (1823); *Cherokee Nation v. Georgia*, 30 U.S. (5 Pet.) 1, 8 L. Ed. 25 (1831); *Worcester v. Georgia*, 31 U.S. (6 Pet.) 515, 8 L. Ed. 483 (1832) and *United States v. Wheeler*, 435 U.S. 313, 98 S. Ct. 1079, 55 L. Ed. 2d 303 (1978). See chapter 14 in this volume for a short history of tribal governance challenges and administrative implications. For a list of federally recognized tribes go to http://www.bia.gov/cs/groups/xopa/documents/text/idc013398.pdf.

[3] Includes dependent school districts, which are under the control of the state, county or other governing body.

Fourth, new pressure to expand cities and special districts occurred during the 1960s with the New Frontier administration of President John F. Kennedy and the Great Society administration of President Lyndon B. Johnson. Federal aid to cities almost doubled during this period. It came in the form of programs for housing, urban renewal, mass transit, education, job training, poverty, model cities, and grants-in-aid (Burns 1994, 62). These initiatives yielded two consequences: (1) They changed the expectations of the role that cities could play in meeting the redistributive social needs of the community. In addition to planning for growth and providing infrastructure, New Frontier and Great Society programs laid the groundwork for a larger community-building role to be played by public administrators. (2) These new programs increased the complexity of local government and placed new challenges of interorganizational and interjurisdictional coordination on local government leaders. For example, transportation planning had to be coordinated with a growing number of local jurisdictions as well as with newly created administrative bodies as a precondition for receiving federal funding. The elected and career officials responsible for these new arrangements found themselves in an enviable position.

The fifth factor that spurred the growth of cities and special districts was the significant increase in state and local taxation during the 1960s. Starting in 1961, taxpayers at the local level experienced the largest increase in taxes since the 1930s (see chapter 10 for a more detailed discussion). This increased burden induced businesses and residents to create new cities and special service districts as a way of avoiding the taxes. New special service districts also gave them options in deciding whether they wished to purchase additional services (Burns 1994, 62). For example, if suburban dwellers wish to live in the pastoral setting of the countryside but still have access to city-level police and fire services, how can they be funded? One answer is to provide everyone in the countryside with a base level of rural/county-level service, with an option to purchase additional levels of police, fire, health, education, or other services through the formation of a special service district. During the decades following the local taxation crisis of the 1960s, special districts grew in number from 21,264 in 1967 to 35,052 in 2007, an increase of more than 60 percent. (As of 2012, post-2007 data were still being collected.)

The expansion in the number, complexity, and role of local government jurisdictions since the New Deal has greatly increased the challenges for those who govern. At an administrative level, they have to coordinate more of their work with other jurisdictions. For example, how many special levies will voters support during any given election? How can jurisdictions coordinate their need for voter support while demonstrating that they are wise and prudent stewards of the community's resources? At a political level, the challenge becomes even greater, as communities balkanize into relatively isolated pockets that are organized by socioeconomic status, race, ethnicity, and business opportunities for employment. Under such circumstances, it becomes difficult for administrators to meet the needs of the community in ways that create a shared sense of common interest; the many boundaries created on the basis of narrow self-interests are hard to overcome.

## THE NEW ENTREPRENEURIALISM AND THE DECLINE OF THE ADMINISTRATIVE STATE (1976–PRESENT)

New Entrepreneurialism reflects a growing distrust of big government in general and a concurrent rise in preference for nonregulatory policy action, delivery of public services through third parties, and market-based solutions to administrative problems. The framework for this era is reflected in both major political parties and their candidates. In creating the National Performance Review on March 3, 1993, President Bill Clinton said: "Our goal is to make the entire federal government less expensive and more efficient, and to change the culture of our national bureaucracy away

from complacency and entitlement toward initiative and empowerment."[9] While reflected in the small government and Anti-Federalist legacy of the founding era, this movement also reflects the sentiments of those founders favoring a commercial republic in which the primary function of government is seen to further the function of business activity. This era's reliance on entrepreneurialism and competition, paradoxically combined with an increasing demand for public goods and services, set the stage for a more complex political economy—a new economy that reflects the rising importance of nonprofit organizations and special districts to meet increasing demands. Public service leaders in this era find the need to add competencies in collaborative governance and other tools of horizontal governance to meet the challenges they face.

### The Rise of New Public Management (NPM) and Emergence of New Public Governance (NPG)[10]

A variety of factors began to coalesce in the 1980s, calling into question some of the basic assumptions of the administrative state. First, there was a resurgence of support for a less intrusive government that reduced the regulatory and financial burden on individuals and property holders. This call for less government surfaced on a variety fronts, including taxpayer revolts in several states that succeeded in putting into place limitations on tax increases and spending (see chapter 10). It surfaced on the regulatory front in the call for reduced restrictions on the rights of property owners to develop their land and on businesses burdened by environmental, occupational safety, health, and employment regulations. The call for less government was also fueled by the belief that the private and nonprofit sectors could provide many government services cheaper and more efficiently.

Second, the call for less government was advanced by those who were worried that the growing national debt and the escalating costs by state and local government for health and retirement plans for employees were going to break the bank.

Finally, the call for less government was fueled by a general philosophical belief that democracy was safer when government is smaller. Taken together, these forces for change have resulted in two movements that call into question the capacity for government to be the primary agent in solving society's problems. The first movement, called *New Public Management* (NPM), took the business or market model as the standard for measuring government success and has applied it in successive waves of administrative reform since the early 1980s. The second movement, called *New Public Governance* (NPG),[11] emphasizes the importance of taking a collaborative approach with partners within and across the public, nonprofit, and private sectors in providing public services. This model is more emergent and bridges communitarian aspects of the nonprofit sector with aspects of the market model. Neither model claims to be exclusive; each one emphasizes different kinds of strategies designed to reduce the size, scope, costs, and inefficiencies of government.

### The Rise of New Public Management (NPM)

There has been a concerted effort over the last three decades to reframe the model of public administration from a rule-centered system of accountability to one that makes government run more like a business. This movement, called New Public Management, strives to make the services provided by government more responsive and accountable to citizens by applying businesslike management techniques with a strong focus on competition, customer satisfaction, and measurement of performance. There is general agreement among scholars and practitioners alike that these efforts to measure what gets done have produced a variety of worthwhile results:

- Measures of efficiency and effectiveness have inspired managers, supervisors and frontline employees to improve their capacity to diagnose and correct operational problems (Ammons and Rivenbark 2008).
- An emphasis on performance measurement has heightened interest in creating systems that improve the overall management and governance of political entities (Hatry 2010, 2002; Moynihan and Pandey 2005; Wholey and Hatry 1992.
- Performance measurement systems have expanded to embrace an increasingly larger array of values, including cost and efficiency measures; various effectiveness measures such as outputs, outcomes, and impacts; and qualitative measures such as satisfaction, responsiveness, and quality of life (Jørgensen and Bozeman 2007; O'Flynn 2007; Stoker 2006).

But there are two major weaknesses of using private-sector business principles to improve the performance of government, regardless of what gets measured. First, there is no common denominator—such as profit, market share, or return on investment—that can serve as the basis for comparison across the wide range of criteria that build trust and legitimacy among citizens in their political institutions. Furthermore, efficiency, effectiveness, and responsiveness to citizens (customers) are not the only legitimating possibilities under consideration. Values like fairness, equity, protection of rights, and transparency play important roles in determining the legitimacy of political institutions, processes, and outcomes (Cooper 2003; Hefetz and Warner 2004; Kelly 1998; Lynn 1998; Moe 1994; Moe and Gilmour 1995; Moore 1995, 1994; Rosenbloom 2003). How do you put these more elusive values on the same plane as those that can be measured more easily, and how do you create a common denominator that allows for meaningful comparisons?

The second weakness of using private-sector models for improving government performance is that the public sector is comprised of increasingly fragmented structures of authority that confound the possibility, and even desirability, of moving in a straight line from goals and objectives to instrumentally and rationally linked performance measures. The proliferation of local governments we described in the previous section, coupled with the entrepreneurial push to outsource public service to nonprofit and private-sector organizations, shifts performance away from a single-minded focus on the efficient, effective, and customer-sensitive achievement of goals and objectives to a focus on achieving and sustaining agreements between and across structures of authority. This has been described as "leading in a power-shared world" (see chapter 12) and is the focus of an emerging body of literature, called New Public Governance (Osborne 2010).

To summarize, the NPM agenda is based on a truncated view of the purpose of government. Government is not simply the agent of accountability to citizens or the agent of efficiency and effectiveness. It is also responsible for collecting the values of the community and creating integrated responses to these values across increasingly fragmented government systems (Kelly 1998; Lynn 1998). When the values of the community are in conflict, or when they are contrary to the interests of significant minorities, government officials have a fiduciary responsibility to make decisions that are in the larger public interest. This kind of accountability model has faded into the background with the emergence of NPM. In a previous day, whether it was the scientific management movement of the early twentieth century or the efficiency and effectiveness initiatives of the Brownlow and Hoover Commission Reports in the 1930s, 1940s, and 1950s, the discussion of performance was framed within a larger discussion of the respective roles of the executive and legislative branches in making the overall system of government work (see especially Cook 1996, 119–120; Stever 1990, 1988). Performance was not stripped down to the simple issue of business efficiency and effectiveness. It was treated as an important part of a larger set of governance issues that were vital to building trust and legitimacy in governing institutions and their leaders. This

larger, more holistic and organic perspective has been missing from the principles of the NPM movement since its inception in the 1980s. These concerns spawned the rise of the New Public Governance (NPG) movement.

## The Rise of New Public Governance (NPG)

Concerns with NPM's narrow instrumental focus generated a countermovement by practitioners and academics to place substantive political values more firmly at the center of the governance debate. This movement emphasizes three trust- and legitimacy-building characteristics of public governance that are ignored and/or undervalued by NPM. First, NPG is value-centered; it argues that the goal of government is to promote the larger common good. Mark Moore has called this new emphasis "the public value approach" (Moore 1995, 1994; also see Smith and Huntsman 1997), while Stoker and others have called it "the collective preference approach" (Alford 2002; Stoker 2006). NPG is interested in advancing the value created by the whole of government activities, not just improved efficiency, effectiveness, or responsiveness in the implementation of a given program. This shift has broadened the objectives of performance measurement and management to include service outputs, satisfaction, outcomes, a wide array of substantive political values, and, ultimately, citizen trust and the very legitimacy of government itself.

A second characteristic of NPG is that it emphasizes the importance of creating government processes that facilitate the generation of implementable agreements among wide-ranging stakeholders who may disagree on what courses of action will produce the maximum public value (Sanger 2008; Yang and Holzer 2006). This is because NPG views politics as the politically mediated expression of collectively determined preferences that the citizenry deems valuable (Alford 2002; Moore 1995; O'Flynn 2007)—a sharp contrast to the philosophy of NPM, which views politics as the aggregation of individual preferences. The consequences of this difference at a practical level are abundantly evident in the major steps the United Kingdom (UK) has taken since 2000 to reform the delivery of its social service, education, medical, and justice services to citizens at the local government level. In recent years, public officials in the UK have chosen to treat government performance not as a set of rationally planned objectives, but as a process of political mediation among contending stakeholders; these stakeholders have very legitimate differences regarding the public values that need to be preserved to ensure the integrity of the larger public good. Such efforts have resulted in the creation of a wide variety of new policy instruments, negotiated agreements, and performance measures that would have been difficult, if not unthinkable, under NPM (Brookes and Grint 2010; Osborne 2010, especially chaps. 16, 19, and 22).

A final characteristic of the NPG movement is that it views the creation of the public good as a coproduction process involving the public, private market, and the nonprofit sectors (see discussion in chapter 2 on intersectoral interdependence; also see Crosby and Bryson 2005; Osborne 2010; O'Toole 1997). Under this model, the role of government is not simply to regulate, distribute, or redistribute public benefits, but to serve as a catalytic agent to invest private and nonprofit stakeholders in shared ownership of the public good. This can take the simple form of community policing programs or a much more complicated form of networked governance such as watershed management over a very large geographic area involving multiple stakeholders and structures of authority. It is important to distinguish NPG's approach and NPM's approach to partnerships with the private and nonprofit sectors: The latter is interested primarily in using the private and nonprofit sectors to deliver a service cheaply, efficiently, and effectively (Osborne and Gaebler 1994), while NPG is interested in enhancing the capacity of local organizations as a means of building civic infrastructure and the overall capacity of a community to be self-authoring (Smith and Lipsky 1993; Smith and Smyth 2010).

The three characteristics of NPG discussed above emanate from a common belief that government performance must be viewed from the perspective of the organic wholeness of a political system in which the public, private, and nonprofit sectors work together to contribute to the distinctive way of a life of a political community. This view emphasizes the synergistic influence of history, institutions, and culture in creating a shared system of values, as well as shared agreement on governance processes and structures, both formal and informal. Over the past two decades, there has been a resurgence of scholarship that uses "polity" or "regime" as the unit of analysis for understanding performance, political change, governance, and leadership development (Elkin and Soltan 1999; Johnson 2002; Lauria 1997; Leo 1998, 1997; Ozawa 2005; Rohr 1989; Stone 1993, 1989). We believe this framework is especially useful in understanding the role of local administrators in building bridges across sectors and organizations to leverage the maximum resources possible for the promotion of the larger good.

## THE EVOLUTION OF PUBLIC ADMINISTRATION AS A FIELD OF STUDY AND PRACTICE

In Exhibit 5.5, we summarize the evolution of the study and practice of public administration through at least five stages of development. We call the first stage *preclassic* because it precedes the conscious creation of public administration as a formal field of study and captures what leaders are expected to do when undertaking nation building and state building. Studies of the role of public administration during these successful founding periods (in the United States and elsewhere around the world) document the importance of administrators who used their discretion to assist founding political leaders in building the trust and legitimacy of the political order. This was the genius of both Genghis and Kublai Khan, who together united China and laid the foundations for the modern world (Weatherford 2004); of the founders of the Greek and Roman city states; of Ataturk, who founded the Turkish Republic (Bay 2011; Mango 2000); of Mao Tse-tung, who founded modern China; of Ho Chi Minh who reunited Vietnam; and of the American founders as well (cf. Green 2002b; White 1948). All of these founders viewed the work of administrators as essential to government performance. They consciously recruited members of their administrative cadre based on their (1) competence in building systems, (2) their sensitivity to the needs and values of local citizens, (3) their ability to increase the reputation and trust in the larger political system, and (4) their ability to create and maintain a shared sense of common values and purpose. In short, the work of administrators was not seen as simply being instrumental and loyal but as being an integral part of shaping the meaning, value, and legitimacy of the political order itself. This makes the work of public administration—from its inception—political, constitutive, and value-centered.

Column 3 of Exhibit 5.5, labeled *classic public administration,* represents the emergence of public administration as a distinct field of study. It has its origins in the Populist and Progressive eras of the late 1800s and early to mid-1900s. Salamon observes that classic public administration theory "posited a new type of institution, the democratic public agency, that would overcome the three major problems long associated with government bureaucracy—that is, excessive administrative discretion, special-interest capture, and inefficiency" (2002, 9). From the beginning, public administration has concerned itself with the business of (1) restricting government agencies to the administration of policy rather than the making of it, (2) the staffing of agencies based on competence rather than influence, and (3) management principles aimed at efficient dispatch of duties.

Represented by column 4 in Exhibit 5.5, *New Public Management* became the dominant paradigm in the 1980s. There is widespread agreement that the NPM agenda has succeeded in

Exhibit 5.5  **Distinguishing Characteristics of Public Administration Philosophies**

| Distinguishing Characteristics | Preclassic Nation Building | Classical Public Administration | New Public Management | New Public Governance | Value-Based Performance Governance |
|---|---|---|---|---|---|
| Theoretical basis | Regime Theory | Political Science, Public Policy, Organizational theory | Rational/Public Choice Theory, Management Science | Institutional, Network, Theory of Agency | Political Economy, Regime Theory, Complex Interdependence |
| Concept of state | Unitary | Unitary | Regulatory and Privatized | Plural and Pluralist | Regime-Dependent |
| Management focus | Nation | Organizational Hierarchy | Organizational Performance | Values that are co-produced by networks and partners | Value-based performance |
| Leadership actions | Nation-building and statecraft | Output management | Coordination | Interest-based conflict resolution | Diplomacy |
| Leadership scope | A people and their destiny | Management within an organization | Coordination among organizations | Forging collective horizontal leadership | Collective vertical and horizontal leadership |
| Leadership results | Institutions and processes of state | Hierarchical and Professional control: efficiency and effectiveness | Customer satisfaction, efficiency, effectiveness | Agreement on actions | Agreement on the nature of the problem and solution |
| Value orientation | Variable | Agnostic values | Explicit values | Limited explicit value conflicts | Unlimited explicit value conflicts |
| Value arbitration | Institutions and processes of state | Hierarchy | The market and classical or neo-classical contracts | Networks and relational contracts | Renewed institutions and processes of the state |
| System orientation | Monocentric | Monocentric; Internal focus | Polycentric; Internal focus | Minicentric; External focus | Polycentric; External focus |
| Performance unit of analysis | Legitimacy | Outputs; Transactions | Outcomes | Conflict resolution | Consensus building, trust and legitimacy |
| Leadership archetype | Visionary | Tactical and operational management | Strategic management | Strategic leadership | Transformational leadership |

*Source:* Adapted and expanded from Osborne 2010, 10.

accomplishing multiple goals, among them increasing government efficiency, improving service access and delivery to citizens, and downsizing government while expanding the private and nonprofit sectors (Brookes 2008, 3). NPM has strengths that are important to preserve for building citizen trust in government, including: (1) an emphasis on customer service; (2) the need to foster professionalism, managerial skills, and accountability in public administration; (3) and the important role of leaders in creating and maintaining high performing organizations.

The critical responses to the deficiencies of classic public administration and New Public Management have spawned *New Public Governance,* represented by Column 5 in Exhibit 5.5. NPG represents a shift in focus from what it takes to make things work in vertical structures of authority to what it takes to make things work in horizontal structures. These horizontal structures are represented by cooperative agreements between and among public agencies, nonprofit organizations and participating entities from the market sector. Joint actions like these require a focus on identifying and reconciling conflicting values with a reliance on different policy instruments and tools than those used in traditional hierarchical structures. Salamon (2002) outlines five key areas of change that result in this transition from classic public administration and New Public Management to New Public Governance: (1) a shift in focus from agencies and programs to the kinds of policy tools and instruments needed to create and sustain network agreements, (2) a shift in organizational form from hierarchy to network, (3) a shift in dynamics from public v. private to public and private, (4) a shift in exercise of power from command and control to negotiation and persuasion, and (5) a shift in orientation from management skills to enablement skills.

## CONCLUSION

We conclude this chapter on the theme with which we began. The history of American public administration is a "History of Sheep in Wolves' Clothing" (Karl 1987). It is the story of a love/fear relationship between bureaucracy and democracy. It is a relationship that has increasingly eroded and obscured a desirable tension between the instrumental and constitutive roles that public administrators play in America's many democratic systems of governance. The New Deal image of public administration as an instrument of a centralized liberal state, operating under the leadership of a politically accountable executive, did much to obscure this tension (Cook 1996). It has been further obscured by NPM, which, like the New Deal model, makes bureaucracy fully subordinate to the elected executive, as illustrated in Exhibit 5.6.

However, at a level of practice, or "theory in action" (Schon 1983, especially chap. 2), the story is quite different, particularly in local systems of government where part-time elected officials rely heavily on career administrators for policy advice and counsel. Public administrators at all levels are expected to take a proactive role in shaping policy agendas that flow from complex and diffuse structures of authority. In fact, in many local jurisdictions, it is frequently the case that career administrators play the dominant role in shaping public policy (Morgan and Kass 1993). This theory in action is illustrated in Exhibit 5.7.

The feedback arrow at the chief executive and administrative levels illustrates the constitutive role that is characteristically played by career public servants, both procedurally and substantively. Policy development and administration in most local jurisdictions is a fluid and collaborative process of exchange. It is difficult to determine where to draw the line between the instrumental role of administrators and the constitutive policy role of elected officials. At the level of practice, elected officials and career administrators are performing both roles without the legitimating authority to do so. This has become even more the case as resources shrink and administrators are called on to take greater initiative in problem solving and in creating new approaches to funding

Exhibit 5.6  **Espoused Theory of Government**

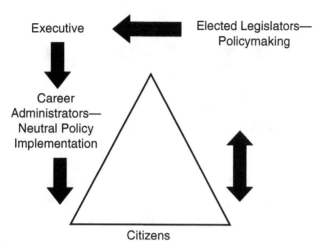

Exhibit 5.7  **Theory of Governance in Action**

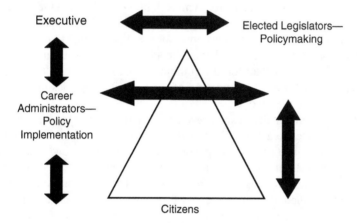

and delivering public services. NPG reflects this call to take a constitutive role, going beyond the official theory in Exhibit 5.6 that legitimates administrative work.

As we pass the first decade of the twenty-first century, we are confronted with an ever-widening divergence between our espoused theories of public administration and the theories we actually use. At the level of espoused theory, we continue to claim that administrators are more like clerks: They simply use their technical, neutral competencies in the service of the policy directives set by the elected officials. This theory maintains a bright-line distinction between politics and administration, as illustrated in Exhibit 5.6.

But to the average citizen, the policymaking and implementation process appears as a free-for-all, in which every special interest has its leg in the match. The difference is that career administrators are viewed by the citizenry as having an inside track. Exhibit 5.8 illustrates this model. It is a perceived theory of democratic governance that puts administrators under a constant cloud of suspicion. Much of what they do or say is not trusted because there is an as-

**Exhibit 5.8   Perceived Theory of Public Administration**

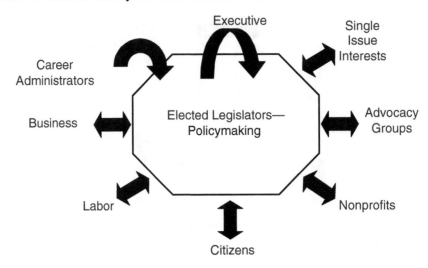

sumption that they simply go through the motions of various administrative processes to arrive at a predetermined result. This is a recipe for cynicism, burnout of chief administrative officers, and avoidance of hard public policy choices by elected officials (Morgan and Kass 1993). In the chapters that follow, we will explore various opportunities that administrators have to cultivate legitimacy and ameliorate the perception that public administration is just another vested interest that operates against, rather than for, the common good. In exploring these opportunities, it is important for administrators to be mindful of the historical legacies they can draw on to inform, guide, and validate their work.

The historical eras covered in this chapter reveal the determination of public officials to amass power and declare mandates to act on behalf of the American people, while claiming to divide and check power by diffusing it across multiple sectors, multiple levels, and multiple branches of government. Each era adds layers and permutations to the conflicts engendered in the founding era debates over how best to preserve a regime of ordered liberty. The Jacksonians wanted to restore the "republican simplicity" of the Jeffersonian and Anti-Federalist vision while drawing on mass appeal and representative politics. Their successes sowed the seeds of their own failures as manifested in the emergence of corrupt machine politics and overbearing executives. The Populists sought to correct these defects by advocating reforms that were focused on democratic responsiveness, direct accountability, and aggressive regulation. The irony is that their measures required a shift in governing power to the federal government to effectively reign in powerful private interests, while their reforms drew away power from entrenched state and local officials. The Progressives preached centralization and strengthening the role of professionals for the sake of efficiency and effectiveness in the delivery of services—and thereby eclipsed institutions steeped in practices of civic governance. The New Dealers refined the Progressive doctrines for a burgeoning administrative state that sponsored the growth and professional transformation of the private market and nonprofit sectors in wake of the Great Depression and World War II. Executive-centered administration bred its own predictable abuses, and the administrative state violated contending norms of frugality, simplicity, grassroots participation, and face-to-face, deliberative-centered governance. Disenchantment with these conditions spawned a return to principles of devolution, privatization, and a renewed spirit of entrepreneurialism. And so the drama of American governance continues.

The historical continuity of these conflicts suggests at least two things: The first is that we cannot understand the activity of public administration apart from the political contexts which have defined its values and practices. The second is that definitive political and administrative solutions are inherently impossible, especially given the complex constitutional and legal structures of America's varied systems of democratic governance. These structures, with their built-in competing values to administrative work, must be continually reexamined and rebalanced to secure the vitality of a regime of ordered liberty. Knowledge of how we have dealt with problems and solutions in the past can help current and future public administrators cope more effectively and with less surprise, and may even assist them in assuming roles that balance contending principles in the pursuit of ordered liberty. That may be the best we can do to achieve a measure of the public's confidence. In the next chapter, we will address how theories of administrative responsibility may hinder or help toward that end.

## STUDY QUESTIONS

1.  What historical role has the nonprofit sector played in meeting the needs of local democratic communities? How does the purpose and role of the nonprofit sector compare to the role played by government? What are the implications of these differences for the ways in which each organizes and delivers its services?
2.  What historical role has the for-profit sector played in meeting the needs of local democratic communities? How does the purpose and role of the for-profit sector compare to the role that government plays? How do the differences between the public and the for-profit sectors affect public accountability and the common good?
3.  How do the contributions of the Populists to a career civil service compare to the contributions of the Progressives?
4.  What are the chief contributions of the New Deal to American public administration?
5.  Drawing on your agency experience and assigned readings, analyze and evaluate the contributions of the Populist, Progressive, and New Deal eras to the theory and practice of American public administration.
6.  What is meant by the "rise of the modern administrative state"? What are the factors that have contributed to this rise? What are the implications for the role of public administrators?
7.  What is the significance of the Brownlow Report?
8.  What are the major influences and developments that have influenced public administration since World War II?
9.  What are the strengths and weaknesses of New Public Management (NPM) in building trust and legitimacy in democratic governance?
10.  What are the differences between New Public Management and New Public Governance (NPG)?
11.  What are the strengths and weaknesses of New Public Governance in building trust and legitimacy in democratic governance?
12.  What lessons do you draw from the historical development of public administration with respect to the tensions between its instrumental and constitutive roles?

## NOTES

1. We have relied largely upon Paul Van Riper's excellent summary of the history of the United States Civil Service (1958) to organize the major eras of development. However, we have distinguished the Populist and Progressive eras here because of the significant differences in goals and objectives.

2. President Jackson opposed the existence of a national bank, which had been established by Congress in 1816. His opposition was based on the belief that a national bank created an exclusive monopoly that benefited privileged stockholders at the expense of the hard-working American people. He ordered the secretary of the treasury, William Duane, to transfer deposits out of the U.S. Bank to 12 designated private banks. When Secretary Duane refused, Jackson dismissed him from office. The protracted battle over the role of the national bank was symbolic of a much larger and more fundamental set of issues that President Jackson set forth in his famous veto message of the renewal of the bank's charter in 1832. "Many of our rich men have not been content with equal protection and equal benefits, but have besought us to make them richer by act of Congress. By attempting to gratify their desires, we have in the results of our legislation arrayed section against section, interest against interest, and man against man, in a fearful commotion which threatens to shake the foundations of our Union" (Richardson 1899, II:1139–1154).

3. These scandals involved typical abuses of the public trust that have their contemporary counterparts. All were variations on the same theme: using your position of public trust for personal gain.

- *Crédit Mobilier* (1872): The vice president of the Union Pacific Railroad, George Francis Train, created a private construction company called Crédit Mobilier of America, which was the sole bidder for certain construction contracts from Union Pacific. The company was paid hefty fees through federal subsidies approved by members of Congress who were provided with cheap shares of stock in Crédit Mobilier.
- *Gold Conspiracy* (1869): The Gold Conspiracy has its roots in the U.S. government's decision to abandon the gold standard during the Civil War. So-called *greenbacks,* the name given to the paper currency issued during the war, were not backed by gold. Two private speculators, Jay Gould and James Fisk, tried to use the unbacked paper money for their own gain by seeking insider information on the gold market in the postwar years. In advance of the government's plan to buy back the greenbacks with gold coinage, Gould and Fisk manipulated the market by hoarding gold, which drove up prices and caused a nasty dip in stocks. This speculator-created financial panic became known as the first "Black Friday."
- *Indian Ring* (1876): President Ulysses S. Grant's secretary of war, William W. Belknap, accepted bribes from companies with licenses to trade on the reservations of many Native American tribes. He was impeached by the House of Representatives but acquitted by the Senate in August 1876.
- *Salary Grab* (1873): Congress gave itself a 50 percent salary increase on the last day of the session in 1873 and made the increase retroactive for the previous two years.
- *Whiskey Ring* (1875): A conspiracy of government agents, politicians, whiskey distillers, and distributors diverted millions of dollars in federal taxes on liquor for personal gain by creating a network of bribes involving tax collectors, storekeepers, and others.

4. These state laws were called Granger Laws, because they were designed to protect the interest of farmers who had organized into local associations, called *granges,* to advance their interests against the monopolistic practices of price fixing by railroads. The laws were overturned in a series of Supreme Court decisions: *Munn v. Illinois*, 94 U.S. 113 (1877); *Budd v. New York,* 143 U.S. 517 (1894); and *Brass v. North Dakota ex rel. Stoesser,* 153 U.S. 391 (1894).

5. See the President's Committee on Administrative Management, *Report with Special Studies* (1937); President's Message to the Congress, March 25, 1971; Mansfield (1969); Nathan (1976); Rohr (1986, chap. 9); National Academy of Public Administration (1983); and National Performance Review (Gore 1993).

6. *U.S. v. Chicago, St. P. and P.R. Co.,* 282 U.S. 311, 324 (1931). The view expressed by Justice George Sutherland in 1931 was much less strict than the version of the nondelegation doctrine articulated by Justice Stephen J. Field toward the end of the nineteenth century: "That Congress cannot delegate legislative power to the President is a principle universally recognized as vital to the integrity and maintenance of the system of government ordained by the Constitution" (*Field v. Clark,* 143 U.S. 649, 692 [1892]).

7. *Panama R. Co. v. Ryan,* 293 U.S. 388 (1935); *Schechter P. Corp. v. U.S.,* 295 U.S. 495 (1935). In addition to changing its view on the nondelegation doctrine, the Court shifted its interpretation of the due process clause. It had interpreted the due process clauses of the Fifth and Fourteenth amendments to prohibit legislative bodies from passing various kinds of economic and public health regulations on the grounds that they restrict property or liberty without "due process of law." Businesses used this interpretation to challenge government market regulation, including efforts to establish standards for wages, hours, working conditions, and competition (Pritchett 1968, chap. 31). The Supreme Court's shift in its interpretation of the due process

clause and the nondelegation doctrine became known as the "stitch in time that saved nine" (*West Coast Hotel v. Parrish*, 300 U.S. 379 [1937]).

8. *Sunshine A. Co. v. Adkins*, 310 U.S. 381, 397 (1940). Judicial deference to administrative discretion has developed over the past 50 years into some reasonably clear standards of review. Although there is evidence that the degree of deference is not as great as it once was (Cooper 2007, chap. 7), the addition of new conservative jurists to the U.S. Supreme Court during the Bush II (George W. Bush) administration may give yet more presumptive weight to administrative action. This issue will be discussed further in chapter 15.

9. William J. Clinton: "Remarks Announcing the National Performance Review," March 3, 1993. See also Gore, 1995.

10. For this section, we have drawn from the following article on New Public Governance: Bao et al. 2012. "Beyond New Public Governance: A Value-Based Global Framework for Performance Management, Governance, and Leadership."

11. The term *New Public Governance* first appeared in print in 1998 (Osborne 2006; Toonen 1998). It has been used consistently to describe new governing structures and processes that include intergovernmental arrangements; partnerships across the public, private, and nonprofit sectors; and policy instruments to promote the common good (Osborne 2010).

# CHAPTER 6

# ADMINISTRATIVE ETHICS AND RESPONSIBILITY

> By suggesting a theory of Public Administration that combines constitutional subordination with autonomy, I hope to preserve the enduring insight of the venerable dichotomy without succumbing to its naïve view of administration as apolitical. Administration is political; but like the judiciary, it has its own style of politics and its distinctive functions within the constitutional order.
>
> *(John Rohr 1986, 184)*

In chapter 3, we examined the nature of discretion in public administration, linking much of its pervasiveness and variety to conflicting political ends that have been at issue since the debates over the founding of the nation. In chapter 4, we reviewed the competing ideas of the Federalist and Anti-Federalist founders with respect to what they believed was essential to preserve a regime of ordered liberty. Their opposing visions resulted from different answers to two fundamental questions: (1) Who should rule, and (2) what is the proper role of government? In chapter 5, we showed how different answers to these questions produced the four problems that needed to be successfully addressed in order to sustain a regime of ordered liberty. The "King George Problem" poses the threat of tyrannical rule, especially by overbearing executives. The "George Washington Problem" reveals the ineffectiveness of predominantly deliberative and responsive governance. The "Shays' Rebellion Problem" raises the specter of tyrannical majorities as a threat to minority rights, and the "Engaged Citizen Problem" emphasizes the loss of civic capacity and self-government in a system that ignores or downplays civic virtue and citizen engagement.

Administrators play a key role in providing correctives to these problems. In chapter 5, we identified four corrective models—interest balancing, entrepreneurialism, systematic planning, and community building—that emerged in nascent form during the founding era and have evolved in significant ways through subsequent political eras. We argue that these models have developed into distinct administrative traditions (described succinctly later in this chapter) that are now thoroughly woven into the fabric of American governance. These traditions reflect conflicting criteria about what constitutes "good" administration; that is, they provide different substantive standards for guiding the exercise of administrative discretion, as well as for determining whom and what public administrators are obliged to serve. Traditionally, such matters are covered under the subject of *administrative responsibility.*

Administrative responsibility forms a cornerstone of public ethics. Theories of administrative responsibility help us articulate the ethical standing of public administration in relation to the public at large, to different sectors of society, to superintending authorities, to guiding principles of the regime, and to the proper scope, nature, and exercise of discretionary power. Understanding these ethical relationships provides important grounding for public servants who possess discretionary authority. Acting on such authority requires astute judgment guided by an informed conscience, as well as an acute sense of accountability. Thus, the subject of administrative responsibility must address matters that are internal to public officials—that affect their *ethical* values and sensibilities—and external to them as expressed in the language of *accountability* to others. However, this distinction between internal and external sources of ethical responsibility is also somewhat artificial. To illustrate, most career administrators take an oath of allegiance to uphold the Constitution and the laws of the land. Is this ethical responsibility best characterized as "accountability to" or "responsibility for"? The answer depends on the extent to which allegiance to the Constitution and the laws have been internalized as part of one's professional role responsibilities. For this reason, we will treat both the internal and external sources of obligation as necessary dimensions of a larger set of ethical responsibilities that are inherent to public service.

In emphasizing the need to integrate the internal and external dimensions of one's ethical obligations, it is important to distinguish the *principle* of accountability from the various political, legal, and organizational *mechanisms* used to ensure accountability. Though related, these accountability mechanisms fall into the category of techniques, tests, and processes, to which we devote greater attention in chapter 14. In this chapter, we will focus our attention on the ways in which the principle of accountability creates a set of ethical obligations for career public servants.

The first part of this chapter examines theories of administrative responsibility in a critical light. Some are commonly held, but also overly simplistic and thus misleading. Their common use contributes to a widening gap between what career officials espouse as their proper roles and what they actually practice. As we noted at the end of chapter 5, inconsistent definitions of *responsibility* often undercut administrative credibility. Other theories may seem more nuanced and complicated, but they provide a better fit with the constitutional realities of our multiple governing systems. In short, they establish a more solid grounding for the four administrative traditions that have become embedded so deeply in American governance.

In the second part of this chapter, we employ a *Balancewheel model* that portrays the four administrative traditions as existing in constant tension with each other. In addition to coping with these enduring tensions, career administrators are ethically obliged to preserve them so that the practices associated with each tradition remain in play. We believe this Balancewheel model can serve as a rough, practical guide to the exercise of administrative discretion at all levels of government. We discuss the advantages and implications of this approach in relation to the foregoing theories, and then apply the model to the library patron case presented at the beginning of Part I.

In the third part of the chapter, we derive from the discussion of administrative responsibility some criteria for distinguishing *public* administration in America from other realms of administrative or managerial work. These characteristics help define a *public morality* that can be used as a body of standards and obligations that shape administrative practices in distinctive ways.

The last section of this chapter addresses some implications of public morality for bureaucratic politics in modern society. Topics covered include the deleterious effects of bureaucratic organization on moral judgment, the pervasive influence of utilitarianism in management thought and practice, the predominance of elite professions in democratic governance, and the pervasive and troubling nature of compromise.

## THEORIES OF ADMINISTRATIVE RESPONSIBILITY

Many political and academic attempts have been made to delineate a clear and definitive theory of administrative responsibility. Some of these attempts fail in practice because they also simplify administrative responsibility by tying it to one superintending institution or principle. In the process, they disregard or even eschew the effects of diffused power in the American constitutional system and fail to comprehend the contending roles prescribed for its administration. Political attempts at establishing simple theories of administrative responsibility are usually born of ambition toward putting the right people or the right institution in charge and establishing clear lines of authority and responsibility to them. In the American regime, such ambition tends to favor either *legislative dominance* or *executive dominance*.

As mentioned in chapter 5, many political executives have followed President Andrew Jackson's claim to a broader electoral mandate than their legislative counterparts, who are elected by specific and more limited constituencies. They typically employ this claim in conjunction with expansive constitutional interpretations of executive power in order to justify broad, or even exclusive, super-intendence of career administrators and their agencies. Under this executive-centered framework, the public administration answers to the executive alone, who then works with Congress to establish sound public policy. President Jackson made exactly this claim to the U.S. Supreme Court in a case involving his postmaster general, Amos Kendall. The Court unanimously rejected the argument in *Kendall v. U.S., ex rel. Stokes* (1838), making it clear that Congress shared power with the executive branch over the subordinate public administration. Congress could, if it chose, fix statutory respon-sibilities in executive branch subordinates, as it had with *Kendall*, or it could, as later courts would confirm, even establish administrative organs independent of executive control.

The Supreme Court's decision supported the Constitution's blending of powers among the branches in order to guarantee a robust system of checks and balances—where ambition would be made to check ambition, even among the subordinate ranks of government. Erstwhile execu-tives bristle at such rebukes and persist in their efforts to offer simpler and politically expedient formulations, as evidenced in the many centralizing reform initiatives of the twentieth century, the more prominent among them being the Brownlow Committee Report (1937), the two Hoover Commission reports, and the initiatives contained in the Civil Service Reform Act of 1978 and the New Public Management movement of the 1990s (see chapters 5, 8, and 15 for more detailed discussions of these initiatives).

Academic theorists have also attempted to simplify administrative responsibility, and some of their theories have enjoyed considerable influence. This is especially true of Progressive Era doctrines on the supremacy of legislative authority. Reform-minded professors such as Woodrow Wilson and Frank J. Goodnow constructed a theory of administration founded upon the principle of legislative supremacy, which had more in common with parliamentary systems in Europe than with the American Constitution (Rohr 1986, 59–89).

For Wilson and Goodnow, the public administration forms part of the executive *function* (as opposed to *branch*) of government and serves in a subordinate role to the legislative authority. According to their theory, the legislative body is the supreme authority of government, who, with the participation of political parties, performs the function of expressing the will of the people. The administration carries it out. In Goodnow's design, the executive function includes executive authorities (such as a governor or president), the courts, and the public administration staffed with nonpolitical experts who "attend to the scientific, technical, and, so to speak, commercial activities of the government" (Goodnow 1900, 45, 85–87). The executive function, therefore, is separate from politics, which is the work of parties and legislatures.

This basic design effectively collapses the separation of powers in favor of a *separation of functions*. The legislature becomes the supreme governing body in place of the people, and the executive institutions carry out their will by the most efficient means. Neither Wilson nor Goodnow liked separation of powers because it encouraged division and conflict in the expression of the public will. How could the public administration take directions if it had multiple masters who disagreed over policy? Under such conditions, administrative efficiency and effectiveness are continually compromised.

Wilson and Goodnow favored constitutional amendments to establish this parliamentary-styled model, but they also realized—to their chagrin—that achieving their goal was politically unrealistic. Since it is extraordinarily difficult to amend the U.S. Constitution, they opted instead to reinforce the idea of a politics/administration dichotomy in practice and to pursue administrative reforms toward that end. As noted in chapter 5, their ideas contributed to the broad movement of Progressive reform, which, not surprisingly, found its purest institutional manifestation in the council-manager form of city government. The city manager works at the pleasure of a city council, in which resides a fusion of executive and legislative powers. The city manager runs the administrative apparatus like a business operation. Public employees are hired on the basis of technical merit or neutral expertise, rather than on the basis of political loyalties. Technically trained, responsive bureaucrats under this system inform policymakers and the public of the best means of implementing public policy.

Given the historical development of local governments in America, it makes some sense that the council-manager form would take root. As indicated in chapter 5, local institutions of governance have always reflected a wide array of forms, many of which fuse powers in their operations. Especially during the nineteenth century, their communitarian principles and organic development encouraged unique administrative arrangements under the protection of state sovereignty. In large part, local governing bodies reflect the fact that separation of powers is an artificial construction that must admit of at least a partial blending of powers at the top levels of government (cf. Federalist Nos. 47–49, 1788/1961), and must comprehend a fusion of powers in many agency and street-level contexts. Local governments reside at the nexus of organic, street-level governance and the downward flow of policy and administration from state and federal governments.

The Progressive reform model, as recalled from our discussion in chapter 5, advocated a new functional approach to the fused powers model, which corresponded neatly with the contemporary literature on scientific management. The management of organizations had evolved into a separate field of study by the early 1900s, and it claimed universal application. It mattered not whether the organization was public or private because the activity of management was the same everywhere. Moreover, the scientific study of the field added an important nuance to the meaning of administration as a nonpolitical endeavor. Not only is management nonpolitical in the sense of being separate from electoral politics, it is devoid of politics altogether. Its character is technical and scientific—and therefore *apolitical*. The infatuation during this period with science as an alternative to traditional ways of knowing led eventually to the idea that scientific knowledge stands in contrast to politics. Politics is local and parochial, while science is universal. This was exemplified in the first city managers, who tended to come from technical backgrounds such as engineering and were expected to bring scientific study to bear on local public functions.

Managerialists joined with other emerging professions in staking a claim for legitimacy on the foundation of science in opposition to politics (Green, Keller, and Wamsley 1993). This approach yielded benefits to scholars in public administration: It justified an institutional niche in modern research universities and garnered significant funding that would never have been awarded if the field were deemed "political" in nature.[1]

Leonard D. White (1926) advanced these conceptions in the field's first textbook. He asserted that management is a practice quite separate from law and politics. Management has a unified and coherent nature of its own and is the same whether employed in government or business. The field of public administration was transforming from art to science. Though White's thinking would change later on,[2] his early work helped shape what is now described as the *orthodox* or *traditional* model of public administration theory (cf. Peters 2001). This model enjoyed wide popularity through the late 1930s and was reinforced with the publication of Gulick and Urwick's *Papers on the Science of Administration* (1937, 13) in which Luther Gulick coined the acronym POSDCORB to describe in a nutshell what the authors deemed the essential and universal features of management work.[3]

Notably, Gulick played an influential role on the Brownlow Committee, which employed the instrumental and scientific view of administration in order to consolidate all administrative power under the *executive branch* (see chapter 5). The efforts by Wilson and Goodnow to make administration instrumental for the sake of legislative supremacy were thus appropriated by advocates of executive supremacy. The desperate conditions of the Great Depression and World War II required national leadership, quick action, strategic planning, and lots of experimentation—qualities that gave clear advantage to executives. Franklin Roosevelt and his university-trained professionals were happy to oblige with both theory and action. The equation of administration with executive power became compelling.

Beginning in the 1940s, however, scholars began challenging these simplistic theories of administrative responsibility with studies that demonstrated a vastly different reality. Political scientists were especially keen to illustrate how career administrators engage in making both law and policy on a routine basis. They pointed out that administrators propose policy, make rules, adjudicate disputes, and redefine policy through implementation, even at the street level. There now exists a rich and extensive empirical literature on bureaucratic politics that explodes the myth of an apolitical public administration.[4] Along the way, an increasing number of normative theorists examined the field and concluded that public administration is an inherently political activity.[5] Dwight Waldo (1948), a political theorist by training, examined the ideas and assumptions of public administration theory and practice, and he concluded that they amounted to a political theory in their own right.

For our purposes, these critical studies highlight the distorted and overly simplistic nature of the early theories relative to our constitutional system of governance. Nevertheless, the espoused theory of a simple dichotomy between politics and administration remains popular among practitioners—partly because more appropriate theories have not yet gained widespread understanding and acceptance in the field, much less with the public. Alternative models are not as amenable to simplified, cogent expression, and therefore not as easily invoked in politically expedient situations. It is still safer, easier, and more acceptable for administrators to claim that they do not make policy, they just carry it out. This is, of course, buttressed by their healthy desire to maintain some independence from partisan influence. Thus, both the theory and exercise of administrative responsibility remain in a developmental stage in the United States.

Despite these difficulties, substantial insight exists in literature and practice that contributes to a sound and distinctive basis for responsible public administration. Ironically, this includes the idea that partisan politics and administration should enjoy some institutional separation, even though both are political. Public administration is highly political, but that does not mean it should be heavily exposed to partisan influence. To understand why, we must begin with *rule by law* as a distinguishing principle of *public* administration in the United States.

## RULE BY LAW

American systems of government operate on the principle that all public officials should rule by law rather than by will. Decisions should accord with standards that are publicly deliberated upon and authorized by representative institutions or by the people directly, through legally established processes. If it is discovered that a decision is based purely on human will or intuition, it can be declared arbitrary and capricious, and reversed. For example, it is unlawful for a police officer to stop a motor vehicle purely on a hunch that the driver is involved in illegal activity. Legal accountability means that, at minimum, police officers and all other officials must articulate reasons for their actions, which can then be examined for conformity to legal standards (cf. *Delaware v. Prouse,* 1979). Fortunately, the constitutional system of checks and balances ensures that decisions can be examined at multiple points in the policymaking and implementation process. This constitutional legal system establishes sources of accountability that are *external* to decision makers, and thereby sensitizes them to norms of democratic responsibility.

## MINISTERIAL VERSUS DISCRETIONARY RESPONSIBILITY UNDER LAW

For some people, the principle of rule by law suggests that laws should achieve the greatest possible clarity and specificity in their standards. The best laws are those that leave no room for discretionary choices by officials. This is called *ministerial responsibility* under law. By this standard, an official must simply obey instructions that require no judgment or skill. He or she serves strictly as an instrument of the law—as a mere clerk. There are situations where this standard is both possible and desirable. For example, in the case of *Kendall v. U.S.* cited earlier, Congress had ordered Kendall, the postmaster general, to pay a specified sum to a contractee, Mr. Stokes, pursuant to existing legal obligations. Under the law, and as affirmed by the Supreme Court, Kendall had no discretion about this and therefore was required to simply carry out his ministerial responsibility. Put yourself in Mr. Stokes's position and you will quickly see the benefit of this kind of obligation. The command is clear, and the compliance is easily monitored. It affords a high degree of predictability and responsiveness. Advocates of instrumental administration favor this strict, ministerial standard in law. Where delegation of discretion cannot be avoided, they argue that standards should be as clear and narrow as possible and subject to intense oversight.

The reach of ministerial responsibility, however, is quite limited, and clarity in standards is not always possible or desirable (cf. Leys 1943). Statutes, rules, and ordinances, for example, are intentionally general in their language because they are prospective in nature—to be adapted to future circumstances. Furthermore, the substantive matters addressed in law are often abstract and ambiguous. For example, most Americans want laws providing for criminal justice, public education, and national defense. These are vitally important things, but they also engender significant conflict over specific meanings and applications, and no single approach proves adequate for long. Diverse schools of thought and practice inhabit each policy arena, ebbing and flowing in the extent of their relative influence.

Moreover, legislators in these arenas often seek to increase legal ambiguities and generalities. This is due in part to the nature of the legislative process. Most bills that pass into law are subject to an elaborate series of compromises over scope and meaning. More interests can be included in a bill with abstract and ambiguous language than can be met in one that is clear, concrete, and specific. An old adage in politics says that "generalities unite, while specifics divide." Such factors leave open a broad field of varying types and degrees of discretion for career administrators

(see chapters 3 and 14). These types of discretion are not completely unbounded. We describe in chapter 14 how they are structured and controlled through administrative law—a body of doctrines, mechanisms, and processes that help articulate the principle of rule by law throughout federal and state governments. Here we examine how administrative discretion is essential to sustain the rule-by-law principle itself.

## FORMAL-LEGAL RESPONSIBILITY

In 1988, John Burke published an important work on bureaucratic responsibility in democratic regimes. He argued, first, that such responsibility must be based upon formal-legal accountability rather than upon the virtue or character of officials. In this, he joined a famous debate carried on in the 1940s by Herman Finer and Carl Friedrich.[6] Finer argued that reliance on virtue poses the danger of discretion run amok and lack of effective means of policing it through external mechanisms of accountability. Formal-legal accountability is thus the only acceptable basis for bureaucratic responsibility. Friedrich, on the other hand, argued that formal-legal mechanisms are inadequate and even interfere in the responsible exercise of discretion by trained professionals. Burke sided with Finer on the point that bureaucratic responsibility must be based on legal accountability in support of popular sovereignty. Legal accountability establishes external responsibility to superiors and to the public at large, whereas virtue or character ethics rests upon trust in individual administrators to do the right thing, every time, based on their own judgments. For Finer and Burke, the latter approach is too risky. And even without the risk of abuse, they argue, reliance on judgment or wisdom in administrative officials ultimately yields a system that is less faithful to democratic rule. It establishes a meritocracy that becomes more aristocratic than democratic over time. Burke thus favors a strict formal-legal approach to bureaucratic responsibility that minimizes administrative discretion as much as possible. This approach "takes seriously the dictates of higher political authorities, and recognizes that bureaucratic office is a domain where politically determined obligations rather than personal preference should prevail" (Burke 1988, 38).

In that context, however, Burke argues that public administrators still require discretionary power that exceeds their formally defined roles. Public officials incur an institutional responsibility for upholding the established "practice of democratic politics and the cause of effective public policy" (42). This is important because it calls attention to the "web of offices, processes, and institutions that define the explicit obligations of official [and democratic] precepts" (42). He outlined three discretionary responsibilities that are inherent to democratic administration under rule by law.

First, every career official is responsible for *propping the duties of other officials*. Colleagues, subordinates, or even superiors may, at times, neglect their duties. It is an implied responsibility of officials who discover this problem to find ways of restoring the errant official to the proper exercise of h duties. This requires discretion, not to usurp the other person's duties, but to induce him or her to do the work properly. For example, a public servant may fail in duties because of family or personal problems. Coworkers, regardless of their hierarchical relation to that person, are obligated to find formal and informal ways through the bureaucratic system to help restore him or her to good-faith service. Solutions may be provided through an employee assistance program, leave time, other employee services, or by a variety of informal means. If the colleague cannot be restored to the proper exercise of office, then the career official is responsible for replacing him or her through transfer, leave, or dismissal.

The second responsibility requires supporting the *integrity of the policy formulation process*. According to Burke, though bureaucrats should not actively promote their own policies, they may justifiably assist policymakers in myriad ways that reinforce policymaking capacity and

fairness in the proper offices. This includes helping or inducing a legislative body to avoid undue vagueness or improper delegations of power in its laws. It may also entail restraining overzealous political executives from initiating programs without regard to resource capacity or assessments of feasibility. Political agendas can easily run beyond human and organizational capabilities, and administrative officials bear responsibility for bringing realistic assessments and solutions to the policymaking table.

The third responsibility concerns *proper and effective implementation of policy tasks* within a bureaucratic milieu that can easily confound such efforts. This requires prudent judgment about the adequacy of resources and the ability to coordinate efforts among participating jurisdictions. Most of all, it requires political sense about how to deal with turf, the incapacities of narrow specialization (referred to as "trained incapacities"), programmed routines, and organizational imperatives that can work at cross-purposes with official policy. Achieving cooperative effort toward policy objectives is often less a matter of organizational engineering than of astute bureaucratic politicking.

Burke's theory provides a useful framework for explaining how some bureaucratic discretion is inherent to a rule-by-law system in a democracy. It adds concern for institutional capacity and integrity to the mix of administrative responsibilities. Burke's theory falls short, however, in explaining additional grounds for discretion that are unique to the American constitutional system. The imperative to support the "background institutions" that comprise our democratic system is greatly complicated for career officials by the realities of divided constitutional powers, as well as by the contending administrative traditions we described in chapter 4. John Rohr (1986) has thoroughly explored the implications of diffused power for American public administration.

## CONSTITUTIONAL-LEGAL RESPONSIBILITY

In his seminal work, *To Run a Constitution* (1986), Rohr develops an elaborate theory of administrative responsibility from the logic of our constitutional system. The theory thus begins on the foundation of rule by law, but it is not restricted to the ministerial standard, with its emphasis on clarity and specificity in the delegation of power. Nor is it confined to the narrow, instrumental relation of policymaking and execution as portrayed by Burke. Rather, it derives robust discretionary roles that require career officials to govern in a similar, though narrower, fashion relative to their superiors. Rohr begins with the relaxed, pragmatic view of separation of powers held by the designers of the Constitution and then draws out the political and ethical responsibilities inherent to this design.

### Partial Agency

In his analysis, Rohr finds that the framers of the Constitution were very pragmatic about blending powers among the branches of government. They knew that the danger of tyranny existed when one branch was capable of usurping the *whole* power of another branch. That would upset the constitutional balance of powers and thereby subvert the system. However, they also understood that a *partial blending* of the powers would be necessary to make the government work. James Madison provided the mechanism that met both concerns. In *The Federalist Papers*, he explained how each branch must enjoy "partial agency" in the powers of the other branches. That is, each branch should possess some of the powers of the other branches in order to prevent encroachment, and yet permit cooperation among the branches for the sake of governing effectively (Federalist Nos. 47 and 48, 1788/1961).

Many provisions in the Constitution establish checks and balances through mechanisms of partial agency. The president, for example, enjoys legislative power through the veto clause. He can veto any attempt by Congress to infringe on executive powers and may also use it to induce cooperation on the substance of bills. Likewise, the U.S. Senate exercises executive power through the advice-and-consent clauses on appointments and treaties, and serves as a judicial body to try impeachments of the president. These powers can be used as checks on the executive branch, but they also enable the branches to join forces on vitally important matters. Rohr uses the clauses on the Senate as textual evidence that the "framers were quite willing to place all three powers of government in one institution where circumstances so required" (1986, 18).

During the first years under the new Constitution, members of the three branches demonstrated a relaxed attitude about the mingling of powers for specific purposes. For example, in the creation of the sinking fund (a fund used to retire national debt), the first Congress established a governing board composed of the chief justice of the U.S. Supreme Court, the president of the Senate, the secretary of the treasury, the secretary of state, and the attorney general (Green 1987, 152, 178). As Rohr indicates, Congress also was willing to conduct investigations through committees that included congressional representatives, executive officers such as the secretary of war, and inferior or subordinate officials (Rohr 1986, 27). So, too, did President Washington request assistance in executive matters from circuit-riding judges (26).

Moreover, Congress willingly combined powers in subordinate agencies for narrowly defined purposes. The Treasury Act of 1789 conferred significant discretion on the secretary of the treasury, permitting exercise of quasi-legislative and quasi-judicial powers in treasury-related and customs-house operations (Green 1987, 178). The first Congress clearly intended to comanage the U.S. Department of the Treasury with the executive branch, and the treasury would, by extension, exercise the powers of all three branches in confined spheres of policy and practice.

Today, the combination of legislative, executive, and judicial powers in public agencies for limited purposes is commonplace, and Rohr's analysis shows that the logic of the Constitution both permits and legitimates this practice. Other scholars, especially Philip Cooper (1988) and David Rosenbloom (2000), give rich descriptions of how the political values and practices of the courts and of Congress are fused to the operations of administrative agencies at all levels.[7] Their studies clearly demonstrate that administrative work is neither exclusively executive, nor merely instrumental in character. Rather, administration reflects the values, methods, and character of all three branches (cf. Rosenbloom and Kravchuk 2002). This reality creates tensions that administrators must hold in a rough balance. If they fail to do so they may eventually have correctives imposed on them. For example, Philip Cooper (1988) illustrates how federal district courts have imposed "remedial orders" on state and local agencies to protect rights and improve services. This reminds administrators that they are *subordinates* in the governing system and as such must try to understand and apply the perspectives of superiors in all three branches (Cooper 1988, 350). At critical points, however, they must also choose sides with one branch or another.

### Public Administration as Balancewheel

Rohr's theory of administrative responsibility obligates administrators to serve as a Balancewheel among the superior branches of government. This means career public officials should resist actions by any superior branch of government that threatens the balance of powers among all three. Thus, like Burke, Rohr emphasizes institutional obligations first. Unlike Burke, however, Rohr's theory of responsibility entails much greater discretionary power because the logic of our constitutional system demands it. Bureaucrats are politicians in their own right, with a legitimate and distinctive

constitutional role to fulfill. That role includes choosing sides, which means they cannot be the sole instrument of any single branch. If they are instruments at all, they are "instruments of the Constitution" (1986, 89).

This is a profound theory because it justifies a significant degree of institutional and professional autonomy for the public administration. It provides a rationale for separating public administration from partisan politics. Without a meaningful degree of separation, bureaucrats could hardly resist partisan measures that threaten the balance of powers among the branches. Moreover, the theory embraces the idea that administration has its own political characteristics, borrowed in part from each branch and melded into the distinct organizational politics of public agencies.

## Refortifying the Executive

Rohr strengthens his case for limited autonomy in the public administration by showing how the modern administrative state compensates for defects in the constitutional design. First, he shows how the Senate failed in its design as an "executive establishment." The founding debates on the Senate reveal that it was intended to serve not only as a representative body but also as a vitally important executive institution. Key provisions in the Constitution give the Senate a share in executive powers. For example, through the advice-and-consent clauses in Article II, Section 2, it shares power with the president in appointing high officials and in ratifying treaties with foreign powers. Senators serve longer terms (six years) in part to gain more expert knowledge and lend stability to the executive branch. Both Federalists and Anti-Federalists agreed that the Senate must become a "permanent body constantly in session" in order to collaborate with the executive in complex policy development and in emergency conditions such as wars and depressions (Rohr 1986, 35).

The Senate's role as an executive body failed to reach its desired potential, however. Very early in its history, the Senate reverted to its role "almost exclusively as a second legislative chamber" (Rohr 1986, 39). Interbranch jealousy of power, partisan differences, and imperatives to represent state rather than national interests made close collaboration with the executive problematic at best. Formal recognition of this reversion to legislative functions occurred in the ratification of the Seventeenth Amendment in 1916. Subjecting senators to direct popular vote was "a wise and long overdue recognition of the democratic spirit of the United States" (39), but it also reflected recognition of constitutional failure. Rohr argues that the creation of the career civil service, especially at the higher echelons, helps compensate for the loss of this senatorial role. Career senior administrators can provide the long duration, stability, and expertise needed for complex policy formulation and implementation.

## Enhancing Representation

The second defect of the original constitutional design involves inadequate representation. Rohr cites criticism, widespread among Anti-Federalist founders, that the constitutional scheme of representation was severely flawed. They believed that "representatives should be close to and resemble the people they represent, but the small number of representatives in the proposed Constitution will make this impossible" (Rohr 1986, 41). The Anti-Federalists viewed effective representation as a matter of thinking and feeling as the people think and feel. This required that representatives be numerous enough to reflect the many diverse communities and interests in political society. In effect, they should form a microcosm of the public. The Constitution, providing no more than one representative per 30,000 inhabitants in the House of Representatives, could hardly achieve

that standard. Furthermore, the location of House members far away in the nation's capital would cause them to lose touch with those at home. They would inevitably begin to favor more general measures that were less responsive to local constituencies.

Most Federalists, on the other hand, emphasized representation that knows the general nature of regional, state, and community interests, yet remains aloof from them in favor of policies that unify these diverse interests into a public interest. They wanted locally representative voices to be restrained and tempered by concern for broader interests. They intended the bicameral structure of Congress to reflect this desire, with the Senate restraining unduly parochial measures in the House. James Madison's constitutional design reflected a desire to "filter and refine" public senti-ments through layers of officials who were in varying degrees insulated from the direct influence of the populace.

These contrasting views of representation have never been reconciled, and neither one has met expectations (Rohr, 44). This became evident as the population increased and our politics became more democratic. Today, each House member represents, on average, more than 660,000 people. They can hardly know or sympathize with the incredibly diverse communities and interests in their districts, much less reflect their character and feelings.

Inadequate representation has spawned a great deal of political disenchantment in our history, resulting in a number of compensating measures and theories.[8] Rohr argues that the emergence of the modern administrative state, with its millions of employees, provides an important corrective in that it more closely approximates the microcosm envisioned by the Anti-Federalists. He refers to the substantial literature on "representative bureaucracy" in support of his argument. When we examine the demographic makeup of our governmental bureaucracies, "we see our sons and daughters, our brothers and sisters," our neighbors, friends, and acquaintances (Rohr 1986, 50).[9] They think as we think, and feel as we feel.

This mass of employees serves as a bulwark against arbitrary power. Administrators are spread across myriad agencies, special districts, and levels of government that often compete jealously for influence over policy. Studies of bureaucracy show that it more closely resembles a vast inter-organizational field of diverse agencies with competing interests than a monolithic edifice (Rohr 1986, chap. 11). Rohr argues that the characteristics of the governmental bureaucracy have more in common with the "extended republic" envisioned by Madison and therefore serve to diffuse and check governing power rather than unify it. Bureaucrats thus contribute to representation in government, even though they are not directly elected by the people.

Direct election, Rohr contends, is not the sole criterion by which representative legitimacy is conferred under our Constitution. He offers as evidence the fact that the Constitution specifies 22 different methods of appointment to office, only one of which is by direct election (185). The variety of appointment methods coincides with Madison's design for a filtered and refined system of competent public officials who would represent the people by pursuing a unifying public interest. In Madison's scheme, all officials under the Constitution share in representation of the people.

Rohr's Balancewheel theory, then, identifies four significant and distinctive responsibilities for public administration that meet the spirit, if not the letter, of the American constitutional system:

1. To integrate and exercise all three governing powers for limited purposes
2. To help preserve the balance of powers among the superior branches
3. To bolster and stabilize executive branch operations
4. To enhance political representation by approximating the microcosm desired by the Anti-Federalists

These obligations, arrayed as they are among a vast field of public agencies, make the public administration much more than a mere instrument or agent of policymakers. Their responsibilities require the exercise of both institutional and substantive discretion, which means they participate fully in governing the democratic republic. Career officials balance, complement, stabilize, inform, and extend the governing activities of the superior branches throughout society, and their professionalism helps meet the need for competence and energy. However, the power and expertise of the professional state stand in tension with the democratic obligation to cultivate citizenship more broadly.

## DEMOCRATIC CITIZENSHIP

The American constitutional-legal tradition may help legitimate a robust role in governance for the public administration, but it also embraces a weak or minimalist view of citizenship for everyone else. The framers emphasized that they were creating a republic rather than a democracy. Following Aristotle (*Politics*, Books III–VII) they viewed democracy as a perversion of popular sovereignty that led ultimately to the excesses of mob rule (the "Shays' Rebellion Problem"). In part, they supported separation of powers and Madison's method of filtering and refining representation in order to mute populist impulses (Storing 1980). The new regime was designed to encourage people to enjoy their private rights with few public obligations. As Rohr (1984) indicates, the Constitution speaks far more to rights of *persons* than to their status as citizens. Some founders, Alexander Hamilton in particular, envisioned a robust commercial republic that would provide diverse pursuits and material benefits to enhance our liberties, while demanding little in the way of civic duty. As described in chapter 4, the preeminence of private interests over public life is what distinguishes American democracy from classical democracies.

But as we have noted, this does not mean active citizenship is irrelevant. America has a long legacy of civic engagement that has taken many forms. These stem from the civic republican tradition described in chapter 4, and they provide important correctives to the excesses of the private rights tradition. The Anti-Federalists criticized the Federalists for designing a hedonistic system that (they believed) would eventually corrupt the morals of the people, thereby reducing the prospects for staffing government with civic-minded officials. As Herbert Storing (1981b) indicated, the Federalists gave no effective rebuttal to this challenge, and they ultimately conceded that even a liberal commercial republic must rely on a modicum of virtue in the people. The Federalists mistakenly took it for granted that the many local communities and social institutions of the country would continue to nurture civic virtue. The reality is that its cultivation requires conscientious assistance from all levels of government and from all sectors of society.

Terry Cooper has made important contributions to our understanding of the responsibilities of the public administration in cultivating active citizenship. In *An Ethic of Citizenship for Public Administration* (1991), Cooper reviews legal and ethical orientations common in the literature on citizenship (see chapter 2). The legal orientation emphasizes formal jurisdictional roles pertaining to obligation, authority, and participation. Obligations are confined to formal governmental arenas, authority is distributed through legal structure and delegation, and participation is treated as a matter of legally defined avenues of access. As expected, the legal orientation confers the most significant responsibilities of citizenship on public officials in the sense that they participate full time in governing the regime. The rest of the citizenry chooses how and when to participate, if at all. Given the constitutional emphasis on rights without corresponding duties, their participation more often reflects the pursuit of narrow self-interests that look askance at even the modest idea of "self-interest rightly understood" (Tocqueville 1835–1840/2000) Interest-group advocacy thus

tends to dominate the channels of direct participation and obscure regard for communal ties and obligations.

Cooper then examines the parallel tradition of ethical citizenship that is informed by Puritan, Anti-Federalist, and Jeffersonian ideas. As we pointed out in chapter 4, these ideas have deep roots in colonial history, and they fed an ardent political opposition that influenced the development of the nation at local levels during the nineteenth century (also see chapter 5). These ideas rest on the assumption that people need the experience of face-to-face civic interaction within communities in order to flourish individually and socially. At the very least, some attention to community is required as a modest corrective to excessive individualism—that is, the weak version of Anti-Federalist civic virtue (see chapter 4).

Cooper's *An Ethic of Citizenship for Public Administration* (1991) recounts how civic associations formed vital, informal adjuncts to the formalized governments during the nineteenth century. Though they often performed in haphazard fashion, the process of drawing immigrants and community members into collective life was as important as any particular goal they sought to achieve. Building associations helped socialize people to collective or political awareness and sealed their dedication to self-reliance and self-government. Melding with Puritan ideals, this dedication underscored the notion of a community covenant richer in meaning than the bare-bones Lockean view of social contract. A covenant connotes commitment to mutual welfare, to the good of the whole, and it requires people to give more regard to the welfare of the community than to their own selfish interests (Cooper 1991, 62–63). This aspect of civic virtue provides a vital social restraint against the divisiveness of faction.

In addition, Cooper describes how the rough and tumble development of community and self-rule was overrun by industrialization after the Civil War. Communities were uprooted as manufacturing towns washed over the agrarian society in feverish economic development. Progressive reformers sought to retrofit political institutions to regulate and support a new and complex political economy that tied the nation together through interdependent corporate markets. The reformers represented an emerging middle class, populated mainly with technocrats and professionals who would rationalize public institutions and supplant democratic participation with rule by experts (Cooper 1991, 107–11). As we noted in chapter 4, the fascination during this period with technical administration by experts was unfortunate in that it diverted attention away from any responsibility by career public officials for cultivating citizenship among the populace and for preserving their communities. As a result, the habits of active civic life withered in the shadow of the professional administrative state.

According to Cooper, this situation can be reversed. Active citizenship and the administrative state are not necessarily incompatible. The acknowledgment in the last half of the twentieth century that public administration is an inherently political enterprise reopened legitimate questions about its role in cultivating citizenship. The field of public administration has been slow to respond, but Cooper and a growing number of administrative theorists continue to press the important point that the public administration shares in the ethical obligation to foster civic engagement (Cook 1996; Cooper 1991; Morgan 1990; Morgan and Kass 1989; Sirianni 2009; Wamsley et al. 1990).

It is important to note that fostering civic engagement is not the same as creating community. Public administrators do not create community; rather, they are part of the political community, a manifestation of its life. Government's role "is to provide a supportive environment in which [a pluralism of communities] may flourish" (T. Cooper 1991, 161). The body politic becomes a "community of communities" and an "association made up of thousands of different small and large communions and groups" (Cochran 1982, quoted in T. Cooper 1991, 161). This process requires attention by administrators to the relation of different spheres of life that sustain the political

community. Public officials are obliged to provide "certain particular common goods such as the building of roads, the enforcement of law and order, the delivery of water, the conduct of public education, and the maintenance of public health . . . in ways that enhance the common good of community life through which character and civic virtue are formed" (Cooper 1991, 161).

Thus, the public administration should provide vital infrastructure for new and existing communities, with an eye toward more than just the economic order and efficient delivery of goods and services. It must pay further attention to how that infrastructure upholds a continuum of relationships that range from personal, intimate, fraternal, and associational spheres of private life to affiliational, organizational-economic, and political spheres of public life (Cooper 1991, 182–85). The public administration bears immediate responsibility for regulating and ordering relationships in the affiliational, economic, and political spheres so that these may provide healthy conditions for both private life and civic engagement. It is not enough to protect rights and interests; these must be augmented with a healthy regard for the prerequisites of the "primary and inclusive dimensions of community" (McCullough 1991).

The primary dimension of community is comprised of the personal, intimate, fraternal, and associational spheres of life that are "prepolitical" in nature (Cooper 1991, 195), and that provide the sheltered environment in which personal life and character are developed. As Thomas McCullough indicates, this dimension of life is dialectically related to the broader, inclusive dimension of the political community.

> Each is nourished by the other, and each is checked and corrected by the other. Only if I am at home in my native community will I have the inner strength and transcending vision to seek the vague and intangible goods of the comprehensive community. And only if I have some vision of the inclusive community will I be sensitive to the provincialism and selfishness of the primary community and have the openness, the patience, and the courage to work for constructive change. Primary communities thus contribute to, constitute, and require the inclusive community of the pluralistic society. (McCullough 1991, 22)

The public administration shares responsibility with elected officials, business leaders, and civic association members for stabilizing the infrastructure of the primary community. This includes community planning that supports the wide variety of familial, educational, and social relations, in addition to economic development that sustains rather than erodes community life. Public administrators should actively include interested citizens and community leaders in codeveloping and implementing these plans. Expertise should serve these groups rather than displace them in this process.

As concerns the inclusive dimension, public administrators bear more direct responsibilities for inclusion of the public in community life. They should seek to empower the public and "produce positive effects with the least control" (Cooper 1991, 197). Paradoxically, this may at times require vigorous regulation of groups or firms that tend to dominate the making of public policy. For example, economic elites, as members of the public sphere, bear social responsibility for mitigating the negative effects of their business decisions on communities. If they fail to do so, government officials should step in to protect the communities. Government officials serve as the "trustees of the interests of the democratic political community, [and are] ultimately obligated to acknowledge and uphold the continuum of relationships that make democracy possible" (Cooper 1991, 196).

The role of trustee in this context requires a different orientation to community than is typical in the modern administrative state. Public officials have to reverse the corrosive effect of govern-

ment stepping in to replace community and social functions that were formerly sustained through shared civic concerns and commitments. They should look more to the conditions necessary for reestablishing civic engagement than to replacing those functions with government programs and expertise (Cooper 1991, 195; Etzioni 1983, 49). Carrying out such a plan entails more facilitation and coproduction than expert, managerial direction. Cooper suggests that this community orientation requires certain virtues in career officials.

The first is *public spiritedness*, which, for public administrators, is "an inclination or predisposition to behave in ways that value and respect the rights and obligations of the citizenry." This includes the ability and inclination to "restrain one's expertise and efficiency" for the sake of interesting the public in making significant, rather than merely symbolic or marginal, contributions to public decisions (Cooper 1991, 163). The content and effectiveness of these decisions may suffer somewhat in the short run, but the civic investment is likely to yield more benefit for the community in the long run.

The second virtue is *prudence*, or *practical judgment*, and it connotes the ability to relate principles to concrete action—to relate good ends to appropriate means (Cooper 1991, 165; Green 1992; Morgan 1990). It "comprehends efforts to give reality to moral commitments and responsibilities" (Dobel 1999, 15). The challenge for public administrators is to "keep technique in its proper relationship to the wishes of the citizenry" (Cooper 1991, 165). Prudence must be made to support rather than trump civic engagement. As mentioned in chapter 2, practical judgment differs from rational-calculative decision making in that it requires a great deal of tacit knowledge. It is more synthesizing than analytical in nature, and looks for proportion and balance among competing priorities (Green, Keller, and Wamsley 1993). It is judgment that assesses when calculation should be used, if at all. Ultimately, prudence is tied to political compromises or outcomes that "gain legitimacy, endure over time, [and] strengthen political community" (Dobel 1999, 199).

The third virtue is *substantive rationality*, which is the ability to "reason about the ends of governmental action and its inherent value assumptions, as well as to engage in instrumental rationality" (Cooper 1991, 166). Preoccupation with instrumental rationality in public administration stems in part from a commonly accepted economic assumption that values are matters of emotive preference, and, therefore, are irrational (cf. Simon 1947). This assumption obscures the fact that most public values are matters of complex moral reasoning. For example, we are inclined to accept without question a person's "preference" for chocolate ice cream, but a statement by that person in support of, say, going to war immediately raises legitimate questions as to why. Public matters are subject to all kinds of considerations worth discussing, and for which it is sensible to expect a reasoned argument. Substantive rationality, then, "is the inclination to engage in both personal and group reasoning about the ends of public decisions and conduct" (Cooper 1991, 167). As such, public administrators bear responsibility for "supporting, encouraging, and participating in the process of social learning about public values" (167). Reasoning with citizens about collectively shared values is a vital aspect of inclusion, deliberation, and civic education. It helps legitimate the public servant's role by improving the quality of civic participation and discourse.

Cooper's framework emphasizes the role of public administration in fostering civic engagement in the American democratic republic. It brings more balance to the tension between representative and direct democracy, it eases the conflict between community and individual, and it provides some guidance for both the application and restraint of bureaucratic discretion in a democratic context. In doing so, it complements and extends Rohr's model of robust constitutional responsibility. It also supports what Brian Cook (1996) describes as the "constitutive" aspect of public administration.

Cook argues that "public bureaucracy is deeply and permanently involved in structuring relations between groups of citizens and in shaping public purposes" (1996, xv; see also Elkin and Soltan 1993, chaps. 1 and 2). Like Rohr and Cooper, he too draws on the legacies of the procedural republic and civic republic traditions of the founding era, using them to illustrate (1) how public administration has participated in constituting the character of American society, and (2) how deeply it has affected the dispositions and abilities of citizens to involve themselves in public life. Public institutions shape the rules and play of the game, and thereby "define the meaning of citizenship" (Cook 1996, 15). Neglect of this constitutive aspect of administration in favor of a strictly instrumental conception skews the balance of administrative responsibilities and, in the process, compromises the dispositions and abilities necessary for civic engagement. Cook, however, bases his theory of administrative responsibility on a much narrower and stricter conception of rule by law than that used by either Rohr or Cooper.

Following the work of Theodore Lowi (1979), Cook reasons that responsible administrative discretion must be strictly limited through clear and more narrowly defined legislative purposes. This "constrains unreasonable demands and expectations . . . on administration," and "also returns liberal democratic politics to the center of the American polity" (Cook 1996, 177). It is "democratic politics, particularly the debate and deliberation associated with legislative forums, that must stand at center stage" (177). Thus, Cook narrows the responsibility equation to a single institution, despite acknowledging "an adequate sphere of constitutionally legitimate independence for administration," as developed by John Rohr. For Cook, an appropriate constitutive role for public administration is confined to, and dependent upon, the responsibility of legislative bodies for passing appropriately clear and narrow legislation. As we have indicated in this and in previous chapters, the pressures of politics in the context of separation of powers at state and federal levels simply have not permitted such strict juridical behavior in legislative bodies. The public administration is thus saddled with much broader agendas and must find other appropriate ways of maintaining the integrity of democratic governance. The four administrative traditions we have identified lend more insight in this regard.

## THE DEMOCRATIC BALANCEWHEEL OF ADMINISTRATIVE RESPONSIBILITY

We began this section with the principle of rule by law as a foundation for administrative responsibility. As Herman Finer argued in 1941, law provides an essential guard against abuse by providing external accountability. John Burke (1988) joined Finer in contending that accountability to politically elected officials must take precedence over the character and competence of officials in a democracy. This does not entirely preclude entrusting discretion to career officials, but confines it narrowly to a formal-legal relationship of subordination and support. Rohr's (1986) theory ties administrative responsibility to law as well, but rather than restricting it to electoral responsiveness under law, he adapts it to our complex constitutional system and its historical evolution. This legal infrastructure significantly broadens the role of public administration, obliging it to perform overtly political functions. It thereby justifies much wider latitude for discretion. Likewise, Terry Cooper (1991) derives normative and fiduciary obligations regarding citizen participation from American political traditions that inform our evolving constitutional heritage. These obligations confer and channel discretion in administration for the purpose of cultivating civic activism in the populace.

The theories of Rohr and Cooper expand the scope of administrative responsibility well beyond the strictures of ministerial models and electoral accountability. They treat administrative profes-

sionalism and limited autonomy as potentially legitimate manifestations of rule by law rather than as undesirable aberrations, and thereby avoid the unfortunate Hobson's choice—that is, no real choice—posed in the Friedrich-Finer argument. They reconcile rule by law with professional autonomy. We find Cook's notion of "constitutive" public administration a good fit with this more robust approach, despite the fact that he seeks to bind it more narrowly to electoral/legislative accountability. The concept is easily appropriated without need of the single-institution tether.

We offer our Balancewheel model as an extension of these theories. Rohr and Cooper derived their theories from America's constitutional tradition, and they have emphasized structural integrity (balance of powers, for example) and civic engagement as vital nerves. In like fashion, we draw on a problematic tension that is inherent to the constitutional system—one arising from four inversely related problems that present grave threats to a regime of ordered liberty. They are inversely related in the sense that an increase in correctives for one problem tends to make the other problems worse. Again, the problems include the following: (1) the threat of too much power in government, making it less responsive to the people and more inclined toward executive tyranny—the "King George Problem"; (2) the threat of too little power in government, making it weak and feckless, as illustrated under the Articles of Confederation—the "George Washington Problem"; (3) the threat of a tyrannical majority to the rights of a minority—the "Shays' Rebellion Problem"; and (4) the threat to civic capacity and self-government posed by a system that ignores or downplays civic virtue—the "Engaged Citizen Problem."

The founders tailored correctives to each of these threats, and these spawned distinct administrative traditions that have evolved through important political eras (see chapter 5) and are now thoroughly woven into the fabric of American governance. These traditions are briefly summarized as follows:

1. The correctives for the "King George Problem" prescribe more direct responsiveness to the people, more deliberation and openness, popular initiatives, privatized alternatives, and smaller, weaker agencies for carrying measures into effect. We have dubbed this set of prescriptions the *responsive governance tradition.*
2. The correctives for the "George Washington Problem" prescribe competent, unified, energetic governance; effective career professionals; efficient customer service; contracting out; and systematic planning. We have dubbed this set of prescriptions the *competent and energetic governance tradition.*
3. The correctives for the "Shays' Rebellion Problem" prescribe enumerated rights, strong legal protection of those rights against overbearing majorities, due process and equal protection standards, individual and interest-group access to decision makers, interest-group balancing, appeals and other accountability protocols, and open-government standards. We have dubbed this set of prescriptions the *minority rights and access to governance tradition.*
4. The correctives for the "engaged citizen" Problem" prescribe enhanced opportunities for citizen participation, cultivation of conditions to support participation, coproduction of public decisions and services, face-to-face interaction in governance processes, local control, and small, frugal venues and jurisdictions. We have dubbed this set of practices the *civic governance tradition.*

Public administrators today may favor one administrative tradition over the others, but in following a single set of practices, they are likely to be confronted by problems that require corrective practices from the other traditions. Exhibit 6.1 presents the main features of each administrative

Exhibit 6.1 **The Democratic Balancewheel**

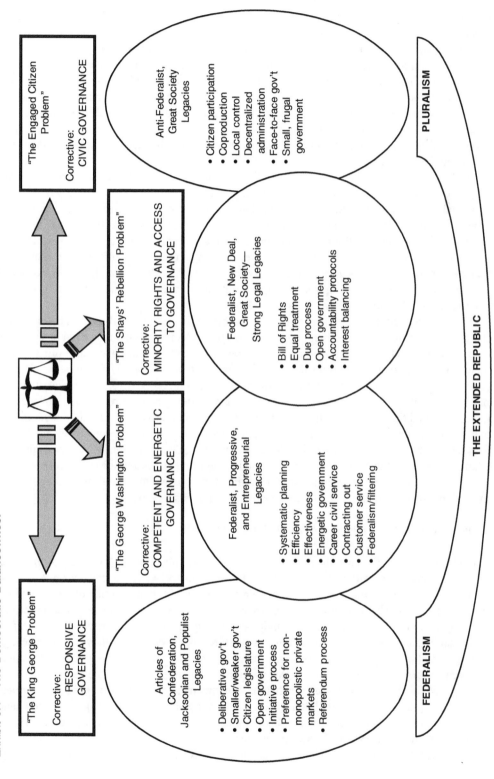

tradition as it has evolved and arranges them as cells on a Balancewheel. Each cell contains elements that have accreted characteristics of various historical eras as legacies that now represent significant aspects or tools of administrative practice for that tradition. As a graphic illustration, the cells may appear more distinct or separate from each other than is reflected in everyday life. The cells overlap slightly as a reflection of this reality. Moreover, all of the cells are joined to an anchor at the base of the model, reflecting the pervasive impact of pluralism and federalism upon the entire American governing system. This is James Madison's "double security" against tyranny (see Federalist #51). The practices of each administrative tradition are affected by the diversity of factions and the interplay of dual sovereignty, which present additional coordinative and mediative challenges.

We find this Balancewheel model compelling and instructive for public administrators in two ways. First, it presents a handy way of organizing and understanding a wide variety of practices commonly found in public administration. Second, the traditions of administrative practice cohere around the obligation to sustain a regime of ordered liberty. They are steeped in the ethos of our evolving constitutional tradition and therefore contribute to responsible administration. But they must contribute in balance to be fully legitimated. No single tradition is sufficient by itself. In effect, each tradition stands as an authoritative source from which administrators may draw for both insight and legitimacy. Drawing from multiple traditions helps define a standard of thoroughness and impartiality in administrative decision making.

The advantage of this model, relative to the theories of responsibility discussed before, is that it accounts for administrative practices at all levels of government—and may even be applied to fused-power models of local governments and special districts. Local governance often evinces a mutability and diversity of forms that reflects community and street-level adaptation. Separate powers must often merge and fuse there in order to accommodate diverse functions that help officials cope with the continua of daily life. Local governments often reflect more of the civic governance tradition as a result, but not without significant counterbalances. The familiar, intimate, and often parochial nature of local control and face-to-face governance processes are obliged to be counterbalanced by the more inclusive (and intrusive) standards and practices of the rival administrative traditions. The Balancewheel model, therefore, bases administrative responsibility in the dynamic tension of these four administrative traditions without requiring strict adherence in local jurisdictions to the federal/state separation of powers model.

## APPLICATION OF THE BALANCEWHEEL MODEL

The relevance of the Balancewheel model can be seen in application to "The Case of the Angry Library Patron," presented at the beginning of Part I of this book. The angry patron, Mr. Jones, expresses his offense at the presence of a certain book in the children's section of the local public library. He wants the book removed from that section, not only for his child's sake, but for the sake of other children. He believes the community shares responsibility for protecting children from such material, and professionals must often stand in for the parents when they're not present.

Cheryl Miller, a library professional, is pressed by growing lines of patrons behind Mr. Jones, but engages him with a stock response that the library encourages responsible parental choice of reading material. She offers assistance in helping him find more appropriate material, but he rejects this, claiming the book is generally unsuitable for kids less than 10 years of age. She then hands him a form upon which he can register his complaint. He files the complaint, and this triggers discussion between Cheryl and the library director, who then hands her a response letter written for another case to be used as a precedent for responding to Mr. Jones. The letter invokes the library's

mission as a democratic institution that promotes the free flow of ideas, many of which conflict. Cheryl experiences this conflict in her own views on the matter. Personally she is sympathetic to Mr. Jones's concerns: She wonders if this might present an opportunity to take up the matter as a policy discussion with the library board, which would likely result in modification of library policy. But she is also pulled by her professional obligations to respect the more inclusive norms of the library mission, and those of her professional code of ethics, which espouses strong resistance to all efforts at censorship of library materials. Censorship issues raise concerns stemming from the inclusive dimension of civic governance, as well as protection of rights and access by individuals who may not fit in with majoritarian views in the community.

One can easily sense the presence of the civic governance tradition in the face-to-face encounter with Mr. Jones. Despite the pressures for maintaining efficient and effective service to other patrons lined up behind him, Cheryl begins a process of engagement that requires some sustained effort by both her and Mr. Jones. This results in an interesting discourse that reveals tensions between protective, nurturing values of the primary community, and the protection of rights and access by the broader community and region under the minority rights and access to governance tradition. The whole process is tempered by career professional and organizational norms of the competent and energetic governance tradition, which remind us that efficient customer services must be abstracted to address "the average child, the normal parent, presumed standards of the community," and so forth. Also evident are norms and practices of the responsive governance tradition, which emphasizes open, deliberative government and direct participation.

Cheryl Miller finds herself positioned in the middle of these conflicting traditions of practice. Understanding the values and evolving practices of each tradition enables her to diagnose the situation in ways that may lead to more than one acceptable solution; the same process will help her identify inappropriate ways of resolving the situation as well. The norms of appropriate process as well as the substantive values inherent in each tradition will help inform her discretionary choices. She should not, for example, simply impose her own personal values on the situation without mediating them through accepted channels of discourse, deliberation, and decision. As a librarian, she is responsible for bringing professional values into the process and articulating their connection to democratic and rights-based norms of governance. Mr. Jones, on the other hand, has every right to bring his personal values to the table, but he will find them mediated through the same deliberative processes as a way of holding him and others accountable for their claims. He has entered the sphere of community governance and must play by its rules. This is a fair claim on Mr. Jones if the process reflects the standards and practices of all four administrative traditions. Public administrators hold substantial responsibility for ensuring that this balance of practices is realistically in play.

This case analysis helps illustrate the relevance of our constitutionally based administrative traditions to modern public administrative practice. They lend a distinct quality to public practice that reflects their grounding in a public morality. Ruling by law requires a public morality that should inform the habits and dispositions of public officials as they exercise discretionary power. Many elements of this public morality can be extrapolated from the theories we have already discussed.

## PUBLIC MORALITY AND PUBLIC ADMINISTRATION

The idea of public morality as being distinguishable from social or personal morality seems foreign and troubling to many people. It raises the specter of moral relativism—and all the abuses associated with it. This concern deserves attention. It is common for students in courses on ethics to assert that

all would be well in public life if people would just follow the basic morals with which they were raised. At minimum, they should be honest, caring, and fair. All people, and especially politicians, should observe the golden rule of treating others as they would like to be treated themselves. These are vitally important social values, but they hardly exhaust the subject of morality or ethics.

When cast in terms of character, ethicists question how these and other values are inculcated in people to form habits or dispositions to behave accordingly. It is not enough to simply know what these values are: They must be cultivated over time. For example, we do not expect young children to be courageous in terrifying situations. However, with a regimen of training and testing over time, we can reasonably expect that they will become courageous as adults. In similar fashion, we know that people can be trained in a variety of careers and avocations that require distinctive habits of mind as well as of body. We may thus speak of vocational excellence or virtue, as well as of general social mores. Both are vitally important to political society. While there is no absolute separation of these moral realms, they are in many respects distinct.

Vocational excellence entails much more than social morality. It develops through disciplined "practices" that yield distinctive moral goods for society (MacIntyre 1984). Terry Cooper (1991, chap. 5) has applied this concept of *practice* to public administration. Practices cultivate "internal goods" through organized efforts that embrace "certain standards of excellence" and "involve technical skills that are exercised with evolving traditions of values and principles." Each practice possesses a distinctive "coherence and complexity." The more one engages in the practice, the more one develops the disposition and ability to apply its internal goods to concrete situations (Cooper 1991, 146). As a practice, public administration includes a variety of internal goods that give it distinct coherence. These goods form part of a broader sphere of morality that pertains to matters of public interest. This is the realm of public morality, and it entails many values and virtues that are not *generally* required in other spheres of life. Three examples will help illustrate the point.[10]

It disturbs our moral sense when a person who has committed a heinous crime is set free because of mistakes in procedural technicalities. Yet, in less trying moments, most people will grudgingly admit that justice (an internal good) should sometimes be sacrificed in specific cases in order to maintain the discipline and integrity of the criminal justice process as it pertains to civil rights (another internal good). If public officials fail to do this, then both civil rights and justice are jeopardized in the long run. These are clearly matters of public obligation that require the support of elaborate institutional practices. Judges, lawyers, police officers, corrections officers, caseworkers, and other professionals working in the criminal justice system must be trained in principles and procedures that condition how they conduct investigations, treat suspects, use force, and generally interact with the public.

It is also common for people to become frustrated when public decisions take days, months, or even years to complete, when in the private sector the same decisions can often be made in a fraction of the time. Yet, when they are brought along in the process, most people immediately appreciate the need for openness and public input regarding many of these decisions. Public access and account-ability (internal goods) require officials to slow down the decision-making process, making it more accommodating and, therefore, more elaborate. Public officials regard this diffusion of power and the resulting multiple points of access as an ordinary condition that shapes their institutional practices. Private-sector managers who enter public life, or try to develop plans or decisions for public benefit, often run afoul of this condition. For example, a few years ago a local chamber of commerce and some banking officials developed a housing plan for homeless people in a downtown retail district of one of our major cities. The plan would relocate the homeless population farther away from a new downtown retail hub. It failed quickly because the proponents neglected to involve service providers, homeless advocates, and other stakeholders at early stages. It was developed (no doubt

very efficiently) in private, and it thereby lost public legitimacy. As one key stakeholder noted, "The process was flawed, people weren't involved." The motives of the private sponsors were immediately called into question because of secrecy and obvious pecuniary interests. From the standpoint of an experienced public manager, it is hardly surprising that details of the plan, however meritorious, were vigorously attacked at its first public airing (Santini 2004).

Finally, consider the responsibilities of a U.S. Border Patrol officer. The officer is required to patrol, apprehend, and process undocumented immigrants for deportation back into the horrid conditions they were trying to escape. The officer may well have been raised in a traditional family setting, marked by religious or social values that obligate him to render aid and care to these suffering people; however, his obligations as a public officer demand that he arrest and process them for deportation. Thus, a tension may arise between his personal obligations and his professional obligations. This example illustrates how public morality introduces an "I-thou" relationship (Buber 1958) and a corresponding set of public expectations that cannot reasonably be evaluated purely from the standpoint of social morality. Public life entails many obligations to act in ways that personal morality, on its own, would not tolerate. As John Rohr (1998, 21) indicates, it is important to "distinguish *in principle* the norms for appropriate behavior in governmental relationships and personal relationships," lest we invite undue cynicism that any morality exists in public life. In other words, public life is suffused with moral content, but it cannot match the standards we hold in our personal relations (see Green 2012 for further elaboration).

## STANDARDS OF PUBLIC MORALITY FOR PUBLIC ADMINISTRATION

The cases discussed in the previous section illustrate that standards of American public morality are sensible and appropriate, and that they set expectations for public management that differ from those for business and household management.[11] Ten of the most basic public standards are briefly summarized in the pages that follow. They emanate from the American constitutional tradition and are deeply embedded in the practices of public administration. Ignoring any one of these standards undermines the legitimacy of administrative work.

### Constitutional Sovereignty

The people are sovereign through their state and federal constitutions. They are the ultimate principals in our governing system, but their will is conditioned by the arrangement of institutions, processes, and powers established in their constitutions. Public administrators are subject to the constitutional diffusion of powers and are obliged to support the balance of powers among the competing branches of government. As demonstrated by the examples above, this is an institutional responsibility that conditions the outcome of many decisions. Public officials must attend as much to preserving this institutional integrity as to making their substantive decisions. They must assess how their decisions will affect the institutions that support the capacity for sound governance in general. In short, they act as institutional stewards (Morgan and Kass 1989).

### Subordination and Autonomy

Although the career public service enjoys a measure of legitimate autonomy, its sphere is bounded through subordination to the constitutional branches and their competition for control of administrative action. Subordinate status engenders an ethos of deference that conditions all administrative agendas, along with all modes of interaction and decision. Deference, however, does not mean

blind subservience to one branch over the others. Administrative politics is thus distinguished in part by the tension between respectful subordination and professional autonomy.

## Representation

As noted earlier, all government officials share in the obligation to represent us. In doing so, they must balance their own judgment with the expressed wishes and interests of the people, and they must subject their decisions to public scrutiny. They also should reflect as much as possible the habits and interests of the populace. Thus, more careful attention is devoted to the demographic makeup of the public service than in any other sphere of employment. Moreover, as representatives, their primary obligations run to their constituents, whether national, state, or local in scope. Government officials are not obliged to protect and serve all of mankind. At times this can create tension between social and political morality. As illustrated earlier, U.S. border guards are responsible for arresting and deporting undocumented immigrants, even if doing so conflicts with a social or religious duty to give aid to people fleeing from horribly destitute or dangerous circumstances. A private person living near the border may understandably render such aid, but border guards are publicly obligated to send illegal entrants back to their home country.

## Civic Engagement and Participation

Public managers are obliged to find meaningful ways to engage the public in civic dialogue about important public issues and to cultivate participation at key points in the development and execution of public policy. Though government may at times properly treat people as clients or customers, their overarching status as legitimate participants in governance should not be overlooked. For instance, the philosophy of community policing has enjoyed renewed interest because police departments noted that policing by well-established professional practices can isolate officers (in their vehicles) from the cares and sensibilities of their own communities. The officers had lost touch with the tacit knowledge of community members and could regain such knowledge only by engaging residents in police practices and coproduction of public safety services.

## Effective Governance

Through various modes of delegation, the public administration is empowered to govern. The powers range in type from direct coercion (as in taxation, arrest, and incarceration)) through various modes of regulation, persuasion, mediation, facilitation, promotion, service provision, licensure, and education. In exercising these powers, career public officials must blend "I-thou" authority with respectful collegiality ("authority-with") in their public encounters. Furthermore, because career officials presume to govern the rest of us, they are held to higher standards of public probity that can affect their private lives. Depending on the nature of their responsibilities, they may be monitored and restricted in such matters as their involvement in party politics, whether they can hold second jobs, their choice of residence, and how they conduct their financial affairs.

## Responsiveness

As public servants, career officials are obliged to respond in a timely fashion to multiple superiors as well as to the public at large. They can seldom refuse to respond to anyone on principle. Significant elements of administrative law require easy access and efficient response. However,

competing demands for responsiveness can compromise quality of service and overall effectiveness. One of the more difficult challenges of democratic public service is determining to whom and to what public servants should be responding at any given time.

## Due Process and Rule by Law

Public administrators are obliged to interpret their policies and decisions within the spirit of due process. This is a much broader responsibility than observance of technical due process under the Fifth and Fourteenth amendments to the Constitution. It means that all policies and decisions must rest on reasoned justifications that are made capable of examination by a wider public audience (not necessarily the general public) for conformance to legally established criteria. Moreover, public officials cannot act on any and every good cause. They may act only on matters that legally fall within the scope of their responsibilities. The principle of limited government would be meaningless without this standard. Public administrators are also constrained by rules of process in achieving public goals. Appropriate means matter as much as appropriate ends do.

## Equity

In addition to fair procedures, public officials must attend to fairness in results. In regulatory and contracting contexts, for example, public administrators must be mindful of disparate impacts of rules and contract provisions on rural versus urban service areas, and they must guarantee special services, such as subsidized air transport, to remedy the disparities (Cooper 2003, 7). Many agencies also develop processes for granting exceptions in situations where the normal functioning of rules and policies creates an injustice or imposes an undue burden on a small number of citizens or clients (Green 2002b).

## Accountability and Open Government

Governmental decisions are much more accessible to institutional and public scrutiny than other spheres of life. Agencies are subject to multiple audits, performance reviews, legislative oversight, review hearings, and extensive reporting requirements. Managers must factor this "fishbowl" condition into almost every decision process. Where decisions are not accessible, public officials are obligated to consider whether a public audience would approve of their actions. Would their proposed actions pass the "smell test"? In addition, the power of an independent and suspicious press looms large over all governmental operations and may expose even the most sensitive matters despite strenuous efforts to prevent it from doing so. In many respects, the constitutional rights of the press make them an integral part of the American governance landscape, and public agencies need to devote substantial time and resources to managing their relationships with the press in ways that promote respect for its role and yet limit its reach in appropriate ways.

## Protection of Rights

Though listed last, protection of rights is the chief concern of our governing systems, and it pervades all decision-making processes in government. In considering any government action, provisions must be made for the effect of that action on individual rights. This makes government decision making and the design of policy and process much more complicated than is typical in other spheres of life.

When taken together, these ten standards provide a coherent moral basis for public decisions. They produce practices and obligations with a distinct character—a pedigree that often confounds those who want to make government more businesslike. Moreover, this pedigree reveals a constitutional genesis that engenders public discourse and argument (not simply results) as the centerpiece of American political life (Arendt 1963, 214; Green, Keller, and Wamsley 1993, 520; Rohr 1986, 9). The Balancewheel model captures the vital center of this debate regarding how best to achieve and sustain a regime of ordered liberty. As participants in this debate, public administrators must understand that their practices rest as much on discourse as on their ability to deliver the goods. Such discourse is seldom a matter of idle or passive conversation, but of high-stakes and high-pressure politicking. The account given by Debbie Ellis in Exhibit 6.2 illustrates how one public servant learned to cope with the tensions between her personal morality and her public responsibilities in this environment.

## ADMINISTRATIVE RESPONSIBILITY AND BUREAUCRATIC POLITICS

The lessons Debbie Ellis draws from Albert Speer are especially important for modern-day career administrators who operate in complex bureaucratic environments. As illustrated in chapter 5, the American republic has evolved into a regime dominated by large, complex organizations. In public life, these organizations are integrated into a pluralist array of agencies, nonprofit organizations, public corporations, special districts, networks, and intergovernmental policy subsystems. Conducting public discourse and responsibly achieving public purposes in this environment requires astute skill in bureaucratic politics, which poses its own distinct ethical challenges. Also, recall John Burke's (1988) point that public servants are obligated to support the integrity of policy formulation and implementation processes. These obligations entail the need to overcome a variety of organizational pathologies and perverse dynamics.

First, Dennis Thompson (1985) has noted the prevalence of two problematic ideas in administrative life—the *ethic of structure* and the *ethic of neutrality*. The ethic of structure refers to the fact that complex organizations require "many hands" to perform their specialized functions, and this diminishes the sense that any single employee has much to do with the end results of those functions. The responsibility for success or failure, for good or harm, is widely dispersed, and therefore often diminished in the minds of officials. It becomes much easier to escape or even deny responsibility than to accept it.

The ethic of neutrality portrays bureaucratic roles as merely technical and instrumental in nature, and therefore devoid of ethical culpability. It is captured succinctly in the phrase, "I didn't make the decision or policy, I just carried it out." In combination, these two ideas convey a strong impression that officials possess very little discretion and that loyalty to the organization is supreme. Moreover, they strongly suggest that if employees cannot go along with organizational decisions and policies, then they should find work elsewhere. The persistence of this kind of thinking tends to breed timid, indecisive, rule-bound, and blindly obedient attitudes among employees. It ignores the fact that they must routinely exercise discretion and judgment, and provides little moral guidance for doing so (Dobel 1999; Mainzer 1964; Storing 1980; Thompson 1985).

The theories of responsibility espoused by Burke, Rohr, and Cooper make it plain that the ethic of structure and the ethic of neutrality are out of place in our constitutional system of governance. The principles of separation of powers and checks and balances countermand the bureaucratic principle of unified hierarchy. They institutionalize distrust of power simultaneously with delegations of power. Diverse lines of accountability from the separate branches mix with rules of transparency and public access in every agency, thereby tending to confound and frustrate blind

Exhibit 6.2   **Administrative Responsibility and Personal Ethics: How I Came to Know the Difference**

*Debbie Ellis*

This is a story of my personal journey as a public servant from viewing ethics as just "being a good person" to now viewing my ethical responsibilities as a matter of personal and public morality in which I must balance democracy with authority (Meyer 1975), and civic engagement with our strong spirit of individualism (Lane 1988). This journey has come halfway through my public service career and is the result of lots of self-reflection promoted by discussions with my Executive MPA colleagues and the readings in the previous sections of this book.

In my current role I serve as a program manager for Parent Information Resource Centers (PIRCs). The U.S. Department of Education created the first PIRCs in 1995 to provide parents, schools and organizations with the training, information, and technical support needed to understand how children develop and what they need to succeed in school. The program was founded on the belief that family engagement is critical to increased student success, reduced dropout rates, increased college attendance, decreased achievement gap, and increased positives outcomes for children. While federal funding for the PIRC program ended in 2012, I am working to keep the program intact through a combination of state, local, nonprofit and fee-for-service funding alternatives.

When I first began thinking about administrative ethics and values, I went to my own internal definition and understanding of morals. Like many in America, my viewpoint was based on my home and religious upbringing, which in my case was an extremely rigid Pentecostal heritage founded on a narrow set of moral principles. I believed I was using my own personal standards of ethics to help me determine what was appropriate and acceptable in my public role. Because these moral standards were so deeply engrained (and so "black and white"), I thought my considerations of ethical principles as applied to my work were almost automatic and unintentional. Upon further reflection, I began to realize that the standards and criteria which I used for guiding my judgment as a public servant were much more complex and maybe not even the same at times. For example, I noticed that my frustration with the performance of some of my coworkers was not always the result of a violation of my personal ethical views of "hard work, honesty, integrity, civility, etc.," but because they did not show proper respect for basic democratic values and legal principles, such as protection of client rights, transparency, citizen engagement and a commitment to equitable processes for resolving client grievances. It was not simply a matter of getting my fellow colleagues to become "nicer human beings." I gradually came to appreciate that my ethical framework encompassed more than just the personal ethics that were the result of my upbringing. They encompassed my stewardship responsibility for basic constitutional and democratic values. This discovery posed two challenges to my newfound locus of administrative responsibility. First, how do I square the conflict between the values taught as part of my upbringing and the values I now hold as a public servant? Second, how do I become better as an ethical public servant?

**Administrative Ethics: Personal Integrity and Public Responsibility**

My ethical framework is founded on both my personal morals and the commitment I have to the common good. Fortunately for me these two sets of values are not in frequent in conflict. But what happens when that is not the case? How do I resolve the conflict? For example, from a young age, I was told how to act, what to say, and what to think and believe—creating for me a much narrower meaning of morals and ethics which took the form of negative "thou shall nots," and Puritanical or Victorian "no-nos" (Diamond, 1982, 40). From the point of view of my family who hold to the strict religious values of their upbringing, I am probably viewed as a moral chameleon—anxious to accommodate others, "temperamentally indisposed to moral controversy and disagreement . . . [ and] quick to modify or abandon previously avowed principles in order to placate others" (Benjamin, 1990, 47). The work of Martin Benjamin has played a significant role in helping me make sense out of the person I have become and to reduce the conflict between my personal ethical values and my moral values as a public servant.

Benjamin argues that there are three approaches to resolving ethical conflicts: an interest-based approach, a principle-based approach and an integrity-based approach. With the interest-based approach, negotiation and compromise are viewed as an ethically good thing. This is because negotiation and

*(continued)*

Exhibit 6.2 *(continued)*

compromise are seen as part of the process of producing a shared common good, which stands on higher ground than the separate interests of the parties. This view contrasts with the "principled-based approach," which organizes life around "a single most important goal to which all others are subordinate" (Rawls quoted in Benjamin 1990, 21). This approach is common among those who use their religious beliefs to determine which values, principles, feelings and intuitions are given serious consideration; while paying little or no attention to competing goals. This is the view that was part of my upbringing. To my family, compromising on any concepts within their single dominant end constitutes a betrayal to themselves and their God.

I have found Benjamin's integrity-based approach helpful in understanding how it is possible to alter one's ethical views while at the same time holding true to a core of ethical beliefs and values that remain with you throughout life. The integrity approach to ethics assumes that our moral beliefs and values are altered by our experience. With each new experience comes a more nuanced understanding of the ethical complexity of a given situation that requires action. Benjamin gives an example of family members and health care specialists standing around a patient who is on life support with no medical data that supports recovery. When someone who is on principle opposed to the withdrawal of life support decides to join in a group decision to withdraw life support, has the individual sold their soul? A principled-based approach would argue yes, while the integrity-based approach would simply ask whether one's integrity remains intact. Integrity is about the moral wholeness of a person at any given point in time, even when this wholeness may be composed of conflicting values that take on urgency at different points in time and where the wholeness itself is composed of different parts in a different order over the course of one's life. It is similar to someone believing in the commandment that "thou shall not kill," but taking another person's life to save a loved one or participating in the medically assisted suicide of a love one. These experiences, while life changing, do not automatically alter ones moral integrity, although they may not square with one's first principles.

Over time, I have learned that, because of my sense of civic responsibility, my strong commitment to equity, and my passion for the work I do and the people I serve, I have reframed the meaning of my previous values to include my values as a public servant. I still have most of the same basic moral values and character traits that my family espouses (integrity, honesty, trustworthiness, respect, responsibility, fairness, caring, etc.), but reframing has enabled me incorporate a more diverse array of values that are essential to the achievement of the common good. In doing so, I would argue that my integrity has remained relatively unchanged over my life course. What is critical to an integrity-based view of ethics is the commitment to a constant process of introspection in which we reexamine our personal moral code and the way in which it can be more closely aligned with the larger stewardship values that are integral to our public service roles.

**Standards of Public Morality: How Do I Become a More Ethical Public Servant?**

Given my integrity-based view of ethics and my commitment to introspection, I believe that we become better in our ethical role as public servants in the same way we become better as moral human beings: It requires practice, not simply thinking morally virtuous thoughts. For me, having a catechism of public values of the kind provided in the previous section of this text serves as a good daily test of whether we are doing all that we can to become morally better public servants. That is why I find it useful to benchmark my work against what I have come to call "The Ten Public Service Commandments." This exercise has been especially important to me in my transitional role of trying to secure the future of my PIRC program by finding alternative sources to the federal funding that has now come to an end.

*1. Constitutional Sovereignty*

Throughout the process of negotiations regarding the future of the Parental Information and Resource Centers (PIRCs), the program directors had to be fully aware of their role as institutional stewards. As a large group, we informed citizens and state officials of the impact of our work and of the proposed changes in legislation—being ever mindful of not crossing the bounds of lobbying for our own efforts. We had to put in place checks and balances to ensure that no government funds were used in any of the efforts to inform the public. Because of our informational efforts, current

legislation is still in place that authorizes PIRCs; although no funding has yet been appropriated for these efforts.

## 2. Subordination and Autonomy

The grant program under which I operated my program was created by a deliberately ambiguous law, which kept us subordinate but also allowed us considerable autonomy. The law was deliberately created this way, in part, as a response to too much government (aka the "King George Problem") with the goal of giving more flexibility and control at the state level. My grant had four main goals; two of which were fairly specific as to the actions required to carry them out and two were quite vague. This discretionary authority allowed us to use a constitutive approach (see chapter 1, 16 and chapter 5, 106) when developing our activities. Based on feedback from clientele during our training workshops, feedback from partner organizations during meetings, and evaluation reports and studies across the state we could adjust our activities to gain trust and legitimacy with our community partners.

## 3. Representation

Due to the exponentially growing population of Latinos, when we first wrote the grant we focused on increased services for Spanish-speaking families. In addition to providing them with services, we hired a staff member who was a Spanish-speaking parent of children who had previously been educated in Mexico. As part of our efforts to retain funding for the PIRCS, citizen groups were informed of the proposed changes to elementary and secondary education policy. They then took their opinions to their state representatives to voice their desire for continued services. In addition, we continue to work with parents (as outlined below) in additional empowerment efforts to assist them in having a voice in the micro level (their own child's classroom) to the macro level (state and federal government).

## 4. Civic Engagement and Participation

At our microlevel of service provision, we are actively engaged in citizen participation. In fact, our main mission is getting families more engaged in their child's education in ways that lead to school and lifelong success. For this, we abide by the philosophy that in order to make lasting/ sustainable change, we must sometimes bypass the "experts" and empower family members to be the driving force behind parental education and advocacy efforts. In order to nurture this type of civic engagement, we have collaborated with parent groups to design and develop their own packages of training materials that they will use with other families in order to understand the school system and to become active participants in the educational processes. For one group, we told them we were just the "administrative conduits" who were taking their words and ideas and putting them into a form that could be used across their district and the state.

At the macro level, we are assisting families and parent-serving organizations to be more engaged in educational policy. Since there is no longer any federal funding or federal/state mandates regarding family engagement, we are working with partner organizations to develop policy guidelines for family engagement that we will propose first to state officials and then to our federal legislators. We have also drafted language regarding family engagement that has been delivered to the state's Education Investment Board in hopes of enhancing their vision of family engagement for the state's public schools. In addition to policy formation, we are using this collaborative effort to map the services currently being provided to the families within the state, determine the gaps in services or service areas, and assess the most effective way to meet the needs of students and their families.

## 5. Effective Governance

The goals of the PIRC are ones of facilitation, service provision, and education. For facilitation, we coordinate school-family partnerships activities among agencies and organizations to ensure that families and schools are served statewide. This facilitation takes place in many of the civic engagement activities outlined above. Our educational services include personal, one-on-one technical assistance activities carried out with families or educators to large-scale statewide conferences. We generally tailor our educational

*(continued)*

Exhibit 6.2 *(continued)*

ventures to the specific needs of the audience and try to engage in long-term educational processes versus the single workshop in order to build sustainable change. Education is one of our services, as well as guidance regarding compliance issues, product development, and technical assistance.

*6. Responsiveness*

In order to meet the needs of the entire state, we structured our services to provide easy access and efficient response. For individuals outside the Metro area, we provided services online so that they could access our products or access technical assistance through email/text communications. In addition, we added toll-free telephone number that was monitored by individuals that spoke English and Spanish. We also created a response system that required us to return a phone call or email within 24 hours of its receipt (during business hours). So that more parents could attend our training sessions and our annual conference, we kept our costs low, provided translation, educational stipends, and a range of other services at no charge. In order to maintain this level of responsiveness in the future, we have incorporated these provisions as a basic part of our proposed service model.

*7. Due Process and the Rule of Law*

Within our grant obligations there was a stipulation that we be governed by a Board of Directors made up of a diverse representation of parents and parent-serving organizations across the state. The Board provided oversight of our activities as they related to the goals of the grant.

*8. Equity*

Equity was a major consideration within all our activities. As stated earlier, we proposed the grant around the needs of the Latino families (and families with limited incomes) in the state. We knew that educational equity issues were a major focus of education reform. The No Child Left Behind act specifically called for the accountability of schools and districts in their services to and outcomes for low income and minority children. In order to achieve both fairness in procedures and in results, the families of these children were targeted (by the federal grant makers) in order to assist them in gaining the information and knowledge that the parents of higher achieving students already possessed. But, in addition to these targeted services, universal services were made available to all families in the state.

*9. Accountability and Open Government*

As a grant-funded organization, we were subject to multiple performance reviews and legislative oversight. In addition, we were accountable to the citizens of the state and responsible for achieving the funds and grant goals supported by our funding. Also, considering our options for future funding, I am very mindful of the impact of the service fees that partner organizations are considering for their administrative services. I take seriously my responsibility to be a good steward of the money we receive so that our clientele receive the most appropriate services at the most reasonable costs.

*10. Protection of Rights*

As I mentioned in the Equity section, protection of rights is a major consideration in all our activities. We proposed the grant around the needs of the Latino families and families with limited incomes in order for them to be more fully able to take part in and secure the educational rights that belonged to their children. Education, in and of itself, is a major component in the attainment of our other constitutional rights of freedom, equity, and property. Without education (and the knowledge it provides), one is not fully able to participate in and secure their rights.

As I continue my efforts to transition the PIRC program to some kind of alternative funding, all kinds of ethical issues are at the forefront of my concern. From a personal point of view, I have a great passion and great sense of civic responsibility for advocating for the type of family engagement that increases the likelihood that children will be successful in life and school. But am I simply substituting my personal

ethical values for my public service duties as an administrator? Certainly, one of these duties is to bring the existing federally funded program to an end in the most successful manner possible. Another ethical responsibility I have is to assist my coworkers in finding other work that fulfills their passions.

But I also have concluded that I have a duty to take the leadership in exploring ways of continuing the program by examining both service delivery and funding models that will galvanize the support and enthusiasm of community partners, state administrators and elected officials. This view is a result of the expansion of my thinking of what it means to be a public servant. I started with the narrow view that was primarily interested in maximizing service to a target population in the most efficient and effective manner possible. But now I see my role as a steward of democratic governance. With this shift in focus I now am more concerned about how I can leverage all of the assets from the private, nonprofit and for-profit sectors to achieve the larger common good of the polity. The notion of polity leadership developed in chapter 12 has transformed the ethical meaning and purpose of my public service role as an administrator. I have come to appreciate the importance of constant reflection on the moral purposes of my work. Without such reflection one can quickly succumb to the plight of Albert Speer, a remarkably gifted administrator who ran the Ministry of Armaments and War for Hitler with great efficiency and productivity, who was sentenced to a life in prison for war crimes. "[I]n the isolation of imprisonment, I learned to look inside myself to study my own weaknesses and strengths and for the first time in my life, I had the leisure and opportunity to read and absorb works of philosophy and theology" (Norden, 1971, 202). The lesson for me from the story of Albert Speer is that as administrators we need to constantly subject the ends we serve to the same kind of rigorous questioning that we apply to the means we use to carry out our work.

obedience. In this spirit, Dennis Thompson (1985), J. Patrick Dobel (1999), Terry Cooper (2004), and Rosemary O'Leary (2006) have urged public administrators to develop and protect channels of dissent as a basic aspect of organizational design and policy. In the same spirit, John Rohr (1989, 164) has suggested that agency managers cultivate a culture of free speech in support of robust discourse about agency values and frank communication about agency problems.

Second, at least since the Progressive Era, most management theories and practices have over-emphasized the role of utility, a form of "means-ends" rationality, in public decisions. This is due in part to the tendency to define public administration exclusively as an instrumental, executive-based function that is preoccupied with delivering services efficiently to masses of people. The principle of utility emphasizes achieving the greatest good for the greatest number of people by the most efficient means. It is most evident in decision models that exhort managers to weigh costs and benefits of alternative solutions. The problem is that such measures can justify virtually any action that most expediently gets the desired results, including the abrogation of individual rights in favor of majority interests. The pressure to do so is especially pronounced in times of emergency, when public passions are inflamed and politicians feel compelled to act. As mentioned earlier, however, our constitutional system is premised first on the protection of individual rights. Rights should trump utility. Public managers are continually reminded of this by lawsuits and other legal and political interventions that compromise the efficiency of their administrative affairs. Rights-based principles condition management practices in important ways. For example, in social service agencies, it is common to see caseworkers routinely consider "lesser restrictive" treatment alternatives for their clients; in addition, one often sees school officials structuring disciplinary practices around basic due process rights of their students. Unfortunately, however, very few management texts treat rights-based practices as an integral aspect of management theory.[12]

Third, the devotion to utility in management practice can easily lead to the problem of paralysis by analysis. Herbert Storing (1980) noted how scientific management and rational-comprehensive approaches to decision making actually promote indecision. Studying all possible decision alternatives and calculating their costs and benefits is a never-ending process. The effort consistently focuses on

the hope of finding information that will make the "right" decision self-evident, when in fact most decisions of any importance require judgments that lack such data, or are inundated with data that cannot possibly be processed for timely resolution. Moreover, as Deborah Stone (1988) explains, the assessment of costs and benefits is continually confounded by the interpretive and contingent nature of the activity. Defining what counts as a cost or a benefit depends on how one defines or structures the problems with which one is faced. This complexity makes definitive calculation impossible, and thereby necessitates advocacy (instead of comprehensive analysis) for one decision or another based in rough estimates and tacit adaptations of institutional capacity, routines, and training.[13]

Fourth, as discussed in chapters 5 and 8, the predominance of professions in modern government poses a problem of self-interested elitism that stands in tension with democratic norms (Green, Keller, and Wamsley 1993; Mosher 1982; Rohr 1998). The autonomy and specialized knowledge of elites enhances their powers and benefits by restricting entry to their ranks. Furthermore, many professionals have successfully dovetailed their career tracks into administrative ranks, and thereby enjoy significant policy-determining powers. It is hardly surprising that they dominate the culture of many public agencies. Their specialized, protected knowledge and elevated status in public life mark them as members of a ruling meritocracy (Green, Keller, and Wamsley 1993; Mosher 1982). Fortunately, however, it is not a monolithic meritocracy.

The diverse number and types of professions that populate public agencies tend to make them pluralistic rivals, and this usually prevents dominance of agencies by any one profession. In addition, lateral entry requirements common in American civil service systems prevent them from creating completely closed career ladders. In recent decades, their top echelons have also undergone significant politicization by removing their civil service protections and blending political appointees into their ranks (see chapter 8). These factors tend to mute the more excessive effects of professional elitism. However, high specialization often works against the responsibilities of public agency professionals as they move into administrative ranks.

As professionals move upward to the strategic apex of organizations, the nature of their work changes from specialized, technical tasks to the coordinative, facilitative, and integrative work of governance. Public administration is more like a supervening profession, one that cannot rely upon specialization to justify its practices (Green, Keller, and Wamsley 1993; Rohr 1989). Its work has more to do with weaving human relationships and organizational dynamics to achieve public purposes (Green 1996). It builds general competencies in organizational and interorganizational processes, as well as in modes of decision making, participation, and patterns of human motivation. Public administrators also play mediating roles between citizens and elected officials, and "exercise a special kind of prudence that enables them to coalesce considerations of workability, acceptability, and fit" in an environment of diffuse, competing organizations and policy subsystems (Dobel 1999; Green 1992; Morgan and Kass 1991, 74).[14] At the career-executive levels, they help sustain cooperative linkages among the competing branches, especially between chief executives and legislative bodies (Fisher 1975), and serve as buffers between partisan and bureaucratic agendas.

These are competencies of generalists, people who can relate the specific to the general, who possess a sense of the whole—of the public interest (Appleby 1952; Herring 1936). Unfortunately, public service reforms have not seriously emphasized the role of administrative generalists, preferring instead to staff senior ranks with specialists. The lack of generalists in the career executive ranks is well documented, despite some weak attempts to the contrary (Heclo 2000, 226–37; Rohr 1998, chap. 7). Institutional supports are necessary for this to change, and so is broad education in the ethical, political, legal, and organizational dimensions of public administration (Green, Keller, and Wamsley 1993).

Finally, the central role of public administrators in balancing conflicting values and powers among the superior branches increases the significance of compromise in administrative practice. Compromise is vital to all collective effort. Public life would be impossible without it. Public argument, bargaining and negotiation, coalition building, systematic cooperation, and competition for power all work primarily through compromise. It helps coalesce and sublimate diverse motives and agendas into common interests. It makes the balance of conflicting priorities possible. A disposition to compromise goes hand in hand with an attitude of civility, in which opponents display some willingness to respect each other's interests. This means that politicians of all stripes (elected and bureaucratic) should not act as zealously for one set of interests as many of their constituents can (and perhaps should). Public officials are obliged to bridge or fuse diverse interests into a broader collective good (Benjamin 1990, 174).

However, as J. Patrick Dobel indicates, the "very activity of compromising can [also] undermine the assumptions necessary to its prudential, political, and principled justifications" (1990, 139). The habitual practice of compromise can slowly obscure the moral bearings and commitments that help one determine when compromise is appropriate. One may begin to compromise impulsively rather than strategically, and thereby yield prematurely to resolutions that do less good than could have been achieved—that promote the status quo over constructive improvement of policy. This tends to happen incrementally, through small compromises that diminish the potential for bigger, more coherent reforms. In the process, officials can easily weaken their own power base as constituents become disenchanted with the results. This, in turn, raises fears about defection, disloyalty, and rivals emerging from the ranks. Jealousy of power begins to blur and subvert commitment to public ideals and purposes delegated to one's office (see Dobel 1990, chap. 7).

The depredations of habitual compromise are common, though not inevitable. Officials can mitigate their effects by attending to some basic conditions of good compromise. First, wholesome political practices demand that officials include others in their deliberations on the propriety and potential effectiveness of compromises. Good compromises require publicity tests that force one to examine basic assumptions, to ask searching questions that may help anticipate weaknesses, and to provide reasoned justifications (Dobel 1990, 167). In the process, officials must avoid the tendency to surround themselves with like-thinking allies or colleagues. They must not shield themselves from critics and advocates who are much more zealous for specific interests affected by the potential compromise (Benjamin 1990). Exposure to critics enlivens the sense of what should be moderated through compromise and what should not.

Second, officials should avoid compromising institutions and values that are designed to uphold the integrity of public decision making. This includes protecting professional confidences as well as decision processes that are designed to ensure public scrutiny and participation. It also means avoiding compromises that violate someone's dignity or fundamental rights. These are matters that, short of the most compelling circumstances, almost always exceed the boundaries of good compromise (Dobel 1990, 166).

Third, compromises that tend to exclude broader interests in favor of narrower interests should be viewed with suspicion. They lead all too easily to the dynamics of "interest group liberalism" (Lowi 1979), wherein private interests use their informal influence with political officials to effectively neutralize agency policies, and even redefine them for their own purposes. Conversely, good compromises link individual self-interests to broader public purposes. Such compromises should draw interests from diverse sources and sustain people's desire to participate (Dobel 1990, 167). Compromise should stimulate rather than enervate civic engagement, and this requires that the parties be empowered and that the resources be distributed in such a manner as to entice commitment. That way, each party will perceive a valid stake in the outcome.

## CONCLUSION

Ethical responsibility, whether viewed personally or as a public servant, requires knowledge of one's moral commitments. This chapter has outlined the distinct public anchors upon which to ground one's administrative obligations. Walking the talk is not a simple matter, despite attempts to make it so. Nevertheless, with careful attention to our constitutional heritage, it is possible to articulate a sensible and legitimate approach to the subject. We have reviewed some theories of administrative responsibility that take us in the right direction and, working from those, have offered our own formulation—the democratic Balancewheel—as a potentially useful model. The challenge ahead is to find cogent ways of expressing and illustrating the value of these approaches in both administrative and partisan political circles. Public managers still tend to shelter themselves under more simplistic claims of neutral expertise, and politicians happily reinforce this for short-run advantages. In the long run, such claims obscure the need for public managers and politicians to formally acknowledge and respect their distinct political roles. There is no quick or easy way to change this situation. It is doubtful, though, that anything of lasting value to political life comes from a quick fix. Efforts to institutionalize these political and ethical insights require time and usually must endure a gauntlet of challenges. Perhaps one way to begin is to illustrate the relevance and usefulness of the Balancewheel model to the traditional functions of public administration. The remaining chapters of this book address these functions in light of our administrative traditions.

## STUDY QUESTIONS

1. What theory of administrative responsibility best describes the approach taken by your organization/jurisdiction? Is this approach executive-centered or legislative-centered? What best explains the approach that is taken (that is, structure of governance, management style, history, and so on)?
2. What theory of responsibility do you most prefer and why?
3. What Balancewheel role does John Rohr believe public administration plays in the American systems of democratic government? Drawing on your experience, readings, and understanding of how our various democratic systems function, evaluate Rohr's argument.
4. What aspects of Terry Cooper's theory of citizenship do you see at work in your organization?
5. How would you put the Balancewheel model in Exhibit 6.1 to use within your organization? If you do not have significant organizational experience, how does the Balancewheel model alter your thinking about the role responsibilities of public servants?
6. Which of the ten elements of public morality discussed in chapter 6 do you think are most important? Which elements, if any, are missing from the organizations with which you are most familiar? What strategies would you suggest for achieving a better balance?
7. What is the significance of Dennis Thompson's distinction between the *ethic of structure* and the *ethic of neutrality?* What are the strategies you might use to mitigate the adverse consequences of these two ethics that operate within public organizations?
8. In the section "Administrative Responsibility and Bureaucratic Politics," we discussed a variety of pathologies that can undermine administrative responsibility, including professional elitism, focusing on means, and excessive reliance on rules. Which of the problems discussed in this section seems most urgent, and what mitigating strategies would you suggest?

## NOTES

1. This insight was given by Paul Van Riper in a personal interview with Richard Green in the spring of 2001. Van Riper indicated that the faculty (including Leonard D. White, Luther Gulick, and Charles E. Merriam) at the University of Chicago knew full well that public administration (PA) was inherently political, but that it had to be portrayed as scientific in order to get funding to support PA education (Van Riper 2001).

2. White subsequently became a student of administrative history and developed a much more sophisticated view of public administration, presented in his classic four-volume history of public administration (1956–1958). The works of White and Goodnow were read widely in their era, whereas Wilson's rather confusing essay was neither read nor cited until after 1940, when academics in public administration resurrected the work as a founding document for the field (see Van Riper 1983).

3. POSDCORB stands for planning, organizing, staffing, directing, coordinating, reporting, and budgeting.

4. Representative of this literature are works by Philip Selznick (1957, 1949), Charles Lindblom (1959), Aaron Wildavsky (1964), and Michael Lipsky (1980). Leonard White's histories also bore significant evidence of the political nature of administrative practice, as did Paul Van Riper's history of the U.S. Civil Service (1958). Van Riper was a later student of White's. Many of White's protégés at the University of Chicago contributed important theoretical as well as empirical works dealing with the political aspects of the field.

5. Cf. Dwight Waldo (1948), Wayne Leys (1952, 1943), E. Pendelton Herring (1936), and Paul Appleby (1952, 1949, 1945).

6. See O.C. McSwite (1997) for an in-depth analysis of this famous debate.

7. Cooper illustrates through analysis of "remedial court orders" how extensively judges become involved in the administrative and budgetary politics of the states. Rosenbloom shows how Congress infuses itself into daily administration of agencies in ways that transcend mere oversight and amount to outright supervision of some agency personnel and processes.

8. Most prominent among these is pluralist political philosophy (cf. Bentley 1935; Dahl 1964; Lindblom 1965), which is based on the idea that formal representation of the populace is greatly augmented by the organization and advocacy of special interests. Individual citizens can greatly enhance their particular interests by joining these groups to lobby formal representatives and influence the policies of public agencies.

9. See chapters 5 and 6 of Rohr's book *To Run a Constitution* (1986). Note that Rohr admits that bureaucrats do not perfectly replicate the microcosm of the broader citizenry. They more closely match the characteristics of the middle class, but this still provides a much broader scope of representation than formally provided for in the Constitution.

10. Some additional examples may help readers understand the specific and distinctive institutional requirements of public agencies that require administrators to adhere to different standards than might otherwise be required of private citizens. First, public officials may have to display more impartiality and emotional distance toward the public as an aspect of consistent and fair treatment. Judges in courts are classic examples. Likewise, public administrators often have to distance themselves from various causes and relationships they would otherwise openly support. Second, police officers and other types of regulatory officers may have to disrupt, inspect, and search private premises, while this would amount to trespass in private life. Third, covert and military agencies may have to confine us to our homes or remove us from our homes in emergencies. Moreover, they may at times have to deceive us in order to protect us.

11. Public office involves what Michael Walzer (1992) calls *separation*, in which one realm has its own moral logic and demands that are not necessarily continuous with, although may be grounded in, the rest of one's moral life (119).

12. A notable exception is Rosenbloom and Kravchuk (2002).

13. This point was illustrated in compelling fashion by Graham Allison in *The Essence of Decision* (1971).

14. J. Patrick Dobel (1999) aptly describes political prudence as encompassing eight aspects of achievement, which can be grouped in three categories: First, leadership capacities—such as (1) disciplined reason, (2) openness to experience and knowledge, and (3) foresight and attention to the long term—must be cultivated. Second, leaders need competence in the modalities of statecraft, such as (4) acquisition of power and resources, timing, momentum and direction, and (5) the proper alignment of means and ends. Third, proper attributes of political outcomes to which leaders must attend are (6) durability and legitimacy of outcomes, (7) minimal violence and coercion, and (8) building and sustaining community and trust.

# PART II

## DESIGNING AND MANAGING ORGANIZATIONAL SYSTEMS

# TUMULT IN PRAIRIE COUNTY: A CASE STUDY

## CASE DESCRIPTION

Erwin Hargrove and John Glidewell (1990) have noted that "some jobs fall at the difficult extreme of so many dimensions that they can legitimately be called 'impossible.'" The situation of Prairie County, described below, deserves such an appellation, not just for a specific job but for an entire town and surrounding county. It is a real story, one in which many public officials face acute and intractable problems that have no immediate solution. At best, they can develop strategies and tactics to help residents and colleagues cope. Sadly, however, the problems are not unique to Prairie County. A significant number of communities across the country share some or all of these circumstances. Readers experienced in state and local social services administration and in local government settings will likely be familiar with many of them. Such cases are, therefore, worth thinking about. The ensuing chapters provide a variety of perspectives and questions through which the case can be analyzed. There are different levels and types of administrative challenges involved that range from internal organizational and personnel issues to matters of strategic assessment and adaptation, interorganizational networking, leadership, and community development.

## OVERVIEW

The chief industries of Prairie County have always been based in agriculture and mining. Agribusiness (related to both crops and cattle) has remained fairly stable over the years, providing adequate employment opportunities and a comfortable pastoral culture. Prairie County's towns are fairly small but viable and pleasant. Historically, mining played a lesser role in the area's economy. Small gypsum and coal mining operations existed on and off since before the county had been established, but this changed dramatically in 2002, when tests indicated the existence of large pockets of natural gas in the area. The resulting mining boom has transformed the lives of everyone and is not likely to abate for at least 20 years, when the gas wells are predicted to run dry.

The natural gas drilling operations brought in droves of tough young men, many with girlfriends or wives and children in tow. With them came skyrocketing problems with drug abuse, crime, housing shortages, inflation, and domestic abuse. Environmental problems also emerged as drilling operations began polluting water wells, and thousands of gas vents polluted the air. Ranchers and farmers had always known they did not own mineral rights to their land, but few ever expected any significant mining activity. Even fewer realized that federal law provided relatively easy access to their lands by

mining companies, with little recompense for the intrusion. Landowners were caught completely off guard by these problems and are now demanding action. Unfortunately, they have few avenues for redress. Their problems pale, however, in comparison to what nonfarming communities in Prairie County are experiencing. The worst manifestations appear in the town of Ward, the county seat.

Ward serves as the major commercial, governmental, and residential hub in this otherwise rural county. Its population grew from 18,000 inhabitants in 2002 to 29,000 in 2006, and is expected to peak at around 40,000 people by 2011. The town is located on a junction of interstate and U.S. highways and has become a convenient stop for hundreds of migrants seeking work. Many of these individuals are of Hispanic descent, and they have become a distinct minority in a town that was almost 100 percent white with strong ethnic ties to Scandinavia and Germany. The town has been surrounded by "man camps" made up of trucks with campers, run-down mobile homes, and hastily built shacks. County planning and building codes were too permissive to stop such ramshackle development. Within Ward, owners of larger vacant lots, lured by the prospect of lucrative rents, quickly converted them to mobile home parks with all the necessary utilities but little in the way of amenities such as small yards with shrubs and trees, storage units, and playgrounds. The city lacked a comprehensive plan and related codes to require such things. The city planning commission has been barraged with demands from adjacent homeowners to impose such standards on these developments immediately. Commission members have proposed new rules, but none have yet passed, due mainly to threats of lawsuits from the mobile home park owners.

Likewise, the city police department (which is unionized) and the county sheriff's office were not prepared to deal with all the changes. Crime rates exploded. Violent crime, once rare, became commonplace. Loud, raucous parties led to fights and drug deals. Quiet local taverns were soon overrun by a rough and surly clientele. Property crimes and juvenile delinquency proliferated. Arrest rates climbed, court dockets swelled, and the county jail overflowed with inmates. Many of the individuals who were arrested spoke little English, while none of the officers spoke Spanish. The ranks of police officers and sheriff's deputies were white, and most had lived in the area all their lives. Many of them resented the influx of outsiders as much as their neighbors did. To compound matters, gang activity developed in Ward, and police discovered the existence of crack houses and meth labs in remote rural areas of the county. Police investigators also confirmed that a Latino gang leader from Los Angeles had purchased two homes in one of the more prominent neighborhoods, apparently with intentions to relocate family members to a safer and more profitable locale.

The schools in Ward and the surrounding county were inundated with new children, many with special needs and difficult family conditions. New teachers were hired, some with fluency in Spanish, and school administrators worked with the local police to place an officer part time in the local high school. The school superintendent also forged an agreement with the field office of the state Department of Social Services (DSS), requesting a caseworker to visit elementary schools routinely in order to identify children in need of social services. Children's needs, however, far exceeded school district and DSS resources. The DSS was overwhelmed with people requesting services and with domestic abuse and child protection cases.

These problems were compounded by the prevalence of methamphetamine ("meth") use. Meth is a highly addictive, cheaply made drug that often stimulates violent behavior in the user. Law enforcement officials in the area attribute 80 percent of recent crime to meth abuse, and addiction is spreading quickly beyond the mining population to the younger traditional population. Worse still, effective treatment for meth addiction requires 18–24 months in a closely controlled environment. Only two facilities in the entire state are prepared for such treatment, and they take very few addicts at one time. Ward has no such facility. Out-of-state facilities are expensive, and state policy does not support the transfer of in-state clients to other states for treatment.

Although the state is taking in significant new revenue from mineral severance taxes, little of it has percolated into the social services system and local school districts. The political culture of the state is fiscally conservative, and its politicians are loath to fund "welfare" programs. They are, however, very tough on crime, and so have begun to allocate additional revenue to law enforcement and criminal courts. School funding operates primarily through county property tax assessments, but these consistently lag behind the booming growth.

Prairie County's social services subsystem is comprised mainly of small nonprofit and for-profit service providers who contract with the local DSS field office to take out-of-home placements of children and provide family services such as anger management, care of infants, and family counseling. Most children who are removed from their homes have been assigned to foster homes, but these cases have declined in number due to the new and extremely difficult nature of the cases entering the system. Group homes, drug treatment facilities, and crisis centers in Ward are overloaded, and statewide capacity is nearly exhausted as well. Ward's mental health provider struggles to keep up with the demand, but it is a powerful actor in state politics and essentially maintains a monopoly power over mental health services statewide. Attempts by local DSS officials to attract competitors and bolster services are consistently repelled by the provider.

DSS coordinates placement, case management, and treatment decisions through multi-disciplinary teams (MDTs) and a child protection team (CPT) staffed by many of the providers, as well as by legal officials such as a deputy district attorney, police officers, and court-appointed legal guardians (called guardians ad litem or GALs). These teams struggle to cope with the excessive caseloads, and the tensions have caused some dysfunction, especially on the CPT, where legal values often conflict with treatment priorities. The conflict has heightened with the appointment of a new district court judge who has been assigned primary responsibility for juvenile cases. Judge MaryAnn Grimes came to the position as an outspoken advocate for tough "law and order" measures to be taken against offenders, both juvenile and adult. She disagrees with the DSS philosophy of "family preservation" as a first priority. Juvenile offenders deserve punishment ("tough love" as she describes it), and should not be coddled by an overly sympathetic social services system. She prefers stiffer penalties, especially out-of-town placements in juvenile corrections facilities (privately owned boot camps and public reformatories). The kids, she argues, need a clear sense of boundaries and need to get out of their dysfunctional family and peer environments in order to get "straightened around." This is especially true, she believes, for kids from "meth families." In her first year, she dramatically increased the number of correctional placements (even for fairly minor offenses) out of Prairie County. The deputy district attorney, Gary Sullivan, who oversees all juvenile cases, desires harmonious relations with the new judge and touts her position at CPT meetings. The GALs are alarmed, but they are even more frustrated with the low pay ($50/hr) they receive from the state for their services. Some have stopped serving as GALs altogether, which has created a shortage of legal representation for children.

All of this has infuriated the local DSS field office director, Susan Webb, who has run the office for eight years. Webb is fully committed to DSS family preservation policy. She feels that Judge Grimes intimidates her caseworkers and has disrupted the priorities of the DSS mission. Webb has lost her temper with Judge Grimes on several occasions, and both have dug in their heels defensively. Relations between the DSS office and district court are now openly hostile.

## PROBLEMS IN THE DSS FIELD OFFICE

The DSS office is structured around three main functions, with a supervisor overseeing each one.

## 1. Benefit Services

Benefit Services (BS) takes applications for services; provides information regarding the range of community services available to eligible clients; determines eligibility of clients according to strict, legally specified criteria; and processes all paperwork and reports pursuant to these tasks. Twelve BS employees work in the Ward field office, with an average tenure of 10 years. Their longevity results in hourly pay that exceeds the salaries of professional caseworkers—a matter of some resentment among caseworkers.

## 2. Child Protection

Eight child protection (CP) caseworkers investigate allegations of child abuse and take steps to prevent further abuse through out-of-family placements or like measures that must be authorized by the district court. They work closely with the child protection team (CPT) to review cases and provide multiple perspectives and raw information about specific cases. CP caseworkers are overwhelmed with cases and suffer tremendous stress, especially since Judge Grimes took office. She berates them in court for inadequate preparation and poor recommendations. The average tenure of CP caseworkers has reached an all-time low of about 18 months. The beginning salaries for CP caseworkers with less than 3 years of experience is about $27,000 per year—with the required bachelor's degree.

## 3. Family Services

Family Services (FS) caseworkers work with families in need of a variety of developmental services and coping strategies. Most services are provided by private or nonprofit vendors in the community, while the local FS caseworkers must coordinate client placement. The caseworkers are members of the MDTs, but their lack of experience relative to professionals working for the vendors leads to friction and sniping on all sides. Twelve FS caseworkers are assigned in the Ward field office, with tenure averaging between 12 and 18 months over the last two years. The stress and working conditions have become unbearable. New recruits receive training in the DSS system and then quickly seek more tolerable positions with social services vendors. Salaries for FS caseworkers with less than three years of experience start at $21,300. Some of these workers are single mothers who actually qualify for DSS services themselves. Others now seek jobs in the mining industry as truck drivers, equipment operators, and office workers, where pay is double or triple a caseworker's salary, and benefits are comparable.

All DSS caseworkers in the Ward field office now average approximately 50 cases each, more than twice the number recommended by federal standards. Benefit Services (BS) workers process more than 1,700 benefits claims each month, up more than 40 percent from the previous year. The state central office has put pressure on the Ward field office to close more cases and keep the caseloads to federal standards. The state faces significant penalties in the form of reduced federal funding for not meeting the standards. The central office also routinely increases reporting requirements and paperwork revisions, usually due to initiatives from political appointees who turn over about every two years, and due to software upgrades and other technical imperatives. The redundant paperwork adds heavily to everyone's duties. The view of local caseworkers is that there are "too many chiefs in the central office, and not enough workers on the street."

The centralized state human resources (HR) recruiting and testing system is slow and unresponsive to local cries for immediate help. The Ward field office encounters great difficulty at-

tracting qualified caseworkers to the area, and recruitment usually takes several weeks or months to complete. DSS caseworkers must have a bachelor's degree, though not necessarily in social work. For example, one caseworker has a degree in business, and another earned one in exercise physiology. The state requires a broad range of training programs for caseworkers, partly as an opportunity for career development in lieu of better salaries. New caseworkers need a lot of in-office, on-the-job training and mentoring; however, the state training itinerary mandates their attendance at a variety of training sessions held at the state capitol and other locations that require traveling long distances from Ward. Caseloads continue to grow while the caseworkers are out of town. They now view most training sessions as interference with their work. Moreover, the per diem for travel is inadequate, so some travel expenses must come out of their own pockets. Many of the caseworkers must also put their kids in day care or hire babysitters while they are away, which they cannot afford.

To cope with the tremendous demands on caseworkers, Director Webb has established four Case Aide positions to handle transport of clients and to assist with case reports. She tries to recruit people who are working toward completion of social work or counseling degrees, but few live in the area, and the state pay range ($9.00 to $11.00 per hour) is no longer competitive in the local economy. Those hired are barely competent to handle the office work, much less transport anguished and occasionally violent clients with complex problems. The potential liabilities are frightening to consider.

Besides these positions, the local field office employs three secretaries, one of whom also serves as office bookkeeper. They experience high stress from:

1. clients with tragic circumstances who enter the office desperate for help,
2. the high number of phone calls to the office,
3. paperwork support for all other functions, and
4. their low status relative to other employee groups.

They currently lack a supervisor, as the position was cannibalized to hire another caseworker. Caseworkers routinely berate them for interrupting their work, and benefit specialists hound them with paperwork.

## DSS MANAGEMENT

Problems in the Ward field office are compounded by poor internal management practices. Director Webb is a task-oriented manager who, when she's in the office, micromanages the employees—and in an extremely passive-aggressive manner. She delegates responsibilities to subordinates and then angrily berates them for making wrong decisions. Subordinates, especially the three supervisors, are reticent to make decisions and keep to their assigned roles because of her actions. Employees hide mistakes and avoid communicating for fear of her unpredictable response. They never know "which Webb will show up" on any given day. The lack of communication only exacerbates problems, which, in turn, serves to heighten Webb's belief that she must constantly police the offices to sniff out trouble. When she sees problems, she often lashes out in vindictive rage—even in front of clients and stakeholders. Later, in a fit of guilt and remorse, she turns overly sweet, lavishing praise on her subordinates, trying to win their confidence and trust—but to no avail. The employees are afraid to file grievances about Webb with the state offices. The DSS field administration director, Dan Oglesby almost always sides with Webb in such disputes, and field office employees have suffered retribution in the aftermath.

The morale in the office has sunk to an all-time low. The benefit specialists have formed a very tight and self-protective clique, controlling all paperwork and rebuffing attempts by the caseworkers and secretaries to gain easier access to benefits determination and related decisions. They treat clients in a cold, officious manner, often appearing to ignore their "stories." They focus almost exclusively on the accuracy of their reports, in large part because more than five mistakes in a year results in a reprimand that goes into their personnel files. The BS supervisor is viewed as untrustworthy because she waffles in her resolve to defend her specialists from Webb's tirades. She tries to temporize, to smooth things over, but she ends up appeasing Webb to the detriment of her relations with everyone else.

Caseworkers despise the benefit specialists for their legalism and refusal to cooperate, and have "gone tribal" in order to protect themselves and garner some power over informal office dynamics. The child protection and family services supervisors have worked strenuously to mediate disputes among the groups, but they have become very discouraged. The CP supervisor has to protect her caseworkers from both Judge Grimes and Webb. She succeeds with Judge Grimes (Grimes respects her) until Webb intervenes to challenge the judge's decisions. She had also managed to buffer her caseworkers from Webb's office tirades until Webb started spying on them, listening in on conversations from down the hall, and then berating them for making wrong decisions. The only redeeming factor in the situation is that, more often than not, Webb is out of the office working with officials in the community.

Webb's real strengths as field office director lie in her ability to work strategically with most stakeholders in the DSS subsystem. Her disastrous relationship with Judge Grimes is a rare exception. She has forged very cooperative relationships with law enforcement officials, social service vendors, and city and county elected officials. She is highly respected in these circles for her knowledge of the social services subsystem, her ability to leverage scarce resources through grants and to induce interagency collaboration, and her insight about the kinds of problems emerging in the area. She has joined Ward's chief of police, the county sheriff, the county administrator, the public health and environmental safety directors, the school district superintendent, and the Ward town manager on an interagency task force to develop recommendations on how to meet the many challenges posed by the mining boom.

## CASE ANALYSIS

The chapters in this section provide the reader with knowledge and insights that will enable them to develop some meaningful solutions to the problems described in this case. As you read the chapters that follow, think about how the concepts, theories, and historical context related to the development of the fields of organizational and human resources management might be used to help the public servants in this case assess and cope more effectively with their situation. Prepare a list of useful measures that could be transformed into an action plan that you would employ if you were a player in this drama. Think about how the differing philosophies and perspectives of various players would affect your plan and how your plan successfully anticipates these differing perspectives.

# ORGANIZATION STRUCTURE AND BEHAVIOR

> Every organized human activity—from the making of pots to the placing of a man on the moon—gives rise to two fundamental and opposing requirements: the division of labor into various tasks to be performed, and the coordination of these tasks to accomplish the activity. The structure of the organization can be defined simply as the sum total of the ways in which it divides its labor into distinct tasks and then achieves coordination among them.
>
> *(Henry Mintzberg 1983, 2)*

> Many of the questions that both analysts and members of organizations confront are fundamentally *political*. That is, they have to do with making choices, allocating benefits and burdens, generating commitment and legitimacy, and coping with conflict, complexity, and uncertainty. This in turn suggests that one approach to understanding organizations is to conceive of them as political systems, or *polities*, that develop structures for channeling political dynamics and performing political tasks.
>
> *(Karen Hult and Charles Walcott 1990, 5)*

We live in an organizational society. Even in our sleeping hours we are embraced by organizations—city police departments, state air quality control agencies, county health departments, nonprofit mental health service organizations, fire districts, utility districts, school districts, and more. In fact, we require a certificate at birth and one at death executed by people working in public organizations. Citizens experience government largely through contact with professionals and administrators who are charged with designing the structures and guiding organizational behavior. Equally important, most people work in complex organizations, whether private or public. For many, personal identity is tied up with their work organizations. Listen to the introductions we make when we meet one another. Notice the way we describe ourselves with organizational references: "I'm a building inspector. I work for the City of Wilsonville."

So much of contemporary life revolves around complex organizations that it behooves us to understand something of their structure and dynamics. A large body of literature now exists on the subject, and this chapter reviews its more prominent schools of thought. The field illuminates many aspects—good and bad—of organizational life and administrative practice. It reveals tensions that arise between treating employees as instruments for organizational purposes and their maturation through organizational life; it also highlights the conflicts that develop between organizational

values and the values of American democratic governance as expressed through the administrative traditions of (1) minority rights and access to governance, (2) civic engagement, (3) responsive governance, and (4) competent and energetic governance.

*Organizations* are commonly understood as intentionally created social collectivities with explicit purposes and relatively discrete boundaries. In this sense, they are clearly designed as instruments—a means to ends. If the things people in society want could be generated by individuals working alone, then organizations would not dominate the social landscape. From running shoes to ballet, from libraries to highways, from clean drinking water to accessible hospital care, the things people want and the things they care about require the coordinated efforts of many people. However, in addition to being instrumental bodies, organizations possess expressive qualities that reflect their surrounding culture and mores and, in turn, define organizational subcultures in which people live out much of their lives. Many organizations take on a life of their own, reflecting identities that are valued for more than the sum of their parts. Their practices, policies, and procedures shape relationships, affect habits and dispositions, and define ways of living that help determine appropriate and inappropriate means for achieving ends. The design of an organization adapts and mutates as these expressive, cultural qualities manifest themselves. Local public schools, public libraries, city halls, state colleges and universities, parks, forestry agencies, military bases, and even prisons come to define integral aspects of community, state, and nation. Philip Selznick (1957) described this as a process of institutionalization within the broader fabric of society (see a more extended discussion in chapter 2).

While we aggregate resources through organizations to produce goods and services, there are some distinct differences in the way this happens in public and private organizations. First, public goods and services are typically underproduced in, or not fully accounted for through, private markets (Ostrom 1990). Such goods require public policy decisions directing their production: clean air, monetary policy, social security, national parks, safe building standards, community safety, and public health. Second, public goods and services tend to reflect ambiguous values and are often rather abstract in nature. For example, though we may see concrete manifestations of law enforcement, the underlying values of policing permit widely varying approaches, no one of which can or should be pursued to the exclusion of others over time. Public organizations, therefore, face more uncertainty and conflict over both means and ends, and this poses unique challenges for organization policy. Third, public organizations require more complex lines of accountability and superintendence through all levels and beyond their boundaries to myriad oversight institutions. Citizens can affect these functions at virtually every stage, from legislative lobbying to delivery at the street level as clients and customers. Fourth, the resources aggregated in public organizations to accomplish the organization's work are public resources. As such, those who manage the resources incur strong fiduciary responsibilities for their stewardship and are often constrained in the ways they use such resources. Public officials are thus more than mere functionaries of production: They are public officials who bear ethical responsibility for proper use of resources in the public square. All these factors affect the design and complexity of public organizations.

The delivery of public goods and services, however, does not stop at the government door. In a mixed political economy, public goods and services are delivered by organizations in all sectors: public, private, nonprofit, and special district. The complexity of our mixed political economy arises from a deliberate constitutional construction that mandates limited government and a wide-open sphere for private life. Accordingly, the U.S. Constitution is permissive regarding a wide array of public and private partnerships for achieving public purposes. Our governments can form quasi-governmental institutions such as government corporations, enter into close contractual relations with private and nonprofit firms, and vest specific governing powers in various kinds of

associations and joint ventures. We are thus able to enjoy a rich diversity of organizational forms and processes for coping with so many public purposes and problems.

## THE MYTH OF UNIFORM ORGANIZATION STRUCTURE

Organizations are familiar to people mainly through lived experience. When asked to describe an organization, most people start by describing one they know—often their work organization. They describe what they do, where they do it, and how they do it. Such descriptions provide a rich natural history of organizations of different forms and levels of complexity. However, when asked to describe their organization's structure, the overwhelming response by both pre-service and in-service students is to present an organizational chart in standard hierarchical form. Their structural description seldom coincides with the stories they tell about their work. People thus think of organizations as natural in terms of what they do and how they do it, but as artificial in terms of overall construction. Interestingly, when prompted for more details about their structural portrait, students typically begin describing a variety of decision structures, work relations, sub-cultures, and informal channels that differ significantly from the hierarchical form. This cognitive dissonance between natural and artificial conceptions is pervasive and leads to real problems in organizational design.

Most of us, when charged with designing an organization in whole or in part, will instinctively adopt the hierarchical organization chart as if it were a universal structural template. In this chapter, we emphasize the point that complex organizations require diverse organizational forms in order to adequately perform various types of work, and to cope with many challenges stemming from uncertainty and conflict that are built into our system of democratic governance. Appropriate structures are contingent upon such factors.

Consider for a moment the situation faced by Prairie County officials in the case study preceding this chapter. In their various organizational capacities, they encountered tremendous changes in their communities that added many additional responsibilities to their plates and forced them to rethink how they should meet their missions. They clearly needed more staff, new expertise, more programs, and new organizational designs to accommodate them. Such changes seem as threatening to employees and citizens as do the problems that confront them. Their first task, it appears, would involve pulling leaders together from key organizations in all sectors to assess needs and to work out the implications for subsequent design and staffing. Thus, their first new structure was more collegial and deliberative than hierarchical in nature.

The dilemma these officials face is a common one. Organizations usually accrete multiple purposes as they evolve. Elementary schools have taken on public and community health functions. Water districts have taken on watershed management as well as the delivery of potable water and the removal of wastewater. Utility districts have moved beyond electricity or telephone services to include a variety of energy conservation and communication services. A current trend in human services is to bundle services into "super" departments to improve the coordination among programs serving different populations. Nonprofits often add service missions as the demands of their clients or funding sources change. State and local emergency managers face an enormous organizational design challenge because of federal policies adding terrorism response to the list of natural and social emergencies historically assigned to first responders. New purposes add complexity, which strains existing designs. Adding to the strain are declining resources, dramatic demographic turn-over in executive ranks, and changing sentiments in society about how public services should be delivered. These internal and external pressures create real tensions and trade-offs in design. It is not surprising to see a growing literature suggesting strategies for adaptive design.

## ORGANIZATIONS AS ABSTRACT UNITS OF ANALYSIS

Studying organizations is complicated, largely because it involves several possible levels of analysis. At the very least, we must consider the individual, the group, the organization qua organization, and the environment surrounding the organization—which entails populations of organizations (the *ecological* or *strategic* level of analysis). Significant insight is gained at every level of analysis. This chapter will move across these levels but will focus primarily on the organization as the unit of analysis. The reason for adopting this focus is that most students of public administration are expected to understand how an organizational entity can be better structured to achieve its purposes. In doing so, however, it is important to remember that there are no bright lines between these four levels of analysis.

For example, individual levels of analysis are typically used in areas of selection, motivation, and individual performance. What is known at this individual level of analysis influences group-level dynamics and shapes leadership at the organizational and ecological level of analysis. Similarly, job design is impacted by the organizational design of work units. Moreover, as organizations are often large and complex, one could choose to carry out an organizational level of analysis of subunits. That is, one could analyze the Forestry Division within the Department of Natural Resources (DNR) as an organization—this would make the DNR part of the organization's (that is, the Forestry Division's) environment. One could also analyze the DNR as an organization, in which case the Forestry Division would be a functional subunit of the DNR. To extend this example, one could also study the executive branch of state government as an organizational unit of analysis, in which case the DNR would be a functional subdivision. Thus, specifying the level of analysis and the unit of analysis in organizational study is a way of abstracting particular entities from their broader context in order to limit one's focus. While this is useful, one must not forget that the abstraction highlights some things at the expense of others in the bigger picture.

## THE STUDY OF ORGANIZATIONS

The early study of modern organizations was based in the rational-legal norms and mechanized production associated with the Enlightenment of the eighteenth century. Adam Smith's *Wealth of Nations,* which frames much of modern Western political and economic thought, begins with a focus on the importance of organization design in a production firm.

> The effect of the division of labor, in the general business of society, will be more easily understood, by considering in what manner it operates in some particular manufactures. . . . To take an example, therefore, from a very trifling manufacture; but one in which the division of labor has been very often taken notice of, the trade of pin-maker; a workman not educated to this business nor acquainted with the use of the machinery employed in it, could scarce, perhaps, with his utmost industry, make one pin in a day, and certainly could not make twenty. But in the way in which this business is now carried on, not only the whole work is a peculiar trade, but it is divided into a number of branches, of which the greater parts are likewise peculiar trades. One man draws out the wire, another straightens it, a third cuts it, a fourth points it, a fifth grinds it at the top for receiving the head; to make the head requires two or three distinct operations; to put it on is a peculiar business, to whiten the pins is another; it is even a trade by itself to put them into paper; and the important business of making a pin is, in this manner, divided into about eighteen distinct operations, which, in some manufactories, are all performed by distinct hands, though in others the same man will sometimes perform two or three of them.

I have seen a small manufactory of this kind where ten men only were employed, and where some of them consequently performed two or three distinct operations. . . . They could, when they exerted themselves, make about twelve pounds of pins in a day. There are in a pound upwards of four thousand pins of a middling size. Those ten persons, therefore, could make among them upwards of forty-eight thousand pins in a day. Each person, therefore, making a tenth part of forty-eight thousand pins, might be considered as making four thousand eight hundred pins in a day. But if they had all wrought separately and independently, and without any of them having been educated to this particular business, they certainly could not each of them have made twenty, perhaps not one pin in a day; that is, certainly not the two hundred and fortieth, perhaps not the four thousand eight hundredth part of what they are at present capable of performing, in consequence of a proper division and combination of their different operations. (Smith 1776/2003, 3)

Smith's account of the pin factory presents a classic study of organizational differentiation and specialization leading to greater efficiency. It describes a key challenge of organizational design— how to properly divide work, and then how to coordinate and control the work once divided. Smith realized that improving efficiency and productivity through division of labor would bring benefits as well as problems. It would create a great deal more surplus value than could be achieved through individual efforts, and this raised the question of how to divide the newly created wealth—a matter that would dramatically affect relations of power within the organization as well as throughout modern society. It also introduced concerns about how division and specialization of labor, and its resulting organizational structures, would affect individuals and their liberties. Smith had seen firsthand how the division of labor in the pin factory could produce dulling psychological and social effects on human beings, and he worried about the implications for broader civil society. Organization theorists have wrestled with this problem ever since. Gross and Etzioni (1985, 5) characterize it as a central challenge of modern organizations. How can we design organizations as rationally as possible while minimizing their dehumanizing effects? Broad and sustained study of this and related problems began in earnest during the late nineteenth century, coinciding in America with the rise of Progressive reforms.

## THE DEVELOPMENT OF FORMAL ORGANIZATION THEORY

Important developments in organization theory marked the turn of the twentieth century. First, in Western Europe, scholars such as Max Weber, Emile Durkheim, and Vilfredo Pareto studied the transformation of work from an individual, craft-based approach to a corporate, complex organizational undertaking. In Europe, large, complex public organizations preceded the emergence of large private organizations (McCraw 1984), all of which preceded large-scale organizations in the United States by at least 50 years. In the United States, the reverse was true—large public organizations followed the emergence of large private organizations. Industrialization of textiles, oil, railroads, food stuffs, and resource extraction (mining and timbering) prompted efforts to understand more systematically how to manage division and specialization of labor in multisite organizations. European scholars began identifying organizational characteristics common to both sectors. Most prominent among them was Max Weber and his *bureaucratic* theory of organization.

In the 1890s, Weber,[1] a German sociologist, studied the emergence of modern, rational organizations around the world. From these studies, he derived what is now considered the classic model of bureaucracy. Weber portrayed his model as an "ideal type," meaning he abstracted from organizational practices those characteristics he believed most logically fit a *legal-rational* structure.

In reality, organizations display other organizing characteristics (traditional, patrimonial, charismatic, and so on) as well, but these seemed to diminish as cultures adapted to industrialization. Bureaucracy seemed more characteristic of the age. Its main features include the following:[2]

- Fixed division of labor by official function
- Offices ordered in a hierarchy
- Reliance on expertise, skills, and experience as the basis for selection
- Formalized rules that govern performance
- Separation of organizational and personal property and resources
- Resources of the organization are free from outside control
- Employment viewed as a career and compensation sufficient for livelihood
- Extensive written records of administrative acts, decisions, and rules

Such characteristics create an organization that is legal-rational in contrast to traditional organizations in history. The traditional organization relied on the personal loyalty and other intimate ties between employees, their employers, families, clans, and their communities. Weber argued that efficiency is gained by replacing this loyalty-centered system with one that relies on specialization, standardization, and formalization of administrative work. Further, he argued that organizations designed on this model create uniformity of organizational action by "purging particularism" (Perrow 1986). Trained expertise ensures competency in each office, and the hierarchical nature of the relationship among offices provides a chain of authority for purposes of control as well as formal pathways of communication for coordination among offices. Oversight is made easier through written rules and standard operating procedures (SOPs) that provide substitutes for individual judgment. All of these characteristics rationalize and standardize behavior in the organization.

Weber believed that bureaucratic organization possessed clear advantages over previous models. It creates clear lines and grades of authority. Its formalized work processes ensure uniform treatment of cases, and full-time employment reduces the risk of self-dealing or favoritism. Perhaps most important, employees hired on the basis of merit—and who are protected from outside influence—can focus their full attention on the achievement of organizational goals.

Despite these advantages, Weber also recognized certain negative aspects of the bureaucratic model. Employees may feel dehumanized, treated as cogs in a machine. Clients may feel much the same, treated as case numbers rather than as distinct individuals with unique needs. The formalism that ensures consistent treatment can constrain the ability of employees to deal with exceptional cases, a condition referred to as *trained incapacity*. Trained incapacity breeds passivity and a lack of creativity needed to adapt to changing conditions. Robert Merton (1957) extended this critical insight by calling attention to the tendency of bureaucratic employees to emphasize consistent procedures to the point that the overarching purposes were lost from view, resulting in *goal displacement*. Weber and subsequent scholars foresaw the dangers involved in putting organizational efficiency above individual needs and organizational goals. Weber also worried that large bureaucratic organizations would concentrate power in new ways, limiting the ability of individuals to affect their own futures—a major concern shared by many subsequent critics (cf. Downs 1967; Merton 1940; Perrow 1986; Scott and Hart 1989).

Weber's work stands as one of the most comprehensive analyses of modern complex organizations ever undertaken, and today it is still considered the most influential work on bureaucracy. Ironically, his work was largely unexamined in the United States until translations became available in the 1940s. However, many European scholars shared similar ideas, some of which influenced American thought. Military thought embraced a general staff model based in large part on early ver-

sions of the bureaucratic model developed in Prussia and France during the late eighteenth century. The American military establishment adopted these ideas in the wake of the Civil War. American corporations adapted them to industrial organization, and their adaptations were commonly identified as the *business model* during the Progressive Era. In this fashion, various manifestations of the bureaucratic model seeped into the fabric of American life. It manifested itself in a variety of academic and professional literature. An important aspect of this story is captured by Frederick Taylor, who looked for ways to improve work outcomes through improving work processes.

Taylor's *Principles of Scientific Management* (1911) stands as one of the most prominent American works in the field. Taylor enthusiastically advocated the use of "time and motion" studies to optimize the work of employees. In one of his shop studies, he pointed out that every person shoveling coal had an optimal shovel size that would help maximize daily output over a day's labor. He surrounded workers with "functional foreman," who would study every aspect of an employee's work process and look for ways to improve on the efficiency of effort and motion. He believed that all types of work at all levels of organization would eventually benefit from this concentrated, systematic analysis.

Taylor insisted that traditional management practices were operating by worn-out doctrines that lacked pragmatic adaptation and systematic study. Thus, he framed his work as a criticism of general management practice. Managers, he argued, needed to carefully study and design *work processes*—and separate this as a function distinct from the doing of work. They were responsible for (1) increasing the productivity of their employees by studying the one best way to divide work, (2) selecting and training workers for carefully designed jobs, (3) coordinating the flow of resources to accomplish the work, and (4) contrary to existing practices, awarding a fair division of the benefits to workers for their increased productivity.

Taylor's contributions anticipated the rise of systems analysis and operations research, out of which emerged commonly known managerial techniques such as Critical Path Method (CPM) and Program Evaluation Review Technique (PERT). His work also influenced organization theorists such as Chester Barnard (1938), who emphasized the importance of systematic coordination in making the internal operations of organizations effective, and Luther Gulick and Lyndall Urwick, who identified core functions of executive management. These theorists focused on higher-level management functions, adapting their ideas from scholars and practitioners of Taylor's generation. For example, Henri Fayol, a Frenchman and contemporary of Weber and Taylor, drew on management and organizational experience to develop principles described in his book *General and Industrial Management* (1949). His principles included the following:

- Division of work
- Authority and responsibility
- Discipline
- Unity of command
- Unity of direction
- Subordination of individual interest to general interest
- Remuneration of personnel
- Centralization
- Scalar chain
- Order
- Equity
- Stability of tenure of personnel
- Initiative
- Esprit de corps

Gulick borrowed heavily from this work to derive his own condensed list of managerial functions. He listed seven executive functions—planning, organizing, staffing, directing, coordinating, reporting, and budgeting—and coined them in the now-famous acronym POSDCORB (Gulick and Urwick 1937, 5).[3]

Taken together, these theories of the classic period of organization theory operated on several key assumptions. First, there is one best way to organize work. Second, organizations are created to achieve specific goals related to production. Third, efficiency is maximized through the division and specialization of labor, planning of work, coordination of work processes, and direct supervision. Fourth, people are motivated to work in such rationalized systems by economic incentives that reflect a fair distribution of the efficiency gains. Finally, the creators of these theories exhibited immense optimism about the promise of their reforms for society as a whole. That optimism stemmed mainly from the incredible technological inventions and changes already evident in society. The era generally reflected high enthusiasm about the ability of science to solve virtually any human problem. Not only could scientific theorists perfect the organizational process, they could perfect the humans who worked in organizations. For example, early behavioral studies focused on the elimination of such problems as worker fatigue, disease, poor health conditions in the workplace, and social-psychological disorders. Out of this work emerged new approaches to organization theory grounded in human relations.

## THE HUMAN RELATIONS MOVEMENT

The human relations approach is rooted in the fact that organizations are essentially human collectivities in which human relations—formal and informal—determine much of an organization's productivity. Whereas Weber's bureaucratic model and Taylor's scientific management model emphasized formal structure and efficient work processes, the human relations movement emphasized social-psychological factors in organizations—factors that motivate people to work. The major study responsible for the growth of this movement was designed as a set of scientific experiments (beginning in the early 1930s) aimed simply at improving worker efficiency at the Hawthorne plants of the Western Electric Company in Chicago (Mayo 1933; Roethlisberger and Dickson 1939).

A series of studies was carried out by a team primarily from Harvard University with the goal of demonstrating that modifications to work process and work environment could improve productivity. The most cited study, called the "illumination study," examined the impact on work output of electrical relay assembly groups by varying the extent of lighting in their work rooms. The controlled experiment showed that the group experiencing variations in lighting (from extremely bright to almost dark) increased productivity regardless of the direction of the variation. Curiously, the study also indicated that production among the control groups, where there was no change in lighting, also showed increases. Light intensity, therefore, could not explain the difference. The scientists decided that what *did* explain the difference was the attention paid to each group by the researchers. This finding has been labeled the "Hawthorne Effect" in social science study. For organization theory, it reinforced the claim of those who believed that paying attention to people is what matters most in creating efficient, productive, and healthy organizations. Motivation is more a social-psychological phenomenon than a physical or economic one. This insight spawned a host of studies relating emerging theoretical insights from the field of social psychology to organizational studies.

A number of contemporary works in organizational studies lent credibility to social-psychological interpretations in the human relations school. Most prominent among them were works

by Mary Parker Follett (1926) and Chester Barnard (1938). Follett, who wrote most of her work during the 1920s, exerted significant influence on subsequent scholarship in the field. She drew insight from work in socially oriented "helping" professions such as social work, nursing, and education, where concepts of mutual adjustment, collaborative leadership, and client-centered analysis prevailed. Her notions of "system" and the "law of the situation" suggested that focusing on collaboration and on problems, rather than on people and their formal status, were more central to organizational productivity. Follett emphasized street-level work as the more prominent aspect of effective organization, provided that workers were committed to the goals of the agency. This concept of relying on the discretionary judgment of first-line service providers grew from her observations of social workers in Boston, and from the work of a growing number of nonprofit organizations delivering basic needs to the poor, the mentally ill, and immigrants. From these studies, she formed the powerful idea that managers must share authority with, rather than over, workers (Follett 1926, 34). This decidedly human-centered approach to management contrasted with the prevailing structure-centered theories of the era.

Chester Barnard, a business executive as well as a scholar, produced one of the field's most prominent works, *Functions of the Executive*, in 1938.[4] In it, he stresses the importance of understanding the informal organization as an essential aspect of effective management and organizational development. The informal organization is the social system that governs human relationships and determines not only how work will be accomplished but the level of effectiveness it will attain. Barnard explained executive leadership mainly as a function of cultivating trust and rapport in an organization's social life. He defined authority in circular terms, arguing that it flowed as much from the ranks of employees as it did from management. He also conceived the idea of an "economy of incentives" that forms within an organization's social system. This phenomenon defines the rules of the game around those motivational patterns that best satisfy a particular group of workers and managers. Barnard showed that employees display significant "zones of indifference" about organizational relations, processes, and goals (1938, 168), and are therefore open to a variety of systematic designs and decision rules that structure incentives as well as work. In short, they will "get along to go along." In this fashion, they can be induced to follow organizational goals defined and articulated by management.

Follett's and Barnard's works drew widespread attention to the social dimension of organizations and prompted further study along social-psychological lines. In 1943, Abraham Maslow published one of the most influential articles ever written on management and human motivation. In "A Theory of Human Motivation," he posited that people are driven by a series of needs and that these needs are hierarchically scaled. Motivation results from the desire to climb from basic physiological and security needs (like safety, food, and shelter) toward social and self-actualizing needs (like self-esteem, sense of personal worth, and fulfilling accomplishment). As needs are met at one level, new needs at the next level emerge and gradually broaden motivational potential. Management can take advantage of this potential by providing organizational benefits (stimuli) that elicit higher-level drives. While there is little scientific evidence to support this notion of a hierarchy of needs (summarized in Exhibit 7.1), Maslow's model has dominated generations of research and is widely used among professionals in fields such as social work, education, public service, business, and public management. It is an intuitively appealing theory, perhaps because of its simple yet compelling imagery, and because it permits multiple ways to meet the needs of people working in organizations (Morgan 2006).

Frederick Herzberg and his colleagues (1959) refined Maslow's theory by drawing a distinction between *motivators* and *demotivators*. Motivators are those factors that help individuals develop a sense of accomplishment, sparking further effort; demotivators, on the other hand,

Exhibit 7.1   **Maslow's Hierarchy of Needs**

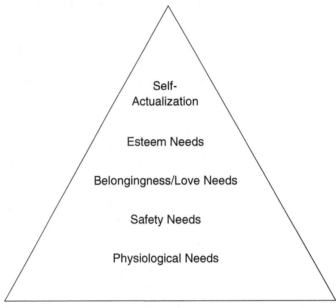

Self-
Actualization

Esteem Needs

Belongingness/Love Needs

Safety Needs

Physiological Needs

*Source:* Derived from Maslow (1943, 370–96).

actually block or interfere with these things. For example, in the difficult circumstances presented in the Prairie County case, pay and training policies at the Department of Social Services (DSS) served as demotivators for field office caseworkers. Managers needed to find ways of buffering or short-circuiting these effects as part of any broader effort to motivate these employees. In short, Herzberg's model emphasizes the importance of distinguishing between two separate scales of motivation: working conditions, pay, and the like, which often demotivate or just satisfy without motivating, and more intrinsic factors such as the challenges of the work itself, which can act as positive motivators under properly managed conditions.

The emphasis on intrinsic motivators led human relations theorists to rethink work processes and content, moving away from narrow, repetitive, specialized tasks designed by others, to code-velopment of complex tasks and enlarged responsibilities. The more challenging the work, the more potential there is for enhanced motivation, as well as greater commitment to organizational goals. This kind of thinking gave great impetus to professional development in many occupational realms and recast the culture and management practices of complex organizations.

Douglas McGregor framed the achievements of the human relations movement through a stark and rhetorically powerful contrast of management styles. In his classic work, *The Human Side of Enterprise* (1960), McGregor describes two basic orientations toward managing people in organizations: "Theory X" and "Theory Y." The Theory X orientation assumes that workers generally dislike work, lack ambition, are self-centered and not interested in organizational goals, are resistant to change, and prefer to be led rather than to take the lead (McGregor 1960). Accordingly, management must closely supervise and control workers lest they run amok.

Then, borrowing from Maslow and other human relations theorists, McGregor developed a much more appealing alternative, Theory Y, based on assumptions that workers have a broad scale of needs that include desires for inclusion, esteem, and fulfilling work. The genius of his dichotomy lies in

the self-fulfilling nature of the assumptions. Workers become indolent and resistive to management when treated in the negative Theory X fashion. Likewise, by adopting Theory Y assumptions that workers possess intrinsic motivation to work and to identify with organizational goals, managers can remove barriers and release more potential for self-motivated accomplishments. Workers will adopt organizational objectives and labor steadfastly to achieve them. Management must provide the proper conditions for this to occur, however, which means that less emphasis is placed on direct supervision, direction, and control, while more is placed on indirect, coordinative, and facilitative functions. Work can be made more challenging ("job enrichment"), and more responsibilities can be delegated to employees ("job enlargement") without much supervision.

The human relations school drew important insights from this kind of work. It spawned a whole new literature on organizational leadership, emphasizing styles over traits, and called attention to the need for more diverse types of managerial roles and practices than those offered by conventional management theory. Much of this leadership theory operated within the framework of human relations theory, focusing on a variety of leadership styles and techniques appropriate to relations within and among working groups inside organizations. This emphasis on the uniqueness of the setting coalesced into contingency approaches to leadership that called for different styles, depending on circumstances faced by different workgroups (cf. Fiedler 1967; Hersey and Blanchard 1977a; Vroom and Yetton 1973), but all emphasized achievement of more robust work relationships through facilitative and participatory practices. Borrowing from this literature, other theorists broadened attention to the interrelation of group-based social systems with the nature of tasks and functions to be carried out. Management practices and organizational designs vary across more factors than just individual needs and social relations among individuals and groups. Indeed, organizations can provide for these without necessarily enhancing their "task effectiveness." Managers must focus on the integration of individuals and groups with roles, structures, tasks, and technologies in order to achieve organizational goals (Argyris 1964; Trist 1981).

## THE CONTINGENCY THEORY OF ORGANIZATIONS

In the 1950s and 1960s, starting in England at the Tavistock Institute of Human Relations, organizational scholars focused on empirical studies of organizations as *sociotechnical systems*. These scholars viewed the technical aspects of organizations, including structure, job design, and task technology, as being interdependent with social aspects such as motivation, group dynamics, and leadership. As borne out in many subsequent studies, a change in technical features of production (such as increased automation) would change peer relationships among workers that could lead to changes in their attitudes toward performance (Gibson, Shinn, and Locklear 1990). Likewise, changes in social or peer relations may affect the ways tasks are perceived and performed. Furthermore, the relationships among these factors are affected by the organization's interaction with its environment (Emery 1959; Emery and Trist 1965; Trist 1981; Trist and Bamforth 1951). Studies of these factors concluded that the idea of a single, best organizational design had to be abandoned in favor of a contingency approach. For example, a more mechanical, Weberian-styled bureaucracy may work in a stable environment with a clear mission and little uncertainty about the tasks to be accomplished, but it would be inappropriate in most other conditions, especially those facing high uncertainty, rapid change, and powerful forces that threaten survival (Emery and Trist 1965).

One can see the relevance of this insight in the Prairie County case. Organizations within the county had enjoyed stable, relatively peaceful conditions over many years, and some of them had simple organizational designs that emphasized hierarchical principles. But their designs and

capacities were suddenly challenged by a host of changing environmental conditions, including the entry of highly exploitive mining companies and all their attendant problems. These immediately affected the nature of managerial and street-level tasks, as well as social relations, especially within the county's public safety and social services organizations. They needed new, varied, and networked organizational designs in order to adapt to the new realities.

**Adaptation and Contingent Managerial Roles**

In 1967, James D. Thompson drew together several streams of literature to develop a much more sophisticated understanding of how organizations adapt to such situations. His book *Organizations in Action* set out a contingency theory of organizational adaptation that heavily influenced an entire generation of scholarship. Borrowing from an emerging systems perspective, Thompson characterized the classical organization and human relations schools as focusing on internal aspects of organization as if they were closed systems. Management work and organization design were conceived entirely as internal matters—focused on mechanics, flow of work, and harmonious work relations. Such focus assumes that factors external to the organization remain stable—something that cannot be safely assumed for long. The necessary inputs and outputs of the organization are affected in myriad ways by environmental conditions (Thompson 1967, chaps. 1–2).

Drawing from the field of organizational sociology, Thompson illustrated the need for an institutional-level perspective through which managers focus on imminent and emerging conditions in the environment of their organization. Their work consists more of diplomacy, cooptation, cutting deals, and cultivating multilateral relationships with competitors, regulators, clients, media, and suppliers (Burns and Stalker 1961; Selznick 1957; Thompson 1967). Managerial work in this realm must emphasize change, adaptation, and evolution. Institutional or strategic managers must adopt an open-systems perspective, much like a biological organism responding to its environment. They spend more time working in the environment of their organization—mostly through meetings, conferences, and other communication-oriented activities—than inside the organization itself. They must anticipate trends, scan for threats, span boundaries, enact changes in the environment that are favorable to their organization, and expand the organization's domain (Thompson 1967, passim).

In light of the marked differences between inward-focused management and strategic management, Thompson then presented middle managers as translators, mediators, and buffers between them. Middle managers must translate the implications of strategic information, decisions, and policy changes for street-level operations (the "technical core" of the organization), and likewise inform strategic managers about the needs and capacities of the technical core in light of environmental factors. They must also mediate conflicts and tensions arising from the internal need for stability and control, along with the strategic demands for flexibility and adaptation. Then, through various coping tactics, they must buffer and smooth the rates and extent of change that affect various parts of the organization. According to Thompson, middle managers perform these functions through *capacity building,* which entails developing a consistent supply of materials and human resources and providing support functions across coordinating subunits, and through *boundary spanning* activities that organize and reorganize the governance structures within the organization to meet new contingencies (Thompson 1967, chap. 3).

Despite their vital and distinct nature, the roles of middle managers are seldom appreciated or understood. Thompson's work did much to illustrate their importance. Douglas Morgan and his coauthors (1996) conducted extensive field research in order to develop a richer understanding of middle-management functions in local government contexts. Their work challenges popular

reinvention reforms that view middle-management functions as sources of unnecessary paperwork and redundancy that can be eliminated. The findings of their study are easily applied across a broad range of public organizations at any level and serve as a caution to those who seek to simplify and devolve organizational functions in search of greater efficiency and effectiveness. Their insights about the vital roles served by middle managers are briefly summarized in Exhibit 7.2.

The differentiation among levels and types of management responsibilities discerned by Thompson and many subsequent theorists drive home the point that management is not a uniform activity. Its practices vary dramatically across all levels and functions of organizational life. Thus, it is not uncommon for a "technical core" (street-level) manager to be promoted into a middle-management position and experience great difficulty adjusting to its tasks and orientation. The same is true for middle managers who are promoted into strategic roles. The tasks and perspectives ingrained at one level of management may actually inhibit the ability to understand and exercise management roles at other levels. As mentioned earlier, this phenomenon is referred to as *trained incapacity* (cf. Merton 1940), and it requires substantial reorientation and training to overcome.

## Contingent Structures for Getting the Job Done

In Thompson's model, complex organizations require varying structural designs in order to cope with their myriad tasks and functions. Different kinds of tasks face different kinds of challenges, depending on the type and extent of uncertainty involved. Complex tasks with a considerable degree of uncertainty as to expectations and/or outcomes require highly interactive, collegial structures (reflecting *reciprocal interdependence*), as illustrated by medical teams working in an emergency room or SWAT teams dealing with a threatening situation. Tasks with more certainty and fairly stable rates of change can be handled more efficiently through hierarchical, linear, and specialized structures. For example, a nonprofit food pantry may assemble meals on an assembly line in which tasks are sequentially interdependent. The work at one stage is dependent on work done at the prior stage. In other cases, the work may involve multiple lines delivering the same kinds of products or services, as illustrated at a motor vehicle licensing office. The staff depends on a common pool of resources (*pooled interdependence*) but provides multiple avenues for accessing them.

Other important dimensions of organizational work involve task variety and task analyzability (Perrow 1986). Low task variety allows workers to focus their efforts on narrowly defined problems, such as how to place test monitors on well heads for purposes of assessing pollution levels. High task variety requires broad training that enables workers to adjust quickly to many different kinds of challenges. Social workers handling family services cases rely on a range of skills and concepts, and they may have to interact with other professionals to render effective aid to their clients. Task analyzability refers to the ability to assess and solve problems in a timely fashion. Low analyzability requires more intensive and interactive work, as exhibited in teaching special education students and case-management work carried out by social services agencies. High analyzability enables standardization of work processes, as exemplified in various benefits determination and dispersal functions carried out by government agencies.

As task structures develop, they must be linked and integrated into the broader organization through various methods of coordination and control. These include more complex approaches involving mutual adjustment among organizational colleagues and different levels of management, as well as simpler approaches such as supervisory or expert-based direction (Mintzberg 1979). Here again, middle managers play a crucial role in developing and operationalizing the working relationships among subunits. As they do so, they also develop compliance mechanisms

Exhibit 7.2    **Vital Functions of Middle Managers**

1. *Interpreting and representing their work unit's interests:* Must articulate needs/interests in allocation of resources for personnel and infrastructure, and develop policy responses to daily issues affecting distribution and definition of work unit tasks and responsibilities.

2. *Lending and securing assistance:* Much time is spent finding areas in which a middle manager's subunit can be helpful to other subunits of the organization, as well as to external entities, and not be hurt in negotiations over turf responsibilities.

3. *Developing organizational relationships:* Must manage interdependent relationships with other work units in the accomplishment of shared tasks (a "linking/spanning function"). This includes fostering routine coordinative relationships with external suppliers, regulators, and clients, as well as with one's own strategic managers.

4. *Leveraging others' time:* Takes on ill-defined tasks and vague mandates to determine their significance for superiors and subordinates, thus saving their time for other work.

5. *Interpreting and negotiating what "good service" means:* Public entities often encounter uncertainty and controversy over appropriate means as well as goals. Middle managers frequently help develop and/or interpret standards that define "good service" at all levels of the agency. They must also help mediate the tensions among competing standards imposed by external regulators and suppliers.

6. *Ensuring accountability in the context of diffused power and authority:* Must translate implications and influence of multiple sources of authority over the organization in coherent, operational terms. Must acquire legitimate authority to act on responsibilities with which the agency is saddled. Authority and responsibility are often incommensurate, which means it must be shared with other agencies and jurisdictions. This requires negotiation, coordination, and integration of intra- and interorganizational tasks.

*Source:* Morgan et al. (1996, 360–364).

---

for monitoring performance and enforcing standards (Gross and Etzioni 1985). The sources of compliance are both internal and external. Typical internal mechanisms include accounting/auditing procedures, standard operating procedures, program objectives, job descriptions, performance evaluations, and consensus building. External controls may include legislative and/or executive oversight, imposed competition with rival organizations, budgetary conditions and restrictions, and procedural regulation. There are also unobtrusive control mechanisms that may actually play more powerfully on employees than direct mechanisms.

Herbert Simon (1947) noted that those who set the premises or parameters of decisions exert tremendous control over those who must make the decisions. Thus, the way new employees are trained, the organizational vocabulary they learn, and the workgroup processes to which they are socialized exert a general but very powerful problem- and process-defining influence on their thought and behavior. Andrew Dunsire's (1979) empirical studies of employee behavior revealed that these unobtrusive factors more effectively guide and structure behavior than monitoring and supervision.

## Organizational Conflict and Controversy

Relative to public organizations, Thompson's contingency model overplays the drive to reduce uncertainty about goals, expectations, and effectiveness for the sake of organizational survival. Karen Hult and Charles Walcott (1990) observe that conflict and controversy are pervasive factors that affect structure and behavior in public organizations. In fact, in the American system of government, conflict is built-in through structures such as separation of powers and elaborate

checks and balances that are designed more for the sake of accountability and representation than of effectiveness. Seeking to reduce these factors in public organizations is therefore not always desirable, especially when so many public purposes are inherently ambiguous and must be held in tension with competing values. Moreover, because public organizations play constitutive as well as instrumental roles in society, they acquire more characteristics of political communities in their own right than do most private-sector organizations. Hult and Walcott thus characterize public organizations as political systems or *polities*. Within these polities, a diverse array of organizational and network designs called *governance structures* may be found. Governance structures assist in coping with widely varying roles and responsibilities and in governing relationships among the citizens in the system (Hult and Walcott, chap. 8). The authors refer to the work of designing and arraying public organizational structures as *organization policy* (139): Different network structures are used to knit organizational subunits together and to link a public organization to other organizations in its environment. Through their studies of public agencies, Hult and Walcott developed a typology of governance structures commonly found in public life. Exhibit 7.3 lists types of governance structures and networks they identified.

## ORGANIZATION POLICY AND THE CENTRALITY OF NETWORKS

Hult and Walcott's treatment of networks anticipated growing interest by scholars associated with the New Public Management and New Public Governance movements of the last decade. These scholars focus attention on the flexibility and adaptability of governance networks in public settings marked by decentralization, downsizing, and privatization (Milward and Provan 1998, 1995; O'Toole 1997; Salamon 2002), and by shared-power settings, multilateral global arrangements, and networked community governance (Osborne 2010) A network perspective views public organizations as intersecting webs that rely on distinctive management and policy "tools" such as contracts, grants, loans, vouchers, insurance, and variety of regulatory techniques. Nonprofit and private-sector organizations play an important implementation role as contract providers of many public services (Salamon 2002). Phillip Cooper (2003, 16) aptly characterizes these trends as representing a shift of *policy from authority* to *governance by agreement.* Networks in this literature appear to supplant programs as the dominant unit of analysis, preferring rapid adaptability and transformation of operations to stable, programmed routines. Thus, as might be expected, the literature emphasizes hybrid forms of networks and collaborative leadership and decision making.

The network literature is also related to an older body of scholarship on policy subsystems (cf. Wamsley 1985), emphasizing interorganizational and interpersonal relationships that cohere around policy fields. Policy implementation in a federal system such as ours cannot be confined to any single organization or agency. One must usually map out a complex set of stakeholders made up of organizations, networks, and key individuals who are linked through interdependence of authority, power, location, and resources. Policy subsystems form a unit of analysis in their own right; much more information about how things get done can be gleaned from policy subsystems than from organization-level perspectives alone. For example, in the Prairie County case, local officials formed a network that linked organizations and other key players (like guardians ad litem) to leverage resources, alliances, expertise, and organizational capacity for more effective solutions and coping strategies. This resulted in a new subsystem of closer, coordinative relationships among criminal justice agencies, schools, mining firms, housing authorities, county and town elites, and youth placement centers across the state. One cannot understand how families and children receive social and protective services without tracing implementation processes through the subsystem.

Exhibit 7.3  **Governance Structures and Networks**

**Governance Structures**[1]

- Hierarchical structures—top-down control, information up the chain, focus on rules and accountability, determinate ends and means
- Adjudicative structures—designed for recurring disputes of win/lose or right/wrong type, with rules of procedure to present views before a neutral decision maker
- Adversarial structures—permits advocacy of more than two points of view before a neutral party
- Collegial-competitive structures—legislative or deliberative bodies, reflecting multiple interests, no neutral decision maker
- Collegial-consensual structures—emphasizes agreement on the merits rather than by compromise, multiple revision of proposals, brainstorming, eliciting opinions
- Collegial-mediative structures—tactical maneuvering of interests, logrolling politics, clarification of positions, facilitation by mediators
- Market structures—undirected interplay of individual groups, minimal coercion, unspecified ends other than self-interest

**Governance Networks**[2]

- Bureaucratic—standardized reporting, hierarchical authority
- Team—collaboration and collegiality, strong membership ties
- Decentralized—interactive, competitive, mutual adjustment
- Confrontational—intermittent clashes, limited participants, arbitrative
- Bargaining—rule-structured compromise and negotiation, votes and vetoes
- Consultative—conveying multiple types of expertise to decision makers
- Appeals—reconsideration of decisions by other bodies via hearings and reviews
- Hybrid—networks embedded within networks, transformation of forms over time

[1]Hult and Walcott (1990, chap. 3, 33–47).
[2]Hult and Walcott (1990, chap. 7, 96–109).

The complexity of policy subsystems and reliance on the delivery of public goods and services through third parties has given rise not only to networks but to the emergence of hybrid and conciliatory organizations. In his research on drug courts, Crumpton (2008) showed how the interactions among parties engaged in the work related to drug courts created relatively routine patterns of interaction that began to resemble an organization. Crumpton found that the emergence of organizational functions moved the relationships among parties beyond those typical of a network structure. Similarly, as delivery of policy has become more fragmented, there is evidence that we are creating additional organizations to coordinate and control the work among organizations. These new conciliatory organizations look rather unique. Take for example the Coalition for a Livable Future, which exists in various forms around the country. Members gather regularly to solve public problems that cut across organizational boundaries, among them low-income housing and community health, or greenspace development and alternative transportation planning. The key characteristic is that the conciliatory organization brings groups together regularly to establish goals, align resources, and create implementation plans. These conciliatory models can be analyzed as networks (Kolibam, Meek, and Zia 2010; Milward and Provan 2006; Whitall 2007) or as organizations (Harrison 1994), but they are really a mixture of both.

While the network and policy subsystem literature adds valuable insights to our understanding of policy implementation, it tends to take for granted that most of the players in these systems require support systems, legal portfolios, and powers typically conferred through an organizational home. The literature tends to stress informal, flexible, and adaptive relationships, and to overlook the need for solid institutional grounding. This is especially true of the network literature. Cooper

(2003, 160–162) notes that contracting through leaner, weakened public institutions "is hardly likely to obtain a good deal for the public," and that contracts are still legal instruments that require an infrastructure of carefully developed standards and resources in order to ensure fidelity to the public interest. The capacity of government for maintaining this infrastructure is already stretched to breaking point, while New Public Management doctrine continues to emphasize deregulation and the elimination of red tape. As Cooper notes, more attention needs to be paid to how contracts are actually managed and what the results really look like (2003, 162). This leads inevitably to concerns about adequate support and organization. Hult and Walcott add that this includes paying more attention to the status and conditions of employees as organizational citizens.

## PUBLIC ORGANIZATIONS AS POLITIES

The varied governance structures identified by Hult and Walcott enable employees to interpret, classify, and process problems, and to cope with them over time. Moreover, the structures are grouped into various kinds of political systems in which organizational citizens work out such matters as issues of power allocation, "the extent and nature of members' participation in organizational decision making, and the bases of the political system's legitimacy" (Hult and Walcott 1990, 113–114). These matters transcend the concern for instrumental control that is so prominent in the field of organization theory (Etzioni 1975; Mintzberg 1983; Thompson 1967).

By treating organizations as polities, Hult and Walcott emphasize politics as a central rather than a peripheral and aberrant activity in organizational life. Though politics may at times interfere with good managerial practices, it also structures and conditions them for effective operation. For example, some organizations may adopt attributes of a collectivist polity that emphasizes equal distribution of authority among colleagues in order to manage complex tasks requiring high levels of interaction. Hospitals, universities, analysis shops, and legal organizations (or subunits therein) are good examples. In others, management work may be conditioned by more plural, competitive relations among colleagues and subunits, and thereby require bargaining and compromising practices among disparate yet confederated members. Local community service organizations, for example, may be comprised of formerly separate nonprofit providers who banded together to leverage resources while continuing to maintain their respective missions. This is an approach well worth considering in the Prairie County case. Other organizations (such as police, fire, and military agencies) may reflect the political characteristics of a command polity, with hierarchical, rule-based management practices (Hult and Walcott 1990, 114–116).

Understanding organizations as polities, then, means that management practices contribute in varying ways to an organization's authoritative allocation of values (Easton 1965) and to the determination of who gets what, where, and when through its political economy (Lasswell 1936; Wamsley and Zald 1973). Management thus constitutes a form of governance, and all employee groups participate in it, regardless of their titles. This becomes quite evident in the dynamics of human resources management, wherein employee groups seek to enhance their status, power, and roles in determining work responsibilities, resource allocation, and organizational conditions (see chapter 9). From this perspective, organization design addresses constitutional elements that include criteria of membership, empowerment, rights and benefits, substantive roles and responsibilities, and status. As such, organization design is not treated simply as a matter of unified, rational effort but as a matter of political evolution through decisions based in compromise, tradition, habit, rules, chance, intuition, and competing forms of advocacy (Stone 1997, 233–256).

A narrower expression of the political nature of organizations is visible in the way goals are set within organizations. *Goals* are the desired future condition an organization seeks to obtain (Gross and

Etzioni 1985). Establishing goals is problematic. Even in organizations with rather straightforward policy direction—for instance, supplying domestic water to a city—goals are multiple and often competing. For example, some goals will be related to the policy outcome, in this example delivering water. Other goals will relate to the maintenance of the organization itself. The expectation is that the water district will maintain the facilities, records, and staff competency to meet the overarching goals. It is likely that the water district will adopt goals associated with meeting safe drinking water standards set by the federal government and perhaps others set at state or local levels. Clearly, such a matrix of goals is not established without value trade-offs, that is, politics. This suggests that within organizations, goal setting is a political activity in which decision outcomes are determined by agreement among members of the dominant coalition in the organization, and limited by external policy and the need to maintain legitimacy. A political approach to organizations emphasizes the development, location, and maintenance of power—in this case, the authority to set goals.

A variety of theories have evolved in political science and organizational sociology that treat organizations as political systems. Herbert Simon (1947), Richard Cyert and James March (1963), and Johan Olsen (2001) developed a branch of administrative science that focuses on decisions as a unit of analysis in organizational life. *Decisions* are not simply isolated, discrete entities: they are typically arranged in routinized patterns called *programs* (Simon 1960). As many readers will notice, this is a term used formally as well as informally to designate many public entities. Programs are designated organizational subunits that must be linked and coordinated to achieve broader organizational goals. However, the process is not simply a matter of conscious, rational design, but of programmed competition and advocacy among coalitions of organization interests (Cyert and March 1963). Simon noted that few decisions are ever optimal in nature. Rather, they are "bounded" by limitations of knowledge, experience, habit, and capacity, and therefore require managers to make decisions that are just satisfactory and sufficient for the moment. He coined the term *satisficing* to characterize such decisions (Simon 1947, 38–41; also see Cyert and March 1963).

From these ideas, Cohen, March, and Olsen (1972) derived a model that describes complex organizations as "garbage cans" of programmed solutions which compete to solve problems. Such organizations are made up of coalitions that offer *outputs* from well-established routines and *outcomes* from political battles and compromises with competitors. Graham Allison (1971) used this schema in his classic study of the Cuban Missile Crisis to illustrate how decision models based in programmed routines and political advocacy reveal a reality that differs vastly from the one that emerges in "unified rational" accounts of such affairs. He showed, for example, that the U.S. Air Force predictably lobbied for surgical air strikes as a solution to the presence of nuclear missiles in Cuba, while the U.S. Navy predictably advocated a blockade. Based in part on faulty information from the secretary of defense that surgical air strikes would be "militarily impractical" (Allison 1971), President John F. Kennedy ultimately announced a naval blockade of Cuba to counteract the missile buildup. Applying the same kind of analysis to the Russians revealed that decisions to move missiles to Cuba resulted more from bureaucratic routines and outcomes of political battles than from a rational master plan.

Similarly, Charles Lindblom (1965, 1959) adapted a pluralist political model to organizational life, and he described decision making as a matter of "successive limited comparisons" that allow agencies to adapt incrementally, rather than of "rational-comprehensive" analyses commonly advocated in the traditional management literature. In their limited capacities, according to Lindblom, agencies must rely on existing patterns of resource allocation and status quo operations, and they must adapt slowly at the margins in response to external pressures. Administrators adopt a variety of political tactics and games to finesse these marginal adjustments. Aaron Wildavsky, another highly influential

political scientist, employed this framework in his classic work *The Politics of the Budgetary Process* (1964) to describe the variety of games played by federal agency officials to win favorable budgetary decisions through congressional and executive branch politics. He also illustrated the usefulness of the approach in explaining how policy analysis works in practice (Wildavsky 1979).

Finally, theorists such as Thomas Sergiovanni and John Corbally (1984), Edgar Schein (1985), Vijay Sathe (1985), Gareth Morgan (2006), and J. Steven Ott (1989) devoted attention to the concept of organizational culture as a useful framework for explaining the dynamics of organizational design and behavior. Borrowing from the sociology of professions, research on organizational socialization, and from work on political symbolism and interpretivism,[5] these theorists viewed organizations as systems of highly ingrained, taken-for-granted assumptions, values, and symbols that affect behavior in largely unconscious ways. Organizational culture provides premises, parameters, norms, and expectations that unconsciously guide or induce people to prefer one method over another, to make certain kinds of decisions over others, and to choose certain groups over others in organizational life. Attention is drawn to shared meanings and assumptions, mental models, established rules of the game, organizational climate, guiding metaphors, and integrating symbols (Schein 1993). These are phenomena of human belief, interpretation, and values that structure political relationships and define appropriate means as well as ends. Every organization displays a collage of these phenomena that define the lived experience of organizational life. They define expectations of what constitutes good work or good management in organizational contexts. They define the proper ways of acting and interacting in the organizational community. They also constitute interpretive systems for determining what is real, what is believed, and what is significant about organizational activities and the environment (Daft 1984; Mogren 2011).

Thus, upon entering an organization, newcomers must look for ways of making sense about what is going on. They must learn the ropes and adopt the organizational vocabulary in order to fit in (Ritti and Funkhouser 1977, passim). They have to acclimate to the organization's political culture and subcultures. Only then will they begin to understand what is meant by proper management and organization design, because these are heavily contingent upon the character of the organizational community. Moreover, organizational members must know how to work within the culture to effect changes that will respond appropriately to external influences. Such adaptation is neither purely instinctive nor purely rational. It is negotiated, interpreted, translated, and mediated, and is marked as much by miscommunication and failure as success. This is the messy world of political life where both means and ends are matters of interpretations that can be debated and misconstrued, and tend to be ambiguous, normative, and paradoxical in nature (Stone 1997).

## PUBLIC ADMINISTRATIVE TRADITIONS AND ORGANIZATIONAL POLITIES

Treating organizations as polities with norms, habits, and traditions lends further support to the idea of administrative traditions. In this respect, the governance structures of public organizations are likely to manifest characteristics stemming from the four administrative traditions described in chapters 4 and 6. One or another of these traditions may dominate a particular agency, but all of the traditions are likely to be present in some fashion.

Consider, for example, the Department of Social Services (DSS) in the Prairie County case. As a state agency, it has an elaborate system of policies and resources intended to provide competent and energetic governance. It provides an extensive array of training for its many specialized, merit-protected employees, and organizes local field offices to provide one-stop processing and assessments for assignment of client services, many of which are contracted to private and nonprofit

vendors. The DSS maintains an elaborate, centralized, and computerized records-management and case-tracking system. It also provides aggressive child protection (CP) measures that are carefully structured and balanced by concerns rooted in the tradition of minority rights and access. Children without adequate parental guardianship are provided a court-appointed guardian ad litem, and all child custody cases are authorized, monitored, and supervised through state district courts. Moreover, the DSS touts a philosophy of family preservation and preference for localized child-placement decisions as its overarching mission. This supports norms and expectations arising from the civic and responsive governance traditions, which entail local control, decentralized decision making, and face-to-face governance. It is reflected organizationally in the establishment of multidisciplinary teams, CP teams, and task forces staffed by DSS stakeholders in each community. Many of their decisions are considered binding on the DSS unless deemed contrary to law.

Finally, although the DSS can hardly be characterized as small government, it is certainly a weak and responsive agency. The state legislature (actually a citizen legislature with very short sessions) provides very weak funding, low salaries and benefits, and has established the state court system as a key decision maker and close supervisor over the most serious matters affecting children and families. The agency must respond to a host of stakeholders and relies upon them to deliberate over local case-management decisions, as well as to provide effective services. While the DSS provides some critical infrastructure as a hub for handling benefit eligibility/referral decisions and resolving cases, its ability to adapt to the crisis in Prairie County is almost entirely dependent upon the web of officials and organizations in the county and across the state. Even in the best of times, the agency is widely considered to be weak and feckless. Thus, it displays some of the best and worst attributes of the responsive governance tradition.

As indicated in chapter 6, the four administrative traditions provide sets of obligating norms or expectations that affect all public agencies in terms of both internal and external relationships. In many respects, the governance structures identified by Hult and Walcott (1990) (see Exhibit 7.3) show a clear relation to one or another of these traditions. Hierarchical structures emphasize the efficiency, standard procedures, and accountability associated with the competent and energetic governance tradition. Adjudicative and adversarial structures emphasize rights and due process, constituent advocacy, robust debate, and impartial judges or mediators—all of which ably reflect the minority rights and access to governance tradition. Collegial-competitive structures provide legislative and deliberative capacities, emphasizing representation of interests, transparency, and compromises associated with the responsive governance tradition.

Collegial-consensual, collegial-mediative, and market structures bolster the competent and energetic governance tradition by (1) presenting different means of interpreting ambiguous standards; (2) exploring proper and effective responses to complex problems; (3) developing and testing strategies for accomplishing broad goals under conditions of significant uncertainty, ambiguity, and controversy; and (4) identifying common interests among diverse parties. They enhance the collegial norms of organizational citizenship, promote face-to-face interaction, and enable decentralized decision making. They also promote ties to broader professional communities and associations that regulate professional practices, rights, and perks within the organizational polity. These aspects of organizational community receive more attention in chapter 9, which addresses human resources management.

## AN ORGANIZATIONAL ANALYSIS OF THE PRAIRIE COUNTY CASE

The usefulness of organization theories reviewed in this chapter can be illustrated in application to the Prairie County case. We begin with James Thompson's model because it integrates many

of the theories discussed earlier into its open- and closed-systems perspectives. We will treat the DSS field office as the host organization, though the fact that it is actually part of the much larger state organization must figure into the analysis as well. In light of the turbulent conditions in Prairie County, what internal changes to DSS field office operations can be made to help its personnel cope more effectively?

**Internal Analysis**

Clearly, some attention is needed to levels of managerial responsibility. Prior to the onset of so many challenging problems, most of the field office personnel, including field supervisors, would most likely have been classified as "technical-core" employees in Thompson's schema. That left the field office director, Susan Webb, to handle most middle-management and strategic responsibilities. But the new conditions require some changes in this arrangement. The supervisors need to perform some important middle-management functions to help buffer their caseworkers and benefit specialists from so much acute pressure. First and foremost, they need to shield them from the director's meddling and passive-aggressive tactics. Though this may be difficult, a few changes could make a big difference. For example, the physical layout of the office might be changed in small ways to make it more difficult for the director to hear or see what is going on among the workers. Supervisors could schedule more closed-door meetings with the director to address task-oriented issues and coordination problems. The objective is to engage Webb in ways that emphasize judgment and advice over intervention. Supervisors can accomplish this by interpreting and articulating the issues their work units face and asking for Webb's opinion on how to proceed. They might also propose to the director that one of them be appointed her internal operations chief in order to leverage her time for working on strategic problems. The new internal manager could then serve as a buffer and translator between the street-level employees and Webb. In addition, it is clear that the child protection supervisor needs to assert herself as a buffer between Webb and Judge Grimes.

Judge Grimes presents a strategic challenge that concerns higher-level DSS officials. Webb needs to understand this and use their concerns to her advantage. The judge is essentially an immovable force in the DSS environment, which means the DSS officials need to work out ways to accommodate her, not the other way around. Webb has compromised her own ability to deal with the judge and must therefore rely on others to fill that role. Judge Grimes clearly trusts the CP supervisor, so she is a natural candidate for representing the DSS office in routine court matters. The DSS field administration director, Dan Oglesby, is a likely candidate for handling larger issues with the judge. Webb trusts Oglesby, who has consistently defended her up and down the hierarchy over many years, and he needs to assure his superiors that the judge is accommodated to some degree of satisfaction.

Additionally, Webb and her supervisors need to examine governance structures in the office to see what advantages might be gained with different arrangements. Currently, for example, the benefit specialists are organized bureaucratically, reflecting the strict state and federal legal-eligibility standards with which the agency must comply. The specialists are now using those bureaucratic norms to unduly insulate themselves from their caseworker colleagues, case aides, secretaries, and clients, as well as Webb and the outside world. Likewise, the caseworkers have closed ranks within a tight collegial-consensual structure. Each employee group is hypersensitive about its status, benefits, and powers vis-à-vis the others in the office. While an organizational development intervention would serve well here to break the ice between these groups, some real structural changes are needed to institutionalize more effective communications and to make each group more aware of each other's status needs and interdependencies.

The field office personnel must develop a collegial-mediative structure in which at least the benefit specialists and the caseworkers are "mobilized . . . to seek areas of shared interest and consider settlement" of their differences (Hult and Walcott 1990, 80). This cannot be achieved mechanically in the sense of just imposing such a structure. The parties must buy into the new structure by seeing its advantages and developing more trust between the groups. Moreover, the existing structures must be retained in substantial form because of their functional advantages. Thus, it may be useful to experiment first with network structures that begin breaking individual employees out of their tight, fearful isolation. It may be helpful, for instance, to assign one or two benefit specialists to the multidisciplinary and CP teams, first to gain some appreciation for challenges faced by the caseworkers, and second to increase interaction with key players inside and outside the field office. One of the caseworker supervisors could conduct debriefing sessions after the team meetings to induce the caseworker and benefit specialist team members to interpret and discuss implications.

In addition, the supervisors could establish bargaining and appeals committees (networks) composed of an employee from each of the groups in the office to represent their interests, communicate perspectives, reach operational compromises, and reconsider past practices and decisions that are deemed by one or more groups to have resulted in inequitable distribution of burdens. In short, these are efforts to engage the field office employee groups in real governance issues that matter to them, and then allow them to attempt resolution through these new structural arrangements. The problems these employees face are daunting, but their outlook and capacity may improve as they come to see each other, and their workgroups, as bona fide colleagues with shared interests and a modicum of power to affect their working conditions. A lot will depend, however, on what Webb and other strategic managers in Prairie County can do to help their organizations cope.

## External Analysis

Because we are treating the Prairie County DSS field office as a host organization in this analysis, it makes some sense to treat the broader state DSS as an external player in its environment. Indeed, field office employees around the state often talk about the DSS head office in such terms—and seldom as an ally! Susan Webb and her superior, Dan Oglesby, face some serious challenges with the head office, as well as with the State Division of Human Resources. Prairie County and its neighboring counties are experiencing extraordinary conditions compared to the rest of the counties in the state. Webb and Oglesby need to join with field office directors from neighboring counties in seeking special exemptions from normal procedures affecting training policies, salary and benefits policies, and recruiting practices. They desperately need greater operational flexibility and more resources to cope with the onslaught. Many other state agencies have adopted differential policies of this sort to accommodate regional disparities in conditions, so it may be feasible here.

Second, Webb and Oglesby need to conduct a stakeholder analysis that identifies all the players in the Prairie County area, including other counties that share vital interests and capacities for dealing with the new circumstances. This has already been done to some extent by Webb, who was instrumental in organizing a countywide task force to begin assessing needs and capacities and formulating plans. Plans of this sort typically entail different levels of strategy. For the longer term, they must develop a legislative strategy that gets the attention of key legislators, lobbyists, and other state-level elites. The entire county governance system needs an infusion of state funds and regulatory support. This may come slowly for the human services subsystem, but the criminal justice agencies, schools, and city governments will likely get state resources more quickly. The state legislators representing Prairie County and its neighbors are thus likely to become regulars with the task force.

The new county task force also needs to get the attention of the mining companies as a source of potential funds and increased cooperation. These firms have very deep pockets, and they typically want to please the state and local authorities as part of their strategy for rapid mobilization and resource extraction. They may be supportive, especially to nonprofit vendors and schools, in helping to establish more drug treatment facilities, building new schools and community centers, and bolstering day care and after-school programs. They may also cooperate on developing improved housing in the county for miners now living in squalid "man camps."

Webb and Oglesby also need to team up with local vendors of human services, the school system, and the police agencies in an effort to persuade the mining companies to police their own employees for drug use, especially methamphetamine. Natural gas mining companies that operate in boom cycles desperately need well diggers—lots of them—and, as a result, they often fail to monitor their employees for unlawful activities such as drug use. Webb and Oglesby's team are unlikely to sway the mining officials unless they present a very firm and united front that may ultimately threaten enforcement interventions, leading perhaps to a temporary shutdown of some well-head operations and public embarrassment for the companies. Cultivating relationships with state environmental-quality officials and tactical use of the press may increase their leverage with the mining companies as well.

In this situation, Webb and her task force need to think of themselves as potential regulators, suppliers, customers, and *citizens* in the mining firms' environment. In modest ways, they may be able to influence the way the companies do business in Prairie County, and thereby help buffer and smooth some of the worst effects of the boom on the social services and criminal justice subsystems. Then, in many respects, they must develop new infrastructure through which they can nurture the formation of a new community and county. For example, Webb and her task force must cultivate relationships with developers, local housing and planning authorities in the county, and city and town councils to begin developing more coherent zoning policies and affordable housing options. And perhaps their most difficult challenge involves reaching out to the new population of mine workers, their managers and professional support staff, and new mining-related businesses to help integrate them into the governance of community life.

Even if many of these newcomers will only be there as long as the mining activity lasts, they will want some meaningful quality of life offered through the amenities of the community. Some of them will want to participate in the governance of one part of the community or another, and they should be encouraged to do so. They become a new source of political and community capital. This is very difficult to achieve because many of the native population will resent attempts by "outsiders" to participate. Also, many of the newcomers are temporary employees, and their involvement in the community will often start on negative terms—being watched closely by law enforcement, treated with cold shoulders in many local establishments, and living in squalid conditions on the wrong side of the tracks. Additionally, the large number of minority employees will stand out and be viewed as a threat to the majority population.

Despite these difficulties, Webb and her associates must try to hire and train the spouses of these newcomers, and even their older children, to fill full-time, part-time, and voluntary posts. They need them to help their agencies more adequately represent, relate, and respond to the new population. In a sense, each must coopt the other for the sake of melding disparate cultures and interests through the American tradition of face-to-face civic governance. When the mining boom passes, as it always does, at least a few of the new residents who have become integrated into the community will stay on because of their new ties and help Ward or other affected communities survive the aftermath. Some communities will simply disappear, becoming ghost towns, but those such as Ward are likely to survive because they house key state, county, and

local institutions, are located on key transportation routes, and still maintain some semblance of an agricultural base. The newcomers will join the old-timers in adjusting to a modest but far less turbulent way of life.

## CONCLUSION

The literature on organization theory and behavior provides important insight for public administrators about the complex yet coherent ways in which people live and work together. Much of the literature is couched in terms of managerial control and task effectiveness, even when dealing with human social relations, giving advice along these lines: "Pay attention to your employees' social-psychological needs and they will work harder for management." In the end, as Henry Mintzberg (1983, 2) suggests, getting the job done is largely an organizational function of opposing tasks: "the division of labor into various tasks to be performed, and the coordination of these tasks to accomplish the activity." However, as the field of organization theory and behavior developed, it could not help but embrace more complex and subtle explanations of organizational life as involving much more than instrumental treatment of its inhabitants. As Hult and Walcott attest, there is great benefit in "conceiving of them as political systems, or *polities*," as communities in which they work out much of their daily lives. In important respects, this insight brings us back to the political philosophers of the Enlightenment who focused attention on modern organizations, especially Adam Smith.

As we mentioned earlier, Smith not only described modern industrial organizations and a free market approach to their development but also expressed grave concern about the kinds of effects these organizations have on employees. Smith was an astute philosopher who understood that industrial organizations must develop in a rich political culture that would restrain them and temper them with countervailing principles, traditions, and ways of life defined by the broader communities of which they were a part. These new organizations should serve the interests of the broader communities, not the other way around. However, the quality of life in these communities was often threatened to the extent that employees' energies and mental capacities were dissipated in mindless, repetitive tasks of industrial organization.

It can be argued that the modern organizations of the twentieth and twenty-first centuries have done much to mitigate the dissipative aspects of work through job enrichment, professionalization, and participative management. Norms of democratic governance have seeped into our organizations through sociotechnical and human relations systems theory, and we have begun to embrace the view that these organizations are polities in their own right. These points have merit, but they do not fully allay the concerns of thoughtful critics. For example, Sheldon Wolin (1960) observed that American life in the twentieth century had become so dominated by complex economic and governmental organizations that politics had become almost entirely sublimated within their recesses. As these organizations became stronger, other forms of community weakened, and this resulted in harmful degrees of homogenization among the populace, along with pluralization of organized special interests. The richness of civic engagement and community life withers in the face of instrumental and professional preoccupation with organizational imperatives. Organizational citizens tend to lose their sense of any broader public good toward which to direct their energies.

William G. Scott and David K. Hart (1989) extended this critique by arguing that the dominance of these organizations tends to create undue dependence on a managerial class and also reduces American life to two roles: job roles and leisure roles, both of which are captured by organizational influences. First, one's job-related life is so consuming that it inevitably bleeds

into one's personal life. Second, individuals find it increasingly difficult to separate their job roles from other identity-giving roles, so they increasingly define themselves in terms of their work. Third, managerial authority over work roles grows to encompass authority over more and more of a worker's life. Scott and Hart view this as a slippery slope toward totalitarianism—the end of liberal democracy where individuals determine their own way in life.

The hope they suggest is not in eliminating the managerial class, but in challenging managers to understand the political significance of their responsibilities and act in reference to the broader principles of our political society. As we noted in chapter 6, *public* managers bear special responsibilities to promote a *public* ethic that transcends specific agencies and organizations. And in the spirit of limited government, they must strive to promote heterogeneity rather than homogeneity among the sectors of political society. In order to accomplish this, public managers should steep themselves in the distinctive pedigree of our public administrative traditions. In this chapter, we briefly illustrated how public organizations can employ governance structures that complement these traditions. The following chapter recounts the evolution of public personnel policy as a history of choosing who governs in American society. The character and competencies of the public service determine in large part our capacity to uphold these traditions or to fritter them away.

## STUDY QUESTIONS

1. Briefly summarize the characteristics of Weberian bureaucracy, and discuss the limits of its applicability in terms of human relations theory.
2. Explain the contingency theory approach to organization structure.
3. Using a public or nonprofit organization with which you are familiar, identify which kinds of governance structures (à la Hult and Walcott) are commonly used there to meet its goals and cope with its challenges.
4. In the Prairie County case, assume the role of chief of police in the city of Ward. Given the daunting conditions and changing demographics in Ward and the outlying county, what internal changes to the police department would you make? Then, what strategic actions would you take with respect to the broader community, county, and state?
5. In the Prairie County case, assume that you run the private mental health firm that exercises a statewide monopoly. Analyze the environmental conditions presented in the case and develop a strategy you think will (a) adequately serve the rapidly growing number of referrals to your Prairie County facility, (b) help the broader human services subsystem in Prairie County cope with the challenges it faces, and (c) maintain or enhance your domain over mental health services in the state. What theories in this chapter helped you in developing your strategy?

## NOTES

1. Weber (1864–1920) identified bureaucratic organizations as the defining characteristic of the modern political economy emerging in the late 1800s. His broad, comparative studies of ancient and contemporary society influenced scholars well before his works were translated into English and made available in America. Weber's analysis of bureaucracy is scattered among a number of his works. The most influential collection of his work was published in a translation by Hans H. Gerth and C. Wright Mills in 1946.

2. Key characteristics enumerated here follow Gross and Etzioni (1985), Perrow (1986), and W. Richard Scott (1992).

3. From Luther Gulick and Lyndall Urwick (1937).

4. In *Chester I. Barnard and the Guardians of the Managerial State* (1992), William G. Scott analyzes the history of this influential circle of scholars in Boston who were funded by newly formed philanthropies that served to reinforce behaviors most appropriate to large organizations—behaviors that were antithetical to liberal democracy. According to Scott, the emerging social sciences served the same organizational masters.

5. On the sociology of professions, see Vollmer and Mills (1966), Becker et al. (1961), and Van Maanen (1976). On organizational socialization, see Kaufman (1960) and Whyte (1956). On political symbolism and interpretivism, see Edelman (1964), Bolman and Deal (1997), Daft (1984), and Berger and Luckmann (1967).

CHAPTER 8

# A POLITICAL HISTORY OF PUBLIC PERSONNEL ADMINISTRATION

> The relation of citizen to public official, of governed to governor, has always posed a central problem of politics, whatever the form or theory of government. When in a democracy the magistrate is declared to be at once both master and servant, the difficulties are only compounded.
>
> *(Paul P. Van Riper 1958, 1)*

It is common to think of public personnel as the ultimate in stultifying, internal bureaucratic practice. Managers envision rigid rules and elaborate procedures that smother them in paperwork and seriously limit their flexibility in hiring, promotion, discipline, and dismissal. It seems impossible to exercise any meaningful prerogatives of leadership. Employees perceive flawed evaluation systems, incentive systems made up mostly of sticks and very few carrots, job classification systems that seem designed to hold their wages and benefits low, and measures to keep their prospects for upgrades and promotions dim at best. The whole field of practice seems mired in legal rules and managerial techniques that boast objectivity rather than effectiveness as their primary virtue. Wallace Sayre's criticism of the field in 1948 still seems relevant despite many efforts at reform: "Techniques triumph over purpose" (1948, 134).

Yet, when we look to its history, we see the field of public personnel administration not merely as an awkward assemblage of bureaucratic techniques but as a matter of high politics. In the quotation at the beginning of this chapter, Paul Van Riper captures an essential governing tension that lies at the heart of public personnel administration: Americans have always distrusted governing power, fearing its abuse (the "King George Problem"), but they also want public officials who will serve them efficiently and govern effectively (the "George Washington Problem"). Moreover, they want officials to think as they think and feel as they feel, while vigorously protecting their rights (the "Shays' Rebellion Problem"). In short, they expect their officials to be both servant and master. Such ambivalence makes public personnel administration a contested field of practice. It infuses the field with cross-cutting purposes that are bound to frustrate both political and managerial agendas.

Attempts at making employees an efficient and flexible arm of management are often frustrated by attempts to protect their rights and avoid improper manipulation. Efforts at making public servants more responsive to political leaders are countered by political opposition and interbranch rivalry.

199

Moves to empower and reward public servants for making decisions on our behalf are inevitably restrained by those who fear waste, abuse, and lack of accountability. And those who seek to fill public offices with the "right" people can expect challenges regarding the proper criteria.

These tensions have conditioned public personnel practice in the United States from the beginning. They persist as matters of fundamental political principle, despite the increasing sophistication of our management theories and the vastly increased size and complexity of our governing machinery. This chapter traces these tensions through the historical development of public personnel as manifested in changing views about proper qualifications for office. We revisit the eras discussed in chapter 5 to see how political leaders determined who was fit for public office. We discuss which criteria were used and illustrate how changes in the character and staffing of the public service came about in pursuit of those criteria.

This history exposes the "inherent politicality of public personnel policy" (Rosenbloom 1985, 3), and thereby sheds light on how to improve its practices. The political tensions that mark the field are not irrational. They do not destine us to create persistently failing systems. Rather, they contribute to sensible and varying explanations of what constitutes an effective public service, and they remind us of the need for balance among competing criteria. Such tensions are coherent and cyclical in their manifestation and thus can be anticipated and perhaps channeled to beneficial effect. At the very least, public officials who understand personnel history can develop better ways of coping with its dynamics.

## WHO SHALL GOVERN?

One of the highest political challenges in any regime is choosing who shall govern and in what manner. The U.S. Constitution provides basic position descriptions for our top officials and arrays them in a structure calculated to frustrate their exercise of power. In other words, job design was not solely intended to achieve efficiency and effectiveness. As noted in earlier chapters, the founders sought to check and balance effective governing power with precautions against its abuse.

The operative principle behind checks and balances is James Madison's concept of partial agency. In *The Federalist Papers* (1788, Federalist Nos. 47–49, quoted in Rossiter 1961), he explained how each branch of government should possess sufficient powers of the other branches to resist their encroachment. For example, the president holds legislative power in the form of a veto, while the legislative branch holds significant executive power over finances, appointments of high officials, and treaties. Paradoxically, it is the partial blending of these powers that ensures a measure of both institutional independence and interdependence. Each branch can stave off encroachments by the other branches, and yet must cooperate with them to effectuate policy. As Madison indicated in the Federalist No. 47 (1788/1961), a strict separation of powers would cause government to grind to a halt, and that would be as bad as the other extreme—the tyranny of unified governing power. Blending the powers helps strike a balance between the extremes.

The effects of partial agency among the branches percolate throughout the subordinate offices of public administration, creating interdependence and competition for influence over agency employees and their decisions. For example, legislatures have historically controlled pay and benefits and induced cooperation on appointments at all levels. The courts have scrutinized employment conditions and practices, protecting managerial prerogatives as well as the constitutional rights of employees. Amidst these pressures, the executive branch has jealously sought expansive administrative power over public employees and has often taken the initiative in defining the character of the public service. This covetous interplay reflects competing views of what is needed most for the successful governance of our multiple democratic systems.

In each of the major eras of our history, the character of the public service has shifted to accommodate changing views of what counts as successful governance. The qualifications can be grouped into four classes of criteria. Each era reflected its own distinctive conceptions of *merit*, of *appropriate character*, of *representativeness*, and of *proper political ideals*. We will show how these have changed over time, and how they affect current personnel policy. For ease of comparison, Exhibit 8.1 summarizes the basic elements of these conceptions by era.

## The Founding Era, 1789–1828

It is no surprise that the founders wanted people of similar sensibilities working in public service. The founding era is accurately described in many personnel texts as the era of government by gentlemen. As former British subjects, most Americans from this era had inherited a strong sense of social class. The American leadership of the founding era displayed strong aristocratic tendencies that required modification for life in a republic. In that spirit, many of the founders subscribed to the idea that republican governments should be staffed with people who possessed natural talents and dispositions for the work of governing. In principle, this "natural aristoi" could come from any class, and that distinguished their approach from the aristocratic societies of Europe, where qualifications were determined by bloodlines. The founders advocated a type of *meritocracy* that they believed could be fitted to a republic. Alexander Hamilton demonstrated this during the Revolutionary War, when he convinced George Washington to make all military enlistees eligible for promotions into officer ranks based on their performance (Mitchell 1957). After ratification of the new Constitution, President Washington established merit as a primary criterion for appointments. It figured prominently in the founders' overarching conception of "fit character" for public office (White 1948). Strategically, merit played a critical role in the founders' attempts to win the loyalty of the people to the new national government. They believed that competent people with adequate powers would conduct administration more effectively than most Americans were accustomed to seeing at state and local levels (Hamilton 1787, Federalist Nos. 17 and 27, quoted in Rossiter 1961). Getting results would impress people.

The founders, however, could hardly avoid defining competence in ways that favored their own elite class. They were, after all, the best educated and best prepared for public life. They viewed merit mainly in terms of their own social and educational backgrounds. Thus, they conceived of it largely as a matter of a liberal arts education combined with experience (Adair 1974; Green and Zinke 1993; McDonald 1985; White 1948). They believed broad learning enabled people to put matters into perspective, to see things in proportion and balance, and thereby to exercise wise judgment. Formal education included political history and philosophy, classical and modern literature, and foreign languages, along with schooling in the modern science of the day. The course of study was extensive, highly disciplined, and largely unavailable to the rest of the American population.

A good education, however, was insufficient unless tested under the pressures and commitments of institutional practice. The founders assumed that a person's judgment would be tempered by the circumstances of public life. Over time, an individual would gain general knowledge of the requirements of governance, specific knowledge of institutional and political contexts, and a sense of the unique requirements of institutional practice. In this fashion, officials would acquire significant decision-making skill. Such skill should not be equated with subsequent notions of technical or formulaic expertise, which are based upon the systematic collection and analysis of data. Rather, it more closely approximated the types of tacit knowledge described in chapter 2,

Exhibit 8.1  **General Qualifications for Office by Political Era**

| Merit | Appropriate Character | Representativeness | Proper Political Ideals |
|---|---|---|---|
| **Founding Era, 1789–1828** | | | |
| • Merit considered primary criterion for appointments<br>• Played critical strategic role in attempts to win loyalty of people<br>• Viewed in terms of founders' social and educational backgrounds, i.e., formal education coupled with experience<br>• Idea of merit similar to Greek concept of practical wisdom | • Calm under pressure<br>• Prudent in decision making<br>• Record of respect and integrity in public life (regard for reputation)<br>• Shunned any actions designed to stir and exploit controversy for political gain | • Mainly strategic concerns<br>• Geographic representativeness was important—critical for winning state support for new national government and bringing local views to administrative agencies<br>• Need for "sharing" government jobs was recognized | • Prospective employees required to be committed to newly created governing system and ideals embodied in the Constitution<br>• Partisanship should be resisted; public officials should stand above factions and pursue an overall public interest |
| **Jacksonian Era, 1829–1869** | | | |
| • Diligence and ordinary common sense were only requirements<br>• Government jobs could be performed by industrious determination | • Loyalty became means of accountability<br>• Proper behavior was spelled out in rules | • Democratic ideals<br>• Political parties and representative bureaucracy aimed to make public office more accessible to average people | • Personal and partisan loyalty viewed as important to achieve a real democracy and political responsiveness |
| **Gilded, Populist, and Progressive Eras, 1869–1921** | | | |
| • Technical merit was primary criterion; open testing for general competencies took place<br>• Took ideas from technical education; idea of "neutral experts" to create effective government (the business model) | • Dedicated, efficient, technically minded, trained public servants<br>• Employees trained for long-term service; "organization man"<br>• Loyalty expected (IMPLIED) | • Strictly representative: Pendleton Act provided for hiring federal employees based on proportions of state populations | • Basic honesty and commitment to ideas of public trust—obligations should transcend partisanship and embrace neutrality<br>• Businesslike efficiency and dedication expected<br>• Public officials expected to be an efficient representative of the people |

## New Deal Era, 1933–1954

- Professional model; university training in technical knowledge, adoption of work standards, professional associations
- Neutral competence expected
- Independent-minded and professional experts

- Collegial, group, and team-based attitude expected
- Dedicated to work; professional
- Deference to hierarchy and formal authority
- Strong faith in expertise and what it could achieve

- Pluralistic, organizational politics—administrators work with many different actors
- Agencies became interest groups in their own right
- Idea grew that public service should represent the various and contending interests of society; geographic representation was no longer sufficient

- Idea of expert-based "systems" and problem solving replaced partisanship
- Public administration centralized and held responsible to the executive; a managerial image

## Civil Rights and the Great Society, 1954–1976

- Public service should be neutral and technically competent

- Shift from "organization man" to democratic individualism; possession of equal rights with all others

- Affirmative action policies followed by a "goals and timetables" approach to reach real equality in the workplace
- Idea of representation expanded to include all historically underrepresented groups in society

- Many distrusted and challenged prevailing authority
- Public administrators should make decisions based on mediation, collaboration, and consensus; should govern "with" rather than "over" the electorate

## Entrepreneurial Era, 1976–present

- Public employees should possess entrepreneurial imagination blended with professional and technical competency
- Should be risk takers, problem solvers, continuous improvers

- Recognition that government employees are no different from private employees in terms of self-interest; blurring of distinctions between public, private, and nonprofit sectors

- Domain-expanding officials replaced by those more sympathetic and responsive to wishes of silent majority
- "Old guard" politicians replaced by those responsive to constituents

- Restoration of states' rights, free markets, and freedom from governmental constraints; governments distrusted and limited government desirable
- Entrepreneurialism is highly valued
- Privatization preferred to public provision of goods and services

such as prudential understanding, transitory knowledge, and critical knowledge. Their idea of merit had more in common with the Greek concept of practical wisdom (Morgan 1990; Spicer 1995) than with modern notions of technical expertise. In modern parlance, they preferred prudent judgment to analytical decision making (Storing 1980).

The founders' conception of merit dovetailed with their idea of appropriate character. They wanted people who displayed proper dispositions for public service. They should be calm under pressure and prudent in their decisions, and they should exhibit a record of respect and integrity in their public lives. They believed such virtues could be cultivated and sustained among those who prized public honor and "regard for reputation" (Adair 1974; McDonald 1979). The founders believed that one's reputation was a person's most prized possession. Damage to reputation meant the loss of dignity—a fate worse than death to many of them. The importance of preserving one's honor is reflected in the famous duel in 1804 between Aaron Burr and Alexander Hamilton, in which Hamilton lost his life at the age of 49 because neither party would back down from a perceived attack on their honor. Douglas Adair (1974, passim) explained that this regard for reputation hinged upon the founders' passion for fame. Fame was distinguished from popularity in that it entailed deep concern for how future generations would view their policies. This required public figures to take the long view of their public actions and measures. Demagogues sought popularity for immediate personal gain or glory, while statesmen sought the high regard of posterity. Most of the founding generation shunned actions designed to stir and exploit controversy for political gain. George Washington epitomized the calm reserve and good judgment sought by his peers. Friend and foe alike noted his intense regard for reputation (Flexner 1969; McDonald 1979).

This founding-era concern for appropriate character played into the design of public jobs. Alexander Hamilton and many of his Federalist colleagues strove to provide benefits suitable to an honorable public service. They argued that officials should have competent powers and sufficient duration in office to see their systematic plans and policies come to fruition (cf. Hamilton 1788/1961, Federalist No. 72, passim). The executive branch should generally exhibit unity in the form of single heads of departments, thereby enhancing individual distinction and encouraging decisive action. Officials should be compensated sufficiently to live in a manner suitable to their station and possess high-quality dress and other symbols of office as a badge of respect and dignity (Green 1987). These attributes and conditions were characteristic of a nascent career system (Crenson 1975; Van Riper 1958; White 1948, 13, 362).

The combination of education, experience, and fit character contributed to mature judgment, according to most officials of the era. The presence of hierarchy did not imply mindless subservience by those occupying positions in the lower ranks; rather, it provided what Lynton Caldwell (1964, 96–97) described as "a working unanimity among the members of an administrative family" without "sacrifice of conscience and judgment" and with "higher duty to the community." Hamilton, writing under the pseudonym Lucius Crassus, argued that the Constitution "excludes the dangerous pretension that [administrative officials are] mere creature[s] of the executive," because they take "an oath of fidelity to the government, but no oath of any kind to the President" (1802). Employees should display a mature and independent perspective about official responsibilities. This formulation seemed to work, as the period is noted for competent and stable governance at all levels (Van Riper 1958; White 1948).

Both the Federalist and Republican administrations of the era recognized that geographic representativeness must be considered as a factor in hiring. They viewed it as critical to winning support among the state populations for the new national government and bringing local views and status to bear in the far-flung administrative agencies. Steady employment was hard to find, and the national government quickly became a significant employer. Any impression of geographic

favoritism would quickly invite schism among the states and hamper effective operation of field offices. Though balance was sought, merit and fit character would occasionally take a back seat to this principle as a matter of political prudence. For a new and shaky republic, it became a significant criterion for recruitment and selection.

Debate over the proper political criteria appropriate for government service coalesced around two problems. The more immediate one concerned whether a prospective employee was fully committed to republican principles and to the Constitution that embodied them. Many Americans lacked confidence that the new national government could succeed, especially given the daunting political and economic problems it faced. They also feared that British loyalists would easily subvert the new government and work to restore the monarchy. Unfortunate episodes with confiscation and sedition laws arose from this threat. Letters of reference would often mention in very polite terms the suitability or unsuitability of an applicant's political ideals, meaning primarily one's loyalty to the new republic.

The second problem ran to the heart of the founders' conception of good government: It addressed the age-old issue of factions. The founders believed officials should stand above factional strife and pursue a transcending public interest. This ideal was reinforced by their focus on public reputation. Public officials should take the long view of things, always keeping matters of immediacy and narrow interest in context. Thus, in letters of recommendation, they stressed assessments of the applicant's regard for reputation, and of factional leanings that might tempt the candidate to compromise public interests.

This mix of qualifications for office served the young nation very well for about 40 years. It could not last, however, as Americans abandoned the elite orthodoxy of the founders. The founders were almost unanimous in their distrust of democracy. For them, it signified the dangers of mob rule and related perversions of the republican form of government. They designed a carefully restrained republic that they hoped would "filter in" the best characters, a "natural aristocracy," for office (Epstein 1984). But their hopes faded in relatively short order. The era of rule by gentlemen soon lost its luster and gave way to populist impulses.

Although the Federalist and Republican eras have been judged very favorably for the quality of their administration, they did exhibit flaws that eventually fed desires for reform (Van Riper 1958; White 1948, 1951). The gentlemanly virtues were plainly elitist in character and resented by increasing numbers of common folk who felt excluded from government jobs. Their bitter sentiments first found expression in state legislative houses and set the stage for interbranch squabbles over every sort of employment condition. Resentment grew over the budding career system. Dominated as it was by lawyers, and with relatively higher pay and benefits of office, it became a symbol of social and political inequality. The reserved stability of the government, achieved by long duration in office, came to symbolize vested rights to office for a privileged and distant few.

Despite claims to the contrary, Federalist and Republican administrations did occasionally manipulate patronage for partisan and familial reasons, and this increased with successive administrations to the point where many viewed the government as being dominated by partisan bias and nepotism. Jefferson tried to restrain these practices when he "devised the useful doctrine that there should be something of an *equal division of the offices* between the parties" (Van Riper 1956, 22, emphasis added). But he preferred to staff the positions with those of gentlemanly persuasion, and so the plan could not last.

Finally, the design of federal policies as a spur to economic development was strongly biased in favor of increasingly powerful regional and national commercial interests. Resentment grew rapidly at state and local levels, stimulating new partnerships between party machines and local businesses. Political parties grew in significance at these levels well before establishing a robust

national presence. They propagated the view that the government of the Federalists and Republicans had lost touch with the broader citizenry. Andrew Jackson, on the other hand, represented a new image and hope for the nation—one suited to feverish, entrepreneurial democracy.

## The Jacksonian Era, 1829–1869

Andrew Jackson entered office as a reformer, though one with a conservative bent. Inspired by Jefferson, he promised to restore "republican simplicity" and "virtue" to the government (White 1951). He asserted that the federal government had become much too large, complicated, and meddling. It needed paring back in favor of states' rights, laissez-faire commerce, and local self-determination. The ranks of government employees were out of touch with the emerging masses of common folk. Their numbers should be reduced, and many of those remaining should be replaced with more representative and responsive officials. Jackson advocated the reform doctrine of "rotation in office" as a means to those ends (Crenson 1975, chap. 1, passim).

The doctrine drew its power from the fateful "decision of 1789," in which the first U.S. Congress ceded to the president the power to remove certain subordinates at will. The immediate decision affected only the secretary of foreign affairs, but the power broadened steadily by assertion and was quickly accepted as custom. Jackson exploited the custom to democratize the public service while greatly expanding presidential power. He rotated many existing employees out of their positions and filled them with his loyal followers. In the process, he proffered new definitions of merit, appropriate character, representativeness, and proper political ideals for the public service.

As we indicated in chapter 5, the principle of *merit* as understood by Jackson emphasized common sense tested by the rough, meager circumstances of common folk. Though the extent of his patronage hiring has been exaggerated (Van Riper 1958; White 1951), Jackson did bring with him a significant number of partisan colleagues whose experience and competencies were shaped in small enterprises and in state and local political offices. Many of his peers had gained experience as entrepreneurs working in small, personal organizations that flourished during the era (Crenson 1975). Having succeeded mainly through force of will and gritty common sense, they believed that government jobs could be mastered in the same fashion. This prompted Jackson's assertion that "the duties of all public offices are . . . so plain and simple that men of intelligence may readily qualify" (Richardson 1899, II:449). This proved very appealing to the masses of immigrants and local political leaders who jealously eyed federal jobs. The image of a proper public service changed accordingly.

The Jacksonian view of appropriate character started with the virtues of simplicity, frugality, integrity, and harmony commonly attributed to Jeffersonians. Jackson touted these attributes and, contrary to popular impressions, demonstrated them with calm reserve and moderation through much of his later political career (White 1951). However, he and his associates also added strict personal loyalty to the mix, and this would unwittingly subvert much of his program and tarnish partisan leadership thereafter.

Jackson introduced a type of personalism in which loyalty constituted the essential glue for his harmonious system (Crenson 1975, 64, 70–85). As Matthew Crenson has shown, the Jacksonians abandoned the distinction between public and private interests: "The units of administration were not offices or job descriptions, but human beings, and it was difficult to bisect a bureaucrat so that his private interests could be held at arm's length from the public interest" (1975, 83). This held true in local contexts, where ties of kinship, association, and community often superseded obligations to public office, and it made public service susceptible to sleaze and corruption on a large scale. In this environment, enforcing strict personal loyalty became the principal means of holding

public servants accountable and muting conflicts among them. If the executive is responsible, his subordinates will be too. This simple logic spawned a new kind of employment relationship, as well as a new kind of presidency.

Ironically, as Crenson illustrates, it introduced an early version of faceless, bureaucratic functionaries who were highly responsive to their patron. They became anonymous agents of the leader's will. A system for policing loyalty also emerged, and part of it entailed writing rules that prescribed minimal standards for compliance. These rules proliferated in short order because so many of the new officeholders lacked much in public etiquette and integrity. Proper behavior had to be spelled out. Despite such efforts, Jackson and subsequent presidents suffered through one scandal after another. Party machines developed to help allocate as well as police the patronage. The public service became increasingly politicized as patronage increased, and the reform spirit of rotation gave way to a greedy scramble for spoils.

The Jacksonians are justly famous for making representativeness in public service more democratic. Paul Van Riper (1958) describes it as the only truly class-conscious change in representation in American history. Though accompanied by corruption and scandal, the partisan/patronage system performed a vital service to the nation by bringing the "ideals of freedom, equality, and political democracy . . . to fruition" through staffing of public offices (Van Riper 1958, 32). The changes underscored Anti-Federalist criticism that the constitutional scheme of representation was flawed and inadequate from the start (Storing 1980). Political parties and a more representative bureaucracy added much needed complements to that scheme and made public office more accessible to the average person.

The political ideals of the period were carried into the routine and daily functions of public service as a result of its partisan and local democratic focus. Personal and partisan loyalty doubled as a political ideal as well as a desired character trait. The new ideal of parties as valid and essential expressions of the will of the people found its way increasingly into patronage removals and hiring. However, in practice, this ideal received only modest attention in Jackson's administration, and in most subsequent administrations a significant number of key posts (especially in the military) remained in the hands of long-tenured officials. In fact, Van Riper characterized the Jacksonian era as a selectively partisan, dual employment system. Those agencies with highly dispersed local offices, such as the postal and customs agencies, were most affected by rotation and spoils practices, while other agencies (or significant parts of them) retained much of their career character. Nevertheless, tinges of partisanship spread throughout all agencies because of generalized fear and uncertainty among employees about their jobs. Partisanship thereby elevated the ideal of political responsiveness in public employment to a high principle of democratic orthodoxy. It lent great strength to the responsive governance tradition, ebbing and flowing in tension with the competent governance tradition established by the Federalists.

### The Gilded, Populist, and Progressive Eras, 1869–1921

Though the Gilded, Populist, and Progressive eras displayed marked differences, they are treated together here for two important reasons. First, with the end of the Civil War (1861–1865) came a steadily growing conviction that the patronage system had to be reformed. The reforms took shape in the Gilded and Populist eras, resulting in passage of the Pendleton Act of 1883 (ensuring government jobs were awarded on the basis of merit) and a variety of electoral reforms that broke up the closed ranks of political parties. These achievements provided the platform for more extensive personnel reform during the Progressive Era. Second, the three eras held in common the emergence of complex organizations and an interdependent national economy as dominant features

of American society. These externally driven forces clashed with Populist forces in ways that made it possible for Progressives to mark out new paths in political and administrative development.

The years following the Civil War were marked by new extremes in patronage abuses and interbranch disputes over control of the public service. Andrew Jackson had helped expand presidential power through patronage in the pre–Civil War years. After the war, however, Congress achieved dominance over the executive and the public service by much the same means. This was inevitable, not only as a reaction to the assertion of new powers by presidents, but also because of the sheer scale of managing growing numbers of political appointments to widely dispersed offices. Members of Congress had routinely inundated presidents with patronage referrals and eventually formed political machines of their own, linking federal operations in their home states with local political machines. Through these machines, they could wield far greater influence over their local constituencies and thereby control the referral mechanisms for most public offices. Without significant staff support (which did not come until after 1939), presidents could do little but acquiesce and appease as a means of bargaining for influence of their own.

During the postwar Reconstruction effort, President Andrew Johnson (in office 1865–1869) sought to expand his powers through what appeared to be a new presidential political machine. Congressional opponents quickly unified to pass the Tenure of Office Act, which limited the president's removal power. The congressional decision of 1789 to cede removal of subordinate officers to the president came suddenly under challenge. Johnson defied the act, and the House reacted by passing impeachment resolutions. The tradition of broad presidential removal power was upheld by one vote in the U.S. Senate trial, but Johnson's victory was Pyrrhic. Congress successfully asserted its dominance over the next several presidential administrations. Patronage practices then descended to mad partisan scrambles for spoils, turning over as much as three-quarters of the employees in some agencies with each new election. The muckraking press made corruption and abuse of the patronage system the constant focus of attention, giving strong impetus for public service reform.

Public personnel reform also became a growing issue of concern because of the rapid growth of large-scale organizations and the need for the expertise to manage them successfully. Since we have already reviewed these developments in chapters 5 and 7, we will simply note that they were important in shaping the thinking about the kind of reform that was needed to eliminate the abuses of patronage politics. While the Gilded Age began with the simple impulse to end the corruption of patronage and bring moral individuals back into government (Van Riper 1958; White 1958), it ended with a broader focus on acquiring the technical competence necessary to make large organizations work well.

The civil service reforms culminating in the landmark Pendleton Act of 1883 had the modest moral goal of providing open, competitive examinations as a merit-based alternative to patronage for selecting lower-level employees and retaining them for a full career of service (Van Riper 1958). But it soon became evident that much more than good test-taking skills was required. The civil service could no longer sustain the simplistic distinction between clerks and politicos of earlier periods. New types of employees were added to the ranks in growing numbers, most of them coming with new technical skills and professional training in emerging specializations. Women too gained entry into these ranks, at first occupying the lower-level clerical and technical grades. By the beginning of the twentieth century, Populist and Progressive reformers pursued far more ambitious goals to open the political process with extensive constitutional and election reform, and to staff governments with people whose qualifications and bearing were fitted to the new social and organizational culture.

The rise of large, complex organizations made technical merit the prime criterion for public office. The interest in a technical version of merit was fueled by two separate impulses. First, the

world of business was awash in the allure of machines, invention, and technical mastery (Johnson 1991). It was commonly assumed that a technically trained, business-minded person was apt to be diligent and efficient, keeping an impersonal, steady eye on the regularity of tasks and functions and avoiding the distractions of politics. Several major educational reforms also spurred interest in the technical version of merit: (1) the passage of the Morrill Acts of 1862 and 1890, which established land-grant colleges dedicated to education in agriculture and mechanic arts; (2) the establishment of public high schools for improved general and vocational/technical education; and (3) the emergence of multidisciplinary universities focused heavily on science, technology, and professional education (Mosher 1982, 47–50).

Bringing technical education and the business ethos to government became an attractive package for the advocates of reform. This blend was used politically to heighten the contrast with the turmoil and dysfunction of partisan spoils. Reformers argued that creating a system based on technical merit would make government so efficient and effective that tax increases would be unnecessary as government grew into its new responsibilities. Business leaders who felt hampered by the waste and abuse of the patronage system found the argument very appealing (White 1954, 297). The combination of technical education and business ethos with the moralistic spirit of reform gave powerful effect to the idea of a politically neutral civil service.

Nowhere was the new technical ethos more prominent than in local government reform. The new council-manager form of government envisioned engineers, not politicians, running the machinery of local governments. All aspects of local public service, from settlement houses to public works departments, should be made over in the compelling image of a harmonious, efficient, custodial state run by diligent and caring technicians. Much of the Progressive reform agenda grew out of grassroots experiments and initiatives based on this assumption.

The criterion of appropriate character followed suit with this image of dedicated, efficient, technical-minded and trained public servants. Like their business counterparts, public employees required new habits and disciplines fitted to large-scale organizations. Reform in public school systems emphasized new habits appropriate to industrial society such as timeliness, regimentation, steady adherence to rules, and efficiency of effort—habits that encourage unquestioning obedience to managers (Eden 1963). Modern universities emerged as socializing institutions for new science-based professions with distinct cultural norms, barriers to entry, and control over development and application of knowledge (Green, Keller, and Wamsley 1993; Mosher 1982). A host of new professions were established in this period, many formed specifically to support governmental functions—forestry, city planning, and social work among them.

One of the most important roles that emerged was that of the *manager*, whom Frederick Taylor (1911/2006) identified as the person responsible for the *planning* of work rather than the *doing* of work. An important unintended consequence of this development was a de-enriching of work for those "doing" the work. More important, this change created a new class of people responsible for the organizations dominating social, economic, and political life. Consequently, as Scott and Hart (1989) point out, a major shift of power occurred in society, cementing the rising influence of organizations in modern life.

These new professionals were trained for long-term organizational service and, accordingly, required reorientation of their loyalties to life in organizational communities. Such reorientation became possible as public servants gained independence from partisan influence and secured longer duration in office. The Pendleton Act prohibited obligations to render political service, to contribute to political funds, or to use one's authority to coerce partisan activity from any covered employee (White 1954, 329). Subsequent presidential orders would prohibit removal from office for any reason but cause (Johnson and Libecap 1994, 67).

In short, a new idea of fit character emerged, and it is perhaps best described as the rise of "organization man" (Whyte 1956, passim). This was Weber's educated functionary, loyal to organization life and process, molded to its purposes, and rewarded with steady pay and a stable career. This new model of character did much more than transform public organizations. It changed the nature of American politics as well. As Sheldon Wolin (1960) described it, our politics was sublimated into organization life and expression. A political sense of the whole, of a "public" good, gradually gave way to pluralization of public policy as expressed through organizational interests (Bentley 1935; Dahl 1961; Dahl and Lindblom 1953; Lowi 1969).

The criterion of representativeness in the public service during this period was bolstered at the federal level by the addition of state-by-state hiring quotas. The Pendleton Act made explicit provision for hiring based on proportion of state population as a more systematic method of representation. In practice, it played out even more effectively than the patronage system and became a matter of some boasting in the battle to reduce patronage practices (Van Riper 1958, 101; White 1954, 302). It reinforced a new argument that party patronage actually frustrated democratic rule by closing access to office and policymaking on the part of the general populace. Under the patronage system, corrupt party elites and their partners in big business controlled governments for their own ends. Accordingly, reform efforts targeted political parties and governments in an effort to make them more responsible and representative.

Partisan opponents retorted that the civil service reforms would create an aristocracy of effeminate schoolboys (Stivers 2002a) and educated elites (White 1954) appointed by examining boards who knew nothing of the particular duties to be performed in specific offices. Furthermore, as increasing numbers and grades of employees came under centralized civil service protection, concern arose that incoming administrations would lose the ability to effectively shape and direct policies in the departments and bureaus. Administrators would lose control over their subordinates because they could not appoint them (White 1954, 295, 319–21). Though perhaps disingenuous under the circumstances, these retorts provided early warning signs of the problems inherent in emerging public personnel systems. At the time, however, they could not stand in the face of the glaring weaknesses evident in patronage practices. Experts, it was argued, would be both more responsive and more competent in their governance.

The proper political ideals for the public service during the Gilded, Populist, and Progressive periods began with restoration of basic honesty and commitment to the idea of public trust (à la Teddy Roosevelt). Public trust entailed obligations to the public that should transcend partisanship and embrace neutrality. It implied the need for party and electoral reform at top levels of government and banishment of partisan practices from the middle and lower ranks of the public service. The egalitarian norms of the Jacksonian era could, ironically, be better preserved and extended through reduction of patronage.

As these moralistic reforms ensued, more progressive ideals were added to the mix. Most prominent was the ideal of businesslike dedication and efficiency in office. The "business model" enjoyed widespread appeal. As noted in chapters 5 and 7 (see especially the discussion of Frederick Taylor), reformers viewed public administration as a new field of business. By the 1920s, federal employees would be rationally organized into job classes (according to the Job Classification Act of 1923), and at all levels, personnel functions were gradually centralized under civil service commissions. The ideals of scientific organization and neutral competence formed integral aspects of the business model and were symbolized in the era's devotion to efficiency.

Likewise, the ideal of economy grew more popular as public agency ranks and budgets increased. Americans had always resisted taxes, even while demanding more governmental services and protections. The burden of inadequate revenue usually fell on employees—meaning few if

any raises and negligible benefits. Public-sector morale had reached new lows in the last quarter of the nineteenth century, and this helped spur union activity. Bringing businesslike efficiency to government would help eliminate the waste and abuse of patronage systems and yield significant economies that would provide much-needed revenue without recourse to extensive taxation. Employees and taxpayers could be mollified without increased taxes. Economies were realized, but they seldom resulted in much benefit to public employees. Government grew so fast, especially during World War I (1914–1918), that savings from economy measures were simply absorbed by the expansion. Rhetorically, however, equating economy with reduction of waste and added efficiencies in public services stuck in people's minds. Neutrality, efficiency, and economy thus emerged as new political ideals for the public service.

Finally, the transition from patronage to merit employment was aided by a combination of factors that centered on the American presidency. In the Pendleton Act, Congress gave the president the power to bring federal employees under civil service protection by executive order. Johnson and Libecap (1994) indicate that many members of Congress grew tired of the heavy demands and costs of managing patronage and needed a way out of the morass at an institutional level, even while individually they found it necessary to continue using patronage to please constituents. With the power of issuing executive orders, presidents—who had engaged vigorously in patronage practices as they entered political office—could play the reform card at the end of their tenure by blanketing into civil service as many of their patronage appointments as possible. This induced fairly rapid conversion to a merit-based federal service. In 1884, about 10 percent of the federal workforce of 131,208 had been covered under civil service. By 1921, about 80 percent of the workforce of 562,252 was so classified (Johnson and Libecap 1994, 48).

The introduction of all these changes by Progressive reformers helped transform America into a complex organizational society staffed by a new kind of employee. They established a template for development that in many ways persists to the current day. They bolstered the competent governance tradition in new ways, while promising to improve the responsive governance tradition in the process. Their successes provided great impetus for a new era that would face some of the most devastating events in world history, reawakening concerns about civic governance, minority rights, and access to the levers of power.

### The New Deal Era, 1933–1954

After World War I, the federal government engaged in extensive retrenchment of public personnel and gave strong encouragement to the private sector to pick up the slack in employment. This worked quite well during the rapid business expansion of the 1920s. The doctrine of laissez-faire had returned to full sway over economic development—so much so that President Calvin Coolidge (in office 1923–1929) could assert confidently: "The business of America is business" (White 1938, 264–65). The growing corporate sector took lessons from the federal government regarding centralization and classification of personnel, and subsequently overtook the field with its own research on employment in industrial settings (Van Riper 1958, chap. 12). The business sector led in organizational and personnel studies for decades thereafter. However, as in the past, the weakening of the federal establishment left the country exposed to the ravages of business cycles, and in 1929 the stock market crash precipitated the deepest and most widespread depression in U.S. history. President Herbert Hoover (in office 1929–1933) struggled with it throughout his term. He possessed remarkable organizational skills, but his economic free market policies (including budget cuts) seemed only to exacerbate the situation. In contrast, his successor, Franklin Delano Roosevelt, offered new ways of thinking and a glimmer of hope for the nation.

Animated by the belief that government must actively intervene in such situations, President Roosevelt brought a whole new cadre of young, university and industry-trained professionals into the higher reaches of government for the first time. With their help, he led the way to creating a host of new government agencies to address the nation's myriad problems. It was a bold agenda, made up of regulatory, employment, social insurance, and public service policies. As the agenda grew, so did the ranks of government employees. The great irony, however, was that in his early terms, Roosevelt was compelled to engage in patronage hiring on a massive scale in order to staff the new agencies.

During the 1920s, the existing civil service system had become rigidified through rationalization and centralization, and employment ranks had been pared drastically through retrenchment. The combination made rapid expansion under the system in the 1930s impossible. Civil service hiring rules emphasizing protection from political manipulation were cumbersome and had to be suspended. Patronage hiring proved more effective in a pinch. However, the hiring did not focus on rewarding partisans and family relations as had been the case during the abuses of the Gilded Age. The speed and scope of hiring was too great for such antics to have much play.

In addition, Roosevelt separated the partisan political organizers from his idea men (Van Riper 1958). The politicos mobilized support for his policies; the idea men supplied the content of the policies. The latter were an entirely new breed, coming mainly from universities. Neither the old-line politicians nor the businessmen of the day offered new ideas or new ways of dealing with the complex issues of public life (Van Riper 1958, 326). Roosevelt therefore introduced a nonpartisan-spirited group of intellectuals to the policymaking system—something not seen in any significant scale since the founding era. These were the middle-class organization men and women of the new era. They were the progeny of Progressive reformers who accordingly sought pragmatic expertise rather than partisanship. In fact, many of them eschewed politicians and politics as being antithetical to professional, scientific modes of practice (Mosher 1982).

Finally, Roosevelt brought highly competent experts into government agencies at all levels to tackle problems of organization, management, and policy. The experience in the new agencies bore this out. As Van Riper (1958, 322) indicates, many of the agencies outshone the older ones in their administrative methods and deftness with policy formulation and implementation.

Roosevelt's patronage practices thus differed substantially from those of his predecessors and raised afresh the notion that patronage and merit might be compatible. Initially, the key to their successful combination lay in the qualities of the available workforce—qualities that were coming to be defined primarily through the norms of professional and technical education and the culture of complex organizational life. Most of the key personnel of the New Deal administration fit the new image of capable, energetic, organized, and professionally trained public servants.

The prevailing standard of merit adhered to the professional model. This required university training in a specialized corpus of scientific or technical knowledge, adoption of work standards and enforcement through professional associations, and articulation of those standards through agencies that controlled criteria over job practices as well as employment and promotion decisions. Each profession, including managerial professions such as public personnel, sought exclusive control over an expanding base of important, substantive work in the agencies, along with clear differentiation of their work from other occupations (Mosher 1982, 117). The work that falls within the profession's province is accorded much higher status than other work, especially over "nonprofessional" or "subprofessional" work.

The professions and their related disciplines colonized the notion of neutral competence and expanded its reach into the highest levels of administration. Even policy development and analysis were reconceptualized as sciences driven by forms of analytic positivism and behavioralism that

were developing in political science and economics. The obedient, responsive technician of the Progressive Era gave way to the independent-minded professional expert who designed policies and organizational systems, developed leadership and management theory, and engineered group processes of interaction. Public agencies would be run as professional meritocracies. The Roosevelt administration moved steadily in this direction during its later terms by blanketing higher ranks under civil service protection. They believed only a small cadre of political appointees would be necessary in the future. By the early 1960s, it had become almost a foregone conclusion that patronage was dying out (cf. Sorauf 1960).

The criterion of appropriate character came to be defined by attributes of life in complex organizations. Employees should be collegial, demonstrating a group or team-based attitude, at least among fellow professionals. They should be dedicated to their work and find personal fulfillment in it. They should generally exhibit deference to hierarchy and formal authority, and display a high degree of loyalty to their employing organization as well as to their professional associations. Furthermore, employees should exhibit a strong faith in expertise and in the systems and processes produced by that expertise. They should generally eschew politics as an irrational phenomenon, yet fully support the political turf of their agency, helping to advance the agendas of their professional associations through interest-group advocacy.

Ideally, these employees would also display a distinct professional character born of socialization through schooling and on-the-job training. There, they would have nurtured commitment and conformance to specific policy agendas and to the expert-based means of achieving them (Kaufman 1960). A variety of personality and leadership tests were developed by organization researchers and theorists to more effectively assess the fit or "integration" of the individual with professions and employing organizations (Argyris 1964, 1957; White 1938). As discussed in chapter 7, organizations were transformed in their cultures to accommodate the needs and interests of professionals. Theories of motivation and leadership changed from an industrial "Theory X" approach that distrusts workers, to "Theory Y" approaches (McGregor 1957) that embrace professional norms of devotion to work and commitment to organizational goals. Under the impetus of the Classification Act of 1923, many agencies distinguished professionals from other job classes, recognizing their rank-in-person status as opposed to the standard rank-in-position system of the traditional civil service. Professional positions were tiered and ranked into the administrative hierarchy to enhance career ladders and incentive systems. Organizational life was made habitable for an emerging middle class that defined its good life in terms of professional and managerial achievement.

Proper political ideals for the professionalizing public service blended skepticism about traditional politics with enthusiastic professional activism in policy and administrative arenas. Career administrators were expected to shape policy and administration through the acquisition of scientifically validated knowledge applied through well-managed organizations. They would establish organizational and expert-based systems for handling every contingency. The idea of the *system* presented an attractive and persuasive image of streamlined organizations and problem-solving processes as sanitized substitutes for the old and dirty partisan methods of administration. As Frederick Mosher (1982, 83–84) indicated, this brought a new dimension to administration not contemplated in previous eras. The public administration was no longer simply an instrument of politicians. Managers and professionals would govern us through their expert operation of public agencies. They ushered us into an era of *technocratic politics* (Beer 1978, passim).

This drive to govern by executive management and expertise was aided greatly by the crisis circumstances of the Great Depression and then World War II. Executives typically exert great power in such periods because they can act quickly and plan systematically, while other governing branches must deliberate, delegate, and defer. Administration became an executive matter, thus

encouraging the view that all subordinate operations of government should be centralized under the executive (Mosher 1982; Rohr 1986). This thinking gained substantial legitimacy when couched in the imagery of "overhead democracy," as characterized by Emmette Redford (1969, 70–71), and touted by a long train of politicians and scholars since the time of Andrew Jackson.

In overhead democracy, the public administration is centralized and held responsible to the executive, who along with the legislative branch is, in turn, responsible to the people. Pursuant to this image, the Brownlow Committee advocated its many centralizing reforms (see chapter 5). These broad, centralized powers could then be safely delegated to the managerial leaders of departments and agencies, who would direct professional expertise to solving the nation's complicated problems. Despite vigorous criticism and political resistance, this managerial image of proper administration took firm root in the minds of most administrators, educators, and professionals. It has been touted in many subsequent reform efforts, especially by the two Hoover Commissions (1949 and 1955), and later found substantial support in the Civil Service Reform Act of 1978 under President Jimmy Carter. The states and localities followed the same path in the 1970s, adopting provisions of the Model Public Personnel Administration Law that embraced the Brownlow/Hoover ideals (Mosher 1982, 102).

The criteria for effective representation in this period emerged mainly from *pluralist* political thought (Dahl 1961; Dahl and Lindblom 1953). As distinct from traditional partisan politics, public administrators were viewed as part of a world of organizational politics characterized by the play of internal and external contending interests. In this world, administrators must negotiate and compete among the interests of clients, employees, congressional committees, suppliers, influential individuals, and bureaucratic factions. Agencies in this pluralistic melee become interest groups in their own right and are factionalized internally by their own employee and programmatic groups. The professions are represented by their own standard-setting associations and seek exclusive control over their work, their hiring practices, and their advancement. As Mosher (1982, 134) noted, a "basic drive of every profession, established or emergent, is 'self-government,' because 'no one outsider—no amateur—is equipped to judge or even to understand the true content of the profession or the ingredients of merit in its practice.'"

Professions must therefore jealously guard their own interests—and do so through specific "channels of professional influence" (Mosher and Stillman 1978, 96). Many professionals, especially lawyers, are elected and/or appointed to high offices and thereby fashion policies and agency practices that coincide with professional interests and competencies. Professionals also tend to dominate the middle- and upper-managerial positions in public agencies, and they often occupy key staff or support roles in agencies where they might otherwise lack dominance. Furthermore, they exercise broader influence through dissemination of professional standards and conceptual frameworks via the media, professional associations, coalitions of related professional interests, and by control of grants-in-aid criteria (Mosher and Stillman 1978, 77–98).

As professionals expanded their influence, many nonprofessionalized employee groups sought improved collective representation and influence through unions and employee associations. Unions had existed in our governments since the early nineteenth century but were not considered a common feature of public employment. Union activity increased dramatically in the twentieth century and by the 1960s had become a significant political force in its own right. Public unions were spurred by support among several state governments, especially in Wisconsin. State administrators there viewed unions as a useful means of managing employee relations. The American Federation of State, County, and Municipal Employees (AFSCME) got its start at their behest, and remains one of the largest public unions in the country. At the federal level, the Kennedy administration issued an executive order in 1962 that gave public unions the right to bargain on

a narrow range of issues affecting working conditions. These and many other initiatives resulted in the growth of public union membership to approximately a third of public employment in the country. Union power varies considerably agency by agency and by level of government, but it is still considered a significant force in public employment. Unions constitute a distinct employment system in many federal, state, and local agencies, and they exist as an option for those who are disenchanted with employment in the traditional civil service system. These tend to be the lower technical, clerical, and blue-collar grades that lack professional status, and view themselves as not being adequately represented by agency management. Such groups add significant impetus to the pluralist dynamic of modern organizational life.

According to pluralist theory, people are more effectively represented through participation in interest groups than they are by elected representatives. A crude public interest is achievable through a balancing of those interests. The weakness, as Mosher (1982), Lowi (1969), and others have indicated, is that this balancing of interests is hardly automatic because some interest groups are more powerful than others and thereby exert gravely disproportionate influence over public agencies and public policy. Some pluralists argue that an elected chief executive can counter this effect through vigorous leadership and oversight of the agencies. This version of the theory complements the ideal of overhead democracy and the "managerial executive." The CEO holds the ship of state on course for the public benefit. While this may hold true in some instances, the reach of chief executives over the vast spectrum of policy subsystems is generally quite limited and subject to significant challenge as an ideal.

An important new approach to representation as a criterion of public office also has its origins in pluralist theory. Though yet nascent in its development, the idea grew that public service should be representative in the sense that the various and contending interests of society should be reflected there (Kingsley 1944; Krislov and Rosenbloom 1981; McConnell 1966; Mosher 1982, 98–101). Geographic representation alone was no longer deemed sufficient as our governments became significant and stable employers. As a matter of constituency building, Roosevelt's New Dealers actively recruited the emerging professional middle class, along with a variety of historically disenfranchised groups, into government ranks. They gradually chipped away at the power of the southern-block Democrats and began reversing discriminatory policies against blacks and other minorities. They attempted significant enhancements for labor unions and employee associations. The changes were slow in coming, with most of the landmark legislation and executive orders occurring during the Kennedy and Johnson administrations, but the groundwork for these changes had been laid over nearly three decades.

It is significant, however, that this pluralistic version of representativeness ultimately works at odds with the harmonious and unified conception of administration envisioned in the Brownlow and Hoover Commission reports. As Mosher (1982) and Long (1962) indicated, the pluralist theory brings conflict to the core of the administrative process, and it works against basic personnel functions such as job classification and recruitment and promotional examination. Moreover, it undermines a uniformly stable career ladder for professionals. In this pluralist model, the lateral entry of new officials is required to adequately represent the various and changing interest-group perspectives.

The Jacksonian principle of "rotation" was thus reintroduced in new garb. It found limited expression with Dwight Eisenhower, America's first Republican president in 20 years (in office 1953–1961). The Eisenhower administration distrusted the huge numbers of New Deal professionals and administrators staffing key posts in every agency. Many of them displayed stubborn resistance to Eisenhower's initiatives. As a result, Eisenhower established a new (and controversial) "Schedule C" class of senior political employees that could be rotated and therefore made responsive to

interests that coalesced under the Republican Party banner. Partisanship still mattered as a means of administrative control, despite confinement to the upper reaches of the public service.

The tensions raised by pluralist ideas and practices provide hints of trouble with the managerial and interventionist orthodoxy of the New Deal era. Challenges to that orthodoxy began early and on a number of important fronts, and, by the 1960s, would culminate in tumultuous social and political change.

## Civil Rights and the Great Society, 1954–1976

Managerialism, professionalism, and the rise of big government in the New Deal era provoked challenges that stemmed from deep-rooted American political attitudes and institutional traditions. Institutionally, the role of Congress in the New Deal had been seriously weakened vis-à-vis the executive branch, and this spurred a slow but steady reaction. In 1939, Congress thwarted movement toward a national executive political machine by passing the Hatch Act, which prohibited most federal employees from participating actively in partisan political management and electoral campaigns. Roosevelt had attempted to sway the 1938 elections through distribution of patronage to those senators and representatives who had supported his policies (Karl 1963). He was defeated in this effort, and the Hatch Act effectively eliminated the potential for such abuse in the future. These actions are a reminder of a central theme of this book: staffing, organizing, and carrying out the administrative work of public organizations cannot be separated from the larger contending constitutional forces at play. This point is made ever more clear in the aftermath of the New Deal and World War II, when Congress sought to use control over the personnel system to reassert its role in the constitutional balance of powers.

In 1946, Congress set in place a framework of legislation that would enable it to compete with the executive branch in policing the new and vastly enlarged agencies—and exert more direct supervision of their administrative affairs. David Rosenbloom (2000) describes in rich detail the 1946 framework and subsequent train of legislation that established "legislative-centered public administration" in the last half of the twentieth century. Congress had to confront the necessity of delegating significant powers to enlarged executive agencies, while trying to gain some control over massive public spending in a growing political economy. It passed the 1946 Employment Act in part to more responsibly control its allocation of public works projects among the states. It reorganized itself via the Legislative Reorganization Act in order to provide more effective control over agency delegation and, through separate titles of that act, shed many of its more cumbersome constituent services to agencies that could manage them more efficiently. Finally, it passed the Administrative Procedure Act in order to regularize administrative procedures and infuse legislative values via rulemaking into administrative practice. In subsequent decades, Congress passed a wide range of laws that would continue to (1) open government agencies to broader public access, (2) extend its supervision of agency decisions, (3) establish analysis and evaluation capacity of its own, (4) limit the negative impacts of agency regulation, and (5) control its budgets (Rosenbloom 2000).

In the 1950s and 1960s, the U.S. Supreme Court under Chief Justice Earl Warren, 1953–1969, began moderating the trend toward judicial deference to administrative discretion by broadening and extending concern for individual rights in the face of pervasive government action. This included growing recognition that public employees had a substantial interest in protection of their basic constitutional rights in the workplace (Rosenbloom 1971). Prior to this time, the public employment relationship had been governed mainly by the doctrine of privilege. This doctrine assumed that "because there is no constitutional right to public employment, there are few or no

constitutional rights which cannot be restricted while the citizen is in public employment" (Rosenbloom 1971, 16). The citizen voluntarily accepts restriction of rights when he or she decides to accept the conditions of public employment. The job is held at the pleasure of the government. However, as the ranks of government employment swelled from the 1940s on, the wisdom of this approach was seriously questioned and finally rejected in the 1960s.

By the 1960s, public employment accounted for close to 20 percent of the total labor force. The rights of this vast population of workers could no longer be unduly restricted on the job without significant legal and political fallout. Cold war–era fears of communist subversion had heightened restrictions of workers' rights through the introduction of loyalty-security regulations, and this spurred many challenges through the courts (Rosenbloom 1971). Public agencies were sued for unreasonable restriction of employees' rights to free speech, thought, association, religion, privacy, and equality of access to public employment. Gradually, government managers were compelled to adopt the more sensible criterion of "job relatedness" in personnel practice as a means of determining when rights could be restricted in the employment relationship. Public managers would have to explain how deprivation of basic rights was necessary to job performance, and to determine if less restrictive alternatives were feasible. Due process protections became a necessary component of employee relations, and public managers were subjected to the risks of tort liability as an inducement to protect employee rights. In this way, the courts successfully intervened as another governing voice over public personnel policy and thereby curtailed some of the power and managerial flexibility sought by the executive branch.

These institutional dynamics unfolded in the midst of broader political movements to expand civil rights, first for African Americans, then for women, and then for Latinos and other groups that had suffered invidious and hurtful discrimination at the hands of both government and society. The black civil rights movement mounted new efforts on a grand scale, due mainly to effective use of legal challenges in the courts and to use of the mass media to draw national attention to their plight. The women's movement received an unexpected (and ironic) boost in 1964, when conservatives sought to kill a civil rights bill by adding gender as a category of discrimination along with race. Southern conservatives believed a rights bill including gender would never pass in Congress. The attempt backfired, and the landmark Civil Rights Act of 1964 passed into law. Latino groups also gained some initial attention in the late 1960s, when President Richard Nixon established the Spanish-Speaking Program in an attempt to bring more people of Latin American ancestry into federal employment.

In the political upheaval of the 1950s and 1960s, women and minorities strove for inclusion in the mainstream of the American political economy. This meant gaining better educational opportunities and increased access to good jobs with equal pay. Civil rights legislation and affirmative action policy followed on the heels of school desegregation efforts. Equal employment opportunity (EEO) policy started in the 1940s, primarily under the pressure of wartime mobilization, but it took civil rights demonstrations and court cases in the 1950s and 1960s to spur it into broad application (Rosenbloom 1977). In 1961, President Kennedy issued an executive order creating the President's Committee on Equal Employment Opportunity. The committee emphasized more aggressive measures to bring historically disadvantaged minorities into the federal service. At first, this meant eradicating legal and administrative barriers to educating, hiring, and promoting minorities. Simply declaring a policy of equal opportunity meant little if the barriers remained; likewise, it did not mean much to those who lacked sufficient education, training, and status to truly qualify for good jobs.

The long history of discrimination left these groups in a horribly disadvantaged condition that required more than a policy of nondiscrimination to adequately remedy. It demanded a compensa-

tory mind-set to overcome significant social and economic barriers to education and employment. The traditional means of redressing public employment disparities through patronage appointments had been outlawed for most of the civil service. An alternative was required, and affirmative action policy emerged to fill the void. The groundwork was laid through a mix of enforcement mechanisms for attacking discriminatory practices, and then through mandated plans for actively recruiting more minorities and women into education, training, and employment. The Equal Pay Act of 1963, the Civil Rights Act of 1964, and the Equal Employment Opportunity Act of 1972 provided statutory foundations and key enforcement mechanisms for attacking discriminatory employment practices.

Beginning in the 1940s, each presidential administration issued executive orders addressing discrimination and equal employment opportunity. These culminated in the 1960s with mandates for federal agencies to take positive steps toward bringing more minorities and more women into higher levels of employment.[1] President Lyndon Johnson's Executive Order 11246 (1965) provided organizational and promotional impetus to affirmative action by transferring responsibility for the federal effort to the Civil Service Commission (CSC). President Nixon's Executive Order 11478 strengthened the CSC mission by requiring use of agency resources for promoting equal opportunity "through a continuing affirmative program in each executive department and agency" (*Federal Register* 34 [August 8, 1969], 12985). These orders set the stage for adoption of agency *goals and timetables* in the early 1970s, the policy that has defined affirmative action, with only modest revision, ever since.

The goals and timetables approach came into practice with pressure from *representationists* who believed the color-blind, equal-opportunity approach had run its course in terms of eliminating formal barriers to employment (Rosenbloom 1977, passim). They wanted more aggressive actions that would attack informal practices and achieve real measures of substantive equality in employment. Accordingly, they looked more to the actual social and demographic composition of the workforce, as well as to specific agency goals and timetables for achieving demographic representation, as the appropriate test of effectiveness (thus earning the label *representationists*). Promises of equal opportunity meant little without evidence of real employment gains for both minorities and women. The efforts of representationists met resistance from CSC officials who, at least initially, viewed goals and timetables as synonymous with quotas—an approach they believed ran contrary to the principle of merit. These *meritists* supported measures for enhancing equal opportunity but balked at more aggressive actions (Rosenbloom 1977, 105–10). At the root of the controversy were two contrasting views of the public service.

The meritists upheld the longstanding Progressive view of the public service as a neutral, efficient, and technically oriented employment force that had successfully replaced an inefficient and corrupt partisan system. But this view "obscured the subjectivity and cultural biases informing the merit principle" they held so dear (Rung 2002, 186). In the minds of meritists, modifying merit practices for any reason posed a threat to the viability of their system. The representationists, on the other hand, viewed the public service more in Jeffersonian and Jacksonian terms—as a political body that must represent the democratic diversity of broader society. They were quick to remind meritists that their system actually had not focused on hiring the most qualified public servants. "Rather, it was directed toward recruitment and promoting to positions of importance the 'best' white males" (Rosenbloom 1977, 71). The merit system did little to prevent segregation and discrimination. It had ignored merit among women and minorities for most of its history, while giving preferences to white male veterans and employing hiring quotas for purposes of geographic representation among the states. Meritists had in fact, for many decades, embraced a castelike conception of merit that presumed minorities and women had inferior abilities (Rung

2002, 8–11). The civil service system gradually abandoned this notion for a more individualistic conception of merit, but the pace of change was much too slow in accommodating these long-disadvantaged groups (11–22).

Furthermore, into the 1970s, the Civil Service Commission had very poorly managed its EEO mission because it had delegated too much responsibility to the agencies, where resistance to EEO was often fierce. The commission successfully resisted goals and timetables until the early 1970s, when serious attempts were made to transfer the EEO mission to another agency (Rosenbloom 1977, 105–10). It then conceded to the goals and timetables approach, though it was continually hampered by frequent reorganization and lack of adequate reporting and evaluation data to assess progress (Rosenbloom 1977, 109).

As affirmative action and equal employment opportunity efforts mounted, questions and accusations arose concerning hiring processes and the prevailing conceptions of merit as applied through testing. That hiring practices among various agencies had been discriminatory was easily demonstrated. In the process, employment tests were challenged for bias, and subsequent scrutiny by experts revealed serious flaws. In all but the most menial types of work, the connections between the tests and successful job performance raised significant doubt. As we noted in earlier chapters (see especially chapters 3 and 7), most government jobs entail varying degrees and types of discretion. Studies revealed that employment tests were quite weak in assessing work-related discretionary judgment (Krislov and Rosenbloom 1981, 41–51). Highly subjective indicators (such as interviews) are more commonly used to assess such matters and are known to be very unreliable.

These problems lent further credibility to claims of racial and gender bias, and fed growing doubts about the technical foundations of merit in public employment. As described in chapters 5 and 6, scholars challenged the claim of neutral expertise with study upon study, and a small but growing number of public administration scholars called for a critical examination of the normative foundations of the practice. They exposed the narrow and conservative nature of instrumental conceptions of administration, and they criticized mainstream scholars and practitioners for lack of attention to glaring social and political problems. A young group of scholars called for a "new public administration" dedicated to social equity and democratic responsibility (Marini 1971). Such an administration would draw upon broader political efforts to make American governments more democratic by enhancing modes of representation and direct participation. Rejuvenation of Jeffersonian and Jacksonian values concerning social equity and democratic decision making challenged the orthodox thinking of "the establishment"—an edifice of political and economic elites served primarily by white middle-class functionaries who were deemed to be unreflective, unresponsive, and patronizing toward the citizenry. The challenges grew in strength with revelations of governmental abuse and misjudgment.

A fairly steady series of mistakes and abuses by government officials unfolded during the period. The McCarthy hearings in the 1950s showed how government power could intrude upon the beliefs and associations of private persons as well as public employees, ruining careers in the process. The U-2 spy plane incident and the Bay of Pigs fiasco showed how governing elites and their experts could make embarrassing mistakes in judgment. The Vietnam War illustrated how big government could spend billions trying to stem the communist tide in Asia, only to discover that our foreign policy and military strategies were based upon mistaken assumptions, flawed theories, outdated methods, and outright lies. As antiwar demonstrations ensued, we discovered that our own community leaders would turn police forces and military troops on white middle-class demonstrators, just as they had on blacks and other disaffected minorities. Such events led many people to question governmental and social priorities.

Grassroots political groups pushed for reforms to enhance civic governance through direct participation and accountability. They sought enhancements to social as well as physical communities through community development programs, urban renewal of blighted areas, environmental regulation, and a host of social welfare programs intended to integrate disaffected populations into mainstream life. Public administrators found themselves pitted squarely in the middle of these conflicts, without much guidance from their political masters.

These events turned the public mind toward broad social reforms that included significant modifications to the criteria for public service. The prevailing professional-technical approach to merit was seriously questioned for its antidemocratic, authoritarian tendencies, and for its neglect of the normative bases of administrative work. Public decision making required more than technical and professional expertise. It required sensitivity and good judgment, which entailed a variety of intangible and ambiguous factors, including commitment to proper ideals, cultural sensitivities, and responsibility to political communities that are broader than any special interest. This led inevitably to the conclusion that merit is always freighted with normative content. The insensitivity of the existing establishment to such matters came glaringly into focus as grassroots political activism increased. At the very least, these challenges helped open more avenues to public employment for women and minorities. In addition, the concept of public service expanded, especially at local levels, to include various types of community activism and development that devolved some governing power to previously disaffected nonprofit groups. Though many of these early experiments failed, the underlying concept would become important later in the effort to privatize public services.

The criteria of appropriate character and proper political ideals melded seamlessly during this period. Appropriate character shifted from that of "organization man" to a neo-Jeffersonian image of a democratic individualist who possessed equal rights with all others and who held an image of society where wealth and social conditions were shared equitably and free and expressive individualism could flourish (Bellah et al. 1985; Rung 2002). This was an era of intense democratic idealism in which many people distrusted and challenged prevailing authority and consequently sought grassroots alternatives to traditional party and interest-group politics (Huntington 1975, 74–75; Lowi 1969; Stillman 1984, 5–24). An increasingly loud call came for smaller, decentralized, popular institutions and programs associated with the responsive and civic governance traditions. According to this alternative view, ideal public administrators should exhibit a democratic leadership style and the ability to cultivate sensitivity among fellow employees to individual, cultural, religious, gender, and ethnic differences. They should embrace programmatic change readily for the sake of responsiveness and inclusion of the public in decision processes. Decisions should emanate more from mediation, collaboration, and consensus than from centralized authority. In the spirit of Mary Parker Follett, public officials should govern *with*, rather than *over*, the public (Follett 1949).

The criterion of representation in public employment expanded in conception to include all historically disadvantaged groups in society. Women and minorities ought to be employed in government as one very significant aspect of democratic participation and access. Affirmative action and equal employment opportunity policies constituted more than matters of compensation for past wrongs; they were a means for bringing about full inclusion in the political and economic community, just as patronage hiring did for the states and their working-class white populations in the nineteenth century. The logic of democratic inclusion also strengthened voting privileges through the Voting Rights Act of 1965 and extended them through the Twenty-sixth Amendment to all citizens ages 18 and over. It was common sentiment in the era that if one could be drafted into military service at that age, then one should certainly be granted full political rights as well.

These criteria helped change the demographic complexion of the lower and middle ranks of public service over the long run. However, in the short run, much of the Great Society agenda lost steam, in part because it attempted too much in one sweep. The intense idealism of this era turned just as quickly to despair and disillusionment by the mid-1970s. The turmoil and change of two decades had exhausted the nation. The rapid expansion of public employment and social programs, combined with the staggering expense of American involvement in the war in Vietnam, prompted fears of financial and economic ruin. The most identifiable trigger point for the rapid decline in public spirit came with the withdrawal from Vietnam without victory at the same time the Nixon-Watergate scandal came to a head.

The retreat and withdrawal from Vietnam embarrassed many Americans and provided only a weak sense of relief to those who opposed the war. The Nixon-Watergate scandal revealed firsthand how a centralized, managerial presidency could abuse power in unparalleled fashion. It shook the confidence of many elites and dispirited the American people in a way that made previous scandals pale in comparison. It also revealed the extent to which a powerful executive could use the personnel system to manipulate and abuse civil servants who were not responsive enough to White House agendas. The notorious *Malek Manual* (1974) provided Nixon's political officers with detailed knowledge of the federal government's personnel systems and of tactics for working them in ways that would have impressed Machiavelli. Though such tactics had been used in past administrations, the extent and viciousness of their application by the Nixon White House surprised even insiders.

In the wake of these events, the generally positive attitude toward government and public activism tilted quickly toward cynicism, reopening the question of what role our governments should play in society. Political conservatives had waited patiently for such an opportunity, and they took full advantage.

### The Entrepreneurial Age, 1976–Present

Conservative intellectuals and politicians had kept alive the historic distrust of centralized power in strong national governments. Their fears and convictions were strengthened by the horrors of World War II, which illustrated graphically the worst excesses of centralized bureaucracies and dictatorial regimes. New Deal intellectuals parried with neo-Hamiltonian arguments for a strong national government, providing evidence that democracy and a powerful centralized government were compatible and that the combination could be safe, more effective, and more innovative than dictatorial regimes (Gulick 1946). The New Dealers prevailed during the long period of national emergency and enjoyed the general trust of the American people into the early 1960s. But conservative intellectuals gradually reasserted themselves in the wake of World War II (Nash 1976). The libertarian wing of this group, described as the Austrian and then Chicago School of economists, advocated a set of alternative ideas that could be used when the abuse and extravagance of big government became evident. Their ideas were hardly new. They reasserted the Jacksonian values of states' rights, limited government, free markets, self-interested rational choice, and competitive, entrepreneurial spirit as the proper foundation of human freedom (cf. Hayek 1948, 1944; Friedman 1962). By the mid-1970s, many Americans were once again receptive to such an agenda.

Jimmy Carter, a conservative southern Democrat, won the presidency in 1976 by campaigning as a moralistic Washington outsider who would clean up the federal government, bring the bureaucracy under control, and check its rapid growth. Carter introduced conservative fiscal policies and brought about the most significant restructuring of the civil service since the Pendleton Act. Taking advantage of the new mood, and following a long train of reports recommending civil service reform, he proposed and won passage of the Civil Service Reform Act (CSRA) of 1978. The act abolished the

Civil Service Commission and divided its missions among separate institutions. Merit protection was assigned to a new Merit Systems Protection Board (MSPB), backed by a new Office of Special Counsel (OSC); public unions came under the auspices of a new Federal Labor Relations Authority (FLRA); and personnel management functions addressing civil service ranks were centralized under the Office of Personnel Management (OPM)—a managerial arm of the presidency.

The centerpiece of the act entailed creation of a Senior Executive Service (SES). The SES represented a new elite structure for senior-level federal administrators. Those who entered it would forfeit civil service protection for the promise of significant incentives that included higher salaries, performance bonuses, and more managerial prerogatives. The stated intent was to recast senior administrative ranks in the image of corporate executives who could be moved among the agencies at will in order to bring generalist management skills to bear when needed. As such, it heralded the resurgence of the corporate model of administration, with the president serving as CEO. President Carter had been an engineer in his earlier career and was enamored with the idea of bringing business methods and engineering-styled efficiency back into government. It also fed into a common executive-branch strategy designed to keep Congress focused on the mechanics of the merit system while the White House reestablished its power and reach over the public service. Patricia Ingraham has noted the attempts by many executives to disguise "questions of power in technical terms" (Ingraham and Rosenbloom 1992, 15).

At a political level, the SES design induced much greater responsiveness to the executive branch by senior administrators. Up to 10 percent of the SES ranks could be staffed by political appointees. For the rest, the lack of job security and the possibility of punitive job transfers pretty much guaranteed fidelity to White House agendas. This arrangement represented a new synthesis of political influence and professionalism for the top echelons of federal agencies. Indeed, subsequent reviews of the CSRA as a whole have concluded that the restructuring largely favored enhanced political responsiveness for the presidency at the expense of real managerial flexibility for personnel in the agencies (Ingraham and Rosenbloom 1992). Merit system protections have actually been weakened due to meager funding of the MSPB. The FLRA suffered from the start with an unclear mission and weak institutional identity. Though designed as a managerial arm of the president, the OPM became instead an arm of partisan ideological persuasion through the punitive use of accountability and control mechanisms (Lane 1992, 105–111). The CSRA did little to improve public personnel policies affecting hiring, promotion, position classification, pay and benefits, and other critical functions. What it did do was prime federal personnel for significant modification or reversal of many agency policies as conservatives mounted their attacks on big government and excessive power in the hands of career administrators. It came quickly with the election of Ronald Reagan as president (in office 1981–1989).

President Reagan played to an immensely popular image of the rugged individual who symbolized the embodiment of the good life in America. He believed Americans needed the freedom to ply their own way, with opportunities to better their conditions without government help. Government did not help solve problems; in his opinion, government was the problem. Government regulation had stymied initiative and entrepreneurialism. Welfare programs stole away the individual's pride and motivation to work one's way out of poverty (Gilder 1981; Murray 1994). By cutting taxes, regulations, and social programs, and by freeing the marketplace for robust competition, the Reagan administration promised to stimulate the private sector into a massive expansion of investment, and thereby bring about real jobs and opportunity for everyone.

Reagan attacked the public service, especially the federal service, as an edifice of bumbling bureaucrats who were far less productive than private-sector workers. He reasserted Andrew Jackson's argument that government jobs were plain enough to be carried out by the average

person, though he applied it with an interesting twist. The plainness and simplicity of government work meant that most tasks and services could just as easily be privatized and delivered more efficiently under the discipline of markets. A burgeoning body of economic policy theory and analysis, based in the Chicago School ideas of radical individualism, rational choice theory, and transaction costing, lent credibility to these beliefs (Alexander 1992; Arrow 1963; Buchanan 1991, 1986; Buchanan and Tollison 1972; Calista 1987; Moe 1984; Niskanen 1994; Shepsle 1989; Tullock 1965). Moreover, even where government work involved some complexity, the prevalence of specialists or "knowledge workers" in both the public and private sectors contributed to the view that the work of government could be done in any organizational setting. Putting more of the work into the business setting would ensure that it was done more efficiently (Savas 1982, 1977). Reagan believed that governments should be downsized, and those left in public employment (at all levels) should become more entrepreneurial in tackling their missions. This required competition and leadership, and business executives were needed to show the way. Reagan packed the political appointee ranks with corporate executives and analysts. Books on business leadership, corporate excellence, effectiveness, and efficiency (cf. Peters and Waterman 1982) quickly became bestsellers, and corporate-styled management and training programs spread rapidly among the agencies.

The Reagan platform set the basic policy and administrative agendas for succeeding administrations (Republican and Democratic alike) and remains firmly in place today. Entrepreneurial management reforms have paraded through the public administration at all levels under such rubrics as *total quality management, reengineering, right-sizing, reinvention,* and *new public management.* They have been accompanied by substantial downsizing of the federal civilian workforce,[2] especially in the lower ranks of the civil service system; the erosion of governing capacity by regulatory agencies; and the significant devolution of powers and resources to state and local governments.

The corresponding efforts at privatization have spawned a large and growing sector of for-profit and nonprofit service providers and turned government contracting into a core administrative function (see chapters 5 and 15 for a more extensive discussion). Significant arenas of public policy (especially human services) are now administered through a loosely coupled system of contracted employment that is haphazardly monitored by public agencies via performance contracts. Employment relations in this system are freed of many of the protections and restrictions placed on governments. However, the obligation to the public for responsible use of public resources for public benefit remains, and a train of revelations about contractor abuses and a general lack of accountability is growing. The implications for employment and oversight in this system are still being worked out, mostly on a case-by-case basis. The reality is that much of our governance is now conducted by proxy (Kettl 1993, 1988), and many institutions, at least in the federal establishment, have been hollowed out (Rhodes 1994). Conceptions of proper personnel practice in the burgeoning contract-employment system are nascent at best and subject to contradictory managerial philosophies (Peters 2001).

The lack of protections and restrictions on personnel practices in this contractual services system is viewed as a great advantage that should be parroted in the government agencies. Cries for a less legalistic and more managerially responsive civil service are a familiar refrain that began soon after the enactment of the Pendleton Act. The fear of patronage abuse and employment discrimination usually overwhelmed such cries, but today these fears seem overblown or distant to many people. Politicians, administrators, and scholars alike want to restructure the civil service system into a performance-based incentive system with broad and flexible position classifications, even though the track record of such systems in the private sector is mixed at best.

The same trend affects state and local governments. In many of these governments, legislatures, governors, and career managers are reducing merit system procedures and restrictions in favor of minimal *for cause* protections for public employees and in some cases expanding or reintroducing *at-will* employment agreements. At-will employment gives managers the power to hire and fire employees for any reason or no reason at all. The practice has always existed in a number of state and local governments and appears to be growing in scope, despite some limitations imposed by case law.[3]

This new entrepreneurial era has brought with it corresponding expectations concerning the proper criteria for public service employment. Ideally, in terms of merit, public employees should possess entrepreneurial imagination blended with professional and technical competencies. They should be industrious risk takers and pragmatic problem solvers, always seeking new and better ways to achieve desired outcomes while remaining highly responsive to elected officials and customers of their services. The managerial skills of public service workers are thus conceived in more instrumental terms, serving to rejuvenate the dichotomy between politics and administration. Responsive entrepreneurial managers should find better and cheaper ways of "rowing," while political leaders should focus on "steering" (Osborne and Gaebler 1992, passim). Along the way, institutional and regulatory impediments to recruitment and promotion of the best workers should be swept out.

Among the managerial ranks, decision-making expertise should reflect a strong bias in favor of economically efficient choices in outcomes for individuals in society. Decisions should follow a general policy and reflect motivational orientation founded in economic theories of *agency* and *rational choice* (Shepsle 1989). New public management and public policy curricula reflecting this economic and rational analysis have expanded rapidly in universities around the country. In essence, these programs have repackaged generic management science and econometric policy analysis as developed in the corporate/industrial setting of the mid-twentieth century, and applied them to public administration (Arrow 1963; Barnard 1938; Buchanan 1986; Buchanan and Tollison 1972; Moe 1984; Simon 1947). They have recast management as an analytic-centered activity, though now with more powerful methodological tools. In the process, the New Public Management and public policy movements have elevated the technical/instrumental conception of merit, while largely ignoring the substantive or normative conceptions that focus on ends and presume a distinctive institutional sense of public office (Pfiffner and Brook 2000). Accordingly, they are leading the way in socializing a new kind of employee for public service.

Appropriate character for public employment in this New Public Management era is founded on the assumption that rational-economic self-interest is universal to the human condition. As in the Jacksonian era, institutional contexts are deemed irrelevant with respect to human motive and temperament. Government employees (including managers) are no different as human beings than private employees. They seek their own self-interest, and this can be harnessed with the right market and organizational incentives for public benefit, regardless of the sector in which they work. This school of thought blurs the traditional distinctions among public, nonprofit, and for-profit sectors. The image is quite attractive to many professionals because it unites career mobility with a sense that they can perform their professional services within any sector. They want to believe that the nature of the work is the same everywhere. Paul Light's book *The New Public Service* (1999a) details the new self-interested character of this workforce.

Based on an extensive array of surveys, Light's conclusion is that these new employees are motivated by challenging work; an opportunity for personal growth and skill development; the chance for rapid advancement; provisions of benefits, security, and higher pay; and the prospect of exerting a lasting impact on specific local and national issues (Light 1999a, 29–30, 45). Profes-

sional idealism may exist here, but it is not tied by loyalty to any sector of employment. These professionals want to go wherever such motivators are offered. Thus, they epitomize entrepreneurial, rational choice. Correspondingly, they are largely devoid of that sense of "office" which "subordinates self to larger normative responsibilities that cannot be captured by a list of job tasks to be performed" (Heclo 2000, 232–233). There is diminished awareness of matters relating to specific institutional arrangements and to the distinctive obligations therein. Light describes this as "the end of the government-centered public service and the rise of a multi-sectored service to replace it." As one might expect, he also notes that it is the private and nonprofit sectors that are attracting most of these professionals, especially those schooled in analytic techniques (1999a, 48). Thus far, our governments have failed to recruit for the best of this talent.

Light's studies indicate that young professionals perceive the private and nonprofit sectors as providing more flexible work environments, where they can more quickly make a difference with their job skills while getting better pay and benefits in the bargain. They want challenging work, and they do not believe that governmental employment systems can provide such opportunity (Light 1999a, 2–5), especially in the short run. Government agencies are viewed as rule-bound hierarchies where promotion into truly challenging and rewarding positions takes many years to secure, if it happens at all.

These perceptions are, of course, heavily influenced by the general cynicism of the era toward government and by specific political efforts to make governmental employment less desirable. Agency budgets do not allow for aggressive recruitment, and most of the career development and training opportunities provided in earlier decades have been drastically cut back. The Volcker Commission, convened in the late 1980s, described an ensuing "quiet crisis" in the federal service (Volcker 1989). The crisis developed as attacks on government led to neglect of pay, benefits, and working conditions. In the 1980s, Congress often refused to fund the bonus and performance pay provisions for the Senior Executive Service. The gap between government and private compensation widened, and employee morale steadily degraded in most agencies. A second Volcker report (2003) indicates that these conditions have steadily worsened. Ten-year and 20-year appraisals of the Civil Service Reform Act of 1978 indicate that the promises of higher pay and better incentive systems, especially for the Senior Executive Service, have not been kept (Ingraham and Rosenbloom 1992; Pfiffner and Brook 2000). No wonder, then, that our governments find it increasingly difficult to recruit committed and competent public servants.

The criterion of representation in this era also bears some resemblance to the Jacksonian era. The Reagan administration asserted that the federal government was dominated by New Deal "tax and spend" liberals and their career civil servants. This edifice of domain-expanding officials had to be toppled and replaced by people who would be more sympathetic and responsive to the wishes of the heretofore silent majority. The message was clear: public servants had better change their mind-set or get out. This precipitated a war among the parties and branches of government that resulted in waves of jarring management and personnel reform (Light 1997).

At the political level, a nationwide movement for term limitations ensued; this movement represented a clear attempt to remove the old-guard politicians (those "tax and spend" Democrats) and make the new ones more immediately responsive to their constituents. The effort was moderately successful, especially at the state level, and contributed to eventual dominance by the Republicans. As they gained dominance, the term-limitation effort ceased, and it is now being reversed. Predictably, conservatives claim that the American people now have more democratically representative leadership and that they should be able to keep it in place as long as they wish. That leadership has been busily altering the civil service with one wave of reform after another in order to transform it into a system that better reflects their ideological assumptions. The Democratic

opposition joined the fray with its own reform measures calculated to frustrate Republican efforts, or beat them to the punch, especially with the Clinton administration's embrace of the "reinventing government" movement in the 1990s. The reascendance of Democrats to control of Congress and the White House in 2008 hinted at a change of attitude toward the public service. President Barack Obama asserted that public employees had endured enough bashing and that it was time to bring more support and encouragement to the public service. It was time to recognize public service as a respectable calling. The attempt fizzled quickly, however, in the intense ideological and partisan strife that continues to this day.

In terms of bureaucratic representation, the conservatives have voiced opposition to affirmative action. Like the meritists of the Great Society era, they view affirmative action as a violation of merit, one that stigmatizes minorities and constitutes reverse discrimination against qualified whites. Despite the distinctions enforced by the U.S. Supreme Court in the famous case of *Bakke v. Board of Regents of California* (1978), which barred quotas but preserved Affirmative Action in principle, conservatives rhetorically equate affirmative action with quotas and seek a return to the policy of passive nondiscrimination. Employment decisions, they claim, should rest on merit alone. Everyone, regardless of race or gender, should have equal opportunity to compete for jobs; individual competencies and experiences will vary, but conservatives maintain that employers and colleges should be free to decide which candidates are "the best qualified."

As indicated earlier, this era marks the restoration of states' rights, free markets, and freedom from governmental restraints as appropriate political ideals. Governments are to be distrusted, and therefore limited. And *limited government* means less government. At the base of these reforms is the American penchant for unrestrained economic individualism combined with the Jeffersonian distrust of large government. Individuals gain vitality through the dynamics of acquisitiveness and competition, and that, according to supporters of the entrepreneurial model, is what makes America great. The shift in political dialogue from addressing citizens to serving customers dramatically reinforces the message (Crenson and Ginsberg 2002). The task of proponents, then, is to recast all of society, including the public service, in this image. The words of Calvin Coolidge, spoken in 1924, ring loudly once again: "The business of America is business."

The Wall Street–induced financial bust of 2007–2008 and the resulting "Great Recession" that persists at the time of this writing has stimulated questions and raised challenges concerning the ideas and practices of the entrepreneurial era. The repeated scandals in the corporate economy (e.g., the savings and loan scandal of the 1980s, the junk bond scandal that followed on its heels, along with the mutual funds scandal, the Enron and Worldcom scandals, the Arthur Anderson accounting firm scandal, the Madoff scandal, and the pervasive mortgage fraud and credit default swap scandals led by Wall Street financial firms) combined with the failure of government to prevent these abuses have shaken public confidence in private and public institutions alike. They have fueled ideological battles that polarize not only the political parties, but society in general. The resulting political and economic instability has brought into serious question the efficacy of "American-style capitalism" and, along with it, "American-style governance" (Rothkopf 2012, 8–9; Stiglitz 2010, 343).

No one knows where all this is heading, but we can be sure that regardless of the direction we take, the issues and policies of the day will be framed in terms set by our constitutional heritage. Laurence Lynn (2010, 119) recently observed that matters of "constitutional governance" have endured and continue to frame cycles of reform and change. "With all that has been new over centuries of state development, what has endured has been those institutions that guarantee the legitimacy of delegated authority: legislatures and judicial bodies along with the norms of public service. . . . Constitutions and constitutional institutions will continue to frame the evolution of states and, as a consequence, their managerial institutions." We couldn't agree more!

## IMPLICATIONS AND CONCLUSIONS

The historical eras described in this chapter have left their mark on public service personnel systems. In them we see the operation of ambiguous and rival political principles that continue to animate public personnel administration. As Van Riper (1958, 66) observed, the public service has always reflected the heated debates about what improves, and what most endangers, democratic government. We conclude this chapter by considering briefly some implications for modern public personnel practice.

### Reframing Merit

Concern for merit has long been a cornerstone of the American system of democratic governance. It is inherent in the founders' beliefs that competent, efficient, and effective administration was essential to preserving a regime of ordered liberty. But it should be apparent that merit entails far more than technical criteria. It is an inherently complex and ambiguous concept. Moreover, as David Rosenbloom has noted, it is "often introduced at least as much in connection with demands for a redistribution of political power, authority, and influence among members of political communities as [it is] to secure better efficiency and economy" (1977, 31). This was as true of the founding era, when American elites endeavored to displace a royalist system of governance, as it was of the Progressive Era, when emerging white middle-class professionals sought to displace the entrenched patronage system. It is happening again in the current era, as entrepreneurial reformers have displaced a public service constituted by reformers of the New Deal and civil rights eras, and the nation now may be on the verge of some new era that will likely displace the entrepreneurial conservatives. It seems inescapable, therefore, that merit is politically defined and deployed—and is periodically reframed to suit new political agendas.

Our history also demonstrates, however, that no matter how merit ends up being defined politically, it should not be overwhelmed by partisan politics. If we learned anything from the Jacksonian era, it is that we do not want to convert the public administration into a partisan machine. Though we need political parties as one mechanism for guaranteeing representation, we also want a governing system that transcends the confines of party agendas and avoids the ravages of spoils. To a significant extent, we want stable organizational capacity, consistent service, and sound regulations that protect our rights, our health, and our safety. We want a public service that possesses the competencies required to achieve these things. Such competencies are inherently political because they are employed to regulate our affairs and support much of our community life, but they must coexist in a rough balance with partisan and interest-group politics. The balance is difficult to sustain because public servants are subordinates in the system, and are thus especially vulnerable to party and interest-group pressure. Precautions in the form of institutional barriers and restraints are necessary.

In the current entrepreneurial era, we are unraveling many of these protections in favor of partisan responsiveness. This is quite predictable, given the contentious and ideological nature of partisanship as of 2012. But we dare not go too far in extending partisan politics into the public administration lest we enervate the public administration's distinctive capacities.[4] We know that responsiveness to the public is crucial to democratic governance. Unfortunately, our history clearly demonstrates that partisan responsiveness is not the same thing. Consequently, we must protect the capacity of governing institutions to respond in nonpartisan ways to public needs (as in the responsive governance tradition). Those who exercise political leadership over the career public service share responsibility for preserving such capacity and for presenting more robust conceptions of merit to the public. But what do such conceptions entail?

According to public personnel history, merit includes knowledge and judgment that is sensitive to the myriad organizational, cultural, and political conditions that influence agency work. A useful classification of these competencies is offered by Lane and Wolf (1990). In addition to technical competencies (basic occupational skills and literacy for completion of tasks), there are "program or agency competencies" and "governance competencies" (Lane and Wolf 1990, 62). *Agency competencies* are "those capabilities required to activate administrative processes which create and deliver programs and execute public policies." These include "intimate knowledge of agency procedures," as well as tacit knowledge of strengths and weaknesses, knowledge of institutional context or history, knowledge of informal relationships that affect the play of power, and other factors that help all officials in an organization to understand motivational patterns and to anticipate decisions and policy directions (63, 69–76).

*Governance competencies* include civic literacy—and the ability to communicate it effectively to citizens as well as colleagues. Most public servants have obligations to cultivate civic literacy and to make civic participation by the general public more meaningful and robust (Cooper 1991). This type of competence also requires "thorough understanding of how governance institutions interrelate with the specific activities of an individual agency" (Lane and Wolf 1990, 76). Public service employees must understand the dynamic relationships among the three branches that supervise their affairs. This requires political skill, negotiating skill, and knowledge of key constitutional principles such as rule of law, separation of powers, due process, and equal protection. These principles govern many decisions, even at the street level.

Since the Progressive Era, the common tendency to view merit strictly in technical terms has obscured these vital components of public work. This is even true for clerical positions. In the formal design of clerical positions, public personnel officers and line managers tend to emphasize technical skills (such as keyboarding and file maintenance). But most clerical workers also carry out important functions such as representing programs to the public. They typically possess critical knowledge of how organizational processes work, how to manipulate those processes formally and informally to give more timely effect to decisions from above, and how to more speedily accommodate the public. They must be able to speak the language of the organization and to translate it to the general public. These abilities are harder to assess in precise, measurable terms, but are more vital than their technical competencies. Wise public managers try carefully to protect such employees, often from the depredations of merit and position classification systems that fail to account for and reward these more vital skills. When personnelists propose revamping the personnel classification system, they should factor these other types of competencies into the new system so that it rewards rather than retards their exercise. Many clerical workers would rise significantly in stature and title with such changes.

Public personnel history also demonstrates that merit is poorly rewarded, at least in pecuniary terms. Calls for better pay and benefits usually fall on deaf ears or are rebuffed with the claim that public employees trade higher salaries for job security. Some periods are worse than others, and it appears that public employees at all levels of government are worse off once again, especially in light of efforts to cut their benefits, union rights, and even their pay as governments retrench in the face of revenue lost or in decline due to the Great Recession. We should try to reverse this situation as best we can, but history tells us that any improvement of a monetary nature will be modest at best.

This long-standing condition implies two things. First, the emphasis in public personnel literature and practice on pay-for-performance and other merit-pay systems seems misplaced. Such schemes are usually doomed to fail because the rewards are almost always insufficient and misapplied in ways that de-motivate employees (Fox and Shirkey 1997; Ingraham 1993a, 1993b;

Perry et al., 2009; Moynihan 2008). At times, such rewards are nonexistent or so low as to be insulting. Merit and pay-for-performance systems also force significant symbolic distinctions of quality and competence among workers into precise monetary terms, while the actual differences among the rewards are negligible. Thus, when merit money is appropriated, managers are caught in the lose-lose dilemma of choosing whether to spread it around as a long overdue cost-of-living adjustment, or give most of it to a few most worthy employees while incurring the ire of all the rest—most of whom are good employees. Unfortunately, the application and mechanics of the merit process, combined with a general lack of funding, pretty much guarantee a cycle of demotivating decisions. Few are satisfied—much less motivated—by such a system.

Second, since pecuniary rewards are generally insufficient, it appears that public personnelists and line managers should focus more on working conditions for motivational potential. The motivation literature has long trumpeted intrinsic and "public service" motivators (Perry et al. 2010), but most public personnel systems fail to take advantage of this research. As Light (1999a) has indicated, professionals and most other classes of workers are looking for challenging work. They want to make a difference. They want power, along with the time and flexible working conditions in which to exercise it. The vast majority of them do not need constant supervision or oversight. They want to be accountable, but they do not want to be stymied at every turn for its sake. Personnelists and line managers need to think about how to redesign working conditions, job classifications, and incentive systems that account for these motives, "allowing their energy to flow" with less interruption, while ensuring effective accountability (Lane and Wolf 1990, passim).

## Appropriate Character in the Public Service

Public personnel history tells us that character matters. It is recognized in some limited ways as an aspect of merit, as evidenced in position descriptions and performance evaluations that address demeanor, manner, attitude, and so on. But on a broader level, it broaches two separate questions: Who is fit to *rule*, and who is fit to *serve*? As long as the exercise of administrative discretion continues to exist, we need the qualities required of both roles. When out of balance, we suffer from smug authoritarianism on the one hand, and from mindless subservience on the other. We have suffered from both extremes, and the oscillation between them lends strength to our penchant for personnel reform. We have seen how both the promise and the excess of the desired character traits of each era can play out.

For example, the founders desired honor, but they brought with it a gentlemanly code ill-suited to a democratically spirited majority. Today, we still want and need a sense of honor, though without the aristocratic tinge. We want honor to ensure that tasks are faithfully executed without constant oversight. Furthermore, we seek honor as a means of preserving the independence and lucidity that enables a public servant to discern when and how one should resist the encroachment of partisans, special interests, and imperious leaders. These qualities seemed in short supply during the years leading up to financial crisis of 2007–2008. It was plain to see in retrospect that large numbers of public servants in the financial regulatory arena had decided to look the other way, or even go along with the gross improprieties occurring and reoccurring in the financial industry over three decades (cf. Green 2012). We need public servants to maintain this sense of honor not just individually, but corporately, as a shared public ethic that can help individual public servants withstand the withering attacks of politicians and powerful interests, and prevent the worst excesses of such corruption. Modern professionalism should help in this regard, by providing individual recognition, pride in well-performed work, and real protection when their standards of good practice are threatened and/ or compromised. Professionals of all stripes, in the private as well as the public sector, have not

acquitted themselves very well in the scandals of the entrepreneurial era, perhaps in part because entrepreneurialism erodes any concrete sense of a public good. We also saw how the Jacksonian era brought the character trait of loyalty to the forefront of public service. This trait was linked to democracy, as in loyalty to the common man—to the masses. It started as a kind of populist public spirit. In practice, however, it served partisan, business, and individual interests of elected leaders and their associates, resulting in powerful political machines. The great problem with loyalty is the tendency it cultivates in people to blindly protect their benefactors, thereby creating a dangerous system of personal influence and subservience. Loyalty and partisanship combined in the Jacksonian era to transform politics into the rawest form of parochialism.

Progressive reformers gradually overturned this system and reintroduced broader conceptions of the public interest as the proper objects of loyalty for public servants. As Rosenbloom (1977, 33) describes it, they "hoped to create a new national politics that inhibited partisan influence as the chief source of parochialism." Their initial tactic for success in this effort lay in creation of a centralized personnel system with powers sufficient to limit the reach of nepotism, parochialism, and partisan meddling. But Progressive reformers also relied on the Victorian spirit of moralistic reform, paired with growing faith in the power of a rational science that would eventually transcend politics altogether. Their resulting fascination with modern rational organization engendered loyalty to groups and to organizational systems. In doing so they contributed to a new pluralistic form of parochialism—later termed *interest-group liberalism* (Lowi 1969). It is a form well matched to the character of employees who spend their lives in complex organizations, whether public or private.

The implication here is that all conceptions of proper character for public office have flaws. It is in our interest, therefore, to keep open the question of which traits we want, and to anticipate the defects inherent to those in ascendance. We want a balance of desired traits mixed with institutional protections that tend to counter excesses, if not within each public servant, then between them and among their varied orders and classes. As noted earlier, in the current era we need to anticipate the downsides to our preoccupation with entrepreneurialism and economic versions of self-interest. Are we cycling into a Jacksonian-styled resurgence of personal influence, now expressed through professional networks, contracts, and consultancies that focus more on short-term results and bottom lines than on institutional capacity and governance? What impact does the current, polarized partisanship have on all this? Is the unraveling of centralized, protected personnel systems opening the door to another period of raw and debilitating parochialism? Should the public service respond obediently to these pressures, or should it play a role in moderating their effects? The historical record seems to indicate that the public interest is better served by the latter.

## On Representativeness

Representativeness must serve as a cornerstone for public personnel policy in a democracy. It has played a prominent role in every political era of American history. What is most notable about it is that we are never satisfied with any single representational scheme. The Anti-Federalist founders rightly criticized our Constitution for an inadequate plan of representation, arguing that our elected representatives could not possibly represent so many people over so vast a territory. Our history is replete with attempts to improve or increase representation by supplemental means, and these too have displayed serious flaws.

As we have seen, much of the conflict in public personnel history centers on the concern for more and better representativeness. At times, it has overwhelmed the competing concern for a competent public workforce, and thereby inflicted some harm as well as benefit. However, the

fear of abuse must not lead us to ignore or undervalue the role that representativeness must play in public personnel policy. The current tendency to trumpet merit as the only sound basis for public service hiring is misplaced and mistaken in our polity. Advocates of merit will inevitably (though perhaps unwittingly) import conceptions of representativeness into their designs. As David Rosenbloom (1977) and Margaret Rung (2002) have indicated, early and mid-twentieth-century meritists carried with them the assumption that adequate representation included only white males for most government occupations. The subsequent battles with representationists over EEO and affirmative action policy in the 1960s and 1970s seriously challenged that assumption. Those who craft and implement public personnel policy must recognize that the positions of both meritists and representationists have intrinsic political and historic value for our democratic republic.

## Proper Political Ideals in the Public Service

If American public personnel history tells us anything, it is that the public service has been re-formed continuously to reflect the ascendant political ideals of each era. This is appropriate given our democratic spirit. It is also apparent that many ideals persist in tension with those that came before. They form legacies or traditions that are now integrated in various ways throughout the public service. In chapter 6, we arrayed these traditions as a Balancewheel of four sets of core values that must be kept in equilibrium in order to preserve our system of democratic governance. These traditions include: (1) responsiveness to citizens; (2) sensitivity to the unique nature of local communities (also known as civic governance); (3) ensuring competent and energetic governance; and (4) protecting minority rights and ensuring access to governance. We argue that regardless of the direction the public service takes, it should find ways to help preserve the balance among these essential core values. Political and managerial zeal will periodically warp or distort this balance. It is a central task of public personnel policy to absorb and mute the attempt.

## STUDY QUESTIONS

1. How do the classic criteria of public office (such as merit and character) apply to agencies with which you are familiar?
2. What factors from each historical era have some impact on current personnel policy and practice?
3. Describe how the four administrative traditions (responsive governance, civic governance, competent and efficient governance, and minority rights and access to governance) affect U.S. public personnel policy generally. Then identify ways in which each tradition comes into play in the Prairie County case.
4. Identify and discuss the different kinds of competence or "merit" that are required to deal with the conditions evident in the Prairie County case.
5. How might representation in employee ranks factor into the Prairie County case? Consider various agencies in Prairie County, not just the DSS field office.
6. How do "proper political ideals" play into personnel issues in the Prairie County case?

## NOTES

1. David Rosenbloom (1977, 59–61) explains that "it was not until the 1930s and early 1940s that a continuing, systematic effort to ensure equal opportunity in the public service became a major feature of federal personnel administration." The Hatch Act of 1939 provided some initial, though very limited, language pertaining to employment regardless of race, color, or creed. The Ramspeck Act of 1940 prohibited

"discrimination against any person, on account of race, creed, or color" in fixing salaries, allocation of positions to grades, and transferring employees, as well as in promotions and other personnel actions. Executive Order 8587 (1940) by FDR amended civil service rules to prohibit discrimination on the basis of race. Executive Order 8802 (1941) established the Fair Employment Practice Committee to help smooth over racial tensions during the war effort and "take appropriate steps to redress grievances" (Rosenbloom 1977, 61). Executive Order 9980 (1948), issued by Harry Truman, created the Fair Employment Board within the Civil Service Commission (CSC), giving it the first real authority to deal with discrimination complaints. Kennedy established the President's Committee on Equal Employment Opportunity, which took more positive actions, though seldom decreed discrimination for fear of needless hostility. The Civil Rights Act of 1964 established the Equal Employment Opportunity Commission, and Lyndon Johnson put it in the CSC. A women's program was incorporated into it in 1967 (see Rosenbloom 1977, chap. 3).

2. Paul Light (1999b, 1–7) reports that as of 1996, federal civilian employment had been reduced to 1.9 million, "down almost 400,000 jobs since the height of the Vietnam War in 1968." (Federal Office of Personnel Management data from 2010 shows federal civilian employment dropped to 1.36 million.) However, Light also explains that the true cost of government must include the rapidly growing "shadow government" made up of nonprofit and for-profit firms that contract with the federal government to provide goods and services. When those employees are counted, government has grown substantially.

3. "At-will" employment is hedged about in public employment by three basic exceptions. First, though rarely used, there is a "public policy" exception that bars removal of a public official for conscientiously carrying out his or her duty to the public in the face of political resistance by superiors seeking to thwart the effort. A second is the "constitutional conditions" exception, wherein a public employee's job cannot be conditioned on the sacrifice of basic constitutional rights unless it can be shown that the agency's interest in effective and efficient implementation outweighs the individual's interest in his or her rights. The third, and most common in both public and private employment, is the "contract exception," where an employer has established an employment policy that modifies the at-will relation by implementation of practices that establish expectations for both employer and employee that are contractually binding. A new wrinkle, developed by some public managers at local levels, is to entice employees to voluntarily waive existing agency personnel policies in favor of an individualized "at-will contract." For an extended discussion of at-will employment history and trends, see Green et al. (2006), Bowman (2002), and Bowman and West (2007).

4. The U.S. Supreme Court has recognized this point in some key cases, noting that partisan concerns are legitimate only when they are job related (*Rutan v. Republican Party of Illinois,* 1990). But the courts cannot adequately protect the public service alone.

# CONTEMPORARY HUMAN RESOURCES MANAGEMENT

The mechanism of inducements is enormously complicated in the polis by the fact that the givers and receivers are likely to be, or to operate in, a collective entity. We can easily imagine a donkey responding to a carrot, but a trainer who proposed to motivate a hundred donkeys with a bunch of carrots would leave us pondering many questions: Should he put the carrots all in one place? Throw them into the middle of the herd? Should he have one carrot for each donkey? Do all donkeys like carrots? Will two or three aggressive donkeys get all the carrots, regardless of how the others behave? Will the latecomers and slow learners get no carrots anyway, and figure it's not worth changing their ways? Might the donkeys stampede the trainer and devour the carrots? And what if carrot distribution policy is decided by a committee of independent-minded, strong-willed trainers? The carrots might be given out according to several different standards, or the committee might be paralyzed and the carrots never given out.

*(Deborah Stone 1997, 265)*

In chapter 8, we illustrated the political nature of public personnel policy through a historical review of the criteria used in selecting employees for public office. As the United States grew, the scale and complexity of public personnel practice increased dramatically. Today, public personnel has evolved into a field with complex functions and responsibilities, and along the way it has adopted new titles to symbolize changes in philosophy and mission. This chapter begins with a brief review of the nature of these changes and the core functions of contemporary public personnel practice—subjects typically covered in greater depth in personnel and human resources texts. The last part of the chapter provides a constitutional framework for understanding the dynamics of public human resources practices. We believe this framework can help administrators cope more effectively with the underlying tensions and conflicts that pervade public personnel practices.

## CHANGES IN MISSION AND PHILOSOPHY

As described in the previous chapter, in the early part of the twentieth century, public personnel specialists led the way in developing a clearly defined system that would ensure legal protection of public employees from improper partisan influence. But these efforts were soon overwhelmed by

the need for greater innovation and flexibility to manage large-scale personnel functions. Having been battered constantly by contending political forces striving to control the public service, it is hardly surprising that personnelists developed a kind of bunker mentality that resisted innovation and cooperation in favor of legalistic protections against partisan and managerial manipulation of covered employee groups (Gawthrop 1969). Legal and technical functions became their only refuge, and in the process they "hemmed in the line operator with restrictive rules governing job classification, appointment, promotion, transfer, salary change, and dismissal of employees" (Rosenbloom 1977, 83). As a result, public managers have long felt compelled to find ways of "gaming" personnel rules and processes to get desired results, and they have often viewed personnel offices with contempt and derision (Ospina 1992).

Throughout the latter half of the twentieth century, continuous efforts were made to reform the legalistic bent of public personnel administration. Personnel professionals in all sectors worked hard to engender more proactive and cooperative roles, and they adopted a new title for their field, Human Resources Management (HRM), to distinguish the formalistic approaches associated with traditional personnel administration from newer orientations to the practice. Borrowing heavily from private-sector practices and in keeping with developments in organizational theory discussed in chapter 7, personnelists shifted emphasis to the development of employees as vital resources for use by managers in pursuit of organizational goals. They developed streamlined recruitment processes, more relevant training and development programs, broadbanded classification systems, improved pay and benefit plans, and expedited disciplinary processes. These measures have increased, at least modestly, the flexibility and support for line managers at all levels of government.

Human Resource managers sit at the interface between organizations and individuals. As Gross and Etzioni (1985) note, we design roles to meet the needs of organizations and then fill the roles with whole people. This inevitably creates strain. The tools and techniques of HRM selection, socialization, and performance control are the means to manage this interface. This puts new behavioral science innovations and emerging personnel law to the classic challenge offered by Chester Barnard (1938) of creating "cooperative systems." Barnard observed that employees enter a cooperative relationship with organizations, essentially agreeing to the managerial authority of the organization over the zone of activity associated with their work role. While part of this agreement is instrumental, as we saw in chapters 7 and 8, part of it is also expressive and developmental for individuals and groups—for example, to support career development, better balance between roles at work and at home, team building, and the like.

The agendas of contending political and managerial forces, however, seem inevitably to confine and truncate these innovations on a cyclical basis. Public managers are given increased discretion over personnel decisions to improve working conditions, to enhance training and professional development opportunities, and to offer a broader array of benefits to public servants, only to have these things withdrawn or seriously modified with the next budget crisis or after the next election. HRM offices are then left to deal with the aftermath. In addition, HRM professionals have to play a difficult balancing act between serving the interests of policymakers and top management on the one hand, and protecting and enhancing the conditions for employees on the other. For example, agency executives must restrain the expansion of personnel costs, while employees try to take advantage of promotional and other career-enhancing opportunities that increase these costs. HR managers are caught in the middle and more often than not must follow the executive agenda. Thus, they are seldom trusted by employees and their supervisors to act on their behalf.

This grim reality has resulted in distribution of many HRM functions to other units. Much of the recruiting for professional positions, for instance, is handled in line departments, while the

paperwork is coordinated by office managers working with HRM technicians. The HRM office is kept at arm's length. Affirmative action and equal employment opportunity (AA and EEO) functions are often split off and placed for symbolic reasons near top executive offices. It seems that most public managers continue to believe that any significant measures for improving the condition of the public service will generally originate elsewhere. And seasoned HRM administrators know that their plans are best sponsored by others in the organization for the sake of legitimacy, and that they will get little credit for their contributions.

Despite these difficulties, HRM professionals remain steadfast in their efforts to improve the field and to bring new conceptions of their practices to the forefront of managerial and political attention. In recent years, this has resulted in a new movement to recast Human Resources Management as *Human Capital Development.* The new title emphasizes the idea that employees are more than replaceable resources to be exploited. Following the current theme of entrepreneurial government, these professionals promote public service as a vital form of capital in which to invest for our long-term benefit. Functions (such as training) that develop the long-term potential of public employees for high performance should therefore be bolstered (cf. Carnevale 1995).

Although the nuances of meaning behind these titles differ significantly, we employ them interchangeably in this chapter. We fully endorse the conception of public employees as valuable capital in which to invest, but we also find that the older titles (and their connotations) remain relevant to the practice. We use the title Human Resources Management most often because it is likely the most familiar to our readers.

## THE CORE FUNCTIONS OF PUBLIC HUMAN RESOURCES MANAGEMENT

Virtually all but the smallest local governments and special districts in the country now have a separate HRM office with specialists to help manage a variety of complex functions. We briefly describe the nature of these functions in order to introduce readers to the topics typically associated with the field. We do not go into detail about them, as this would require a full-length text, and there are many such texts already available.[1] These functions have evolved from management theories prevalent in both the public and private sectors, and they are performed with widely varying results. The reader will see parallels between these HRM roles and the evolving theories of organizational design discussed in chapter 7. Changing political eras (described in the previous chapter) and organizational conditions affect their performance in dramatic ways.

### Employment Status, Protection, and Process

*Employment Status*

It should be apparent from the previous chapter that providing legal protection and process for public employees remains a vital function of public HRM for many reasons. First, we do not want public employees unduly interfered with or harmed for performing important and lawful public services. Second, the public sector is obligated to respect the rights of all persons, and this includes employees. An extensive variety of rules govern the treatment of public employees, and many derive from employment status. Employment status refers to the legal nature of the employment relationship in a governmental entity. A variety of employment *systems* are associated with each type of legal status.

*Civil Service Status*

Civil service systems are governed by independent or quasi-independent *commissions*, whose members are usually appointed by an elected chief executive to a fixed term. Commissions control the application, referral, and disciplinary processes of agencies under their jurisdiction. Their primary mission focuses on fair and equal treatment of employees and avoidance of undue manipulation by elected officials and public managers. Commissions are typically disliked by managers for their legalism, their exercise of control over job design and classification decisions, their expensive and time-consuming disciplinary processes, and their lack of appreciation for the needs of line managers. What is gained in fair and equal treatment via rigid rules is lost in managerial flexibility to select, deploy, reward, and discipline employees as needs dictate. The power of civil service commissions comes through their independence from agency management, combined with a narrow, legalistic focus on protective and objective employment processes. Their distance from day-to-day management conditions in the agencies makes their objectivity arid and unresponsive to managerial needs. Since the late 1970s, civil service systems have been gradually eliminated in favor of merit systems controlled directly by the executive branch.

*Merit Status*

Widespread and long-standing frustration with civil service systems led the federal government and many state and local governments to replace them with *merit systems.* Typically, merit systems are controlled directly by chief executives but still provide protection for employees through a legal "for cause" standard and elaborate "step-and-grade" classification systems that structure promotion and disciplinary processes. Employees covered under merit systems may not be removed from office (once they pass their probationary status) except for grave infractions (such as committing a serious crime, insubordination, or violence on the job) or through a gradual process of progressive discipline for not performing adequately on the job. Merit systems give more flexibility to executives and managers for some aspects of job design, transfers, and promotions, but still rigorously control pecuniary rewards and employee disciplinary processes. They are generally preferred to civil service systems, yet they do not escape serious criticism. For example, the process of progressive discipline is still slower than many managers would like and requires sustained attention to difficult and often painful matters. Progressive discipline refers to the required practice of applying disciplinary action proportionately to the seriousness of an infraction. If subsequent infractions occur, they are punished with increasingly severe sanctions. This process often requires a lot of coordinated action, careful and sustained recordkeeping, elaborate appeal procedures, and consistent treatment over substantial periods of time. Few managers seem able or willing to maintain these requirements successfully through the process. The problems compound when new managers inherit a disciplinary problem midstream.

In addition, as evidenced in the Prairie County case, personnel functions in merit systems are often centralized under the chief executive and not considered as responsive or flexible as subordinate managers would like. The HRM office becomes a tool of control for senior managers, and this often leads to an "us versus them" mentality among subordinate managers and their employees. These problems frequently lead to a cycle of devolution of HRM responsibilities to line offices in order to accommodate their needs more efficiently, and then recentralization as new chief executives endeavor to regain control. A swing in this cycle occurred in Utah state government in 2005. Governor Jon Huntsman (elected November 2004) persuaded the state legislature to devolve the cabinet-level Department of Human Resources into an "office" under the Department

of Administrative Services, but with the HRM director answering directly to the governor. In the process, all HRM officials in line agencies were transferred to the new central office in order to enhance the control of senior management over state personnel policy. Many agencies were, of course, very unhappy about losing the close and influential relationship they had with their HRM officers. The responsiveness of the HRM function is always contested through these cycles.

*At-Will Employment Status*

A small but growing number of public employees are employed in an *at-will* employment relationship. This relationship provides the fewest protections. At-will status means that employees may be removed from office for any reason or no reason at all. Typically, it is applied to political appointee positions that lack fixed terms and to staff positions that require a close and confidential working relationship with managers and executives. However, in the wake of the Civil Service Reform Act of 1978, which created an at-will Senior Executive Service in the federal government, many state and local governments have expanded their at-will systems to include senior- and middle-management positions. Georgia state government converted all new state hires to at-will status (Condrey 2002), and Florida converted 16,000 supervisory positions (Bowman 2002; Bowman and West 2007). The attraction stems from the desire to achieve much greater political responsiveness and accountability, as well as to enhance managerial flexibility. The drawbacks lie in the exposure of employees to political and managerial manipulation of the worst kinds, and to the loss of job security as one of the few and most meaningful attractions for public employment (Bowman and West, 2007; Green et al. 2006). That said, some limitations still remain on the use of at-will prerogatives. These involve constitutional rights as they affect conditions of employment, as well as a few legal exceptions recognized in common law. However, the reach of these protections may be insufficient to prevent most of the abuses that civil service and merit systems were created to prevent. Thus, widespread conversion to at-will status presents a potentially radical change in public employment status, with tremendous political, ethical, legal, and managerial implications (cf. Bowman 2002; Green et al. 2006).

*For-Cause Employment Status*

A stripped down *For-cause* employment status represents a newer and relatively untried modification to merit and at-will systems that attempts to combine the advantages of both. It dispenses with the highly structured merit system, leaving much greater flexibility to line managers and executives to tailor incentives, disciplinary processes, and job design to the particular needs of divisions and programs. In principle, it still affords protections for employees from arbitrary discipline and dismissal. However, the due process afforded them is very truncated, usually stopping at the agency door, with no appeal allowed to an independent authority. The system is intended to accommodate simpler performance-based decisions about pay and promotions. Perhaps its greatest potential lies in the ability to flexibly deploy public employees in new ways to accommodate more networked and ad hoc work arrangements with personnel in contracted private and nonprofit systems. Job classifications are minimized or written in broad language for the sake of flexibility and evolving responsibilities. This may also present real advantages in tailoring work for younger generation workers whose motivational sets are oriented more to changing and challenging work projects than to stable but slow progress through agency career ladders (Bordia and Cheeseborough 2002; Hammill 2005; Light 1999a; Stefaniak and Vetter 2007).

There may be significant disadvantages to this system, however. More flexibility in rewards and discipline can lead to unfair disparities in treatment of employees across an agency.

Truncated due process means there are fewer opportunities to discover hidden or disguised discriminatory practices and favoritism by managers, and the system is more susceptible to political manipulation. Nevertheless, the potential for accommodating the design of more adaptable public agencies and workforces is being explored. Some state and local governments are currently experimenting with, or considering moving to, for-cause employment systems.

*Union Employment Status*

About a third of all government employees are covered by union contracts that require collective bargaining over working conditions and, in some state and local agencies, over wages and benefits. During the 1960s and 1970s, public employee unions grew rapidly. Their numbers have since leveled off and are beginning to decline, while union membership in the private sector has declined precipitously from around 38 percent to just 18 percent of the private workforce. As of 2012, 28 states required collective bargaining for some public employees, and of the 22 remaining *right-to-work* states, all but five permit collective bargaining for some employee groups—most commonly police and fire personnel. Right-to-work states have "meet and confer" provisions, which allow some group identity (primarily through employee associations), but only require managers to take advice rather than enter into binding agreements with employee groups. Union contract provisions protect covered workers in much the same way as merit and civil service protected systems, and they stipulate specific hiring, promotion, and disciplinary practices. Where union contracts apply, both management and the union are bound by the terms of the negotiated contract. Such contracts are limited to matters defined by state or federal laws that describe the "scope of bargaining." Agency managers, for example, typically enjoy a significant number of "prerogatives" that in many cases cannot be bargained away.

Recent controversies in Wisconsin and Ohio have thrust unions and labor to the center of partisan politics once again. Scott Walker of Wisconsin campaigned for governor against unions and collective bargaining rights, arguing that they were bankrupting the state. Upon his election, he worked with legislative Republicans to pass a new law rescinding the collective bargaining rights of many public employees. This prompted heated demonstrations and a petition drive generating almost a million signatures calling for the governor's removal from office. These efforts, coincidental with the "Occupy" demonstrations, have sparked a reaction to the pro-business policies of governments over the last 30 years. The results of the 2012 election may reveal the significance, if any, of such efforts.

*Contract Employment Status*

A different kind of contract system has burgeoned in recent years. Contracts for temporary workers and individually negotiated employment contracts are becoming more popular. For instance, it is increasingly common for employees who retire or are laid off to be called back to work under an individual contractual arrangement. These are often hemmed about with restrictions on the time and manner of employment in order to avoid widespread abuses. Seasonal or cyclical hires are also common; these usually entail minimal or no benefits beyond an hourly wage or capped compensation for services. The provisions of these contractual agreements vary widely, and few entail protections concerning discipline or firing. The agency usually retains the option to cancel the contract for any reason.

*Employee Rights and Restrictions*

As indicated earlier, public employment was at one time considered a privilege rather than a right. By the 1960s, however, constitutional case law recognized that public employment could not be conditioned upon the sacrifice of rights enjoyed by all other persons unless the nature of the job required it (Rosenbloom 1971). Managers must be prepared to defend any deprivations of rights as reasonably "job related." This means that some employees, especially emergency employees (police officers and firefighters, for instance), may have substantial limitations imposed on their freedoms, such as where they may live, what they may wear, when and how they may be searched, and what they can say.

Public employees are also deemed to have a "substantial interest" in their jobs, at least as these affect their reputations and careers. These rights are protected under the due process clauses of the Fifth and Fourteenth amendments. Since the 1970s, the range of these protections has varied rather inconsistently with evolving case law and new civil rights statutes. The prevailing legal judgments today seem to favor the interests of the agency over the rights of employees, but they have not wholly returned to the pre-1960s doctrine that a public job is a matter of privilege. Legal doctrine imposes a "balancing test" between agency interests and employee rights that prevents total capitulation to one extreme or the other, yet poses significant uncertainty as to determining the proper balance in specific cases (cf. *Cleveland Board of Education v. Loudermill* 1985, 562).

Public employment is further protected under the equal protection clause of the Fourteenth Amendment, as well as by a number of related civil rights statutes that prohibit various forms of discrimination and harassment based upon race, ethnicity, religion, gender, and sexual orientation. A variety of affirmative action and equal employment practices have also been mandated pursuant to this constitutional standard. Other protections exist through statutes such as the Fair Labor Standards Act (FLSA) and the Occupational Safety and Health Act (OSHA), which regulate compensation standards, overtime provisions, worker safety, and environmental conditions.

Finally, although the freedom of association is constitutionally protected, the right of many civil service and merit service employees to participate in political campaigns has been restricted in the federal government and in most states. The federal Hatch Act of 1939 spawned a number of "mini" Hatch acts among the states, and these restrict types of participation in campaigns, party management, and fundraising that have the potential to compromise impartiality and lead to the formation of party machines. Some modifications have been made to these acts over the years, especially the 1993 revision of the federal Hatch Act, which restored some rights to many federal employees to participate in political party activities in limited fashion.

The wide range of legal standards and regulations affecting employees present a formidable challenge to HRM officials. They must balance them with the managerial needs of their agencies and educate managers in the best practices that they engender. This is difficult to achieve, in part because the case law of the courts changes fairly rapidly and the evolving standards are often difficult to understand and apply with confidence. Amid all these laws, it is not uncommon to face conflicting legal mandates from different authorities. Even specialists in personnel law find it difficult to maneuver among them. For example, it is common to receive Department of Labor (DOL) opinions on cases that do not jibe with provisions of the FLSA, and then to encounter court opinions that change the meaning of existing standards. HRM officials often get conflicting advice; ultimately, they must rely upon their own judgment in difficult cases. Thus, it is prudent for public managers to know at least the basics of constitutional and statutory protections afforded employees, and to err on the side of caution when employees' rights are affected by agency policies.

## RECRUITMENT AND SELECTION

Recruiting for public jobs in a democracy requires standards of openness, fair consideration, and equal opportunity that can draw out the length of the process considerably. Elections and political appointments dominate the top ranks of most government agencies, and it can take months or years of campaigning before candidates are finally chosen. Elected officials then take many more months, and even years, to make all their political appointments.

In merit, for-cause, and contract systems, managers and HRM professionals must determine appropriate and viable sources of recruits (internal and external to the agency), while also assessing whether the open positions should be redesigned and/or redeployed. Furthermore, they must assess the competitiveness of salary and benefits, along with any unique qualities or challenges about the job that will affect the success of the recruitment effort. Managers must assess the broader economic conditions that may affect availability and interest of qualified applicants. For example, during the "dot-com" boom of the late 1990s, it was extremely difficult to recruit information technology (IT) employees into government positions. Agencies simply could not compete on salaries and benefits, so they were forced to hire less-qualified people. The situation reversed itself with the dot-com crash a few years later and now provides a rich talent pool for public employment (see study question 1).

Given the complicated nature of many public jobs, it is also quite difficult to design recruitment processes that will help a manager effectively identify, attract, and hire the right person for a given job. Despite ongoing attempts to specify relevant knowledge, skills, and abilities (KSAs), a significant degree of subjectivity pervades all hiring decisions. As we indicated in the previous chapter, the four broad types of criteria (fit character, merit, representation, and proper political ideals) traditionally applied in public employment do not lend themselves to precision. Moreover, their application to specific hiring decisions is often more tacit than explicit. In any hiring process, one must pay as much attention to informal and unspoken cues as to objective indicators. For these reasons, it is usually wise to include other colleagues, subordinates, and superiors in the recruitment process. They sense different things about candidates that should factor into the ultimate hiring decision. Additionally, the interview process often requires more than a single encounter with applicants in order to adequately assess their qualifications and fit with the agency. In the end, the manager or managers charged with making the final decision commonly sense that their judgments still involve a considerable degree of luck.

These difficulties help explain why finding the best employee usually takes far more time and expense than managers desire. They face serious pressures to fill positions quickly—such as market competition for the same applicants, looming budgetary threats that could freeze hiring, and reallocation of positions to other divisions in the agency. Because of these factors, managers jealously guard their open positions and try desperately to fill them as soon as possible. In this light, it is easy to understand why bureaucratic politics concerning recruitment and selection is heated, and why HRM offices face the ire of line managers for trying to do their jobs as conscientiously as possible. Recruitment and selection is inherently difficult, requiring a balance of thorough preparation and process with expeditious timing. Managers who try to juggle the process by themselves usually fail to maintain this balance and end up making many bad hiring decisions.

Although recruitment and hiring processes vary significantly, it will be useful to review a list of steps commonly followed by public managers to recruit merit and contract employees. These are provided in Exhibit 9.1. This summary of steps illustrates the complexity of the HRM function and the need for experts to play a significant role in working with managers to balance the needs of the organization with the special criteria that arise from work in the public sector.

Exhibit 9.1 **Common Steps in Recruitment and Selection Processes of Public Agencies**

1. Administrator notifies HRM office and affected line employees of new positions, resignations, transfers, etc.

2. Assemble committee of staff, colleagues, and HRM officials to assess whether the current job description (KSAs) needs revising according to changing job conditions, and to assist in setting up the rest of recruitment and selection process. What certifications, licenses, etc. are required? (Job analysis and evaluation.)

3. Assess market pool versus targeted (in-house) recruitment options with HRM office. Must determine when/if promotion ladders and seniority issues pertain.

4. Set schedule for recruitment process.

5. Assess AA/EEO/diversity needs of affected job classes (AA/EEO office maintains labor pool demographic characteristics and hiring goals/deficits of affected offices). Factor in accommodation for veterans' preference and for ADA-affected applicants.

6. Assess salary/benefit capability and comparability of affected positions. May require salary/benefit surveys conducted by either the affected offices or by HRM if it has the staff/capacity to do so. Salary ranges and benefits may be governed by grades and steps of classification system, or by contract provisions in union settings.

7. Get commitment from relevant authorities to fund and fill open lines.

8. Determine selection criteria and process (may want to consult with external reference or clientele groups for advice on proper criteria and process). What are the minimum and preferred qualifications? What types of tests and background investigations are necessary/desirable and affordable? What kinds of interviews and assessment exercises are necessary/desirable and affordable? What phases of application and screening/testing process will be handled by the HRM office or by a contracted HRM service? Enlist relevant participants, determine appropriate locations, and schedule accordingly.

9. Determine extent and type of recruitment strategy needed. What are the best sources for recruiting the best talent? What is the appropriate market for recruitment (e.g., local, statewide, regional, nationwide, international)? What sources are best for targeting minority and women applicants? What steps have been, or should be, taken to cultivate a diverse applicant pool?

10. Design job announcement with relevant and required elements (in consultation with HRM office). Must determine appropriate application period and appropriate venues (publication sources, collegial networks, conference recruiting, etc.) for advertising the position.

11. Determine membership of committee that helps make final selection.

12. Review applications to develop list of qualified applicants in the pool, and then to develop a short list of most qualified applicants. Determine if applicant pool meets selection committee expectations for acceptable candidates. If it does not meet expectations, assess feasibility of canceling recruitment and starting over at appropriate time. Budgetary cycles may factor heavily in this decision.

13. Conduct interviews of short-list candidates (first phase may include phone interviews or meetings at professional conferences). The final interview process may include a series of interviews with relevant officials, colleagues, and staff. It may also include informal social gatherings. Extent of process is contingent upon levels and types of expertise/judgment required in the position.

14. Determine which short-list applicants are worthy of a job offer, then rank them. Determine bargaining strategy for job offer. Make the offer.

15. Upon acceptance of offer, process all appropriate records and forms, and schedule orientations with HRM office. Prepare with colleagues and staff for transition of new hires into positions and for performance evaluation during probationary period.

## HRM Position Planning, Management, and Design

Planning for human resource needs in public agencies is made difficult by the diffusion of authority among the political branches at all levels of government. Political agendas and bargaining often determine more about the allocation of positions than rational analysis of workforce needs. Public managers in the current era commonly face the reality of privatization, budget cuts, and political reallocation of functions to other agencies. Political modifications of salaries, benefits, work schedules, and other perks affect the ability to plan and recruit, and they can aggravate problems with increased turnover and absenteeism.

For example, the Utah State Legislature decided in 2005 to rescind a sick leave policy it had instituted 15 years earlier, and the change prompted a large number of state workers to retire early. The policy had rewarded employees for not using sick leave by exchanging eight sick leave hours for one month of health insurance after retirement. In the eyes of many legislators (and the governor), rising health insurance costs turned a cost-effective sick leave policy into an unfunded liability. With the change, those workers who had banked many months of health insurance would lose most of the benefit at the end of the year unless they retired. State HRM officials and agency managers (those who were not retiring) were left to cope with the aftermath.

This does not mean that workforce planning is a waste of time. Much can still be done to anticipate broad trends that will affect the ability to recruit, motivate, and sustain a qualified workforce. HRM officials often track turnover and retirement rates for agencies to help with succession planning. Workforce characteristics can be tracked to plan for modifications to benefit plans. For instance, the entry of large numbers of women into the workforce has prompted managers to restructure work schedules and develop alternative work provisions, including day care policies, family leave policies, and job sharing arrangements. Changing technology, especially information technology, has allowed many agencies to consider work-at-home programs and to plan for reallocation of positions away from clerical job classes to other agency functions. Continuing budget cuts have prompted planning for temporary and volunteer worker programs. Contingency plans are often developed to deal with hiring freezes, reductions in force, work furloughs, and work reassignments. The aging of the workforce has prompted reassessment of benefit plans to include long-term care, different types of medical coverage, leave policies, and semiretirement provisions.

## Job Analysis, Design, and Classification

Even small public agencies lacking HRM specialists engage in job analysis and design, if only on an informal and haphazard basis. At the very least, broad judgments must be made as to the content and qualifications of positions. Small jurisdictions often hire consultants to help them rethink the design of key positions. Such activities usually accompany broader studies of organizational capacity for both growing and downsizing agencies.

For larger agencies, job analysis and design become part of management planning and are conducted systematically with the help of HRM specialists. Job analysis leads to the creation of job descriptions, which then enable the creation of job classifications. This is achieved mainly through a process of judging the similarities and differences among various positions. We emphasize that efforts at classification are more a matter of judgment than rigorous technical analysis. Analysts can identify many specific components of positions and still miss the essence of what a specific job is really all about. This can happen inadvertently or by design. The example of clerical positions, mentioned in the previous chapter, illustrates the point: Clerical positions tend to be analyzed and categorized by use of technical terms and criteria that emphasize lower-status

skills and training, and therefore lower pay grades and benefits. Yet, many clerical positions play central roles in representing the agency in a politically astute manner, maneuvering informally through complex layers of bureaucratic process and politics to assist superiors in expediting all kinds of decisions, and even allocating resources and managing processes on their own. In job analysis and design, these vital roles are often relegated to vague and marginal categories such as "other duties as assigned," or "coordinate and maintain office processes."

This example makes it clear that effective job analysis and classification involves careful assessment of both formal and informal dimensions of work. Centralized HRM offices are most adept at analyzing formally acknowledged job elements but are limited in their ability to assess the informal roles that may substantially differentiate one position in a traditional job class from another. Battles over which roles and elements will be formally acknowledged constitute a significant aspect of HRM politics (see study question 2).

Formal job analysis and classification began with the creation of protected merit systems. Early analysts emphasized fitting employees to rationalized job descriptions through a bureaucratic *rank-in-position* system that provides information to legislatures and executives for purposes of control over numbers of jobs, managerial efficiency, and cost. Rank in position means the officeholder carries no rank between jobs and is identified only by job title and functions. This contrasts with *rank-in-person* systems typically associated with professionals who carry their rank with them into different jobs. Military officers, medical practitioners, clergy, tenure-track faculty, lawyers, and many other formally recognized professions enjoy rank-in-person status.

The difference is rather dramatic in terms of job classifications. Rank-in-position job classes are typically broken into narrow, specialized job duties bounded by rigid procedures and rules. Job tasks are standardized and routinized, and pay is pegged to specific steps and grades that mark marginal increases in job tasks and complexity. Emphasis is placed on entering at the bottom and working up in very small steps, though sometimes exceptions are made. Rank-in-person positions typically enjoy a broader and simpler system of ranks that are often determined by the profession itself through professional associations. This system permits lateral entry as well as much better pay and extra job perks at each rank. At various times, both systems have been lumped into common pay and job classification schedules (such as the federal government's General Schedule), which tends to obscure the significance of different ranking systems. Most governments adopt multiple schedules to reflect different kinds of employment or agency status.

Since the early 1990s, many governments have considered adopting more flexible approaches to the classification of rank-in-position jobs. Traditional step-and-grade systems are notorious for high levels of legalism, rigid bureaucratic steps for promotion and job reclassification, technical complexity, and weak performance evaluations that focus on quantity rather than quality of work. A variety of efforts at simplifying HRM processes have been tried, including consolidation of various job grades into broadbands that permit more flexible movement among jobs and job assignments as well as pay adjustments. Some decentralization of HRM functions to line agencies has also occurred in order to enhance the ability of managers to reallocate job functions, make their own classification decisions, and tailor HRM processes to more of the informal characteristics of their agencies. As noted earlier, however, such changes are often cyclical and depend upon the ambitions of politicians who may seek recentralization to enhance their influence.

## Compensation and Benefits

On average, compensation and benefits make up more than 80 percent of public agency budgets. It is hardly surprising, therefore, that taxpayer associations and legislative bodies concentrate a

lot of attention on these matters in an effort to control costs. Nor is it surprising that employee associations, managers, and HRM offices constantly seek to acquire more resources and flexibility to attract and retain a talented workforce. The resulting pressures subject pay and benefits policy to the most contentious and dispiriting politics. Sadly, the compromises that emerge from this cauldron do little to motivate public servants. This reality is seldom acknowledged by management theorists and practitioners, many of whom remain wedded to the belief that economic incentives are primary motivators for employees in any sector. The compensation systems imposed on the public service rest largely on this belief, despite a host of factors that immediately compromise their intent and design.

### Compensation

Intuitively, we all want to believe that employees can be paid fairly for the work they do, and thereby make enough on which to live. The old adage "A fair day's pay for a fair day's work" still seems to capture the essence of what most people mean by "merit pay." Indeed, the principle of fairness or "equity" runs through the heart of all compensation plans. It seems so simple, but unfortunately it is not. A major problem lies in discerning the true merit of people involved in organized, collaborative efforts, and matching that to an appropriate level of pay. A brief review of a few systematic pay plans used in the public sector will illustrate the complexity involved in deciding what principle to use for determining compensation.

*Longevity pay systems* presume that employees gain valuable insight, expertise, and institutional memory as they rise in seniority and rank. They invest much of their lives and loyalties in the employing agency, and this should count for something. Moreover, longevity pay tends to reduce turnover costs, as this investment is slowly but steadily rewarded. Longevity systems exist in various forms among some hourly wage earners and salaried professionals—police, teachers, firefighters, and nurses among the most common. However, these systems are also subject to intense criticism, first because some long-term employees do not live up to the merit presumption. They perform at minimally acceptable levels, while younger, lower-paid employees shoulder the extra burden. Critics, therefore, tend to see longevity as an inequitable and dispiriting system because raises go for time served rather than relative performance. Second, the system's stability also makes it more rigid—more resistant to the change and adaptation that is sometimes necessary to improve work (Wamsley 1997). Supporters of longevity systems point out, however, that the technicians and professionals who are subject to these policies are, as a group, among the most satisfied and productive workers anywhere.

Alternatively, traditional *merit pay systems* attempt to link pay to individual performance. Some tasks entail more valuable work and therefore deserve better pay relative to other tasks in the same agency. This concept is known as *internal equity*. These rankings are usually tested as well for comparability with other similar or competing organizations, a concept known as *external equity*. At the same time, better performance in any job deserves more pay. Accordingly, merit pay systems first structure pay through hierarchies of grades and ranges that, ideally, permit pay disparities based upon work value and performance. Then, each year, either percentage increases to the base or onetime bonuses in varying amounts are awarded to those who perform at or above minimum expectations.

Merit pay systems routinely fail in the eyes of employees and managers alike. First, they are inordinately complex because they require constant analysis and diversification of job tasks and analyses that must be linked to pay levels and ranges. Second, they require more precise distinctions among individual performers than the nature of complex and collaborative work generally

allows. They force managers to attach dollar values to work elements that, in most jobs, defy such discreet measures, and that are also dependent upon the collaborative performance of colleagues and supporting staff. Third, merit systems assume that managers who award merit can and should monitor their subordinates closely enough to make such precise distinctions. Few workers could tolerate someone standing over their shoulder for this purpose, and most managers would not want to do it in the first place. So, at best, managers must rely mainly upon indirect and incomplete performance indicators. Fourth, public merit systems rely upon political branches to adequately fund merit rewards. As personnel history demonstrates, legislatures and executives rarely do so (cf. Ingraham 1993a, 1993b). This violates a basic principle of *expectancy theory* upon which merit systems are based—namely, that merit raises must be sufficient to motivate employees, to meet their expectations for the work performed (Perry 1986). Politicians find it expedient to withhold and renege on pay raises and pay-for-performance incentives in order to avoid tax increases. Because of this failure, many managers recognize that when merit raise funds are available (a haphazard prospect at best), they will function more as a cost-of-living adjustment than anything else. This is accompanied by an inevitable tendency to collapse merit assessments into simple pass/fail distinctions that treat most employees alike. Managers will seek to equalize the raises as much as possible by rating the vast majority of employees as "meeting or exceeding expectations" (Fox and Shirkey 1997). Only those employees who clearly do not meet expectations may be denied merit raises. Fifth, fluctuations in job markets can undermine the established order of pay grades and ranges among some jobs, forcing managers to "market-adjust" pay levels with merit funds that would otherwise go to all job classes. This further inflames resentment among employees.

Finally, merit systems often fail because they emphasize pay as the primary motivating factor for workers. Studies indicate that, for public employees, pay is less of a motivator than intrinsic factors that affect the quality of the work. A large number of employees join public service because it involves serving the public and because the work is challenging and important (Bright 2003; Perry and Wise 1990; Perry 1996; Perry et al. 2010). With all their other failings included, merit systems not only miss the point, they typically operate in the most dispiriting and demotivating fashion.

Despite these serious failings, merit pay systems remain prevalent in public agencies. It is very hard for people to distinguish between the principle of merit (which no one wants to abandon) and the flawed dynamics of merit pay systems. HRM professionals try to innovate with new merit schemes, such as pay broadbanding, skill-based pay, and gainsharing. Though more flexible and team oriented, these schemes ultimately suffer for lack of support from politicians. Pay broadbanding permits more discretion and flexibility for line managers to reward teams as well as individuals, but it also tends to escalate the fixed costs of the system, which legislators in the current era strenuously resist. Skill-based pay focuses on paying for skills acquired by employees rather than on tasks associated with the position, but this depends heavily on adequate opportunities for training and development. As stated earlier, these opportunities are among the first to be cut when budget shortfalls occur. Gainsharing encourages employees to work together in teams to save the agency money through improved efficiency and performance. The surplus is then supposed to be rewarded back as bonuses or reinvested in their group work projects and work environment. Short-run pilot tests of this approach have demonstrated some real successes, but these are seldom expanded into a full-scale pay system. Politics again intrudes in ironic and disappointing ways. For example, it is common practice for politicians to cut the savings achieved by such schemes from agency budgets. The results of efficient performance get reinterpreted as "fat" to be cut away under the pressures of cost containment. It reminds one of the old adage that "no good deed goes unpunished!" (See study question 3.)

*Benefits*

Benefits policy is also complex and filled with snags, though its motivational power is far greater than merit pay incentives. Many people seek public employment initially because they value stable benefits over the higher pay that accompanies riskier employment settings in the private and nonprofit sectors. From an HR manager's perspective, however, the task of managing and sustaining these benefits is complicated, and it is becoming more problematic.

First, benefits make up anywhere between 15 and 40 percent of total personnel costs per agency, and are therefore as much a matter of fiscal concern to politicians and interest groups as compensation. Many benefits are sponsored and defined through a combination of federal, state, and local legislation and thus are managed through intergovernmental relations and contractual agreements. For example, some mandatory programs such as unemployment insurance and workers' compensation are run through a network of programs established by federal and state legislation.

The variety of benefits and the array of benefit options add to cost and complexity. For instance, retirement benefits may consist of a combination of Social Security (also known as Old-Age and Survivors Insurance Trust Fund, or OASI), Supplemental Security Income (SSI), a state or local retirement plan, and individualized investment retirement accounts that are managed in-house or by contracted vendors. Health care benefits can include a variety of plans tailored to individual needs. Because of rapidly escalating costs, traditional fee-for-service plans now involve substantial employee co-pay requirements, and many states and localities have abandoned them in favor of preferred provider organizations (PPOs) and health maintenance organizations (HMOs) to help manage costs. The range of health benefits varies widely among the programs. Rural states have great difficulty attracting health insurers and providers, which means their employees have few real choices but are still required to shell out high co-pays.

Beyond these traditional benefits, many public agencies provide a range of programs to help employees manage the interaction of their personal and professional lives. Typical among them are flextime, compressed work schedules, telecommuting, job sharing, family leave programs, vacation leave, sick leave, fitness and wellness programs, employee assistance programs, and tax-sheltered flexible-spending accounts. Many of these programs entail little monetary cost but add significant administrative burdens. Managers and HRM officials must continually assess the needs among employee groups for these kinds of programs. Simply providing them does not guarantee that employees will use them. It takes a great deal of notification and orientation among employees to learn how to use them effectively. Employees can also become quite reliant on some benefits and will strenuously resist any efforts to modify them for the sake of organizational needs. Many of these benefits constitute key elements of employee working conditions that may be subject to collective bargaining or intense meet-and-confer sessions with management.

One common method used by HRM officials to manage a wide range of benefits is to offer them in a *cafeteria plan*. Employees are allocated a fixed-dollar amount for benefits, and then they choose among items on a menu of benefit options and programs. When too few employees subscribe to a program, it becomes a target of elimination. HRM officials try to contain the costs of these programs through various risk-management strategies that focus on avoiding injuries, preventing chronic health problems, and reducing liabilities. This can require statistical forecasting and analysis of turnover rates, sick leave use, typical medical conditions, vacation usage, and injury rates. Training programs are then developed to help employees reduce high-risk behavior. However, such efforts can become intrusive and, in some cases, may even threaten basic rights. For example, some employers have attempted to get rid of employees with high medical risks and even tried to genetically screen applicants for medical risks as a means of containing future health

liabilities. This may help meet some organizational imperatives, but it crosses some disturbing ethical lines and is highly intrusive to the private lives of those affected. Public-sector organizations are expected to protect these privacy rights and even become a model employer for others in the private and nonprofit sectors. Under such expectations, it becomes especially problematic for public organizations to compromise the interests of individual employees for the sake of the effective functioning of the organization.

In the current era, rapidly rising benefits costs and tight budgets have forced many governments into austere reforms of benefit programs, especially at state and local levels. The financial crisis of 2007–8 and the ensuing "Great Recession" changed many people's attitude toward generous benefit plans for public employees, leading to substantial modifications and cuts in many state and local governments. The longstanding expectation of lower wages, balanced by good and stable benefits, no longer pertains to many public employees, and this is likely to reduce the attractiveness of public employment significantly. As long as unemployment remains high, public employers will retain and attract employees, but that could change dramatically when the unemployment rate falls.

## Training and Development

Since the New Deal era, governmental training and development programs in the United States have been the envy of the world. Public agencies have developed, or helped sponsor development of, specialized professions that serve nonprofits, private industry, and governments worldwide. Training and development have traditionally been viewed as a necessary and desirable social investment as well as specific support to public agencies. However, the public attitude toward social investment has declined severely in the current antitax, entrepreneurial era, which now emphasizes individual responsibility for funding and developing professional and technical competencies. Public funding for higher education and agency training programs has diminished accordingly, prompting alarm among those who promote human capital investment. As of 2008, only about 1.3 percent of most agency personnel budgets was allocated to training and development, when a minimum of 3 to 5 percent is recommended (cf. Pew Center on the States 2012; see also Winter Commission 1993).

In many cases, responsibility for training programs has been decentralized to line agencies, with HRM offices retaining only the agencywide training functions. It is difficult for line managers to carve out time and resources for training when they are already short of employees and program funding. Moreover, they may not control the types of training they really need in these difficult circumstances. As illustrated in the Prairie County case, human service agencies experience frequent mismatches in the types and levels of training required for caseworkers. Turnover among caseworkers is typically very high in local field offices, which means more introductory on-the-job training is needed. However, HRM training funds usually are allocated across a full range of training for such positions, often in compliance with state and federal mandates. Much of this training occurs in central locations, or even out of state, and this pulls new employees away from their on-the-job training. Orientation time is thereby extended, caseloads mount up, and both managers and employees begin to view training as a frustrating distraction—especially when performance standards are tied to resolution of cases.

This kind of problem highlights tensions that make the training and development process increasingly difficult. The basic process entails three phases. HRM officials and managers must first collaborate to assess training needs, then design and deliver them, and then try to evaluate their effectiveness. All agree that good training is vital to effective performance, but training needs far exceed the available resources (see Exhibit 9.2 for list of typical training needs).

Exhibit 9.2    **Typical Training Needs for Public Agencies**

This list is only suggestive, not exhaustive. HRM offices manage or coordinate many, but not all of the suggested training programs. Public organizations sponsor hundreds of training sessions and opportunities each year and must forecast training needs many months and years ahead.

1. New employee orientation
2. On-the-job training: vestibule training, mentoring, internships, immersion programs, apprenticeships, job rotation, etc.
3. Professional development: certification and licensing, continuing education requirements, training for promotion and advancement, etc.
4. Preventive training programs: illegal discrimination and harassment, constitutional rights, legalities of recruiting, ethics/conflict of interest codes, injury prevention, safe equipment operation, emergency and disaster preparedness, etc.
5. Employment relations and development: conflict resolution, bargaining processes, performance appraisals, rewards and promotion process, diversity training, educational advancement, fair labor standards, service contracting, etc.
6. Management training: leadership, supervision, system design, operations management, coordination of systems, improving communications, incentive systems, appraisal systems, strategic planning and assessment, organizational development and planned change, problem solving, etc.

When resources are scarce, the big question arises as to which types of training are most needed. Line managers tend to emphasize immediate, task-oriented training needs, while middle- and senior-level executives want to focus on coordinative, preventive, and strategic needs. HRM officials try to achieve a balance among these. Inevitably, however, a greater portion of training budgets goes to the technical and operational skills while development of generalist skills (leadership, interpersonal skills, and conceptual abilities) is sacrificed. This stems in part from the fact that training in technical and operational skills is more easily evaluated. Evaluation of training programs is hard to justify under tight budget constraints, and it is the most neglected phase of the process. However, when it is mandated, the effort will usually go toward measurable assessment. It is inordinately difficult to measure the increased value that leadership or interpersonal skills bring to agency programs.

The heavy preoccupation with measurable assessment of outcomes further skews the bias of training and development programs. It presents some serious problems for succession planning. The World War II baby boom generation is rapidly approaching retirement age. Many of these employees have reached highly responsible middle- and upper-management levels in public agencies. The most important skills at these levels are generalist in nature, while training and development programs are geared more toward technical and operational skills. One hears a lot of talk among HRM officials about succession planning, but legislatures and political executives seem unready and ill prepared to support it in even a meager fashion. Everyone wants efficient and productive performance, but few seem ready to support and develop the kinds of public performance now most in need.

**Performance and Appraisal**

The attention to performance of public employees is strongly linked to our penchant for accountability. As described in the previous chapter, much of the history of public personnel development is about democratic accountability. We attend first to the qualifications for office to help

ensure that public servants reflect and serve the values of the broader political community. As we have seen, these vary and are contested over time. With the changing eras, new reform leaders attack the competency, character, responsiveness, and political ideals of the entrenched public service. Appraisal systems are developed and applied in this politicized context to help induce change among the ranks of employees. The current era is no exception. Political leaders of the entrepreneurial era attack "bloated, unresponsive bureaucracies," first through privatization and downsizing, and then through measures designed to police their efficiency relative to preferred (announced as "new and better") modes of public service delivery—as in competitive markets, contracted services, lean networks, and the like. The improvement of analytical techniques for tracking outcomes and individual performance serve these purposes quite well. However, they do little in any objective sense to meet managerial purposes of assessment. This is the sad irony of performance appraisal.

Despite decades of study and innovation, every method of managerial appraisal tried has been found wanting. Private- and public-sector studies consistently verify that most managers and employees believe their appraisal systems are ineffective, unfair, or not related to their ostensible purposes (cf. Daley 1988; Halachmi 2011, 1995; Ilgen and Favero 1985; Ingraham 1993; Pearce and Porter 1986; Perry 1991; Schellhardt 1996). Insightful analysts of organizational processes and employee motivation have warned against focusing appraisals on individuals and tying them to rewards and incentives (Balfour 1992; Deming 1982; Gabris and Mitchell 1988; McGregor 1957). Behavioral studies of professionals and other trained workers have demonstrated that once the premises of their jobs are defined and programmed through training, the vast majority work steadily without need of much supervision or appraisal (Cyert and March 1959; Dunsire 1979; March and Simon 1958; Simon 1957). Apart from their broader political mandates, then, why would managers bother with appraisals?

Intuitively, people want managers to meaningfully assess the performance of employees in terms of their job descriptions, in terms of their performance relative to fellow employees in the same positions, and in terms of how they contribute to broader agency goals and objectives. And we want the managers themselves evaluated on the same basis. We expect appraisals to be fair. The promise of carefully designed, scientifically objective evaluation processes lures managers into believing that fairness is achievable and that the processes will safeguard their judgments against legal challenges. Decades of research and experimentation have been devoted to improving these aspects of performance evaluation; yet, time and again, when managers and employees experience the actual process, they come away perplexed, frustrated, and often offended. The following discussion illustrates why.

First, given what we have already learned about the failures of public pay and benefit systems, it should be clear that tying them to performance evaluations is a huge mistake. Pecuniary rewards will never match expectations because they are too small and too infrequent in the public sector. Second, tying performance to monetary benefits is troublesome because even the smallest difference (that is, a few dollars a month) in rewards among fellow employees will spark an inordinate amount of resentment. Monetary increments force a regimented and symbolic precision on the often nuanced and idiosyncratic judgments managers must make among performing employees. Third, mistakes in these judgments are likely, given that managers usually monitor performance sporadically from afar and indirectly, and because so much of public work is interactive or collaborative. Most organizational tasks are inherently interdependent, and many are also abstract— of a communicative and interpretive nature. Discerning the relative merits of individual workers in this context is bound to be difficult. Moreover, performance evaluation tied to incentives introduces a competitive element that can undermine the pressing need for cooperation. Setting

employees against each other on the basis of precise, differential rewards is hardly conducive to teamwork. Fourth, it is common that managers do not share the same professional backgrounds and competencies of the people they supervise (Halachmi 1993). Managers cannot effectively evaluate these subordinates, so they rely instead on peer evaluations that use professional rather than organizational criteria. Finally, many of the criteria established for employee assessments are determined by higher authorities who seek to control the direction and priorities of the organization. These authorities may well have agendas that do not favor the work being done by whole subunits of an agency. They may lack power to eliminate the disfavored subunits, but they can certainly retard their effectiveness through imposition of inappropriate assessment criteria that will make the subunit look bad (Thompson 1967); so much, then, for objectivity.

Given these factors, it is generally wiser to separate performance evaluation from flawed reward systems if anything constructive is to come from the effort. In fact, it is probably the case that most public managers and employees engage in off-the-record evaluations, where they can mix constructive criticism with compliments that are not compromised by mismatched pecuniary awards. Most public managers are probably more interested in buffering their employees from the vicissitudes of formal appraisal systems, and some may even provide an informal or shadow evaluation practice that focuses on system problems and quality work rather than on people (Deming 1982; Fox and Shirkey 1997).

The glaring failures of formal appraisal systems will not likely dissuade politicians or managers from continuing to use them. They are, after all, still useful as political tools for enhancing appearances and power. Agency managers will no doubt strive diligently to deflect or mute the harshness of these systems, gradually turning them into simple pass/fail evaluations that preserve a roughly equal distribution of meager pecuniary incentives (Fox and Shirkey 1997). Performance appraisal systems thus induce a cyclical drama that all public officials must endure.

## UNIONS AND COLLECTIVE BARGAINING

Unions emerged during the Industrial Revolution of the eighteenth and nineteenth centuries as a response by tradesman to the deskilling and standardization of their work in mass production facilities. They had enjoyed substantial political and economic power through trade guilds, but the guilds disappeared quickly as industrialization transformed society. Working conditions in the new manufactories were horrible and dangerous, and workers were paid extremely low wages for long hours (often more than 80 per week), seven days a week. Worse, they were deemed expendable because jobs were simplified and regimented, and a surplus of labor was available. In short, workers lived at the whim of their employers, and their entire lives were transformed by this extreme new form of dependency. This drove many into unionizing activities that faced severe private and public resistance but eventually won substantial concessions on wages and working conditions, as well as some political support for their beleaguered industrial neighborhoods. Early successes at unionization were achieved largely without state sponsorship or protection. Important legislation, such as the Wagner Act of 1935, which established private-sector rights to unionize, did not emerge until unions had achieved informal political and industrial clout. Industrial unions did much to improve wages, benefits, and working conditions, not only for themselves, but for nonunion workers across the country. Their successes provided a baseline for satisfactory standards of work life, making it possible for blue-collar workers to establish modest, livable communities beyond the workplace (see chapter 5 for a more expansive discussion of the processes of industrialization and their consequences for public service).

Public-sector unions developed even more slowly but emerged out of the same adversarial labor-management culture. Mechanics and laborers unionized in the 1830s, and postal workers

successfully organized in the 1880s. Local police and firefighters organized themselves in the late nineteenth and early twentieth centuries. Strong resistance to public unions persisted, however, in part because they were viewed as a threat to governmental sovereignty over public policy. Opponents of public-sector unionization argued that labor strikes had the potential to shut down parts of government and that union contract negotiations would be conducted by appointed rather than elected officials, thus tying the hands of legislative bodies.

Despite these objections, public unions began to grow due to increased political support for private-sector unions during the New Deal era. At the state and local level, Wisconsin led the way in 1959, with the state legislature requiring local governments to bargain with organized employees and subsequently authorizing state employees to organize in 1967. Dennis Dresang notes that the American Federation of State, County, and Municipal Employees (AFSCME), now the largest public employee union, formed out of the Wisconsin State Employees Association and was supported by local and state government managers "as a way of managing conflict between employees and their supervisors" (Dresang 2002, 307–310). (Note the irony, then, that Wisconsin's current governor, Scott Walker, would lead the charge in rescinding collective bargaining rights for these employees.) Many other states then followed suit. State and local unions grew the most in subsequent decades. As of 2008, 28 states had extended bargaining rights to all public employees, nine states covered selected workgroups, and 14 failed to cover any workers. It is notable, too, that many employee associations that lack collective bargaining rights, operate in much the same manner as unions, often wielding substantial informal bargaining power.

Federal employees received their first broad support for unionization from President John F. Kennedy (in office 1961–1963) when he issued Executive Orders 10987 and 10988 (both in 1962), which allowed workers to bargain collectively, but only over a narrow range of working conditions and grievance procedures. (This is referred to as a narrow "scope of bargaining.") To this day, federal unions cannot formally bargain over wages and benefits. Statutory support for collective bargaining finally came in 1978, with the passage of the Civil Service Reform Act. This act established the Federal Labor Relations Authority (FLRA) to provide mediation and arbitration services and to certify unions as bargaining agents.

Membership in public unions grew rapidly during the 1960s and 1970s, peaking at around 45 percent of the workforce, and then slowed down in the 1980s. A variety of factors such as privatization of public jobs, downward wage restructuring in the private sector, and resurgence of antiunion sentiment have led to stagnation and decline in public union ranks to around 35 percent overall. Private-sector union membership has declined much more significantly to around 16 percent, as the corporate sector downsized and globalized union jobs in an effort to control labor costs. Although public unions are again under attack, they remain an extremely significant factor in public HRM, especially at state and local levels. The reasons for their continued viability have much to do with the lack of identity, power, and status in the lower civil service systems of our governments. Unions provide unifying symbols of collective power vis-à-vis other employee classes in the public employment community. Understanding public agencies as employment communities explains much about the political dynamics of human resources management.

## THE PUBLIC SERVICE AS POLITICAL COMMUNITY

In previous chapters, we described how modern, complex organizations of the twentieth century transformed society, molding work life to their ways and purposes. Employees have become educated functionaries, loyal to organizational life and process, and they spend much of their lives within them (Whyte 1956). These organizations have engendered new expressions of political

life and, in many respects, possess attributes of political communities in their own right (Wolin 1960). The political tensions inherent in the various functions of public HRM make more sense when portrayed as aspects of such communities.

Political communities display a variety of features that are relevant to this analysis. A vast literature exists on the subject, but we rely primarily on Deborah Stone's "polis model" because she presents it in contrast to "rationalist" explanations of society that presume a "market model" of collective life (Stone 1997, 7–9 and chap. 1, passim). Many HRM practices employ a means-ends rationality based on the market model. Individual workers seek to maximize their own self-interests, and employers harness these interests with economic and psychological incentives to meet organizational goals and objectives. This individualistic and competitive view of organizational life overlooks significant insight from more robust models of community that help explain how and why public employment relations works the way it does.

Political communities are places where people collectively find meaning and develop various dimensions of their lives. They involve issues of membership, roles, culture, and conferral of status, rights, and privileges that define a way of life. They stimulate associations of shared commitment and common interest that shape patterns of motivation. They provide a "sense of order and of fair play" through a variety of governing processes (Stone 1997, 21). They mediate "commons problems" in which "self-interest and public interest work against each other" (22). They emphasize ideas, influence, cooperation, persuasion, socialization, and communal education. They are mired in passionate differences of opinion, and in expressions of loyalty, as well as parochial exclusion. They cultivate a sense of tradition and legacy—an appreciation of their origins as well as an awareness of what they will pass on to posterity.

Community members have allies and enemies, long memories, and are constantly aware of the play of power. They engage in policymaking not only to solve problems but also to affect "how groups are formed, split, and re-formed." Thus, they help constitute the orders and structures of the agency, thereby shaping the allocation of priorities, powers, and resources (Stone 1997, 27). Budgets, for example, are allocative devices that help agencies meet goals, but they also determine status and power among competing divisions and programs. Buildings, office space, and equipment are not simply rational tools of implementation—they constitute vitally important symbols of rank and influence in the agency community. Even the relative size of office cubicles (not to mention real offices!) and their accoutrements matter tremendously among employees and managers alike. In short, agency policies define or "constitute" ways of living and working together (Cook 1996), and these yield distinct organizational cultures and subcultures (Ott 1989; Schein 1993).

In agencies, as well as in broader communities, goals are ambiguous, fraught with paradoxes, and defined more through strategic advocacy than rational search for efficient alternatives (for a more detailed discussion, see chapters 3 and 13 of this book and Stone 1997, 1–13). Within this milieu, information is "interpretive, incomplete, and strategically withheld" in order to garner power and cultivate influence. The acceptance of "knowledge" depends heavily on who is presenting it, the means by which it is presented, and how it is interpreted (Stone, 28). Furthermore, communication is not simply a matter of sending and receiving "data": It is a recursive and rhetorical process that depends as much upon timing, emotional conditions, and cultivation of communal dispositions to accept the message as it does on the substance of the message (Green and Zinke 1993).

These characteristics are found in all complex organizations and are especially prominent in public agencies. They explain much about the nature of public service and the dynamics of employment relations. The public service is all about membership—who gets in and who fits in, what qualifications one must possess, what status is conferred, how rights and powers are granted, and what rules of interaction should take precedence. Selection criteria are communally devel-

oped and contested. Employees are socialized into groups that form distinct work cultures and employment strata in which patterns of motivation vary considerably. Frederick Mosher (1982) illustrated many of these membership characteristics through a typology of American personnel systems. These do not correspond neatly to the formally defined employment systems typically established by law and presented in personnel manuals. Rather, they are sociological types that are useful for tracing informal practices and roles in agency governance (Mosher 1982, 144–146). This is most apparent in the distinction he makes between the "general civil service system" and the "career system" (Mosher 1982, 144). These two systems are often covered under the same formal rules and treated as part of the same classification system in many governments, but they differ dramatically in practice.

*General civil service systems* are populated primarily with lower ranked white-collar employees whose jobs are rigidly and formally defined. They hold rank in position, with very limited career steps. Their pay and benefits are tied closely to formal merit evaluation processes, which, as already indicated, are more often dispiriting than motivating. Emphasis is placed on standard operating procedures, routinized tasks, skills testing, and open competition for hiring. Hiring processes are determined mainly by centralized referral from personnel offices that are deemed by workers as an arm of management.

Discretionary powers in this system are narrowly circumscribed and technically driven. As a result, the most significant tools of power these employees wield are rules and procedures. In organizational life, these employees hold low status, not unlike enlisted military personnel relative to the commissioned officer corps. It is hardly surprising, then, that predominant patterns of motivation are structured around rigid legalism and bureaucratic routine—their only real sources of protection and power. Employees tend to police the allocation of tasks through their job descriptions and induce cooperation from above and below by controlling paperwork and bureaucratic processes. Many live by the clock and may adopt a strong quid pro quo attitude about their work contributions relative to organizational inducements. Most significant, because this system strongly discourages collective identity and offers few avenues for exercise of group power, many of its employees seek advancement into the professional career system through professional education, or they form collective bargaining units in defiance of the system. Most prefer the collective power of professions because such status wins far more legitimacy and mobility in and out of the agency, and because many states and localities limit collective bargaining rights to just a few types of employee groups (see the concluding section in chapter 3, "Discretion, Organizational Culture, and the Varieties of Bureaucratic Sensibility," for further discussion of the impact of employee sensibilities on the exercise of administrative discretion).

By contrast, the *professional career system* covers a wide variety of professions that form the middle and upper classes of agency communities. These include policy and scientific professions, staff professions, and administrative professions (Mosher 1982, 110–142). Professionals typically hold their rank in person, carrying it (and the accompanying status) from one position to another. They are selected for a career, not just a job (Mosher 1982, 158). Thus, they enjoy individualized career plans and promotional ladders that are formalized in the agency personnel system. Their professional associations develop, protect, and enhance professional education as well as employment qualifications. Professionals exert substantial control over what is deemed the "authoritative knowledge" of the agencies. Professional schools socialize and train recruits to professional norms. They help foster "a sense of unity, cohesiveness, and homogeneity" that stands in contrast to the stark life in general civil service systems (Mosher 1982, 161). Agency professionals typically control the specification of minimum and desired job qualifications in the agencies, and they conduct the recruitment and selection of colleagues at all levels. These workers

are "uninhibited by [the strictures of centralized] position classification," and enjoy substantial independence from the formal HRM system (Mosher 1982, 162). In terms of discipline, they are largely self-policed. Though sanctions can be significant, they are rarely applied in comparison to disciplinary actions in the general civil service system. The disciplinary process is far less rigid, and very tolerant, readily according each professional the benefit of any doubt.

The professional career system typically enjoys more robust training and educational opportunities due in part to certification and licensing requirements. This enhances career mobility as well as advancement. Moreover, professionals maintain their power by extending career ladders into the administrative and policy-determining ranks of the agency. They garner more trust, more discretion, and empowerment. In terms of motivation, therefore, "Theory Y" norms tend to prevail (McGregor 1960). Professionals commit strongly to organizational missions—and even help define them. They work until the job is done, rather than by the clock. They enjoy privileges and benefits that enhance their working conditions, and they exert substantial power through the strategic and tactical application of their expert knowledge. Their work lives are stimulated by interesting challenges and are thus intrinsically satisfying.

The substantial contrast between professional career systems and general civil service systems often leads to resentment, envy, "difficulties of communication, and low morale with and among other personnel of the agency" (Mosher 1982, 161). There exists a fairly distinct sense of the haves and the have-nots, of those who count and those who do not. Furthermore, political rivalries exist among the professions themselves, much like clans vying for influence in the agency community. One or another profession may dominate, while others play supporting or rival roles. Together, they form a pluralized, agency middle class that attracts many aspirants from the other employment systems. This has resulted in attempts to establish professional and paraprofessional status for many other occupations, HRM professionals among them. In many respects, attempts to reform public personnel systems are influenced by the attraction to the career-professional model. Management reforms that embrace the entrepreneurial principles of reinvention and New Public Management have targeted general civil service systems in many jurisdictions. As this proceeds, the distinctiveness of the traditional civil service system and the professional career system has blurred somewhat (Mosher 1982, 158–164).

Career systems in public agencies have been weakened significantly by the entrepreneurial (market model) ideals of the current political era. Politicization, budget cutting, privatization, and resulting reductions in force have conditioned many professionals to move among the public, private, and nonprofit sectors, with less commitment to specific agencies (Light 1999a). In the process, administrative professionals have gained more power vis-à-vis other professionals because they manage the retrenchment and contracting processes. Most professions, however, retain the distinct advantages of protective associations and more flexible career options than encountered in other employment systems.

Professionals are thus able to remain as viable participants in the broader policy community, while adapting to the competitive market model that is gradually transforming public life. For example, in state social services arenas, psychologists, social workers, and related professionals frequently move among private, nonprofit, and public organizations to take advantage of competing career opportunities and better working conditions, as well as to increase their influence over particular policies and practices within the system. In the Prairie County case, DSS caseworkers actively sought caseworker positions with nonprofit and for-profit vendors, where the pay was better and the work pressures much more tolerable. They had meaningful options in the human services subsystem. Such advantages contrast with the fortunes of the collective system which struggles to adapt.

The *collective system* is marked by an adversarial ethos that often frustrates the desire of managers and politicians to achieve a harmonious and efficient administration. It stands in contradiction to the individualistic norms and unilateral authority of rationalized merit systems, though it is not opposed to the principle of merit (Mosher 1982, 188–190). Unions seek collective influence over the determination of how merit should be rewarded and how working conditions contribute to meritorious performance. In short, they want their members to have some say in the governance of the personnel system. They want a role for their members as significant and respected citizens who share in rule over the agency communities they inhabit. Given the low status of many union jobs and the history of labor relations in general, unionized workers had little recourse but to stake this claim in an adversarial manner. Despite the initial turmoil, union-management relations typically develop in rather predictable fashion.

First, there is vigorous assertion of collective rights to unionize by employees who wish to form a bargaining unit. This is usually accompanied by strained rhetoric and high emotions about poor labor-management relations in the employing organization. Second, the formation of the bargaining unit—usually through a legally stipulated process—establishes quid pro quo bargaining over terms of a contractual relationship that includes managerial prerogatives, disciplinary processes, and workers' rights. This colors all subsequent employment relations. Third, the new relationship between management and the union develops through strict adherence to the terms of the ratified contract. Over the years, this process becomes ritualized, making the conflict more predictable and manageable for both sides, and this often results in the adoption of longer-term contracts (three to five years instead of one to two years).

This process, established collectively by union members, managers, and political authorities, puts organized workers on a new footing that means a lot to them, even if the scope of their bargaining powers are narrowly circumscribed. Mosher (1982, 207) noted that "the powers and weapons of labor unions in the public sector . . . are primarily political rather than economic." Their numbers, with their families, comprise a significant political constituency for elected politicians. The threat of work slowdowns, sick outs, and strikes (even if illegal) can induce compromises that workers would not otherwise achieve. Strikes or slowdowns, combined with media campaigns by union leaders, can publicly embarrass politicians and administrators. Most blue-collar and low-level white-collar employees who join public unions have deep roots in their communities. The hiring pools for their jobs are usually local rather than regional or national. As a result, they form communities and neighborhoods with strong ties that bridge into their employing agencies, and this affects their patterns of motivation in the workplace.

Traditionally, most blue-collar and low-level white-collar workers view their positions as jobs rather than as careers. Observers note that workers in these categories see their jobs as a means to other avocations and satisfying activities outside of work (Green et al. 1993; Mosher 1982). They may have little desire to self-actualize on the job, especially since so much of their work is heavily regimented and policed. They are likely required to punch a time clock or submit hourly work sheets, and this further induces a transactional approach to their jobs. They expect to give "a fair day's work for a fair day's pay," and no more than that without substantial inducements such as overtime pay or generous comp-time provisions. Like their civil service counterparts, they may become legalistic about workplace rules and standard operating procedures and will strictly police the provisions of labor contracts that reflect hard-won concessions from management. Unions help workers enforce these norms and provisions and enhance their sense of identity and status in the process.

Internally, unions allocate status and governance responsibilities for routine as well as strategic matters such as collective bargaining. They form their own political cultures—cultures that are

all about representation, group identity and loyalty, protective rights, fairness in decision-making processes, good-faith bargaining, agenda building, good citizenship (for example, sharing burdens and taking one's turn at various assignments), equitable rotation of plum assignments, seniority, and fair compensation.

Ironically, many of these characteristics have also hampered the ability of unions to adapt to the changing public employment environment in the entrepreneurial era. Their tight-knit cultures are inherently conservative. They fight hard to preserve their gains and rigidly maintain established labor-management processes. Their adversarial tradition aggravates the already difficult process of cutting budgets in lean or depressed fiscal environments. Some HRM scholars have advocated adoption of more collaborative, *participative decision making* (PDM) relationships based on mutual trust and respect, a flexible scope of bargaining, and diligent search for win-win compromises (cf. Kearney 1995). Unfortunately, the ever-looming threat of privatization, attempts to scale back employees' rights and protections, years of negligible raises, and cutbacks in benefits are hardly conducive to establishing such relationships. Unions tend to dig in their heels in the face of these threats, and it often makes them look bad because so many other employees are already coping with such losses. On the other hand, they have little else to bargain with in the public employment community. For their members, job mobility usually means losing union membership and protection, as well as severe cuts in pay, benefits, and the quality of working conditions.

Public unions suffer further because their private-sector counterparts have lost so many members to workforce restructuring that replaced formerly high-paying industrial and commercial jobs with lower-paying, lower-skilled service work. This has devastated many blue-collar communities by cutting incomes, forcing many residents to relocate, and breaking many of their political bonds in the process. The power base for both private and public unions steadily erodes in this environment, and the dislocations lead to higher crime rates, broken families, and less appealing communities for everyone. Union culture stands opposed to the individualistic norms and managerial ethos of the entrepreneurial era. It asserts participative rights in agency governance through collective unity and adversarial process. But with an eroded political base, unions are likely to see more losses than gains for some time to come. It will be interesting to see in the coming months and years whether the push-back by unions in Wisconsin and Ohio results in a broader movement to reverse the trend. In the meantime, however, those workers (unionized or not) who face privatization or are driven out of public service by other means may find themselves moving into a new and rather amorphous system of employment by individual contract, where power, identity, and status are heavily weighted in favor of the employer.

The *contractual services employment system* has grown rapidly in the last 20 years as a private- and nonprofit-sector adjunct to public agencies.[2] The employing organizations perform public services and produce public goods via performance contracts with sponsoring public agencies. A new kind of employment community emerges here, coalescing more with policy subsystems than with single public agencies. Policy subsystems are comprised of networks and subnetworks of organizations, associations, interest groups, politicians, and other influential individuals. Relationships among these "citizens" vary from tight, symbiotic marriages to loosely coupled associations. Employees in this system bear many public responsibilities in the performance of their work, but are often paid less, receive fewer benefits, and are typically employed on an at-will basis. Some professionals in this system, however, may win higher salaries in lieu of fewer benefits, depending on how badly their expertise is needed. The working conditions in this system vary widely. Pay, benefits, and discretionary powers may be substantial in some sectors, such as in the military-industrial complex, while conditions in human services policy subsystems are bleak—with low salaries and high burnout. Again, as illustrated in the Prairie County case, many employees move

frequently among employers in this system, seeking marginal improvements in pay and benefits, along with better working conditions.

Although this employment system exists separately—at arm's length from formal employment in governmental agencies—public HR managers are increasingly involved in fashioning individualized contractual relationships, especially with former employees whose experience and expertise are still needed. In many respects, this process substitutes for lack of formal succession planning. Widely varying contractual arrangements have emerged, requiring more planning and development of accountability factors, performance assessment, risk management, liability bonding, and so forth.

The networks of contracted workers create new policy neighborhoods and communities of officials who work closely with each other. They vie for influence over policy decisions and more stability in the flow of resources to their employing organizations. In essence, a political economy develops to allocate authoritative priorities and to articulate equitable criteria for distribution of resources among the subsystem players. Contract offices become surrogate HRM functionaries as well as regulators of the allocation process. Life in these systems can be lean and haphazard, and lines of accountability for policy development and implementation are easily muddled. Much of the contractual system remains in flux as it grows in scope and significance. Its networks are now a subject of intense interest among public management and policy scholars (cf. Hall and O'Toole 2004; Meier 2006) as a unit of analysis independent of host organizations, which lends evidence to their having taken on a life of their own. As they do so, questions of public service identity, legitimacy, issues of representation on important boards and committees, loyalty among members, and other characteristics of political community will continue to manifest themselves.

In some respects, these changes entail "decomposition of the civil service"; employer identity is blurred and/or disaggregated across multiple jurisdictions and private firms (Cooper 2003; Rosenbloom 2005, 555). Many public employees' jobs and pay are supplied by diverse jurisdictions, and their identification as "public servants" is blurred or dissipated through privatization and careerism. An emerging and especially troublesome issue involves the question of whether private contractors and their employees should be subjected to constitutional/legal standards in the performance of public services. The problem was highlighted in the events surrounding the Blackwater security firm, whose employees were involved in reckless, even deliberate, killings of Iraqi civilians while escorting American diplomats during the Iraq War. By law, the contractor and employees are immune from prosecution, while American soldiers caught doing the same thing would be prosecuted by a military tribunal. Similar issues arise in privatized prisons, where cuts in training as well as staffing lead to erosion of prison conditions and protection of prisoner rights. There is no easy answer as to when and whether we should "outsource" constitutional/legal norms to privatized employers (Cooper 2003; Rosenbloom 2005, chap. 13), but the implications are serious if we are to ensure accountability for the actions of those who perform public services on our behalf and with our tax dollars.

Finally, the *political appointee system* represents a diverse, elite class in the public employment community. Ironically, its top echelons—the political executives—are temporary employees, serving only about 18 months to two years on average. Most serve at the pleasure of elected officials, though some (such as members of commissions and boards) enjoy fixed terms in order to preserve some independence in judgment and policy development. A few, including city managers, are able to negotiate contracts with golden parachutes to compensate for the risks of short-term employment.

Those who serve at-will do not expect to serve for long, and therefore they assume a very limited window of opportunity to make an impact on policy and practice. Some are employed as change

agents who bring external perspectives to bear on their agency. They often possess substantial policy knowledge or professional expertise that buys them some legitimacy in the agency. In other cases, they are close political associates of their elected superiors and are given appointments as rewards for their campaign efforts and partisan loyalty. Most political appointees at this level come from business or from professional fields such as law or economics. They typically expect to return to more lucrative and stable pursuits at the end of their political appointment (Mosher 1982, 177–180). The attraction to these posts is stimulated by an ambition for power over significant policy arenas and by an opportunity to affect or achieve political ideals, to display personal and political loyalty, and to fulfill a sense of duty or professionalism. In addition, many executives feed on the charisma and intrigue that pervades politics at this level and may develop powerful aspirations for elective office.

Below the political executives exist echelons of political appointees who form a community of regulars and specialists; they move from one appointment to another and move back and forth between career and political appointments. A few are generalists in administrative and organizational matters, while more are highly experienced specialists. These ranks have grown substantially as personnel reforms among the states have converted even middle managers to appointee status on the premise that they wield policy-determining powers or affect agency practices statewide. The trade-off has often come in the form of higher salaries, or at least the promise of such incentives in the future, as well as prospects for enhanced powers. These appointees generally enjoy longer tenure in their posts and have "almost complete confidence of continuing work somewhere in their field of specialization" (Mosher 1982, 182).

However, as partisan conflict has escalated, so too has the politicization of these ranks. This has been especially evident in the federal Senior Executive Service (SES), where noncareer appointees are steadily replacing career executives. As this occurs, the ability of managers to buffer agency communities from political turmoil decreases. It disrupts existing patterns of incentives, expectations, representation, loyalties, relations of power, and career ladders in the agencies. Existing competencies, roles, and organizational cultures are challenged. While such changes may be desired by new political leaders, the extent of the change at the street level may come back to haunt them. It appears, for example, that radical changes in the Department of Defense (DoD), in the Central Intelligence Agency (CIA), and in the Federal Emergency Management Agency (FEMA) during the administration of President George W. Bush (in office 2001–7) led to exile or exodus of significant numbers of career officers, and this compromised the field operations and capacities of all three. The poor performance of FEMA in the early days of the Hurricane Katrina disaster (2005) was widely attributed to this problem.

It is apparent that relations among the partisan political cadre and the upper ranks of agency communities are anything but stable. The short tenure of most elected and appointed officials presents a structural incentive for them to act as change agents, and for career officials to resist or mute their attempts. The history of public personnel policy and human resources management is rife with such conflict. However, the intensity and extent of conflict between these political groups varies substantially over time, depending on the extent to which members of each side understand and respect their mutual roles. Louis Fisher (1975) noted that productive relationships between agencies and their superior branches rely extensively on tacit agreements between career and political officials about the ways conflict and cooperation are handled, and that such agreements require knowledge and appreciation of the incentives, values, roles, and culture of each institution. Mosher (1982, 184–185) describes the echelons of political appointees and top career officials as terraces on a farm that may slow or buffer the destructive tendencies born of "irreconcilable differences in ideology." These terraces "may be the best bridges we have yet devised to connect politics and administration."

In order for this system to work, however, officials on the terraces must cultivate some important competencies and perspectives. Public administrators must know how to adapt their agencies to changing partisan agendas without perverting the legal mandates imposed on them. This requires in-depth knowledge of the dynamics of party politics, as well as of the ambiguities and paradoxes inherent in both politics and law, in order to reach tolerable compromises. Moreover, it requires frank assessments of how to stimulate and manage organizational change in agencies that are more like communities than rational, flexible tools. Formal-rational explanations convey the misimpression that policy, organizational, and HRM changes occur in linear and technical fashion. Since this is not the case, career professionals need to orient politicians to the communitarian realities of agency and subsystem politics. At the same time, politicians and their high-level appointees must openly acknowledge that career administrators cannot be mere instruments of their designs. The constitutional principles and structure of American government work against such extensive, unilateral responsiveness. Administrators must respond to decisions of all three branches of government and thereby balance the conflicting pressures for responsiveness, effectiveness, and protection of rights through a system based on rule by law. That system engenders agency communities with diffuse powers and structures of their own. Overall, then, politicians and careerists must gain greater appreciation for the often conflicting political roles, competencies, and imperatives of the other, while developing an etiquette that openly respects and sustains them.

## CONCLUSION

The communitarian aspects of public service discussed here may be viewed by some as detracting from the efficient pursuit of public purposes. Reformist rhetoric tends to emphasize a strictly instrumentalist view of administrative process, promising politicians and taxpayers the "best bang for the buck," above all else. Everything else is expendable. This reform doctrine is propagated for the sake of political expediency, despite decades of research demonstrating its insufficiency. Since at least the 1940s, organization theorists have emphasized the productive tension between the pursuit of task effectiveness on the one hand, and development and maturation of individuals in organizational contexts on the other. Job enrichment, employee empowerment, and career enhancement serve both ends. Group dynamics, participative decision making, and democratic styles of leadership figure prominently, not only as pragmatic elements of organizational effectiveness but also as normative principles appropriate to democratic life.

The literature on organizational culture has broadened our understanding of complex organizations by looking at underlying values, assumptions, and symbols that shape people's views on what, how, and why things are done in an organization, irrespective of rational-instrumental explanations. These insights point to other important dimensions of daily life that suffuse and transcend organizations. Human beings may find great meaning or value in work, but they also exhibit sociality, family, convention, religiosity, tradition, ritual, political affiliation, and community. Work life, especially in complex organizations, cannot exist in complete isolation from these phenomena, nor should it.

The communitarian aspects of organization call attention to the play of ideas, power, authority, status, rights, and entitlement in the administrative process. They emphasize the propriety of means as well as ends in defining who we are as a people, and beyond that, define ways of living together in the face of ambiguous and conflicting values. American government embraces conflict and tension as inherent characteristics of governance, and it institutionalizes them through a multitude of checks and balances, legal-political jurisdictions, and various decision processes based in opposing administrative traditions. These dynamics engender quasi-autonomous centers of power divided

among levels of government, among competing agencies and programs, and among governing powers ceded to private, economic, and social spheres of life. The public service reflects this richly diverse and complicated plurality of forms, processes, and powers. Public servants are not mere instruments of society but fully active members of a political community who live out much of their lives in its governing institutions, exercising their own shares of power.

It is the role of human resources managers in this system to mediate among the conflicting centers of power in order to help preserve the viability of the public service. Thus, they cannot serve exclusively as extensions of an executive branch but must operate betwixt and between the full array of superintending principalities and powers. They must strike a balance between competing interests, rights claims of employee groups, and the imperatives of managers and politicians to control costs, effectively reform programs, and deploy personnel for new initiatives. The tendency to place more HRM functions under the direct control of elected executives inevitably shifts the balance in favor of executive and managerial agendas. While this plays to the competent and energetic governance tradition, it too often weakens support for the other traditions. Employees thus view HRM offices as an arm of management, and they may distrust their claims to fairly consider employee interests, especially in the resource allocation process. Despite this structural bias, HRM professionals work hard to represent all sides. The pressures of their work continually remind them of the enduring tensions between effectiveness, responsiveness, participation, and the protection of rights. Human resource administrators play a key role through the exercise of their discretion in maintaining a workable balance among these conflicting values that are inherent to the daily work of all of our public organizations.

The ability to balance these tensions can be enhanced by paying attention to the organizational structures and processes that exist within the executive branches of our governments. HRM offices, for example, can be structured to provide more independence of function and judgment. Offices tasked with protecting employees' rights are often separated from other HRM functions and organized as a quasi-judicial or adversarial body. Employment relations functions can be separated and organized into collegial-mediative structures or as organs designed to accommodate internal advocacy groups that bolster the participation rights (the civic governance tradition) of employee groups in decisions that affect salaries, benefits, and working conditions. HRM offices should assist and support the development of dissent channels through which agency employees may safely express opinions about substantive policy and administrative practice as well as personnel matters. At the same time, agency managers and employees must build and sustain responsive linkages to legislative bodies that nurture deliberation and education about the dilemmas and dynamics of employment relations. Legislators are too often relegated to an arm's length relationship with each agency, in deference to claimed executive prerogatives regarding personnel issues. Yet, as we have seen, legislative values and practices do much to unravel the personnel policies of executives. Legislators always share substantial influence over personnel policy. In short, HRM offices should be allowed to differentiate their functions sufficiently to accommodate the diverse powers and factions that shape agency communities and thereby reflect the logic and spirit of our constitutional system.

## STUDY QUESTIONS

1. Regarding the Prairie County case, what can be done to improve the prospects of the DSS field office for hiring and retaining qualified caseworkers?
2. In the Prairie County case, it is possible that the demands on the position of DSS field office director, currently occupied by Susan Webb, are impossible for one person to handle

effectively. Assuming that this is the case, design a new position that you believe will help mitigate the problems in the office. What difficulties do you expect to encounter in the state personnel system as you seek to establish the position?

3.  In the Prairie County case, DSS caseworkers are professionals and are paid by salary. Benefit specialists in the DSS office are not professionalized and are paid hourly. Because of high turnover among the social workers, the benefit specialists—who average 10 or more years in their position—make more per year than most caseworkers. This has deepened resentment among the caseworkers. Susan Webb, the DSS field office director (and a former caseworker herself), is embarrassed by this and has repeatedly complained about it to the state DSS director. The state director has offered to call the disparity to the attention of the state HRM office but warns Webb that they are just as likely to reclassify the benefit specialists downward to correct the disparity. What options does Webb have? What might you do to placate the caseworkers if you were in Webb's position?

4.  In workgroups, discuss which aspects of the communitarian model seem to apply to the Prairie County case, and answer the following questions:

    a.  How is the communitarian model discussed in chapter 4 manifested in the local DSS office and as part of the broader state agency? What steps would you take to ameliorate the extreme conditions in the office?

    b.  How might the model apply to the local police department and sheriff's office, especially in light of the demographic changes in the county? What are the implications for recruitment, training, and motivation of law enforcement employees?

    c.  How might the model apply to the nonprofit organizations in the human services subsystem? What role, if any, should recruitment and training of volunteers play in coping with the severe problems they face? To what extent should these organizations share employee resources, or work together, and with DSS, to address dreadful working conditions?

## NOTES

1. For example, see Berman et al. (2012), Dresang (2002), Patton et al. (2002), and Robinson-Hickman (2000).

2. The contractual services employment system developed after Frederick Mosher's work in the early 1980s, though he did anticipate some of its emerging characteristics.

# PART III

## FINANCING AND BUDGETING FOR THE PUBLIC'S BUSINESS

# THE CASE OF THE MEDLER SCHOOL SYSTEM

## CASE DESCRIPTION

Medler is the largest school district in the state, with a total enrollment of 48,300 students, 109 schools, 3,600 teachers, and an overall staff of 6,800 employees. This also makes Medler the third largest governmental entity in the state. The budget totals $868 million, consisting of $470 million in discretionary general fund support, with the balance consisting of U.S. and State Department of Education funding (mostly for target populations) and nondiscretionary grants. The federal and state funds are required to be spent for limited and specific purposes. The seven elected members of the school board, who are chosen for a four-year term and serve part-time without compensation, face some significant financial challenges. Three of the seven members of the school board are up for reelection in May—just about the time the budget is required to be formally approved by the board. A number of factors increase the challenges that the board and the district face:

- The district is facing a $58 million shortfall as a result of the expiration of two local option levies and decline in enrollments. School-age population has been on the decline from a high of 80,000 students in 1984 to a current level of 48,000 students. The population is expected to continue declining to a low of 44,000 students by 2012 largely due to increasing costs of housing and a lower birthrate among urban dwellers. Each decline of 1,000 students results in a loss of $5 million in state funding.
- A recent study of Medler's facilities concluded that the district has approximately 33 percent more capacity than the national average for similarly sized districts. In addition, the district's buildings average 62 years of age, compared to the national average of 42. The district spends about 40 percent less on maintenance than other districts of its size.
- Because of a stagnant economy and growing costs of building and managing prisons to accommodate mandatory sentencing requirements, the state has been unable to provide K–12 schools with the funding necessary to keep up with cost increases. Based on current state budget projections and current enrollments, Medler expects to receive $15 million less in funding next year from the state.
- Health care costs have increased an average of 10 percent per year for the past three years and are expected to continue increasing at that level for the next three years. Health care is negotiated as part of the bargaining process with four separate unions. In order to balance the budget and prevent the early closure of schools, teachers in the district (unionized teachers)

265

worked for 10 days without pay last year. In the past, teachers were given health care benefits in lieu of salary increases, which has resulted in teachers in the district being "below market" on pay, but "above market" on health care benefits.

- Medler spends approximately $15 million per year on mandated program for students with disabilities, for which it receives no federal or state reimbursements.
- Nearly 85 percent of parents in the Medler District send their children to public schools, one of the highest rates in the nation for an urban school district. However, only 26 percent of the electorate has children in Medler's schools.
- The voters of the state successfully used the initiative process to pass a constitutional amendment that requires local tax measures to obtain a double majority. This means that a tax measure passes only when a majority of the voters from the last presidential election show up at the polls to vote, and the measure receives a majority of those voting. In the last special election, supporters spent $800,000 on a campaign that succeeded in passing the measure by 56.5 percent with 50.3 percent voting. There is concern that with the large influx of young and new voters in the last presidential election, it will not be possible to meet the double majority requirement when the special levy expires next year.

This combination of circumstances presents the board with some daunting choices. They have just hired a nationally renowned superintendent who has launched a series of educational reforms to close the achievement gap between high- and low-performing students. For the first time in seven years, the district staff, teachers, and the larger community are enthusiastic about the direction in which the district is moving. The school board wants to find a way of dealing with its serious fiscal and budgetary challenges in a manner that continues to build the confidence of the community in their schools and in the leadership of the district. This will be difficult to accomplish in the light of the estimated $54 million shortfall—about 12 percent of the general fund budget. This is equivalent to closing the schools for 50 days or laying off 750 teachers.

## CASE DISCUSSION: TOUGH CHOICES

Board members are split on the strategy they should follow. Some favor a revenue-centered approach, which emphasizes the importance of filling the various gaps in the district's revenue stream. Others point out the growing citizen hostility to increased taxation and emphasize the importance of a budget-centered strategy, which focuses on cutting costs, especially those that will result in permanent long-term savings. The following tables list some revenue and budget strategies that are under consideration, along with their consequences.

### 1. Budget-Cutting Strategies

| Advantages | Disadvantages |
| --- | --- |
| Strategy: | |
| **1. Reduce the school year by 50 days.** | |
| 1. Will achieve the budget target | 1. Will seriously compromise the educational mission of the district |
| 2. Will visibly demonstrate the seriousness of the problem | 2. Will undermine confidence of businesses, parents, and elected officials in the public school system |

3. Will be opposed by the teachers' union, which favors a higher student-faculty ratio than lower pay for teachers
4. Won't do anything to provide a long-term solution

## 2. Increase the student-faculty ratio from 25:1 to 30:1.

| | |
|---|---|
| 1. Will achieve the budget target | 1. Will result in laying off 750 teachers |
| 2. Will visibly demonstrate the seriousness of the problem | 2. Will undermine the momentum to close the district's achievement gap |
| | 3. Will anger parents who may move their children to private and charter schools or nearby growing suburban districts |

## 3. Undertake "hard-line" negotiations with unions to reduce health care benefits.

| | |
|---|---|
| 1. Estimated savings of $8–12 million annually | 1. Would engulf the community in a bitter battle with unions |
| 2. Additional steps still necessary to balance the budget | 2. Would require some offsetting salary increases to make teachers "market competitive" |
| | 3. Would likely undermine long-term efforts to build a collaborative relationship with union partners, which is important for carrying out the superintendent and board's educational reform agenda |

## 4. Contract out services.

| | |
|---|---|
| 1. Estimated savings of $10 million per year on a permanent basis if custodial services were contracted out | 1. Would engulf the community in a bitter battle with unions |
| 2. Would not be sufficient to balance the budget | 2. Would detract attention from positive focus on the educational mission of the district |

## 5. Establish an outcome-based school performance system, with the goal of closing schools that do not meet criteria.

| | |
|---|---|
| 1. Estimated savings of $400–$600 thousand per year for each school closed | 1. Would engulf the parents in a bitter struggle to save their schools |
| 2. Would demonstrate "good faith" effort that leadership is committed to dealing with long-term problems | 2. Would likely result in closure of schools in poorer neighborhoods, where standardized test scores tend to be lower and parent constituents lack the organization and power to resist such measures |
| | 3. Would not be sufficient to balance the budget |

## 6. Require all organizational units to take a 10 percent cut in expenses.

| | |
|---|---|
| 1. Would be viewed as fair | 1. Would result in major inequities, particularly at the school site level |
| 2. Would be easiest to implement | 2. Formula could not be applied to about half of the budget, which is covered by dedicated funds |
| | 3. Would require major reductions in teaching staff |

## 7. Create a priority ranking system and continue making cuts to balance the budget.

| | |
|---|---|
| 1. Would meet expectation of making thoughtful and rational decisions | 1. Would take extensive time |
| 2. Would produce conflict | 2. Would produce conflict; would eliminate existing discretion of principals and site councils to prioritize |

## 2. Revenue-Based Strategies

| Advantages | Disadvantages |
| --- | --- |

Strategy:

**1. Ask local voters for additional supplementary support through some kind of tax increase.**

| | |
| --- | --- |
| 1. Will provide a longer-term solution<br>2. Can earmark funding for specific purposes to demonstrate accountability to voters | 1. Key pollsters argue this is high risk and unlikely to succeed without parents suffering from the consequences of cuts<br>2. Will require costly and time-consuming campaign<br>3. Will not address the capital needs of the district<br>4. Will not address declining school enrollments |

**2. Lobby the governor and legislature for more adequate funding of schools.**

| | |
| --- | --- |
| 1. Will locate responsibility where it legally resides<br>2. Will allow the district to build coalitions with other stakeholders throughout the state | 1. Likely to be only partially successful in light of the large state budget shortfall<br>2. Will not address declining enrollments<br>3. Won't address the capital needs of district, which have to be funded locally |

**3. Seek legislative support for dedicating a portion of state lottery revenue to education.**

| | |
| --- | --- |
| 1. Could potentially add $15 million annually in new state revenue to the Medler School District<br>2. Allows the district to ride the coattails of a private initiative of parents and school lobbyists supporting this solution | 1. Will compete with business owners and social service providers who are lobbying for a larger share of lottery revenue<br>2. Won't address the need for district to deal with declining enrollments<br>3. Won't address the capital needs of district, which have to be funded locally |

**4. Seek a loan against the district's investment in the State Retirement System, which has generated more income than is necessary to fund projected retirements.**

| | |
| --- | --- |
| 1. Could potentially generate $50 million on a onetime basis<br>2. Avoids the immediate need for a special election to renew the income tax surcharge | 1. Uncertain outcome, since issue has never been raised before<br>2. Won't address need for district to deal with declining enrollments<br>3. Won't address the capital needs of district, which have to be funded locally<br>4. Won't address long-term funding needs |

**5. Convert some school programs to a fee-based system.**

| | |
| --- | --- |
| 1. Provides a long-term revenue enhancement<br>2. Could free up as much as $5 million in existing revenue annually and generate another $2–3 million in new revenue from the fees | 1. Can only contribute to reducing the shortfall by a small amount<br>2. Creates inequities for students from low-income families |

**6. Expand school foundation (501c3) funding for select programs.**

| | |
| --- | --- |
| 1. Could provide as much as $10 million annually<br>2. Increased flexibility in use of funds<br>3. More buy-in from the community | 1. Takes teacher/staff time away from the classroom and from routine administrative work to do development work<br>2. Funding stream is highly variable<br>3. Donors want more direct influence over targeted programs |

**3. Case Decision: If you were the chief administrative officer of the Medler School District, what combination of strategies would you recommend for adoption by the elected board?**

In considering what to do, it is important to keep in mind the following lessons this case illustrates about public finance and budget issues in the public sector:

- While the delivery of services may be fragmented, citizens experience their taxes as part of an integrated whole. This requires government officials to coordinate the interjurisdictional interface at the local and state levels in order to develop and implement successful revenue and budgeting strategies for public agencies. For example, the choice of strategies selected by Medler will be greatly affected by the decision of the city, county, and special districts to ask the voters for additional tax support in the next election.
- The American system of government was borne out of a concern for the power to tax without representation. Levying taxes and spending the taxpayers' hard-earned money is one of the most fundamental and important functions carried out by public administrators.
- Because the stakes are so high, budgeting and finance issues are governed by numerous legal and technical requirements, which expand as well as limit the discretionary authority of public officials and administrators.
- The selection of a given combination of budget and finance strategies cannot be separated from other conditions necessary for realizing the additional long-term goals of an organization. For example, in the Medler case, building the confidence and trust of the community in the school system may be more important than short-term budget considerations. An important part of this trust-building strategy may involve the development of a cooperative working relationship with the unions—especially the teachers' union, whose hiring, assignment, and transfer policies play an important role in accomplishing the district's student achievement goals. Strategies that undermine these relationships for the sake of achieving success on the revenue and budget front pose some agonizing trade-offs.
- It is nearly impossible for local government decision makers to maintain a bright-line distinction between policy development and policy implementation. The superintendent and members of her leadership team in charge of finance, budgeting, student achievement, and human resources management cannot make their recommendations without extended talks with individual members of the board. Administrators and policymakers need to work as a collaborative team.
- It is impossible to separate the forces that shape the private marketplace from the forces that shape the allocation of resources in the public sector. The two realms are mutually interdependent.

CHAPTER 10

# PUBLIC REVENUE AND FINANCIAL MANAGEMENT

Tax laws have in vain been multiplied; new methods to enforce the collection have in vain been tried; the public expectation has been uniformly disappointed, and the treasuries of the States have remained empty. The . . . popular government, coinciding with the real scarcity of money incident to a languid and mutilated state of trade, has hitherto defeated every experiment for extensive collections and has at length taught the different legislatures of the folly of attempting them.

*(Hamilton 1788, Federalist No. 12, quoted in Rossiter 1961, 92–93)*

To judge what sacrifices democracies know how to impose on themselves, we must therefore await a time when the American nation is obliged to put half of the revenue from goods into the hands of its government, like England.

*(Alexis de Tocqueville 1835–1840/2000, 213)*

The early days of the republic taught a very simple but hard lesson: without adequate power to lay and collect taxes, the fate of democratic governance hangs in the balance. The founders developed the U.S. Constitution in part to address this problem. And while our legislative bodies now possess considerable authority to raise public revenue, the power is jealously guarded by the people and gingerly exercised by public officials who act on their behalf. There are two reasons for this jealousy: one rooted in the psychology of taxation itself, and the other rooted in the American political tradition.

At a psychological level, each of us can easily calculate the *costs* of increased taxes to ourselves, but we cannot so easily calculate the *benefits* to us from taxes. This is because the benefits are frequently spread over a large number of individuals and occur gradually over an extended period of time. It is difficult to appreciate the broad benefits of education, of a clean environment, of public transportation, or of land-use planning when the tax bills come due. The costs of taxes, on the other hand, are specific in nature and usually well known at a personal level. This cognitive dissonance between the known costs of taxes and the corresponding uncertain and indeterminate benefits makes taxation a controversial subject.

But there is an additional reason why taxation is problematic, and it is deeply rooted in the American political tradition, beginning with the Anti-Federalists and continuing with the Populists

271

and modern-day proponents of smaller government. Many Americans share a deep distrust of government, as well as a belief that private markets are more efficient in the allocation of scarce resources. The issue of distrust has often centered on the financial affairs of our governments. In the founding era, very few people had any knowledge of public financial matters, and financiers were often viewed as magicians or tricksters who conjured up schemes to defraud people. Their fears were not unreasonable, for many in Europe and the Americas had lost fortunes in speculation booms, bank failures, and flawed paper money policies spawned in part by public financiers. Furthermore, colonial Americans had long experience with being taxed by the Crown to help fund the British Empire and its entrepreneurs and aristocrats, with little say or benefit in return. The charge of "taxation without representation" constituted a major grievance in our Declaration of Independence. The dramatic events of the financial meltdown of the mortgage market 2007–2009 mark the most recent American experience with financial speculation and its far-reaching implications. According to the National Bureau of Economic Research (2010), the U.S. business cycle contraction began in December 2007 and ended in the second quarter (June) of 2009. During this period, many Americans experienced a deep unease with the federal government's intervention into the private banking and financial system and support for automobile manufacturers. For many, the federal Troubled Assets Relief Program (TARP) represented efforts to provide relief to wealthy industries at the expense of struggling small businesses and homeowners facing foreclosure.

The long-standing American suspicion of finance and taxation is reflected in the civic governance and responsive governance traditions (see chapters 4 and 6, especially the discussion of the Democratic Balancewheel in chapter 6), which demand smaller and weaker governments, local control, and direct participation. Government must be open and immediately accountable for the taxes it does levy and spend so that people can watch vigilantly over the public treasury. Watchdog groups such as local and state taxpayer associations routinely police government taxing and spending policies, raising alarms at the slightest hint of tax increases and new spending priorities. Fiscal conservatives focus public attention on balancing the public checkbook as the supreme priority.

These concerns are matched, however, by a compelling interest in sufficiently funding our governments to carry out their assigned functions with some effectiveness. The competent and energetic governance tradition reminds us that too much fiscal conservatism can result in wasteful and ineffective policies that present as much danger to democracy as overly concentrated power. Alexander Hamilton championed this cause and set in place a system of public finance that immediately stabilized America's economic system and made it possible to develop the robust political, economic, and administrative practices that continue to serve us today (Green 1993). Public officials face the challenge of melding this concern for funding effective government with standards of responsiveness, intense civic suspicion, and resistance to taxation.

How can public leaders be responsive to the will of a citizenry that dislikes taxes, while at the same time generating the necessary revenue to meet its demands for services? In the Medler School District case, how can local school board members expect to generate community support for additional school revenue when only 26 percent of the voting population has children in public schools? How does the board please those who want more money for roads and prisons rather than for lower student-teacher ratios, special or remedial education needs, or English as a Second Language programs? The problem intensifies when we add the sentiments of those who believe that charter or private schools are a better alternative than public education. As the Medler case and this chapter illustrate, a variety of financial strategies and instruments are used in managing these pressures.

Governmental structure in the United States is more complicated than in most countries. The federal government and state governments operate under separate constitutions, and at the local

level, cities, counties, boroughs, and special districts enjoy varying degrees of legal autonomy ceded by the states of which they are a part. Each level has its own authority to levy taxes and collect revenues to support the delivery of its services. The transfer of funds between levels, especially from the federal and state governments, provides an important source of revenue for local service delivery.

In the context of these multiples layers of autonomous taxing authority, we find a wide variety of policies to generate revenue. Governments, like individual citizens, have complex strategies for financing the needs of the community. These strategies have important consequences for the capacity of citizens to control the affairs of their community. Some of these strategies—such as floating revenue bonds for a new water treatment facility—give citizens little choice over their future. Others—such as the imposition of user fees to support parks, golf courses, and similar amenities—give citizens direct control over whether to patronize these services, though they may have only indirect say over how the fees are set and at what amount. Property and income taxes fall somewhere between these two extremes.

Extensive involvement of the nonprofit and for-profit sectors with government in governance and service delivery adds another level of complexity to revenue generation for public services. As we pointed out in chapter 5, the reality behind the popular public perception is that contractual linkages, dominant donor relationships, and formal partnerships closely bind many nonprofit social service providers with government agencies into a community network. Such contracts and partner relationships often force transformations in nonprofit structure, culture, and sense of purpose. However, the complement of government funding with direct donations channeled from citizens and donors through nonprofit partners can often result in a diversified set of revenues that can sustain a public service program in good times and bad. Charitable giving of small donations and strategic philanthropy of large donations provide citizens with an alternative mechanism for supporting public services. In contrast to the coercive nature of taxation and the limited choice of paying user fees for specific public services, nonprofit organizations offer donors a direct choice of whether to support an organization or service. The voluntary option of supporting and sustaining nonprofits appeals to those citizens who prefer nongovernmental, entrepreneurial approaches to the delivery of health, social, educational, and family services. Rather than support a seemingly large, distant, conflicted, and coercive government, or a private for-profit enterprise, nonprofit organizations provide supporters with the option of relying on a unique combination of motivating principles that include self-help, voluntarism, and philanthropy. In making donations to a nonprofit organization, donors can align their personal values with the values and mission of the organization and acquire a sense of ownership in shaping the destiny of the community in which they live.

We write this chapter with local governments as the primary focus, but we would argue that much of what we say also applies to nonprofit organizations that share the "public good" mission of governmental entities. A careful study of government revenue and budgeting systems demonstrates common principles of revenue diversification, a similar need for fiscal transparency to gain public and donor support, and common principles and practices of budgeting, accounting, and organization management control. Further, both government and nonprofit administrators must have a full grounding in the political systems and dynamics that surround their programs.

As we will see in the remaining sections of this chapter, financing the public's business is an integral part of democratic governance. Too frequently, citizens and even career administrators consider public finance the esoteric work of specialists. The purpose of this chapter is to disabuse readers of this notion, and to shed some light on the processes available to government agencies and nonprofits for financing the work of their communities. As we examine the variety of finance

strategies that we rely upon to fund our many public projects, we will see how these strategies comport with our contrasting administrative traditions (see chapters 4 and 5).

Raising revenues for public services has always been challenging, but the recent economic downturn and its continuing fallout have made the task even more difficult. With a requirement for balanced governmental budgets at the state and local levels, reduced government funding translates into smaller programs, reduced staffing, and less money available for grants and contracts with nonprofit organizations. Tax and spending limitations placed on state and local governments before the economic downturn may further limit the availability of revenues in some states. Recent efforts by the national government to reduce the federal deficit have added uncertainty to state and local government revenues. All of these factors have left government and nonprofit administrators in a new world of extremely limited resources.

The economic downturn of 2007–2011 generated both short-term and longer-term effects. The financial meltdown and institutional failures of the fall of 2008 brought immediate shocks and high levels of uncertainty to the U.S. and world financial systems. Faced with severe lost value in the investment financial markets, consumer spending fell steeply and state and local sales and user fee revenues fell accordingly. Charitable donations to nonprofits fell steeply. New hiring by employers froze, as did wages; the unemployment rate increased sharply. This quickly affected federal, state, and local income tax revenues. The unraveling of complex credit instruments threatened the existence of major financial institutions and major banks, while quickly deflating housing prices in real estate markets across the country. The sale of existing houses and new residential construction came to a standstill. Reduced housing values lowered property tax revenues in some states and jurisdictions, while tax limitation regulations dampened the effect in other states. Depressed markets for residential and commercial construction resulted in dramatic declines in planning and construction permit fee revenues, real estate transfer tax revenues, and new infrastructure development charge revenues. To further aggravate the situation, the frozen capital markets in short-term commercial paper prevented borrowing by governments, and long-term borrowing for capital infrastructure investments became severely depressed.

Over the last months of 2008 and through 2009, intervention by the federal government helped to stabilize the downward spiral of the economy, but uncertainty remained in most local housing markets. A recovering economy and strong stock market in subsequent years has helped the recovery of tax and fee revenues to local governments and charitable giving to nonprofits. However, difficulties in resolving residential housing foreclosures have left property values uncertain, real estate markets jittery, and new construction at low levels. Unemployment numbers remain high in many parts of the country several years after the business downturn supposedly ended in 2009 (National Bureau of Economic Research 2010). The composition of regional and local economies varies widely across the United States, which has led to varying levels of economic recovery. Broadly however, weak housing values, tenuous economic growth, and high unemployment continued to plague many regions of the country well into 2012, and revenues to governments remained low.

Likewise, support to local governments from the states and the federal government has become less than certain. Faced with reduced tax and fee revenues, state governors and legislatures have carefully reviewed intergovernmental payments to local governments. These once protected transfer payments have been reduced and limited in many states. Federal payments under the American Recovery and Reinvestment Act of 2009 (ARRA, "Recovery Act," P.L. 111–5) helped state and local governments blunt and delay the extended effects of the economic downturn. The funds affected the 2009 and 2010 fiscal years but were subsequently eliminated. While coping with weak revenues, state and local government struggle to balance their annual budgets. Furlough days of

closed schools and government offices have become common, and government-sector employment per capita has fallen steeply since early 2010 (Greenstone and Looney 2012).

State level tax and spending limitations (TELS)—typically enacted before the economic downturn—continue in force for many local governments. One class of TELS limits one or several parts of the property tax equation by capping the tax rate, prescribing the valuation procedures, or limiting the total tax imposed. Another class of limitations sets maximum spending levels or requires super-majority votes (either in the state legislature or on citizen ballot initiatives) to raise revenues. Almost all states have enacted some form of tax or spending controls that limit the ability of local governments to raise the funds needed to meet program needs.

The combination of repeated economic downturns since the early 1980s and the ongoing effects of antitax and spending limitations create the prospect for a prolonged fiscal crisis for state and local government officials. This condition helped spawn the national political movement called New Public Management (NPM; see chapter 5 for additional discussion). Leaders of this movement argue that an entirely new approach is called for in developing strategies for public finance and expenditure (Osborne and Hutchinson 2004). These strategies include discontinuing some services altogether, contracting out other services, expanding user fees, and relying on various management incentives to encourage public administrators to think and act more like the owner of a private business. We will return to these strategies at the end of the next chapter.

This chapter assumes that the future of local government budgeting and finance will reflect the complex conditions illustrated in the Medler School District case study. Successful management of public resources will increasingly depend on: (1) becoming more conscious of revenue strategies as part of budget development, (2) educating taxpayers about the benefits they are receiving from public expenditures, and (3) developing public-private partnerships to fund public goods.

We begin this chapter by examining governmental revenues and their sources. Taxpayers must have confidence in revenue collection systems. In the pages that follow, we first examine the key attitudes and relationships that condition citizen willingness to pay taxes and fees to government for services. We then examine taxation as a public revenue source, including the major types of taxes. Related to taxes, we summarize tax and expenditure limitations as a means to limit government revenues. We also consider how government uses tax expenditures to lessen or omit tax burdens to achieve desired social outcomes. Fees and charges for service provide an increasing share of state and local government revenues. We review this source of dedicated revenue and the potential to increase fee revenue in an antitax climate. Revenues from state lotteries provide a source of growing, noncompulsory revenue, and we review the strengths and drawbacks of this revenue category as well. We then review intergovernmental revenues as a major source of funds for county, city, and state governments. This leads to a short discussion of *unfunded mandates*. Finally, we examine borrowed funds as an important source of revenue for major capital investments such as facilities and large equipment.

The chapter continues with a review of revenue generation in the nonprofit sector. Much like government, nonprofits must demonstrate legitimacy in their program and purpose and accountability in their use of donated funds. We summarize the importance of donor confidence in an organization, and recognize a distinction between charitable and philanthropic giving. This leads to a summary of the major types of revenues collected and used by nonprofit organizations. Fundraising techniques are undergoing major changes with the spread of the Internet, and we take a brief look at some of those changes. Finally, we consider the larger polity and its integrated financial resources that support both the governmental and nonprofit sectors. We consider an approach to integrated revenue assessment that provides a basis for networked service delivery and community decision making.

At the heart of revenue generation and program planning is the art and craft of forecasting. We sketch the importance of revenue forecasting for program planning purposes, but also discuss forecasting of the financial environment of midterm revenues and costs as the basis for a structurally balanced government or nonprofit budget. The chapter concludes with an overview of the accounting funds that structure government and nonprofit budgets. The accounting fund approach complies with professional practice and helps to ensure accountability and public confidence in revenue receipt, allocation, and use.

## SPENDING IS CONSTRAINED BY AVAILABLE REVENUES

Public budgeting, or the act of deciding how to spend the community's money, cannot occur without first identifying the revenue sources that can support it. Then, public officials must cultivate the willingness on the part of the citizenry to allow these sources to be used. Except for the federal government, most state and local governments in the United States cannot deficit spend. Like individuals, governments may borrow money, but they cannot do so without pledging a specific revenue source or arranging a payment schedule that ties the debt payment to the jurisdiction's long-term stream of unobligated revenue. Similarly, the program responses by nonprofit organizations to community problems must reflect the widespread interest and support of citizen donors, or the support of larger community foundations. In short, public service organizations of all kinds must carefully balance existing and future monetary resources against existing and future expenditure needs. Governmental, for-profit, and nonprofit organizations address this balance in different ways.

For state and local governments, the available revenue limits spending for tax-supported governmental services. This idea stands in contradiction to the popular notion that by adjusting complex formulas, governments can arbitrarily raise the level of taxation to meet ever-higher levels of program spending. State laws and regulations establish limits on any annual local government tax increases, and only through a vote of the people or their representatives can governments raise revenue above established levels. Once a government entity settles on the available level of revenue, a predictable political dynamic begins to unfold. On the one hand, agency staff and their constituents will view available revenues as falling far short of the true demand for governmental services. For this group, revenue levels are limits to be challenged. On the other hand, taxpayers and many elected officials view available revenues as all that is available to allocate among competing programs. From this perspective, revenue levels demonstrate a commitment to only the most important needs of the community. The public budgeting process provides a procedure for reconciling these differences. Should sufficient political and community support emerge, the government may ask the voters to allow a higher level of revenue to support a higher level of programs and services. Where such political support and voter acceptance is lacking, the available level of revenue will determine program size for the coming budget year.

When the actual collection of revenues falls far short of expectations, city councils, school district boards, county commissions, state legislatures, and nonprofit boards must reconvene to adjust spending downward. This is always a serious and troubling occasion, since it may require immediate program reductions and employee layoffs. On the other hand, when economic conditions improve and revenue collections unexpectedly increase from the previous year, administrators and elected officials may face an uncomfortable windfall of resources. When this occurs, government administrators and elected officials are caught on the horns of a dilemma: Do we return funds to the taxpayers, admitting our failure to forecast accurately, or can we credibly demonstrate a valid reason for the use of extra revenues? Less open to public scrutiny and with donor-driven missions,

nonprofit boards and executives typically have greater flexibility to focus unexpected revenues on the seemingly endless needs of community health, social, and family service problems.

Governments do operate a limited number of programs on an entrepreneurial, quasi-business model. For local cities and towns, these programs are typically constrained to municipal public utility monopolies such as water, sewer, and in some jurisdictions electricity and Internet access. Special district governments provide hospital services, seaport and airport services, and bridge and road use services on a fee-for-service basis. Rates for these services are set by public process to recover operating and investment costs, and service areas are clearly defined and limited. Government monopoly of these services is understood to be in the public benefit and more efficient than competing private providers. Private for-profit and nonprofit corporations also provide these services, and often stand ready to compete for service area customers, but state regulators constrain service territories. Beyond public utilities and monopoly services, government has traditionally been restrained from entry into the commercial market. Government enterprises must find careful limits between providing needed public services and displacing the competitive for-profit sector. Blending governmental and for-profit enterprises into public-private partnerships provides one way to span this economic sector boundary.

The notion that revenue levels set limits on government spending contrasts with perceptions and practices in the for-profit commercial sector. In the for-profit sector, revenues can often be adjusted to meet expenditure needs. If a private company projects revenues below anticipated expenditure levels, the first goal is to generate more money through sales and advertising before resorting to laying people off or cutting budgets. For the public sector, including many nonprofits, the opposite strategy is usually followed. Revenue estimates are developed first, which then serve as the basis for deciding the levels of expenditure and program service.

Nonprofit organizations stand as a hybrid to the governmental and for-profit strategies. Many nonprofits budget and operate against the limits of their major sources of revenue. Nonprofit service providers typically receive a defined level of grant or contract funds from their government, foundation, or federated intermediary partners. This defined level of funds sets a base program level. Like the for-profit sector, however, nonprofits have the entrepreneurial potential to generate additional income. Nonprofits can generate business income known as *earned income*. Profits from auxiliary enterprises such as gift shops and bookstores, health clubs, ice cream stores and snack bars, or used clothing stores provide substantial revenues that can fund service programs. Continuous and larger income earning activities cause the nonprofit to behave much like entities in the for-profit commercial sector. Increased advertising and increased sales of products and services can result in increased revenues to the organization, ultimately leading to higher levels of programs and services.

Because of the fixed nature of governmental and nonprofit revenues, revenue identification and forecasting is a critical basis for all public budgets and financial plans. Accurate revenue forecasting allows for the development of appropriate program, funding, staffing, and contracting levels, while helping to maintain the trust of public employees and the confidence of the taxpaying public. An underestimation of revenues leads to reduced spending that may fail to meet critical needs, while the overestimation of revenues leads to program and service cutbacks partway through the budget year. Either situation results in citizen and employee disenchantment with the organization. Developing and agreeing upon revenue estimates requires both political and technical skill.

Unfortunately, public budgeting in the government sector typically separates the development of plans for program spending from the activity of revenue forecasting and generation. In larger government organizations, the budgeting and program development, as well as the revenue forecasting tasks, are specialized enough to warrant different staffs. This separation is especially evident at the federal level, where deficit spending is legally permissible. Congressional com-

mittee structure divides responsibility for government financing from budget development and appropriations spending, in part because the size and complexity of the federal budget makes it impossible to do otherwise. In local jurisdictions, deficit spending is illegal, but separate departments frequently undertake the tasks of revenue forecasting and budget development. Even when this separation does not occur, departments funded by general fund dollars have little influence over revenue generation (see the section on revenue funds later in this chapter).

*General fund* revenue is a reserve of money that may be used for any purpose authorized by law, and it often comes from a wide variety of sources that have nothing in common with the spending program. For example, a jurisdiction may collect various kinds of building and inspection fees that end up lumped into the general fund with property tax revenue. This pot of revenues is available to be redistributed to support a variety of government services. Even if a department budget analyst has knowledge of immediate departmental revenues, he or she likely has little understanding of the full tax and revenue picture faced by the jurisdiction.

As a consequence of this separation, many department and agency budget analysts may place relatively little emphasis on the revenue context surrounding their spending estimations. For example, if you are the chief of police, and 95 percent of the expenses of running your department are supported by local property taxes, you may have little interest in the complexities and finer points of revenue estimation and generation. You simply assume that you will be given some "fair share" of a relatively fixed pot of revenue. In short, there is nothing to encourage you as a manager to link your budgeting decisions to revenue issues over which you have little control. In the end, program administrators, executives, analysts, and elected officials must depend on accurate forecasts of revenues as the basis of budgeting and resource allocation for the coming fiscal year. Effective revenue and cost forecasts into the six- to ten-year midterm help to assure the structural solvency of the government or nonprofit organization.

## REVENUE TYPES IN GOVERNMENTAL BUDGETING

A variety of revenue sources contribute to the government budgeting process. State and local governments may generate their own revenues through taxes and fees. Intergovernmental revenues come from other levels of government as direct grants or on a matching basis. For some states, lottery funds have become an important source of revenue; however, lottery funds are not usually directly available to local or special district governments. Revenues from the sale or rental of resources provide still another source of income. Various borrowing and debt instruments are used to generate the revenue necessary for capital projects such as water and sewage treatment facilities, transportation infrastructure, public buildings, and recreation facilities. In many jurisdictions, unspent funds may be carried forward for spending in the new fiscal year.

Ideally, a combination of several different sources of revenue will provide a balanced, stable flow of resources to support governmental operations. An effective blend of revenue sources allows sufficient stability to build the organization, develop and retain expert staff, and plan the program activities necessary to effectively address public problems and issues. Under a balanced blend of revenues, a temporary increase in one source of revenue will help offset a cyclical or temporary decline in another source. For example, during a period of economic downturn, revenue generated by property taxes and taxes for liquor, cigarettes, gaming, and gasoline do not decline as rapidly as individual and business income taxes. In a growing economy, revenue from sales taxes and from personal and corporate income taxes tends to increase while fees and value-based property taxes remain relatively stable. An effective public budget should forecast revenues far enough into the future to support program continuity and efficient service delivery in the context of these cycles.

In the following paragraphs, we will review the most common sources of state and local government revenues, including: (1) taxes, (2) user charges and fees for services, (3) sale of products and assets, and rental revenues, (4) lottery and gaming revenue, (5) intergovernmental transfers, (6) debt instruments, (7) balance carried forward, and (8) other miscellaneous revenue sources. Each revenue source is governed by its own unique set of legal restrictions.

## Taxes

Most states collect a personal income tax, a corporate income tax, and a retail sales tax. In addition, many states allow counties and cities to impose a local sales tax on top of the state tax. A group of states allows local cities and townships to impose income or wage taxes on residents and commuters who work in the jurisdiction. Property taxes provide a major source of revenues for special district governments and a significant portion of the revenue for counties, cities, townships, and other general-purpose local governments. Tax limitations have placed constraints on property tax increases in many parts of the United States. Other major tax revenue sources include per-gallon fuel taxes, highway use taxes and fees, tobacco and alcohol taxes, natural resource and timber severance taxes, insurance taxes, gift and inheritance taxes, hotel and lodging taxes, and a variety of local business taxes. Real estate transfer taxes cover county recordkeeping costs in some states, but in others they provide substantial revenue for new local infrastructure and systems development.

## User Charges and Fees for Services

Increasingly, governmental jurisdictions at all levels are looking for new ways of generating revenues by charging for the services they provide to the public. The most significant characteristic of fees for service is that they cannot be used to fund *general* government services. Instead, the revenue from each fee goes into a *dedicated* fund that can be used to support only the activity for which the fee is collected. For example, land use review fees collected from developers must reflect the actual cost of the planning activities, and the money collected must be dedicated to performing the land-use review. User charges and fees reinforce the concept that the user pays for the service. Fee-for-service arrangements tend to position citizens as customers rather than as governing members of the community. At the local level, jurisdictions charge fees to utility and communications corporations for the privilege of having access to county and city residents, while city or water district residents pay water and sewer fees to cover infrastructure and water/sewer provision.

In some states, local governments charge developers and builders systems development charges to cover the cost of the infrastructure needed to support new development. Many state agencies generate revenue from fees and charges. For example, most states charge post-secondary education tuition and fees, commercial fishing license fees, state court fees, driver's license fees, vehicle title fees, state park recreation use fees, and fees for hunting and fishing licenses. Governments also charge other agencies, local governments, and other entities that may purchase services under intergovernmental agreements.

Revenues generated by the sale of permits and licenses represent a special case of fees for government service. Governments collect these fees under their regulatory or recordkeeping authority. Revenues from licenses and permits are especially important to local governments, which may choose to dedicate these funds for special purposes or allow them to be collected and distributed as part of the general fund. License and permit revenues typically contribute a small share of total local government revenues.

## Sale of Products and Assets/Rental Revenues

A number of government programs generate revenues through the sale of products and commodities. Other programs generate rents through the lease of properties. As examples, a percentage of state-controlled sales of alcoholic beverages contribute to the state general fund. In some western states, the sale of timber from state-owned forests provides revenues to help support K–12 education, and some counties generate revenues through the sale of forest products and other natural resources from their county lands. Rents from state facilities such as docks and utility corridor right-of-ways also generate rental income.

## Lottery and Gaming Revenue

Until 1964, lotteries were illegal in every state in the country. Today lotteries operate in 43 states, in the District of Columbia, and in several U.S. territories. Profit from the lotteries to their parent governments totaled over $17.8 billion by 2012 (National Association of State and Provincial Lotteries 2012a, 2012b). Net proceeds from lotteries are used to support job creation and economic development, public education, protection of the environment, public health, and a multitude of other public activities.

## Intergovernmental Transfers

The transfer of funds from one level of government to another, or between governments on the same level, is described as an *intergovernmental transfer* or *intergovernmental revenue*. Intergovernmental transfers provide a substantial portion of the resources for many state, county, and local governments. As examples, federal transfers to the states contribute major resources to human services, medical, housing, transportation, and environmental programs. State government transfers to county governments provide major resources for human services and public safety programs. Federal transfers also support worker training, community services, children's health and family services, and public health programs at the county level.

Other federal transfers are tied to federal landownership in a jurisdiction, or to a percentage of the revenue generated by federal natural resource management activities in the jurisdiction. In the past, these transfer payments provided a major source of income to many rural western counties and school districts. Federal payments of this sort are intended to compensate counties for the loss of local property tax revenues.

Intergovernmental revenues are packaged in a variety of ways, including:

- direct grants with few restrictions
- direct grants to support the performance of a particular service or activity, often referred to as categorical grants
- matching funds at a given ratio and as a condition of a particular service or activity
- reimbursement of local jurisdictions for the loss of property tax revenue
- resources funneled through a government to another level of government, as when the federal government transfers money to the states to fund a major portion of local health service programs, social service programs, and education for disabled and poor students

Accessing and using many of these federal and state grants requires the spending of state and local matching funds. These combined funds are then transferred to counties, boroughs, and other local jurisdictions for the actual delivery of services.

## Debt Instruments

Borrowing funds through the sale of bonds or other financial instruments is a vitally important source of revenue for state and local governments. While borrowing opens governments to debt liability, long-term financing provides an effective means of funding capital projects and other major purchases. For example, states use various forms of debt financing to fund higher education facility construction, pollution control grants and loans, highway construction, low-income housing construction and renovation, and mass transit construction.

## Balance Carried Forward

Nearly all governmental jurisdictions require that general fund monies be spent by the close of the fiscal year. General fund revenue is distinguished from dedicated revenue by the requirement that governments spend it for "the general good" of the jurisdiction. General fund revenue may be spent on any purpose under the control of the local government or district. Authorized purposes include familiar governmental services such as elections and document recording; program operations including public safety, public health, libraries, and parks and recreation; pension and benefit payments; and to supplement revenue from bonds for capital and equipment purchases. Dedicated revenue, in contrast with general funds, must be spent for the specific program purpose for which the revenue is raised. General funds are often used to supplement the minimal dedicated charges and fees collected by programs.

In most states at the local level, the majority of routine governmental spending must be spent, or reserved for spending, within either an annual or biennium time frame. Local jurisdictions typically must maintain a general fund reserve that complies with state requirements. This reserve makes certain that the total budget at the end of the fiscal year does not experience a deficit. The tendency to underestimate revenue and to overestimate expenses frequently results in a positive year-end net balance in the general fund. Whenever this occurs, this balance is carried forward into the next budget year as available revenue. Local governments may label this balance as the *beginning balance* or the *available fund balance*. While governments as a matter of policy try to minimize this carry-forward balance, it may reach sizable amounts, especially when it is used as a source of revenue for meeting financial obligations prior to the receipt of property tax revenues. Since property taxes are often paid by citizens in biannual or quarterly installments, a jurisdiction's revenue frequently lags behind its expenditures.

## Other Miscellaneous Revenue Sources

Several other minor sources of revenue contribute to government finance. Fines and forfeitures provide a small but steady source of revenue to local jurisdictions. Fines from traffic and parking regulations are included in this category. Interest on invested funds also generates a small addition of governmental revenues.[1]

## Varying Balance of Revenue Sources

Using the eight major categories of revenues discussed above, jurisdictions rely on quite different combinations to fund their public services. For the sake of illustration, Exhibit 10.1 presents the blend of revenues used to support a sample state budget. By contrast, Exhibit 10.2 presents the revenue blend for a sample county for the same fiscal year. Compare this information with your own state or local jurisdiction.

Exhibit 10.1   **Sample State: All Revenues from External Sources**

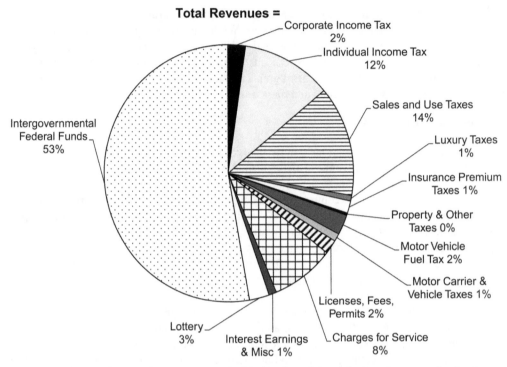

*Source:* The sample state chart was prepared with data from Arizona budget documents for fiscal years 2010–2013. General fund base revenues from State of Arizona 2012b, 31. General fund revenue detail and other appropriated fund detail from State of Arizona 2012a, 392–400. Federal funds from State of Arizona 2011. Similar budget documents for earlier and subsequent fiscal years are available at the Arizona Governor's Office of Strategic Planning and Budgeting, www.ospb.state.az.us.

Exhibit 10.3 provides a comparative summary of tax sources that are relied upon by the 50 states. As one can see, considerable variation exists in the revenue combinations used at each level of government.

## TAXATION AS A REVENUE SOURCE

For better or worse, taxation binds together all citizens of a nation, state, or jurisdiction. The contribution of personal resources toward the common good represents a major element of citizenship, although most citizens do not regard the payment of their taxes in quite the same way as they view their citizenship duties as voters or petitioners. This is because paying taxes is thought of as something we have to do—but have little control over.

In contributing to the general welfare, taxes provide a powerful tool for the achievement of public policy. Taxation can be used as the means to redistribute income across society, such as requiring people with more wealth to pay a higher tax rate. It can be used to discourage or encourage desired behavior, such as taxing alcohol or tobacco products, or providing tax credits for energy efficient appliances. Taxation can also be used to redress the hardship of a particular industry, class, or group, such as giving the elderly or a depressed industry some kind of discount

Exhibit 10.2  **Sample County: All Revenues and Resources**

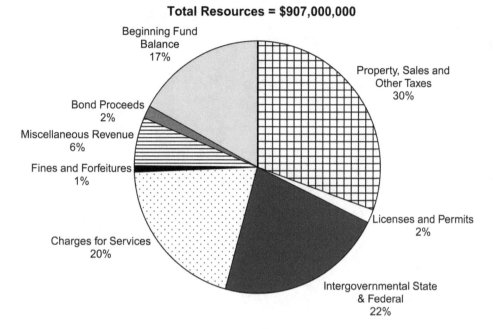

*Source:* Clark County, WA, provides the data for the sample county pie chart. Data for this graph were accessed from Clark County, Washington 2011a, xi; 2011b, 93.

on their tax liability. Finally, for some citizens, taxation represents an intrusion of the community into the development of private wealth and success.

Since the application of a tax has obvious political, economic, and administrative ramifications, imposing and raising taxes presents a major political challenge. Many citizens and politicians are inclined to view new tax proposals as the product of government inefficiency or of the unquenchable thirst of career administrators and clients for new government resources. As a result, the burden of proof is always on the proponents of tax increases to convincingly demonstrate that the increases are justified. Such justifications include: a widely and clearly communicated demonstration of need; a guarantee that waste and abuse will be avoided; and a linking of revenues to specific projects, purposes, and performance criteria. Thus, proposals to increase taxes require significant political capital in the form of trust, confidence, or at least citizen tolerance, all of which are usually in short supply.

### Tax System Design Principles

Since tax systems are designed with a wide variety of purposes in mind, careful design and forethought is required to generate citizen acceptance and to avoid numerous unintended consequences. This is especially the case when a tax system is intentionally designed to shift wealth or to retain wealth in a given group.

At the center of all discussions of taxes is the principle of fairness or equity. A distinction is commonly drawn between two types of equity—vertical and horizontal. Vertical equity refers to

Exhibit 10.3  **Rankings of Per Capita Tax Burden for Selected Major Tax and Charges Categories by State Including the District of Columbia (2008–2009), with U.S. National Average**

| State | Property Tax Ranking | General Sales Tax Ranking | Motor Fuels Tax Ranking | Alcoholic Beverage Tax Ranking | Tobacco Tax Ranking | Individual Income Tax Ranking | Corporate Income Tax Ranking | Charges and Fees Tax Ranking | All Taxes and Charges Tax Ranking |
|---|---|---|---|---|---|---|---|---|---|
| Alabama | 52 | 32 | 24 | 2 | 40 | 39 | 29 | 5 | 44 |
| Alaska | 11 | 48 | 52 | 1 | 3 | – | 1 | 3 | 1 |
| Arizona | 34 | 10 | 30 | 38 | 30 | 43 | 33 | 50 | 50 |
| Arkansas | 51 | 9 | 11 | 23 | 29 | 32 | 23 | 43 | 48 |
| California | 16 | 20 | 48 | 43 | 45 | 9 | 7 | 11 | 10 |
| Colorado | 26 | 18 | 31 | 45 | 35 | 22 | 43 | 10 | 24 |
| Connecticut | 3 | 27 | 21 | 31 | 11 | 5 | 22 | 51 | 6 |
| Delaware | 45 | – | 28 | 21 | 2 | 12 | 8 | 7 | 15 |
| District of Columbia | 1 | 5 | 51 | 42 | 25 | 2 | 2 | 52 | 3 |
| Florida | 14 | 13 | 6 | 11 | 47 | – | 31 | 13 | 27 |
| Georgia | 36 | 25 | 47 | 12 | 48 | 31 | 41 | 37 | 45 |
| Hawaii | 37 | 3 | 35 | 6 | 22 | 18 | 45 | 15 | 8 |
| Idaho | 42 | 36 | 19 | 48 | 41 | 33 | 35 | 18 | 49 |
| Illinois | 10 | 31 | 26 | 22 | 28 | 34 | 17 | 46 | 21 |
| Indiana | 33 | 22 | 32 | 46 | 16 | 24 | 20 | 25 | 32 |
| Iowa | 24 | 26 | 17 | 50 | 17 | 20 | 37 | 4 | 16 |
| Kansas | 21 | 16 | 13 | 5 | 37 | 19 | 18 | 12 | 17 |
| Kentucky | 48 | 43 | 14 | 15 | 32 | 17 | 24 | 36 | 46 |
| Louisiana | 47 | 4 | 23 | 30 | 42 | 36 | 16 | 29 | 28 |
| Maine | 12 | 39 | 7 | 32 | 5 | 15 | 28 | 49 | 26 |
| Maryland | 29 | 42 | 29 | 49 | 20 | 3 | 19 | 44 | 13 |
| Massachusetts | 9 | 45 | 44 | 35 | 10 | 4 | 5 | 32 | 9 |
| Michigan | 17 | 28 | 45 | 28 | 6 | 37 | 42 | 17 | 30 |
| Minnesota | 22 | 30 | 18 | 25 | 15 | 7 | 13 | 22 | 12 |
| Mississippi | 43 | 17 | 15 | 27 | 44 | 41 | 26 | 8 | 40 |

| State | | | | | | | | | |
|---|---|---|---|---|---|---|---|---|---|
| Missouri | 39 | 33 | 37 | 47 | 51 | 28 | 46 | 41 | 47 |
| Montana | 25 | – | 3 | 13 | 9 | 30 | 11 | 40 | 39 |
| Nebraska | 18 | 21 | 8 | 24 | 38 | 23 | 27 | 21 | 22 |
| Nevada | 23 | 12 | 20 | 29 | 36 | – | 4 | 31 | 31 |
| New Hampshire | 4 | – | 43 | 40 | 1 | 44 | 4 | 47 | 34 |
| New Jersey | 2 | 24 | 50 | 33 | 12 | 8 | 6 | 33 | 5 |
| New Mexico | 49 | 6 | 46 | 18 | 50 | 42 | 39 | 42 | 43 |
| New York | 6 | 11 | 49 | 34 | 19 | 1 | 3 | 20 | 4 |
| North Carolina | 40 | 34 | 9 | 8 | 46 | 16 | 32 | 23 | 38 |
| North Dakota | 31 | 15 | 1 | 36 | 39 | 40 | 10 | 9 | 7 |
| Ohio | 32 | 35 | 12 | 41 | 14 | 11 | 47 | 28 | 29 |
| Oklahoma | 50 | 19 | 40 | 16 | 21 | 35 | 34 | 26 | 42 |
| Oregon | 30 | – | 42 | 51 | 23 | 6 | 40 | 16 | 35 |
| Pennsylvania | 27 | 40 | 10 | 14 | 18 | 13 | 15 | 38 | 25 |
| Rhode Island | 8 | 38 | 38 | 37 | 4 | 21 | 30 | 48 | 19 |
| South Carolina | 38 | 41 | 41 | 9 | 52 | 38 | 48 | 2 | 33 |
| South Dakota | 35 | 8 | 16 | 20 | 13 | – | 44 | 45 | 51 |
| Tennessee | 44 | 7 | 25 | 4 | 33 | 45 | 21 | 34 | 52 |
| Texas | 15 | 14 | 34 | 10 | 26 | – | – | 39 | 41 |
| Utah | 41 | 29 | 27 | 26 | 49 | 27 | 36 | 14 | 36 |
| Vermont | 7 | 47 | 22 | 7 | 8 | 26 | 14 | 30 | 11 |
| Virginia | 19 | 46 | 39 | 17 | 43 | 10 | 38 | 19 | 23 |
| Washington | 28 | 2 | 4 | 3 | 24 | – | – | 6 | 14 |
| West Virginia | 46 | 44 | 2 | 44 | 27 | 29 | 9 | 35 | 37 |
| Wisconsin | 13 | 37 | 5 | 39 | 7 | 14 | 25 | 27 | 18 |
| Wyoming | 5 | 1 | 36 | 52 | 34 | – | – | 1 | 2 |
| U.S. National Avg. | 20 | 23 | 33 | 19 | 31 | 25 | 12 | 24 | 20 |

*Source:* Original data from U.S. Census Bureau 2011b, 2001d. Population estimates from: U.S. Census Bureau 2011a. There are numerous variations on this type of burden and ranking analysis. The National Council of State Legislatures and the Tax Foundation provide representative examples. See also Ford 2012.

the fairness of a tax for both the rich and the poor. The following three terms are used to assess the vertical equity of a given tax:

- *Regressive:* places the greatest tax burden on those with the least wealth to spend beyond necessities, and with the least ability to pay
- *Proportional:* sometimes referred to as the *flat tax*, distributes the tax burden as a percentage of income or wealth across all groups
- *Progressive:* places the greatest tax burden on those with the greatest wealth and ability to pay

Whether regressive, proportional, or progressive in impact, there is the further question of whether a tax exhibits horizontal equity. This refers to whether taxpayers who are similarly situated pay similar amounts of tax. For example, if a small upholstery business pays significantly higher taxes than the small electronics repair store next door with about the same gross revenue, then the tax would violate the principal of horizontal equity. Both horizontal and vertical equity are necessary in generating the public's support and compliance.

In addition to equity concerns, there is the question of whether a tax policy places an undue burden on the population. The tax burden is frequently measured by calculating the effective rate of the tax payments as a percentage of income. Exhibit 10.4 provides a summary of the tax burden of citizens in the United States compared with their counterparts in other industrialized nations.

In the design of taxation systems, the *ability to pay* principle becomes a vitally important criterion. Under this principle, those with the greatest ability to pay contribute the most tax support. In contrast, the adoption of a *benefits received* principle places the greatest tax burden on those receiving the greatest program benefits, regardless of income. For example, under the benefits received principle, citizens with school-aged children are required to carry a greater load of education-related taxes. This often seems more equitable to those who do not have school-aged children, but it also raises questions about whether all of us benefit from having an educated populace, and whether families with school-age children possess the ability to pay the greater share of education costs.

In addition to the political aspects of taxation, tax system design has tremendous economic implications. The imposition of a tax adds to the price of a service or good, thus raising costs for everyone participating in the market. Consequently, tax systems in the United States are almost always designed to minimize burdens on markets. But equally important, especially at the federal level, the success of a tax policy is frequently judged by its ability to support and stabilize economic development and growth. At the federal level, this commitment is reflected in the adoption of the Full Employment Act of 1946 and the Full Employment and Balanced Growth Act of 1978, which establish a full employment economy as a national goal (15 U.S.C. 1021; 15 U.S.C. 3101–3152). At the local level, the commitment to economic development is reflected in tax breaks offered to major businesses, either to encourage them to locate within the jurisdiction or to prevent them from leaving.

Finally, the administration of a tax system carries costs. The tax must be applied in a nonarbitrary, fair, and transparent manner. Citizens in similar circumstances must receive similar treatment under the tax policy. Administering a tax system to meet these criteria requires meticulous recordkeeping, precise management of processing and notification, and systematic enforcement. Different tax systems carry a different proportion of administrative costs, but ultimately the goal is to keep these costs as low as possible. To reassure citizens of the fairness in tax administration, jurisdictions and revenue collection agencies must make the tax system easily understandable.

Exhibit 10.4  Comparison of Citizen Tax Responsibility in 2009 for 20 Selected Nations

| Country | Relative Rank Total Tax Receipts as % of GDP | Relative Rank Personal Income Tax | Relative Rank Employee Social Security Contribution | Relative Rank Taxes on Goods and Services (Sales, Use and VAT) | Relative Rank Other Taxes Including Property Tax | Relative Rank Disposable Income of Average Single Worker (% of gross pay) |
|---|---|---|---|---|---|---|
| Australia | 14 | 2 | 20 | 13 | 5 | 9 |
| Canada | 11 | 4 | 14 | 17 | 4 | 8 |
| Denmark | 1 | 1 | 19 | 7 | 16 | 19 |
| France | 3 | 15 | 11 | 16 | 2 | 14 |
| Germany | 9 | 11 | 3 | 11 | 17 | 20 |
| Greece | 13 | 19 | 6 | 6 | 13 | 11 |
| Ireland | 12 | 8 | 18 | 5 | 12 | 3 |
| Italy | 4 | 9 | 16 | 15 | 3 | 13 |
| Japan | 17 | 14 | 4 | 19 | 6 | 4 |
| Korea | 18 | 18 | 7 | 8 | 1 | 2 |
| Mexico | 20 | 10 | 5 | 1 | 20 | 1 |
| Netherlands | 5 | 13 | 2 | 9 | 8 | 18 |
| Poland | 10 | 20 | 1 | 4 | 19 | 17 |
| Portugal | 8 | 17 | 10 | 3 | 18 | 7 |
| Spain | 7 | 12 | 17 | 12 | 9 | 5 |
| Sweden | 2 | 6 | 15 | 14 | 15 | 16 |
| Switzerland | 15 | 5 | 8 | 18 | 14 | 6 |
| Turkey | 19 | 16 | 12 | 2 | 11 | 15 |
| United Kingdom | 6 | 7 | 13 | 10 | 7 | 12 |
| United States | 16 | 3 | 9 | 20 | 10 | 10 |

*Source:* OECD 2009.

**Major Types of Taxes**

Most forms of taxation are derived from one of the following three sources: income, wealth, or consumption. Each source forms a tax base. Every taxing jurisdiction must carefully delineate the content of the tax base it will rely upon for revenue generation. In order to ensure a stable, consistent, and continuing flow of revenues, taxing jurisdictions must blend multiple tax bases and multiple kinds of tax for each base. The following is a summary of the major types of taxes, their bases, and their uses.

*Personal Income Tax*

Income taxes are designed to apply to citizens and to corporations. For citizens, the income tax base includes salary and wages, but may or may not include interest income, income from investments (capital gains), and income from other sources. A series of adjustments, exemptions, and deductions refine the income tax burden to each citizen's situation. The income tax rate structure determines the actual burden carried by each payer. In many states, legislatures have linked state tax rules on income adjustments, exemptions, and deductions with the corresponding federal regulations.

The income tax can effectively combine all forms of income under a tax with efficient administration. An income tax may be applied to large areas or jurisdictions. By requiring employers and financial services companies to administer the tax withholding, tremendous effectiveness is achieved in the administration of the tax.

Income tax revenues are subject to the swings in economic cycles. In a strong economy, income tax revenues often exceed forecasts, while in a declining economy, income tax revenues drop. In inflationary times, taxpayers may be pushed into higher tax brackets before the government can make adjustments. Indexing for inflation or changes to deductions can help to compensate for inflation-driven "tax-bracket creep."

The federal and state governments make extensive use of the income tax for purposes of revenue generation. Assuming it is legal under state law, counties and cities may also levy an income tax or an income-related tax. For example, Michigan cities are authorized to levy a city income tax upon adoption of a uniform ordinance prescribed by the legislature. The tax levied is a flat tax at limited rates on income. The city of Philadelphia, Pennsylvania, has a wage tax on compensation earned by nonresidents working in the city and on residents of Philadelphia working anywhere. In the Medler School case, local income taxes are used to supplement the inadequate levels of property and business tax revenue.

*Corporate Income Taxes*

The tax base for a corporate income tax is often defined as corporate net earnings. Refinements to this general base include deductions for capital losses, depreciation of capital investments, and spending on research and development. In Washington state a business and occupation tax (B&O) makes a contribution similar to that of corporate income taxes. In practice, corporations can pass the costs of an income tax on to consumers through higher prices, reduced wages to workers, or reduced dividends to shareholders. The corporate tax structure and corporate tax rates may also encourage or discourage corporations from locating in a state or local jurisdiction. Elaborate games are often played in balancing "acceptable" levels of corporate taxation with corporate incentives. Local governments, and even states, find themselves at a disadvantage in these games vis-à-vis large corporations, whose enterprises are spread across the nation and

the world. Corporate discretion regarding the location of their enterprises can often make or break state and local economies.

*Property Taxes*

Property taxes rely on a tax base of accumulated wealth. As property owners build new buildings and improve existing ones, property values increase. Generally, whenever local governments improve the level and quality of services—that is, water/sewer service, transportation, housing, or parks—property values increase. The property tax captures this increased value of wealth. Property taxes apply to both citizens and corporations. For citizens, property taxes typically apply to the real property of land and improvements, such as homes. In some states, a property tax is also applied to personal property, including automobiles, trailers, and farm vehicles. Corporations often pay property taxes on land, buildings, and equipment.

The property tax rate is usually expressed in *mills*, or one-tenth of one percent of the real market value or the adjusted assessed value. A one mill rate yields $1 dollar of revenue on $1,000 of assessed valuation. Often, the same property is assessed by several districts for varying services. These overlapping districts include counties, cities, schools, and special service districts (fire, hospital, library, water/sewer, vector control, etc.), among others. Each district or government levies a tax on the value of the property within its boundaries. In most states, the county assessor summarizes these multiple levies into a single tax bill covering all component jurisdictions. Each owner's assessed property value is multiplied by the summed millage rate to compute the tax incurred. The total levy for the jurisdiction is the total assessed value of property in the district multiplied by the jurisdiction's tax rate.

County and local governments rely heavily on the property tax. Relatively insulated from economic cycles, the property tax can provide a stable stream of revenue under most economic conditions. Unlike income and sales taxes, decision makers can precisely set the property tax rate to meet proposed spending requirements, as long as the maximum limit set by law is not exceeded.

Property tax is generally regressive in its impact. Lower-income citizens who own property will pay a larger percentage of their available resources as property tax than citizens in a higher income bracket. Taxable thresholds, exemptions, and financial payment strategies are used to help elderly citizens and citizens on fixed incomes comply with property tax assessments. Property used for religious and charitable purposes is commonly exempted from property taxes altogether.

*Property Tax Limitations*

As one of the earliest forms of taxation in the United States, property taxes have never been especially popular with citizens. Part of the reason for this is that American governments were created to protect private property from the excessive reach of government and fellow citizens. For some, the taxation of private property represents a fundamental attack by government on the rights of the individual. This philosophical hostility to property taxes is reinforced by the practical difficulties of administering a property tax system, which requires assessors, collectors, and administrators. Keeping up with the changing value of taxable wealth is difficult. In many cases, the tax base may not match the actual use or value of the asset. Farmland situated within an urban area provides a common example. Similarly, identifying taxable financial and other intangible assets may be especially difficult in an age of computerized, global transactions. In short, inequities in valuation are common, an administrative apparatus is required for collection, and annual or biannual tax bills

demand major lump-sum payments. The inclusion of property tax payment as part of a monthly mortgage payment helps to hide the property tax and to smooth out its burden.

Tax limitations on property taxes appeared in the 1880s, but the most recent round of limitations began in the 1970s and 1980s. California's Proposition 13 in 1978 has become the most famous, but limitations on property taxes and government spending have been adopted in 41 states. Many of these limitations continue to restrict the flow of revenues to local governments. Voters in some states have adopted multiple citizen initiatives that have resulted in a confusing, uncoordinated combination of controls. For example, through the initiative process, some states like Colorado and Oregon have placed restrictions on the amount of increases in property taxes from one year to the next, along with limitations on increases in government expenditures. The actual effect of a property tax and spending limitation varies by the starting assumptions, limitation mechanisms, and current and recent economic conditions.

California's Proposition 13 is representative of property tax limitations. This voter-adopted constitutional amendment reduced property taxes by about 57 percent through a measure that prohibits property tax rates from exceeding 1 percent of the property's market value, and further prohibits valuations from growing by more than 2 percent per annum above the 1976 base assessment, unless the property was sold. In addition, Proposition 13 requires that all state tax-rate increases be approved by a two-thirds vote of the legislature, and that local tax rates also be approved by a vote of the people. In the words of one of Proposition 13's primary advocates, Howard Jarvis, "in the finest tradition of the Boston Tea Party, California taxpayers stood up and said 'No more!' to excessive taxes."[2]

Adoption of Proposition 13 by California voters had several implications. In the face of a sudden and severe decline in local tax revenues, state government backfilled some of the lost local revenues (McCaffery and Bowman 1978; Mathews and Paul 2010). This kept many services functioning but shifted control of local finances to the state. Additionally, over time, the Proposition 13 tax structure created two unequal classes of taxpayers—those owning property at the time of adoption, and those who afterward purchased property or built property. For those who owned property at the time of passage of Proposition 13, property taxes were rolled back to grow at a limited annual rate. But new property owners were forced to pay a much larger share of the property tax levy because of a booming economy and steeply rising real estate prices. Inequitable tax burdens are a by-product of property tax limitations in other states as well.

Property tax limitation mechanisms work in three primary ways and are directly related to the method of property tax computation. First, the assessed value of a property may be adjusted. Some states have retained market value as the basis for assessed property values, but others insert a mechanism to revise or roll back the assessed value to a previous year's reduced value. The annual growth of assessed or reduced value is then capped and allowed to grow slowly—for example, the 2 percent increase per year in Proposition 13. A second tax limitation strategy is to cap the overall tax rate. This approach limits the property taxes collected to the specified capped rate. For example, the state of Washington limits the combined tax rate on government and special districts to $5.90 per $1,000 value. If the tax rates from all applicable jurisdictions exceed this cap, "junior" districts take a proportional cut to bring the total under the cap. A third group of limitations caps the growth of an individual property owner's annual tax. The tax is allowed to grow by a specified percent annually. The percent cap on the growth of individual property owners' taxes is similarly applied as a percent cap on the total tax levy imposed by the jurisdiction. Thus, Washington imposes a 1 percent annual limit on the growth of the total tax levy imposed by a jurisdiction on its property owners. It is important to note that in some states, voters—by either a sufficient majority or a super-majority—may override a limitation by local ballot measure.

*Sales Tax*

Sales taxes derive revenues from consumption. The general sales tax has become an important, if not the primary, vehicle for revenue generation in all but five states. In most cases, the general sales tax is levied at a single point in the economic exchange process, usually at the retail level between the retailer and the consumer. In contrast to the lump-sum annual payment of a property tax, a general sales tax applies a small incremental rate at each transaction. This spreads the burden over a large number of transactions for each person, thereby making it more tolerable to taxpayers. Because the sales tax is regressive in impact, many states exempt certain basic items, like food and prescription drugs, from this tax. To further compensate for the regressive nature of a general sales tax, state legislatures may also provide refunds for low-income residents. States have opted for special-purpose sales taxes, or excise taxes, that tax the sale of specific items such as gasoline and diesel fuel, air travel, cigarettes, tobacco products, and alcoholic beverages.

State law and regulation define the structure of retail sales and use taxes in each state. A state level sales tax allows the equalization of resources across wealthy and poorer areas of a state. The location of the stores and shopping districts that generate sales may be distant from the areas in need of government services, and applying the tax at a state level helps to redistribute funds across a state according to need and the state budget. Commercial centers near state boundaries present special collection problems because of interstate disparities in sales taxes. For example, the state of Washington has a general sales tax, while Oregon has none. It is quite easy to escape the effects of a sales tax by simply crossing the border to make purchases. This is much easier than moving your domicile or relocating your employment in order to escape the effects of property or income taxes.

State law typically allows most local jurisdictions to piggyback a "local option" sales tax onto the state sales tax. This authority allows local jurisdictions to gather revenues from local residents for local services, or to augment service levels above the state-funded minimum. However, the retail sales tax and other sales-related taxes such as hotel/motel, restaurant, and motor fuels taxes effectively capture revenues from tourists and other visitors as well as from local residents.

The burden of sales tax collection, however, falls to merchants. Computerized checkout equipment that can quickly identify exempted items has eased implementation of the sales tax for in-person transactions. Nevertheless, sales and use tax regulations have varied widely from state to state, and U.S. Supreme Court decisions in the *National Bellas Hess* (1967) and *Quill* (1992) cases have severely limited the tax collection responsibilities of businesses selling by mail or telephone to consumers in other states. Congress too has refused to act to support nationwide collection of sales tax revenue on interstate purchases. These constraints challenge revenue collection from businesses operating in multiple states and selling across state lines. The recent and strong emergence of e-commerce (the practice of selling through the Internet) has exacerbated state efforts to collect sales taxes from interstate commerce. Projections indicate that the nationwide loss to state and local governments of uncollected e-commerce sales tax revenue by 2012 would be as high as $11.4 billion (Bruce et al. 2009). As a result, 24 states with sales taxes have adopted harmonized tax codes and joined the Streamlined Sales Tax system under which cooperating states will collect tax due and remit it to the state in which the consumer resides (National Conference of State Legislatures 2010; Streamlined Sales Tax Project 2011; Streamlined Sales Tax Project 2005). Forty-four of the 45 states with sales taxes have been involved with the Streamlined Sales Tax Project.

In many states, sales tax systems have limited capacity to tax and capture revenues from the service sector of the economy (Edwards 2006). In the 1930s, when sales taxes were first

implemented, the service sector was relatively small, and collection from the sector was costly. Doctors, attorneys, and accountants resisted the imposition of taxes on their services. This constraint has increased in importance as the service sector has grown to become a major portion of the U.S. economy. Three states—Hawaii, New Mexico, and South Dakota—have comprehensively integrated services into their sales tax programs. Other states have tried to expand taxes on services with mixed results. Finally, collecting taxes on the barter and exchange sphere of the economy (encompassing domestic help, swap meets, farmer's markets, garage sales, and the like) remains difficult.

To summarize, most state governments rely on a combination of income, sales taxes, and some property taxes to generate a diversified, consistent stream of revenues. Local governments rely on property taxes, general sales taxes, fees for services, and intergovernmental transfers to generate a similar diversified balance in revenue flow. Sales and income taxes reflect the fluctuations of the state economy. Because property taxes are based on accumulated wealth, they are relatively insulated from economic cycles.

## TAX EXPENDITURES: LOST REVENUES OR INTENDED POLICY DECISIONS?

The structure and implementation of a tax code at any level of government serves not only to raise the necessary revenues, but to bring about public policy decisions and to influence citizen and corporate behavior. Exceptions to a tax code provide relief from taxes to certain segments of society. Such targeted relief from taxes is known as *tax expenditure*. For the recipient beneficiary, a government decision not to collect tax revenue is equivalent to direct government spending for their benefit—hence the name *tax expenditure*. Exemption from taxes serves to encourage a particular behavior by corporations or citizens.

Granting a tax expenditure signals a policy decision by government either to shift the remaining tax burden to nontarget groups or to broadly forego revenue. Tax expenditures take a variety of forms, including, deductions, exclusions, deferrals, preferential tax rates, and tax credits. Some tax expenditures are widely recognized, such as the federal mortgage-interest deduction for a primary residence on income taxes. The behavioral incentives of this expenditure encourage homeownership and the stimulation of the banking, real estate, forest products, home construction, and home furnishings industries.

Tax expenditures are frequently criticized as an inappropriate public policy instrument for several reasons. First, a tax expenditure aids a limited group of corporations or citizens. Second, the creation of a tax expenditure may be the result of a deliberate policy decision, but more frequently it results from quiet legislative action that is buried in the arcane details of tax and revenue bills. The policy impacts and effectiveness of many tax expenditures are rarely reviewed or debated for broad public benefit. Third, tax expenditures tend to erode general taxes. Once one group receives relief, other groups desire equal or relatively more favorable treatment. Fourth, tax expenditures are often liberally granted during times of economic stress without regard for their impacts on government revenues and public policy.

Tax expenditures have become quite common—so much so that 32 states require them to be reported on a systematic basis. In the absence of such reporting, tax expenditures can accumulate incrementally over time and add significant impact to the overall revenue flow of a state. For example, for the 2011–2013 biennium, the Oregon Department of Revenue identified 378 tax expenditures. Of these, 123 were related to local property taxes, and 217 were related to personal and corporate income taxes. The remaining 38 expenditures were related to various

state taxes. More than half of the 217 income tax expenditures were tied to the federal tax code. While linkages with the federal tax code may have an impact on state revenues, it makes citizen and corporate compliance with the state income tax code much easier. State income tax collection and administrative costs are greatly reduced. The total cost of tax expenditures for the 2011–2013 biennium was an estimated $31.3 billion for the state of Oregon. This compares to the roughly $27.2 billion that the state and local tax districts expect to collect over the same period (State of Oregon, Department of Revenue 2010a and 2010b).

On the positive side, carefully designed and vetted tax relief is an important tool for economic development. Local governments can often grant relief from property taxes to attract new businesses and to retain existing businesses. State governments may grant full or partial exemptions from the state corporate income tax.

Tax expenditures also define and subsidize the nonprofit sector. Nonprofit tax relief first began with the Wilson-Gorman Tariff Act of 1894, which included federal income tax exemptions for charitable, religious, and educational organizations. The act was declared unconstitutional in 1895, but the exemptions for the same set of organizations reappeared in the Revenue Act of 1913, which implemented the new federal income tax. The Revenue Act of 1917 established the federal income tax deductions for giving to tax-exempt charitable organizations (Arnsberger et al. 2008). Federal tax policy continues these exemptions to the present. Though the details vary by state regulations, religious and charitable nonprofit organizations typically receive relief from state and local government retail sales taxes, property taxes, and corporate income taxes. As described above, local governments across the country are suffering from deep losses in tax and intergovernmental revenues. These fiscal pressures have caused some of these governments to carefully review their property tax exemption regulations for local nonprofits in an attempt to better define charitable activities and potential tax revenues (e.g., in North Carolina, see Anderson et al. 2003). Threats to local property tax exemptions for nonprofits occur on a fairly regular basis, including those from a statewide ballot initiative in Colorado in 1996 (Anderson et al.) and in a Minnesota Supreme Court case in 2007 (Randolph 2007).

## THE GROWING TREND OF FEES FOR SERVICE

User charges, often labeled as fees or fees for service, provide an important source of revenue at all levels of government. Unlike taxes that raise discretionary revenues to broadly fund government, user charges and fees cover the cost of providing a specific government service. Revenue from government issued permits and licenses, which allow the consumer to perform a regulated activity, is very similar to fee revenue. In practice, the customer perception of user fees, licenses, and permits blends together. Permit and licenses, however, provide a mechanism for regulatory enforcement. For example, a county or city building permit first allows home construction or remodeling, but secondly, the permit results in the follow-up service of building code and safety inspections. While often listed separately in public budgets, user fees, licenses, and permits are similar in that the citizens and businesses using the service are the ones responsible for covering their costs.

Over the last several decades, fees and charges for service have increased as a share of county and other local government revenues. This growth responds in part to the property tax limitations and other revenue limitations imposed in many states (Mullins and Pagano 2005; Bartle 2003). Increasing fees and user charges is often less politically sensitive than increasing taxes to cover the same service. Resistance to tax increases has become so extreme that state legislators have increasingly turned to fees as a means to cover the rising cost of government services. In one

western state, user charges increased from 10 percent of the state revenues in 1992 to nearly 13 percent in 2002. On a per capita basis, these charges leaped from $248 per person in 1992 to $534 per person in 2002 (Franzen and Mayer 2008; Mayer 2005). The changes reflected an unconscious shift away from general fund support of government. This particular state legislature has only recently acknowledged the increasing importance of user fees as a source of state revenue. From a citizen's perspective, an endless stream of "nickel-and-dime" user fees results in a covert accumulation of financial burden. This contrasts with the overt clarity of a unified tax bill.

In principle, user fees enable citizens to choose the services they want and pay the matching user fee. In this sense, user fees reinforce one aspect of fairness—the consumer pays for the services rendered, and the cost is not subsidized by other taxpayers. This approach allows government to provide a specialized service for a minority of the population without doing so at the expense of the general public. However, many government activities provide basic social benefits or services of lower preference and last resort. For example, mass transit with extended rides and multiple transfers may provide the means of transportation for low-income workers. Similarly, sewer fees and trash collection under a franchise system result in mandatory government fees. In these circumstances, there is little difference between fees and taxes.

An implication of the fee-for-service approach is that the payment of a user charge results in a clearly defined service or outcome. Local special district governments tend to reinforce the selective aspects of the "user pays" concept. Special district governments rely heavily on user fee revenues, including seaport cargo tonnage and passenger use fees; airport passenger and cargo fees; hospital and medical use fees, and parks and recreation district fees. Fees are an effective revenue form for these governments because the link between the service and the payment is clearly defined and dedicated. Some governments establish separate enterprise accounting funds to separate fee revenue and to demonstrate the business nature of providing the particular service. Port districts, and local government water, sewer, and electric utility departments often follow this practice. The clarity of fee revenues and dedicated funding contrasts with the numerous and often poorly defined expenditures covered by a government's general fund.

Lost in this quest for fairness and clarity is the notion that the government services covered by user charges and permits result in a broader public good. For example, an exclusive user fee approach would demand that students at public universities cover the full cost of their education through tuition and building fees. Yet, broad and equitable access to higher education carries many external social benefits to the community, including social mobility, economic viability, an educated workforce, and even political civility. The presence of a highly educated workforce benefits the community in its economic development effort and assures employers a labor pool of quality workers. The use of general fund resources to cover at least a portion of the service costs recognizes that many government activities are more than a simple purchase of a service by citizens.

For county and city governments in some states, fees and charges related to the development of residential and commercial property is a substantial source of revenue. These fees cover all or part of the cost of building new roads and installing street lights, sewer and water systems, and parks and recreation facilities. Fees of this type include systems and traffic development charges, and traffic impact fees. Development fees may be assessed on a per house, or per business basis which can result in inequitable burdens relative to pre-existing taxpayers. The development fee approach also places the burden for development on new residents and new property owners. This is especially true where the fee covers all of the systems development costs. Some municipalities recognize the broader community benefit of the new infrastructure, and set the fee to cover a specified percentage of the total infrastructure cost, with tax revenue covering the other portion of the cost.

The design of the fee structure and the fee rates raise implications concerning consumer affordability and fairness. Governments and government agencies set the rates for fees and charges through public notice and comment processes. Governments can set fees (1) to break even and exactly cover costs, (2) to generate a profit to subsidize other government services through a general fund, or (3) to only partially recover costs. This last situation provides a subsidy to the citizen consumer and may be useful in supporting social, health, and educational services to low-income residents.

## LOTTERY AND GAMING REVENUES: PARTIAL REPLACEMENT OF OTHER REVENUE SOURCES

States have increasingly approved various forms of gambling activity as a source of revenue. While the contributions of gaming revenue to a governmental entity's overall revenue are relatively small, they can be used at the jurisdiction's discretion or earmarked for specific program purposes. Exhibit 10.5 shows the dramatic growth in the revenue-generating capacity of lottery and gaming activities. However, lottery contributions to state budgets are modest. In 2000, total net returns after prizes and expenses revenues from the 37 state lotteries amounted to just over 2 percent of state tax revenue. This revenue of $12.3 billion in 2000 was of the same order of magnitude as alcohol tax revenue ($4.1 billion) and tobacco tax revenue ($8.4 billion) (Fink, Marco, and Rork 2004). By contrast, state general sales taxes and income taxes each averaged one quarter of all general revenue collected by states (Clotfelter et al. 1999, 31; c.f. Exhibit 10.1).

Because lottery participation is voluntary and not a compulsory "tax," elected officials often find it easier to offer a lottery rather than to impose a tax increase; however, lotteries as a revenue source are similar to a tax because, after expenses and prize payments, the profits are available to state governments for any authorized purpose. The annual fluctuation in lottery revenues can be volatile, but a lottery can contribute to the diversification of a state's revenue portfolio (Szakmary and Szakmary 1995). Analysis by Fink, Marco, and Rork (2004) indicates that lottery sales may reduce general sales and excise tax revenue partly because of displaced sales but also may increase income tax revenue.

Lotteries are a regressive revenue source because they place a greater proportional burden on the wealth and income of low-income individuals. Moreover, as lotteries and gaming become more common, the need for social and mental health programs related to gambling addiction grows. This raises an ethical dilemma for state and local government. Is it fair to place some citizens at risk for behavioral and social problems in order to benefit the larger state or community? Aggressive advertising by state lottery and gaming commissions may further aggravate the impact on citizen and community health. In response to this threat, state lottery commissions may channel a small percentage of lottery profits into treatment programs, research, and advertising for gambling addiction (Hooper 2005). County and city governments often receive a portion of the state gaming revenues, which is fitting because county mental health departments provide one of the first lines of response for citizens struggling with gambling addiction.

## INTERGOVERNMENTAL TRANSFERS, FEDERALISM, AND UNFUNDED MANDATES

As mentioned earlier in this chapter, the transfer of funds from one level of government to another, or between governments on the same level, is described as an intergovernmental transfer or intergovernmental revenue. Intergovernmental finance in the United States differs from arrangements

Exhibit 10.5  **Growth in U.S. Lottery Sales** (in billions of dollars)

|  | Number of State Lotteries | Total Lottery Gross Sales |
| --- | --- | --- |
| 1973 | 7 | $1.97 |
| 1987 | 23 | $17.55 |
| 1997 | 38 | $36.40 |
| 2007 | 43 | $51.48 |
| 2010 | 43 | $53.10 |

*Sources:* Clotfelter, Cook, Edell, and Moore 1999, 26. Originally published and adapted from Clotfelter and Cook 1990, 100 (Table 1). U.S. Census, Annual Survey of State Government Finances for 2010 and 2007, http://www2.census.gov/govs/state/ (accessed June 12, 2012).

in countries with unified governments. For example, in France, local administrative units receive funds that are transferred from the central ministry for the purposes of administering services at the local level. In the United States, the states are legally independent, which means that in some instances states or recipient units of government may refuse to participate in a program, refuse offered funds, or petition for a waiver of requirements to make acceptance of the offered funds more palatable.

Within the states, the independence of county governmental units varies with each state. Home rule charters increase the independence of county and city governments: In some states, county governments stand as a virtually independent level of government. In other states, counties are perceived as semiautonomous, local extensions of their state government. The degree of state control and restrictions binding intergovernmental transfers between state and county governments reflects these differences in independence.

Estimates of intergovernmental revenues as a share of all state and local revenues were fairly consistent—at about 33 percent—throughout the 1990s (see Exhibit 10.6). These revenues included federal revenues to states and local governments, state revenues to local governments, and local revenues to state governments. The percentage of intergovernmental revenues is a function of a combination of conditions, among them the state of the economy, state revenue conditions, and major state and national emergencies. For example, following the 9/11 attacks, federal funds to the states and to local governments increased to improve homeland security. These funds eventually fell off and the intergovernmental revenue percentage reverted back to the general range of 33 percent, which was the norm during the 1990s. The economic downturn of 2007–2009 brought reduced revenues to states and to local governments, while federal intergovernmental dollars increased due to the American Recovery and Reinvestment Act of 2009 (ARRA) stimulus dollars. Tax and expenditure limitations in some states also worked to limit state and local revenues. This combination of reduced state and local revenues and increased federal funds resulted in an exceptionally high intergovernmental percentage of 49.7 percent in 2009 (Exhibit 10.6). With the end of the ARRA programs and grants in 2010 and 2011, and the strengthening of local economies, the percentage of intergovernmental revenues should fall toward historical levels.

Intergovernmental transfers come in a variety of forms, including:

- revenue sharing or direct grants with few restrictions;
- direct grants for the performance of a specific service, program of services, or defined range of services;
- matching funds at a given ratio as a condition of expenditure on a specific program of services;

Exhibit 10.6    **Intergovernmental Revenues as Share of Total State and Local Revenues, 1992 to 2009**

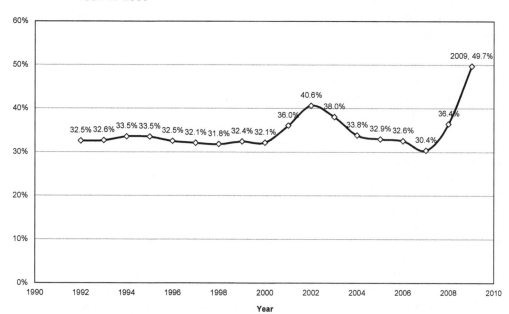

*Source:* Original data from U.S. Census Bureau 2011c, 2011d. The data captures estimates of federal payments to states and direct federal payments to local governments, state payments to local governments, and local governments to states. The data likely underestimates payments between local governments.

- resources funneled through one level of government to another level;
- revenues shared with local governments as a consequence of federal programs and land management activities; and
- reimbursements to local jurisdictions for the loss of tax revenues.

This last category reflects the substantial federal ownership of land, property, and facilities throughout the nation. As reimbursement for lost property tax revenues, the federal government makes annual payments in lieu of taxes to county governments, specified city governments, and specified territorial governments. In a related arrangement, the federal government shares a percentage of the revenues generated by federal natural resource management programs with local counties and school districts. In both cases, these transfers represent grants of unencumbered revenues to the local governments. From the local perspective, these transfers are discretionary revenues.

Federal intergovernmental revenues provide substantial revenues to state governments and local communities, including the SNAP food and nutrition program, the WIC (Women, Infant and Children) program, Medicaid administration and provider reimbursement, mental health services block grants, substance abuse block grants, and the Children's Health Insurance Program. Other major federal intergovernmental transfers include funds for unemployment assistance, worker retraining, community development block grants (CDBG), community services block grant, HOME investment partnerships and the Section 8 low-income housing programs, U.S. Department of Justice public safety competitive grants, U.S. Department of Homeland Security grants, transit and transportation infrastructure construction grants, environmental infrastructure, and education assistance programs.

In certain program areas, the federal and state governments must work together to effectively provide services to citizens. Under many federal statutes, authority is granted to the federal agency to involve the states in regulatory activities and service delivery. Federal revenues may provide incentives leading to state participation in the program. Other federal payments may serve to cover state costs. In many cases, federal law and regulations set policy directions for the administering federal agency, yet counterpart state agencies may face state legislative and gubernatorial direction that affect and even redefine regulatory behavior and service delivery (Scheberle 1997). These circumstances can lead to complicated funding and oversight relationships between the states and the federal government. For example, federal laws restrict grants to libraries that meet certain computer filtering requirements, while state laws may not impose similar restrictions. This leaves agencies in the position of deciding whether to accept federal money with restrictions that may not be in conformance with state policies.

Federal oversight provides an effective consistency in program intent and outcome. State and local implementation of federal mandates provides the opportunity to make adjustments that fit local conditions and needs. State and local implementation of regulatory programs puts a more familiar local face on a broad national intent. Gaining effective results out of these joint delegated programs requires close coordination and cooperation between federal agencies and their partners at the state and local levels.

Unfortunately, the burden of federal demands on the states and on local governments has far outstripped the resources provided by Congress. In the school district case example at the beginning of this section, part of Medler's budget crisis is caused by an additional $15 million of expenditures per year that result from mandated federal requirements in serving students with disabilities. For many state and local governments, the lack of federal resources has resulted in an intolerable burden of unfunded mandates. Between 2004 and 2008, the National Conference of State Legislatures (NCSL) estimates that Congress has shifted over $131 billion in unfunded burdens to the states (NCSL 2010a, 2010b). Unfunded or partially funded federal legislation contributing to this burden shift affects all states. Examples of unfunded mandates include an increase in the federal minimum wage; a preemption of state authority to tax Internet sales and transactions; and a requirement for public transit and rail carriers to conduct security assessments, employee background checks, and training. Unfunded mandates and cost burden shifts result from several legislative situations such as (1) the establishment of new mandates packaged as conditions of grant aid; (2) the reduction of federal program funds to states, or a reduction in the federal contribution to a matching rate; (3) the extension of an existing or expiring mandate; (4) the establishment of a compliance date after which states and local governments lose aid; (5) the preemption of state and local authority, creating a loss in state or local revenues; (6) mandated coverage of certain groups without the provision of adequate resources or full reimbursement; and (7) the creation of an underfunded national expectation, for example in homeland security (NCSL 2010a). County governments have also noted that increasingly limited federal resources have resulted in a shifting burden to state and local governments without corresponding funding (National Association of Counties [NACo] 2011).

Efforts by Congress and other national political actors (e.g., National Commission of Fiscal Responsibility and Reform [NCFRR] 2010) to balance the federal budget and to eliminate deficit spending will place federal intergovernmental revenues to the states and to local governments in question for years to come. Most intergovernmental transfers originate from the discretionary, nonmilitary portion of the federal budget. These budget functions and accounts are subject to the annual congressional appropriations process and are legislatively susceptible to reduction. County government advocates have argued that Congress cannot reach a balanced budget solely

by reductions in discretionary spending; they also make the case that federal spending should support local employment and that deficit reduction should not impose unfunded mandates on the counties (NACo 2011). Traditionally, returning federal funds and grants to states and congressional districts stood as a success criterion for members of Congress. However, political initiatives to balance the federal budget and increase fiscal responsibility have challenged this notion of political success. Maintaining federal intergovernmental transfers in the future will require active advocacy by states, counties, and other local governments; by constituent groups and program advocates; and by interested citizens.

Reductions in federal intergovernmental transfers to the states will have ramifications on state budgets and transfers to local governments. Almost all states operate under balanced budget requirements. Reduced federal intergovernmental payments, coupled with reduced tax and fee revenues following the economic downturn that began in 2007, have made it increasingly difficult to balance state budgets. In the face of extremely limited revenues and resources, some state legislatures have reconsidered intergovernmental payments to counties and local governments. Some of these once-consistent payments are now in jeopardy of reduction or elimination. Again, local governments, their advocates, and citizens will need to advocate for intergovernmental revenues.

## DEBT INSTRUMENTS AS A REVENUE SOURCE

Earlier in this chapter, we established the importance of borrowing funds through the sale of bonds and other financial instruments as a source of revenue for state and local governments. Clearly, borrowing opens up governments to debt liability, but long-term financing provides an effective means of funding capital projects and major purchases. In emergency situations, governments can use short-term borrowing to smooth out gaps in cash flows. However, extended and excessive reliance on borrowing reduces the jurisdiction's credit rating and increases borrowing costs. One of the central principles of public debt management is that governments should not use borrowing to finance routine spending for operations.

The financial community has developed two primary forms of long-term debt financing for the public sector: guaranteed debt and nonguaranteed debt. *Guaranteed debt* commonly takes one of two forms: One form consists of "full faith and credit" obligations packaged as *general obligation bonds,* which receive the full backing of all the revenues and resources of a state or local jurisdiction. The second form of guaranteed debt is backed by more narrowly defined revenue sources. These are called *revenue bonds,* and they are backed by a specific stream of revenues and resources generated by a particular project, program, or new facility. For example, a water department or special district may issue revenue bonds to build a new facility, pledging its water rate revenue to secure the debt. In order to secure a stream of future revenues, many governments integrate commercial space into new facilities. This blending of different kinds of space usage often results in the government undertaking complex ownership and leasing arrangements. Finally, a jurisdiction may borrow on a short-term basis to meet payroll and similar operating expenses by pledging anticipated income or property tax revenue that has not yet been collected. This type of borrowing is known as tax or revenue anticipation borrowing.

*Nonguaranteed debt* is financed in a manner similar to the way we personally finance our homes or cars. Instead of backing our loan with either a stream of income or a fixed fund of revenue, we are charged interest at a rate that represents the amount of risk the lender is taking. This kind of borrowing in the public sector takes the form of *bonds,* which can be issued either as term or serial bonds. With term bonds, the issuing jurisdiction makes periodic interest payments on a regular basis and must pay off the principal in a lump sum after a set period of years. With serial bonds,

the jurisdiction makes periodic interest and principal payments on a regular basis from the time of issue to full repayment. Many jurisdictions budget a debt service fund or a sinking fund to build up reserves to meet debt payments.

Determining the limits of borrowing by a state or jurisdiction is a complex task. Debt is used primarily to finance capital projects and major purchases. Capital projects are usually understood to be relatively expensive, with long-term returns and a permanent, physical presence. Capital investments include buildings and facilities, as well as large equipment such as fire engines. For some smaller jurisdictions, the purchase of police cars would be considered a capital investment. Traditional accounting practices require that the useful life of a purchase should exceed the debt repayment period.

Setting the level of borrowing by the state or a local jurisdiction reflects a balance among the following complex set of considerations: (1) community needs, (2) repayment ability reflecting recent revenue flows, operating expenses, and borrowing, (3) the strength of the economy, (4) the value of the real estate property tax base, (5) public opinion, (6) a willingness to accept higher interest costs because of a reduced credit rating, and (7) the essential purpose of the capital project. The development of a public budget with a capital investment schedule provides the forum for making conscious decisions on these trade-offs. The chief executive officer of the jurisdiction plays a key role in framing this debate with the debt proposals in the recommended budget. The credit rating granted to a state or jurisdiction by the bond market community can play an important role in shaping whether local officials are willing to ask their voters for authority to borrow money for public facilities.

## NONPROFIT REVENUES AND FUNDRAISING

No matter the need and value of their public service offerings, nonprofit organizations will cease to exist without revenues. New revenues and resources on hand must be sufficient to meet operational, administrative, and capital investment expenses. Foundations, federated intermediaries, service providers, religious organizations, and member-serving organizations must take the time, effort, and resources to generate sufficient revenues to sustain their organization. Family foundations and organizations drawing from endowment revenues stand as the possible exception to the fundraising obsession. However, for endowment dependent organizations, donations and earned income provide a welcome supplement to endowment investment revenue. Major sources of nonprofit revenues include private giving (donations and membership dues); earned income such as fees for service; grants, contracts, and reimbursements from governments and other nonprofits; investment income (Salamon 2012, 1999); and borrowed funds (Dropkin, Halpin, and LaTouche 2007). Much like governments, nonprofits attempt to diversify revenue sources to obtain a consistent flow of resources over changing economic conditions.

Raising donations and dues revenues takes place in a competitive environment of donor choice. Donors have options of where, when, and how to give their money. Nonprofits must make themselves known to donors, and distinguish their performance, services, and products from those of their competitors. In addition, nonprofits must demonstrate to donors that they have the organizational capacity to effectively and efficiently use donations for their intended purposes. Donors also expect an organization to have the effective leadership and administrative systems of a trustworthy organization. The scale of private charitable giving varies. Small-scale charitable giving covers small opportunistic giving as well as routine giving through annual dues and pledges. Philanthropic giving represents a larger scale of major gifts, which is normally guided by a strategic plan (Frumkin 2010) to gain maximum effectiveness with the recipient organization or

community. Philanthropic giving of major gifts is often channeled through foundations or other intermediary nonprofits, which in turn make grants to service organizations.

Fundraising, donor development, and resource development are ongoing organizational tasks for almost all nonprofits, and fundraising stands as a primary duty of the executive officer of most nonprofits. Nonprofit board members also support the development of the fundraising network and donor contacts. Large nonprofit hospitals and universities employ an executive at the senior level to organize and implement fundraising programs and strategies. A small staff may assist this individual with administrative and research tasks. The staff maintains files of past and potential donors, and helps to organize and implement fundraising activities. In smaller nonprofits, the executive director often takes primary responsibility for fundraising, while other middle- and senior-level staff members contribute to the effort. To apply for and win foundation and government grants and contracts, many nonprofits retain professional grant writers on staff.

Fundraising is an integral element of an organization's strategic plan, mission, and branding. The revenue base used by an organization helps to define it among the population of nonprofits and service providers. Organization goals and objectives for fundraising define the fundraising campaigns, events, tactical marketing, and administrative tasks needed to raise revenue. Obtaining larger donations often requires a team effort of persistent contacts over an extended period. The nonprofit executive director, the fundraising or development director, board members, the grant writer, and the program manager may all be involved in the effort to secure a major grant.

Fees and charges for services are a major source of nonprofit revenue that complements private giving and donations. Nonprofit administrators and board members have some control over the rate structure for fees and charges. Rates may be set on a cost recovery, profit, or sliding scale basis as best expresses the organization's mission. For example, a private university might set tuition rates to recover administrative, instructional, and facilities costs. A nonprofit hospital might set charges on a sliding scale of partial cost recovery in order to effectively serve low-income, unemployed, or homeless patients. A nonprofit might operate a health club and sports facility to generate a profit that can then subsidize and support services to youth and low-income clients. Once the purpose of the fee or charge has been established, the analysis and development of a rate schedule is not unlike that used by governments.

Grants and contracts from governments, foundations, intermediaries, and other nonprofits provide a major revenue source for many nonprofits. Grants and contracts are typically awarded on a competitive basis, and applicant organizations must distinguish themselves from competitors based on performance and organizational capacity. Government grants and contracts of multiple years' duration or with annual renewal potential have the benefit of bringing stability to a nonprofit's revenues and financial planning. However, political and citizen efforts to limit the growth of government agencies and services can affect the government funds available for contracts and partnerships. Nonprofit managers must understand the circumstances that their government-agency counterparts face in trying to obtain funding for their joint programs. The government-related content of this and the following chapter sets the foundation for building such an understanding. By following the progress of annual or biennial budget proposals and legislative debates, nonprofit administrators can begin to predict the level of government revenues that will be available for the coming fiscal year.

Like government organizations, nonprofits borrow funds for major capital investments in land, buildings, and equipment. Nonprofits may arrange lines of credit or loans from banks or other lenders, or they may sell bonds for major capital investments. Nonprofit use of credit ranges from a local church taking out a mortgage to fund construction of a new parish hall, to a major nonprofit hospital building a new wing. Most state governments have a financial agency that gives nonprofit organizations in the state access to the tax-free municipal bond market.

Building a dependable and balanced funding base is a challenge for most nonprofits. Revenues from different sources should complement each other in terms of timing and durability over economic cycles. Heavy dependence on a single funding source, such as a major government grant or donor, may have deep effects on a nonprofit's staff structure, grant administration and accounting load, service operations, and performance standards. Accepting a major grant or donation requires that the board, executive, and members of a nonprofit thoroughly consider the downstream impacts and the changes it will bring to the organization and its relationship to its target population.

While nonprofit organizations constantly work to raise funds, intermediary organizations have limited funds to distribute. An intermediary nonprofit organization is an organization that raises and collects funds but does not deliver services; these organizations are intermediate between the donor and service provider. Federated campaigns run by intermediary organizations solicit donations across many employers or member organizations to generate a substantial volume of revenue that can then be allocated to community needs. Religious intermediary organizations coordinate fundraising across local churches, synagogues, mosques, or branches and then distribute the combined donations according to mission priorities. Other national health and research organizations collect donations from local chapters for centralized health and disease research efforts. Community foundations also act as intermediary nonprofits. Foundations gather donations and philanthropic gifts into a combined pool of resources. Some of these resources may be invested into the foundation's endowment, while other funds may be distributed to purchase service delivery. A foundation program manager typically allocates funds and makes grants according to the foundation's mission or the needs of the community it serves. Corporate foundations express a business's support for the community, while family foundations draw from endowment investment income to distribute funds according to the expressed desires of the family member's priorities (Frumkin 2010). Financial market performance and economic cycles affect financial returns and the level of investment income available annually for distribution from foundations.

Like any donor, the major community intermediaries and community foundations have limited resources, but they are faced with a broad array of funding requests from across the community. These circumstances often create extremely fierce competition for funds from intermediaries and foundations. Intermediaries and foundations are increasingly conditioning funding on efficient and effective organizational performance. This performance-based approach contrasts with past practices in which community collections and federated intermediary organizations, such as local United Way chapters, granted each member organization a relatively certain annual "fair share" of the total combined collections. Nonprofit administrators operating under the fair share model were, like governmental organizations, somewhat insulated from the details of revenue estimation and generation.

## TRANSITIONS IN NONPROFIT FUNDRAISING

The World Wide Web is transforming long-standing pathways and institutions of charitable giving. The web allows donors to research and verify a nonprofit organization's credentials, its programs, and its finances in minutes. Online research can quickly reveal reports from third-party evaluators and ratings from state government consumer agencies. Donors can use the research to support traditional giving pathways of pledge campaigns, employer paycheck deductions, or hardcopy payment, or they can move directly to online donation.

The web and social media software also provide a powerful tool to solicit donors and to present the nonprofit organization both inside its community, regional, state, or national home territory, and outside to an audience of new donors. The web can provide donors with timely information

on emerging needs locally and globally; it is especially effective in emergency and disaster relief situations. The global reach of online giving creates the opportunity to generate funds from outside the immediate home territory, but this also raises concerns of external donor control of local nonprofits and their program content.

Online giving is also transforming the organizations that support community philanthropy. Instead of relying on federated intermediary organizations for a structured giving campaign, many employers are turning to online employee-giving systems. These online programs allow employees to give directly to the charities of their choice without involving an intermediary. This directed-giving approach has long been a common practice, but it has accelerated in the online environment. There are several consequences of reliance on the web for revenue generation. First, intermediary organizations are in less demand to provide organized solicitation, community research and planning, need prioritization and resource allocation, and project monitoring. In some cases, these organizations have reinvented themselves as community research, planning, and coordination organizations. A second unintended consequence of directed giving is that it may result in a loss of flexibility for meeting community priorities. This is because donors often do not have a full understanding of comprehensive community needs and dedicate their funds as best they can under partial information. Community foundations that have a more comprehensive view of community needs may get bypassed by donors who can direct their larger donations with minimal professional oversight (Frumkin 2010, 148).

## POLITY LEVEL PERSPECTIVE ON REVENUES

Historically, each government and nonprofit organization raised funds and budgeted its resources independently of others in the community. A government or special district would impose taxes and fees and advocate for state and federal intergovernmental revenues; then, government in-house staff would use those resources to deliver services. Similarly, each community intermediary organization or foundation raised funds from donors and investments, and then distributed those resources to its members or favored service providers. A segregated approach to raising revenues was sufficient to support stove-piped pathways of service delivery. However, networked service delivery and community-centered planning and issue response demands a broader, integrated polity-level perspective on resource development and public budgeting. Intergovernmental agreements, public-private partnership agreements, grant provisions, and contracting arrangements with subcontractors provide some order to the allocation of resources and performance management across the policy network. Further, each primary government or intermediary member of the network may have individual policies on how to respond if another member fails to provide resources. Efforts to assure the survival and growth of individual organizations can conflict with the broader goals of network-level efficiency and effectiveness. Similarly, short-term financial needs of network members may conflict with the longer-term goals of the network. Without conscious coordination and awareness on the part of the network members, governmental and charitable resources could quickly be wasted or inefficiently used.

The network level creates a broader perspective on community resources and public revenues. Revenues from property taxes, sales taxes, government fees and charges, nonprofit fees for service, charitable donations, and philanthropy all originate from a common metropolitan or regional economy. Though the levy and collection mechanisms are different, governments and nonprofits draw revenues from a common economic base. Decisions on taxation and tax expenditures in the government sector often have ramifications in the resources citizens can devote to charitable giving. The accumulation of wealth and the health and growth of the economy is critical to growing

resources for the polity and its networks. The health and growth of the state economy is critical to the flow of intergovernmental revenues from state programs to local governments and nonprofit service providers.

In urban areas with large service networks and sufficient resources, community intermediary organizations have taken on the financial planning tasks of assessing and tracking the flow of revenues from different sources. Such analyses demonstrate the historic and current relative contribution of government, foundation, and intermediary revenues to the community programs and initiatives. With an understanding of the historic flow of resources, changes in revenue streams become evident. Network members can then make more informed decisions of when to add or withhold resources for a given set of programs. Governmental and nonprofit administrators must continue to raise resources for their own organizations, but they must also be aware of the flow of resources through the community networks in which they partner.

## THE ART AND SCIENCE OF REVENUE PROJECTION

The amount and availability of future revenues defines the scope of programs that a government or nonprofit can provide. Thus, the estimation of revenues becomes a critical foundation of public budgets, program development, and citizen expectations. The estimation of revenues expected in the coming fiscal year or biennium, and the forecasting of the financial context of expected revenues and costs over the near to midterm, are critical first steps in building a budget. If analysts overestimate future revenues, governments and nonprofit entities must scramble to cut back operations in the middle of a fiscal year, seriously undermining the administrative efficiency and effectiveness of the organization in the process. If the opposite occurs, and analysts underestimate future revenues, governments and nonprofit organizations are left with an embarrassment of revenues. Governmental jurisdictions are especially vulnerable as they seek to explain why they have "overtaxed" the citizenry. Like the temperature of baby bear's porridge in *Goldilocks and the Three Bears,* the goal is to rely on a combination of mathematical and statistical tools and judgmental skills to get the estimate "just right." Using this combination of tools and skills to figure out how regional, national, and global economies might evolve and affect future revenue elevates revenue estimation from a predictive science to a professional art.

Even though revenue estimation relies heavily on quantitative, statistical, and economic techniques, it is also important to create a revenue forecasting process that has the confidence of the participants (Barden 2000). This may be difficult, especially when there are large numbers of participants who have different priorities. But without some agreement on the size of the pot of money, it will become nearly impossible later on to make much progress in deciding how the pot should be divided. Regardless of how technically accurate the work of revenue forecasters may be, if their work does not have the faith and confidence of participants in the budget process, it will be ignored. For this reason, revenue forecasters have to be mindful of the larger political backdrop that includes policy visions, political agreements, impacts on interjurisdictional and interorganizational relations, and citizen support. Revenue forecasters play a major role in building and maintaining the trust and support of elected officials, taxpayers, attentive stakeholders, and clients.

For governmental organizations, the revenue forecast is a public document, which means that the budget actors and citizens must find the forecast process credible and the revenue estimates accurate. While technical committees of revenue specialists typically perform the actual detailed forecasting work, a broader review by stakeholder groups is usually necessary to build the larger credibility necessary for this technical work to have its maximum impact. More often than not, both the technical and the broader review processes are open to the media and to the general public

in order to ensure that no single sector, group, or individual monopolizes control of the process or the forecast. This openness also plays an important part in building the larger political legitimacy necessary to resolve the inevitable conflicts that arise when allocating scarce public resources.

In addition to being open, the revenue forecast must be easily understandable to all of the budget process participants. Full understanding includes both knowledge of the forecast results, and the concepts and general procedures used to develop them. The techniques that are familiar and appropriate to the revenue forecaster may easily appear as a mysterious "black box" to the general public and elected officials. Revenue forecasters must therefore make a special effort to translate their approaches and processes into lay terms. This plain-language standard arises primarily from the responsive governance tradition and is critical to sustaining the legitimacy of the forecasting process. In the same way, elected decision makers must be aware of the basic assumptions and reasons behind the forecast. All of the key participants in the budget process must understand the likelihood that the forecasts may underestimate or overestimate the actual amount of revenue ultimately collected. Based on this understanding, elected officials, administrators, and interest groups can deal with the consequences of likely outcomes. Revenue forecasters also must be able to explain the probability and impacts of any significant reductions in revenues; for example, the inability to explain a 10 percent reduction for a given category of revenue will quickly lead to lost credibility.

Confidence in a revenue estimate rests on several additional criteria. First, a revenue estimate must be consistent with the revenue forecasts of comparable jurisdictions. While revenue forecasts for state or local governments may be marginally different, any major differences in techniques, assumptions, and estimates must be easily explained and defensible. Second, a revenue forecast must be accurate. Accuracy is often measured in terms of the percentage deviation of actual revenues from the forecast. This is sometimes quite difficult when there is too little time and money to be equally thorough and systematic in making estimates for each revenue source. Even small jurisdictions must track several sources of tax revenues, intergovernmental transfer revenues, revenues from fees for service, licensing revenues, and opening balances. Each source of revenue represents a different level of importance to the overall revenue picture. Accordingly, a key concept of revenue forecasting is to focus time and attention on those revenue sources with the greatest contribution and impact to the budget. A forecast that predicts revenue within two percentage points of anticipated expenditures is considered within the acceptable margin of error as a best practices standard.

Finally, revenue forecasting is an art as much as it is a science. No forecaster or forecasting group knows for certain what revenue numbers will look like a year or two into the future. Because of this, consistent matching of forecasts and actual revenues rarely occurs, and a cushion always needs to be built into the revenue and expenditure balancing equation. When this cushion results in having a higher positive net balance at the end of the budget year, how does one explain it to the public? Even with the best technical work, public distrust remains. The only antidote is to make every effort throughout the process to be sincere and transparent in communicating with the public.

## REVENUE FUNDS ORGANIZE THE GOVERNMENT BUDGET

Each source of revenue used by a government or jurisdiction brings a different degree of flexibility in its use and in its accountability requirements. Following accounting standards, a government budgeting process must effectively separate revenue sources and revenue uses. This separation into "funds" ensures that spending meets the intent and requirements set by law or by the granting

source. The budgeting process and subsequent accounting during budget execution must support effective reporting on how funds were used. The creation of separate funds, the establishment of routine accounting practices to maintain control of these funds, and a follow-up audit at the end of the budgeting cycle becomes central to maintaining administrative accountability (see chapter 12).

Nonprofit budgeting and accounting uses relatively few fund types to relate revenues and resources to expenses. As mentioned, sources of nonprofit revenues include fees for service, annual membership dues and paid pledges, investment income, endowment income, grants, and contracts. Other nonprofit income categories include nonmonetary donations and contributed services. Donor and contract sources of income are classified as either *unrestricted* and available for all uses, or as *restricted* and dedicated to a particular activity or program service. Degrees of restrictions on revenues range from permanent to temporary, depending on the circumstances (Herman and Associates 2005, 470–476). Unrestricted funds, which may be used for any purpose, are equivalent to a government general fund. The fund structure for nonprofit, for-profit, and government hospitals is highly complex (Finkler 2010, 436).

Governmental budgeting and generally accepted governmental accounting practices typically recognize the following ten different types of public-sector budget and accounting funds: (1) general funds, (2) special revenue funds, (3) debt service funds, (4) capital project funds, (5) enterprise funds, (6) internal service funds, (7) expendable trust funds, (8) nonexpendable trust funds, (9) pension funds, and (10) agency funds. The first four of these 10 fund types are considered governmental funds. Governmental funds support programs and activities not normally found in private-sector business.

As explained earlier in the text, in governmental budgeting, a *general fund* gathers all revenues without spending restrictions. General funds may be used by the entity for any legal purpose. Because of their flexibility, general funds are often labeled as *discretionary funds*. General funds provide for large portions of general government operations, including fire, police, parks, and library services. In addition, general fund revenues are often used to provide the local supplement or "dollar matching" that is required to receive special dedicated funds. Revenues raised through property, sales, and other general taxes, fees paid for services, and fines are the main sources of revenue that make up the general fund.

In contrast to the wide discretion of general fund revenues, *special revenue funds* are collected for a specific purpose or program. These funds carry restrictions on use and accounting practices that require separation from other resources. They are often categorized as *dedicated funds*. At the federal level, the Federal Highway Trust Fund, supported by federal motor fuel taxes, provides an example of a special revenue fund. Similarly, at the state level, revenues from gasoline taxes are dedicated through a special revenue fund for highway construction and repair activities. Local jurisdictions may have a parks fund that is supported by user fees.

*Capital project funds* are dedicated revenues collected and managed for the construction of buildings and facilities, or for the purchase of major types of equipment. Revenues for capital project funds may originate as a transfer from the general fund, intergovernmental revenues, or from bond sales paid by general fund revenues. In a similar use, *debt service funds* provide the dedicated resources to meet interest and principal payments on general long-term debt. Again, general fund revenues may be transferred to this fund to make payments and to meet accounting needs.

*Proprietary* or *enterprise funds* operate in a businesslike manner, separately from the rest of the government activities, budgeting, and accounting. Revenues collected from water and sewer services, public electricity provision, road and bridge tolls, and the sale of timber from state or county lands are often managed as enterprise funds. The use of federal funds may require the

establishment of a proprietary fund to ensure dollar matching and effective accounting during spending. In a related use, *internal service funds* set up accounts that describe a "business" function within government. For example, a general motor pool, a common equipment pool, human resource services, or public affairs services may operate as an internal business, with each operational department paying general fund revenues for services. Payments for these services would be recognized as an *interfund transfer* in a public budget.

*Fiduciary funds* provide a means to separate unique assets from the general functions of government operations. In holding these funds, governments act as fiduciary agents for other government programs, agencies, or client groups. At the federal level, the Social Security Trust Fund provides a major example. At the state level, public employee retirement funds are normally treated as a fiduciary fund. In several other examples, revenues from the sale of timber and forage from state lands, along with rents from the use of leased state lands or facilities, are frequently funneled into a special purpose fund designated for school support (*common school funds*). The earnings from state lotteries may specifically contribute to special funds for education, economic development, and parks and natural resource programs. Locally, school districts hold student club and activity funds in fiduciary accounts.

Revenue categorization by funds reflects both the sources of the revenues and the revenues' potential uses in government spending. While many special revenue funds and fiduciary funds receive revenues exclusively from a dedicated source, some funds may receive revenues from several sources. A general fund may receive any unencumbered revenues. General funds and lottery revenues often supplement or leverage special revenue funds, capital project funds, and debt service funds. Some federal revenues have dedicated sources, uses, and fund designations. Other federal funds may be relatively unencumbered and, in practice, replace general fund dollars. Each jurisdiction creates its own major categories of revenue and establishes rules governing their use subject to supervening jurisdictional requirements. The creation of these revenue funds and the rules governing their use play an important role in maintaining democratic accountability and in limiting the discretionary authority of public officials.

The definition and organization of funds has several implications beyond the control of revenues. Funds also serve to link revenues to specific spending accounts and thus to the delivery of a specific set of services to citizens. In this way, funds form the basic structure of state and local government program accountability. In addition, in many local governments, a department and all of its programs may be supported by one fund or only a few funds. This approach reinforces the structure of the organization and provides internal linkage of its operating divisions and programs. To summarize, funds provide for both program and organizational accountability, in addition to revenue accountability.

## CONCLUSION: GOVERNING MEDLER SCHOOL DISTRICT THROUGH FINANCIAL EXIGENCY

The Medler School District case illustrates the role public finance plays among our contending traditions of governance. School districts display some of the most personal and intense aspects of community politics. Parents rightfully expect the careful nurture and education of their children in a safe school environment, and they are often acutely interested and concerned about any changes that may affect their local schools. Many of them get involved in local school governance through site councils and PTAs, and help coproduce education and support services through volunteer efforts. They know teachers and principals personally. The civic governance tradition thrives in this environment.

And yet, this case involves a very large bureaucratic district run by professional administrators with large staffs and thousands of teachers who belong to a powerful and well-organized union. The district's revenue requirements run into hundreds of millions of dollars per year. Responsive and accountable financial management requires the expertise of financial analysts, budget analysts, contract officers, accountants, and a hierarchy of line administrators. Unions represent the teachers in personnel-related decisions within and among the schools, including bumping rights in the case of layoffs. (If a qualified school district employee is faced with drastic cuts to working hours, bumping rights allow that employee to "bump" or displace a less-senior employee from his or her position and then take it over.) School administrators and the elected school board must account for the interests of the broader community as well as the interests of parents with children in their schools. These senior officials operate primarily under the norms of the competent and energetic governance tradition, sitting awkwardly alongside the neighborhood schools and their more intimate community settings while a fiscal crisis looms ominously over all.

How, then, should these administrators respond to the expected revenue shortfall? From a strategic standpoint, school administrators face two glaring problems: declining enrollments and a strong resurgence of antitax sentiments and measures. Now consider the strategies presented in the Medler case. Calls for a tax increase and lobbying for more state funding from the legislature are not likely to receive serious consideration without at least the articulation of a plan for gradual retrenchment. Borrowing from the state retirement system represents a risky precedent, first because it opens the door to subsequent loan requests by other state and local institutions and thereby threatens erosion of a vital fiduciary fund, and second because it is a temporary expedient for a situation that entails longer-term fiscal and demographic problems. Increases in federal grants may help to offset some revenue losses but are unlikely to help very much because of their categorical or dedicated nature. Converting certain school programs, such as theater and sports programs, to a partially fee-based system will generate some offsetting revenue, but not nearly enough to cover the shortfall. Moreover, this approach would likely eliminate these services for students from lower-income families. Given the extent of expected revenue shortfall, these limited financing options make a compelling case for adopting more of a budget-centered strategy that includes a combination of seven options.

One obvious strategy for reducing expenditures is to cut the school year by 50 days, but this is, at best, a temporary expedient. More important, cutting school days threatens to undermine the confidence of the district's most vital constituency—its parents—and seriously compromises the educational mission of the schools. As we learned earlier, effective public finance is built on public confidence in its institutions. If this is lost, little hope remains for viable solutions later on. The question remains, however, whether a shorter school-day reduction period (perhaps one or two weeks rather than ten) might not erode the public's confidence while contributing to a multi-pronged strategy for coping with longer-term reductions.

Increasing the student-to-faculty ratio from 25:1 to 30:1 poses many problems, not the least of which is undermining the student-achievement initiatives introduced by the new superintendent and the political fallout from laying off 750 teachers. This option does, however, meet the budget exigency head on, and for the longer term. Recruiting more volunteer teacher aids could mitigate some of the negative effects on achievement, but such efforts seldom result in consistent staffing and quality. Some increase in the student-to-faculty ratio will likely be necessary in order to deal effectively with the revenue shortfall, but such a steep increase may not be needed if other measures are also adopted.

Negotiating for a significant reduction of health care benefits with the teacher unions will likely be viewed as a heinous betrayal, since the benefits had been maintained in past years in lieu of salary increases. Such action would likely undermine labor-management trust and cooperative

relations achieved by the new superintendent. At best, the administration may get away with no raises in salaries or health benefits in the coming year or two as labor's concession to revenue exigency, but the savings would be temporary.

Contracting out some school district support services may be viable despite union animosity, but this too will only partially meet the revenue shortfall. Moreover, contracting out usually results in less savings than anticipated because of increased costs of contract administration and compliance. There may be some opportunities for actually generating revenue through corporate vendors who want to market goods to schoolchildren and adolescents, but this is a controversial practice from which some school systems are now backing away.

Closing schools (in league with layoffs) may have to form part of the district's strategy, but doing so through an outcomes-based performance system will likely invite extreme divisiveness and claims of socioeconomic discrimination. Such a system also entails serious problems with assessment, both in terms of design as well as effects—such as inducing teachers to "teach to the tests" instead of teaching students to think abstractly and to cultivate the imagination. Another option is to close schools in low-enrollment neighborhoods. This often affects upper-middle-class and aging neighborhoods and is difficult to accomplish because of their political clout.

Requiring an across-the-board cut is a common approach for two reasons: It is relatively simple to implement, and it appears fair in the sense that all receive the same percentage cut. However, flat-rate cuts have a disproportionately regressive effect on poorer schools and are likely to compromise the new achievement program as a result. Nevertheless, some level of across-the-board cuts is likely to occur in league with other revenue-saving measures.

Finally, creating a priority ranking system for ongoing cuts to keep the budget balanced seems like a rational-comprehensive approach to analyzing the school district's fiscal affairs. However, as we noted in chapter 7, organizational analysis and decision making entail incredible complexity, uncertainty, and controversy, especially under the circumstances faced here. In this context, decisions and analyses are conducted more through political advocacy by organizational subunits in league with constituents and other stakeholders (Stone 1988), and through incremental methods that reflect compromise at the margins (Lindblom 1959). A 10 percent revenue shortfall in one year is hardly incremental, but the means of dealing with it will likely occur through a web of smaller compromises and revenue offsets. The school board, working with their superintendent and staff, must include a variety of stakeholders in the process of determining and ranking priorities. The priorities and the process will be negotiated among face-to-face communities such as site councils and the PTA, unions and other organized interests, and principals who jealously guard their powers and roles in the system.

The administrators in this system play a critical role in managing the process, as well as maintaining viable powers and roles. They must try to keep the weaker stakeholders in play with the stronger ones, maintain the focus on the exigencies at hand, and not lose sight of the "internal goods" of educational practice that define the district's mission. They must work closely with elected officials who possess well-developed political skills of listening and assessment of public sentiment, and who can provide an important legitimating anchor in a world of conflicting citizen expectations. At the same time, administrators must deploy analysts and other specialists to assess the viability and implications of various revenue- and budget-cutting alternatives and weave this information into the political process. They also must carefully articulate their assessments of changing family demographics, local school capacities, and infrastructure issues that affect school closure alternatives. And finally, administrators must cultivate broader assessments of community intent, usually conveyed through various stakeholders' tacit knowledge of moods, values, and perspectives.

This is where school principals play what is perhaps the most vital role of linking the larger system, dominated as it is by professionals and organized interests, with local site councils, parents, volunteers, support staff, and teachers who identify more with the civic governance tradition. The principals are in a position to translate between the street-level community and the strategic level of district governance. They must represent their schools in the budgetary melee, and some of them are likely to mobilize neighborhood resources and elites to help buffer their schools from the more drastic measures that are likely to be adopted. This is the heart and soul of budgetary politics. Understanding the political dimensions and dynamics of budget practice is vital to every administrator's success in this process, and we turn to this topic in the next chapter.

## STUDY QUESTIONS

1. City, county, and special district governments in many states must refer property tax increases to the voters. What ethical constraints limit the participation of public administrators in communications with the public over the proposed tax changes? Contrast these limits with those faced by elected officials. What constraints should limit employee union participation in levy campaigns? Which groups should take the lead in proposing and advocating for proposals to raise government revenues?

2. Many American citizens possess low levels of confidence in their governing institutions. How can public administrators manage and respond to this suspicion during the public discussion of tax levies and other revenue-generating actions?

3. With the failure of a local property tax levy, should public administrators encourage elected officials to scale back programs and discontinue services, or should they advocate stretching staff and services to cover funding shortfalls? How should administrators communicate the impact of funding shortfalls on the community?

4. Multiple forms of taxation and revenue sources help to ensure a stable flow of revenues across a range of economic conditions. A small number of states have no general sales tax. Another group has no income tax. How must these states design their revenue and budgeting systems to compensate for a missing source of tax revenue?

5. How would you assess your local jurisdiction or nonprofit organization in possessing a "balanced" revenue portfolio?

6. Raising revenues through increased fees and payments for defined government services provides an out for politicians opposed to general tax increases. What are the ramifications of heavy reliance on fees for the service user and for community governance?

7. How can the fund structure of an accounting and budgeting system enhance citizen confidence that fees for service will in fact support only the intended services?

8. Should the size and scope of government programs expand or contract to follow regional economic cycles of growth or recession?

9. Economic development packages often include tax limitations and rebates on local property and state taxes. Are the revenue provisions in these packages tax expenditures? What should be the criteria in awarding economic development incentive packages, especially in weighing the loss of immediate tax revenues and the alterations in the tax burden against the longer-term economic advantages to the community?

10. Intergovernmental revenues provide a substantial source of revenues for most state and local governments. These funds often support local corrections, social services, and educational programs. With the transfer of these funds, how much oversight and control should the source government exert on local governments? Should local governments

comply with state or federal laws and mandates if the accompanying funds are completely inadequate to the performance requirements?

## NOTES

1. There is a growing trend for many public-sector organizations to supplement their increasingly constrained public resources. For example, at the local level, public school systems have encouraged the creation of school foundations, both systemwide and school specific, to raise money that can be used to provide art, music, and physical education programs not supported by the public sector. At the federal level, the U.S. Forest Service (National Forest Foundation), the National Park Service (National Park Foundation), and the Bureau of Land Management (Mustang Heritage Foundation) have all championed the creation of foundations to generate additional revenue to supplement their funding. Although new and growing, these agency-linked foundations do not yet provide a significant source of revenue to governmental entities; however, they do illustrate the growing erosion of the traditional bright-line distinction among the sectors. In chapter 15, we provide a case example of an initiative taken by local administrators to create a new nonprofit organization to coordinate countywide delivery of social services by the private, public, and nonprofit religious, philanthropic, and civic organizations.

2. Details on Howard Jarvis's views on Proposition 13 are available at the Howard Jarvis Taxpayers Association's website, www.hjta.org/index.php.

CHAPTER 11

# BUDGET FORMATION AND RESOURCE ALLOCATION

Political rationality is the fundamental kind of reason, because it deals with the preservation and improvement of decision structures, and decision structures are the source of all decisions. . . . There can be no conflict between political rationality and . . . economic rationality, because the solution of political problems makes possible an attack on any other problem. . . . In a political decision . . . action is never based on the merits of a proposal, but always on who makes it and who opposes it. . . . Compromise is always a rational procedure, even when the compromise is between a good and a bad proposal.

*(Paul Diesing 1982, 198, 203–204, 232)*

In a democratic society, the division of resources between the public and private sectors is roughly determined by the desires of the electorate. But because it is such a complex and time-consuming task to acquire adequate political information, the electorate is chronically ignorant. . . . This ignorance causes governments to enact budgets smaller than the ones they would enact if the electorate possessed complete information. . . . The resulting misallocation of resources becomes more and more serious as the economy grows more complex.

*(Anthony Downs 1960, 76)*

The budgeting of public resources is a delicate balancing act. It is partly a matter of collecting good technical information and using it to make data-based decisions that succeed in balancing expenditures with available resources. It is also a matter of mobilizing political influence and using it to pressure decision makers to address citizen and societal needs. How do we strike this balance in the public budgeting process between the need for high levels of technical expertise and the need for accountability to the electorate and their chosen representatives?

Alexander Hamilton, in his 1791 "Report on Manufactures," established a precedent for striking this balance: "budget to a plan" (1791/1966). Hamilton, in his role as secretary of the U.S. Treasury, presented an elaborate, well-argued, and well-documented plan to U.S. Congress as the cornerstone of his strategy for obtaining members' support for public funding. On its face, this makes perfect sense. Why should anyone support a request for the expenditure of public funds without having a clear plan of what the expenditures will accomplish? Despite the good sense of budgeting to a plan, public expenditures are frequently approved based on who supports what,

rather than on a clear understanding of what exactly the expenditures will accomplish. Even when there *is* a clear plan for the allocation of resources, Paul Diesing's observation at the beginning of this chapter reminds us that mobilizing information in the service of a plan is a political act, not simply a technical one. In this chapter, we will explore how this tension between the need for responsiveness and accountability and the need for technical expertise manifests itself and gets resolved in the public budgeting process.

The Democratic Balancewheel metaphor outlined in chapter 6 will serve as the central framework for this chapter on public budgeting. Career administrators play a critical role in balancing the competing claims of efficiency, effectiveness, equity, and fiscal accountability that come into play during the budgeting process. As we shall see in the sections that follow, public budgeting is not about esoteric techniques, knowledge, and numerical calculations; rather, public budgeting is really about balancing competing democratic values and the appropriate amalgam of participation, expertise, and decision-making processes in order to best achieve the larger public interest. In short, we argue that public budgeting is not about numbers and computations; it is about making democratic governance work. Thus, this chapter assumes that those with budget responsibility—whether in large hierarchical state and federal governments, in small local city and county governments, in special districts, or in community nonprofits—participate actively in shaping what "the public good" means.

Taxation and public expenditure issues were one of the driving forces leading to the creation of America's complex system of separation of powers and checks and balances. Today, various state and local democratic constitutions give the executive branch the power to propose a budget and to collect taxes, but the power to authorize and appropriate funds is lodged in the legislative branch. *Authorization* entails the act of passing a law that enables the future spending of public money on a given set of activities, usually with a stipulated upper limit. *Appropriation,* on the other hand, entails the additional act of approving the actual expenditure of funds. At the federal and state levels, this two-step procedure is clearly divided, with one group of specially designated and separate legislative committees in charge of program authorization and budget construction, and another group in charge of fund appropriation. Some states even organize their legislative sessions so that authorization activities occur every other year, with budget appropriation activities occurring between authorization sessions. At local levels of American government, the line between appropriation and authorization is not drawn quite so brightly. Even then, however, there is a well-defined "budget season" during which an identifiable set of processes is in place to create and approve the allocation of a jurisdiction's or organization's resources.

In contrast to the defined roles and processes of government, nonprofit boards and executives do not clearly separate program authority from budget approval. Both activities are frequently loosely coupled, with the board and the chief executive officer centrally involved. The exact balance of authority and power between the executive and the board is unique to each organization. In larger nonprofits, the preparation and adoption of an annual budget is a formal process with clearly defined roles for the organization executive, the finance officer, and the board. In contrast to the openness of government budgeting procedures, nonprofit budgeting is typically less open to broad public scrutiny. This reflects the role of nonprofits as private organizations that act for the public benefit.

The formality and public nature of the government budgeting processes remind us that budgeting is an inseparable part of a jurisdiction's general governance activities, not simply a mechanical process performed by technicians. Once we view public budgeting as part of a jurisdiction's larger structure of authority, the practical task of developing a budget becomes a window to the community's heart and soul. The budgeting process is the focal point for debating the roles of experts

and citizens and the questions of whose views should be given primary weight in deciding what is in the public interest. More fundamentally, it is the primary means by which local citizens give expression to the kind of community they wish to create.

This chapter is divided into three sections. Section I examines the following four foundational elements critical to understanding why the budgetary process works the way it does: (1) the historical pattern of governmental budget development in the United States, (2) the competing purposes served by a public budget, (3) the government budget cycle and its impact on the behavior of its participants, and (4) the conflicting perspectives of the budget actors. We again focus the discussion primarily on state and local governmental budgeting and finance with attention to the differences in the nonprofit experience. However, the common and central question raised in this section is: What is the best way to manage the allocation of scarce resources in the face of diverse opinions on complex issues that have to be decided in a short period of time? This is the basic question that all public budgeting processes must answer, government as well as nonprofit.

Section II briefly explores a variety of budget formats that governments and nonprofit organizations use to help solve the resource allocation problem that emerges from the process explained in Section I. Budget formats such as *line-item budgeting, program budgeting, performance budgeting,* and *zero-base budgeting* represent different decision criteria and what counts as valid evidence in decisions resolving the allocation of resources. At the heart of this discussion lies the question of what kind of influence budget analysts, finance officers, and program managers should have in the budgeting process as compared to the roles of citizens, elected officials, and nonprofit board members.

Section III offers some final reflections on how the governmental budgeting process and the roles of its participants contribute to the overall functioning of our systems of democratic governance. We argue that our legal tradition of checks and balances and the separation of powers necessitates a strong role for career administrators, citizen activists, elected officials, and technical experts. This view does not do much to help resolve conflicts in the government budgeting process, but it reframes the conflicts so that they are seen as a natural and necessary by-product of our peculiar form of democracy. We believe this reframing exerts a sobering influence on expectations. By viewing conflicts as an important process of our system of democratic governance, participants are less likely to see them as artifacts that can be made to disappear through the magic of budget reform, restructuring, or changes in personnel.

## SECTION I: FOUNDATIONAL BUILDING BLOCKS OF PUBLIC BUDGETING

### The Development of Governmental Budgeting: Lessons from History

Governmental budgeting as we know it today is a surprisingly recent invention. Prior to 1900, it was common for each agency or government commission to approach the legislature separately to request funds (Schick 1980). The chief executive officer (CEO; president, governor, or mayor, for example) was left with only informal control, and the legislative body was faced with an uncontrolled and uncoordinated flood of requests. As with most reforms, experiments with budget accountability began at the state and local level.

One of the first and most important efforts at more systematic budget accountability was undertaken by the New York Bureau of Municipal Research. Created in 1907 to advance the Progressive movement's emphasis on "good government," the bureau sought to increase government efficiency by establishing a functional budget, by activity, and with measurable tasks such

as street cleaning and sewer maintenance. Computation of unit costs for each of these activities allowed total project costs and productivity information to be calculated. The overall goal was to make government more businesslike and, in the process, improve both the quality and efficiency of government service (Schiesl 1977, 128).

The first major effort at budget reform at the national level was undertaken in 1910 by President William Howard Taft (in office 1909–1913), who created the Commission on Economy and Efficiency (often referred to as the Taft Commission). The Taft Commission's report, entitled *The Need for a National Budget,* was presented to Congress in 1912 (Commission on Economy and Efficiency 1912). Its recommendations laid the foundations for many of the following modern-day principles of public budgeting (Cozzetto, Kweit, and Kweit 1995, 20–21):

1. The president should prepare a comprehensive budget covering all agencies and programs and present it to Congress (the concept of an *executive budget*).
2. A budget message should accompany the budget and should outline policy proposals of the president as well as include summary financial information.
3. The secretary of the treasury should submit a consolidated financial report to Congress.
4. Each agency should submit to Congress an annual financial report.
5. Agencies should establish and maintain a comprehensive accounting system.

The Taft Commission's recommendations became the foundation for the Budget and Accounting Act of 1921, which established a comprehensive executive budget for the federal government and laid the foundation for present-day budgeting at the national level. The 1921 act accomplished several important purposes. First, it ensured accountability for all money that was allocated to public projects and activities. By establishing line-item accounts with assigned numbers for personnel, materials and supplies, and capital outlay, it became difficult to divert money from its intended purposes (see example in Section II of this chapter). Those reformers who were primarily interested in controlling graft and corruption saw the act as a major step in maintaining financial accountability.

As the size and complexity of government increased during the late nineteenth and early twentieth centuries, other reformers became interested in increasing government efficiency by consolidating fractured government commissions and agencies under strong executive leadership. The executive budget combined these two visions (preventing corruption and increasing efficiency) into a single tool for government reform. As the 1920s came to a close, the federal government and many states and cities had adopted a formal process of public budgeting as an essential governmental activity.

Toward the end of the Great Depression and the beginning of World War II, civil service procedures, purchasing controls, and budgeting reforms had resulted in an increasingly professional government service. With spending control institutionalized, the purpose of public budgeting—especially at the national level—began to shift away from accountability, focusing instead on the efficiency and the effectiveness of government operations. As this shift toward performance began to occur, professional public administrators became increasingly important members of agency budget staffs. It is important to note that the presentation of efficiency information in budget documents raised the visibility of "performance" issues with legislators and executives.

Since 1953, there has been a steady and consistent growth in government spending at the national level as a percentage of gross domestic product (GDP), rising from 16.1 percent in 1956 to a peak of 25.2 percent in 2009, and then falling to 24.1 percent in 2011 (U.S. Office of Management and Budget 2012). Military spending, expansion of social service programs, economic stabilization and

stimulus following the housing mortgage market crash 2007–2009, and infrastructure spending have all resulted in a steadily expanding budget—and a corresponding concern by many citizens that government growth is increasingly unchecked.

This concern for growth and control over the budget was first reflected in new initiatives undertaken at various levels of government. Secretary of Defense Robert McNamara and his "whiz kids" undertook an early initiative to gain control over budget growth at the national level. When McNamara became the secretary of defense for President John F. Kennedy in 1961, he immediately became concerned about how best to decide among the competing and growing weapons systems requested by the various branches of the armed services. He brought with him a system he had used at the Ford Motor Company, along with his experts who used computers to design systems that would integrate planning, program development, and budgeting. This approach, dubbed PPBS (planning-programming-budgeting systems), enabled Secretary McNamara to integrate the various branches of the armed services around a unified defense policy with clearly defined programs and budgets that would, allegedly, contribute more effectively to achieving the national defense goals of the United States and avoid unconstrained growth in the military budget.

When Jimmy Carter became governor of Georgia in 1971, he too turned to the private sector for guidance in determining how best to force reconsideration of what government was doing. Peter Pyhrr at Texas Instruments had invented zero-base budgeting (ZBB) in the late 1960s (Pyhrr 1974). Pyhrr's goal was to create a decision-making mechanism that would help Texas Instruments remain competitive in a rapidly changing set of market conditions. He believed this could best be done by putting managers in the position of constantly asking what they were doing and why. To accomplish this goal, he created ZBB, which forced managers to start from scratch each year, justifying every business decision from the ground up. Pyhrr's assumption was that this approach would generate more innovation and new product lines, thus ensuring the company of constant marketplace preeminence. Governor Jimmy Carter adopted Pyhrr's philosophy and system in Georgia. When Carter became U.S. president in 1977, he introduced ZBB to federal agencies.

At this same time, as part of its larger effort to reassert legislative control over the executive branch as well as to create greater internal self-control over the budgeting process (Rosenbloom 2000), Congress passed the Congressional Budget and Impoundment Control Act of 1974. This act established separate budget committees in each house of Congress to prevent members from adding expenditures without at the same time making offsetting budget cuts. It also established its own Congressional Budget Office (CBO) to undertake the technical analysis necessary for Congress to operate independently from the executive branch's Office of Management and Budget (OMB). In the end, these efforts at self-control failed to achieve the desired goal. The federal debt continued to rise, and resources continued to be allocated to programs without clear performance accountability.

The failure to control spending at the federal level gradually created a backlash among a growing number of citizens and legislators who called for an entirely new philosophy of government. In addition to structuring the budget process in ways that forced participants to "live within their means," many argued in favor of replacing the old philosophy of liberalism with what came to be called *neoliberalism*. Advocates of this new philosophy favored market-sector approaches to meeting public needs over approaches that favored government as chief regulator and service provider. This new philosophy had its first major impact at the federal level with the election of Ronald Reagan as president in 1980 (in office 1981–1989). The express goal of the Reagan administration was to stop the growth and expansion of federal programs. This did not occur. In fact, the U.S. deficit grew to its largest amount in history during this period. While government outlays as a percentage of the gross national product remained relatively constant, the deficit grew

from the previous high levels of the Carter administration (U.S. Census Bureau 1989, 301, 303). Nevertheless, the Reagan years set the stage for a fundamental change in public philosophy.

Since then, all levels of American government have experienced growing concern by citizens for more accountability of public expenditures and the need to make "tough choices" in an environment of more tightly constrained resources. As indicated in the previous chapter on public finance, the public mood has undergone a decided change over the past several decades with respect to government spending. This change has put agencies on the defensive, not only to justify the efficiency and effectiveness of their public expenditures but also to defend why existing levels of expenditures and programs should remain unchanged. These continuing public concerns have brought performance budgeting and systematic planning back to the center of the public allocation process.

If history is to serve as a prologue to the future, we can expect challenges as part of popular efforts to keep government spending under control, and to link government spending to clearly defined goals. Why is this so? Part of the answer, of course, is politics: Constituency interests have overpowered the political will of elected officials to budget with clear goals, with a clear sense of priorities, and with a strong sense of discipline. This is illustrated by the Tea Party revolution, which in the 2010 congressional elections brought into office a large number of new Republican members of the House of Representatives who pledged to cut federal spending. But in the ensuing months, efforts to reduce the budget were transformed into a debate over tax increases and reductions of subsidies for high-income citizens and corporations versus tax cuts that would adversely affect the poor and middle-income Americans. The debate over balancing the federal budget was quickly changed into a political question of "fairness." However, it would be far too simplistic to treat the issue of controlling government spending as a problem of partisan politics. As the following discussion of budget purposes will illustrate, the development of a public budget reflects the competing purposes of government itself, which make it difficult to measure the success of a budget by a single standard.

### The Multiple Purposes of a Public Budget

In every governmental jurisdiction throughout the United States, the development, adoption, implementation, and reconciliation of a public budget reflects disagreement over the proper balance to be struck among (1) funding programs that are responsive to constituent wishes, (2) demonstrating financial accountability, (3) funding programs that are effective in accomplishing their goals while being cost efficient, and (4) using the budget to ensure a healthy economy. Frequently, these purposes reflect differences of opinion about using the budget to meet short-term versus long-term needs. For example, elected officials and program clients are often much more concerned about the short-term consequences of a public budget than policy experts and program managers, who are more inclined to view the budget from a longer-term perspective.

Budgeting in nonprofit organizations follows a similar set of purposes. Nonprofit board members have the responsibility of developing a budget that furthers the organizational mission, ensures compliance with law and regulation, and builds and sustains organizational capacity. The variations in nonprofit budgeting processes reflect the very wide diversity in the size, complexity, and purposes of nonprofits themselves. Small nonprofits may follow an abbreviated budget process that summarizes and reduces expenses and revenues to a single page. In these small nonprofits, volunteer officers may receive little professional support. As nonprofits increase in size, the board and executive director may rely on, or retain, finance and accounting professionals to ensure quality and to generate confidence in the organization's budget and finances. Medium and large nonprofits,

including foundations and financial intermediaries such as the federal combined campaigns and United Way chapters, typically designate and staff a chief financial officer position. In these and other larger nonprofit organizations, budgeting responds to a set of needs similar to those found in government: (1) funding programs to match community needs; (2) meeting donor expectations for performance, efficiency, and effectiveness; (3) demonstrating fiscal accountability, transparency, and stability; and (4) meeting tax and corporation filing requirements. In terms of issues and debate, adoption of a budget for a nonprofit organization also reflects issues of balancing between short-term operational and cash flow needs, and longer-term strategic goals.

### Public Budgeting as a Governing Tool to Test Political Responsiveness

The budgeting process is an opportunity to test responsiveness to community desires. For public organizations, the desires are those of the voters and taxpayers. For nonprofits, the desires are a blend of community needs and donor priorities. The "responsiveness test" results in budget expectations and outcomes that change only incrementally from year to year for both public and nonprofit organizations. Traditionally, the amount of revenue for public organizations has not changed dramatically from one year to the next, which accounts for incremental changes from year to year. For nonprofit organizations, multiyear contracts and grants, annual renewable contracts and grants, continuing donor relationships, annual combined donation campaigns, and continuing community needs reinforce the incremental nature of nonprofit budgeting. New major contracts or grants may have the effect of forcing a reexamination of incremental budgets.

For government agencies, the budget process also presents an important political platform upon which to make changes in the selection of policy choices and in the allocation of resources to support those choices. Almost all jurisdictions place responsibility on the CEO to prepare a balanced budget and to present it to the legislative body for review and approval. The CEO's proposed budget provides an opportunity to array and prioritize all the functions and needs of the jurisdiction. In its final presentation, the executive budget represents a unified policy statement of the jurisdiction's services.

The opportunity to use the budget to make fundamental and important policy changes is especially important to elected officials and interest groups who seek to acquire the funding necessary to support programs important to their interests. The perspectives and needs of elected officials and interest groups may often conflict with the values and hopes of public administrators who need to balance competing program priorities. Understanding these contrasting perspectives is a useful key to understanding the budget process.

Elected officials operating within our representative system of government face a different set of performance evaluations than their administrative counterparts. Elected officials must respond to their constituents' needs and demonstrate a record of leadership. Even the most junior legislator must demonstrate an ability to control or use government to solve problems in the home district. Survival as an elected official rests on this ability. By contrast, civil service professionals rely more on agency and professional values to guide their sense of action and accomplishment. For example, program managers, direct service providers (social workers, police officers, civil engineers, foresters, and so on), and budget analysts for agencies are primarily committed to acquiring the resources necessary to maintain the continuity of program services to clients and the stability and continuity of the organization. They place less emphasis on delivering on promises to constituents. Sometimes, clients are constituents and vice versa, but there is a fundamental difference between "service delivery" to clients and "delivering the goods" to constituents. The former requires attention to issues of efficiency and effectiveness, while the latter is primarily a

matter of responsiveness. The budget process provides recurring leadership opportunities to bridge and reconcile these competing perspectives.

The chief administrative officer (CAO) of each state and local jurisdiction faces special challenges. Whether the executive is elected directly by the people or serves at the pleasure of the legislative body, the promises made during an election campaign must be translated into policies and programs quickly. The campaign goals and visions must be translated into legislation and directives that reorient administrative agencies to the goals of the newly elected officials. If the CAO is appointed, he or she becomes the immediate contact point for all of the pressures placed upon newly elected officials by various constituency groups. In leading the transition to a new set of policy directions created by an election, there are two reasons why the CAO must proceed with caution: one is economic and the other is structural.

The implications of budget choices within the context of an existing set of economic conditions first become evident only with the compilation of an integrated budget. Good economic times generate strong revenues and provide a chance to strengthen the fiscal health of the budget. When acting against the backdrop of a recession, the CAO must limit spending to match revenues. For all the hopes and promises of new programs and services, a downturn in the economy may make spending cuts and reductions a necessary order of the day.

In addition to economic considerations, there are structural factors built into the process that require the CAO to exercise caution in using the budget to make fundamental policy changes. The CAO's budget is reviewed and modified by legislative institutions and processes to meet the needs of the political leadership of that branch of government. Legislative bodies range from special district, corporate, and nonprofit boards of directors, to city councils and county commissions, to much larger state and federal legislatures. When the branches are divided along partisan lines, compromise is usually necessary to meet a twofold constitutional duty shared by the executive and legislative branches: (1) the CAO must present a balanced budget to the legislature, and (2) the legislative branch in most state and local jurisdictions is constitutionally required to enact a budget.

Finally, a jurisdiction's or organization's budget process provides a means for interest groups to raise and debate issues. Nonprofit organizations can make a special contribution in this regard. Nonprofit service providers often have the clearest conception of community needs and the costs of services to meet those needs. As independent organizations, nonprofits can advocate for changes in service programs during local government budgeting processes. Moreover, in many situations, local governments have limited capacity to structure and to administer social service programs (Berry and Arons 2003). These conditions place nonprofit organizations in a particularly influential role, especially if they have become a single-source supplier. However, excessive advocacy or pressure on the part of nonprofits, especially those with a past contractual partnership with the government, may be interpreted by the public as unethical and self-serving behavior.

Legislative proposals and votes on proposed funding levels and spending directions represent the setting of priorities and purposes for the jurisdiction's government. It is the one time and one place on an annual or biennial basis that the goals of government are given concrete expression with an opportunity for citizens to express their views. A public budget process must increasingly provide an opportunity for citizens and interest groups to be involved, especially as budgets are reprioritized to make adjustments to shrinking revenue. For major community nonprofits, the annual budgeting process provides an opportunity to revisit community priorities, community strategic visions, and community values. But unlike the open government budget process with internal controls of checks and balances, donors offering extraordinarily large-sized grants may, in essence, coerce nonprofits and their dependent partners into particular policy and program choices. The decision to accept such

extremely large donations sometimes forces nonprofit boards to make difficult choices between organizational growth and survival on the one hand, and policy and program choices that are in alignment with their organizational mission, on the other. Even for smaller donations, many donors expect to see program outcomes that meet their particular vision of the public good. Such visions may conflict with the larger political preferences and needs of the community.

*Public Budgeting as Financial Accountability*

A second purpose of the budget process is to ensure financial accountability. This accountability is achieved in a variety of ways, including:

- limitations on spending via the use of accounting codes and regular monitoring of expenditures;
- statutory and/or constitutional limits on spending;
- ongoing legislative oversight;
- postexpenditure audits at the close of the budget cycle;
- a legal requirement that the CAO's Recommended Budget and the Legislative Adopted Budget be balanced;
- a legal requirement that the legislative body enact a budget; and
- a requirement that the CAO comply with the expenditure obligations set forth in the Adopted Budget, rather than use discretion to implement other priorities.

Taken together, these accountability requirements ensure that elected officials will provide public documentation of how citizens' tax dollars are being spent and that the expenditures will not exceed the collected revenues.

Budget preparation and implementation for nonprofits provides the means to demonstrate financial accountability and to build donor and public trust. The wide variation in the purpose and size of nonprofits results in widely varying capacities and resources for monitoring and demonstrating financial accountability. Small nonprofits may have little professional support and few resources to bring to bear on financial issues, while larger nonprofits typically retain accounting and finance professionals in recognition of the need for a full set of financial controls to build public and donor support.

New federal and state laws have revised the structures for demonstrating financial accountability. The Sarbanes-Oxley Act of 2002 was enacted into law in response to abuses and major financial scandals in the for-profit corporate sector (e.g., the Enron and WorldCom scandals). The act requires publicly traded corporations to increase internal financial and accounting controls with personal certification by the chief executive and chief financial officers; to increase external controls through enhanced audit committee responsibilities and auditor independence; and to support evidence protection and whistleblower protection. Following the adoption of the Sarbanes-Oxley Act, the U.S. Congress, several state attorney generals and state legislatures considered extending similar policies to nonprofit organizations. California became the first state to adopt state-level accountability controls with the California Nonprofit Integrity Act of 2004 (California Senate Bill 1262). This California law requires nonprofits receiving gross revenues over $2 million annually to prepare yearly financial statements that are subjected to an audit by an independent certified public accountant; in addition, nonprofits must appoint an audit committee and make annual financial statements available to the public (Oxholm 2005).

Nonprofit compliance with the Sarbanes-Oxley Act has varied greatly, largely reflecting nonprofit size (Ostrower and Bobowick 2006). Although the act does not apply to nonprofits directly,

larger nonprofit organizations, including hospitals, universities, and financial intermediary organizations, have moved to comply with part or all of Sarbanes-Oxley. Nonprofit board members drawn from the private-corporate sector bring their experiences and expectations of compliance with the Sarbanes-Oxley Act. The adoption of Sarbanes-Oxley by organizations of similar stature tends to establish a best-practice standard that other nonprofits feel compelled to meet. Board members may hold concerns that failure to comply might expose their organization to legal liability.

Adoption of the Sarbanes-Oxley standards ultimately speaks to building donor and public trust. Donors, insurers, and bond-rating agencies may also consider compliance with Sarbanes-Oxley in their decision making (Dreier 2005). However, the decentralized structure of many large nonprofits may make compliance with Sarbanes-Oxley especially time consuming and costly. Nonprofits may need to make a special effort and investment to reach compliance with certain provisions of the act, but accounting requirements for managing federal grants and enhanced tax reporting may already leave many nonprofits in compliance with other Sarbanes-Oxley standards.

The budget preparation and implementation processes provide the tools to demonstrate nonprofit integrity. Today, the extensive partnering between nonprofit organizations and government agencies through service contracting effectively blurs the boundary between the nonprofit and government sectors. Nonprofits and government together must work to build donor and public trust.

*Public Budgeting as Managerial Accountability*

Throughout this book, we have emphasized the distinct perspective of those who manage programs and have the responsibility of making government work on a day-to-day basis. This has some important implications for the budget process. Program managers are uniquely situated to provide two kinds of information important to various stakeholders in the budget process. One kind of information focuses on the best way to organize a coordinated response across organizational boundaries in the delivery of governmental services to the citizens. This role has become increasingly important as the public calls for a more responsive and accountable government that organizes and delivers its services with a common and coordinated sense of customer service.

A second kind of information that managers are uniquely suited to provide involves ways to enhance productivity. With the spending information from repeated budget cycles, program managers can develop unit cost trends and other productivity measures. The growing public concern for productivity enhancement has increased the burden on managers to provide this kind of information to the decision makers in the budgeting process. For example, in the Medler School District case introduced at the beginning of this section, school board officials decided to allocate additional staffing above a preexisting base level for low-achieving schools, establishing a clear understanding of the expected student achievement results that these new positions would produce. Similar kinds of productivity-based measures can be established for a wide range of public services.

Similarly, nonprofit organizations often must demonstrate performance and accomplishments. Grant and donor performance requirements often stipulate measurement and accomplishment criteria. The following discussion of PPBS and performance budgeting formats provides a means to integrate donor performance requirements into an organization's annual budget.

*Public Budgeting as an Influence on the Economy*

The spending and taxing policies of public jurisdictions, regardless of size, have economic impacts. Of course, the federal government, with its $3.69 trillion budget in 2011, 2.8 million civilian employees, and its capacity to deficit spend, has far more impact on the economy than a state like Illinois,

which had a $ $26.9 billion budget for 2012, 78,000 employees, and a constitutional requirement to present a balanced budget. To provide additional perspective, a typical top-five Fortune 500 company will generate $200–400 billion of annual gross revenue and have 350,000 employees. Most local jurisdictions have budgets that pale in comparison, yet they do affect their local economies.

State and local spending and taxing policy is important in attracting an expanding and qualified labor pool, and in competing for growing businesses whose incomes add to the jurisdiction's revenue stream. Federal matching dollars add to state and local economies, primarily through federal entitlement programs and transportation infrastructure. In turn, state grants complement county and local government spending, all of which spurs economy activity. Finally, local economies are significantly affected by government facilities and activities, which can include military facilities, prisons, federal forests, parks, and rangeland management.

From a business economist's point of view, a jurisdiction's budget must:

1. fund social service programs and contracts for those in need, thus increasing the demand for private-sector goods and services;
2. fund the transfer of welfare benefits that redistribute income and provide entitlement payments including Medicare, veterans' benefits, and Social Security;
3. reflect tax policy that favorably affects business and individuals;
4. reflect and fund the enforcement of commercial, transportation, land use, and environmental regulations that affect the business climate;
5. fund education and other training programs that enhance the jurisdiction's human and economic resources;
6. fund the direct and the contracted production of goods and services (with benefits ranging from the sale of state timber and other resources, to higher education, to the delivery of law enforcement and correctional services);
7. fund routine purchases and capital projects that stimulate economic activity;
8. serve to redistribute wealth across the jurisdiction's residents;
9. fund economic development efforts to attract and help distribute economic activity within the jurisdiction; and
10. provide significant employment opportunities for citizens.

A final factor that influences the economic health of a community, but is usually taken for granted, is the overall integrity and competence of those who manage the budget and financial forecasting processes. If revenue and expenditure estimates are continually off the mark, and employees lose their jobs, negative signals are sent to the larger financial community. When there is a structurally sound budget that matches recurring revenues with recurring expenses, lenders and financial analysts are encouraged to grant more favorable credit ratings and reduced interest rates to the jurisdiction. Structural soundness includes adequacy of resources to fund retirement programs, supplementary medical benefits for employees, Social Security, Medicare, and similar kinds of expenditures that can have a cumulative adverse impact over a multiyear period. Those preparing the budget have a responsibility to provide the public and elected officials with clear and honest projections that take into account the hidden or unforeseen cumulative costs of doing public business.

*The Consequences of Multiple Purposes of Public Budgets*

The public budgeting process provides a necessary meeting ground for the many competing claims that are at play in our systems of government: responsiveness to interest groups, admin-

istrative concerns for operational efficiency and program effectiveness, taxpayer discontent over excessive spending, citizen concerns for greater accountability, the equitable distribution of services and programs to those in need, and contending ideologies about the proper scope and limits of government's reach into the lives of its citizens. Following is a summary of these enduring conflicts.

*Summary of Enduring Conflicts Regarding the Purpose of a Public Budget*

A. What ends should the budget serve?

1. Responsiveness to clientele interests
2. Financial accountability
3. Program effectiveness and efficiency
4. Promoting a healthy economy
5. Meeting the needs of those with little or no political influence

B. Who should decide?

1. Experts and career professionals
2. Elected officials and appointed board members
3. Citizens
4. Clients

## The Government Budgeting Cycle and Process

Public budgets are structured to provide resources and accountability for a defined period of a fiscal year or biennium. The period of the fiscal year captures all expenditures and revenues reserved within a defined 12-month period. In some states, jurisdictions operate on a 24-month biennium. The federal fiscal year begins October 1 of each year and ends September 30 of the next year. State and local governments often use a July 1 to June 30 fiscal year. Still other jurisdictions use the calendar year as the budget year. Regardless of the fiscal year dates, each jurisdiction, from the federal government to the smallest local service district, must have a budget prepared and adopted into law when the official budget year begins. The structure of the public budget process assures this readiness. Similarly, nonprofits define a fiscal year for operational, financial, and tax filing purposes.

Over the past 75 years, the public budgeting process has gradually evolved into a predictable pattern, with a set of characteristics that are common throughout most political jurisdictions in the United States. The cycle can best be viewed as a "season," which, like most seasons (mushroom picking, skiing, flower growing, and fishing seasons, for example), has distinct phases with clear expectations about the work to be done, those responsible for doing it, and a time frame within which the work has to be completed. These phases for local government and service districts are summarized in Exhibit 11.1.

This cycle possesses some unique characteristics and generates behaviors that set the budgeting process apart from almost all other governing activities: (1) the cycle requires extensive lead time with incomplete information and overlapping budget responsibilities; (2) the process is executive centered but gives the legislative body the right to approve; (3) the complexity and predictability of the process have resulted in some generally accepted rules of public budgeting.

Exhibit 11.1  **Phases of the Budget Cycle**

| Preparation of dept./agency requests: 2–3 months |
| --- |

| Compilation of government-wide recommended budget: 2–3 months |
| --- |

| Legislative review and adoption: 2–3 months |
| --- |

| Agency/dept. implementation: 12 months |
| --- |

| Audit, reconciliation: 2–3 months |
| --- |

*Extensive Lead Time with Incomplete Information and Overlapping Budget Responsibilities*

The full budgeting process is a two- to three-year undertaking. It takes six months to a year of preparation to develop a budget, another year to implement it, and another three to six months to close the books in preparation for a final audit. The repetitive flow of budget cycles also results in overlap of activity related to different fiscal years. For example, participants may find themselves simultaneously preparing next year's budget while monitoring the expenditures of this year's budget and participating in the audit of last year's budget.

During the preparation phase, participants are sometimes working blindfolded: They may not know the outcome of union contracts; they may not know the amount of revenue that will be available; they may not know the exact costs of materials and supplies; they may not know the revenue that will be provided by other jurisdictions upon whom they are dependent to run many of their programs (such as revenue sharing, Medicare, Medicaid, and school funding). Despite these uncertainties, the process has to be completed in a relatively short period of time, with the requirement that the legislative body approve a budget by a specified legal deadline. At the federal level, when this deadline is not met, Congress often resorts to passing what are called continuing resolutions, which authorize administrative agencies to continue spending at the level approved by the previous year's budget. Few states and no local jurisdictions have this luxury. If the legislative body has not adopted a budget, administrative agencies must shut down. Budgeting laws in each of the 50 states set forth the specific requirements and deadlines that must be followed by all governmental jurisdictions.

*Executive-Centered Budgeting with Legislative Right to Approve*

The executive branch of government has the primary responsibility for the creation of a budget and for presenting it for approval by the legislative branch of government. In addition, the executive branch is responsible for implementing the budget once it is approved. This puts the executive in the driver's seat, but not without continuous backseat scrutiny from legislative officials. Such a process makes some sense, given the complexity and detailed knowledge required to assemble a budget and to implement it once approved.[1] Most elected officials at the local level, and many at the state level, have limited expertise in preparing a budget because of term limits, little or no staff support, and lack of experience. For that reason, the budget process begins at the executive level

with the preparation of program-level, department- and agency-level, and executive-level requests for the coming fiscal year. The legislative body then considers the chief administrative officer's recommendations, adopts a final budget, and appropriates funds by agency and by program for the coming fiscal year or biennium.

Once the legislative body approves the budget, administrators then establish financial controls, develop work plans, and implement the budget. Over the course of the fiscal year, the agencies and departments expend funds and fill staff positions. Computerized accounting systems keep close tabs on these activities, often through monthly or quarterly reports. At the end of the fiscal year, all expenses are tallied and matched against resources. At this point, the fiscal year is officially closed; soon after, auditors review agency and departmental spending to determine whether correct financial procedures have been followed based on professionally accepted accounting practices. Other auditing sometimes examines whether agency and department programs made effective progress in accomplishing prescribed goals and objectives. In most instances, year-end auditing results are quietly folded into the budget data for the coming budget cycle. However, concerns may be raised by audits, which can quickly become fuel for groups that choose to use the negative audit information to serve their political ends. In addition to the audit oversight that is built into every jurisdiction's budgeting process, the executive and legislative branches of government exercise additional levels of accountability through monitoring and legislative oversight hearings.

### Some Common Rules of Public Budgeting

The public budgeting process results in numerous balls in the air simultaneously; therefore, it requires considerable coordination from participants. Under these pressing circumstances, the time allotted to complete budgeting-related activities is never enough to meet fixed deadlines. This is not only because the season is short but also because many participants must keep up with other duties that are not directly connected with their seasonal budget responsibilities. In addition, there is usually too little or too much information that, in either case, causes delay.

The budgeting cycle imposes some order, predictability, and certainty on a process that would otherwise be chaotic—filled with nearly uncontrollable conflict among competing interests. Still, this disciplined ordering does not eliminate the need to take shortcuts. The most important shortcuts used in the budgeting process are reliance on the principles of *base budget* and *fair share*, which tend to foster incremental changes from year to year in agency and department budgets. Heavy reliance on base budget and fair share principles has led some scholars to characterize the public budgeting process as inherently incremental in nature (Wildavsky 1984, 1978). In Section II of this chapter, we will discuss *incrementalism* in greater detail, including various reform efforts to overcome the tendency. In the meantime, it is important to understand the forces arrayed in the budgeting process, which predispose participants to take an incremental approach and make alternative approaches difficult to implement.

*Base Budget.* All agencies, programs, and participants in the budgeting process begin with a presumption that they will be able to obtain support for an existing base of services without providing extensive analysis and justification. What constitutes the base may change from one jurisdiction to the next and from one year to another. In some cases, the base may be fixed at some reduced percentage of last year's authorized budget (see discussion of zero-base budgeting below). In other cases, the base may be what was authorized last year, increased by some inflationary factor. The existence of a base from which to operate greatly simplifies

what has to be examined with care and what will serve as the primary focus of debate. The principle of a base budget helps to solve the time-intensive problem of building a budget from ground zero each year, thereby reducing the strain this places on participants in the budgeting process.

*Fair Share.* A second important shortcut that reduces conflict and the need for extensive analysis in the budgeting process is the norm of fair share. It is normal in the budgeting process for the collective requests from programs and departments to exceed available resources. When this occurs, cuts have to be made. What criteria should be used in funding some programs over others? This question can be answered by accumulating much information and undertaking extensive analysis. But this is not always possible within the tight time frame of a budget cycle. The use of the principle of fair share, like the notion of a base budget, provides a norm that is easy to apply and to implement. Usually the norm of fair share is applied by asking for across-the-board cuts from all departments and programs, sometimes even from enterprise fund agencies (see chapter 10) that aren't supported by general fund revenues (such as property taxes, income taxes, and some fees). When you hear requests being made for an across-the-board cut in budget requests, you know that the principle of fair share is being used rather than relying on extensive analysis. Reliance on the principles of a base budget and fair share results in a process that produces only incremental changes from year to year.

*Incrementalism.* There are several ways that the incremental features of the budget process surface during the budget cycle. First, as already noted, most requests begin with an assumption that everyone will request a little more this year than they did last year. Second, there is an assumption that there are likely to be cuts in the original request, but normally these will be small. These two assumptions about a relatively fixed base with small departures from year to year grow out of and reinforce a third source of incrementalism: the desire to keep past political agreements intact. Once you achieve agreement among various constituency and clientele groups outside the organization and various career administrators and elected officials within the organization, it is difficult to renegotiate these agreements afresh each budgeting cycle. For example, in the Medler case, if there is agreement between the school board and superintendent to undertake cost-cutting measures that spread the pain over a two- or three-year period, it is important to keep this agreement intact from one budgeting cycle to another.

Taken together, the principles of fair share and a base budget make it easier for participants in the budgeting process to simplify complexity, avoid exhaustive conflict, and complete budget preparation in a timely fashion. The process can be completed with enough good will for the participants to engage one another in a civil fashion in the next cycle, which is always just around the corner. Building from current political agreements speeds the development of future agreements. The incremental approach also provides continuity in budget decision making and in the routine funding for each agency. And incremental decisions provide stability in another manner: When one or two programs among many in an agency receive relatively large adjustments, incremental decisions at the larger agency level help to maintain the relative structure and balance among the remaining programs within the agency, as well as the balance from one agency to another. While incrementalism has the virtue of maintaining continuity and predictability over time, it is criticized because it does not require the budget allocation to be subjected to hard questions about the efficiency, effectiveness, and the appropriateness of maintaining the status quo. These criticisms are dealt with in Section II.

**Budget Actors: Conflicting Perspectives**

The process of developing and adopting a budget places agencies and programs in competition with one another for scarce resources. The structure and steps of the budget process provide the tools to manage and channel this competitive behavior. Both formal and informal rules outline the behavior of each actor in the budget process. Formal budget instructions provide explicit schedules, requests for products, and budget preparation formats for all budgetary subunits within a jurisdiction. The informal culture of local jurisdictions and their legislative process may be even more important for passage of a budget, as these reflect myriad long-standing agreements about what is done and how. Most important, the citizens of each jurisdiction expect the budget process and its actors to manage any conflicts in allocation priorities in a manner that results in the successful adoption of the jurisdiction's budget.

There are three major factors that shape the nature of the interaction among the major participants in the budgeting process, enabling a budget to be adopted: (1) their respective roles within the budgeting structure, (2) their professional orientation, and (3) the amount of uncertainty, complexity, and potential for political conflict each actor faces at various stages of the process. Since these factors are common to all public budgeting processes, there is considerable predictability in the outlook of the major actors across jurisdictional boundaries and types of governance structures.

*Role Responsibility*

Budget decisions and products move from one set of actors to the next, building the agreement necessary to proceed through the next stage of the process. Participants at each stage have an opportunity to use their authority to pursue the goals that are important to their assigned role. For most agency divisions and programs, the budget process provides the opportunity to obtain the critical resources necessary to provide services to clients. For CAOs and their centralized budget and management divisions, issue/policy priorities and the fiscal integrity of the jurisdiction's budget are of the highest priority. For legislators, managing the role of government and meeting constituent needs is the highest priority.

To add to this complexity, many actors find themselves playing several roles. For example, budget bureau analysts review department and division budget requests with an eye toward two different types of questions. First, does the budget request make good fiscal sense? The concern for fiscal integrity requires budget analysts to critically examine agency/department budgets for both internal consistency and historical patterns of change over time. Equally important is the concern that requests meet the elected executive's policy priorities. The budget submission process by the agencies is especially important from a policy point of view. It is the point of greatest leverage by the elected executive to obtain policy compliance by agency heads. Once the executive's review is complete, the budget analyst then prepares to defend the agency's request as it becomes an integrated part of the executive's recommended budget to the legislative body. The analyst first plays the role of critic and then turns to play the role of advocate.

Members of federal and state legislative appropriations committees stand in contrast to the generalist role of most elected officials. Backed by the technical expertise of professional staff, members of these legislative committees develop a degree of detailed expertise on the annual budget requests; support from external interest group analysts reinforces this scrutiny. As a result of this immersion in the details of agency budgets, legislative committee members become

knowledgeable experts upon whom their colleagues in the larger legislative body can rely. When the committee review is complete, members find themselves in a situation similar to the central budget office analysts. The committee members and their staff first scrutinize the executive's request but then act as managers and advocates as the budget moves through the various stages of the legislative process.

The budget process is structured to channel political competition for resources into a set of final budget allocations. If strong political forces lead the budget process, it is likely that competition, tensions, and dissension will submerge behind a unified front. For example, once an executive decides on a budget request, the directors of agencies and departments are expected to join ranks in support of a unified position. In short, the roles created by our system of separation of powers and checks and balances encourage a modicum of unity that usually tempers and mediates some of the competition and dissension inherent in the budgeting process. Exceptions to this unity usually reflect extraordinarily strong political pressures and a willingness to take serious political risks.

*Professional Versus Political Orientation*

The budget preparation process requires input from both administration and finance professionals, and appointed or elected officials—the latter playing a more political role than the former. Conflicts between these two perspectives are inevitable, and result from differences in the notion of what counts for budget success. Financial analysts, accountants, and career public administrators reflect the traditions and standards of their professions. Their perspectives on the budget process are filtered, focused, and constrained by these standards. For instance, those preparing budget requests at the individual program level are focused primarily on meeting client needs. Building this base requires a strong analytic capability and the ability to organize large amounts of detailed information. Reworked into a different form, this same information may be very useful for program managers, for other financial analysts, and for auditors.

In contrast, elected officials must meet the needs of voters and constituents to demonstrate legislative success. Out of competing constituent needs, elected officials must select priorities and reach some understanding of a larger public good. To accomplish this goal, most elected officials work at an information level of gross aggregation and limited detail. For legislators, the context and the political implications related to budget proposals are as important as the actual values of the numbers themselves. Sometimes, elected officials find themselves caught between competing political goals in the budget process. They may be interested in reducing the size and role of government in the market economy, but this may come into conflict with their own programmatic agendas for their districts. It is common for elected officials to generally favor unfettered competition in the private marketplace while also favoring specific programmatic protection of a particular industry that is important to their constituent base.

In order to provide the most value for elected officials and other generalists, financial analysts must be able to drastically simplify their findings into clear concepts and a few key numbers. By way of illustration, consider the best strategy for dealing with the budget shortfall in the Medler example at the beginning of this section. The chief finance officer and the central budget office director will favor strategies that make the greatest cuts in the short run and preserve the maximum amount of reserves to cover the uncertainties of the future. On the other hand, elected officials will want to deal with the cuts in a manner that tempers the adverse impact on constituency groups. This pressure to spread the cuts out over time and to use reserves becomes even greater when board members are in the midst of a reelection campaign.

Ironically, despite the differences in perspective, elected officials and financial professionals often pursue a common goal. Both groups perform an oversight and control function over the bureaucracy. This oversight plays an important role in maintaining public confidence.

*Uncertainty, Ambiguity, and Potential for Conflict*

While the budget process defines a relatively predictable flow of events, uncertainty surrounds most of the steps involved in carrying it out. This uncertainty often translates into seemingly unpredictable or inexplicable behavior by the process actors. Uncertainty surrounds the state of the economy and the generation and forecasting of the revenues that support budget spending; it also surrounds the actual needs of constituents and program recipients. Political pressure from the legislative leadership, constituents, and interest groups introduces uncertainty into the behavior of legislators, while tense relationships at the state level between the governor and the legislature may add another element of uncertainty into the development and adoption of an annual or biennial budget.

One of the consequences of this conflict, uncertainty, and ambiguity for the process as a whole is that it predisposes the participants to *satisfice* (i.e., to make sufficient allocation decisions that minimally meet multiple requests or needs), to focus on small changes from year to year, and to emphasize dollars rather than programs or performance because dollars can be divided in more finite ways than can programs or performance. These pressures for greater flexibility increase as one moves up through the process and outward toward constituency interests and elected officials. For example, since elected officials frequently experience multiple and conflicting pressures, they are more inclined to want as much discretion as possible in dividing up the budgetary pie. This contrasts with a more performance- and program-based focus of career administrators and the target clientele they serve. The central budget office is caught in the middle, usually with the need to find ways of cutting back on agency and department requests in order to present a balanced budget for legislative review. In short, conditions of uncertainty, conflict, and ambiguity create a common motivation to preserve maximum discretionary authority at each level of the process. Program managers want discretion to adjust programs and service levels to best meet clientele needs; central budget office managers want discretion to adjust the budget to achieve the maximum policy priorities of the chief executive; and legislators want discretion to adjust the budget to meet constituency interests.

*Summary of Budget Actors and Their Role in Democratic Governance*

With such a variety of professional backgrounds and process goals, it is not surprising that tensions and misunderstandings arise among the various actors during the budget process. However, because these tensions occur within a deliberately crafted system of separation of powers and checks and balances, some of the resulting conflict is tempered by role expectations. It is assumed, for example, that the legislative perspective will differ from that of the program manager and the CEO, both of whom are expected to be responsive to different clientele and constituency influences. These intentionally created role expectations render the information needs and behavior of one group of actors distinct from the needs and behavior of other actors in the process. Exhibit 11.2 summarizes the multiple purposes and actors that are part of the public budgeting process. By matching the kind of information that is needed to carry out these purposes with the expertise required, one acquires greater appreciation for the multiple sources of conflict that are inherent in almost all public budgeting. In the next section, we will see how the distinct contributions of these actors in the budget process are expressed and mediated through various budget formats.

Exhibit 11.2   **Summary Overview of Budgeting Purposes, Actors, and Conflicts**

| Purpose | Kinds of Information/Expertise | Who Provides Information |
|---|---|---|
| 1. To implement rational plans | Information on mission, goals, objectives | Department heads; program planners who have program and clientele-based knowledge |
| 2. To allocate scarce resources | Little information if based on principles of "base" and "fair share" | Citizens/stakeholders |
|  | Considerable performance information regarding efficiency and effectiveness if done according to model of rationality in number 1 above | Analysts; program managers and first-line supervisors; clientele served |
| 3. To achieve accountability |  |  |
|    a. Monetary/ financial | Detailed financial tracking and control system | Analysts; accountants; auditors |
|    b. Effectiveness | Performance information regarding achievement of goals | Managers and analysts at all levels of the organization |
|    c. Efficiency | Cost-benefit information | Analysts and program managers who have expertise in designing systems for assessing benefits and measuring costs |
|    d. Political | Public opinion and stakeholder/ interest-group preferences | Elected officials; senior administrators; managers who have contact with clientele groups; clientele and interest groups |
| 4. "Right thing" for government to do | A value question in the first instance; also a question of consequences of government intervention | Citizens; elected officials; analysts; career administrators; interest groups |
| 5. To create commonly shared organizational/ community values | Value preferences of participants | Citizens; administrators; elected officials; stakeholder groups |
| 6. To regulate the economy | Surrogate indicators for "healthy economy" | Economists; elected officials; interest groups; analysts |
| 7. To redistribute wealth | Citizen perceptions; interest group opinions; economic information on impact of policies | Analysts who provide economic information on impacts of policies; elected officials |

## SECTION II: BUDGET FORMATS

> For the forms of budgeting, let fools contest,
> That which is best administered is best.
>
> *(Morgan and Robinson 2000, 58)*

To paraphrase an old line from the eighteenth-century English poet Alexander Pope, one might argue that budget formats, like forms of government, are less important than how well they are administered. But there is an important difference with budgeting formats: They not only establish the rules by which the budgeting game is played (the decision rules), but they also create the standards by which success is measured (rules of evidence). Because budgeting formats create both decision rules and rules of evidence, they play a central and perhaps even decisive role in public budgeting. When we speak of budgeting formats, we are talking about the way in which budgeting information is structured, the kind of information that is required to justify budget requests, and the kind of questions that are asked during the budget review process. For purposes of discussion

in the sections that follow, we will focus on line-item budgeting, program budgeting, performance budgeting, and zero-base budgeting as distinctly separate formats. In practice, most jurisdictions make use of several of these formats as part of their process.

Historically, the evolution of public budgeting formats is the story of ongoing efforts "to speak truth to power" (Wildavsky 1979). Aaron Wildavsky argued that the development of new budget formats reflects a common and persistent attempt to discipline the forces of interest-group politics by subjecting them to the systematic gathering and analysis of information. The goal of this disciplined analysis is to raise questions that normally do not get asked when interest groups lobby for allocation of money to support their favorite activities. Are we spending the taxpayers' money efficiently? What are we accomplishing with the money we are spending? Should we be spending the taxpayers' money on more important programs that affect the public interest? These are the central questions that performance, program, and zero-base budgeting formats seek to raise and answer. In short, budgeting formats should be viewed as a way of structuring the conversations during the budget-making process to encourage participants to address the "right questions." Our review of the budgeting formats will focus on how information is collected, used, and applied to answer different questions "right" in the budget development process.

### Line-Item Budgeting (Object Code)

*Line-item budgeting* is technically known as object code or expenditure code budgeting. A typical example for a portion of a county-level corrections unit is provided in Exhibit 11.3. As the example illustrates, the major categories of expenditure—personnel, materials and supplies, and capital outlay—are assigned code numbers, with each of these major categories further broken down into as many subcodes as a jurisdiction wishes to create. Because of its high value in promoting financial accountability, line-item (object code) budgeting has become the most durable and commonly used budget format throughout the public sector. Line-item budgeting forms the base for many types of financial analysis. This type of budgeting almost always underlies or is used alongside other budgeting formats.

Not much programmatic or managerial expertise is needed to successfully carry out object code budgeting. In fact, this is its chief advantage. You do not need to know how pencils are going to be used in order to budget for pencils. If you used 100 pencils last year, and your overall workload has not changed significantly, and the number of your full-time employees remains about the same, you can with some confidence assume that you will need enough money with inflation to buy 100 pencils for the next budget year. This is why line-item budgeting is frequently linked with what has been called incremental budgeting, in contrast to program, performance, and zero-base budget approaches. The reason for the term *incremental* in this context is that line-item budgeting enables you to prepare a budget for the upcoming year by simply adding an increment for inflationary increases to what you had last year. You do not need to have clear program goals or any measures of efficiency and effectiveness to successfully carry out line-item budgeting. You simply start with an existing base budget and make marginal (incremental) changes up or down each year based on changes in workload, some inflationary assumptions, and a notion of fair share. You do not need to know the programmatic nexus between pencils that appear in an object code and the contributions the pencils make to the overall achievement of program goals and the mission of the organization. In fact, the fuzziness of this connection is one of the advantages of line-item budgeting. By assuming that what you have been doing will likely continue to be done next year with some exceptions on the margin, you can then concentrate your limited time and energy on analyzing and planning these marginal changes. This reduces complexity and allows

Exhibit 11.3  **Line-Item Budgeting Format**

| Object Number | Description | FY I Actual | FY II Actual | FY III Actual | FY IV Adopted |
|---|---|---|---|---|---|
| 242 | CORRECTIONS DEPT. CODE | | | | |
| 2429 | COMMUNITY CORRECTIONS: ADMINISTRATIVE DIVISION CODE | | | | |
| | Personal Services | | | | |
| 51110 | FULL TIME REG SALARIES | 148,396 | 157,163 | 123,948 | 148,597 |
| 51220 | TEMPORARY SALARIES | 16,026 | 1,638 | 0 | 0 |
| 51901 | OTHER SALARY & BENEFITS | 85,609 | 87,423 | 51,093 | 53,816 |
| | Total Personal Services | 250,031 | 246,224 | 175,041 | 202,413 |
| | Materials and Supplies | | | | |
| 52110 | OFFICE SUPPLIES | 325 | 815 | 153 | 0 |
| 52210 | PROFESSIONAL SERVICES (CONTRACTED) | 0 | 0 | 800 | 800 |
| 52311 | TRAINING & EDUCATION | 2,820 | 1,382 | 1,250 | 600 |
| 52318 | OTHER MATERIALS AND SUPPLIES | 16,377 | 12,610 | 8,509 | 7,637 |
| | Total Materials and Supplies | 19,522 | 14,807 | 10,712 | 9,037 |
| 53399 | Total Capital Outlay & Other Expenses | 0 | 68 | 0 | 345 |
| 69999 | Total Interfund Expenses | 11,816 | 30,917 | 35,292 | 20,679 |
| 2429 | TOTAL ADMINISTRATIVE DIVISION | 281,369 | 292,016 | 221,045 | 232,474 |

for the budget to be assembled without endless (and expensive) hours of analysis, without pouring over reams of spreadsheet information, and without spending hours in meetings with others in reexamining everything that is currently being done.

In addition to the efficiency it offers in putting a budget together, the line-item approach to budgeting reduces conflict. It lets sleeping dogs lie. Whenever managers and employees are asked to reexamine what is currently being done, they normally become defensive. At the point where this reexamination begins to create priorities for funding, internal and external conflicts begin to rise exponentially for the organization. With line-item budgeting, when there are more requests than resources available, the budget can be brought into balance by cutting dollars, usually by relying on formulas like across-the-board cuts or some similar notion of fair share. By shifting the universe of discourse to dollars—and away from programs and activities—budget balancing obscures the impact of cuts on services, thereby reducing conflict in the budgeting process. Dollars can be cut and divided in far more ways and in much smaller increments than programs can. In short, line-item budgeting and its reliance on formulas (like base budgeting and fair share incrementalism) tends to keep the conflict and complexity in the budgeting process within manageable bounds. However, the advantages of line-item budgeting are also mirror images of its chief defects.

Because line-item budgeting can proceed without knowing the purposes or accomplishments of expenditures, questions regarding efficiency, effectiveness, and future priorities are not systematically addressed. While there is nothing in line-item budgeting that prevents these issues from being examined, the format itself does not require it. In fact, in order to justify requests for increased expenditures, it is common practice under line-item budgeting formats to incorporate a wide variety of quantitative information, such as workload measures, activity indicators, and so on. But the inclusion of such information is not intrinsic to the approach, and the information usually raises the question of the larger purposes these measures are intended to serve. Program budgets address this weakness.

## Planning-Programming-Budgeting Systems (PPBS) and Program Budgeting

*Planning-programming-budgeting systems (PPBS)* and *program budgeting* organize the traditional categories of expenditure used in line-item budgets into larger units of activities performed by an agency, program, or nonprofit organization. The purpose of program budgeting, as the name suggests, is to highlight the units of activity that the object codes support. Planning constitutes the essence of program budgeting. Budgets may carry a program budget label, but unless there is a concrete plan that connects program expenditures to a set of objectives, which in turn are connected to goals, a true program budget does not exist. Budgeting to a strategic plan is especially important for nonprofit organizations. Without statutory guidance or market signals, nonprofits must rely on thoughtfully developed strategic plans to set visions, goals, and objectives that effectively respond to community needs. Many agencies organize their budget into functional categories or sets of activities; however, without knowing the plan behind these functional categories and activities, it is difficult to tell what purposes the functional categories are intended to serve. Exhibit 11.4 provides an example of program budgeting.

The example illustrates how goals and objectives are causally and hierarchically linked to the achievement of a concrete set of ends. The instrumental nature of this linkage process cannot be accomplished without careful and time-consuming planning. This planning encourages administrators to ask the following kinds of questions each year as the budget request is assembled:

- What are we trying to accomplish? Do we have clear goals and objectives? Are they stated with clarity and precision, and are they linked together in a causal and controllable fashion?
- How are we organizing our work to accomplish our goals and objectives?
- Should resources be shifted between programs or activities to de-emphasize an overstated objective or to enhance an understated objective?

Answers to the above questions enable decision makers and citizens to explain how tax dollars are being spent and what is being accomplished. Program budgeting offers different advantages for decision makers at each level of the organizational hierarchy.

For managers at the bottom and middle levels of the organization, a program encourages clarity of purpose, which helps everyone better understand how the work of their particular unit contributes to the work of the organization as a whole. The top-down hierarchical PPBS/program budgeting framework also provides executives and elected officials with a means to focus and align their organization with external political priorities.

For example, senior leaders can revise the organization mission and goals to include a new mission emphasis that better reflects the critical themes of an executive or political agenda. The goal- and activity-centered nature of PPBS/program budgeting allows the integration of staff and resources from different departments from across an organization in support of comprehensive programs or a major new initiative. From an interagency perspective, the PPBS/program framework can effectively describe, schedule, and organize the resources for multi-organizational and multi-jurisdictional initiatives and projects. From a community-level perspective, a PPBS budget provides an umbrella mission and a set of goals under which all polity partners can align. Under a common mission and goals, local governments, schools, community foundations, religious organizations, and service nonprofits can independently set annual objectives, develop programs, and contribute resources toward an integrated outcome or extended community initiative. But the advantages that come from rationally and systematically connecting means to ends and dollars to programs have some disadvantages.

Exhibit 11.4 **Program Budgeting**

Following is an example of program budgeting. It illustrates how goals and objectives are causally and hierarchically linked to the achievement of a concrete set of ends. The instrumental nature of this linkage process cannot be accomplished without careful and time-consuming planning.

Mission: To provide safe and productive incarceration for citizens who have been sentenced to prison or released on parole.

Goal #1: To rehabilitate clients on parole and probation so they can return as productive members of society.

1. Objective: To increase FY II employment references of clients by 10 percent more than FY I with no budget increase over what was allocated for these activities in FY I.

2. Objective: To double total mental health consultations experienced by clients in FY II compared to FY I at a cost of 1.0 FTE Mental Health Nurse.

3. Objective: To limit FY II parole and probation violations to 15 percent of Corrections clientele by introducing a bracelet-monitoring program at a cost that does not exceed the total budget allocation expended in FY I for parole and probation monitoring.

Goal #2: To provide a safe incarceration environment for inmates.

1. Objective: To reduce the number of violent incidents by inmates by 10 percent in FY II at a cost increase that is no more than 5 percent more than FY I.

2. Objective: To reduce the possession of illicit drugs by inmates by 15 percent in FY II at a cost increase that is no more than 5 percent more than FY I.

The lack of detailed, line-item, historical information can obscure frequent subprogram changes and information on the efficiency of a program's operation. This is especially the case in larger units of government, where the definition of "program" may be so broad that it covers most of a unit's activities. Changes within these units may be significant over time, but they may never show up in the budget process because the name of the program and total dollar amount being spent from year to year appears not to change very much. Another disadvantage is that program budgeting limits the flexibility of managers to shift dollars from one program to another. Over time, programs build up strong constituency support, which means that any program cuts may attract strong external opposition. Program budgeting has been likened to buying uniquely matching outfits of clothing—it is difficult to interchange parts of one outfit with parts of another. In addition to limiting flexibility and increasing the potential for conflict, true program budgeting is quite time consuming and expensive.

## Performance Budgeting

*Performance budgeting* is a term that applies broadly to any format that relies on a measurement of past results as an important consideration in the allocation of future budget resources. These results can consist of workload, efficiency, or effectiveness measures. *Workload measures* are the most common ways of assessing performance. They are frequently used by supervisors and serve various operational purposes but indicate little about the quality of the work. Example:

- Number of traffic lights installed

*Effectiveness measures* focus on how well the goal or objective is accomplished—independent of cost. Examples:

- Percentage of improved neighborhood locations in which through-traffic is no greater than 1,000 vehicles per day one year after improvement
- The average number of highway deaths from drunken driving in FY II compared to the average rates in FY I

*Efficiency measures* focus on how well resources are utilized, not on the amount of service output produced in relationship to the amount of resources required. Examples:

- Cost per participant in the tuition reimbursement program
- Cost per million gallons of wastewater processed
- Cost per installation of traffic control devices

Exhibit 11.5 provides an illustration of performance budgeting. It builds on the corrections unit example used in the previous section to illustrate PPBS and program budgets. As shown in Exhibit 11.5, performance indicators are the natural and final step in the preparation of goals and objectives. Unlike program budgeting, where the goal is merely to assemble and budget to program objectives or goals, performance budgeting systematically incorporates *measurement* into the budgeting process. The results of these measurements are used to allocate scarce public resources.

Performance budgeting has obvious advantages, especially to managers who need some way of determining what is being accomplished with the money they are receiving. Taxpayer revolts over the past several years have heightened the interest in performance measures as a way of demonstrating to citizens what their taxes are purchasing in the way of both outcomes and efficiencies (Osborne and Hutchinson 2004). One way of viewing the politics of performance budgeting is to see it as a struggle between a "constituent service" perspective and a "taxpayer" perspective, with the latter more interested in performance measures than the former. Also, performance measurement is more popular with those units of government that can clearly measure what they are doing, and where increased demonstrations of performance normally result in the acquisition of additional resources. The concepts and measurement tools of performance budgeting have been embraced by governments and agencies as tools in contract administration and performance management. Performance style measures often provide a quantifiable measure to objectively assess the performance of contractors and grantees. Using performance measures has the added benefit of ready translation into agency budget goals and objectives.

But there are many units of government that find it difficult to measure outcomes, especially in the short run. For example, there are a variety of social service programs for children, addicts, battered women, and the mentally ill that encounter difficulty crafting adequate, valid, and reliable longitudinal measurements. Even when such measurements can be constructed, the time and expertise required to do so reduce the resources available for direct service. Finally, some public programs are not nearly as popular as others. When this is the case, program supporters and advocates argue that high measures of performance will not fundamentally change the support they are likely to receive from the general citizenry. For example, there is abundant evidence that building more prisons and expanding mandatory punishment for various categories of criminal activity will not reduce the crime rate or do much good for the incarcerated. Despite this performance information, the general public has supported incarceration over treatment or rehabilitation. At the heart of this debate is what should count for performance: Should it be the number of criminals

Exhibit 11.5  **Performance Budgeting**

Compare this example to the program example in Figure 10.4. The difference between the two examples illustrates the difference between program budgeting and performance budgeting. In the following example, performance measurements are added and used as the basis for allocating scarce public resources.

Goal: To rehabilitate clients on parole and probation so they can return as productive members of society.

1. **Objective:** To increase FY II employment references of clients by 10 percent over FY I with no budget increase over what was allocated for these activities in FY I.

   **Performance Measures:** (1) Number of employment references in FY II is at least 10 percent more than FY I (2) at a total cost that is equal to or less than what was allocated in FY I.

2. **Objective:** To double total mental health consultations experienced by clients in FY II compared to FY I at a cost of 1.0 FTE Mental Health Nurse.

   **Performance Measures:** (1) Total mental health consultations in FY II is double the (2) total mental health consultations in FY I and (3) costs no more than 1.0 FTE Mental Health Nurse: Level III $63,203.

3. **Objective:** To limit FY II parole and probation violations to 15 percent of Corrections clientele by introducing a bracelet-monitoring program at a cost that does not exceed the total budget allocation expended in FY I for parole and probation monitoring.

   **Performance Measures:** (1) FY II parole and probation violations are 15 percent or less than (2) the FY I parole and probation violations and (3) the total costs do not exceed what was allocated in FY I for the bracelet program.

---

incarcerated or the number of criminals rehabilitated? The debate turns on differing notions of justice as well as of the larger public interest. For these reasons, public budgeting formats are inseparable from the larger issues of democratic governance.

Performance budgeting and performance analysis has been established at all levels of government. President Barack Obama abandoned the performance system introduced by his predecessor, President George W. Bush. The establishment of the Government Performance and Results Modernization Act of 2010 (GPRMA) by Congress and the Obama administration changed the focus from grading programs as "successful" or "unsuccessful" to requiring agency leaders to set priority goals, to demonstrate progress in achieving those goals, and to explain performance trends (Kamensky 2012, 2011). GPRMA calls for each agency of the federal government to make a strategic plan available on its public website. The plan must contain a comprehensive mission statement covering the major operations of the agency; general goals and objectives, including outcome-oriented goals; a description of how the goals and objectives are to be achieved; and an identification of key factors external to the agency that could significantly affect the achievement of the goals and objectives, among others. The act also calls for the establishment of a balanced set of performance indicators to be used in measuring or assessing progress toward each performance goal, including customer service, efficiency, output, and outcome indicators. The means used to verify and validate measures must be described, along with how the agency will ensure the accuracy and reliability of the data. An additional effect of GPRMA is that it requires states receiving federal funds to measure their performance with those funds and report on a regular basis to the responsible federal agency.

At the state level, Washington, Utah, Texas, Virginia, and several other states have enfolded performance budgeting into their budget development, management, and audit systems (Barrett and Greene 2008). Executive-centered performance systems such as the Washington state GMAP system (State of Washington 2006) provide a tool for executive performance oversight, evaluation of program effectiveness, and budget decision making. Executive-centered performance systems, however, tend to rise or fall from use and importance with a governor's term in office. The application of performance budgeting and performance management at the local level varies by state. In Washington state, all state agencies and local governments are subject to performance audits. This requirement was established by citizen initiative and has encouraged the development of performance measures and performance information by all local governments and special districts (Municipal Research and Services Center of Washington 2010).

## Zero-Base Budgeting

As mentioned earlier in this chapter, *zero-base budgeting (ZBB)* was first introduced into the public sector in 1971 by Jimmy Carter, then governor of Georgia, as a way of encouraging managers and elected officials to ask a fundamental question that seldom gets answered in the budget-making process: Should we continue doing what we have done in the past? In theory, zero-base budgeting forces this question to be addressed by requiring all managers to justify their budgets from the ground up. In practice, however, the difficulty of doing this every year has resulted in a modified version of ZBB known as the *reduced level budget (RLB)*. This modified version asks managers to reduce their budget to a specified level (typically 75 to 90 percent) from the previous year's base. Exhibit 11.6 provides an example of an RLB for a small county-level department of corrections. A variation on ZBB called *target budgeting* uses a defined dollar amount to set the reduced level as a spending ceiling. For example, an incoming mayor may propose to reduce public works spending by $2.5 million, which would define the RLB spending level.

After preparing an RLB, managers are then asked to develop "add back" requests in the form of discrete decision packages. Exhibits 11.7 and 11.8 provide examples of RLB decision packages for the community corrections unit featured in Exhibit 11.6. The development of decision packages is intended to provide managers with the freedom to shift resources from one program area to another. The technique further requires managers to prioritize the packages they are requesting for approved funding. While ZBB encourages managers to put some existing programs in competition with new programs, the modified approach to ZBB saves managers the severe strain of justifying all programs from the ground up.

Modified zero-base budgeting has become a common practice in many governmental jurisdictions throughout the United States. It has mainly taken the form of "add" and "cut" packages in the submission stage of the budget process, where managers of governmental programs are forced to reduce their appropriation requests from the existing base budget by 10 to 20 percent. Decision packages are then used to provide managers with an opportunity to reconfigure their existing activities into new decision packages that may bring their total budget request up to 110 or 115 percent of what they received the previous year.

This modified process provides an occasion for managers to try something new. It also puts the organization on notice that it cannot assume the status quo. ZBB provides an alternative to the assumption that there will be annual growth in the budget base, at least by the amount of the annual inflationary cost increases.

Like other formats, ZBB comes with its share of disadvantages. To begin with, those employees who find themselves included in a program labeled as "cut" in a decision package may become

Exhibit 11.6  **Zero-Based Budget: Reduced Level Budget**

Dept. _Community Corrections_                                    Reduced Level Budget ___X___

Org. Unit/Code ___FUND BO___                                     Decision Package Number _____

Org. Unit/Code _____

| **Description: Community Corrections 80% Reduced Level Budget** |
|---|

| Purpose: To operate Community Corrections Department at a funding level of 80 percent of last year's adjusted budget. | Methods: Discontinue Restitution Center. Add 4.0 FTE Parole and Probation Officers. Retain 1.0 FTE casework Supervisor from Restitution Center. |
|---|---|
| Alternatives: Contract out Restitution services to private sector.<br><br>Contract with other relevant public agencies in nearby jurisdictions.<br><br>Negotiate with Public Safety Department to assume some responsibilities for parole and probation. | Impact: Restitution Center is now performing many nonessential functions to Community Corrections. It is being used in large part as a low-security jail by Public Safety.<br><br>Retaining Center would force Dept. to make drastic cuts in more essential services.<br><br>Eliminating Center allows Dept. to focus more effectively on department goals and objectives. |
| Measures: Inmate referrals to Restitution Center jumped from 406 in FY II to 1,200 in FY IV. We predict an increase to 1,350 in FY V. Case management numbers have remained nearly constant at 1,700 during the same period. With the 11 percent increase in FTEs within the Com. Corrections Program, we will seek to achieve a 20 percent increase in case management. | Budget:                                    FTE: 45.5<br>Personnel Services  $1,549,375  General Fund:<br>Materials & Supplies     251,175  4%                  80,014<br>                                                Federal        1,439,266<br>                                                Other             595,111<br><br>                              Total Request  $2,114,391 |

permanently disaffected, even if the cut is not ultimately made. In addition, ZBB is often very time consuming to carry out, requires extensive data and information, and it has limited applicability in the public sector for those activities that are legally mandated (see Exhibit 11.9).

A recent variation on ZBB emphasizes the prioritization of programs, services, and activities. "Priority budgeting" asks executives, department heads, and program managers to prioritize all the programs, activities, and service levels under their purview according to critical community need and return on each dollar spent. Effective prioritization requires taking a good hard look at all of these elements to establish which services, activities, and service levels are of the most critical need—and affect the greatest number people in the community. Alternatively, prioritization should identify programs that deserve funding because they generate large impacts in the community for a relatively small investment. Establishing priorities provides guidance to executives, the central budget office analysts, elected officials, and board members as to how best to disassemble the organization under reduced funding. Strategic disassembly of programs and service elements helps to maintain professional expertise, information systems and procedures, and core service capacity in the face of reduced funding and reorganization. Similarly, prioritization of services gives guidance on how to configure services and capacity through ZBB "add back" packages and additional funding. Recent budgets from the City of Chandler, Arizona, have applied priority budgeting as part of a program and performance formatted budget (City of Chandler, Arizona 2010). The State of Oregon has also developed program and service priorities to help guide legislators during budget deliberations (Barrett and Greene 2008).

## Exhibit 11.7  Zero-Based Budget: Decision Package 1

Org. Unit/Code _____

| | Description: |
|---|---|
| | **Restitution Center** |

| | |
|---|---|
| **Purpose:**<br>To maintain capacity to housenondangerous offenders while providing assistance in obtaining education, training, and employment. | **Methods:**<br>To maintain operation of the Restitution Center, a minimum-security housing and training center for offenders. Operate at FY IV staffing and funding levels. Drop addition of 5.0 FTE community Corrections as outlined in RLB. |
| **Alternatives:**<br>Allow Public Safety Department to operate Restitution Center.<br><br>Buy back some housing space and operate reduced program. | **Impact:**<br>Retaining the Restitution Center allows operations of program to continue at previous year level.<br><br>Eliminating program creates need to find other methods to provide services to further the rehabilitation of offenders. |
| **Measures:**<br>Track number of inmates housed in Restitution Center and compare recidivism rate to comparable record of inmates who do not have access to Restitution Center. | **Budget:**            FTE: 15.0<br><br>Personnel Services  $401,908  General Fund:<br>Materials & Supplies    76,877  64%        337,050<br>                           Federal      51,474<br>                           Other      140,074<br><br>                           **Total Request**  **$528,598** |

## Exhibit 11.8  Zero-Based Budget: Decision Package 2

Dept. ___Community Corrections___

Org. Unit/Code _____242_____

Reduced Level Budget _____

Decision Package Number ___2___

Org. Unit/Code _____2421_____

| | Description: |
|---|---|
| | **Job Development Coordination** |

| | |
|---|---|
| **Purpose:**<br>To expand the capacity of the Community Corrections Dept. to rehabilitate offenders and make them selfsustaining, productive citizens. | **Methods:**<br>Add 1.0 FTE Job Development Coordinator. Fund through reduction of department budget for professional services (line item 2219). |
| **Alternatives:**<br>Drop Parole and Probation Aide FTEs equivalent to cost of new positions. | **Impact:**<br>Addition will lower parole/probation violations by estimated 10–15 percent.<br><br>Without this position, only 0.5 FTE Mental Health Worker is available and no staff expert on duty for work placement. |
| **Measures:**<br>Track percentage of violations of successfully placed compared to those who are not placed. | **Budget:**            FTE: 1.0<br><br>Personnel Services  $23,900  General Fund:<br>Materials & Supplies       0  80%        19,920<br>                           State/Federal     0<br>                           Other       6,980<br><br>                           **Total Request**  **$23,900** |

Exhibit 11.9  **Budget Format Comparisons**

| Purpose? Central Question? Problem to be Solved? | Chief Characteristics | Central Actors | Conditions for Success | Strengths | Weaknesses |
|---|---|---|---|---|---|
| **Line Item/Object Code/Incrementalism** | | | | | |
| Financial accountability: prevent misappropriation of funds | Focus is on past, with last year as the "base" | Accountants and central office budget managers interested in balancing the budget | Minimum amount of staff time and expertise is needed to create and track the budget | Works well when time is short, there is considerable complexity, multiple stakeholders, and high potential for conflict | Not good for dealing with questions of efficiency, effectiveness, future and/or neglected and future priorities |
| Is the money being spent according to intention? | Use of formulas, like "fair share," to balance the budget | Constituency advocates and elected officials | | | |
| **Program Budgeting (PPBS)** | | | | | |
| Program accountability: ensure effective outcomes | Focus is on program plans, goals, and objectives | Program managers and program analysts | Requires the resources necessary to develop program plans, goals, and objectives | Provides clear linkage between program activities and budget allocation | Requires considerable investment of resources |
| Program effectiveness: Is the program achieving its goals and objectives? | Requires budgeting to a plan | | | Links parts to whole and present to future | High potential for conflict |
| **Performance Budgeting** | | | | | |
| Program efficiency/ effectiveness | Measurements are created for workload activities, efficiency of resource allocation, and effectiveness | Program managers, first-line supervisors, and street-level bureaucrats | Requires considerable resources to develop reliable measures | Provides objective ways of documenting accomplishments | Time-consuming and expensive |

| Focus / Question | Description / Level | Requirements | Advantages | Disadvantages |
|---|---|---|---|---|
| Is the program cost effective? Is the program effective?<br><br>Seeks to measure what is being accomplished | | Requires time to develop confidence of those needed to create performance measures | | High potential for resistance because of fear of measures being used to penalize |

## Zero-based Budgeting (ZBB)

| Focus / Question | Description / Level | Requirements | Advantages | Disadvantages |
|---|---|---|---|---|
| Priority and appropriateness of what is and should be done | Systematic reexamination of some portion of current program activities from the ground up<br><br>Depending on the primary locus of authority, ZBB can be done at any and all levels of the organization | Requires considerable time and resources to reexamine activities from the ground up | Provides opportunity for existing assumptions and activities to be reexamined | Places a high burden on organizational resources |
| What should we be doing? Are we giving appropriate priority to current programs/activities? | | Requires self-confident staff and managers | Provides opportunity to reallocate resources | Is threatening, usually creating resistance |
| Deciding whether to continue doing what has been done in the past | | | | Difficult to achieve comparability across org. units |

## Conclusion Regarding Budgeting Formats

Since the creation of line-item budgeting at the turn of the twentieth century, there have been repeated attempts to supplement it with other budgeting formats in order to broaden the definition of what counts for democratic accountability (see Exhibit 11.9).

Line-item budgeting does an excellent job of ensuring financial accountability, but it does not provide information that answers the following questions: What are we achieving with the expenditure of tax dollars (PPBS/program budgeting)? How efficient and cost effective are we in the expenditure of these resources (performance budgeting)? Should we be doing this at all, or should we spend tax dollars on $X$ rather than $Y$ (ZBB)? All four budgeting formats examined in this section attempt to bring these questions to bear on budget deliberations by restructuring the decision rules and the kinds of evidence necessary to make a good case in the budget allocation process. It is obvious that no single budget format is sufficient for ensuring all the desired types of accountability, or for managing effectively within an environment of increasingly limited resources. A blending of budget formats is necessary to assure that government is fully accountable while meeting multiple standards of performance.

## SECTION III: PUBLIC BUDGETING AND THE FUTURE OF DEMOCRATIC GOVERNANCE

> So long as political dissensus prevails, bureaucrats will remain the flak-catchers of American society. . . . The public service will then become both more important in carrying on government and more vulnerable to attack on the basis of opposed visions of what its members ought to be doing. The survivors should be a hardy breed.
>
> *(Aaron Wildavsky 1984, 755)*

> Now the traditional means of coping with uncertainty appear inadequate, while the uncertainties themselves are multiplying to an unprecedented extent. . . . The task of public budgeting has become infinitely more complex, complicated and worrisome.
>
> *(Naomi Caiden 1981)*

Public budgeting represents one of the most complex tasks of democratic governance. In part, it is a process that requires reconciliation of competing public goals in a context suffused with a mix of professionally oriented administration and parochial political pressure. Public budgeting is also a mechanism for political control—a means to direct, focus, and track the purposes of government agencies. It enables public monitoring of staff and agency performance, and it serves as a method for influencing the performance of the economy. The history of public budgeting has generated a wide variety of rational analytic approaches that seek to bring more insight and data to bear on the process, but all present serious trade-offs in terms of costs, timeliness, and effectiveness. Despite all these difficulties, it is remarkable that thousands of governments across the United States continue to produce an annual or biennial budget on time and in balance. The ability to do this, however, is now subject to intense political strife, much of which is rooted in shifting perspectives about how we achieve ordered liberty.[2]

Many conservatives challenge the tradition of competent and energetic governance as manifested in the professional state. They want smaller, weaker governments, more robust market and nonprofit sectors, and the accountability of local control and face-to-face governance. In

the process, they have learned to appropriate and tailor budgeting formats and processes to help achieve their ends. It was no mere coincidence that ZBB accompanied the resurgence of fiscal conservatism as manifested in President Jimmy Carter's administration, and then became refined to a high art as the Reagan administration and the entrepreneurial era ensued. David Stockman, President Reagan's budget director, is credited with perfecting a computerized budget monitoring system that red-flagged attempts by domestic agencies to raise their budget allocations. The president's purpose was not to improve agency performance, but simply to preside over the systematic reduction of domestic programs in the spirit of smaller, weaker government as exemplified in the responsive governance tradition. Stockman expressed extreme frustration at not being allowed to apply the system to the military side of the budget (Greider 1981). On that side, the Reagan administration acted more like high spenders and believers in the competent and energetic governance tradition. As pointed out earlier, when this military spending was combined with their successful antitax campaign, the Reagan term ended with the highest public debt to that point in American history.

The story at the state and local government levels reflects more consistent adherence to the responsive and civic governance traditions. Strong antitax sentiments, balanced-budget requirements, and line-item budgets overlaid with ZBB-styled budget reduction processes prevail across many jurisdictions. These factors impose austere conditions such as those experienced in the Medler School District. Career public servants are forced to innovate in finding new ways to cope with their responsibilities. It induces them to rethink their assumptions about what things should be done, and by what methods. As we have indicated before, most public values and functions are inherently ambiguous and fraught with paradox, which means that attempts to resolve them in one direction or another will eventually provoke problems and division. Notably, this has occurred throughout the history of education policy.

Providing a "good" education means a lot of different things, as the Medler School District case illustrates. We experience ambiguity and uncertainty about the proper means and ends of education, and this inevitably subjects the practice to periodic convulsions in educational philosophy and methods. The conflict is all the more severe because it involves our children. Their lives, their character, and their values are heavily influenced by whatever educational philosophy and method we employ. Education, therefore, is one of our most sensitive political institutions. It must be responsive and nurturing, as well as effective at integrating our young into civil society. The battles we fight over how this should be done are inevitably manifested in our public budgeting, where educational priorities also face stiff competition with other public purposes.

The fiscally conservative mood of the current era can only go so far, however, before all educational and other public purposes suffer debilitating effects. Conditions as of late 2012 severely challenged the abilities of the best administrators and street-level bureaucrats, which means that the rest were hard put to cope at all. At some point, many public institutions and their budgetary processes will fail, at first haphazardly and then more generally. As the public grows more disenchanted with these failings, many will begin to question the wisdom of smaller, weaker public institutions, and the Democratic Balancewheel will again begin its turn toward concern for more effectiveness, more energy, and more egalitarian treatment in public life.

## STUDY QUESTIONS

1. What forms the basis for the allocation of resources across government to different agencies, or at the local level between departments and programs? How do these criteria contrast with economic price criteria in the marketplace?

2. Public budgeting serves a number of purposes in democratic governance. List the major purposes and benefits of building a public budget. How should public administrators take leadership to balance the emphasis on the different purposes of the public budget?

3. In the planning and preparation phases of the budget process, how can elected officials exert influence on the budgeting method used and the ultimate budget outcome? How aggressively should public administrators contextualize, channel, redefine, and influence efforts by elected officials to control the budget process and budget content?

4. Do the professional motivations and standards for success place public administrators and elected officials consistently at odds throughout the budget process? Discuss.

5. How do the budgeting shortcuts of the base budget, incrementalism, and fair share define the political behavior of participants in the budgeting process? How should public administrators respond to these budgeting shortcuts?

6. How does the cyclical nature of budgeting affect the technical preparation of the budget and its review at various stages of the budgeting process?

7. Line-item budgeting responds to what governance issue? What are the limits of line-item budgeting? How do the other budget formats respond to these shortcomings? At what point in the budget process should public administrators take leadership for selecting and integrating budget analysis perspectives?

8. How does zero-base budgeting (ZBB), either in its original form or in modified form, check the momentum of a base budget? What are the political ramifications of this analytic strength of ZBB?

9. How can public administrators use the technical aspects of the budget process to enhance citizen confidence in the process and in the ultimate budget decisions?

10. Most jurisdictions require the submission of a balanced budget request and the adoption of a balanced budget. How can elected officials assure that a budget is "structurally balanced" over a multiyear period? How can public administrators help to assure that a budget is structurally balanced?

11. Budgeting as practiced in the United States is a partially open governance process. How well do the budget processes described in this chapter effectively capture citizen concerns, recommendations, and even decisions? How would you revise the process to better incorporate citizen involvement? How might these changes conflict with other goals of the budgeting process?

## NOTES

1. The executive-centered approach to budgeting can sometimes leave members of the legislative branch feeling vulnerable and uncertain about the terms of a budget, the underlying assumptions of the budget makers, and the long-term financial consequences of their decisions. These factors led the U.S. Congress in 1974 to pass the Congressional Budget and Impoundment Control Act. As the title suggests, the purpose of the act is to provide Congress with greater control over the budgeting process (1) by creating a Congressional Budget Office that does analytic work for members of Congress, and (2) by establishing new committees in the House and Senate to oversee the budget allocation process on behalf of Congress.

2. There is growing recognition that the existing rate of growth in Social Security and Medicare/Medicaid expenditures at the national level is unsustainable. Former comptroller general of the United States, David M. Walker, was an early "Paul Revere," sounding the alarm that the United States will be unable to fund Social Security and Medicare beyond 2040 unless major changes are made (Walker 2007; see chapter 15 for further discussion of the future fiscal condition faced by public servants).

# PART IV

STRATEGIC MANAGEMENT OF
PUBLIC ORGANIZATIONS

# EAGLE ROCK: THE CASE OF THE PEREGRINE FALCON

## CASE DESCRIPTION

Eagle Rock is a 600-foot outcropping located along Washington State Highway 14 in the Columbia River Gorge. Just under an hour's drive from Portland, Oregon, the Rock is located in a state park operated by the Washington State Parks and Recreation Department. It has a trail access to the top, where spectacular vistas are available to both hikers who use the trail and climbers who use the rock wall to make their ascent. In addition to being located along a well-traveled state highway within a popular state park, Eagle Rock is situated within a few hundred yards of well-used railroad tracks carrying freight east and west along the gorge.

### First-Year Closure

In 1996, two climbers complained to Eagle Rock State Park officials that they had been attacked by birds on their ascent up the rock face. Upon further investigation, the park officials concluded that the birds were a pair of peregrine falcons, which are listed as an endangered species by both the state and federal governments. Park officials contacted the State Fish and Wildlife Department, which recommended closure of the Rock to climbers. State park officials agreed to comply with this recommendation by the Wildlife Department; they closed the Rock to climbers but left the trail open to hikers.

During the first year of the closure of Eagle Rock to climbers, the State Parks and Recreation Department initiated a process to develop rules for climbing in parks throughout the state. The department hired a climber as a consultant, contacted users for their opinions, notified other state and federal agencies of their plans, and held hearings throughout the state. This process resulted in a conclusion by the State Parks and Recreation Department that conditions were so unique from one park site to another that each park should undertake a process to develop its own rules, subject to review and approval by the state park officials housed in the state capitol.

### Second-Year Plan Development

The park ranger for Eagle Rock State Park initiated a process to develop a site-specific plan for access to the Rock. During this process, the ranger established the following guidelines for collecting and evaluating information:

1.  Eagle Rock would remain closed to climbers until a plan was put into place by the State Parks and Recreation Department.
2.  The State Fish and Wildlife Department would be required to participate in the process of developing the plan, but the final decision would be made by the Parks and Recreation Department.
3.  The park ranger established an Eagle Rock Advisory Committee consisting of representatives from the local climbing organization (with a membership of over 3,000), the Access Fund (a group advocating maximum access to public lands), and other climbers not affiliated with any official organization.
4.  State officials from the State Parks and the Fish and Wildlife departments agreed to hire a peregrine falcon consultant who was employed by the U.S. Forest Service in California and who also had climbing experience. The consultant took personal leave time to engage in his consultation work.

**Relevant Facts**

The following relevant pieces of information surfaced in the public hearings and testimonial process:

1.  The Climbing Association suggested only a partial closure of the Rock to climbers on the grounds that:
    *   No evidence had been presented to show why climbing at a distance far removed from the nesting site was any more disruptive to the nesting falcons than the noise from highway and train traffic or the presence of hikers using the trail.
    *   Partial closure of the Rock would allow the Climbing Association to help enforce the regulatory requirements put in place by the State Parks and Recreation Department.
2.  The Access Fund argued that partial closure would spread the burden of restricting access equitably across various user groups.
3.  The climbing consultant advised the Parks Department to establish a "buffer zone" that would keep climbers away from the line of sight of the nesting falcons and at a distance that was at least equal to the distance of hikers on the trail to the top of the outcropping.
4.  The peregrine falcon consultant from California supported a permanent closure of the Rock to climbing. He argued that we know too little about the kind of external disturbances that peregrines will tolerate to engage in "experiments" with partial closures to climbing.
5.  Under the administrative rules governing state natural resource agencies, administrators have the discretionary authority to make exceptions to mandatory actions by creating "buffer zones," but it is not clear whether the "buffer zone" exception was meant to apply in a case involving climbers and peregrine falcons.

**Recommendation**

Based on your review of the evidence and the processes that were followed, what recommendation would you make to the Eagle Rock park ranger? In reaching a recommendation, please take into consideration the following questions:

1.  Would collecting more cost and benefit information be useful in helping to decide this case? If so, what kind of information would you suggest and what time frame would you need to carry out the necessary analysis?
2.  What policy framework/models seem most applicable in making sense out of this case?
3.  What is the best course of action to ensure administrative accountability?
4.  What values should be given primary consideration in determining the best course of action to be taken?

## STRATEGIC MANAGEMENT OF PUBLIC ORGANIZATIONS: CONFLICTING ROLES AND PURPOSES

The Case of the Peregrine Falcon is typical of the kind of problems that public-sector managers are increasingly facing in the exercise of their discretionary leadership authority. Problems of scarcity have created an expanding regulatory environment where multiple stakeholders and competing authority structures must be successfully reconciled without fully adequate information, time, and money. Laws may be ambiguous, constituency interests conflicting, and organizational resources limited. Still, decisions must be made in a timely fashion, backed by justifiable analysis, and implemented in a manner that meets the multiple tests of democratic accountability.

In the chapters that follow, we will explore how to meet these challenges with success. In chapter 12, we examine the various theories of public-sector leadership and decision making that assist public managers in meeting the many challenges they face. In chapter 13, we review the role of administrators in the policy process with a special focus on the initiatory leadership responsibility they hold in partnership with elected officials. Finally, in chapter 14, we examine the many mechanisms used to ensure administrative accountability, with special attention given to the importance of administrative law and the role of administrative rulemaking.

# PUBLIC SERVICE LEADERSHIP IN A SHARED-POWER WORLD

We live in a world where no one is "in charge." No one organization or institution has the legitimacy, power, authority, or intelligence to act alone on important public issues and still make substantial headway against the problems that threaten us all. No one is in charge when it comes to the greenhouse effect, AIDS, homelessness, the federal deficit, declining inner cities, drug abuse, domestic violence, or a host of other public problems. Many organizations or institutions are involved, affected, or have a partial responsibility to act. . . . As a result, we live in a "shared-power" world. If we are to survive and prosper, and if our children and grandchildren—and their children and grandchildren— are to enjoy the benefits of our ability to make the world better, we must find ways to think and act more effectively in a shared-power world.

*(John M. Bryson and Barbara C. Crosby 1992, xi)*[1]

At century's end, the United States is confronted with a host of complex problems that touch every segment of society. The nation's urban communities are in crisis as homelessness, crime and severe poverty continue to take their toll. Once again, our public education system is under attack. The embarrassing discovery that millions of adults are illiterate has stoked the fire of education reformers who believe that massive changes are needed for America to compete successfully in a rapidly changing, increasingly interdependent world. The number of Americans who lack adequate health care . . . has become a national disgrace. . . . The nature and scope of these and countless other problems, and the perception that public and private institutions are ineffective in solving them, have sparked a renewed interest in leadership.

*(Larry D. Terry 1995, 1–2)*

In a world characterized by diffusion of power in policymaking, regulation, and delivery of public services, administrative leaders play critical roles in accomplishing the work of democratic governance. As we have argued throughout this book, no single person or jurisdiction is in charge of the fractured world administrators inhabit. Heads of agencies, directors of nonprofits, and executives of special districts are in charge of a mission, a program, or a project, and they carry

responsibility for managing these as part of a broader public good. But these leaders rarely have the ability on their own to define a problem or have access to all parts of a solution necessary to deliver the public goods and services they are charged with providing. In short, public service administrators occupy what Barbara Crosby and John Bryson (1992; see also Bryson and Crosby 2005) characterize as a world of *shared power.*

Leading in a shared-power world requires many traditional management skills, such as planning, directing, and coordinating, but it also requires the addition of a different set of skills that focus on collective efforts—skills that include collaborative decision making, brokering deals, and bridging resources. This is "boundary-spanning" leadership; it places a premium on the ability to work in the midst of an undefined structure with a loosely coupled group of participants, assist them in creating a sense of shared meaning, and support them in maintaining direction. This is more like navigating a sail-powered tall ship than driving a sports car. So much depends on circumstances, on elements outside of one's control, and on the willing cooperation of others working in concert. In short, leading public service organizations today requires increased collaborative skill in choosing priorities and bringing them to fruition with partners who are devoted to a shared vision of the public good.

This chapter helps readers understand the significant challenges faced by the current generation of public service leaders: the enduring tensions enumerated in earlier chapters, the nature of our mixed political economy, and the forces of globalization that disconnect people from place. While leadership has been a dominant theme in the popular press and a topic of consistent attention in academic literature, many of the espoused theories of leadership envision leaders who take charge, who unilaterally marshal people and material resources within their organizations to meet exigent circumstances. This is not the world that public administrators inhabit, whether at the front line, in middle management, or at the executive levels of organizations. In fact, it has never been the world public administrators have inhabited.

There are those like Crosby and Bryson who argue that the world today presents new challenges of dispersion and balkanization—challenges that threaten our sense of commonality and common good while vastly complicating our interdependent relationships at home and abroad. The world today may be more fragmented, or perhaps fragmented differently than in the past, but we do not believe that the need for a leadership model that helps us deal with leading in a shared-power world is different today than it was over 200 years ago, when our dispersed-power model was established in our constitutional systems of governance.

This chapter presents a model for leading in shared-power contexts based upon the constitutional Balancewheel described in chapter 6. We believe this model is well suited to the diffuse and rapidly changing conditions of the modern world. Our approach to leadership shares much in common with Crosby and Bryson (1992; see also Bryson and Crosby 2005) but is more institutional and constitutional in focus, and therefore one that is attuned to things we hold in common as a distinct political community. The following sections of this chapter address the current challenges to leadership, the inadequacy of conventional leadership theories, and how the requirements of constitutional governance affect and inform leadership. We then present a legacy model of leadership and illustrate its operation in practice.

## THE LEADERSHIP CHALLENGE: ACHIEVING RESULTS IN A SHARED-POWER WORLD

Many of the challenges that public administrators face have been aptly characterized as "wicked" or "chaotic" problems" (Rittel and Webber 1973; Snowden and Boone 2007). Such problems are exemplified in efforts to reform and effectively regulate a global financial system, in the emergency

responses and security issues faced by the U.S. Department of Homeland Security, in efforts to manage watersheds and community public health, in the disputes over curricula in public education, and in managing the effects on our communities and labor force of an increasingly globalized world. These problems defy simple solutions and single organizations. They necessarily transcend sectors and political jurisdictions. Even seemingly straightforward problems such as delivering clean drinking water, establishing a library, or creating effective kindergarten programs are likely to involve dozens of organizations, policy actors, and interest groups. Gareth Morgan illustrates the complexity of policy problems through maps, as exemplified in Exhibit 12.1 (2006, 268) and Exhibit 12.2 (2006, 269).

The problems of mad cow disease and maintaining electrical power supply illustrated in these maps are typical of problems faced by those in positions of both political and administrative leadership. Educational attainment, child hunger, transportation planning, emergency preparedness, drinking water supply, health insurance, and the development of vital cities all have maps at least as complex as those in Exhibit 12.1 and Exhibit 12.2. These maps help us realize that multiple organizations, associations, and individuals acting both in their personal and organizational capacities play important roles in helping to solve or cope with any given problem. Some of this complexity lies in the nature of the problems addressed. For example, national security, law enforcement, education, public health, and transportation planning are inherently complicated. But the ways in which we deal with them are also complicated by our governing principles, structures, and processes.

The founding principles of the U.S. Constitution provide a good starting point for understanding why leadership in the United States has always been a shared-power activity. America's governing system provides for a mixed political economy in which neither the marketplace nor the political arena exercises complete hegemony in the allocation of resources, or in the generation of regulations, goods, and services. Its federal (national/state/local) design guarantees that there are multiple levels and venues for political action. The size and diversity of the republic, and the liberties it encourages, guarantee the proliferation of factions or interest groups that frustrate unifying leaders (see Madison 1787, Federalist No. 10, quoted in Rossiter 1961). Checks and balances curb authority by distributing power among various branches. It may surprise some readers that our state and national constitutions evince profound mistrust of leaders. The founders feared demagogues who would manipulate passions and prejudices for personal gain at public expense. They believed the rights of minorities would be trampled upon easily through exploitation of majoritarian politics, and that the rule of law might too easily fail without structural precautions that moderate the temptation to demagoguery—the pursuit of narrow interests by ambitious and charismatic leaders.

These structural characteristics ensure that no leader, nor unit or branch of government, is solely in charge of public policy. Our constitutional structures at the federal and state levels anticipate, even build in, an element of conflict as an integral safeguard against overbearing leadership. Moreover, the limited powers of our governments leave ample room for private and nonprofit sectors and enable proliferation of special districts, all of which play significant roles in addressing public problems. When combined with the trends toward greater privatization of public services and globalization of our economy, it is not difficult to see why administrative leadership and capacity are diffuse and indeterminate, and why no one seems to be in control of policy processes and outcomes.

There are also some less obvious though important ways in which the American constitutional system poses leadership challenges for public servants. First, at a basic cultural level, Americans are at once committed to individualism and deeply suspicious of those charged with public leader-

Exhibit 12.1   **The "Mad Cow" Phenomenon**

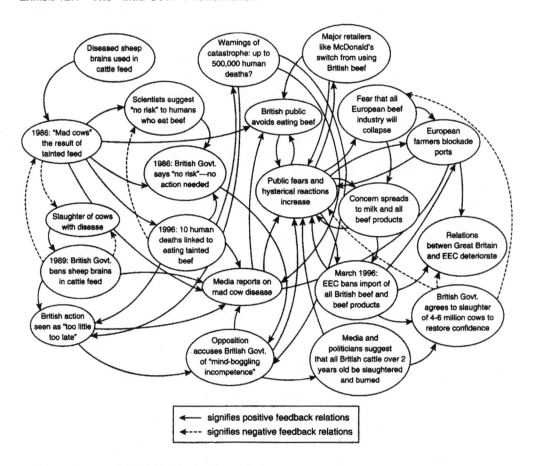

*Source:* Morgan (2006, 269). Used with permission.

ship. Second, the commitment to individualism has spawned a multiplicity of interests that make it difficult for leaders to create agreement among competing groups. And finally, multijurisdictional responsibilities make it difficult for leaders to address problems that require collaboration across political boundaries. Each of these challenges requires some elaboration to fully appreciate them.

### Individualism

The problem of public leadership has deep roots in the American political tradition. As discussed in chapters 4 and 5, our political and economic systems share a common root in classical liberalism, which asserts that authority rests first with individuals. Governmental power is derived as a grant of authority from those who want their rights protected through a social contract. Similarly, in a market economy, the idealized actor is the individual who exercises autonomous choice in pursuit of his or her material self-interest. It is through the aggregation of individual preferences and actions that political society and its economy are formed. This presents a rather stark view of society as a mere collection of autonomous strangers interacting only as they are motivated to

Exhibit 12.2  **Positive and Negative Feedback in the Power Industry**

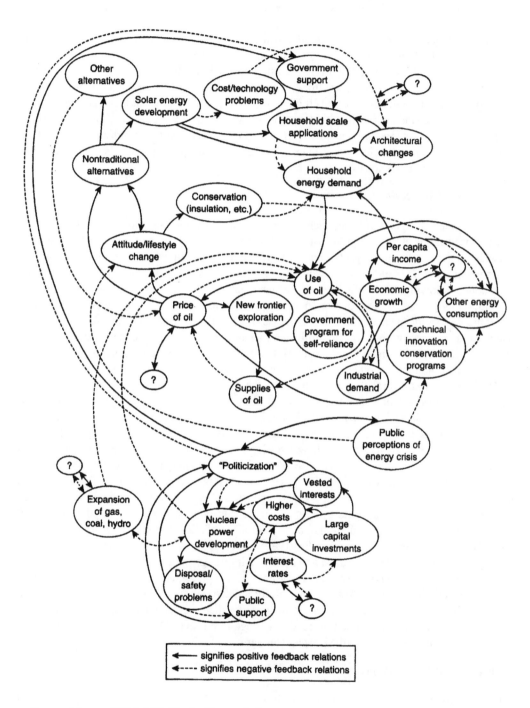

*Source:* Morgan (2006, 269). Used with permission.

advance their mutual interests. Such a view minimizes the role of community and government—and therefore also of public leadership. However, people are much more complicated than this stark, individualistic image depicts.

While Americans express strong individualistic preferences, they also express a desire to live in communities with a real sense of identity and commitment to a larger common good. For example, when asked where they would like to live, most choose vibrant communities that work—where schools function, where potholes are filled, where the perception of a high quality of life exists, where public services are effective and efficient, where people are known and respected, and where the public, private, and nonprofit institutions join in fashioning community identity and spirit (cf. Bellah et al. 1985). Successfully managing this tension between libertarian individualism and our more communitarian aspirations constitutes a key standard against which public service leadership is measured, and it is not an easy standard to meet.

### Multiplicity of Interests

A well-documented outcome of our penchant for individualism is the rise of increasingly specialized interest groups. The pluralist tradition of special-interest-group advocacy teaches us to pursue our individual interests through organizations and associations that will advocate for us in the halls of government. We do not entrust such work solely to our elected representatives because they are incapable of knowing the diverse interests of such a large and heterogeneous population. People join advocacy groups, professional associations, labor unions, and political action groups that target highly specific measures, and then they search for political candidates who support them. In many instances, these groups will faithfully carry an individual's views into the political arena and effectively advocate for his or her interests. However, even within such specialized organizations, it is likely that intense differences among members on key issues will still arise.

The interest-group pluralism that is inherent to the American extended republic creates circumstances where disaggregated interests profoundly disagree with each other, not only among groups of people, but within each group as well. Groups easily splinter into a fury of single-minded commitments and passions. When this occurs, leaders are faced with the condition of hyperpluralism, where coalitions of interests are exceedingly difficult to organize in the service of broader collective purposes. For example, a diverse array of special interests may be able to coalesce around a narrow issue but not be able to extend this agreement to a larger common interest. This is reflected in efforts to ban tobacco advertising, preserve endangered species, create national scenic areas, legalize medical marijuana, regulate pollutants in the environment, and a host of other issues that cut across organizational, jurisdictional, and sectoral boundaries (see Abbott, Adler, and Abbott 1997; Bryner 1995; Fritschler and Hoefler 1996; Yaffee 1994). Furthermore, rather than people sorting out what they care about most and affirming it through civic engagement, interest groups step into their place, speaking for them as professional representatives (e.g., the National Rifle Association and the American Association of Retired Persons). As a result of this group-oriented approach to public affairs, many citizens gradually lose their capacity to engage civilly in public arenas—they lose the temperament needed to engage in politics. The potential for responsible, democratic leadership suffers in the process (Putnam 2000, 49–51).

### Multiplicity of Jurisdictions

While hyperpluralism results in a world of divisive single interests represented by professional advocates in the policymaking process, the implementation side of the process is also fractured. Multiple political and legal arenas make it likely that normal implementation processes will result

in conflicting outcomes. For example, a local community may vote to develop plans for more green space that follows watercourses to connect their town with remote rivers and open spaces. The town's new "green necklace" plan will likely face some daunting challenges. For example, the state legislature may decide to decrease funding for parks and open spaces in order to meet higher state priorities on funding education, criminal justice, or transportation. The federal government may complicate things with expensive environmental regulations or incentive programs that heavily skew or derail the community's plans. Other political entities are also likely to exercise jurisdiction over portions of the watercourse or associated lands. Parts of the land may be held by any combination of counties, private landowners, or states that have jurisdiction over navigable waterways up to the high-water mark. In some settings, Native American tribes or the federal government may hold significant portions of the watercourse.

The green necklace plan envisioned by the town thus depends on the action of multiple jurisdictions. Making such a plan actually work, therefore, requires administrators to coordinate actions across many organizational boundaries and jurisdictions, with each facing different legal, organizational, and political imperatives. Exhibit 12.3 illustrates how this might look.

Although the green necklace plan may appear as a typical program management problem that requires coordination of multiple participants, the difference is that program management—as it is typically understood and applied in the private sector—does not assume that participants have equal and independent governing authority. This means that "what counts for success" may not be defined by the project requirements, but may be defined by larger governing principles, structures, and processes that are in conflict.

Another complication arises from the way in which multiple jurisdictions deliver their services. Development and implementation of the green necklace plan will require a series of land use ordinance changes, alterations to public landowners' management plans, and some land exchanges with willing sellers to balance private with public interests. The constellation of jurisdictions affected by the new plan may require the services of a local land trust or a special-purpose intermediary such as the Wetlands Joint Venture or the Nature Conservancy to focus collaborative efforts on achieving a workable land exchange. Furthermore, private landowners may not be interested in selling their lands, but they might be willing to condition them with easements or other legal mechanisms. If this happens, questions arise about who can or should hold the easement, with options ranging from the local governments to a nonprofit trust or a homeowners' association. Creating the desired policy outcomes thus requires familiarity with a wide variety of coordinative mechanisms to accommodate a multitude of jurisdictions, the business and nonprofit sectors, and dozens of interested individuals and groups.

The conditions described above explain why power sharing is especially relevant to the work of American public administrators, and why public leadership will always be frustrated. However, despite all the impediments, leadership is still possible, still viable, and still necessary. There are many kinds of leadership and many theories of leadership, all of which are useful in the right contexts. Few theories, though, take the shared-power context of public life fully into account, and most overlook the distinct institutional qualities required in American constitutional governance.

## Leadership Theories and Their Inadequacies

An extensive literature exists on leaders and leadership.[2] It draws from a variety of professions, including public administration, business administration, education, and social work, and from academic disciplines such as history, political science, psychology, social psychology, sociology, and anthropology. It is hard to consolidate, summarize, or distill this literature around any

358

Exhibit 12.3   **Green Necklace Parks Plan by Ownership**

WASHINGTON COUNTY
(NE Quadrant- Ross Lake)

| | |
|---|---|
| ┼┼┼┼ | Railroads |
| — — — | Roads and Highways |
| | Rivers, streams and lakes |
| | Urban areas |
| | Private – Rural 1 and Rural 2 Zones |
| | Blue Heron Park District –Greenspaces |
| | County and State Parks |
| | US. DOI Bureau of Land Management |
| | State Forest |
| ━ ━ ━ | Green Necklace Planning Area |

North

1   2   3   4   5   miles

single theme or principle. For our purposes, we have organized this literature around its focus on individual, group, and organizational levels of analysis. We do this for two reasons: first, the literature lends itself to this kind of analysis; second, in our own leadership development work with practitioners, we have found that the knowledge, skills, and competencies needed for these varying types of leadership are quite different. We briefly review the characteristics of these three approaches and identify a variety of inadequacies. We end our analysis with an examination of the implications of the various approaches for the kind of constitutional governance that administrators are required to undertake.

*Trait-Based and Individual-Centered Theories*

Leadership inevitably focuses attention on the unique qualities of individuals who assume the mantle of leadership responsibility. Advocates of this popular approach look for traits or characteristics that distinguish leaders from followers (Boyatzis 1982; Kirkpatrick and Locke 1991; Yukl 1981). Until recently these traits have been associated with the "great man" approach to leadership, emphasizing distinctive qualities in settings traditionally dominated by men. People are fascinated with the qualities they believe make great leaders, especially those who shaped our own history, whether they are presidents such as George Washington, Abraham Lincoln, and Franklin Delano Roosevelt, or successful entrepreneurs such as Andrew Carnegie and Bill Gates. Charisma, courage, energy, wisdom, and other traits have been studied as a basis for distinguishing these leaders from their followers. More recent research has explored traits among women, such as compassion, emotion, affinity, and other qualities that yield a distinctive "relational" approach to leadership (Gilligan 1993; Regan and Brooks 1995). An accompanying literature summarizes individual characteristics of women leaders (cf. Farrel 1996; Fisher 1999; Helgesen 1990; Martin 1996; Rosenthal 1998).[3] However, as appealing as these studies of men and women leaders may be, individual trait theories fall short of explaining leadership success.

Analyses of trait-based studies and their supporting literature have found no clear distinction between leaders and nonleaders in terms of the many dozens of traits explored (House and Aditya 1997; Kirkpatrick and Locke 1991). Little consistency and predictability can be found in relating any given trait to successful leadership (Jennings 1961). Recent research using bundled personality characteristics suggests that some traits are related to leader emergence, but they are not reliable in predicting leader success (Judge et al. 2002). While trait-based theory explains some dimensions of leadership, the failure of this approach to explain or predict effectiveness has led researchers away from individual traits to the importance of contextual influences within particular settings.

One group of scholars has focused attention on the dynamics that occur within small group settings, while another group has focused on the larger external factors that shape what counts for "good leadership." Together, these group- and contingency-based theories have helped to broaden the leadership lens to focus on those factors that are distinctive to successful leadership in the public sector. An analysis of this broadening focus of leadership follows.

*Group-Centered Theories*

Sociologists have taken the lead in focusing attention on the dynamics of leadership within group settings. For example, Guy Swanson (1970) observed that when people find themselves in groups, they engage in formative social processes that are interpretive and deliberative in nature. Leaders emerge through the group's search for substantive meaning and direction. Leaders test ideas in relationship to group members. Group members array themselves in association with the people

who are expressing ideas that resonate with them. The intricate dance between leader and follower builds the shared meaning of the group and inculcates a sense of purpose from which specific goals emerge. This social process matures as leader-expressed meanings and actions become vested in the group as a whole. The group-formation literature underscores the interaction necessary for groups to take ownership of expressed values, and how work roles are sorted out and defined over time (Wilson 2002; Yukl 2012, chap. 11). The process is interactive and recursive, meaning that leadership roles are redefined and reassigned as group values evolve and group solidarity ebbs and flows.

Group theory introduces another level of sophistication through its attention to ideas and meaning, as well as roles. Leadership does not depend entirely upon manipulation of psychological needs or upon a person's management style. Leaders emerge, evolve, and devolve within groups over time, in part due to the normative saliency of their ideas and their ability to inculcate or cultivate shared meaning. As shared meaning coalesces, work roles develop that define expectations and appropriate relations among members. People grow or adapt to the defined roles, which shape attitudes and norms about proper leadership. Good leadership is defined in large measure by the content of, and relationships among, institutional roles. These aspects of group theory embrace the idea that leadership functions exist in many group roles, that there are multiple leaders, and that intergroup dynamics have as much of a formative influence on groups as internal dynamics.

Group theories have had an important influence on our thinking about organizations. For example, some organizational sociologists describe complex organizations as conglomerations of workgroups that evolve around common means as well as purposes (Weick 1979). Organizations engender patterned relationships that constitute structures, within which there is order and role definition. The complexity arising from the development of these multiple patterns of relationships within organizations is now known as contingency leadership theory.

*Contingency Theories*

In the 1950s and 1960s, social psychologists began to focus on leadership as a manifestation of group functions and dynamics in corporate organizations (Blake and Mouton 1964; Hersey and Blanchard 1981, 1977a; Hersey, Blanchard, and Johnson 2001; McGregor 1960). Their research found that effective leadership depends upon an appropriate match between organization/group conditions and leadership style (Fiedler 1967; Fiedler and Garcia 1987; House 1996, 1971; House and Mitchell 1974; Vroom and Yetten 1973). Robert Blake and Jane Mouton (2005 developed a popular leadership grid along two primary dimensions, one focusing on "concern for task" and the other on "concern for people." The grid, presented in Exhibit 12.4, displays a range from 1 to 9 along each dimension, reflecting varying degrees to which concern for task and concern for people yield varying leadership styles.

William Reddin (1970, 41–47) refined the grid into quadrants that yield four basic leadership styles: supporting, coaching, delegating, and autocratic. These styles emphasize the importance of sizing up what is most appropriate to the needs of a given group before determining what type of leadership will be most effective.

A variety of contingency models exist in the literature. All follow the same basic logic and strongly resemble each other. They improve on trait and group theory approaches by suggesting that leadership can, at least to some extent, be trained and adapted to varying circumstances to enhance effectiveness. For example, emergency conditions may call for more directive, task-oriented leadership, while leading a problem-solving team through an emergent, poorly defined,

Exhibit 12.4  **Blake and Mouton Grid**

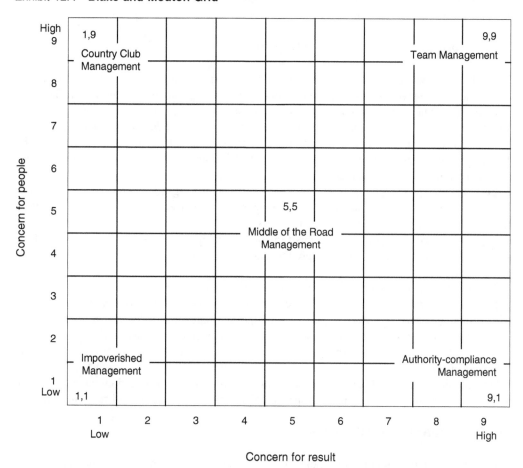

*Source:* Based on Blake and Mouton (1985) and Blake and McCanse (1991).

and long-term situation may require more attention to relationships and process skills. In a public sector marked by frequently conflicting values, these skills are especially important.

However, the inadequacies of the contingency model are evident in its exclusive focus on workgroups and organizations with simple superior/subordinate relationships. It presumes a single, formal leader, or at least a clear hierarchy of formal leaders within a single organization. Such assumptions should not be made—especially in public service contexts where subordinates often have multiple superiors and many workgroups have collegial membership across several organizations. Moreover, legal authority and personnel protections in public life are likely diffused among subordinate as well as supervisory positions. The absence of clear hierarchy and multiple legal obligations means that subordinates bring more independence to the table than is presumed in the corporate contexts of contingency models. Contingency theorists are likely to claim that their models still apply but must be tailored to the differing circumstances of each sector. While there is some merit in this argument, their research methods consistently ignore sectoral differences in favor of a workgroup model based in generic social-psychological theory. Philip Selznick (1957,

1949) built on these insights to fashion an institutional approach to leadership that recognizes the significance of the organization as the unit of analysis.

*Organizational and Institution-Centered Leadership Theories*

Selznick begins with the organization as his unit of analysis. He argues that leadership at organizational levels is a process of weaving and coopting narrower group interests into a broader organizational community of mutual interests and common vision. His classic study of the Tennessee Valley Authority (TVA) (Selznick 1949) illustrates how federal officials bargained, cajoled, and coopted a diverse array of community and business leaders into long-term collaboration with the TVA that would bring electricity to the valley, control flooding, and promote economic development of a primitive region. Selznick emphasizes leadership in this context as an institution-building process that transforms instrumental group and organizational agendas into larger communities of shared meaning, capacity, and purpose (see chapter 7). He describes how institutionalization emerged over time through a gradual and successive process of tying the work of the TVA more deeply to the partners in the region. This type of leadership presumes a sense of the whole, a sense of proportion, of how disparate groups and interests in the institution's environment can be knitted together.

Selznick's work has been criticized for its preoccupation with the cooptative nature of leadership of large-scale, conservative, and monolithic institutions of the post–World War II era. Although this critique has merit, his work represents an important precursor to "new institutionalism," a school of sociology-oriented scholars who, in the 1980s, rejuvenated the focus on institutions as the primary unit of analysis. These scholars emphasize the fluid, interpretive, adaptive, and dynamic nature of institutions (cf. Douglas 1986; Elkin and Soltan 1993; Powell and DiMaggio 1991). Selznick's pioneering work and the "new institutionalism" that followed drew attention to the unique characteristics of public institutions where powers are intentionally diffuse and shared.

## LEADING PUBLIC INSTITUTIONS

Since the mid-1970s, a number of scholars have focused their attention on the uniqueness of the public sector and the implications this may have for the exercise of leadership. One of the more influential theorists, James McGregor Burns (1978), developed a leadership dichotomy that adapted much of the previous literature for use in political settings. He posited that leaders generally adopted one of two general methods of leading. Many leaders use a "transactional" approach that relies on a sense of reciprocity or exchange between leaders and followers. Politicians, for example, make campaign promises to constituents in exchange for their votes. While this is a common approach to leadership, it lacks much in the way of synergy needed to cultivate and sustain a common vision or shared sense of the public interest.

For Burns, the more attractive type of leadership is "transformational," which he defines as the ability to raise the consciousness of followers regarding common and higher values that transform mere aggregations of interests into a shared commitment to a larger common good (Burns 1978, 141–254). This kind of leadership changes people, affects their outlook on individual and collective life, and draws them together with a new identity and shared meaning. For all its claims, however, Burns's work rejuvenates an individual level of analysis, as evidenced in his biographical treatments of exemplary transformational leaders, and fuses it with the modern social-psychological literature. It is an appealing fusion, but from a normative and constitutional perspective, it creates the potential specter of demagogues—leaders with immense charisma who

manipulate the social-psychological dimensions of motivation through charm and propaganda to consolidate power toward their own ends. Communities of "true believers" who construct a solidarity of shared meaning may be transformative, but they may not be very interested in or respectful of the constitutional system of governance and the competing values it seeks to hold in dynamic balance. We believe Burns's emphasis on the social-psychological dynamic of leadership gives insufficient attention to institutions and roles defined in part by norms and structures inherent to America's constitutional system of governance.

Another influential author, Jeffrey Luke (1998), developed the concept of "catalytic" leadership. Luke argues that successful leadership results from the proper timing of speech and actions that catalyze others to employ resources, information, and positions for collaboratively determined purposes. Control over formal authority, resources, or information is less important than being able to make sense out of the complexities of a community or policy subsystem, and having a sense of proper timing of one's actions. In Luke's catalytic model, effective leaders identify critical points for action (thinking strategically), cultivate key relationships among powerholders and operational groups, and maintain constancy of purpose that inspires others (leading from passion and strength) to achieve appropriate ends.

> With catalytic leadership, individuals and groups convene multiple stakeholder groups, and facilitate and mediate agreement around tough issues. We live in a complex world of interconnections in which take-charge leaders are less successful than individuals and groups who provide the spark or catalyst that truly makes a difference. (Luke 1998, 4)

Implicit in Luke's approach is the idea that leadership is not necessarily a matter of constant effort, repeated exhortation, and monitoring by leaders. Rather, effective leaders know how to wait—how to time words and actions for full rhetorical effect. They sense when groups are more or less ready to hear a message, to engage in meaningful discourse, to reach consensus, and to act. This kind of leadership helps cultivate conditions of trust and interaction that lead to fruitful communication and discourse about things that matter to everyone involved. It also respects followers for their own judgments as political actors who bring their own contributions to the effort (Green and Zinke 1993).

John Carver's work (1990) has also made an important contribution to our thinking about the distinctiveness of public leadership. Carver focuses on the challenge of leading in a world of shifting coalitions and rapid organizational change. In the nonprofit world, for example, leaders often run organizations that depend on shared commitments and causes among staff, volunteers, and partners whose organizational identities are tenuous at best. Their host organization may radically change in scale of operation as well as in its linkages to related nonprofit organizations and public agencies. Leaders must maintain constancy of the binding purpose or mission in the face of severe organizational instability. Preparing employees, whether paid or volunteer, for such conditions presents a leadership challenge in its own right. For example, a local community and educational services nonprofit recently experienced severe cutbacks in a critical service due to reductions in federal grant funding. Two paid staff positions were threatened as a result. The director of the nonprofit had prepared the employees well in advance for this contingency, and worked with them to find alternative funding from a local organization to continue their services with some modifications. This included converting the staff members to employees of the paying organization, while retaining them at the same site to preserve service integration.

Crosby and Bryson have extended Carver's work on the distinctiveness of public sector leadership. They have synthesized the work of a generation of scholars and reflective practitioners

on leading in public organizational and community settings where no single person is in charge. They argue that the conditions of modern life require "a new understanding of power" (2005, 17) whereby agencies, organizations, and other entities must learn to share resources, authority, and activities to meet common goals. Achieving concerted action requires a variety of leadership capabilities. From their research, Crosby and Bryson derived a list of the following capabilities:

- Understanding the social, political, and economic givens as well as potentialities
- Understanding and deploying personal assets on behalf of beneficial change
- Building effective workgroups
- Nurturing humane and effective organizations
- Creating and communicating shared meaning/vision in forums
- Making and implementing decisions in legislative, executive, and administrative arenas
- Sanctioning conduct and adjudicating disputes in courts
- Coordinating leadership tasks over the course of the policy change cycle (2005, 34–35)

No leader possesses all of these capabilities. Rather, they are exercised by "a number of people leading at different times and in varying ways over the course of a policy change effort" (Crosby and Bryson 2005, 36). Crosby and Bryson thus emphasize that leadership is itself a collaborative enterprise. We characterize the methods and techniques they and their colleagues use in this enterprise as matters of *conciliatory practice,* because they are designed to win accord—to move from hostility or distrust to agreement, even if only for a short time.

## PUBLIC LEADERSHIP: CONSEQUENCES FOR CONCILIATORY PRACTICE

The various leadership theories we have reviewed presume a distinctive set of skills necessary to make them work. For example, trait theories assume that one must possess or develop the traits necessary to be an effective leader. Group theories assume that individuals must learn the skills to keep the group "on task," while also attending to the social needs of individual members of the group. Contingency theories emphasize the need for leaders to possess the kinds of knowledge and sensibilities to understand the nuances of context, setting, and place. Public-sector leadership is similar in many respects but differs in one significant way. Group and trait theories do not require leaders to serve as stewards, "keepers" if you will, of a set of public values, governing processes and structures that have been legitimated by previous constitutional and legal decisions (see chapter 6). It is important to remember that conciliatory leadership practices in the public sector occur within a legal framework that imposes parameters on what is acceptable and what is possible; therefore, conciliatory leadership requires an understanding of these substantive and procedural values, which we have discussed in chapter 6.

Within the framework of acceptable possibilities, leaders who use conciliatory practices in public settings build toward shared meaning by helping "constituents think about the relationships between individuals and their communities, the groups whose well-being is most crucial, the content of the common good, and means of achieving it" (Crosby and Bryson 2005, 193). This is often a messy process, marked by struggle and conflict where parties selectively use and withhold information in different forums and arenas to increase their advantage. The process may take on characteristics of a game that yields winners and losers, and where new players join in midstream while others withdraw. Out of this "organized anarchy" (Kingdon 1995), leaders try to elicit enough shared meaning to craft a vision, however limited, of a common good. The process relies on an implicit

Exhibit 12.5  **The Recursive Nature of Conciliatory Engagement**

Vision                          Enlarging Support for the Vision                          Institutionalization

assumption that leaders can articulate and exploit the interdependence of self-interested players such that it broadens their receptivity to more common interests. As agendas broaden, so does the capacity for developing a working consensus through coalition building.

The process for achieving consensus and action is recursive, often cycling through the same phases. What started with an initial sense of "the problem" or "vision" that incited group formation subsequently requires revisiting as new players join. As the nature of the problem or vision is redefined, the menu of plausible solutions changes (Stone 1997). We illustrate this recursive process in Exhibit 12.5. The process of engagement begins with a leadership initiative that is carried forward by a single or small number of leaders who engage stakeholders. In the process of engagement, the definition of the problem and range of plausible solutions are redefined, and the support necessary to move on to the next stage enlarges. This continues through stages until sufficient clarity and agreement is reached and the processes of institutionalization can begin to take place. It may start with an organizational solution that establishes a mission, creates a structure of authority, assigns roles, allocates resources, and establishes oversight mechanisms to ensure that the work gets done. As this process continues to build support, the organization may eventually become a community institution. We see this transformational process occur at the local level in the support for sports, education, civic vitality, the environment, and other activities that generate community solidarity and organization.

This recursive process of engagement is illustrated at the organization level with the Prairie County case presented in Part II of this text. The definition of the inciting problem changed as law enforcement agencies, courts, and social service providers brought their particular challenges to the table. It is also illustrated with the peregrine falcon case at the beginning of this section of the text. In both of these cases, the proper solution varied as a result of the process of engaging multiple and competing perspectives. Solutions, therefore, do not typically arise in the abstract. Rather, they are advocated by participants in the process based upon their specific values, capacities, and needs, as well as by the structure of specific forums and arenas that determine how negotiations and compromises will be reached.

As leaders stimulate this process, they must attend to group formation processes as well as to the task of substantive decision making. This entails choosing whom to involve, keeping track of

values, facilitating group dynamics, ensuring individual commitment to the process, and arranging necessary steps for decision making (cf. Behn and Vaupel 1982; Crosby and Bryson 2005, chap. 5; Miller, Shinn, and Bentley 1994). Each element of the conciliatory process requires the use of important tools or practices (Shinn, Hallmark, and Singer 2012). While it is not within the scope of this text to provide a detailed description of these tools, we have illustrated their nature in an extended endnote to this chapter.[4]

Leading through the exercise of conciliatory practices is well suited to shared-power contexts. The practices play an integral role in cultivating civic dialogue and institutionalizing political as well as administrative processes. As such, they are compatible with some important aspects of American governance, especially the responsive governance tradition of bringing plural interests together on an issue, and then maintaining discourse among them until common agreement and action is possible. They also reinforce the civic governance tradition, which emphasizes face-to-face communication and assumes that differences among individuals and groups can be bridged through facilitation, conflict resolution, and civic dialogue.

However, as we have noted in chapters 4 and 6, these traditions also have their inadequacies and require balancing with other traditions (see Democratic Balancewheel outlined in chapter 6). While the conciliatory practice model reinforces the values of responsive governance and civic dialogue, it can come at the expense of the competent government and minority rights traditions. For example, civic dialogue may do little for groups that are at a standoff as a result of fundamentally different worldviews of what is right and just. In such cases, the parties may not be able to reconcile their differences through dialogue and may need to be protected through a legal system that guarantees equal rights and due process. At the opposite end of the spectrum, where groups or interests are not well articulated and formed, it may be necessary to validate the existence of these groups and the interests they represent prior to undertaking conciliatory practices. Finally, conciliatory practices are not as effective when there is a need for high levels of technical knowledge that have to be applied quickly to solve an urgent problem. Emergency management represents an extreme example of this kind of issue, and yet even here we find an ongoing need to cultivate trust and legitimacy that is essential for effective emergency response and subsequent accountability for those actions (Svedin 2012).

To summarize, conciliatory practices associated with the civic governance tradition work best when the groups and individuals involved have a history of working together through time and over tough issues. Such groups can benefit from the streams of engagement, with each succeeding point of engagement benefiting from the achievements of the past. This kind of historical focus works best for participants who are rooted in the community where they have accrued substantial tacit knowledge of community relations, values, and ways of proceeding, and where they can be held to account for their roles and participation through the civic dialogue (McCullough 1991; Svedin 2012). When these conditions do not exist, conciliatory practices require more work. As Robert Putnam has observed, both bonding and bridging capital are important for creating a shared sense of community and sustained common action (Putnam 2000, 22–24, 362–63). In their absence, a greater burden is placed on leadership to create the conditions through deliberate intervention processes.

## PUBLIC LEADERSHIP AND CONSTITUTIONAL GOVERNANCE: A LEGACY MODEL

Earlier in this chapter, we explained why and how the American constitutional system deliberately diffuses power and balkanizes the political landscape through checks and balances, separation

of powers, and federalism. It does so in large part out of distrust of leaders. It is significant that the leadership theories reviewed here seldom mention the possibility or even the likelihood that there is a lot of bad leadership in political society that needs to be thwarted. We are not referring simply to leadership failure, but to leadership that perverts the public good through pursuit of personal or single-minded values at the expense of the balance and processes needed to preserve our regime of ordered liberty. In addition to the problem of what the founders called the "impulse of popular passions," administrative leaders increasingly face the "impulse of popular fads." Most people are aware that political and managerial movements frequently spread as fads over American society, and that political and entrepreneurial leaders try to exploit them for both good and bad reasons. Those with substantial experience in public life know that these movements inevitably fade, but not before they do as much or more damage as they do good. The founders understood this, believing that every good is alloyed with attendant evil.

The legacy leadership model employed here takes this insight seriously. The model emphasizes the stewardship functions that administrative leaders play with respect to the traditions and attendant values of the American constitutional order as presented in chapters 4 through 6 (also see Morgan 1998, in Shafritz 4:2140–2143). Second, they assume responsibility for developing a process of engagement that successfully accommodates change without sacrificing the integrity of the core values or governing design. Finally, they serve an educative and advisory role to both citizens and elected officials. We elaborate on each of these stewardship roles in the paragraphs that follow.

## Protecting Substantive Values and the Governing Design

According to the legacy model, the first and primary role of administrative leaders is to attend to the substantive and conflicting values inherent in the foundations of the American constitutional system and in the administrative traditions that have developed around these values over more than 225 years of history. Again, these traditions are presented in the Democratic Balancewheel model as responsive governance, competent and energetic governance, minority rights and access to governance, and civic governance. As we indicated in chapters 5 and 6, these values stand as counterweights or correctives to each other's excesses. The nature of their relation is captured concisely in the "Founding Beatitudes" introduced in chapter 4 and revisited here.

### The Founding Beatitudes

Too much power begets usurpation, to which majority rule is a corrective;

Too much majority rule begets majority tyranny, to which separation of powers and checks and balances is a corrective;

Too much separation of powers and checks and balances begets incompetent government, to which unity at the center is a corrective;

Too much unity at the center begets usurpation, to which civic engagement is a corrective. (Morgan 2001, 156)

Most governing systems in the United States are designed to perpetuate these correctives and any resulting tensions through a complex structure of authority that separates powers, creates a

system of checks and balances, and divides governance between the federal and the state structures of authority. This governing structure is embedded in a complex rule-by-law system enforced by powerful reviewing courts. Public leaders must operate within this governing framework, and some are exasperated by it, seeking to resolve the troublesome tensions in favor of the tradition that serves their agenda best. Many reforms spring from such efforts but are eventually confounded by those who, for whatever motives, wish to assert rival traditions. This continuing cycle is perplexing, especially to the many officials and citizens who do not understand the governing design. Their frustration contributes to cynicism about politics and the governing system as a whole. One important aspect of good public leadership, therefore, entails acting as a steward of the system as it manifests itself in specific governance settings.

As we have argued throughout this book, career public servants are well situated to exercise this kind of leadership, first because of their longevity, and second because of their relative insulation from partisan pressure. Their longevity allows them to accrue valuable knowledge and experience working at the intersection of these contending traditions as they carry out political, administrative, and technical responsibilities. This makes them an indispensable resource for political leaders, most of whom have comparatively short careers. Politicians rely on career officials not only for information but also for guidance on maintaining institutional integrity and for playing roles that elected officials cannot always perform under the partisan pressures that pervade their work. Politicians may have to take a position on a policy issue or assert a particular prerogative or practice due more to partisan or constituent agendas than to their own preferred approach, and they may rely on career officials to resist, compromise, or remedy the matter for them. Though the career official's insulation from partisan pressure is only partial, it is sufficient to enable him or her to play a steward role where others cannot.

Officials at the middle and street levels share in these responsibilities as well. For example, many public servants must firmly protect rights and access in the face of powerful pressures to ignore them. Police officers, prosecutors, and courts operate by elaborate rules and professional training designed to protect the accused, and even the convicted, against ill-tempered, spiteful, and ill-informed judgments of public servants. Police administrators must also ensure that their street-level officers are trained to restrain themselves in order to protect suspects from improper or excessive police enforcement actions, while at the same time not unduly compromising effectiveness. Other administrative officials must design procedures for open government, deliberation, access, and participation without unduly compromising timely and effective decision making. Still others must seek ways to devolve or privatize public functions while retaining a meaningful degree of accountability. These balancing responsibilities often occur under serious pressures to ignore them. It takes leadership and a lot of risk taking to stand up to these pressures and enlist others in the effort. At times, it may even require that subordinates stand up to superiors—to lead from below.

Rosemary O'Leary (2006, 70–89) illustrates this in a case involving a U.S. Forest Service employee in Indiana's Hoosier National Forest who used every internal procedure and many external political and legal tactics to resist changes made by his superiors. The changes involved off-road vehicle (ORV) policy that seriously violated the agency's own mission and legal standards. The employee in question was loyal, dedicated, and a well-liked personality in the Hoosier Forest area. In the controversy, he protected fellow employees from any culpability resulting from his actions, while eventually enlisting environmental interest groups, the press, local community elites, and national political figures in his efforts. At the height of the controversy, he even joined in a lawsuit against his own agency. He was later fired for his efforts, but then vindicated in a subsequent hearing, followed by reversal of the ORV policy. O'Leary describes this as a case of "guerrilla

government," which from the standpoint of the employee's superiors is an apt characterization. But from the perspective of constitutional governance, the employee led responsibly in the service of open, accountable government and the rule of law. In doing so, he helped to preserve and protect the integrity of the U.S. Forest Service policy and practice.

**Facilitating Change**

The second function of stewardship in the legacy model is to accommodate the need for change without sacrificing core values or the integrity of the governing design. Public administrators face constant pressure to change, whether it is to "run government more like a business," to "steer rather than row," to contract out the delivery of services to the private and nonprofit sectors, to reduce bureaucracy and red tape, to become more client centered, or to administer "faster, cheaper, better." Administrative leaders must sort out which changes are worth embracing and which should be resisted. They need to know how to structure and administer processes of engagement that enable change to occur over time. Exhibit 12.2 in our discussion of conciliatory practices illustrates the model of change we have in mind.

In working through each phase of change—creating a vision, enlarging support, institutionalizing the vision—administrative leaders employ skills in visualization, communication, group facilitation, political organizing, and organization management. They must exercise a blend of skills and techniques based on personal abilities, organizational strengths and weakness, and on assessments of events, social conditions, and political pressures. They must "read the tea leaves," "size up the situation for action," and, in the words of the great hockey player Wayne Gretzky, "skate to where the puck is going to go." As each of the three phases are completed, the results become increasingly stable and resistant to modification.

The legacy model treats leaders as stewards of core constitutional values and governing processes, as well as catalysts to the process, generating in their followers a common ownership and understanding of the issues, fashioning effective means for delivering the goods, and carrying the vision into the future. As leaders and followers work through the phases, they often become increasingly aware of new perceptions and expectations, and of the need to redefine the situation requiring action. This process provides the grounding for more durable and responsive policy solutions as it develops the capacities of the participants which subsequent leaders, in turn, can leverage for future policy changes.

In addition to bringing the appropriate skills to bear in facilitating change, the legacy leadership model requires leaders to take risks. This occurs each time a public official tells others what they do not want to hear, or stands against those who are sacrificing the well-being of workers, the environment, health and safety, the education of children, or individual rights for the sake of their own agendas. A telling example of this kind of leadership was exemplified in the actions of Brooksley Born, an attorney who served as the chairperson of the Commodity Futures Trading Commission (CFTC) in the late 1990s. She led the CFTC in an effort to regulate over-the-counter derivatives practices of investment bankers and hedge fund operators that she feared were defrauding the American people of trillions of dollars, and who were not even being monitored, must less regulated. Top government officials, including Alan Greenspan (Chairman of the Federal Reserve), Robert Rubin (Secretary of the Treasury), and Lawrence Summers (Deputy Secretary of the Treasury) ridiculed her and tried to intimidate her into refraining from regulation, but she pressed ahead. Though these top officials eventually prevailed with the aid of congressional leaders in halting her efforts, her warnings about the dangers of the derivative market proved true in subsequent years, and led to her playing a more important role in reporting on the failures of the

regulatory system as a whole, and in reforming it in the wake of the 2007–2008 financial crisis (cf. Green 2012). If only we'd had more such risk-taking leadership! The legacy model sets an expectation of conflict as a built-in feature of American public life, which means aspiring leaders must prepare themselves for it, be ready to engage it, and perhaps suffer losses in the short run in hopes of achieving longer run measures that improve rather than stymie good governance.

## The Educative Function of the Legacy Model

The third function of legacy leadership involves the educative and advisory role that administrators play in routine interactions of senior administrators with elected and appointed officials, or in bureaucratic encounters of citizens with middle managers and street-level public servants. In these various roles, public officials provide indispensable information about institutional missions, capacities, procedures, and the nuances of bureaucratic politics. Just as important, they can educate and advise these officials and citizens with respect to the interplay of our administrative legacies—of the recurring and conflicting values that should come into play with particular policies and decisions.

Elected political leaders want to bring their vision or agenda to bear on public institutions; administrators play vital roles in making this happen or not happen. With their knowledge of departmental, agency, or local government dynamics, administrators filter political agendas through phases of institutional planning and implementation and, along the way, educate stakeholders about issues, capacities, and processes. In doing so, these administrators have an opportunity to exhibit a real understanding of the governing legacies that will inevitably affect this process, or they may simply react to such legacies as they impinge upon the process. If they are aware of them ahead of time, they can build consideration for them into the process and educate other participants accordingly. If they are ignorant of them, then they, along with many of their colleagues and superiors, will feel victimized and compromised when others foist them on the process from afar. Knowledge of the four administrative traditions outlined in chapters 5 and 6 can help guide stakeholder analysis and process development. They provoke questions critical to this process, examples of which are provided below.

*1. Responsive Governance Questions*

- To whom will proponents of a new policy need to be responsive?
- What avenues of access by stakeholders and citizens already exist or need to be provided?
- What groups are left out of the process and what needs to done to include their voice in the processes of decision making?
- Will or should initiative/referendum processes impact the new policy, and if so, which stakeholders will likely be involved?
- What role should market-styled incentives or privatization play in the policy? What vendors can effectively provide the services or products? What kind of accountability mechanisms need to be built into both the contract approval and contract oversight processes?

*2. Competent and Energetic Governance Questions*

- How will this program be implemented to ensure that it is both efficient and effective?
- What kind of employees—civil service, merit, or contracted—are needed to make the program work?

- What kind of organizational capacity and structure is needed to ensure effective implementation?
- What powers are needed under the new policy for effective implementation?
- At what level of government will the most effective implementation occur?
- Which agencies will have an impact on the design and implementation of programs?
- Which employee groups should have a say in the design and implementation of the policy?
- How will the program be evaluated? How will success be measured?

*3. Minority Rights and Access Questions*

- Whose rights are affected by the new policy or agenda, and which advocacy groups need to be involved as a result?
- Is due process of law needed, and if so, how much, and who should manage it?
- Are there equal protection issues involved? Who needs to be part of the design and implementation processes as a result?
- What accountability protocols should be developed for the new policy or program?
- Which oversight agencies or offices need inclusion in the design process?

*4. Civic Governance Questions*

- What processes of face-to-face interaction are important to the success of the new policy or program?
- Does this program trump nongovernmental (nonprofit, for-profit, individual) missions and responsibilities? Should it do so? If so, who needs to be involved in the design and implementation phases?
- Should the program be more decentralized to facilitate tailoring and flexibility at local levels?
- What avenues and processes of citizen participation or engagement and coproduction should exist under the new policy?
- How many different levels of government need to be involved, and how can this involvement be carried out in ways that are respectful of their separate domains of authority?

Administrators who perform this educative and advisory role become indispensable to their political superiors and wield substantial influence on policy design and implementation as a result. They become both process- and substance-centered leaders, guiding themselves and others by substantive values that affect the legitimacy of vision, process, and outcome.

Officials who exercise substantial discretion as they interact with people on the street have opportunities to educate and advise the public in ways that can foster appreciation for, and improve engagement in, American governance. The venues and occasions for this kind of interaction vary widely. An important question that arises here is whether one is dealing with "single-shot players" or "regulars." Single-shot players encounter governance only sporadically, and often in very short episodes. They typically know little about governance principles and processes, and the opportunities for educating them are quite limited. Nevertheless, occasions do arise when there is time for substantial discussion around a specific concern. In community governance, for example, it is not unusual for individuals to contact their local department of public works to demand that a stop sign be posted near their home to slow traffic in the area, or to request more police presence in their neighborhood. These citizens are commonly referred to traffic safety advisory committees and community policing programs, where they can work through the details of their concerns. In

the process, they usually learn a lot about what can realistically be achieved with traffic signs, and how they can work with community policing officers to improve the security of their neighborhood. And, if community officials are attentive, they can easily find moments to illustrate, in words and actions, how values and processes associated with responsiveness, face-to-face civic governance, rights and modes of access, and effective measures can be used to meet their concerns.

To illustrate further, one can easily see how the librarians in the angry patron case (see introduction to Part I of this text) had opportunities to educate the disgruntled patron about the competing values they must balance as they manage their library collections. They have the chance in these kinds of "bureaucratic encounters" (Hasenfeld, Rafferty, and Zald 1987) to help patrons understand the inherent difficulties in determining appropriate acquisitions and in providing meaningful book and periodical collections for a wide variety of community patrons. The patron's interest and attention is already engaged, and he may well seek changes at higher levels of appeal, so the potential for significant education about the administrative legacies involved is very ripe.

The "regulars" are people who interact with governments on a predictable basis, and many of them represent organized interests. These people may be knowledgeable of governance processes and fully engaged for purposes of access and influence. They are probably articulate about their interests and about selected values within one or more administrative traditions. They may be entrepreneurial, seeking economic advantages and administrative processes that advantage their agendas. Others may be rights oriented, or reformers seeking more governmental efficiency or accountability. Even "regulars" are unlikely to be receptive to abstract discussions about conflicting values or traditions. Attention is focused on their agendas. And yet, opportunities still exist for cultivating a dialogue about competing interests that are missing from the process. The officials who involve these individuals can keep track of which ones advocate from which administrative tradition, and consequently, officials can usually find voices for most or all of them. The process of public education occurs when the participants are drawn into extended or "deep" dialogue with the contending groups (Cummings and Worley 2005; Miller, Shinn, and Bentley 1994).

The peregrine falcon case presented at the beginning of Part IV helps illustrate how the educative process can work. Discovery of the endangered peregrine falcons on Eagle Rock triggered a cascade of legal and bureaucratic mandates upon the Washington State Parks Department that required quick and effective action. Following the recommendations of the State Fish and Wildlife Department, the state parks director immediately closed Eagle Rock to climbers and then initiated statewide hearings that led the Parks Department to conclude that a site-specific plan was the best way to deal with the situation. The department hired a climber and a falcon specialist as consultants and established an Eagle Rock Advisory Committee consisting of representatives from the local climbing organization (with a membership of over 3,000), the Access Fund, and other climbers not affiliated with any official organization. From the standpoint of a legacy education process, the advisory committee holds the most promise. Initially, it provides a venue for educating the climbing community about who should be involved in developing an acceptable plan for Eagle Rock.

The committee already consists of regulars (organized groups) and single-shot players with a stake in the outcomes. Parks Department officials should facilitate a stakeholder analysis (refer again to note 4) with these members so they can participate in assessing who else should be involved, whether as members or as consultants, and on what basis. This is where criteria from all four administrative legacies can come into play as more than an abstract discussion. Advisory committee members want to know who will likely affect the content of the plan (e.g., whose values and powers are at stake), what rules and processes should be followed and why,

and which parties currently have decision-making authority. Parks officials can assess the extent to which committee members are themselves invoking values or criteria from the administrative legacies, and whether other criteria are being neglected. It is not necessary that all four legacies be equally prominent in developing the site plan, but it is important that their principles and values receive consideration. This improves the educational potential of the deliberations while building legitimacy for the resulting plan in the eyes of affected stakeholders. There is, however, no formulaic answer to the question of how one knows when a successful balance of competing values is achieved. Doing this work is like making bread: the basic ingredients may remain the same from recipe to recipe, but the baker must take into consideration the local setting and conditions to decide how to adjust temperature, timing, and quantities of ingredients to make a good loaf of bread every time. Even then, there will be contending standards by which interested parties wish to judge the loaf.

## CONCLUSION

Leadership in American public life is intentionally frustrated by diffusion of powers among many public officials and among multiple sectors of society. It is intentionally weakened out of fear for its excesses. Ironically, this condition sometimes provokes intense desire for just what we fear most—the charismatic leader who charms us with articulate and emotional pleas, who supplies winning ideas and achievements that fascinate us. We have had many such leaders, some achieving fame well beyond their generation, most often for leading the American people through the most trying circumstances. Others achieved more notoriety than fame, and they remind us of the perils and fickleness of relying on charismatic leadership in public life. The founders taught us the wisdom of taking precautions against the free play of such leaders. They established a system of governance that encourages us to rely on more modest types of leadership.

   Much of the leadership theory we have reviewed in this chapter is of this modest sort. It focuses on leadership of groups for more routine matters of task effectiveness, concern for maturation and professional development within organizations, conciliatory practices designed to draw citizens into public discourse and engagement, and on the stewardship roles of subordinate career officials. We have focused on leadership in shared-power contexts, first because this is the kind of leadership that is most amenable to responsible exercise, and second because it is the kind of leadership increasingly needed in daily life—for the maintenance of regular affairs, for our education as citizens, and for the preservation of our public institutions in an increasingly fragmented world.

## STUDY QUESTIONS

   1.  Explain why the American founders distrusted leaders.
   2.  What factors contribute to conditions of fragmented power in American society?
   3.  Summarize the strengths and weaknesses of trait theories, contingency theories, and group theories of leadership.
   4.  What are the strengths and weaknesses of conciliatory leadership?
   5.  How does the legacy leadership model differ from the other theories of leadership?
   6.  Conduct a legacy-based stakeholder analysis (see note 4 for further details) of the "Tumult in Prairie County" case at the beginning of Part II of this text. What conciliatory practices can be applied to this case? What other leadership theories or roles apply?

## NOTES

1. This chapter cites the first and second editions of *Leadership for the Common Good: Tackling Public Problems in a Shared-Power World.* Complete publication information for both editions follows:

Bryson, John M., and Barbara C. Crosby. 1992. *Leadership for the Common Good: Tackling Public Problems in a Shared-Power World.* San Francisco, CA: Jossey-Bass.

Crosby, Barbara C., and John M. Bryson. 2005. *Leadership for the Common Good: Tackling Public Problems in a Shared-Power World.* 2d ed. San Francisco, CA: Jossey-Bass.

2. Literature related to leadership is extensive. Several of the social science disciplines have handbooks published periodically with a section on leadership. These are good places to start for a systematic review of leadership. The bibliography included with this volume also provides a good starting point for those wishing to conduct their own study of the literature.

3. While there is an early literature on women who lead, much of the research and theory development has occurred in the last 25 years. The literature cited in this section provides examples, but it is not comprehensive. Applied areas such as health and nonprofit leadership have developed a related literature. Similarly, there is a growing body of literature that focuses on both public- and private-sector leadership related to women. Also, since the early 1990s, a number of centers for the study and promotion of women in leadership have been created. For example, the National Education for Women's "Leadership Oregon" is a Hatfield School program associated with a Rutgers-based national network of such programs.

4. The following is an abbreviated summary of some of the tools we believe are important to carrying out public leadership roles. These tools are intended to facilitate conciliatory problem solving in a scarce resource environment, and to enlist the continuing support of the necessary stakeholders. The tools are organized around the central questions that conciliatory practices are intended to answer.

### How Do You Choose Whom to Involve?

This is an exercise in "stakeholder analysis," which raises important questions that affect the design as well as the outcome of the process. Typical questions used to conduct such an analysis are listed below (also see Miller, Shinn, and Bentley 1994, chap. 6):

- Who shares authority in the decision setting?
- Who shares power and capacity (with or without authority) to get the job done in the affected setting?
- What jurisdictions are involved with the policy issue, problem, or setting?
- Who will be saddled with significant aspects of implementation if an agreement is reached?
- Who is the group allegedly representing?
- What key values are at stake, and what groups are most sensitive to them?
- Who will be affected by the outcomes of the process?
- Which groups or individuals have historically been left out of the process, but should be involved?

This exercise should be carried out by an initial group staffed with people who are sensitive to those who may oppose outcomes from the collaborative effort, or who may be disenfranchised by it and lacking a voice. No group should be excluded from the eventual collaboration on principle. This helps ensure that the collaborative process passes appropriate "publicity" and "participatory" tests. In addition, as the process unfolds, it is important to assess who, or which parties, will be critical to holding the agreement together through the subsequent implementation phase. This may not be obvious at the start of the process.

Finally, in conducting stakeholder analysis, it is often useful to construct a stakeholder map. The map's design can help visualize the array of stakeholders by the intensity of their power,

their direct versus indirect relation to the process and desired outcomes, their degree of interest, their access to resources, their relation to the initial leading group, and/or their organizational identities. Such maps also help participants visualize the pattern of institutional relationships that define their community or policy subsystem. There is no single best way to design such maps, and a collaborative group may end up constructing more than one for different purposes. Two common designs for such maps include (1) concentric rings with a core group or organization at the center, with other stakeholders arrayed at different levels around the core; and (2) a networked array or constellation with no core group or organization. More elaborate stakeholder charts and diagrams are offered in the literature (cf. Crosby and Bryson 2005, 83–84, 203–5, 262, 283), but we think workgroups should tailor such visual aids in their own way and strive for a balance between simplicity in visual presentation and comprehensiveness in order to preserve their usefulness.

### How Do You Manage Conflicting Values?

Conciliatory practices entail keeping track of value differences that participants care about. This is a leadership task of the highest order. First, those who wish to lead must reflect on and articulate what matters most to them in the collaborative process. Second, they must understand and promote respect for what other participants really care about—what draws them into the collaborative process (Crosby and Bryson 2005, 37–42). Through use of group facilitation techniques such as periodic brainstorming, nominal-group, and values clarification exercises, leaders must keep track of emerging values as they are discovered in the process. Many participants will prioritize criteria differently. Conciliating practices do not disregard these differences; rather, they promote respect inclusion for them. Exhibit 12.6 illustrates a framework developed by the Rural Resource Management team (Behn and Vaupel 1982; Miller, Shinn, and Bentley 1994) for tracking multiple interests and values.

As the decision process moves forward, participants may say, "I cannot support that alternative because. . . ." Such statements often articulate meanings not adequately captured in enumerated criteria. Exploring and reflecting upon these meanings contributes to a richer understanding of relevant values, thereby enhancing the "problem structuring" phase of the process. The way a group defines its values affects the definition of the problems or issues the group wishes to act upon and helps focus the group on particular kinds of decision outcomes (Stone 2002). This aspect of conciliatory practice is usually untidy and open-ended, often provoking suggestions about reweighing criteria and offering new alternatives or variations of existing alternatives.

A task-oriented leader may see these efforts as distractions from the "real" work of decision making—as "politics" in a negative or irrational sense. This is often a mistake, because it presumes that such leaders have already adequately defined the problem, and that they really do not care to listen and cultivate dialogue through which broader commitments and consensus may be built. Moreover, it is common to discover new values or see new alternatives that had not manifested themselves in participants' minds in earlier stages. In the process, people with varied interests may discover a truth greater than either party carried into the debate, or at least identify one that each party finds worth holding in common. This is what civil discourse is all about. Keeping track of values offers a way for seemingly disparate individuals and groups to find and articulate common ground upon which some decisional agreement becomes feasible. The results may not be "optimal" in the traditional managerial or economic sense, but they are likely more politically palatable and sustainable.

Exhibit 12.6   **Keeping Track of Values/Decision-Making Framework**

**Decision-Making Framework**

|              | Alternative A | Alternative B | Alternative C |
|--------------|---------------|---------------|---------------|
| Criterion 1  |               |               |               |
| Criterion 2  |               |               |               |
| Criterion 3  |               |               |               |

*Source:* Based on Miller, Shinn, and Bentley (1994).

## How Do You Keep Everyone Committed to the Process?

Drawing in affected stakeholders and keeping track of values are necessary functions for sustaining and facilitating group interaction and commitment. The players must continually perceive an interest in staying in the game and believe that the process is, on balance, fair and equitable. Ensuring this involves looking for opportunities to reframe or modify alternatives and make concessions that satisfy the priorities of multiple groups. This can be achieved in part through a "rolling alternative" strategy. It is similar to the negotiation strategy of writing umbrella statements, or statements that capture the interests of contending parties such as business and environmental groups in regulatory contexts (cf. Fisher et al. 2011; Ury et al. 1988). Keeping track of what the players care about also enables leaders to identify potential agreements or political solutions to apparent conflicts. For example, it may be possible to identify trades sequenced across time—business concessions (immediate timber harvests) at one point, and environmental concessions at another (land exchanges that enhance conservation).

Conciliatory practices yield varying levels of agreement on specific issues, ranging from no agreement to complete consensus. An important aspect of such practices includes recording patterns of agreement and disagreement. For example, an ad hoc stakeholder advisory group recently presented a management plan to the Oregon Fish and Wildlife Commission. They had developed the plan through a collaborative process that did not come to complete consensus on the preferred alternative. The group decided that they had gone as far as they could on the issues, and that the plan preferred by most group members should go forward as the recommendation of the group. The preferred plan was then improperly characterized in public as representing complete agreement by the advisory group, rather than as a plan with substantial agreement and some dissent. The political backlash that ensued could have been forestalled by recording and presenting the nature of both the agreement and the disagreement. Those who disagree must be given their due. Recognizing the dissenting parties helps sustain their commitment to the process and reinforces the idea that the process provides opportunities to revisit issues subsequently. This helps build trust in the integrity of the process, and thereby raises the level of civic capacity.

Another aspect of sustaining commitment and healthy group dynamics means taking the complexities of public problems and the reality of multiple leaders seriously. Leaders must know their own limitations as well as their strengths and seek out other leaders who can compensate for the weaknesses. In some situations, at least, the leader must learn to become a good follower—sometimes referred to as leading from behind (Blanchard, Randolph, and Grazier 2005). Furthermore, the most able leaders may not be the best persons to serve as facilitators of group deliberations. Nor may a leader with the most expertise on a subject be the right person to represent a group during deliberative and coalition-building phases. Rather, such leaders may be more effective playing supportive or advisory roles. In many institutional contexts, it is common to hear people say that it's not what you know, but who you know, that matters. Such statements invoke ethical relationships defined by status rather than by expertise or ability. Such status may be formal or informal, and it may confer considerable influence, authoritative opinion, and credibility. It is critical that leaders identify and involve group members who possess such status, and, when appropriate, defer to them as leaders in their own right.

### How Do You Manage Decision Making in Conciliatory Processes?

In public contexts, arranging the steps necessary for decision making and implementation can be extraordinarily complicated. The multiple, overlapping jurisdictions involved in the process all have their own procedures, requiring multiple sets of meetings and forms of official ratification. At state and federal levels, administrative procedure acts dictate notice of proposed rules and widely varying procedures for conducting hearings and adjudicating disputes. These are explained in some detail in chapter 14. Limits may also exist on the degree to which public officials can delegate authority. This often conditions the circumstances for when and how to include others, and can easily stymie consensus-building dynamics. Local or community-based decision processes are generally more fluid, but are hardly bereft of their own procedures, rituals, and structures. In fact, the lack of standard procedural rules and the proliferation of special districts amid county, city, and town governments makes the coordination of decision making even more difficult. The differences in urban and rural governance also present challenges. Rural governance activity is usually much more informal, downplaying (or even ignoring) formal legal standards and professional norms in favor of community ties that include friendships, clans, religious affiliations, fraternal clubs, and so forth.

The complexities of decision-making steps in a shared-power world can make specialized tracking and coordination a necessity. It may require establishment of a coordinating body with the expertise, and perhaps with some authority of its own, to effectively manage such processes. In Oregon, the establishment of Oregon Solutions (http://www.orsolutions.org) provides a robust example. The Oregon Solutions approach to problem solving arose from the commitment of Oregon governor John Kitzhaber (in office 1995–2003 and 2011– ) to address the challenges of finding community-based solutions to a range of problems. Oregon Solutions uses a community governance system that has the following elements: a community-defined problem or opportunity; a governor's designation of the project and appointment of a community convener; creation of a solutions team of federal, state, local, or other government entities, businesses, nonprofits, and key citizens; development of an integrated solution; and a declaration of cooperation and commitment signed by the resulting solutions team. Oregon Solutions staff members facilitate projects addressing dozens of public problems, ranging from transportation planning disputes to alternative energy and job training initiatives.

CHAPTER 13

# THE ROLE OF PUBLIC ADMINISTRATION IN PUBLIC POLICY AND ANALYSIS

The true politician . . . takes human nature . . . as he finds it, a compound of good and ill qualities, of good and ill tendencies—imbued with powers and actuated by passions and propensities which blend enjoyment with suffering and make the causes of welfare the causes of misfortune. . . . He will favor all those institutions and plans which tend to make men happy according to their natural bent, which multiply the sources of individual enjoyment and increase those of national resource and strength—taking care to infuse in each case all the ingredients which can be devised as preventives or correctives of the evil which is the eternal concomitant of temporal blessing.

*(Alexander Hamilton 1795/1973, 19:59–60)*

The supposed sequence by which solutions are found for preexisting problems, as if they were fixed in concrete, should give way to the notion that man-made solutions also create man-made problems.

*(Aaron Wildavsky 1979, 23)*

The very categories of thought underlying rational analysis are themselves a kind of paradox, defined in political struggle. They do not exist before or without politics, and because they are necessarily abstract (they are categories of thought, after all), they can have multiple meanings. Thus, analysis is itself a creature of politics; it is a strategically crafted argument, designed to create ambiguities and paradoxes and resolve them in a particular direction.

*(Deborah Stone 1997, 7)*

In its broadest sense, public policy is a reflection of how people in political society define a good life, and how they try to achieve it through their political institutions. Public policy thus comprises substantive perspectives and values that characterize a regime, mixed with institutional processes for realizing them. In a political society that prizes liberty above all else—and toward that end diffuses power among branches, levels of government, and sectors of political society—the policy process is bound to entail confusion and contradiction. In the United States, public policy can be none other than a host of "continuities in conflict" (MacIntyre 1984).

This is why American public policy is so difficult to understand and study. It defies the dominance of any one theme, typology, framework, theory, or model of explanation. This does not mean, however, that attempts at explanation are useless. They are in fact quite useful, as long as one recognizes that each explanation may obscure as much or more as it explains. For these reasons, it is important for leaders of the policy process to be armed with a variety of models in order to compensate for the limitations of any single approach. This becomes even more important within the context of America's constitutional systems of governance, which seek to balance competing values.

In this chapter, we first address the character of public policy in the United States in light of constitutional history and the Democratic Balancewheel model of public administration presented in chapter 6. Public policy is shaped in significant ways by the content and evolution of many constitutional values and doctrines, as well as by the evolution of the governance traditions which now inform administrative practice. Following the discussion of how our constitutional systems of governance shape the policy relationships among the private, public, and nonprofit sectors, we review some commonly used models of the policy process and policy analysis in the contemporary literature, and highlight their strengths and weaknesses in understanding how policy is developed and implemented. Throughout the chapter, we emphasize the pivotal roles played in the policy process by the public administration.

## THE CHARACTER OF AMERICAN PUBLIC POLICY

As described in chapters 4 through 6, the American constitutional tradition revolves around the belief that ordered liberty is a central principle of a good life, and that a republic is the best governing form for achieving this goal. Students and practitioners consistently affirm this belief. Beyond that, however, agreement begins to fray. The founders were no different. Their visions of the "proper" republic ranged from Alexander Hamilton's feverish commercial republic, to Thomas Jefferson's modest agrarian republic, to the Puritans' covenantal republic. Their views of good public policy varied accordingly and have been evident in the struggles over public policy ever since. The four governance traditions identified in our Democratic Balancewheel model in chapter 6 evolved from these struggles and continue to inform policy debate in distinct ways. For example, our governments cannot effectively design and implement a policy without including procedures for access and input by affected interest groups, and without building in protections for individual rights that may be adversely affected.

Moreover, considerations regarding policy effectiveness must include assessments of administrative responsiveness to the public as well as to policy oversight bodies. Effectiveness is also conditioned upon assessments of feasibility, capacity, and the anticipation of political and organizational pathologies that may compromise it. Thus, the four governance traditions we described at the end of chapter 4 affect our judgments of what makes good policy. With each of these models, as we summarized in Exhibit 5.1, there is a complementary administrative role that ensures successful implementation of the governance model. For example, the Hamiltonian strong executive model requires administrators to take greater responsibility for policy design than is the case with the Jeffersonian model, which assumes high levels of citizen engagement in shaping policy initiatives. On the other hand, the Madisonian model presumes administrators will play a central mediating role in managing conflicts among competing interest groups who are the major drivers of the policy process. While all of these models are in play in the policy development and implementation process, they are not in play in equal balance. Rather, the character of public policy is skewed by the dominance of one vision of a proper republic or another over time. This

reminds us that policy debates most often reflect different visions of what is best for a system of ordered liberty.

In chapter 5, we reviewed the historical periods that gave greater shape and focus to each of the various democratic governance models that are embedded in our constitutional foundations. For about a century, public policy reflected the character of Jefferson's agrarian republic, with elements of covenantal republicanism weaved throughout. From the Gilded Age forward, the character of public policy shifted to reflect the evolution of a commercial republic, with a heavy emphasis on Hamiltonian concerns for efficient and effective administration to counterbalance the proliferation and dominance of interest groups. We documented this history in considerable detail in chapter 5 and remind readers here of its relevance as a framework for thinking about public policy development and implementation in the United States.

## CONSTRUCTING A COMMERCIAL REPUBLIC

The failings of government under the Articles of Confederation led the founders to rethink the stimulative and regulatory roles of the national government over the country's economy. In addition to the reorganization of government, the new U.S. Constitution established national authority and uniform standards to regulate commerce among the states, to protect the sanctity of contracts, to establish and value currency, to establish a national postal system, to grant patents on new inventions, to establish uniform bankruptcy laws, to fix standards for weights and measures, and to levy excise taxes on the fruits of trade. It established the coast guard and the navy primarily to police harbors and protect sea lanes of commerce. It also structured a more uniform environment for social policy and citizen behavior: records and judicial proceedings in one state were recognized in all others, and the privileges and protections granted to citizens in one state were extended to visiting citizens from other states. These protections and greater uniformity were reinforced by the adoption of the due process and equal protection clauses in the Fourteenth Amendment (1868), which resulted in the application of many federal rights and powers to the states. The subsequent liberalization of corporate charters by the states, along with the elevation of corporations to the status of legal persons by the U.S. Supreme Court, cemented the commercial republic into a dominant place in American society. This historical development is reviewed in greater detail in chapter 5.

The U.S. Constitution thus gave the federal government significant policy tools with which to promote and regulate commerce, and the states and their communities have since followed suit with policies that strongly favor economic development as their first priority. The combination of federal and state commercial policies provides a vast infrastructure of laws, transportation systems, communication systems, and community structures that support and subsidize the business sector. Economic life flourishes as a result. It is hardly surprising, then, that commentators on the Constitution characterize it as an economic document as much as a political one. Indeed, the new science of political economy emerged as an integral aspect of the Enlightenment and heavily influenced the American founders. The Lockean belief in acquisitiveness as a fundamental human drive to be promoted rather than suppressed informs Federalist thought as well as modern economic theory and practice. It is now sewn deeply into American life, so much so that the market—the means by which the acquisitive passion is inflamed—now serves as the dominant model of society (not just of the economy) for many Americans.

> Society is viewed as a collection of autonomous, rational decision makers who have no community life. Their interactions consist entirely of trading with one another to maximize

their individual well-being. They each have objectives or preferences, they each compare alternative ways of attaining their objectives, and they each choose the way that yields the most satisfaction. They maximize their self-interest through rational calculation. (Deborah Stone 1997, 9)

This image now pervades all spheres of American life, especially politics, where people speak of votes being traded, services bought and sold, customers served, and where public policy "produces" outputs as if from an assembly line. The idea of a complex administrative state that efficiently polices markets and produces benefits and services for its citizens logically accompanied this image in tandem with the rise of industrial markets. And management thought has developed in league with it (see chapter 7). As illustrated below, market life also strongly influences our models of policymaking, implementation, and analysis.

Much of modern policy study is organized by economic themes such as regulation of firms and market behavior; distribution and redistribution of income, goods, and services; and even self-regulation through restructuring of market incentives (see discussion in chapter 3). Most students of public policy are now heavily schooled in economic approaches to policy analysis. In fact, most policy analysis texts treat government action as simply (and desirably) a matter of intervention to correct the operation of markets where normal market dynamics break down or are not present. According to this model, government action should be the exception rather than the rule. This kind of thinking takes for granted the massive infrastructure put into place by our governments to support and subsidize a complex array of markets with widely varying structures and dynamics. This is a mistake analogous to focusing only on the annual operating budget while taking for granted the huge capital budget that undergirds it.

The public is occasionally reminded of the larger reality of government support for the economy when controversial business projects are proposed that involve significant outlays of public money and resources. In Salt Lake City, Utah, for example, a prominent businessperson recently led a campaign to build a professional soccer complex in the metro area to boost support for his new Major League Soccer team Real Salt Lake. He sought support from state, county, and local governments to purchase land and build infrastructure, arguing that well over $100 million in public support would yield even greater economic benefits over the long term. When the Salt Lake County government refused to support the project, citing flawed income projections in the project proposal, leading state politicians stepped in quickly to redirect county tax money and appropriate state funding to support the project—this despite strong public opposition to the massive appropriation of tax dollars for an obviously risky venture. At the national level, we have all witnessed the massive bailout of commercial and investment banks that were deemed "too big to fail," and who brought themselves as well as much of the global economy to its knees during the 2007–8 financial crisis. Though extremely controversial and dispiriting, without the massive bailout and subsequent economic stimulus plan implemented by the federal government, credit for operating many businesses and farms would have frozen solid, leading to widespread market failures and a depression far worse than we have already experienced.

One quickly surmises from these cases how blurred the line really is between public policy and private-sector business and nonprofit activities. Public support comes not only through direct financial subsidies but also through other broad institutional influences established in our constitutions and laws. For example, property rights, binding contracts, tax exemptions for nonprofit organizations and tax subsidies for private firms, social and economic insurance, and monetary and fiscal policy are established by governments to stimulate market exchanges and to maintain as much predictability about the future as possible. In essence, markets are places where people

engage in the voluntary exchange of goods and services only when certain amounts and types of risk are adequately hedged, some costs are subsidized, and a stable infrastructure is established to support the exchanges over the long run.

In all but the simplest of exchanges—as in bartering, where services or material goods change hands—conflicts about exchange are settled outside the transaction itself. For example, the value of a dollar bill is not determined by the exchange itself, and it is only partly determined by the aggregation of exchanges over space and time. Much of the value of any given transaction is an artifact of a uniform currency and of monetary policy conducted by the U.S. Federal Reserve System. What ensures the durability of exchanges over time is a commitment to enforce property rights, including contractual obligations—whether implied or literal—by courts. And market fluctuations are buffered substantially by fiscal stabilization policies at federal and state levels. These public institutions must function effectively before markets can produce goods and services in a satisfactory manner.

## PUBLIC AND PRIVATE GOODS

Once the public infrastructure is put into place, markets can then be relied upon to signal production levels and allocate resources as *private goods*, while governments produce *public goods*. In many economics and public policy texts, public goods are treated as those goods and services that, because of their nature, are underproduced in the marketplace. Exhibit 13.1 presents a common typology of economic goods.

On one axis is tenure or excludability; on the other is consumption or rivalry. Private goods are those over which an individual can have complete ownership. The owner can exclude others from their use or appropriation. Private goods are consumed individually, and thus entail rivalry over consumption. An apple, an article of clothing, or a bottle of soda are typical examples of private goods. In contrast, public goods are those for which excludability is low, and for which one person's enjoyment has no effect on another's enjoyment (hence, no rivalry). A view of the mountains from a housing subdivision qualifies as a public good, as does law enforcement, defense, and clean air. The typology identifies other common goods as well. *Toll goods* are characterized by a lack of rivalry in consumption and the ability to exclude others. For example, all who can pay the toll may enter and travel on the same toll road. *Common-pool goods* are characterized by rivalry in consumption and low levels of excludability, such as fish in the ocean, timber in the national forests, or animals grazing on public lands. The low excludability of these goods makes them susceptible to degradation unless carefully regulated and managed. Failing to regulate such goods results in their unintended depletion—a condition known as the "tragedy of the commons" (Hardin 1968).

Most public, toll, and common-pool goods are provided or regulated by government jurisdictions because market incentives alone cannot lead to their efficient production and/or allocation. Only private goods that are exclusive and whose consumption promotes rivalry are ideally suited to freely functioning markets. Thus, the public sector does not simply build and manage much of the economic infrastructure for markets; it also takes responsibility for producing public goods, regulating the commons, and equitably managing toll goods. Those who work in public life cannot ignore this "visible hand" of government support for the private sector (Chandler 1993; Moss 2002).

Another dimension of this visible hand exists in the world of government contracting. Some markets exist solely because governments directly sponsor the production of certain goods and services. The vast military-industrial complex in the United States clearly reflects this arrange-

Exhibit 13.1    **The Nature of Economic Goods**

| | | | |
|---|---|---|---|
| **Rivalry in consumption** | Low | Common Pool Goods (Fish in a pond, hiking trails in a national park) | Private Goods (Bottled water, your house) |
| | High | Public Goods (National defense, view of your favorite mountain) | Toll Goods (Highway, municipal drinking water) |
| | | Low | High |
| | | **Excludability** | |

ment, as do large construction firms that live mainly from one public road or highway project to another. The expansion of the nonprofit sector in recent decades is also due in large part to increased government contracts for social services. Whole industries and service systems exist because of government sponsorship.

## THE RATIONALE FOR ECONOMIC REGULATION

Given the close relationship between government and the economy described above, it is easier to see why economic regulation is necessary. Markets do not function well without a lot of public infrastructure, and regulatory policies form an integral part of that infrastructure. Exhibit 13.2 outlines the most common justifications for regulation of markets.

Despite these justifications, however, regulatory policies remain subject to serious criticism and have been under active attack since the late 1980s (Cooper 2009). Critics complain that regulation interferes with market efficiency, resulting in higher costs and prices, excess profits, and restricted choices for consumers. They argue that regulatory agencies are easily captured by special interests, that the regulatory rulemaking process is dominated by these "insiders," and that regulators cannot effectively anticipate all the innovative and aberrant behaviors of firms in finding loopholes and ways around regulations. Accordingly, they advocate alternatives to regulation wherever possible, and in ways that enhance rather than retard market principles. Exhibit 13.3 briefly summarizes the more commonly advocated alternatives.

While the criticisms of and alternatives to regulation have merit, they rest on an overly simplistic claim that markets are generally efficient and will effectively police themselves because of the discipline of market competition. This of course presumes that markets are "naturally" competitive, and that consumers have sufficient knowledge of their products, practices, and prices to purchase the "best" products and services. Unfortunately, these ideal market conditions rarely if ever exist in the real world. Businesses often conspire to restrict competition and information, and when they succeed, intervention is needed to correct the ill effects. In many cases, we want our governments to prevent them from succeeding in such efforts in the first place.

Exhibit 13.2   **Common Justifications for Government Regulation**

1. **Need to regulate "natural" monopolies and concentrated oligopolies.** Sometimes monopolies or oligopolies (where a few large firms control the vast majority of a market) are the most efficient and stable structure for an industry. Utilities are the classic example. Most or all people must be served; the infrastructure is massive and expensive to maintain; and there is a public interest in standardization of the service. However, the controlling firm(s) must not be allowed to unfairly restrict the supply of the utility good or service in order to raise prices, and oversight is needed to ensure quality of service.

2. **Equity concerns:** (1) due to universal entitlement to some basic good or service regardless of ability to pay; (2) some sources of income/profit (windfalls) are undeserved and should be redistributed through regulation; and (3) other types of income/profit are especially deserving (minimum wage standards, some price supports, especially for food staples such as milk) and should be increased by regulation.

3. **Efforts to encourage proper use of natural resources.** Short-run profit outlook in some markets is highly wasteful of common resources (the protection of wild lands and natural habitat, for example).

4. **Need to ensure that participants in the marketplace take account of externalities or "spillover" effects of their actions.** Most control for pollution and other harmful external effects of market development are justified by a concern for the "spillover" effects.

5. **Problems of unavailability, inadequacy, or fraudulent information about health, safety, financial services, or other matters of critical public concern.** Market firms often strive to restrict or distort information about products or services to their advantage, thus reducing consumers' ability to make informed and efficient choices.

6. **Prevention of destructive competition and anticompetitive behavior.** Aggressive firms often engage in predatory practices in attempts to limit or destroy competition, or to seek unfair advantage in the marketplace through tying arrangements and other types of collusion that limit entry by new firms into the market. Ironically, free or unfettered markets often lead to behaviors that will destroy competition. Thus, it is often important to distinguish "free" markets from competitive markets!

7. **Protection of consumers from sharply rising prices and windfall profits.** Dramatic fluctuations in some markets can cause immense social/economic disruption that governments must deal with in order to stabilize social and economic conditions and protect consumers. Market fluctuations (and manipulation) that cause debilitating changes in the price of staple goods such as food or basic utilities (water, power, etc.) are classic examples.

8. **Efforts to promote or preserve key industries.** At any given time in history, a nation-state has key industries that are regarded as vital to its economic and political well being (e.g., transportation, communications, finance, defense) or supply critical raw materials that might otherwise be debilitated or squandered under free-market conditions.

9. **Decisions to provide service to special groups through the use of cross-subsidies.** Markets favor lucrative, densely populated areas, and will often not serve rural areas and small communities. Firms must often be required to cross-subsidize services to these areas, or government must take over this aspect of the market entirely. The classic example is the U.S. Postal Service.

10. **Control of competing industries.** Markets are often short-sighted in maintaining a wider range of alternatives in key industries—such as energy, transportation, and technology. If left to their own devices, markets would tend toward monopoly of one industry, and kill or retard alternative industries.

11. **Preservation of established property rights.** Public practices such as licensure help protect property rights that support key industries and professional practices. Without them, these markets would collapse due to erosion of those rights. Hence, the need for licensing of television stations, medical practices, etc.

12. **Controlling to perverse incentives.** Using the financial industry as an example, regulating reserve requirements of banks, limiting leverage practices, preventing conflicts of interest, and insuring deposits helps avoid perverse behaviors that lead to panic bank runs, sell-offs, frozen credit, and destruction of the industry.

Exhibit 13.3  **Commonly Advocated Alternatives to Regulation**

1. **Tradable Permits.** Firms buy/sell/trade permits for scarce resources or to emit pollutants ("emissions trading"). The cost of permits limits entry to the market and/or incentivizes corrective action (i.e., reduction of pollution).
2. **Economic Incentives.** Employ user fees, price caps, earnings sharing, corrective taxes, grants, subsidies, vouchers, or tax credits as behavioral incentives in place of regulations.
3. **Self-Regulation.** Use of industry associations and voluntary standards to guide and supervise market practices in place of direct government regulation.
4. **Enhanced Competition.** Removal of barriers to market entry or limits on the services that may be provided by those already in the market in order to reduce costs and improve the quality and diversity of products and services.
5. **Replace Performance Standards with Engineering Standards.** Replace regulations that specify means of compliance, with specified targets that regulated organizations can meet in the manner they think best.
6. **Convert Regulators into Information Providers and Educators.** Regulatory agencies de-emphasize coercive and intervening roles, and instead provide helpful information about standards and practices across industries and let firms use the information as they see best.
7. **Regulatory Tailoring.** Regulations are tailored to characteristics of markets. For example, regulations designed to control large corporations may be inappropriate or impose undue burdens on small businesses. Regulations designed for large, dense urban areas may be inappropriate for small rural areas with highly dispersed populations.

Furthermore, although government regulation often has its flaws, the flaws are frequently overstated. Steven Croley ably demonstrates "that the cynical view of regulation shows far too little attention to the actual processes through which administrative agencies regulate, and that such inattention is largely responsible for the dominant, jaundiced view of regulation" (2008, 4). The actual study of the legal and institutional processes of regulation reveal "more optimistic assessments" of the nature and efficacy of regulation in a variety of policy contexts. Croley's "administrative process theory" emphasizes a much wider field of autonomy (from political manipulation) gained primarily through administrative law for regulators to actually pursue broader public interests than the cynical view of regulation permits (2008, 53–76). For instance, he demonstrates through real case studies that administrators can, and "often are motivated by concerns for general, public-oriented interests" (73, and see chapters 10–13). He also notes how it is quite possible for agencies to "attenuate the advantages that more powerful interest groups enjoy over less powerful interest groups in the legislative arena" (74).

Perhaps an even more persuasive case for regulation is made when we examine the abuses that occur when regulation is absent in markets. The Wall Street scandals that were revealed in the wake of the 2007–8 financial crash arose because most of the regulatory infrastructure for the banking and investment industry had been gutted over thirty years. Commercial and investment banks (which includes hedge fund firms) operated in what had become a "shadow banking industry" that was purposely devoid of any regulation or oversight (Financial Crisis Inquiry Commission, 2011). The industry was rife with conflicts of interest, fraud, and abuse. It became a tightly concentrated oligopoly of firms that were "too big to fail," and manipulated and contrived highly complex financial instruments that were designed to fool consumers as well as fellow investors. These firms, through their wide latitude of corporate discretion, shifted their missions from serving the financial needs of other markets and clients (firms, countries, municipalities, and individuals), to serving themselves at everyone else's expense—violating fiduciary relationships and the public trust across the globe. Even many insiders to these firms wondered in amazement how governments had turned a blind eye to these destructive practices (Green 2012).

## EXCESSES OF THE COMMERCIAL REPUBLIC

The Greek philosopher Aristotle observed that regimes tend to die from an excess of their own virtues. This insight was not lost on the American founders. Many Anti-Federalist founders warned that the Constitution's strong commercial bent would encourage luxury and licentiousness, and thereby gradually corrode civic virtue in the people. People can lose their capacity for political and civic engagement as they focus more of their energy on commercial and consumer activity, and as economic thought and behavior intrude upon other spheres of life. The Anti-Federalists argued that the loss of civic virtue would endanger the future of the republic by depleting the numbers of people willing and able to serve in public life, and by enervating the sense of a public good that is more than a mere aggregation of private interests. Their concerns resonate with many critics of American society today and call attention to the need for policies and administrative practices that bolster civic commitment and development.

As noted in chapter 5, the civic governance tradition weakened with the rise of an industrial political economy dominated by expert professionals in both the private and public sectors. It is weakened further by the free mobility of business interests in the economy, especially at local levels where the civic governance tradition works best. Firms with substantial capital and large numbers of employees are free to leave communities when it suits their bottom line. Such actions can devastate communities for decades, and some never recover. A variety of public policies— including job training programs, unemployment benefits programs, community development funds, and a host of human and social services programs designed to help individuals until they find new jobs—exist to help communities cope with the worst effects. Local politicians and career public servants devote tremendous energy trying to attract new businesses, diversify the local economy as a buffer against such disruptions, and seek federal and state aid for redevelopment. In effect, they must rebuild or readjust the local economy not only for the sake of commerce, but as a viable infrastructure for civic life. However, the need for nurturing civic governance as part of this redevelopment effort often gets overlooked because local governments are so balkanized, often desperate for revenue, and thus unable to exert much leverage over the large firms and well-heeled developers who dominate development policy and process.

The interests of longtime residents of traditional neighborhoods and communities are often ignored by these powerful players, and the disruptions to civic life are as radical as they are to the local economy. The growth of gated residential enclaves and exclusive commercial districts symbolizes the fiscal and social isolation of community groups, one from another, and the loss of a sense of interdependence and common good of a broader community. From the civic governance perspective, the great challenge lies in rekindling that sense of interdependence and mutual obligation to a common good in the context of the commercial republic. Chapter 12 describes a variety of conciliatory practices that can help toward that end (see especially note 4); however, it is unlikely that local leaders can achieve this without some attention by state and national leaders to what Hamilton called "preventives or correctives of the evils" which naturally accompany the opulence and success born of our commercial bent (Hamilton 1795/1973).

Hamilton, while an ardent advocate and designer of our commercial republic, also sought aggressive regulation and restraint on commercial practices deemed injurious to communities and markets. He was well aware that economic wealth would also become a source of tremendous political power wielded for the sake of private interests that can be injurious to the public good. Thus, what we promote with one hand, we must regulate with the other. Similarly, Aaron Wildavsky, a renowned scholar of public policy, urged policymakers and analysts to adopt "the notion that man-made solutions also create man-made problems" (Wildavsky 1979, 23). We see

in these insights a basic policy principle which shares the same kind of dynamic tension as the Democratic Balancewheel model of public administration. The good we achieve through a set of commercially oriented policies must be restrained and balanced by corrective or ameliorative policies that protect and nurture civic capacity and engagement.

In this light, it is desirable to implement federal and state measures that (1) enhance the powers of local governments over planning and zoning policy, (2) increase the fiscal stability of local governments in the face of economic cycles and business mobility, and (3) promote the growth and stability of the nonprofit sector, or at least do not retard development of civic associations, advocacy groups, and religious organizations. Agriculture policy designed to promote local agriculture and viable family farms are consistent with these larger efforts to prevent the market system from unduly eroding local civic life and institutions. Market dynamics naturally favor urban populations; this requires balancing with statewide transportation, communication, and commercial policies that preserve viable rural communities, natural resources, and agrarian life. Policies such as these promote richer interaction—a sense of reciprocity among people in social and political life—and thereby increase awareness of interdependence with one another. As Wildavsky once suggested, "The object of social policy is to make interdependence a facet of everyday individual decision making" (1979, 260). He further argued that if this is done successfully, then citizens become policy analysts as well because they engage in discussion and argument about both the ends and means that affect their daily lives: "Citizenship and analysis are united by the desire to bring people together so that interaction will facilitate learning" (Wildavsky 1979, 261).

We would add, with Thomas McCullough (1991), that *civic* learning also entails holding each other accountable for both *what* we say and do in public life and the *way* we say and do it. Face-to-face dialogue and argument over policy are vital to civic governance; this kind of interaction and the rising sense of interdependence help cultivate more respectful attitudes toward each other, thereby fostering a public etiquette that tempers the conversation.

Attending to the concerns of civic governance through public policy can help us curb the excesses of our commercial republic and increase awareness of the conditions needed for cultivating public leaders with a sense of the common good. Achieving these goals is no easy matter, and a person entering public life for any purpose must be prepared to negotiate an elaborate policy process. Understanding this process is critical.

## WAYS OF UNDERSTANDING PUBLIC POLICY

The policy process entails much more than formal policymaking conducted by legislative bodies. It involves the interaction of citizens animated by a concern or issue they believe deserves public attention. It involves interest groups, agency officials, courts, and politicians who carry the concerns into multiple venues in an effort to get them on agendas where they will be heard and acted upon. And then, if policies are adopted to address the concerns, they must be implemented through organizational processes that can easily pervert the intentions of the policy, fail altogether, or produce consequences no one anticipated. The disparity between intended policy goals and consequences on the ground means that we need to pay attention to policy choices, policy outputs, and policy impacts. Exhibit 13.4 presents a graphic representation of this process.

### Policy Choices

The first step in making policy choices involves deliberating about what we intend to do collectively. Should we do something about the homeless, about the environment, about declining

Exhibit 13.4  **Policy Dynamics**

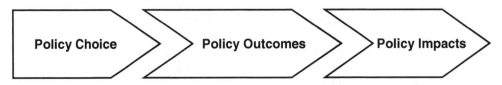

**What we decide  >     What we do >    What the effects are of what we do**

achievement in our public schools? Once a decision is made that something should be done about an issue, then more specific questions arise, which include two dimensions—what we intend to do substantively and how we plan to accomplish that intent. Substantive issues or problems are defined by strategically crafting arguments about their nature and significance (Stone 1997). Words loaded with emotive and symbolic meaning are employed to characterize the problem as one requiring public action, but the range of actions to resolve it is limited. Thus, whoever succeeds in defining the problem exerts tremendous influence over how it is dealt with during implementation. For example, in education policy, those who succeed in making student achievement the focal point for action, and who do so in terms of the performance gap that exists along lines of race and class, will likely dominate the agenda during the process of crafting and implementing solutions. Groups have become much more attentive to monitoring and influencing policy implementation than in the past because they know administrators also exercise considerable discretion in shaping the meaning of policy. Little progress may be made if administrators do not allocate staff and resources that are in alignment with defined objectives.

Policy choices also entail decisions about how authority will be allocated to effectively address the issue or problem. Authority enables the concentration of resources and sets the mandates for action. Policy choices determine how such authority will be allocated across levels of government or among the different sectors of society. Effective policy decisions anticipate how to coordinate governmental and intersectoral mechanisms into integrated delivery systems. They also define paths of accountability and distribute responsibilities. Finally, policy choice must consider how to develop public and constituent support that will help sustain and institutionalize the policy effort. In attempts to close the student achievement gap, for instance, success will depend on how each school principal organizes resources, manages the curriculum, and builds partnerships with parents and stakeholders in the external community.

Additionally, policy choice includes determination of how the choice will be implemented. Traditionally, public goods and services have been directly produced and delivered by governments. The federal government produced and delivered national defense. State governments ensured regulation of fish and wildlife. Local governments provide for streets, sewers, and parks. However, over the last half century, we have seen the emergence of a dizzying array of "tools" to deliver public policy. (This is an issue we cover in greater depth in the second half of chapter 14.) Salamon (2002) argues that a revolution has taken place, and at its heart is a rapid increase in the indirect delivery of policy through an ever-increasing variety of policy tools.

Direct delivery of policy by governments now accounts for well under half of all public policy action, with the larger portion being delivered through indirect means: loans, loan guarantees, grants, contracts, regulations, underwriting bonds, tax expenditures, and more. Delivering public goods and services through nonprofit organizations, special districts, or via contracts with private firms are all parts of policy choice. Each of these types of tools implies different competencies for

administrators and potential effects in outputs and impacts. As Larsen (2008) points out, even the same tool (i.e., a procurement contract for a private vender to provide specific services) can be written in several ways. The U.S. Forest Service, for instance, is experimenting with stewardship contacts where vendors modify the terms and amounts of receipts to deliver a bundle of services over time. Larsen points out that these and other contracting tools can be administered in ways that increase (or fail to increase) the democratic content of the exchange. In summary, policy choice includes consideration of the what, who, and how of policy implementation.

## Policy Outputs

A second way of thinking about policy is to focus on what is produced. Good intentions do not always result in desired outputs. Even with the best planning and implementation, policy outputs may not match expectations. The characteristics of the target population may change, or the methods of program implementation may be compromised. For example, a city council could decide to reduce neighborhood crime related to drug use by increasing community policing activity in certain neighborhoods. The new deployment may induce drug dealers to simply relocate their operations to another neighborhood. Or, as part of the new program, the public safety director might reassign some officers from car patrols to walking or biking neighborhood beats. Patrol officers may view this as an undesirable, low-status assignment and resist using the tactics that will make walking or biking advantageous, and thereby doom the experiment.

Policy outputs may also vary from intentions because bureaucratic routines in the implementing agencies or organizations create trained incapacities for dealing with the new policy problem. Military organizations are notorious for fighting new wars with routines and practices established in previous wars, even when their leaders have mandated the adoption of new warfare strategies and tactics. Outputs can also vary from intentions because of political compromises that make effective implementation impossible. A legislative body may vote to underfund a policy or restrict an agency to ineffectual means of implementation as a concession to powerful interests. For example, one of our colleagues once headed a federal regulatory agency that was not in favor with the president's policy agenda. Instead of seeking to withdraw the agency's legal authority, the president made certain that agency vacancies were never filled; eventually the agency staff shrunk so low that it did not have any capacity to carry out its mission. With the rise of antiregulatory sentiment, it is not uncommon to see legislatures and political executives shift regulatory agency resources away from enforcement functions to information and educational functions in the hopes that firms and organizations will self-regulate.

## Policy Impacts

Policy goals and outputs may be fully aligned but still not produce a difference that matters on the street. For this reason, students of public policy are interested in assessing the impact of policy. Are streets in the neighborhood actually safer? Does a treatment regimen for drug offenders really work? If so, is it more effective than punitive measures such as more prison time? Does allocating more funds for education actually produce children with better education? It might lower student-teacher ratios, but does this really improve educational quality? These are the kinds of questions citizens and policymakers want policy analysts to study.

The distinctions between policy intentions, outputs, and impacts call attention to policy processes. How do we move from good intentions to the right results? As we have noted, policy processes are complex and have tremendous impact on everyday life. It is vital that public servants

understand them in order to improve the prospects for policy success. Scholars and practitioners have developed a variety of policy models that can help us improve our understanding of how these processes work. We review some typical and useful models below.

## MODELS OF THE POLICY PROCESS

Policy models extract some aspect of the policy process, simplify the dynamics, and clarify our thinking about the way policy is made. They are, therefore, abstract representations of empirical reality and are useful for exploring policy processes and their outcomes. Every model has an underlying theory that provides an explanation of how the policy process works. The following is a description of common types of models helpful in understanding policy process.

### Process- and Cycle-Centered Models

Perhaps the most common policy model is a linear policy stage or cycle model that accounts for the various steps in the policymaking process. This model assumes that the most important thing to know about the policy process is that a predictable set of activities occurs in a series of predictable steps or stages over time. These steps, while not discrete, are roughly sequential and can be looped back at the end to create a cycle model, as illustrated in Exhibit 13.5.

*Agenda Setting*

The first stage in this model is agenda setting. In all policymaking settings, an idea about what should be done must get "onto the table." This is no small task, and a number of scholars have focused their research on how this occurs (cf. Baumgartner and Jones 1993; Birkland 1997; Kingdon 1995; Lasswell 1936). Policy ideas are often generated through election campaigns and partisan platforms, advocacy organizations, trade and professional associations, administrative agencies, courts, the press, private think tanks, and academia. In some cases, they are generated by individual citizens. In local government settings, for example, it is not unusual to see a committed citizen with lots of energy and perseverance agitate successfully for new or changed policies. The media often play a vital role in calling attention to policy ideas and can drive an otherwise failing initiative onto the agenda (Dearing and Rodgers 1996). However, most policy ideas fail because the timing is off, the conditions or "window of opportunity" are not ripe, or the ideas are not presented in a compelling way to the people who decide what ends up on the public agenda.

*Policy Formulation*

In the second stage, policy ideas are debated, along with different means to accomplish them. If the goal is to reduce teen pregnancies, what are the best means to accomplish this—abstinence programs, educational programs, family planning programs? Should these be family based, community based, agency based, or contracted out through third parties? Is a single approach warranted, or will a mixed strategy work better? Should this be handled at the state level or the federal level? Always accompanying such discussions are questions of budgets and finance. Questions of governance arise concerning whether a matter should be dealt with by governments, by nonprofits, or through the marketplace. Lobbyists and administrators frequently

Exhibit 13.5  **Policy Stage Typology**

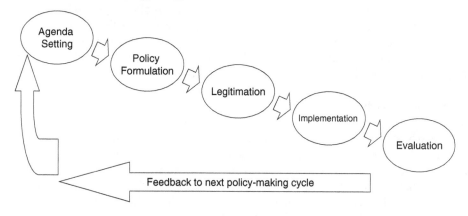

weigh in on problems and solutions during this phase, and policy analysts supply information generated by their studies.

*Policy Legitimation*

Duly elected or appointed decision-making bodies lend legitimacy to new policy through approval processes that culminate with voting. In New England town meetings, the townspeople vote. In council-manager governments, elected council members vote. Nonprofit boards and special district commissioners vote. State representatives, tribal councils, and members of Congress vote. In states with initiative and referendum processes, all voters can make their mark. Legitimacy, however, is not guaranteed through voting. Votes may be cast in the heat of passion, on prejudicial grounds, due to deception, or in violation of legal or political principles. As we indicated in chapter 6, the legitimacy of public measures rests in part on their congruence with authoritative sources manifested in our traditions of governance, and career officials play pivotal roles in establishing and maintaining a balance among them. Their input during the policy formulation and ratification process helps build these considerations into policy content.

*Policy Implementation*

This is the stage commonly equated with public administration—where policy ideas pass to the agencies responsible for making them operational, whether through their own machinery or through other levels of government and contract organizations. All of the functions, processes, dynamics, and roles described in this book come into play in this phase. Public policy means little if it cannot be implemented, and its meaning is continually renegotiated, revised, and redefined through its administration. At this stage, the cyclical nature of the policy process becomes evident as public servants continually interact with the public and their superiors.

*Evaluation*

The final stage entails review of policy intent relative to implementation. Evaluation closes the policy cycle loop with feedback that often sets the agenda for policy change. This could be as

dramatic as "ending welfare as we know it," or as mundane as changing auto emission testing from one measuring device to another. The evaluation process is often triggered by clients or opponents of the policy as it is currently implemented. Legislators and political executives employ staff evaluators to conduct audits of agency implementation on periodic as well as sporadic bases. Internal agency evaluators will test programs for flaws and successes, the results being reported for purposes of accountability as well as increased effectiveness.

### Interest-Based Models

In contrast to process- and cycle-centered models of policymaking, interest-based models assume that the interplay of organized interest groups is the most critical influence in determining policy outcomes. Interest-based models attempt to explain how and why the policy process works the way it does rather than simply describe its stages. The interest-based model offered in Exhibit 13.6 synthesizes the work of a number of scholars, including Theodore J. Lowi (1972), James Q. Wilson (1989), and Randall Ripley and Grace Franklin (1991). This approach assumes that those who are interested in either the politics surrounding a policy issue, or the nature of the policy that is likely to result from the politics, should look at the distribution of interests. The key to understanding the model presented in Exhibit 13.6 is to begin by asking if the benefits of a policy are widely or narrowly distributed in society. Do almost all people benefit, as with national defense or clean air policy, or are the beneficiaries rather narrowly determined, as with dairy price supports or college student loans? The second critical question reflected in Exhibit 13.6 is how widely or narrowly the burden of the policy falls. Is the burden felt directly by a narrow segment of society, as with auto fleet gasoline efficiency standards (CAFE standards), according to which automobile manufacturers must modify engine designs, or does the burden fall broadly on most of society, as in a federal gas surcharge for highway construction? These two dimensions of benefits and burdens create the following four combinations of outcomes: (1) interest-group politics that produce redistributive policy, (2) clientele politics that produce distributive policy, (3) majoritarian politics that produce constituent policy, and (4) entrepreneurial politics that produce regulatory policy. Each of these will be elaborated more fully in the paragraphs that follow.

*Interest-group politics* occur when benefits or burdens of a proposed policy are narrowly distributed. When disproportionate negative impacts of a policy fall on one of these organized groups, they are stimulated to act. For example, increasing taxes on gasoline and cigarettes creates burdens that fall on clearly identified interests who predictably organize in opposition. Tax breaks often represent instances where benefits are narrowly enjoyed. As long as the burdens are widely shared, there may not be an interest group that opposes the policy. However, this is seldom the case, as large coalitions of interests form to stand guard over the burdens created by seemingly small changes in the benefits for the few. The chief characteristic of interest-group politics is that it produces a zero-sum game where those who benefit do so at someone else's expense. That is why interest-group politics produces *redistributive policy.*

By contrast, *clientele politics* arise where only those who benefit are motivated to participate in the policy process. This is commonly referred to as "pork barrel" or "log-rolling" politics and results in what has been characterized as *distributive policy.* Legislators are both famous and notorious (depending on who benefits) for building compromises into appropriations bills that allocate funds for pork projects in their respective states or districts. They curry great favor with specific constituencies as a result. Dairy price supports are a good example. These aid farmers in making a profit on milk while not unduly burdening the paying public. As a consequence, few

Exhibit 13.6   **Distributions of Political Interests Model**

Burdens

|  | | Narrow | Wide |
|---|---|---|---|
|  | | Redistributive Policy | Distributive Policy |
| Benefits | Narrow | Interest-Group Politics | Clientele Politics |
|  | Wide | Entrepreneurial Politics | Majoritarian Politics |
|  | | Regulative Policy | Constituent Policy |

*Sources:* Shinn (1992), following after Wilson (1989). Also Lowi (1972); Ripley and Franklin (1999).

citizens feel compelled to protest the measure. Dairy associations, on the other hand, jealously guard their benefit.

*Majoritarian politics* involve "front door" issues, where prominent political leaders from all parties, both chambers, executive and legislative branches of government, and multiple factions of the policy community line up publicly to advocate for policies that broadly distribute benefits and burdens. National defense, monetary policy, public health policy, and homeland security policy are typical examples. Such policies are *constituency based* in the sense that benefits to large aggregates of voters serve as the yardstick for assessing their success.

*Entrepreneurial politics*, the final quadrant of the typology, typically generates *regulatory policies* in which burdens are narrowly distributed and benefits are broadly distributed. These characteristics produce groups that are highly motivated to oppose the proposed policy. For legislation to pass under such circumstances, the broadly dispersed benefits need a champion, often manifested as a "public interest" entrepreneur. Ralph Nader played this role in early clean air debates. The value to society is apparent but at low intensity relative to those feeling the burden. The policy entrepreneur catalyzes broad public opinion into a strong voice for the general public over and against narrow interests that would compromise everyone's benefit.

### Actor-Based Models

Ripley and Franklin's policy-actor model (1991), presented in Exhibit 13.7, assumes that the most important factors in determining policy outcomes are the people involved and the types of roles they fill in the process. By identifying the types of actors involved in a particular policy issue, we can understand the likely dynamics. For example, when prominent political officials are involved, the politics are likely to be out in the open, or "front door" in nature. When agency administrators, legislative committee or subcommittee members, and a small number of policy community leaders are involved, the politics are likely to be of the "backroom" variety and are often referred to as "iron triangle" politics (Anderson 2003; Kingdon 1995; Lowi and Ginsberg 2000; Meier 2006; Rourke 1984). The term *iron triangle* was coined to reflect the tight-knit relationships among three types of key backroom decision makers involved in new policy initiatives: vested stakeholder/lobby interests, representatives of the key administrative

Exhibit 13.7  **Policy Actor-Based Model**

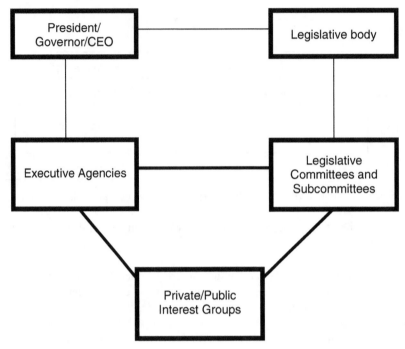

*Source:* After Ripley and Franklin (1991).

agency, and the relevant subcommittee political leaders. The term *backroom* suggests that these decision makers meet at the subcommittee levels of government to hammer out agreements that are simply approved by higher-level political leaders in the policy process; "backroom" is not code for "private deals"; rather, the term calls attention to the fact that decisions may be made at very low and invisible levels of the process.

In the late 1950s, President Dwight D. Eisenhower (in office 1953–1961) warned the nation of the "military-industrial complex," where a few industry leaders enjoyed privileged relationships with a few select congressional committee chairs and key defense department officials. They could set policy quietly in the backrooms of committee chambers, agency shops, and corporate offices. While the idea of a few individuals meeting in a smoke-filled corner of Washington, DC, to set policy has captured the popular imagination, iron triangle politics is hardly universal. It is hard to imagine, for example, that a cozy triangle of players gathers to set wetlands policy. When President George H.W. Bush (in office 1989–1993) invited all the agencies with responsibility for wetlands to discuss his "no net loss" policy, more than a hundred people gathered. Some came from the Environmental Protection Agency (EPA) and the U.S. Department of Agriculture (USDA). Others came from the Department of Transportation and the Department of Defense, and they were joined by independent statutory groups like the Council on Environmental Quality (CEQ). More than a dozen congressional committees exercise jurisdiction over some aspect of wetlands policy; in fact, the entire wetlands policy community would fill a football stadium. Although iron triangle relationships do exist, the more common pattern of relationships resembles that of "policy subsystems" or "policy communities" that cluster around different sets of issues (Cohen 1994; Wamsley 1985).

Scholars have employed a number of metaphors to capture the complexity and dynamism inherent to policy communities. They have described these relationships as power clusters (Ogden 1989), subgovernments (Ripley and Franklin 1991), issue networks (Helco 1978), policy subsystems (Wamsley 1985), and advocacy coalitions (Sabatier and Jenkins-Smith 1993). Ogden refers to power clusters to emphasize the insularity of policy groups in one community from those in other communities. Sabatier and Jenkins-Smith describe advocacy coalitions that form through ongoing interaction among different policy groups; policy outcomes are modified as these groups coalesce.

Policy models that emphasize subgovernments and policy subsystems share the same core assumption: Policy results from a set of relationships that can range from tightly coupled, routinized relations to loosely coupled, sporadic relations (see Exhibit 13.8).

Sometimes the groups driving the process are insular and removed from public visibility. At other times, the groups are visible, large, and fully accountable. But it is fair to conclude that over time, policy communities at the federal level develop governance and resource allocation systems that amount to full-blown political economies (Wamsley 1985) and take on a life of their own. This is less the case at local levels of governance, especially those that have high levels of civic engagement.

### Intergovernmental Relations (IGR) Models

The division of powers among national, state, and local governments establishes the need for intergovernmental relations (IGR). This presents difficulties in assigning policy authority and coordinating policy implementation. For example, the Clean Water Act and the Safe Drinking Water Act devolve differing degrees of authority to the states (Scheberle 2004). Sometimes the preponderance of authority drifts from one level to another, as with the doctrine of local control over schools, which has been eroded by the increasing influence of state and federal education policy. Since the late 1950s, state education departments have set professional standards for teachers and standardized school curricula. The federal government has mandated school policies on race and discrimination, special education, meal programs for needy children, and national achievement standards and testing. The mandated student achievement standards have been among the most controversial (No Child Left Behind 2001). They required annual testing by nearly 14,500 local school districts with targeted student achievement goals. If the goals were not met, districts lost their federal funding if they did not follow mandatory reorganization policies required by No Child Left Behind. However, steady opposition to No Child Left Behind since its passage in 2001 resulted in decisions by the U.S. Department of Education to allow states to gradually "opt out" by developing their own federally approved implementation plans. By 2012 only half the states were still operating under the governance authority of the 2001 law. These kinds of changes create considerable confusion on the part of citizens as to what level of government is responsible for the various aspects of any given policy.

Theorists offer a variety of models for explaining intergovernmental relationships, three of which are presented here. The first reflects the fact that policy increasingly emerges from policy communities which span jurisdictional lines horizontally and vertically. Goggin et al. (1990) and Daniel J. Elazar (1987) describe the interconnectedness of policy implementation across these dimensions and emphasize the interorganizational and networked characteristics which emerge as a result. Morton Grodzins (1960) depicts the varying patterns of these relationships as something akin to a "marble cake," a phrase intended to capture the notion that both the national and state governments exercise overlapping but separate responsibilities. For example, in the areas of

396

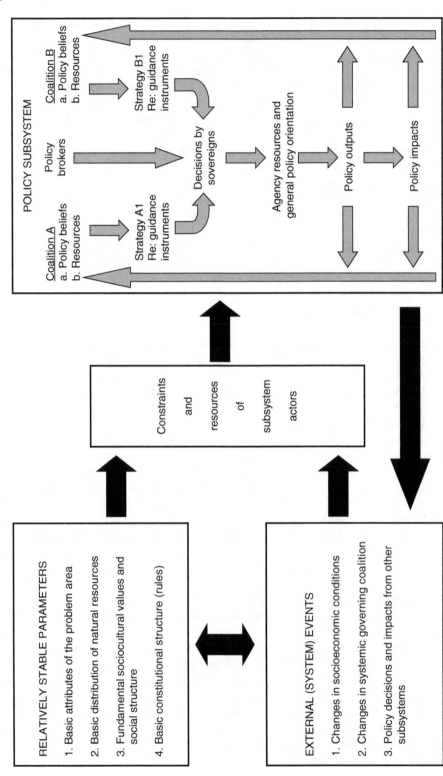

Exhibit 13.8  **Advocacy Coalition Model**

*Source:* From Sabatier, in Sabatier and Jenkins-Smith (1993).

welfare, health, highways, education, and criminal justice, both the state and federal governments exercise independent responsibilities.

A second IGR model emphasizes close vertical relationships among policy arenas which, when mapped, resemble a "picket fence" (Wright 1988). For example, professionals working in housing policy at the county level are likely to have tighter relationships with their state and federal counterparts than they do with their county colleagues in community health or public safety. Working relations within each "picket" are not simply hierarchical. Rather, they are often collegial and reciprocal, with varying capacities and roles played at each level. The local level may exercise substantial discretion and carry more weight on many policy formulation and implementation issues. The amount and kind of discretionary authority is determined by or negotiated with federal professional counterparts. Basic variations in the relationships are depicted in Exhibit 13.9.

The third IGR model is "hierarchical," with the federal government exercising far-reaching authority and power over the policy domain. Environmental regulation is a classic example. States, for instance, implement federal guidelines for the maintenance of clean water through the creation of State Implementation Plans (SIPs) and serve mainly as agents of federal regulatory criteria.

In summary, policy models focus our attention on different facets of the policy process. Their selective focus improves our understanding of different aspects of policy domains, especially in terms of political and economic relationships among multiple players. Politics in these systems is about arbitration of value differences in determining who gets what, when, and how. Governance is about who gets to decide what, when, and how (e.g., what rules, relationships, and processes). Studying policy processes helps us keep track of what we decide to do (policy choice), what we actually do on the ground (policy outputs), and what effects our decisions have in the everyday world (policy impact).

## THE RISE OF POLICY ANALYSIS AND THE CHALLENGE OF "SPEAKING TRUTH TO POWER"

The development of policy analysis as a specialized field of study and practice is part of a long history of attempting to bring the "truth" of disciplined data collection, analysis, and evaluation to the formal decision-making process. The rise of the administrative state in the twentieth century heightened interest in reconciling expert policy development and implementation with the growing demand on the part of citizens for increased predictability and accountability. The Progressive Era played an important role in heightening this tension with reform efforts to rationalize government budgeting, finance, and program performance. The massive growth of the federal government during the New Deal, along with the close ties between academia and the Roosevelt administration, increased the acceptance of rational analysis as part of the policy development process.

In the wake of World War II, social science scholars vastly expanded the use of applied mathematics and, with the advent of computers, revolutionized its application first to large-scale industrial management, engineering, and production economics, and then to the analysis of governmental projects and programs. Through these developments, influential scholars such as Herbert Simon brought economic and technical rationality to bear on public decision making. Management science attracted large numbers of professionals in business, industry, and government. President John F. Kennedy's administration (1961–1963) boosted recognition of these experts, dubbing them the "best and brightest" and aggressively recruiting them into public service. The Kennedy era rejuvenated the Progressive movement's optimism about attaining new heights of achievement through applications of science in industry and government. As spoken before a joint session of

Exhibit 13.9  **Decision Matrix**

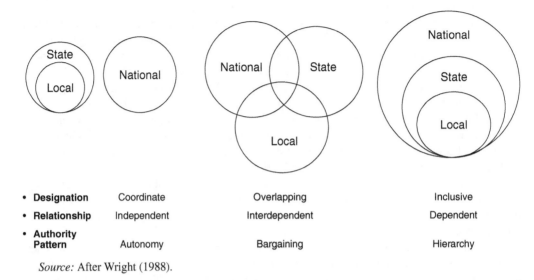

| | | | |
|---|---|---|---|
| • **Designation** | Coordinate | Overlapping | Inclusive |
| • **Relationship** | Independent | Interdependent | Dependent |
| • **Authority Pattern** | Autonomy | Bargaining | Hierarchy |

*Source:* After Wright (1988).

Congress in 1961, President Kennedy's challenge to send a manned rocket to the moon and back symbolized the preoccupation with finding technical solutions to many public problems.

By the mid-1970s, public law required additional levels of technical analysis. Agencies were required to produce project alternatives (as in the Army Corps of Engineers' cost-benefit analysis requirement), comprehensive planning strategies (in agencies such as the USDA's Forest Service and the Department of the Interior's Bureau of Land Management), and formalization of policy and decision analysis to guide policy implementation in such arenas as environmental protection. Economists, decision scientists, and statisticians joined the faculty ranks of professional schools in the 1960s, and by the 1970s most schools of management and public administration had introduced curricula emphasizing computer-aided techniques of analysis for decision making and project management. Today, the technical or "rational" decision-making model is treated by most disciplines and professionals as the preferred approach to management decisions and policy analysis. Current best practice requirements for undertaking policy analysis include the following sequential steps:

- Identify and clarify goals
- Identify problems that hamper achievement of goals
- Identify alternative solutions to the problems
- Measure the costs and benefits of alternative solutions
- Choose the optimal solution

Many well-known policy and program planning methods such as planning-programming-budgeting systems (PPBS), management by objectives (MBO), and zero-base budgeting (ZBB) were developed on this model. As mentioned earlier, this approach to decision making arises from the market model of society, which is based on the philosophical value of utility—achieving the greatest good for the greatest number of people. As such, its most obvious bias is majoritarian in nature, which puts it in tension with rights-based policies or those that may serve narrow target populations. Less obvious

are its emotive, instrumental, and short-run biases. Utilitarianism presumes that values are emotive in nature—stemming from the emotions—and thus are matters of irrational, individual preference. The rational model assumes that preferences are not amenable to reason: they are simply stated or given, and in need of clear expression. The task of policy analysis under these circumstances is to discover majority preferences, state them as clear policy goals, and then analyze alternative means for achieving them based on their relative costs and benefits. In theory, this is an instrumental process because the means of achieving the goals are based solely on whether the benefits exceed costs of the policy. Thus, there is no constraining principle within this instrumental approach to prevent choices that may be regarded as immoral. Any means will do as long as it is helpful in achieving the desired results. Finally, this model is geared toward short-run results because there is less uncertainty about the impact of costs and benefits. Discounting of future costs and benefits is one of the first techniques taught to policy and decision analysts. This means that the long-term benefits to future generations or the environment are given short shrift.

In addition to its biases, the rational decision model exhibits some rather serious problems in implementation. First, it is very time consuming and expensive to conduct thorough cost-benefit analysis of a full range of alternatives. In the abstract, an unlimited number of plausible alternatives exists, which means that arbitrary limits must be set on the number that will be analyzed. The time and expense involved require that the range of alternatives be cut further, usually to two or three at most.

Second, the cost of alternatives is usually easier to determine than the benefits, in part because the costs are incurred first, and also because the benefits are often more abstract, long term, and difficult to measure. This is especially true with prevention programs. For example, how can one really know how many crimes are prevented by a crime-prevention program? Does the analyst look for a reduction in crime rates or a slower growth rate of crime? Do these measures adequately reflect all that is prevented or not prevented? As a result of this difficulty, analysts often modify cost-benefit analysis into "cost-effectiveness" analysis. This approach compares the costs of alternatives relative to a standard deemed acceptable to key reference groups. It thus tries to minimize costs without a precise measure of benefits.

Third, the specification of clear, measurable goals and objectives is hampered by the inherent ambiguity of public values. Most values are capable of multiple meanings. As such they can be reasoned about, interpreted, and argued over rather than treated as irrational impulses. Each definition or meaning attributed to a public value brings different kinds of plausible policy goals and solutions to light, while obscuring others. This was exemplified in chapter 8, with the evolving definitions of merit in public personnel policy. Personnel policy changed as different meanings of merit were adopted.

These problems make the rational model of analysis extremely difficult to apply, which explains why policy planning methods based on it (PPBS, MBO, ZBB) have not worked very well, if at all. The rational model, it turns out, enjoys far more attention as an espoused theory of policymaking than it does as a theory in use. As a result, most students of public administration are treated to a very attractive and practical alternative—*incrementalism,* discussed in chapter 11.

Made famous by Charles Lindblom's article "The Science of Muddling Through" (1959), the incremental approach foregoes the attempt to comprehensively analyze alternative policy solutions in favor of adjusting existing policy at the margins. Adjustments at the margins involve a process of comparing current funding levels, operations, and capacities to those in the previous budgetary cycle and adjusting them by increments to changing conditions on the street. Analysis is thus restricted to tracking information on existing policies from year to year for the sake of comparison and the assessment of policy failure.

Although this approach is inherently conservative because it preserves the status quo, it strikes most students as eminently sensible and realistic. It is not, however, the only alternative mode of policy decision and analysis that is common in public life. Exhibit 13.10 lists many other policy deciding modes commonly used in public life. With the exception of intuition and impulse, these modes embrace a variety of analytic methods suited to the nature of the situations they address. These include historical analysis, reasoning by analogy from case to case (casuistry), voting analysis, deductive analysis, analysis of feedback, analysis through debate, analysis of trade-offs among rival criteria, and so forth. Procrastination may result as much from "paralysis by analysis" as from lack of analysis.

## ANALYSIS THROUGH ADVOCACY AND ISSUE FRAMING

We have noted through each of our chapters public decision making typically occurs under cross-cutting political pressures. As this chapter's opening quotation by Stone indicates, even the rational decision model is a "creature of politics." Its biases reveal its value-laden assumptions and its vision of what constitutes a political community. Thus, each and every method of analysis presents a way of framing or defining issues that predisposes the analyst to entertain certain kinds of solutions. For example, Stone (1997, 6) shows how courts in the United States have wrestled with the question of whether surrogate mother contracts are simply a means for "selling babies," or for "sales of a socially useful purpose." Contracts for selling babies are prohibited for many good reasons, but contracts for socially useful purposes are eminently sensible and perfectly legal. One can see merit in both constructions, as well as in their mutually exclusive solutions. Choosing one definition means abandoning the other. In this sense, defining problems means engaging in "strategically crafted arguments" that seek to "resolve ambiguities and paradoxes in a particular direction" (Stone 1997, 7).

Moreover, the task of defining or framing a problem necessarily involves arguments about "membership," about what should be included and excluded under the categories deemed relevant for application. For example, in choosing to analyze disability in society, one is first asserting that disability is significant enough politically as well as economically that it warrants analysis and some kind of public policy response. But to do so means that disability must first be defined, and that is a task filled with ambiguity. Note that under current federal policy, the definition of *disability* is grounded in a clinical concept of impairment and the use of medical evidence by medical experts. But, as Stone explains, the medical concept of disability

> remains very loosely defined, and the mechanism for determination of disability offers many opportunities for purposeful manipulation. The assignment of citizens into work-based and need-based distributive systems remains a highly political issue which is not easily resolved by the creation of formal administrative schedules or the delegation of decision making to the medical profession. . . . Thus, there is a constant struggle over the boundaries, which manifests itself in shifting pressures for expansion and contraction of the disability category. (Stone 1984, 140)

Defining disability differently would change the nature of policies affecting disability benefits, while raising concerns about how to craft policies that address different (and currently ignored) classes of disability. In short, the problem of defining meaningful policy categories that can be translated into administrative systems is a political issue, not a technical issue that experts alone can decide.

Exhibit 13.10  **Common Modes of Policy Decision and Analysis**

Voting—group, nonconsensual

Consensus—group deliberation

Rules/standards—formal or informal

Orders—executive or judicial

Tradition—customary practice, precedent

Chance—lotteries, flip of coin

Habit—trained response

Analysis of feedback—reactions of those
  impacted

Voting analysis—what kinds of citizens
  care and with what intensity

Deductive analysis—reasoning from a
  given major premise and known/assumed
  minor premise to reach a conclusion

Analysis of trade-offs among rival criteria—
  comparative evaluation

Procrastination—nondecisions are decisions

Mediation/arbitration—by third party

Bargaining—individual or collective

Trial or hearing of cases

Intuition—that "gut feeling"

Impulse—unthinking, untrained reaction

Authoritative opinion—by leader or reference group

Analysis through debate—adversarial engagement
  that surfaces pros and cons

Reasoning by analogy from case to case (casuistry)—
  comparing relevant similarities and differences

Historical analysis—what has been the case in the
  past

*Source:* Derived from Stone (1997, 232).

---

Policy analysts who seek "impartial" analysis must account for these ambiguities and present their implications for the consumers of their reports. Not all analysts are impartial in this sense. Many simply weigh advantages and disadvantages of authorized policy or of the policies their organizations advocate. Thorough, balanced reports will weigh advantages and disadvantages in terms of the different ways various contending groups frame the issues. This approach risks the ire of superiors or sponsors who want reports that support their positions. "Speaking truth to power" can be hazardous. As we have continued to emphasize, analysis is a political act in its own right.

Because policy analysis is an integral aspect of the political world in which we live, there is always a debate over the objectivity and independence of those who are hired to do this kind of work. The worst charge is that analysts are just hired guns who make the best case for decisions already made. While this certainly occurs, it does so with a high likelihood that it will be unmasked by the activity of analysts working from a different set of assumptions or a different worldview. Such unmasking results in a significant loss of legitimacy and, for that reason, is not as common in administrative venues as one might expect.

There are a variety of ways to prevent policy analysis from being captured by the political forces at play in the policy process. These include structuring job descriptions, reporting requirements, peer review processes, oversight committees, professional training, and emphasis on high standards of professionalism. The Democratic Balancewheel model also plays an important role in structuring and legitimizing competing standards for measuring the success of the democratic enterprise and the policy it produces. The model's governance traditions (responsive governance, competent and energetic governance, minority rights and access to governance, and civic governance) embrace contending values which lead proponents of each to define public issues and policy solutions very differently. Public agencies that purposely build these multiple perspectives into their analyses are likely to fare better with policy design, implementation, and legitimacy than agencies that do not follow this design strategy. Often, however, elected officials follow a narrower

strategy for evaluating public policy. For instance, legislators frequently submit proposed bills for legal analysis, or they direct their evaluation staff to audit an agency or program in order to induce more responsiveness to policy agendas. Political executives often direct their policy staff to conduct cost-benefit or cost-effectiveness studies to assess the efficiency of proposed or existing programs. Many state and federal agencies are required by law to conduct regulatory impact analyses and to meet with clients and citizens to solicit feedback about programs. Legislative process and provisions of administrative law guarantee access by interest groups, many of whom add their own policy analyses to the mix.

Policy analysis is now a thoroughly institutionalized practice. Whole organizations like the Congressional Research Service (CRS), the General Accountability Office (GAO), the Council of Economic Advisers (CEA), and many state counterparts are established to provide policy analyses. Various agencies have their own analysis and program evaluation shops. In the nonprofit sector, many advocacy and interest groups, labor unions, political parties, and trade associations employ policy analysts. Professional associations and universities maintain institutes and programs staffed with policy analysts. At local levels, many county, city, and special district governments have less capacity to perform policy analysis, and so rely more on local universities, consultants, and small think tanks. Amidst this wide array of approaches to systematic analysis, policy "wonks" may spend as much time analyzing each other's studies as they do conducting their own. As they parse the values, assumptions, definitions of problems, and proposed solutions of these rival studies for their principals, they contribute to policy dialogue. As political resources, they can play a powerful role in framing and guiding a policy debate.

## AN OVERVIEW OF POLICY ANALYSIS TECHNIQUES AND METHODS

Many policy analysts draw pragmatically from an array of disciplines and employ a variety of analytic techniques and methods. Others are specialized and integrated into a multiphase process that includes a series of analyses conducted by different kinds of specialists. Thus, a proposed policy may be subjected to legal analysis, feasibility analysis, impact analysis, cost-benefit analysis, and client-based analysis. The techniques and methods vary accordingly. Some of the more commonly used approaches and techniques are reviewed here.

### Stakeholder Analysis

As indicated in chapter 12, leaders need to know whom to involve in sorting out policy ideas and solutions. How many people care about an issue and why? Some laws and administrative rule-making processes require the notification of people with known interests in a policy domain. Stakeholder analysis helps assess who must be involved and who can affect the policy design and outcomes. In cases in which the issue is well developed and positions are crystallized, the task of identifying stakeholders is relatively straightforward; in other instances, it is a more complex job. Simplistic stakeholder analysis of policy issues conjures up the image of a tug of war, where stakeholders line up on one side of an issue or the other. However, in the world of iron triangles, policy clusters, and policy subsystems, the pattern of interests is bound to be more complicated. It is likely that interests will be arrayed in a variety of directions, as illustrated in Exhibit 13.11. This is important because modest reframing of proposed alternatives might induce significant realignment in the pattern or constellation of interests affecting an agency. The varying intensity of stakeholder interests, and the kinds of political resources they wield, also matters. The issue at hand may constitute the raison d'être of an advocacy organization but be only one among dozens of issues for the government

Exhibit 13.11   **Stakeholder Interests in Multiple Directions**

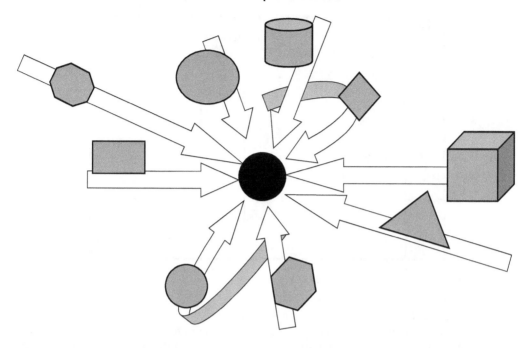

agencies involved. Mapping the significance of the players and ways they are arrayed on an issue will affect the way agency leaders interact with them in the policy process.

**Policy Process Analysis**

It matters how specific policy processes unfold and function. For example, a head librarian may need to know the processes involved for determining land use and acquiring building permits to expand a library facility. A state transportation official may need to know at what stage a permit approval is needed for modifying the edge of a wetland that drains into a navigation channel. The manager of a nonprofit that contracts with both state and county governments to provide services to mentally handicapped adults needs to know how well or poorly state and county policies mesh. These situations require a working analysis of legal procedures and substantive regulations. Process analysis often entails the use of linear planning models and critical path mapping. Failing to adequately analyze these processes can jeopardize contracts, compromise missions, and incur legal liabilities.

**Decision and Cost-Benefit Analysis**

Improving decisions through decision analysis is one of the most commonly taught forms of policy analysis (cf. Behn and Vaupel 1982). There are a number of approaches, but the most common is illustrated by the decision matrix in Exhibit 13.12, which divides the policy process into key decision stages. At the point in the process where decision criteria and policy alternatives are fully developed and agreed to by decision makers, analysts can provide the technical information about the effects of alternatives on the various criteria. This kind of analysis can significantly improve the quality and timing of decisions.

Exhibit 13.12   **Decision Matrix**

| | | Alternatives | | |
|---|---|---|---|---|
| | | 1 | 2 | 3 |
| **Criteria** | A | | | |
| | B | | | |
| | C | | | |
| | D | | | |

*Source:* Miller, Shinn, and Bentley (1994, 158).

Policy analysts have also been called on to summarize the results from a decision matrix into an estimate of overall comparative value. The most common approach for doing this is cost-benefit analysis (cf. Dunn 2004; Stiglitz 2000; Weimer and Vining 2004). In cost-benefit analysis, the values reflected in a decision matrix are assumed to be reducible to economic values.

Once reduced, the benefits and costs can be summarized. Typically, the benefits are divided by costs to determine a benefit-to-cost ratio. A ratio of greater than one (> 1) suggests a positive outcome. The alternative with the largest benefit-cost ratio is considered the optimal choice. A number of federal and state laws require this kind of analysis prior to authorizing new rules or proceeding with implementation. Cost-benefit analysis can be useful for projects involving large expenditures for material improvements (e.g., transportation corridors, public buildings, or expensive equipment) or for projects that involve high-volume, low-unit-cost products (such as immunization programs) where the range of alternatives is narrow. It is much less helpful in determining the value of more abstract public goods (clean air, education, defense, and so on), or in comparing the relative value of unrelated programs (building a highway versus immunizing children).

### Decision Tree and Network Analysis

Decision trees and network analyses provide additional approaches to informing decisions and are especially useful in exploring risk and uncertainty. Exhibit 13.13 illustrates how decision trees can be used to project alternative action steps, explore the potential consequences of those steps, and determine the value associated with their outcomes. They can help estimate the subjective utility of an alternative and its likely effects.

Network analysis provides similar insight by tracking processes, decision steps, and plausible outcomes through a maze of network relationships that defy the either-or structure of decision trees. It also more ably captures the dynamics and competing priorities of interorganizational networks. Here again, stakeholder maps can add greatly to the analysis.

Exhibit 13.13  **Decision Tree Analysis Model**

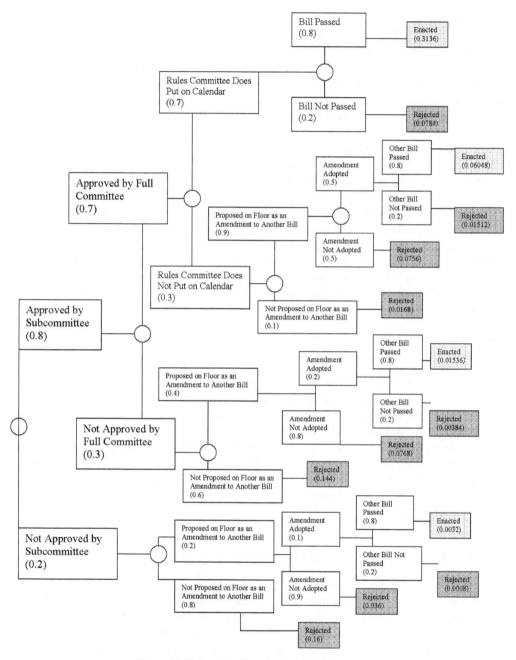

Figure 12.10: Decision Tree Analysis Model

*Source:* After Behn and Vaupel (1982).

## Case Analysis

Case analysis is the use of single or multiple case studies that are rich in detail and thus helpful in understanding the dynamics of cause and effect in a specific type of setting (Yin 2003, 1984). Social statistics on educational attainment provide an overall basis for predicting the likely future of a student or class of students. Based on the laws of probability, we can say with some confidence that children from families of higher socioeconomic status, two-parent households, and households where parents have high educational attainment are likely to do well in school themselves as measured by years of schooling completed. However, such an overall picture does little to inform us about the case where a child does well in school despite the fact that he or she comes from a disadvantaged background. What explains success in such a case? Case analysis that takes a close and comprehensive look at the experiences of a few children and parents may reveal important characteristics or conditions that help explain the factors associated with these children's success.

Case study research is also helpful in understanding success or failure in complex administrative settings. Studying the dynamics of policy failure or institutional transformation can illustrate how processes declined, how values changed, and how roles played by various actors were redefined. Such analyses can be indispensable in guiding reform or institutionalizing new missions. One must be careful, however, not to generalize or formularize the application of insights drawn from a case study. Case studies highlight unique combinations of characteristics, criteria, and policy solutions that can fail miserably when carelessly transplanted to other settings.

## Historical Analysis

Historical analysis brings another rich source of insight and evidence to bear on important policy questions. It provides vital biographical and contextual knowledge that helps trace how current policies emerged and how traditions and practices evolved. Knowing the history of an agency is much like knowing the life and character of a person: Such knowledge is rich in tacit understandings and nuanced interpretations of events that enable analysts and leaders to identify key moments or windows of opportunity to affect policy change. Historians draw on many sources of insight, including interviews, policy and program records, personal logs and diaries, secondary sources, and multiple interpretive sources to provide balanced and well-rounded analyses (Neustadt and May 1988; Yaffee 1994). Like case studies, historical analyses provide insight based on unique characteristics and processes of change. The insight is valuable for insiders and for the contrast it provides with other histories, not as a blueprint for standardized solutions.

## Experimentation and Quasi-Experimentation

Experimental methods can also be useful in policy analysis (Campbell and Stanley 2005; Cook and Campbell 1979). Quasi-experimentation typically entails a "before and after" comparison of the passage and implementation of a law and the effect it has on a dependent variable. Seat belt laws have been subject to such analysis. Exhibit 13.14 illustrates the use of experimental design to test the relationship between the use of seat belts and the number and kinds of automobile crash injuries. The exhibit shows the relationship of the effect of seat belt laws to personal injury in aggregate data. This same logic can be used in time series, as shown in Exhibit 13.15, which illustrates Oregon's land-use law. The expressed goal of the law was to reduce the rate of conversion of farmland and forestland to urban and suburban development. The time-series graph provides strong evidence of the effectiveness of this law.

Exhibit 13.14   **Seat Belt Use Rate and Hospitalization**

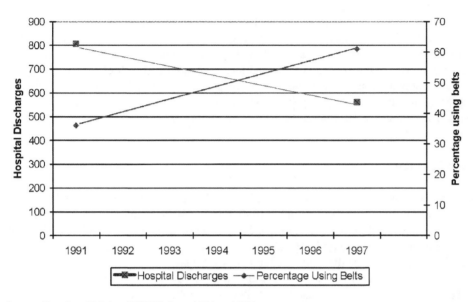

*Source:* Results of Maine CODES data, 1991 to 1997.

Exhibit 13.15   **Land in Farms in the Willamette Valley, Oregon, Before and After Passage of Senate Bill 100, Oregon's Land-Use Planning Law, in 1973**

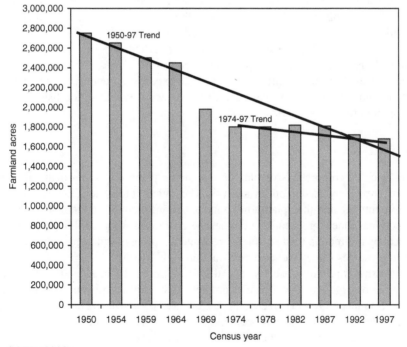

*Source:* SOER (2000).

Policy experiments can also be carried out by using naturally occurring treatments or by actively creating treatment groups. For example, one could test the effectiveness of public education curricula on influencing recycling behavior. Neighborhoods could be randomly selected for public education fairs, each of which employs a different curriculum. Each neighborhood's current recycling efforts would be assessed (perhaps by volume or weight of materials collected by recyclers) prior to the education fairs, and then compared with subsequent recycling efforts across all treatment groups. A common hazard in such study arises in the creation of treatment groups. Individuals may change their behavior simply because they are in the study (a result of what is known as the Hawthorne Effect). More unobtrusive assessments may be required to overcome the effect.

## Survey Research

Survey research is a well-developed method for collecting information on people's attitudes, behaviors, and positions on issues (Babbie 1990; Fowler 2001). Opinion surveys provide critical information on perceptions of issues and on the public acceptance of various policy options. While expensive to conduct, they provide feedback from important reference groups who help define effectiveness and influence the legitimacy of policy agendas.

Used within an appropriate theoretical framework, survey research can test hypotheses about the likely effect of policy actions and the distribution of political values and preferences. Survey research depends on people reporting things about themselves. There are limits to the ability of people to do this authentically. These limits have less to do with sample bias and methodological issues of how questions are written and sequenced, and more to do with the fact that people will respond differently in different social settings. Most people are surprisingly willing to respond to survey questions. They typically respond regardless of how well versed they are on the topic under study. This is problematic in policy study. In the early stages of policy formation, the policy and its implications are usually not well developed. People engage in a discovery process akin to fishing for answers as they consider or talk about a particular policy issue. The less familiar people are with the issue, the more important this concern becomes. Careful and skillful design can reduce the extent of such problems. The ease and expense of conducting survey research has improved dramatically with web tools such as SurveyMonkey, but so too has the potential for proliferation of unreliable surveys.

## Planning

Techniques such as comprehensive planning, strategic planning, action planning, and project management are widely used in policy analysis. They attempt to systematically consider desired or alternative futures, and then plan how to move toward them more efficiently. Planning is an intensely political endeavor, because it defines the conditions for good living and seeks ways to achieve them by redirecting the use of resources and adopting new designs (physical and social) for living. It presumes some level of dissatisfaction with the status quo.

*Comprehensive planning* is usually related to land use, land management, and area development, examples of which include a state's comprehensive land-use planning system, the USDA's Forest Service national forest management plans, and a city's downtown development district plan are typical examples. By their nature, comprehensive plans determine zones of development or preservation, establish criteria for the kind and quality of development allowed within each zone, and set a long-term schedule for bringing the plan to fruition. Commonly, however, as the steps in

the plan are implemented, people in the community change their priorities and force modification of the political agreements that authorized it.

Another difficulty arises due to the technical and professional orientation of trained planners who bring their analyses, judgments, and methods to the planning process. They study planning trends and typically adopt one or another planning philosophy with accompanying methods. Their work often resembles an engineering design exercise more than a useful policy tool that enables citizens to actively explore and plan the future of their communities. More often than not, the real planning in communities occurs with land developers who buy up tracts of land and design their own plans for tract development or redevelopment as suits their vision and profitability. Large developers often hire their own planning staff to help with the design and planning process. The larger developers are usually able to secure variances from a comprehensive plan to accommodate their designs. The planning process is marked by many compromises as a result. Nevertheless, comprehensive planning at least provides for a general pattern of development and can guard against the ravages of spot zoning and other haphazard developments that can harm neighborhoods and compromise aesthetic qualities.

*Strategic planning* is similar to comprehensive planning. However, rather than intending to capture all elements comprehensively, these planning exercises help set direction and address broad policy goals. Strategic planning helps groups and organizations analyze the range of means viewed as acceptable or appropriate by those involved in the exercise. It offers a flexible strategy for working toward particular goals rather than preparing a trip map. The strategic planning process is useful for reexamining an agency mission and for working out the implications of changing the mission for various organizational roles, criteria of success, and policy content.

*Action planning* and *project management* are commonly used in settings where coordinated action is required by multiple individuals or groups, and where actions must be systematically linked to achieve the outcome. Action planning involves enumerating the steps necessary to accomplish a task, deciding who is responsible for which tasks, establishing when the tasks should be completed, and assessing the impact of completed tasks (Miller, Shinn, and Bentley 1994). Action planning steps help to focus people's efforts and provide a sense of structure and concrete achievement. Project management generally entails multiple action plans, a master schedule, and a variety of subcontracting relationships to bring a project to completion. Project review and analysis occur routinely to avoid large deviations and to deal with unanticipated events.

## THE FAILINGS OF POLICY ANALYSIS

Despite all the advancements in tools and methods of policy analysis, the practice remains highly problematic and contested. People generally dislike seeing their policies and practices subjected to analysis, in part because politics and governance are such messy and morally clouded activities. If one looks closely, it is easy to find flaws, discover failures, and dispute the value of proposed and established policies. The probing policy analyst and program evaluator pose potential threats. As a result, public officials at all levels try to control analysts—to set the terms of their inquiries, to define the problems they are assigned to analyze. Most analysts try to maintain their impartiality and the integrity of their methods, but this is contingent upon their degree of independence, as well as the degree of commitment they may bring to any given policy. Like their administrative colleagues, they must continually think about who and what they serve. And even with a substantial degree of autonomy, they cannot fully escape the pressure of events, powerful actors, and the inherent limits of their own enterprise. Policy analysts are thus prone to some common failings.

In a classic treatment on policy analysis, Arnold Meltsner (1976, 302–309) identified "seven deadly sins" that are common to the enterprise. They are worth reviewing because they can induce a measure of humility in those who take them seriously. All politicians, administrators, and analysts should memorize them.

First, analysts must try to avoid "getting in a rut." It is easy for officials and clients to get locked into a solution due to the lull of routine, or the insistence on adhering to "inappropriate goals or beliefs," or because the consensus of policy opinion is so strong that few can think or question outside the box (Meltsner 1976, 302–303). For example, the drive to privatize public services has been strong and sustained for over 25 years and has resulted in many unwise contractual arrangements that are now beginning to haunt us. Critical analysis of these projects was virtually nonexistent for much of this history, and it remains sorely lacking.

Second, the "sin of distant advice" arises from being too far from policy on the street, or by relying too much on general data that do not reflect the specific application of policy. This often occurs because the general data are easy to obtain without going into the field, or because the analyst's "theory and underlying conceptions of causation can be too global or too refined" (Meltsner 1976, 303). This is the classic academic problem of trying to solve problems in general.

Third, the lack of timely analysis and advice can be deadly. Analysts may try to be more thorough than the time and circumstances permit. The nature of the problem may only need a rough analysis, at least initially, to orient a client to the proper range of actions. Late advice is of little value, the effort made futile. The analyst must "understand the situation that confronts the client" in order to balance the need "between accuracy and being on time" (Meltsner 1976, 304).

Fourth, according to Meltsner, is the fact that advice is sometimes superficial, given too quickly, "off the cuff, and not based on enough digging into the roots of the problem." As Meltsner indicates, most reorganization studies suffer from this problem (1976, 305–306), largely because they are used to disguise other objectives. Some studies were never intended to be so thorough. Analysts become mere pawns in such circumstances, and they had best be aware of how they are being used and for what.

Fifth, a common and costly sin occurs when analysts join in overreacting to crises—real or imagined—and when they and their organizations focus too much on current events. Inflamed fears of flu pandemics, terrorism, and the like can "lead to a kind of fire-house mentality, advice on the run" (Meltsner 1976, 306). This is a syndrome of sorts that leads easily to superficial analysis and hasty conclusions. The focus on current events is akin to not being able to see beyond one's nose, and this can lead clients and their organizations into real disasters. Analysts must try to provide strategic advice about the long run, to see trends and developments down the road.

Sixth is the sin of "capricious advice," or the tendency to induce change for its own sake. It is hard for analysts to say "just leave it alone" (Meltsner 1976, 307). The temptation to tinker is almost irresistible. After all, the presumption of analysis is that one expects to improve things or find something to fix. Meltsner's example is as relevant today as it was when he first wrote it: "Consider our primary and secondary schools. Probably I am telescoping things, but I cannot remember a time when someone was not criticizing them and someone else was not suggesting a panacea" (308). In some policy arenas, everyone needs to take a breather.

Seventh, Meltsner calls attention to a problem we have dealt with at length throughout this chapter. This is the tendency of analysts to treat politics as irrational and antithetical to their craft. They often assume that their craft is apolitical, as though there is a separation of "policy" from "politics." This results in constant misapplication of analyses to the situations they address because of the tendency to ignore the political constraints and dynamics that drive analytic work. As Stone (1997, 7) has so cogently illustrated, policy analysis is "a creature of politics" with its own biases, its own view of the world, and its own attempts to define problems and propose solutions.

## CONCLUSION

We end this chapter with a sober reminder that the craft of policy analysis cannot be separated from the art of governance. While the practice of policy analysis is important, its value is not limitless. The goal of policy analysis is to improve policy outcomes while not becoming paralyzed with the obsession to develop the next cycle of data gathering and to extend the analysis. At the end of the day, policy analysis and policy analytic techniques do not make decisions. In fact, as Herbert Storing (1980) indicated, the modern fixation with rational analysis tends to make decision makers weak and passive in the drive to find that next bit of data that will make the right decision self-evident. This fixation ignores the need for officials to be courageous and decisive, to use their judgment in the face of mountains of incomplete information. Analysis can provide relevant information. It can influence politics and policy choice, but in the final analysis it can neither manufacture a political agreement nor fashion a wise decision. That is the work of those who govern.

Viewed as an integral part of the larger process of governance, policy analysis in America will ultimately be judged by the extent to which it enables communities (1) to weave together a shared sense of the common good, and (2) to sustain that agreement in the face of important "drivers of change," which we discuss in greater detail in chapter 15. We have argued throughout this chapter that the history of public policy is a history of dependence by the private sector on the policy infrastructure provided by the public sector. But as we look to the future, one of the themes of this book is that self-governance requires much greater attention to the underlying fabric of civic life than has been the case (Shinn 1999). This underlying civic fabric is now widely viewed as a matter of critical importance and in need of intervention to restore its vitality (Putnam 2000; Sirianni 2009). We end this chapter with a challenge to those who do policy work to focus more of their attention on helping us better understand the role that civic infrastructure plays in supporting the political health of democratic governance, and the role administrators might play in keeping this infrastructure intact.

## STUDY QUESTIONS

1. What factors have influenced American development as a "commercial republic," and how does this affect public policy?
2. Consider the discussion about regulation. Write an essay that provides a rationale for government intervention in the economy by regulation and provides an argument for limiting the degree of regulation in the economy.
3. Distinguish between policy choice, policy outcome, and policy impact. Provide an example of each.
4. Review a recent public action that has taken place in your community in terms of policy choice. What is the choice? What is the structure of authority implied in the choice, and who will implement the policy action? Finally, consider the choice(s) made among the tools governments have available for use today. What criteria are appropriate for guiding such choices and evaluating the impacts of such choices?
5. Peruse a regional newspaper and identify a policy issue in the news. Use the policy cycle model to describe the status of this policy issue in terms of where it is in the policy process.
6. Choose a policy issue with which you are familiar, or one you find described in the newspaper. Make a list of all those interests you think are involved, and use the distribution of benefits and burdens model to identify (a) the nature of the politics involved, and (b)

the type of policy likely to emerge from the political arena in which this issue is being contested.

7. Consider a substantive policy issue of interest to you, such as health care access, transportation planning, affordable housing, or habitat restoration. Use the three models of intergovernmental relations ("picket fence," "marble cake," and "hierarchical") to identify the governments and the structure of authority among those governments.

8. Explain why policy analysis is inherently a political practice. Use examples to illustrate.

CHAPTER 14

# POLICY IMPLEMENTATION AND ADMINISTRATIVE LAW

To simulate initiative, even at the risk of mistakes, must nowadays never be lost sight of as a task in making the government's services responsible. An official should be as responsible for inaction as for wrong action. . . . In matters of vital importance the general public is entitled to the views of its permanent servants. Such views may often provide a check against partisan extravagances.

*(Carl J. Friedrich 1940, 4, 23)*

If the community does not command, there is no call for technical knowledge whatever; and, however magnificent the grasp of technical knowledge and the desire to use it, it must be declared irresponsible whenever it becomes operative except under a direct or implied obligation [to the legislative body]. Many a burglar has been positively hated for his technical skill. . . . [Carl J. Friedrich's doctrine of administrative accountability] is surely to set up the official against the political parties, to make the official the instrument of conflict between the general public . . . and the legislature.

*(Herman Finer 1941, 347, 349)*

Whatever we do, the point has increasingly been to move away from the use of mechanisms of authority and toward governance by agreement, whether that means negotiated arrangements with regulated enterprises, service contracts with profit-making or nonprofit nongovernmental organizations, interjurisdictional agreements with other agencies of government at any level, service agreements with citizens, or internal performance agreements with personnel within a government organization. . . . In this proposed operation the contractor would be responsible not only for operating the program but also for determining the eligibility for services. Would the firm take a draconian attitude toward eligibility determinations as a way to maximize its own profits under the contract and also to curry favor with state politicians?

*(Phillip J. Cooper 2003, 47, 3)*

413

The American policy process entrusts government career administrators with an extraordinary responsibility for the implementation of public policy. On the one hand, they are constrained by a rule-of-law system that structures the exercise of their discretionary authority through a highly developed rulemaking process and myriad other forms of political and legal control. But, on the other hand, they frequently have the interpretive opportunity to decide among conflicting and equally authoritative masters in the guise of courts, legislative bodies, and the executive branch of government. Each of these institutional masters, in turn, is composed of individual legal actors who have vague, ambiguous, and sometimes conflicting public policy intentions. This leaves career public administrators in the catbird's seat with respect to policy implementation. They must do something to implement a law and, usually within a specified time frame, but often without a clearly defined path forward. Under such circumstances, they are left to do the best they can to decipher legislative intent, create effective administrative structures, staff and organize the work in the most efficient manner possible, and assiduously adhere to all of the legal requirements under which administrative agencies are required to operate. Policy implementation is ultimately decided through the action taken by street-level bureaucrats, not in deliberative forums where broad directions are discussed and decided.

At the heart of these street-level democratic encounters is the principle of accountability. As we observed in chapter 6, accountability emphasizes the dependence of administrators on external actors, be they legislators, executives, judges, for-profit and nonprofit contractors and partners, intergovernmental partners, the press, or the citizenry. Correspondingly, the principle of responsibility calls attention to the considerable discretion that governmental, contractual, and partnered administrators have in the policy implementation process. As administrative discretion in the governing process expands, administrators bear an increased burden of responsibility to legitimate the exercise of this discretion, to demonstrate that it meets the tests of accountability, and to ensure that it is consistent with democratic values (see chapters 4 and 5). But what are these tests? Chapter 6 focused on a general discussion of the principles of accountability and responsibility. This chapter focuses on three specific systems that have been put in place to ensure accountability: policy systems, organizational systems, and legal systems (Exhibit 14.1). As *policy* agents, administrative agencies are used to carrying out the political agendas of both the elected executive (if one exists) and the legislature. But as *managerial* agents, administrators ensure that programs are implemented as efficiently and effectively as possible. Both roles entail multiple tests of accountability that require ongoing renewal of relationships and agreements by administrators with multiple institutions and actors in the democratic system. These actors include the executive branch; the legislature; the courts; the press; and the citizens in their multiple roles as voters, as members of oversight/advisory committees, and as general citizen-activists.

The control systems summarized in Exhibit 14.1 undergo change over time and express themselves differently through the specific functions that administrators are delegated to perform, including policy development and interpretation, budgeting and programming of resources, organizational culture and values, and the design and delivery of services to clients.

With the rise of New Public Management (NPM) over the last two decades, governments at all levels have moved extensively to using service contracts and partnerships with external actors to efficiently and effectively deliver programs and services. Government and the private sector view the accountability challenge differently. In the private sector, for-profit businesses and nonprofits negotiate agreements to purchase and to provide services. Contract law and commercial codes govern these horizontal relationships which are private in nature, subject to competitive limitations, and not available for public scrutiny. In contrast, government accountability applies vertical, hierarchical oversight and intense public scrutiny to assure accountability to public values.

Exhibit 14.1   **Types of Bureaucratic Accountability**

| **Organizational Accountability** | **Political Accountability** | **Legal Accountability** |
|---|---|---|
| • The formal structures of bureaucratic authority<br>• Creation of special organizational structures and process focusing on policy implementation oversight<br>• Continuous legislative oversight through required evaluation and reporting requirements<br>• Citizen boards and commissions | • External accountability to executive and legislative branches<br>• Political history and tradition<br>• Electoral structures and processes<br>• Political parties<br>• Citizen-centered processes like the initiative, recall and referendum<br>• Role of interest groups | • Rulemaking: formal and informal<br>• Advisory committees<br>• Negotiated rulemaking<br>• Alternative dispute resolution<br>• Mandatory productivity and efficiency requirements<br>• Open meetings law<br>• Conflict of interest prohibitions<br>• Professional codes of ethics |

Accountable performance in government contracts, grants, and partnerships requires bridging and managing these two conflicting perspectives (Cooper 2003, chap. 1).

In the first part of this chapter we focus on the political, organizational, and legal controls that are used to maintain accountability in traditional vertical structures of authority. In the second part of the chapter, we discuss how these mechanisms are used to maintain accountability in horizontal structures of authority, where government is doing "more steering and less rowing" as a result of relying on the private and nonprofit sector to be direct service providers.

## POLITICAL ACCOUNTABILITY

Political accountability normally is taken to mean that administrative agencies are subject to the supervening authority of elected officials. Typically, this political accountability includes dual responsibility to the elected chief executive, who provides ongoing administrative oversight of the agency, and to the legislative branch, which creates the original legal and budget authority for the agency to carry out its mission and conducts periodic oversight through reauthorizations, committee hearings, and in some cases direct supervision (Rosenbloom 2005, 2000). Serving two political masters at the same time can obviously pose policy implementation problems for administrators. These problems will not arise as long as the legislative body has internal agreement on what needs to be done, provides administrative agencies with clear policy guidelines, does not have a hidden agenda, and is in fundamental agreement with the executive branch on the philosophy that should guide the agency. Even under these conditions, however, there is extensive administrative discretion that needs to be kept accountable.

Among the less favorable circumstances that create challenges for administrators in the policy implementation process are the following: (1) the executive and legislative bodies are polarized along party lines, (2) the legislative body has a hidden agenda or is politically divided, (3) the legislative body is very unclear about what the problems and solutions are, and (4) the legislature is oblivious to the operational barriers to implementing its legislative intent. To the extent these

conditions prevail, administrators are left with the challenge of figuring out what is to be done and to do so in ways that meet tests of political accountability to both its executive and legislative masters.

## Political Accountability to the Chief Executive

The classical model of political accountability makes career administrators subordinate to the hierarchy of authority within the executive branch of government. This model is represented in Exhibit 14.2. The model is the most widely used structure of authority for maintaining administrative accountability at all levels of government in the United States. Whenever a new chief executive officer assumes his or her position, there is an expectation that administrative agencies will be responsive to any new changes in policy and administrative directions initiated by the new leader.

The chief executive officer, whether elected or appointed, has enormous leverage over administrative agencies, even when those agencies have been in existence for decades, have their own independent constituency support, and are numerous, large, and difficult to control. The chief executive officer has a wide variety of mechanisms available to exert centralized control and accountability, including: shared budget authority; power over personnel decisions, management directives, and monitoring systems; influence over rulemaking; access to the media; and a direct pipeline to members of the legislative body and the larger voting public. The executive office, as Teddy Roosevelt observed, can be used as a "bully pulpit" to drive the course of administrative affairs in a given direction, despite great obstacles. This can be done successfully, even when the bureaucracy itself is the direct target of change. President Bill Clinton's effort to fundamentally alter the style and philosophy of the entire administrative apparatus of the federal government is a case in point.

One of President Clinton's goals was to bring to fruition an initiative first undertaken by President Ronald Reagan: to reverse the federal regulatory culture that had dominated the public landscape for nearly 50 years. Clinton wanted to create a culture that cast doubt on increased regulation as the initial solution to a perceived public problem. He used the federal budget process, executive orders, and the media to help accomplish his goal. Prior to Clinton's plan, President George H.W. Bush, in his last year as president, presented a federal budget for FY 1992 that included the information in Exhibit 14.3. The information on first glance is shocking. Federal regulatory efforts are extraordinarily costly. Whether the information contained in Exhibit 14.3 is accurate, or paints a fair picture of the federal regulatory environment as a whole, is not the point for purposes of discussion here.

Viewed in the larger context of the National Performance Review Initiative (discussed next), the information in Exhibit 14.3 is part of larger systematic campaign by a president to alter the implementation of public policy in the United States. A cornerstone of this campaign was Executive Order 12866 (1993), the key provisions of which are summarized in Exhibit 14.4. This order sets out a new philosophy intended to guide the work of federal administrative agencies.

The philosophy embodied in Executive Order 12866 puts all federal administrators on notice that they bear a much heavier burden in justifying all regulatory activity than had been the case in the past. It clearly expresses the countervailing values that should be given increased weight in the regulatory balance: protecting the private marketplace from unnecessary rules, reducing the costs of government regulations, placing higher priority on the role of states and Native American tribes, reducing paperwork, improving the readability of rules, and providing greater attention to the liberty and privacy interests of those being regulated.

Exhibit 14.2  **Espoused Theory of Government**

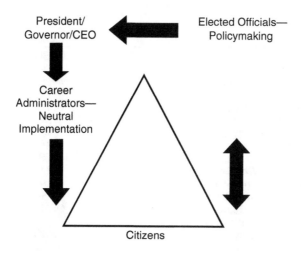

Another step in Clinton's campaign to change the implementation philosophy of administrative agencies was the designation of Vice President Al Gore to implement Executive Order 12866 and carry out what came to be called the National Performance Review Initiative.[1] This initiative received widespread media coverage and formed an important cornerstone of Gore's subsequent campaign for the U.S. presidency. Taken together, the executive order, the National Performance Review Initiative, and the systematic media campaign succeeded in significantly altering the implementation of public policy at the national level. The performance focus of the Clinton initiative has been carried forward into subsequent presidential administrations. President George W. Bush used the Office of Management and Budget to create a new Program Assessment Rating Tool (PART) that facilitated the establishment of performance measures across federal programs. President Obama abandoned this approach and replaced it with the Government Performance and Results Modernization Act of 2010, which changed the focus from grading programs as successful or unsuccessful to requiring agency leaders to set priority goals, demonstrate progress in achieving goals, and explain performance trends.

While the executive-centered approach to policy implementation and accountability is the dominant model at the federal level, there are at least five considerations that make this model overly simplistic. First, at many local levels of government, there is no clear and official "executive" branch of government. Many local jurisdictions have a chief executive officer who serves at the pleasure of the legislative body. These systems resemble parliamentary forms of governance, which blur or even unify the legislative and executive functions of government. This is the case with both strong and weak mayor systems as well as with city manager/county administrator forms of government, where the chief executive officer serves "at the pleasure" of the legislative body.

A second consideration that confounds the model represented in Exhibit 14.2 is that many jurisdictions in the United States have multiple elected chief executive officers, each of whom is responsible for his or her own separate administrative structure of authority. This is the case with jurisdictions that elect an auditor, clerk, district attorney, sheriff, mayor, board chair, and so on. Even at the state level, there may be a separately elected treasurer and comptroller, secretary of state, superintendent of public instruction, and auditor. In these instances, there are many executive branches of government.

Exhibit 14.3  **Cost-Effectiveness of Selected Regulations**

| Regulation | Agency | Cost per Premature Death Averted ($ millions 1990) |
|---|---|---|
| Space Heater Ban | CPSC | 0.1 |
| Aircraft Cabin Fire Protection Standard | FAA | 0.1 |
| Auto Passive Restraint/Seat Belt Standards | NHTSA | 0.1 |
| Steering Column Protection Standard | NHTSA | 0.1 |
| Underground Construction Standards | OSHA | 0.1 |
| Trihalomethane Drinking Water Standards | EPA | 0.2 |
| Aircraft Seat Cushion Flammability Standard | FAA | 0.4 |
| Alcohol and Drug Control Standards | FRA | 0.4 |
| Auto Fuel-System Integrity Standard | NHTSA | 0.4 |
| Standards for Servicing Auto Wheel Rims | OSHA | 0.4 |
| Aircraft Floor Emergency Lighting Standard | FAA | 0.6 |
| Concrete & Masonry Construction Standards | OSHA | 0.6 |
| Passive Restraints for Trucks & Buses (Proposed) | OSHA | 0.7 |
| Crane Suspended Personnel Platform Standard | NHTSA | 0.7 |
| Children's Sleepwear Flammability Ban | CPSC | 0.8 |
| Auto Side Door Support Standards | NHTSA | 0.8 |
| Side-Impact Standards for Autos (Dynamic) | NHTSA | 0.8 |
| Low Altitude Wind Shear Equipment & Training Standards | FAA | 1.3 |
| Electrical Equipment Standards (Metal Mines) | MSHA | 1.4 |
| Traffic Alert and Collision Avoidance (TCAS) Systems | FAA | 1.5 |
| Trenching and Excavation Standards | OSHA | 1.5 |
| Hazard Communication Standard | OSHA | 1.6 |
| Side-Impact Standards for Trucks, Buses, and MPVs (Proposed) | NHTSA | 2.2 |
| Grain Dust Explosion Prevention Standards | OSHA | 2.8 |
| Rear Lap/Shoulder Belts for Autos | NHTSA | 3.2 |
| Benzene NESHAP (Original: Fugitive Emissions) | EPA | 3.4 |
| Radionuclides in uranium mines | EPA | 3.4 |
| Ethylene Dibromide Drinking Water Standard | EPA | 5.7 |
| Benzene NESHAP (Revised: Coke By-products) | EPA | 6.1 |
| Asbestos Occupational Exposure Limit | OSHA | 8.3 |
| Benzene Occupational Exposure Limit | OSHA | 8.9 |
| Electrical Equipment Standards (Coal Mines) | MSHA | 9.2 |
| Arsenic Emission Standards for Glass Plants | EPA | 13.5 |
| Ethylene Oxide Occupational Exposure Limit | OSHA | 20.5 |
| Arsenic/Copper NESHAP | EPA | 23.0 |
| Hazardous Waste Listing for Petroleum Refining Sludge | EPA | 27.6 |
| Cover/Move Uranium Mill Tailings (Inactive Sites) | EPA | 31.7 |
| Benzene NESHAP (Revised: Transfer Operations) | EPA | 32.9 |
| Cover/Move Uranium Mill Tailings (Active Sites) | EPA | 45.0 |
| Acrylonitrile Occupational Exposure Limit | OSHA | 51.5 |
| Coke Ovens Occupational Exposure Limit | OSHA | 63.5 |
| Lockout/Tagout | OSHA | 70.9 |
| Asbestos Occupational Exposure Limit | OSHA | 74.0 |
| Arsenic Occupational Exposure Limit | OSHA | 106.9 |
| Asbestos Ban | EPA | 110.7 |
| Diethylstilbestrol (DES) Cattle Feed Ban | FDA | 124.8 |
| Benzene NESHAP (Revised: Waste Operations) | EPA | 168.2 |
| 1,2 Dichloropropane Drinking Water Standard | EPA | 653.0 |
| Hazardous Waste Land Disposal Ban (1st 3rd) | EPA | 4,190.4 |
| Municipal Solid Waste Landfill Standards (Proposed) | EPA | 19,107.0 |
| Formaldehyde Occupational Exposure Limit | OSHA | 86,201.8 |
| Atrazine/Alachlor Drinking Water Standard | EPA | 92,069.7 |
| Hazardous Waste Listing for Wood Preserving | EPA | 5,700,000.0 |

*Source:* From the U.S. Budget for Fiscal Year 1992, Table C-2, Part II, 370.

Exhibit 14.4  **Executive Order 12866**

Regulatory Planning and Review
September 30, 1993

The American people deserve a regulatory system that works for them, not against them: a regulatory system that protects and improves their health, safety, environment, and well-being and improves the performance of the economy without imposing unacceptable or unreasonable costs on society; regulatory policies that recognize that the private sector and private markets are the best engine for economic growth; regulatory approaches that respect the role of State, local, and tribal governments; and regulations that are effective, consistent, sensible, and understandable. We do not have such a regulatory system today.

With this Executive order, the Federal Government begins a program to reform and make more efficient the regulatory process. The objectives of this Executive order are to enhance planning and coordination with respect to both new and existing regulations; to reaffirm the primacy of Federal agencies in the regulatory decision-making process; to restore the integrity and legitimacy of regulatory review and oversight; and to make the process more accessible and open to the public. In pursuing these objectives, the regulatory process shall be conducted so as to meet applicable statutory requirements and with due regard to the discretion that has been entrusted to the Federal agencies.

Section 1. Statement of Regulatory Philosophy and Principles

(a) The Regulatory Philosophy

Federal agencies should promulgate only such regulations as are required by law, are necessary to interpret the law, or are made necessary by compelling public need, such as material failures of private markets to protect or improve the health and safety of the public, the environment, or the well-being of the American people. In deciding whether and how to regulate, agencies should assess all costs and benefits of available regulatory alternatives, including the alternative of not regulating. Costs and benefits shall be understood to include both quantifiable measures (to the fullest extent that these can be usefully estimated) and qualitative measures of costs and benefits that are difficult to quantify, but nevertheless essential to consider. Further, in choosing among alternative regulatory approaches, agencies should select those approaches that maximize net benefits (including potential economic, environmental, public health and safety, and other advantages; distributive impacts; and equity), unless a statute requires another regulatory approach.

(b) The Principles of Regulation

To ensure that the agencies' regulatory programs are consistent with the philosophy set forth above, agencies should adhere to the following principles, to the extent permitted by law and where applicable:

(1)    Each agency shall identify the problem that it intends to address (including, where applicable, the failures of private markets or public institutions that warrant new agency action) as well as assess the significance of that problem.
(2)    Each agency shall examine whether existing regulations (or other law) have created, or contributed to, the problem that a new regulation is intended to correct and whether those regulations (or other law) should be modified to achieve the intended goal of regulation more effectively.
(3)    Each agency shall identify and assess available alternatives to direct regulation, including providing economic incentives to encourage the desired behavior, such as user fees or marketable permits, or providing information upon which choices can be made by the public.
(4)    In setting regulatory priorities, each agency shall consider, to the extent reasonable, the degree and nature of the risks posed by various substances or activities within its jurisdiction.

*(continued)*

Exhibit 14.4 *(continued)*

(5)  When an agency determines that a regulation is the best available method of achieving the regulatory objective, it shall design its regulations in the most cost-effective manner to achieve the regulatory objective. In doing so, each agency shall consider incentives for innovation, consistency, predictability, the costs of enforcement and compliance (to the government, regulated entities, and the public), flexibility, distributive impacts, and equity.

(6)  Each agency shall assess both the costs and the benefits of the intended regulation . . . [and] adopt a regulation only upon a reasoned determination that the benefits of the intended regulation justify its costs.

(7)  Each agency shall base its decisions on the best reasonably obtainable scientific, technical, economic, and other information concerning the need for, and consequences of, the intended regulation.

(8)  Each agency shall identify and assess alternative forms of regulation and shall, to the extent feasible, specify performance objectives, rather than specifying the behavior or manner of compliance that regulated entities must adopt.

(9)  Wherever feasible, agencies shall seek views of appropriate State, local, and tribal officials before imposing regulatory requirements that might significantly or uniquely affect those governmental entities. [A]s appropriate, agencies shall seek to harmonize Federal regulatory actions with related State, local, and tribal regulatory and other governmental functions.

(10)  Each agency shall avoid regulations that are inconsistent, incompatible, or duplicative with its other regulations or those of other Federal agencies.

(11)  Each agency shall tailor its regulations to impose the least burden on society . . . taking into account, among other things, and to the extent practicable, the costs of cumulative regulations.

(12)  Each agency shall draft its regulations to be simple and easy to understand, with the goal of minimizing the potential for uncertainty and litigation arising from such uncertainty.

A third challenge to the simple model of executive accountability is the existence of independent commissions that may have extensive oversight responsibility for the development and implementation of agency policy. These commissions are of two kinds. The first category are *regulatory commissions,* which function in ways similar to the Federal Trade Commission, the Federal Energy Regulatory Commission, and utility and rate-setting bodies at the state level (see Exhibit 5.2 of chapter 5 for further examples). The chief characteristic of these kinds of bodies is that they have the independence to make policy (such as setting rates, promulgating rules defining fair competition and unfair labor practices, and the like). In addition, they have authority to adjudicate the grievances of individuals that arise from the application of the rules promulgated by the commission. The second kind of commission are *governing* bodies which provide policy, personnel, and budget oversight of a defined set of administrative activities. These governing commissions are especially common in western states, where the Populist and Progressive movements had their greatest impact at the turn of the nineteenth century. Such commissions usually consist of five to seven citizens, appointed by the governor, but holding a four- to seven-year term of office. Commission members usually can be removed from office only for "cause," which means that they cannot be removed simply because of policy or political differences with the chief executive officer.

Extensive use of the commission system of governance severely restricts the authority of the chief executive to provide a common policy and administrative direction for all administrative agencies within the jurisdiction. For example, a governor who wishes to develop a common statewide plan for the recovery of an endangered species may find his or her goals severely compromised by the existence of Fish and Wildlife, Parks, or Water Resources commissions, each having independent oversight of a key agency necessary to develop and implement the governor's plan (Morgan 2005).

A fourth consideration that undermines the simple model of executive accountability is the argument by many American scholars that career administrators are responsible to the Constitution

as a whole, not just to the particular policy or partisan political agenda of a given chief executive officer.[2] Support for this argument is found in the oath of office taken by many career administrators to uphold and defend the Constitution of the United States, which is a superior authority to the chief executive officer or any of his or her lieutenants.

There have been some dramatic examples of what would be considered "executive insubordination" in the name of a higher duty to the Constitution. For example, in 1969, then-president of the United States, Richard M. Nixon, ordered the U.S. Justice Department to petition the courts on behalf of southern school districts to delay court-ordered busing. President Nixon invoked his policy of New Federalism to argue in favor of a desegregation implementation program that would be controlled by citizen committees at the local level. This precipitated a civil disobedience letter from 65 Justice Department lawyers, who asserted they had a constitutional duty to press forward on the court desegregation orders (Greenburg 1984, 8).

A final factor that clouds the simple model of executive accountability is the scale, complexity, and diverse organizational structures of many public agencies—all of which defy a simplistic hierarchical model. Most agencies of any size will have collegial, quasi-judicial, and competitive subunits that are relatively insulated from much of the agency hierarchy (Hult 1987). Professionals in agencies often benefit from strong professional associations that promulgate and enforce external standards for decision making. This is the case for auditing, financial accounting, purchasing, contracting, engineering, and a host of other government standards and practices. Quasi-judicial units also enjoy degrees of independence from chief executives. Parole boards, police oversight committees, dispute resolution bodies, and tenant rights committees all illustrate the quasi-judicial role of executive functions that temper the ability of a chief executive to exercise arbitrary, capricious and uninformed power. While the opinions and recommendations of the aforementioned kinds of bodies can be reversed by the executive, it cannot be done in many cases without formal judicial review and certain political opposition from community leaders. Officials running special enterprise units may also enjoy significant legislative protection from manipulation by the executive. Moreover, the dizzying array of different policy subunits of the agencies can severely limit control by chief executives. These policy subunits often form networks with other agencies and with powerful interest groups that can limit executive control and even transform agency missions over the long run. For example, Admiral Hyman Rickover's work with the Atomic Energy Commission (AEC) in the 1950s led to significant changes in U.S. naval policy. Rickover, working closely with the AEC, helped spur development of the minireactors that could be used on naval vessels (Rockwell 1995; Natchez and Bupp 1973).

For all of the above reasons, the executive-centered model in Exhibit 14.2 oversimplifies the problem of administrative accountability. A model that is more reflective of administrative reality is provided in Exhibit 14.5. This model is especially characteristic of the structure of authority at local levels of government, where career administrators work in partnership with elected officials to craft policies that cannot be separated easily from their implementation (Morgan and Kass 1993, 1991). The two activities of policy development and implementation are frequently an integral part of a larger strategic whole—one in which administrators and elected officials work together in ways that obscure any bright-line distinction between policy development and implementation activities.[3]

## Political Accountability to the Legislature

Legislative accountability runs close to the heart of the American system of democratic governance. In its most extreme form, legislative accountability can mean (as it did for Herman Finer,

Exhibit 14.5  **Theory of Governance in Action**

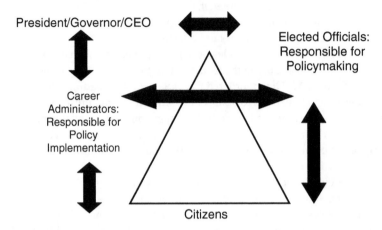

who was quoted at the beginning of this chapter) that it is irresponsible for administrators to use their technical expertise unless and until there is a direct command to do so by the democratically elected representatives of the people. There are many good reasons for taking a strict legislative-centered view of administrative accountability.

Theodore Lowi, one of the most tenacious and articulate defenders of this "strict construction-ist" view, reminds us why implementation should always be guided by the clear direction of the legislative body. Like James Madison in *The Federalist Papers* (Madison 1787 and 1788, Federalist Nos. 10 and 51, quoted in Rossiter 1961), Lowi accepts the necessity of interest groups but argues that legislative supremacy is absolutely central to holding these interest groups accountable for the public policy consequences of their actions. His argument rests on the simple observation that "politics gravitates to the points of greatest discretion" (Lowi 1993, 151). If large amounts of dis-cretion are lodged in administrative agencies, then that is where organized interests will exercise pressure to get what they want out of the process. Whenever this occurs, citizens' rights to access and the openness of government are compromised. The policies produced in these administra-tive and subgovernment forums do not receive the same kind of open and vigorous public debate characteristic of larger legislative bodies. As a result, we end up with programs and laws without really knowing or debating the policies these programs and laws are intended to serve. For these reasons, Lowi is equally critical of a legislative system that delegates large amounts of substan-tive policy discretion to its committees and subcommittees. Democracy is twice the victim of such practices, whether they occur at the legislative or administrative levels of government. First, democratic processes are undercut; second, public policy outcomes are frequently self-serving to a narrow range of well-organized and well-financed interests. Both of these consequences increase cynicism and undermine the legitimacy of democratic governance (Lowi 1979, 1967).

In the final analysis, the argument in favor of making the legislature the centerpiece of ad-ministrative accountability rests less on the pathologies that need to be avoided and more on a particular theory of what makes government democratic. The defenders of a legislative-centered view of administrative accountability are Jeffersonian in their belief that public deliberation is at the heart of democratic governance.[4] They regard the legislative body as the most encompassing of all democratic forums. This is where the deliberative process of government is best focused, and where there is an open opportunity to reconcile and balance the many competing interests and values that are inherent to our diverse system of democratic governance. When the legislative

body loses this deliberative capacity to join and reconcile differences, democratic governance loses its raison d'être and ends up encouraging the many pathologies in democratic processes discussed here.

What are the implications of the legislative-centered model for how administrators should think about and conduct their policy implementation work? Answers to this question vary considerably, usually depending on one's willingness to accept the consequences of legislative ambiguity and inaction. The most conservative end of the spectrum is represented by Herman Finer, who argues that no action should be taken by administrators to implement a policy until they have command-like clarity from the legislative body. But this commandlike clarity may be slow in coming at state and federal levels of government. For example, it is typical for administrative agencies to work with more than one committee, being given, for example, substantive policy guidance by a legislative committee that created the authority to act, and a set of legislative guidelines (perhaps contradictory in nature) by the appropriation committee that approves the agency's expenditure of annual funds.

At the other end of the spectrum from Finer's legislative-centered model is Carl Friedrich's model (1940; also quoted at the beginning of this chapter). Friedrich argues that administrators need to initiate action to solve problems, relying on their professional expertise and "personal sense" of the public will. Between these extremes are those who favor high levels of administrative initiative but rely on the various organizational and legal mechanisms discussed in the following sections to maintain accountability.

The legislative-centered model of administrative accountability, like its executive-centered counterpart, is very difficult to carry out in practice. The realities of the legislative process make it nearly impossible to provide administrators with discretion-proof policy implementation strategies. Recall our discussion in chapters 3 and 13 of the different kinds of public policy settings and the implications for the exercise of administrative discretion. For example, distributive (sometimes called "pork barrel") policies tend to put administrators in the position of using their professional competence and technical discretion to build the dam, construct the bomber, improve the water-way, and so on. With these types of policies, elected officials assume that they need not worry very much about what administrators do to carry out their will. Once a decision has been made to authorize a project and to appropriate the funds, administrators are generally trusted to get the job done. Included in this category are local infrastructure projects such as transportation maintenance, water and sewer systems, and routine licensing and inspection activities. But what may start out at the state or federal levels as a merely technical issue can turn into a major controversy at the local level of policy implementation. For instance, legislative authorization to expand a spillway or to provide funds for dredging a harbor may be seen by environmental advocates as an adverse action to an endangered species. Consider the peregrine falcon case introduced at the beginning of Part IV. Is this a case that technical expertise can ultimately be relied upon to decide? Probably not.

While technical discretion plays a central role in implementing most distributive public policy, this is less the case with regulatory policy discretion. Regulatory policies are represented by efforts to ensure safe foods and products for consumers, the protection of the environment, maintenance of workplace safety, balanced land-use planning, fair competition in the marketplace, and protection from terrorist attacks. The definition of the ends these regulatory activities should achieve is often a matter of considerable disagreement among legislators and the citizens in whose name they act. While there may be a common desire to create secure working environments, clean air and water, safe foods, and maximum protection from the risk of a terrorist attack, given the uncertain state of our knowledge, there can be strong disagreement over exactly what is harmful. Even when there is agreement that a certain substance is toxic or that a terrorist risk exists, the level of risk we are

willing to assume varies from one person to the next, and the price for controlling the risk may compromise other important values. Therefore, administrators are frequently left with the task of deciding both what is harmful *and* what constitutes an acceptable level of risk.

The challenge for administrators in charge of the implementation of redistributive policy may be equally difficult, but for slightly different reasons. As we indicated in chapters 3 and 13, when deciding redistributive policy questions (questions concerning taxes, poverty, gender, and race), politicians create conditions of discretionary administrative authority—not because they are uncertain about what the problem is, but because a proposed solution may well create enemies politicians cannot afford to make. For example, in the case of access to increasingly scarce environmental resources, there is not much political advantage for elected officials in deciding among those who want to use the forests for timber, hiking, snowmobiling, hunting, rock climbing, or a pristine wilderness experience. The legislative task is simplified when elected representatives mandate administrators to manage the scarce resource for "multiple use" without providing any further guidelines. But it becomes ever more difficult when the legislative body requires that administrators manage the conflict among competing groups in ways that are "customer-oriented" and the least intrusive on the rights of private property owners.

To summarize, a legislative model of policy implementation, like its executive-centered counterpart, is problematic for a combination of the following reasons:

1. *Uncertainty:* The legislature may be deliberately ambiguous regarding the policy intent and detail of a piece of legislation because the problem and/or its solutions are not clear.
2. *Ignorance:* The legislature may be unaware of the operational conditions necessary to implement its policy objectives.
3. *Partisan Disagreement:* The legislature may be so closely divided that it is forced to craft vague language that satisfies all sides to the controversy.
4. *Symbolic:* The legislature may pass a piece of legislation as a symbolic gesture to show support for a point of view rather than to demonstrate serious intent to solve a problem. In addition to the obvious advantages this may have for reelection, there are other times when the larger goal may simply be to have the "constitutionality" of the legislation tested by the courts.
5. *Hidden Agendas:* Members of the legislative body may have hidden agendas that are never fully disclosed, even to colleagues who work closely with them to pass a given piece of legislation. It is common practice, for example, for members to support one another to pass legislation even when the reasons for doing so are not clear.

The legislative-centered model of administrative accountability is even more problematic for those who disagree with the foundational premise upon which the model rests. As we have observed in chapters 4 and 6, many scholars believe the deliberative principle of democratic governance represented by the legislative body needs to be supplemented by other equally necessary principles, such as energetic and efficient administration of public policy, direct responsiveness to the citizenry, and the protection of minority rights. These additional principles are as important to democratic governance as a vigorous deliberative process. If administrators have an obligation to the entire structure of constitutional authority and all of the multiple principles that are in dynamic tension, these scholars ponder why the legislative-centered model should be given primacy over other values equally important to the health of democratic governance. For these students and scholars of the administrative process, the burden of maintaining bureaucratic accountability is a

multipronged undertaking that includes reliance on organizational and legal processes, in addition to political accountability to the two major branches of governance.[5]

## ORGANIZATIONAL ACCOUNTABILITY

In addition to direct political control over the bureaucracy by the executive and legislative branches of government, administrative accountability is maintained indirectly through organizational structures and processes, professional values within the organization, and the institutional momentum of organizational memory and practices. The most frequently used mechanism of administrative accountability is reliance on formal organizational structures and processes. In fact, much of the reinvention of government and the New Public Management movements rely on alterations in the structure of organizations: They aim to achieve greater personal accountability through flattening organizations and increasing the discretionary authority at the lowest levels of the administrative hierarchy.

In chapters 7 through 9, we discussed the importance of creating personnel and organizational accountability through appropriate structuring of administrative processes and systems. These, in addition to organizational design and operations, play a central role in achieving administrative accountability in the policy implementation process. We will simply highlight some of the major organizational controls that are relied upon to achieve this result.

### Centralized Policy Control

One way of creating administrative accountability in the implementation process is to rely on policy coordination and control. Chief executive officers, such as governors and the president of the United States, can do this by establishing a centralized policy advisory committee, which may consist of department directors or personal policy advisers. The president's Domestic Policy Council and Council of Economic Advisers are examples of such a practice (Warshaw 1996). The larger and the more complex the administrative structure, the more common it is to rely on a group of internal policy advisers to help advance the chief executive officer's policy agenda through the aegis of administrative agencies. The most centralized form of control is for the chief executive to appoint a deputy chief of staff in charge of a given policy domain with the requirement that department heads need to obtain clearance from the deputy chief of staff or the policy advisory committee to undertake major new initiatives. What constitutes a major new initiative usually becomes clear over time as a result of ongoing interaction with those in charge. The management function of the Office of Management and Budget (OMB) performs this review and coordination role for the president at the federal level.

Local levels of government tend to rely on a strategic plan or long-term business plan that is revisited soon after each major election and is updated annually between elections. The strategic plan sets forth the priorities of the jurisdiction, thus assisting department heads and their subordinates in educating employees and clientele groups about what to expect in the way of policy and budget support from the jurisdiction.

### Centralized Budget Control

The most common mechanism of organizational control is exercised through the budget process. The president's Office of Management and Budget (Warshaw 1996)—as well as the functional equivalent at each jurisdictional level of government throughout the United States—provides or-

ganizational control over administrative agencies to ensure that there is budget and management accountability to the priorities of the chief executive officer. As we discussed in chapter 11 on budgeting, the chief executive officer for most jurisdictions in the United States has the responsibility to organize and present an integrated budget request to the legislative body for deliberation and approval. This responsibility enables the chief executive officer to maintain accountability of the administrative agencies by controlling the initial request for their annual operating budgets.

But budgetary control is not limited to the chief executive officer. Since no public agency can spend any money without legislative appropriation of funds (usually on an annual basis), the legislative body plays an important role in using the budget to maintain organizational accountability during the policy implementation process.

### Centralized Personnel Control

Administrative accountability cannot be maintained without control over the individuals who carry out the work of organizations. In chapters 8 and 9 we discussed in some detail how this process works in the public sector, especially with the existence of professional civil service or merit systems at most every level of government, and influential public unions in many parts of the public sector. Both of these institutions help to maintain accountability by ensuring that individuals within the civil service ranks are hired, promoted, and disciplined for reasons related to the formally defined requirements of the job, not for personal or political reasons of individual managers.

In addition to the continuity and predictability that the civil service/merit systems and public unions play in the policy implementation process, it is also important that agencies be responsive to the most recent political will of the electorate. This is an important part of what accountability means. But this cannot occur unless the chief executive officer can appoint department heads and their major deputies. How far this discretionary authority extends is specifically defined by each jurisdiction. As we discussed in chapters 8 and 9, there has been a gradual historical trend in human resources management that severely limits the ability of the newly elected party or political officials to make large numbers of appointments at lower levels of the administrative hierarchy. These constraints consist of a combination of the following conditions that are especially powerful at our local levels of government: civil service protections, union contracts, the existence of independent commissions, and nonpartisan elections. These constraints are the product of the powerful antipolitics and professionalization movements that dominated the history of public administration during the twentieth century (reviewed in considerable detail in chapters 5 and 8).

One of the consequences of the professionalization of the public service and the limitations on political influence in the appointment of administrative officers is that much greater care is now taken in the review and vetting of selections for agency appointments at the executive- and mid-level positions of organizations. In addition to the increased care taken in the selection process, at the federal level an entirely new category of senior administrators (the senior executive service, or SES) was created in 1978 to serve at the will at the president. They can be assigned anywhere or sit in limbo until a position of trust is found for them. The establishment of the SES and the careful consideration taken in making senior-level appointments signify that accountability to the elected political leaders is a first principle of democratic governance.

### Centralized Organizational Control

Most jurisdictions rely on a centralized organizational structure to maintain accountability in the policy implementation process. For example, many states have an executive department, an

executive office, or a department of administrative services, the purpose of which is to maintain administrative oversight of the work of all administrative agencies. The OMB performs this function at the federal level (Warshaw 1996). This office and its state counterparts can sometimes set quite severe requirements on departments in the name of ensuring administrative accountability. For example, some presidents have instructed OMB not to allow administrative agencies to make any proposed changes in their policies or administrative rules without first obtaining clearance from OMB. Even speeches and testimony before Congress must be cleared and coordinated across departments by OMB.

In states with weaker traditions of administrative independence, this organizational control may not be so bureaucratic. In most local jurisdictions, centralized organizational control over administrative agencies is assumed to be an inherent part of the jurisdiction of the office of the chief executive (the city manager, chief administrator, mayor, or the like). This assumption begins to lose some of its presumptive weight in those jurisdictions that have multiple elected officials, elected administrators, or powerful and full-time legislative bodies.

Despite the best organizational and political efforts to maintain accountability over administrators during the policy implementation process, we have not eliminated the need for the exercise of extensive administrative discretion. The growing recognition of this necessity has shifted attention away from relying on mechanisms of external political and organizational accountability to those that depend on the bureaucracy to police itself based on a set of broad legal rules established by the legislature. As we will see in the section that follows, these rules replicate legislative process and provide opportunities through quasi-judicial processes for disaffected parties to appeal their grievances upward and outward to elected political officials.

## LEGAL ACCOUNTABILITY

The following case illustrates the many ways that administrators exercise discretion within a legal framework that is constrained by the legislative, executive, and judicial spheres of government.

### Case Illustration of Multiple Legal Constraints on Administrative Work

The Department of Environmental Quality (DEQ) received a call from a Mr. Quick complaining that the oil recycling business run by his neighbor, Ms. Pole, was polluting the environment. Ms. Pole runs a small business that recycles used crank case oil collected from automobile repair shops. The DEQ staff frequently receives similar calls and typically responds by making a phone call to the business, a site visit, and a follow-up with the neighbor. During these conversations, the staff uses a variety of negotiating skills it has learned from professional training programs. Through these negotiations, Ms. Pole agreed to change some of her storage practices to allay the neighbor's concerns.

Ms. Pole wanted more than informal assurances from the agency staff that her efforts to address the agency's concerns would be accepted and not result in fines or other adverse legal actions. She asked the agency for a declaratory ruling. Under this procedure, the interested person asks the agency to issue a binding ruling on the application of agency law to a certain set of facts. The agency head believed a declaratory ruling was appropriate in this case and so issued a ruling that found the operation did not violate the law. As required by law, the ruling was limited to the specific description of the operation submitted by Ms. Pole in her request for the declaratory ruling.

After several years, Ms. Pole modified her operation. Mr. Quick complained again about the operation, and the agency staff looked into the matter. The staff concluded that the new operation

did violate the law. Rather than file a formal complaint, the agency offered to speak with Ms. Pole regarding her business. Ms. Pole was convinced that her new operation was within the law. Although the negotiations were conducted in good faith, the agency and Ms. Pole were unable to reach an agreement.

At that point, the agency determined the oil recycling operation constituted a danger to public safety. The agency issued a notice asserting that Ms. Pole was in violation of the law, directing her to cease operations and assessing a monetary penalty.

Ms. Pole answered by claiming that the operation was being conducted legally and requested a hearing, as provided under the state's administrative procedures act. The matter was set for review before a hearing officer. Ms. Pole was represented by her attorney; an assistant attorney general represented the agency. The hearing officer suggested that Ms. Pole and her attorney sit down with the agency staff before the hearing and at least try to reach an agreement on the facts at issue. They did so and found that their dispute was over the agency's interpretation of the law. They stipulated to an agreed-upon set of facts and avoided the need for a formal "contested case" hearing.

The hearing officer issued a proposed order finding that Ms. Pole's recycling operation was in violation of the law. Ms. Pole's attorney filed exceptions to the findings of the hearings officer. After reviewing the proposed order by the hearing officer and Ms. Pole's exceptions, the agency issued a final order adopting the hearing officer's conclusion.

The agency's decision was controversial. A number of persons in the same business as Ms. Pole would go out of business under the agency's ruling. On the other hand, many members of the public supported the ruling because it protected them and their businesses.

Since there were a limited number of interest groups, the agency thought there might be a way to modify the rule so that Ms. Pole could operate and the other members of the public would be protected. Because the agency believed that development and implementation of a new rule would be most effective if it were based on agreement of all the interested parties, the agency decided to use a negotiated rulemaking process authorized by the legislature. The agency hired a convener to begin forming a negotiated rulemaking committee. With the help of the convener, the agency developed an agenda, scheduled a first meeting, and published a notice of the committee's formation. The committee met, selected a facilitator, and developed ground rules. The facilitator assisted the committee by conducting a brainstorming session, which generated an idea to use a new alternative technology. Ms. Pole determined that she could modify her operations to employ the new technology. The committee investigated the idea and presented a final report to the agency, proposing that the current rules be modified to allow the use of this new process. Because the agency believed the committee's suggested rule was reasonable, the agency did not appoint a rulemaking advisory committee, but merely issued a notice of intent to adopt administrative rules. The proposed rule was so popular that no one requested a hearing. The rule was put into effect.

This DEQ case example is repeated on a daily basis throughout every administrative agency at the federal, state, and local levels of government and across a wide range of subjects, including child custody cases, social service eligibility, regulatory violations, land-use approvals, pollution mitigation, habitat and wildlife protection, transportation planning, and licensing requests and renewals. The DEQ example, even with the storybook ending, illustrates some important characteristics of the policy implementation process that we have emphasized repeatedly throughout this book:

- Despite our best efforts to control and structure the policy implementation process, administrators are left with extraordinary amounts of discretion.
- The implementation discretion of career administrators has far-reaching impacts on the daily

lives and activities of citizens. The work that administrators do at the street level plays a dominant constitutive role in defining what quality of life means for every citizen. Equally important, these bureaucratic encounters provide the affected citizens with an example of what democracy means in everyday practice.

- Administrative agencies possess a wide array of tools and strategies to solve problems and enforce the law. In the case example, the agency used an informal negotiation, a declaratory ruling, a contested case, a negotiated rulemaking committee, and the actual rulemaking process. The requirements for all of these processes and other additional options are set forth in a set of procedures called the administrative procedures act. These procedures are discussed in greater detail in the section that follows.

## Administrative Rulemaking

The United States has long been known to operate on a rule-of-law system. In practice, this means that government and its political and administrative agents must be able to find a law, rule, or constitutional provision to justify their actions. Exhibit 14.6 provides an overview of these legal sources of authority. In the remaining sections of this chapter, we will focus on administrative-centered legal controls, especially administrative rulemaking and adjudication.

In chapter 5, we reviewed the major factors that have shaped the development of public administration in the twentieth century. One of the most important characteristics of this development is the rapid expansion in the number and size of federal administrative agencies, largely in response to the Populist and Progressive pressures for increased regulation and New Deal efforts to restore economic vitality and then to carry out the subsequent war effort. This expansion raised a fundamental question of accountability: How can administrators be given extensive discretion to use their professional expertise to solve public problems, while simultaneously ensuring that they always act within clearly defined legal guidelines? The answer is administrative rulemaking, an entirely new American invention that one student of the administrative process has characterized as "one of the greatest inventions of modern government" (Davis 1971, 65).

The invention simply consists of the legislature establishing formal legal guidelines that administrative agencies must follow whenever they try to fill in the gaps necessary to implement a legislative policy. These legislative guidelines are called administrative procedures and can be found in the codified statutes at the federal and all state levels of government. The federal guidelines were established by the Administrative Procedure Act (1947). By the 1960s, every state in the union had adopted similar acts to guide the discretionary activities of state agencies.

The administrative procedures in place at the federal and state levels of government share the following characteristics:

- They require that all agencies regularize their reporting of proposed rules, usually in a formal publication. This publication is called the *Federal Register* for all federal level agencies. Each state has a counterpart publication.
- The procedures require opportunities for "notice and comment" by potential parties affected by a proposed rule. Depending on the specific provisions of the state law, these opportunities can take the form of public hearings or can simply consist of written responses. The "notice and comment" requirement is usually divided into the following three stages: notice that a new rule or a change to an existing rule is being considered; a specified time period to comment on the proposed change or new rule; and notice of the promulgation of the final adopted rule.

Exhibit 14.6  **Sources of Administrative Legal Authority**

| Federal | State |
| --- | --- |
| **Legislative—Bills, Laws & Statutory Codes** | |
| U.S. Public Laws http://www.gpoaccess.gov/plaws/index.html | State Laws (state government websites) |
| U.S. Statutes-at-Large, Government Printing Office, PO AE 2.111 | Lexis-Nexis Academic Universe/Legal Research |
| U.S. Code Annotated (U.S.C.A) West Group | State Revised Statutes (state government websites) |
| U.S. Code Congressional and Administrative News (USCCAN) West Group (proprietary version of U.S. Statutes-at-Large) | http://www.findlaw.com/casecode/#statelaw |
| U.S. Code, http://www.gpoaccess.gov/uscode/index.html http://www.findlaw.com/casecode/uscodes/ | |
| Lexis-Nexis /Congressional Universe and Academic Universe/ Legal Research | |
| **Administrative—Executive Orders, Administrative Rules & Codes** | |
| U.S. Code of Federal Regulations and index (CFR) GPO AE2 106/3 | State-level Administrative Rules and Executive Orders (state government websites) |
| Federal Executive Orders, proclamations and other presidential orders located in Title 3 of the CFR | State-level executive orders most likely found on state governors website |
| Federal Register GPO J1.A2 | Lexis-Nexis /Academic Universe/Legal Research |
| Lexis-Nexis /Congressional Universe and Academic Universe/ Legal Research | http://www.findlaw.com/casecode/#statelaw |
| Code of Federal Regulations, http://www.gpoaccess.gov/cfr/index.html | |
| Federal Register, http://www.gpoaccess.gov/fr/index.html or http://www.findlaw.com/casecode/cfr.html | |
| **Judicial—Cases** | |
| West's Supreme Court Reporter | State-level Court Reports |
| United States Reports GPO | Lexis-Nexis Academic Universe/Legal Research |
| West's Federal Reporter (Appeals Courts) | http://www.findlaw.com/casecode/#statelaw |
| West's Federal Supplement (District Courts) | |
| Federal Court Decisions http://www.lib.lsu.edu/gov/fedgov.html#judi | |
| http://www.findlaw.com/casecode/ | |
| Lexis-Nexis Academic Universe/Legal Research | |

- The guidelines provide for the appeal of adverse decisions by administrators against individuals (for example, the denial of a license or permit). These provisions are considered to be adjudicative rather than rulemaking, since they involve an individual case and something that has happened in the past. Rulemaking, by contrast, is intended to apply to large numbers of individuals in the future.

There are two major questions involving the rulemaking process, the answers to which dramatically shape the nature of accountability achieved by a jurisdiction's administrative procedures:

1. What is the required burden of proof on administrators before they can adopt a rule?
2. And what is a rule, as opposed to an internal set of managerial guidelines, procedures, or policy clarifications?

*Required Burden of Proof*

Accountability is a function of the openness of the rulemaking process and access by citizens to it. Additionally, accountability dictates whether agencies have to listen to the testimony and evidence that is presented. The amount and kind of attention that is paid by administrators to verbal and written testimony is largely determined by the burden of proof that is required before administrators can promulgate a rule. Burden of proof has to do with the amount and kind of information that is needed to make decisions based on less than complete information.

There are a couple of simple ways to understand the importance of the burden of proof. One is to compare it to the approach used by the scientific community, which tends to view certainty as a yes/no choice that demands a high degree of assurance and considers only several variables at one time. For example, we are familiar with the notion of a 95 percent statistical confidence level that is often used by the scientific community to express the degree of uncertainty in a given situation. Another approach—one used by courts—relies on a sliding scale of certainty that allows a lower degree of certainty and considers the totality of the situation. These sliding scales include "beyond reasonable doubt" used in criminal cases and "preponderance of evidence" used in civil cases. A third approach is the one used by professionals who combine science, personal experience, historical information, expert opinion, and knowledge of the unique factors of the setting to arrive at a professional judgment. Exhibit 14.7 summarizes the differences among these three different kinds of approaches to the problem of providing enough evidence in order for a fair decision to be made.

As the summary makes clear, the standard of proof for administrative rulemaking ranks on the lower end of the burden-of-proof hierarchy within the legal frame of reference. Administrators are required to meet the test of "substantial evidence," based on the record taken as a whole. This standard is similar to the "preponderance of evidence" test used in civil cases. The justification for a standard that ranges in the 50–75 percent range is based on a recognition by courts that administrators need the flexibility to weigh a wide variety of factors in crafting solutions to policy implementation problems: cost effectiveness, efficiency of administration, the number of clients served, the reasonableness of burdens placed on clients and those regulated, and the risk and costs of making mistakes.[6] These considerations resemble the kind of considerations taken into account in the professional approach to uncertainty outlined in Exhibit 14.7.

The general trend over the past 50 years has been to increase the burden of proof on administrators, not by abandoning the "substantial evidence" standard but by redefining what constitutes "substantial." A couple of examples will illustrate the subtle but powerful importance this has for the work of administrative agencies.

One of the best examples of changes in the meaning of the "substantial evidence" requirement is illustrated by Executive Order 12866, discussed earlier in this chapter (see Exhibit 14.4). Through this order, the president of the United States redefined what the "substantial evidence" requirement means for all federal agencies promulgating new regulatory rules. Henceforward,

Exhibit 14.7  **Comparison of Frameworks for Standards of Proof**

*Source:* Haas (2003). Copyright 2003 by the Security of American Foresters. Reproduced by permission of Society of American Foresters in the format textbook via Copyright Clearance Center.

these agencies were required to give greater weight to the following considerations than had been the case in the past:

1. Federal agencies are required to include a statement of the need for a rule and how the rule meets the need. Agencies should not promulgate a regulatory rule if the desired behavior can be achieved through alternative means.
2. Agencies need to demonstrate that a regulation is the best available method of achieving the regulatory objective.
3. Agencies must demonstrate that they have designed their new regulations "in the most cost-effective manner" to achieve the regulatory objective.
4. Each agency shall assess both the costs and the benefits of the intended regulation . . . [and] adopt a regulation only upon a reasoned determination that the benefits of the intended regulation justify its costs.

5.  Each agency shall base its decisions on the best reasonably obtainable scientific, techni-cal, economic, and other information concerning the need for, and consequences of, the intended regulation.

6.  Each agency shall identify and assess alternative forms of regulation and shall, to the extent feasible, specify performance objectives, rather than specifying the behavior or manner of compliance that regulated entities must adopt.

7.  Wherever feasible, agencies shall seek views of appropriate state, local, and tribal officials before imposing regulatory requirements that might significantly or uniquely affect those governmental entities. . . . [A]s appropriate, agencies shall seek to harmonize Federal regulatory actions with related State, local, and tribal regulatory and other governmental functions.

8.  Each agency shall avoid regulations that are inconsistent, incompatible, or duplicative with its other regulations or those of other Federal agencies.

9.  Each agency shall tailor its regulations to impose the least burden on society, . . . taking into account, among other things, and to the extent practicable, the costs of cumulative regulations.

10.  Each agency shall draft its regulations to be simple and easy to understand, with the goal of minimizing the potential for uncertainty and litigation arising from such uncertainty.

The cumulative consequences of these executive-level guidelines significantly altered the meaning of "substantial evidence" by requiring administrators to broaden their consideration of the factors that need to be taken into account before promulgating a rule.

A second dramatic example of changes in the meaning of "substantial evidence" is illustrated by a case involving court review of an administrative rule promulgated by a city land-use planning department. The City of Tigard, Oregon, approved a building expansion and improvement permit for a local hardware store on condition that the owners dedicate a portion of their property for streamside mitigation for an adjoining creek that perennially flooded and for a bike path along the stream bank. These conditions were imposed under an earlier rule the planning commission had adopted. The administrators assumed that their transportation and flood control rationales were sufficient justifications to meet the "substantial evidence" test. The case eventually was appealed to the U.S. Supreme Court and—much to the surprise of land-use planners throughout the United States—the Court announced that local land-use planners were wrong in their application of the substantial evidence test to cases involving the rights of property owners. Traditionally, land-use planners could impose conditions on private landowners for a larger public good as long as they demonstrated that there was "a reasonable relationship" between the conditions they imposed and the public purposes to be achieved by these conditions. Based on the "reasonable relationship" test, the conditions imposed by Tigard land-use planners were permissible. Clearly, it was reasonable to assume that parking and flood control problems would be helped by requiring the property owners to dedicate a portion of their property to bike path and streamside mitigation.

However, the Court used the occasion to announce a new "rough proportionality" test that needed to be used in the future in deciding on the reasonableness of conditions imposed on pri-vate landowners in making property improvements: "Although there is no mathematical calcula-tion required, the city must make some form of individualized determination that the required dedication is related both in nature and extent to the impact of the proposed development."[7] In other words, administrators had to provide concrete evidence of the amount of flood control and decreased automobile traffic that would be achieved as a result of the private property that was taken to reduce flooding and the volume of traffic. In addition, the amount of public good achieved

has to be "roughly proportional" to the amount of private property that was taken. Since the city planners had provided no evidence of this "rough proportionality," the action was judged to be in violation of the Fifth Amendment constitutional prohibition against taking property without just compensation. While this case leaves unchanged the "substantial evidence" burden-of-proof test used in deciding the constitutionality of an administrative rule, the decision significantly alters the meaning of "substantial evidence" in all cases involving administrative rules that affect the rights of private property owners.

Our discussion of the burden-of-proof standard used in judging the promulgation of administrative rules has thus far focused exclusively on the federal rulemaking process. Each state's administrative procedures act is accompanied by language and a history of application that may have important implications for understanding the meaning of the "substantial evidence" standard used to determine the legality of an administrative rule. For example, the state of Oregon permits agencies to use a very low threshold of evidence to justify the promulgation of a rule. They simply have to demonstrate a need "that the rule-proposing agency *perceives* a need for the rule."[8] "Perceived need" is a much easier standard to meet than one based on objective, scientific proof.

*The Definition of a Rule*

The formal definition of a rule under the administrative procedures act, like the burden of proof, is also critically important in determining the amount and extent of administrative accountability that is achieved through the administrative rulemaking process. For example, public agencies undertake numerous actions that provide employees with guidelines on what policy means, how to set priorities, and how to interpret and apply their discretionary authority. Are all of these management activities governed by the administrative procedures act? To illustrate the practical significance of this question, let us take two very common hypothetical examples.

The director of a state's police force issues a directive that gives first-order priority to drug trafficking and second-order priority to missing persons or the recovery of stolen property. Does this priority setting qualify as rulemaking, or is it simply an appropriate exercise of managerial prerogative to make the highest and best uses of scarce resources? Or consider the simple question of whether a state Department of Environmental Quality administrator in the far rural reaches of a state can allow a solid waste operator to cover disposal debris with dirt only once a week in contrast to a DEQ administrator in the largest metropolitan area, who may require debris to be covered daily. The amount of debris, the density of the population, and the prevailing winds may create quite different health hazards at the two separate sites. Where is the line between administrative rulemaking and routine management oversight and control?

One end of the spectrum is represented by the U.S. Administrative Procedures Act, which draws a clear distinction between substantive/procedural rules on the one hand, and interpretive rules on the other. The latter are explicitly exempt from the notice and comment requirements of the Federal Administrative Procedures Act.

The other end of the spectrum is represented by the state of Oregon. Oregon's Administrative Procedures Act defines a rule to include "directive, standard, regulation or statement of general applicability that implements, interprets or prescribes law or policy or describes procedure or practice requirements of any agency" (see note 8 at the end of this chapter). This very broad and all-inclusive definition of a rule means that Oregon administrative agencies have very little discretion in deciding what a rule is. The State Attorney General's Office has taken the position that rulemaking procedures for the state of Oregon are to be followed in all cases where management practices and policies "substantially affect the interests of the public."[9] In the state police and

DEQ examples cited above, the directors of both agencies would be required to follow Oregon administrative rulemaking requirements as a state employee, but they would not be required to do so if acting as a federal employee.

There are some unintended consequences of defining a rule so broadly that it precludes administrators from using internal management guidelines and interpretive rules without going through the formal rulemaking process (Morgan 2005). First, it severely restricts the ability of an agency to accommodate local conditions and special circumstances, thus making agencies appear rigid and bureaucratic to citizens who are demanding more user-friendly, case-by-case approaches to policy implementation. Second, it creates incentives for agencies to engage in techniques that avoid the extra expense and time delay (two to five months) of making rules. For example, some agencies may draw a distinction between "employee guidelines" and "policies." The former are considered employee supervision and management issues, thus avoiding the need for rulemaking. Finally, some agencies simply may engage in the practice of issuing rules without going through the formal rulemaking process. Smaller agencies often do not have the staff necessary to promulgate all of the rules that may be required. For others, it may be worth the risk of operating with unpromulgated rules in order to save money, preserve managerial discretion, and provide geographic flexibility. Agencies also vary in their motivation to write rules. For example, some agencies, like departments of correction, have clearly defined and well-organized constituencies who will readily sue the department if there is the slightest departure from required protocols. In other agencies with little or no well-organized external constituencies, there may be more incentive to operate with unpromulgated rules.

Lest the reader become unduly alarmed over the wide variation in rulemaking practice, as well as the failure of some agencies to fully use their rulemaking authority, consider all of the rules, procedures, and practices of local cities, townships, boroughs, counties, fire districts, water districts, local school boards, and thousands of other special districts throughout the states. In nearly all of these cases, most rules, procedures, and practices have never been officially promulgated through any formal rulemaking process, and for those that have, it may be difficult for citizens to locate them. This is because most local jurisdictions have not enacted administrative procedure acts that set forth guidelines for the formal promulgation of administrative rules. The major exception to this is local land-use planning, where there are usually established administrative procedures for making changes in existing land-use rules.

Does the absence of formal administrative rulemaking processes in local governance pose a serious threat to administrative accountability? If more accountability is needed, which rulemaking approach do you prefer? Do you prefer one that allows administrators considerable leeway in exercising their managerial prerogatives to distinguish between an interpretive rule and a substantive rule, as is the case at the federal level? Or do you prefer the much more restrictive approach represented by the state of Oregon? Where you stand on these kinds of questions ultimately turns on your particular theory of democratic governance. Is responsiveness to the public more important than efficiency and cost effectiveness? Is the possibility of arbitrariness by government officials a greater danger to democratic liberty than the failure of administrators to take aggressive action to anticipate and solve future problems?

This debate over the appropriate breadth and reach of local rulemaking mirrors the two opposing views of administrative responsibility presented at the beginning of this chapter. We may be no closer today than we were in the 1940s in deciding whether the view of Herman Finer or that of Carl Friedrich is most needed to best serve the American democratic system of governance. However, if we see this debate less as an either-or choice about options and more as a conundrum that requires equal attention to both views, then the administrative rulemaking process provides

an opportunity to serve a multitude of potentially conflicting needs of the American democratic systems of governance.

1. It can be used to obtain useful information that will broaden and deepen an understanding of a given problem and the appropriate range of solutions.
2. It can be used to legitimate the processes of governance by providing opportunities for participation.
3. It can be used to provide a check against the arbitrary and capricious exercise of governmental authority.

Whatever we may ultimately conclude about the need for more or less rulemaking at the various levels of government, as the following sections will remind us, rulemaking is only one of a very broad array of legal mechanisms Americans rely upon to ensure administrative accountability.

### Administrative Adjudication

In addition to their rulemaking authority, administrative agencies frequently perform the same function as courts in their adjudicative role in deciding individual cases. For example, whenever an agency revokes a license from a driver, liquor owner, or any professional possessing a license to practice; or removes children from the custody of parents; or revokes a person's parole or probation, the agency is engaged in administrative adjudication. It is deciding the outcome of an individual case by applying and interpreting existing rules rather than developing new rules for future general application.

Since justice for the individual is the focus of an administrative adjudication (as it is for all American court proceedings), the main concern is to ensure the appropriateness and correctness of the decision. These concerns are reflected in a set of procedural requirements that set forth the right for an individual to appear in person, the right to present written and oral testimony, the right to have access to the information on which the decision is based, the right to contest the information, and the right to be represented by counsel. The specific guidelines governing these adjudicative applications of existing rules vary from one jurisdiction to another and are specifically outlined in the administrative procedures act for the jurisdiction or agency in question.

### Use of Advisory Committees and Negotiated Rules

One of the most unique and recent developments in the administrative process is the provision for formal, consensus-based approaches to create rules and negotiate disputes after rules have been made. These processes are sometimes referred to as collaborative decision making, hybrid rulemaking, and negotiated dispute resolution (Cooper 2000, 153–161). Once begun, the parties commit to abiding by the results of the process, although any party has the right to withdraw from participation while the process continues. The purpose of these processes is fourfold: (1) to reduce the time, money, and effort expended on developing and enforcing rules; (2) to reduce the time for policy implementation; (3) to create higher compliance; and (4) to develop more cooperative relationships between agencies and the parties affected by agency rules and policies.

For agencies that have used collaborative decision making and negotiated dispute resolution, the experience has been a good one. A few agencies have been reluctant to use this new statutory authority because they believe it reduces their managerial discretion by creating pressures to accept a result that may not be in the larger public interest. Others believe that one can accomplish

the same result with the existing rulemaking process through the use of hearings, advisory committees, and conflict resolution techniques (Morgan 2005).

## Open Records Laws

Another significant feature of administrative accountability involves open access to government records and data by individuals, groups, and the press. The federal government enacted the Freedom of Information Act (FOIA) in 1966 in order to enhance public access to executive agency records. The law was passed in the wake of revelations that public agencies, especially law enforcement and intelligence agencies, were collecting information on many citizens for political activities protected under the First Amendment freedom of association (cf. *NAACP v. Alabama*, 357 U.S. 449, 1958). The law greatly enhanced both the ability of individuals to examine many kinds of records held by agencies about them specifically, and the ability of the individuals and the press to access general government information about many agency decisions, actions, analyses, and so forth.

Most states have followed suit with open records and data privacy laws that apply to state and local government agencies. These laws adopt the general presumption that government records are open to public access unless otherwise exempted. Typical exemptions include information on ongoing law enforcement investigations, proprietary secrets, many intelligence agency and national defense records (sometimes for stipulated periods), regulatory data on financial institutions, and some personnel records.

The scope of open records laws has been subject to ongoing controversy and revision, especially at the federal level on issues involving intelligence data, presidential records, and the like. Open records laws pose challenges to public agencies that must balance the public's interest in transparency for the sake of accountability with concerns for protecting sensitive information on institutions and individuals who might suffer real damage if made public. The explosion of social media and news media through the World Wide Web has greatly exacerbated this challenge. One example will illustrate the nature of the problems agencies face. Private websites now exist for publishing mug shots of people who are arrested on suspicion of having committed criminal offenses. The website owners often use formal records requests to get these mug shots from police departments and jails. The problem is that suspects are not convicted criminals, and subsequently may not even be charged or are acquitted through investigations and/or trials. The mug shots nevertheless remain on the private websites until the affected individual discovers it (if at all), and then must pay a hefty fee for its removal. And there may be many such websites publishing the mug shots. The damage to people's lives—their reputations and employment opportunities for example—can be severe.

## Ethics and Professional Accountability

Other important tools for maintaining administrative accountability include a variety of legal provisions that prohibit career administrators from engaging in various kinds of conflicts of interest—broadly defined to include using one's official position or personal knowledge for private gain. These mechanisms include postemployment prohibitions that prevent certain administrators from working for agencies as lobbyists or consultants within a specified period of time after leaving public employment; accepting funds or gifts while employed; and requiring public disclosure of assets and business/personal relationships that may conflict with their official duties. One of the concerns raised by the proliferation of these "self-disclosure" provisions is the adverse impact they may have on attracting the "best and brightest" to public service careers (Rohr 1981).

In addition to the statutory constraints placed on administrators to ensure accountability, increasing emphasis has been placed on the internal standards of accountability that arise from viewing public administration as a profession. Like doctors who are accountable to the Hippocratic Oath, many scholars and practitioners argue that career administrators are obligated by virtue of their profession to "internalized standards of conduct." One way of understanding what this means in practice is to read the Code of Ethics for the American Society of Public Administration (ASPA).[10] This professional code sets forth at least half a dozen standards by which we can judge administrative accountability and responsibility. A major problem with these kinds of professional codes, however, is that they tend to embrace clear technical and legalistic standards overseen by legal officials, or they are so broad as to be largely unenforceable. While the ASPA Code has been criticized for its unenforceability and generality, there is a core consensus that it does a good job of memorializing the values at the core of American public service and the potential for conflict among these values (ASPA National 2011). The code thus shifts our focus away from debate over what should be on our list of public service values to a debate over the kind of framework that is needed to balance and reconcile conflicts among these values (see chapter 6 for the development of this argument); the latter discussion is necessary to facilitate the translation of the principles in the code into practice.

## MAINTAINING ACCOUNTABILITY IN EXTERNAL RELATIONSHIPS

Driven by the efficiency themes of New Public Management (NPM) and the federal National Performance Review (NPR), governments at all levels have embraced contracted and partnered services delivery. These external, interorganizational relationships cover a wide range of forms, including government-to-government intergovernmental agreements (IGAs), short- to medium-term contractual relationships, long-term public-private partnerships, and collaborative network partnerships. These arrangements allow governments to gain efficiencies and to increase effectiveness in service delivery. Contracts and partnerships with nonprofit and for-profit providers allow governments to access specialized technical and managerial expertise, to take advantage of efficient service delivery systems already in place, to benefit from economies of scale in supply and service delivery, and to obtain access to capital equipment use time and service support (e.g., cranes, dump trucks, bulldozers, aircraft, and other large equipment). The ability to procure and partner to access these services prevents governments from having to maintain full-time in-house staffs and make large investments in little-used equipment. Long-term public-private partnerships often give governments access to private financial capital that can supplement tax and fee revenues. Contracting and partnership arrangements have become so integrated into government procedures that in many instances, government expertise and staff capacity to deliver services has completely disappeared.

Federal and state agencies, county governments, and large city governments may procure hundreds of millions of dollars of professional services annually. These include social services, engineering and construction services, veterinary and medical services, language translation services, information systems and technology, and service support as part of equipment purchases. A number of small- to medium-sized city governments have taken contracted services to the extreme by purchasing most major city services from external providers (cf. City of Sammamish, Washington). Administration by city in-house staff is limited to the minimum required by state law. Typically, fire and emergency services are purchased under intergovernmental agreement from a regional special district or neighboring jurisdiction; police and law enforcement is purchased under intergovernmental agreement from the county sheriff or adjacent police force; and routine

public works functions are contracted from private-sector providers. Drinking water and waste-water provision is contracted to regional providers, and solid waste and recycling are provided to residents by private contractor. Information technology and information services often are purchased as well. These jurisdictions take pride in their limited staff costs, low-cost procurement rates, and efficient use of tax dollars.

Another approach that has grown in importance in recent years is reliance on collaborative agreements to meet community needs. Such agreements may include local governments, state and federal governmental agencies, nonprofit foundations, federated intermediary nonprofits, religious organizations, nonprofit service providers, and citizen service nonprofit organizations (Bardach and Lesser 1996). These agreements can produce large multiple networks of organizations providing service on a variety of fronts, such as afterschool programs for students, summer programs for disadvantaged youth, and social service programs for those in need. In such cases, it is often the case that no one major provider organization has complete control over the service delivery organization, and a single nonprofit service provider in the network may hold contracts and grants from two or more major resource providers. The levels of dependence between primary and secondary support organizations in the network may vary widely.

The challenge in all of these loosely coupled networks is to ensure accountability in meeting community goals and in the use of public and donor funds. Who is the agent and for whom does the agent act (Williamson 1981)? In a contractual relationship, the contracted nonprofit or for-profit company often acts on behalf of and in place of government staff. In a long-term public-private partnership, the private-sector partner acts as a virtual presence of the government agency. In an intergovernmental agreement, the government providing services acts on behalf of the purchasing government. In each of these contexts, the purchasing government must control the outside agent to ensure efficient and appropriate service delivery. Even with the most responsive and conscientious of agents, monitoring and controlling an agent costs money and staff time is a major responsibility. Such administrative costs come on top of the cost to actually purchase the desired service. The difficulty and cost of maintaining accountability increases as the number of partners in a network grow in number and the network agreement rests on collaborative agreement that does not have legal teeth.

We have already noted that "what counts for accountability" differs among the sectors. Nonprofit and for-profit contractors and partners are independent organizations that compete for donor funds, contracts, and grants in the commercial marketplace. Of necessity, public service values and the ethics of the Democratic Balancewheel typically take a secondary priority to financial survival (Cooper 2003, chap. 1). Getting private-sector contractors and partners to honor public service values is an important aspect of serving as a government agent (cf. Krugman 2012). Deciding to contract or partner raises the issue of the cost of maintaining in-house staff capacity that can deliver a service with the desired public service values, versus purchasing the service from a vendor who acts under different values and interests but with high efficiency. Ensuring the professional skills, responsiveness, and performance consistency of a contract or partner agent requires effective procedures and diligent, sustained oversight efforts. Failure of either the government or partner to adequately perform may lead to legal liability, penalty costs, delayed service delivery, and compromise of public service values. Notwithstanding the visions and hopes of idealistic elected officials, contracting and partnering for services does not guarantee increased efficiency and lower costs.

In addition, governments entering into contracts, grants, partnerships, and collaborations open themselves to several forms of risk. These risks include performance risk, financial risk, and legal risk. For the thousands of government contracts, grants, and partnerships successfully completed annually, a share fail to deliver as intended. Failure of a provider to perform includes delivering services below a prescribed quality level, failure to deliver the volume of services, or failing to

deliver services on time. Compounding performance risk, the contractor or partner may have engaged one or more subcontractors to perform particular aspects of the work. The subcontractor's relationship is with the contractor or partner, not the government, which makes it difficult for the government to gain responsive performance. Procurement regulations and procedures typically structure the contribution of subcontractors in the larger procurement relationship.

A contractor or partner may fail to fully perform, but if the contracting government or intermediary nonprofit has failed to provide support as promised, the liability may fall on the government or be shared by both parties. Failure of a contractor or partner to perform opens the purchasing government to financial risk. Often, performance failure results in the inability to generate expected revenues. The loss of revenues may affect both the purchasing government and the contractor. For government, the loss may prevent payment of expenses or the loss of resources to other programs and departments in the government. Additionally, the government has invested funds in a procurement process which may have taken hundreds of staff hours and months of time. The purchaser has invested in training and orientation for the contractor or partner, only to lose that investment. In the face of a failed procurement, the purchasing government is still accountable for delivering the service. Typically at higher cost, purchasers must make other arrangements to buy services or make arrangements to provide services with in-house staff. Critically, there may not be a single provider that can fill the capacity of the failed provider. The purchaser may need to run a new procurement process to select a replacement provider at added expense. Governments entering into contracts and partnerships may require bidders to carry performance bonds and other forms of performance insurance to cover performance risks. On the opposite side, the contractor has lost production time and equipment operating revenue when a contract fails. Failed performance and financial losses quickly point to legal liabilities, but litigation takes time and costs money. These are resources that could have gone to service delivery and improvements in productivity. The failure of a contract or partnership causes embarrassment for the parties involved, costs extra tax dollars or donor funds, compromises service delivery, and shakes public and donor trust in the organizations and their procedures.

Much like local governments, community foundations and federated intermediary nonprofits must rely on contractors and partners to implement programs and services. Governments strictly follow detailed procurement procedures to ensure fairness and equal opportunity to all bidders and applicants. Foundations and intermediary nonprofits use most of the same steps and procedures as in governmental procurement, but often with less formality. Foundations and intermediary nonprofits are private-sector organizations who may select service providers based on their own procedures, criteria, and preferences. However, to maintain legitimacy with the provider community, donors, and the public, foundations and intermediaries often use open advertisement, evaluation, and selection procedures for grants and contracts. Foundations and intermediaries face the same challenges ensuring performance from contractors, subcontractors, and partners.

External relationships in the form of intergovernmental agreements, contracts, grants, partnerships, and collaboration networks provide a major means of service delivery for local governments and government agencies. These arrangements increase the efficiency of government programs and often lower public costs. But obtaining efficient and effective services requires effective accountability and control mechanisms (see Larsen 2008, chap. 5). These mechanisms fall into five broad types: (1) organizational, (2) political, (3) legal, (4) negotiation and communication, and (5) market. Each of these types of control responds to different aspects of the contract, partner, or collaborative relationship. To better understand how these mechanisms integrate and complement each other, we next apply the different controls to five different external relationships: intergovernmental agreements (IGAs), sealed-bid defined-service contracts, grants and negotiated contracts, long-term public-private partnerships, and networked collaborations between community partners.

Ensuring accountability in each type of relationship requires a different blend of accountability mechanisms, but in the end the purchasing government or nonprofit is working to gain the lowest costs and maximum efficiency without losing control of performance quality and public service quantities.

## Accountability in Intergovernmental Agreements

*Intergovernmental agreements (IGAs)* between governments or government agencies range from service procurement arrangements to nonbinding collaboration agreements. Many IGAs are formal, ratified documents, but many others are informal or based on interpersonal relationships and good will. IGAs between two or more local-level governments are termed *interlocal* agreements. Jurisdictions establish interlocal IGAs to gain efficiencies, to respond to boundary-spanning issues, and to respond to fragmented governance authority. Interlocal service procurement agreements between cities, counties, and special service districts have been established for sewer and water utility services, storm water management and environmental services, fire and emergency management services, and law enforcement services (LeRoux, Brandenburger, and Pandey 2010; LeRoux and Carr 2007). An example of a nonbinding collaborative interlocal agreement might include a small city police department and parks and recreation department representatives regularly collaborating with the local county sheriff on youth gang enforcement issues and prevention programs. IGAs may also flow vertically between federal, state, and local and tribal governments. For example, a state forestry agency may establish an intergovernmental agreement with a federal land management agency for wildfire suppression services, and then sign a second agreement with a local rural fire district.

The efficiencies of IGAs appear in three ways. First, where a government has excess capacity in its organization, an intergovernmental agreement may provide an efficient means to capture and use slack in the organization. For example, a county sheriff has an ample patrol staff of deputies, a solid training system, and available equipment. The extra capacity might easily and efficiently provide law enforcement services within the desired response time for an adjacent small city. Further, the sheriff's special services teams for 911 communication, aviation, traffic enforcement, crash reconstruction, investigations, and special weapons and tactics may have excess capacity that again allows efficient sharing with adjacent jurisdictions. Sufficient payment by the city from its general fund helps to cover the sheriff's department costs.

A second efficiency reflects the benefits of a common constitutional and regulatory framework. In our sheriff-small city example, both the city and county fall under a common state constitution and regulatory framework for local governments. The taxation and revenue system for local governments is the same. On the professional side, law enforcement training is centralized at the state level to a common state standard. The constitutional and regulatory framework establishes common legal controls, including procedures and interpretation of code or regulation. Oversight and action by local elected officials and administrators can refine the standard code to local expectations.

In a third efficiency, intergovernmental agreements allow governments to purchase services from each other on a cost recovery, not-for-profit basis. Similarly, in states with a sales tax on services or a gross income business tax, intergovernmental agreements allow governments to buy services on a tax-free basis. All of these cost benefits respond to accountability concerns of government efficiency.

Partner governments commonly use a *memorandum of agreement (MOA)* to define the terms and specifics of an intergovernmental agreement. In essence, the MOA serves as a contract between the partner governments. An MOA typically defines the issue situation and need for action

or services; establishes the authority for action; outlines what each government will contribute in terms of funding, organization, and capital equipment and facilities; defines the duration of the agreement; defines performance standards; defines oversight and review mechanisms; and sets procedures for breaking the agreement. MOAs provide the organizational mechanisms to control performance by the partner governments. In contrast, *memorandum of understanding (MOU)* agreements are often used as nonbinding statements that provide joint guidance to the partner governments. While legally unenforceable, MOUs may effectively guide policy and performance through negotiations, interpersonal efforts, and institutional traditions and momentum. MOUs may serve as trial agreements prior to adoption of a formal MOA (Wisdom and Brooks 2001).

The authority and procedures to establish a formal MOA reflect the level and size of the governmental partners. In small governments, agreements are authorized by the city council, county commission, or district board of directors. Strong executive local governments may give authority to the mayor, executive director, or popularly elected county sheriff to enter into an agreement, but the city council, commission, or board may be required to give concurrence to executive action. In larger governments, authority to enter into agreements may be delegated to the governor, agency executives, and to appropriate line officers within an agency. Establishment of authority and its definition in an MOA should create a political and broad organizational framework of accountability between the government partners. The success of an agreement requires effective communication between the parties regarding the interpretation of policy, expected patterns of performance, and levels of delivered services. For example, under an interlocal MOA, where a small city purchases law enforcement services from the county sheriff's office, the city council might rely on the city manager or a staff director for routine administration of the agreement. However, the city council itself periodically reviews the sheriff's performance relative to community expectations of enforcement priorities, interpretation of the criminal code and its standards, conformance to the expected levels of service, the availability of secondary special teams and laboratory resources, and the sufficiency of city funding. The elected county sheriff, and even the county commissioners, could play a similar oversight role for the county.

### Accountability in Sealed-Bid Defined-Service Contracts

Governments, intermediary nonprofits, and foundations often have need for a clearly defined set of services. Administrators in these situations are fully knowledgeable of their needs and can clearly describe them in detail. These services typically have evident quality and quantity service outcomes that lend themselves to accurate performance measurements. With a full understanding of needs and outcome quality, administrators are faced with the task of generating maximum cost effectiveness and efficiency for public or donor dollars spent. The competitive sealed-bidding procedure provides a tool for using market competition between vendors to gain such efficiencies (LeRoux 2007). In a competitive sealed-bidding procedure, the government broadly distributes an advertisement of the clearly described work requirements and contract provisions, and requests bids from responsible and responsive bidders. Responsible bidders must demonstrate they have the basic staff qualifications and skills, hold financial bonding and insurance, and have sufficient business capacity; a responsive bidder must fully meet procedural deadlines and contact requirements in a timely manner. Because the purchasing government or nonprofit has fully and completely described the needed tasks and performance requirements, price becomes the only assessment variable. Bidders typically bid a unit rate for services and a total cost for services in a sealed, written bid returned to the purchaser. The lowest cost responsible and responsive bidder wins the competition, is awarded the contract, and once accepted becomes the contractor for the project.

Government purchasers retain numerous mechanisms for assuring accountability to administrative and democratic values. A properly conducted bidding procedure with several competitive bidders helps to ensure responsiveness to the administrative value of efficiency. Because the winning bidder sets a firm unit rate price and total price for services, the contractor in the sealed-bid contract assumes the financial risk of inflation and rising prices for labor and materials. In reverse, should prices fall, the government may need to rebut charges of paying too much for services. To assure fairness to all applicants, governments must carefully follow highly prescribed procedures for advertising bid requests, communicating information on the needed service and the contract provisions, collecting bids from vendors, evaluating and scoring bids against objective selection criteria, and selecting and awarding the contract to the winning bidder. Scrupulous attention to detail and procedural compliance ensures fairness, curbs protests from aggrieved bidders, and limits the government's legal liability. A portion of work contracts designed for small business and set-asides for minority- and women-owned businesses provide a means in many states and in the federal government to ensure justice in the distribution of contracted work.

Relying on contracted service delivery opens the purchasing government or nonprofit to the risk of poor performance or nonperformance by the contractor. Organizational accountability procedures and controls help to ensure contractor performance. Structured by highly defined task quality requirements, delivery schedules, performance incentives or penalties, and effective contract administration, a contractor has little to interpret regarding policy, product definition, or quality. Performance evaluations and grading during contract administration provide a narrow opportunity for the purchaser and contractor to refine the interpretation of product quality.

Purchasing governments and nonprofits rely on a series of formal notification and response techniques, incentives, and penalties to maintain and encourage improved contractor performance. Obtaining and ensuring performance in the sealed-bid context can become adversarial between the purchaser and contractor, which tends to reduce productivity and performance. While the sealed-bid approach is still used, governments increasingly use negotiated service contracts and a partnership approach to encourage additional contractor performance.

## Accountability in Grants and Negotiated Contracts

The strict definitions and narrow performance criteria of the sealed-bid defined-service contract quickly become inadequate to the ambiguous tasks of professional service delivery and complex public service projects. These complex projects require extensive professional knowledge, creativity, and judgment in evolving situations. Complex procurement examples include information system development, installation and training; environmental assessment and impact analysis for planning and license applications; and delivery of entire social service programs. But addressing complex situations place the grantee or contractor in positions of interpreting government policy or intent, setting service prioritization, and making resource allocation decisions. Procurement procedures, contract structure, and contract administration must all work to gain professional expertise while at the same time maintaining accountability at the lowest possible cost. Grants for professional services provide a means for governments and nonprofits to purchase the expertise of certified professionals. Procurement procedures using competitive negotiation and multistep bidding techniques provide a stronger response to these complex situations (LeRoux 2007). For this overview, we will limit our discussion to the competitive negotiation bidding procedure, but this still allows us to address the larger questions of government and nonprofit accountability when outside professionals enter into service delivery.

The term *grant* is used with variable definition. Some governments and nonprofits use it interchangeably with a *contract* for services, but many purchasers structure a grant to procure some aspect of professional services and to give discretion for professional judgment to affect the service outcome. Professional certifications and credentials provide a standard for expected performance and public accountability. Some grants may be administered with tight performance evaluation, while other grants receive little oversight, allowing the recipient to exercise broad professional judgment and practice as the basis of performance. Whether by contract or grant, local governments purchase an array of professional services to support their operations. For example, service delivery nonprofits receive grants to provide youth services or social services. Foundations provide grants to school districts to try new educational approaches or student support. County animal shelters contract for veterinary services, and county jails and corrections programs contract for doctor, nursing, and therapist services. Many local governments contract for professional engineering and design services, or for public works management services. In both grants and professional service contracts, the purchasing entity is inviting the professional into the definition of the services needed and into the delivery process.

The procedures for competitive negotiated bidding are structured to evaluate professional experience, service quality, and price (LeRoux 2007). These procedures are again grounded in organizational and legal accountability controls. Unlike the sealed-bid procedure, the lowest bidder is not necessarily awarded the contract. Competitive negotiation works well when the purchasing government or nonprofit cannot fully describe the needed work, or when professionals can take different approaches to the work task. The quality of the service or the provider qualifications are often a more important issue than the price. Additionally, the package proposed by a bidder may need to be adjusted through negotiation to a changing situation and available funding (LeRoux 2007, 37). As in the sealed-bid process, governments use extremely detailed and rigorous bidding procedures to ensure fairness to all bidders. Nonprofit intermediaries and foundations typically follow similar procedures but may opt for less formality.

Government procurement staff and program administrators make their best estimate of the program situation, needs, and costs as a first step in the bidding process. If administrators have limited knowledge, or if the field is fast changing, government purchasers may release a request for information (RFI) to the vendor community. Vendors respond to this request with general explanations and possible approaches to the program situation and need. The RFI is one way governments and intermediaries can learn what services and remedies are available in the market. Based on this and other information, governments release a request for proposals (RFP). The RFP presents the situation and need for services, details the procedural deadlines and requirements for bidding, requests the bidder's statement of qualifications, requests a technical proposal for meeting the situation and providing services, and may request a price for services. The RFP summarizes the purchasing government's expectation of the performance outcomes, service levels, and service qualities delivered under the contract.

In response, bidders respond to the questions in the RFP to develop a bid package. Bidders must deliver their bid to the government offices by the specified deadline or face rejection of the bid. Government staff then reviews, scores, and ranks the bids. Negotiations begin with the highest-ranked bidder based on qualifications, the project scope, content, and cost. If the government and the highest bidder cannot reach an agreement, negotiations begin with the second-highest-ranked bidder. Negotiations move down the ranking until agreement is reached with a bidder and the contract can be developed (cf. LeRoux 2007, 37).

The competitive negotiation bidding process carries the same financial, legal, and performance risks described earlier for competitive sealed bidding. Performance risks remain a major concern,

as does the assumption of financial liability. But competitive negotiation opens government and nonprofit purchasers to an additional series of risks and accountability issues. In competitive negotiation, the government does not have strong or complete knowledge of client and program needs. The RFP asks professionals and firms for their recommendations on how to frame and define problems, what professional skills to apply, and how to develop a service response. Bidders work through these issues as they prepare their bids and make their best recommendations to the purchaser. Purchasing governments and nonprofits then review and rank the bids. Review of the bids focuses on the desired service outcomes and outcome quality. Within the broad contours set in the RFP, bidders may offer many different approaches and levels of service to generate service outcomes. Subsequent negotiations allow the government a chance to learn more about the bidder's strategy, program priorities, and values. Negotiations work to reconcile bidder expectations with the organization's values and priorities. However, the negotiated adjustments to the winning bid package represent a compromise between the purchasing government's needs and values on the one hand, and the bidder's priorities and values on the other. One element of this compromise is that the bidder must make a sufficient financial return in addition to meeting performance obligations and public values (Cooper 2003, chap. 1).

The negotiated competitive bidding procedures allow for greater involvement of the bidder in defining the issue situation, work products, quality of the workmanship and customer relationships, and performance measures. This involvement stretches governmental control of service delivery quality. Purchasers can insist on contractor staffing with certain qualifications and levels of training, and the bidder's professional qualifications and certifications provide a measure of accountability to these concerns. Agreement on performance outcomes, quality requirements, and performance measurements also add control structures to the final contract package. Professional standards and practices set objective standards that help to define program content, quality, and levels of service. Effective enforcement of the negotiated contract helps to ensure that the government attains the desired program outcomes. The basis of enforcement is often a graded performance score and a scheduled due date, but the professional nature of the services makes communication of the rationale for difficulties and nonperformance especially important to fair evaluation. As with the sealed-bid defined-service contracts, the government or nonprofit purchaser retains almost all responsibility for contract accountability and program performance. Oversight of the contract provisions and performance by elected officials provides a means to demonstrate success or diagnose the reasons for poor performance to the public. Oversight by elected officials also provides the opportunity to demonstrate political accountability for the contract and project.

## Accountability in Public-Private Partnerships

Sealed-bid defined-service contracts and competitive negotiated service contracts are structured to place the balance of control, risk exposure, and accountability with the procuring government or nonprofit. The negotiation process in a negotiated contact may modify this balance to some degree, but the primary burden remains with the government. The government agency or intermediary nonprofit—not the contractor—must answer for a failed contract or poor performance. A public-private partnership changes the balance of control, risk exposure, accountability, and time frame. A public-private partnership establishes an agreement between a government and private-sector firms in which all parties share the financial, entrepreneurial, and other forms of risk (Forrer et al. 2010). Additionally, in large construction projects, public-private partnerships bring private-sector funding to public projects and infrastructure construction. The contribution of financial resources further raises the stature and authority of the partner organization. Unlike

the short to medium fixed duration of defined services and negotiated contracts, public-private partnerships typically last for extended periods or span completion of major infrastructure projects. Public-private infrastructure projects usually involve both the government and the private partner in policy interpretation, decision making and project planning, project engineering and design, construction management, operations and revenue collection, and maintenance. After a sufficient time frame for the private partner to recover its financial investment, often decades, the ownership of the project transfers to full governmental control (cf. Williams 2003).

Entering into a public-private partnership presumes that the government does not have the knowledge, experience, and capacity to deliver the good or service and thus needs the expertise that the private partner can provide (Forrer et al. 2010). Public-private partnerships also assume that the private party is willing to share its capacity and will enter into a joint agreement (Forrer et al. 2010, 476). Based on these conditions, private entities in a public-private partnership are at least equal parties to an agreement. In these partnerships, the government and private parties become deeply joined, and breaking the partnership is costly financially and legally. Nisar (2006) argues that private-sector involvement in public-private partnerships signals an increase in public value through a transfer of significant risk away from the government. Market accountability becomes a strong control mechanism on public-private infrastructure in which the private party contributes substantial financing. To support the partnership, the private party must "sell" the project to pension funds, mutual funds, and other investors with large capital reserves (Ghere 2001). Private financial analysts review the proposed project and partnership before any private money is committed. This provides another control on the project and its partnership.

Public-private partnerships contrast with defined-service and negotiated contracts in that the vertical, organization-based controls imposed by governments or government agencies have limited effect. Public oversight, financial controls, and performance administration remain important but are insufficient to ensure the accountability of extended partnerships. Control in a public-private partnership falls to horizontal mechanisms of negotiation, renegotiation, collaboration, and consensual decision making. Both parties must be involved, but the public organization should demonstrate the dominant role (Forrer et al. 2010, 479). Forrer and his colleagues argue that accountability in public-private partnerships require the following:

1. understanding and appropriately allocating the different forms of risk to the party that can best manage the form of risk;
2. identifying all costs and benefits including opportunity costs, life cycle costs, and operations and maintenance costs in the short and over the long term;
3. identifying, planning for, and managing social and political impacts where identification includes social equity issues of which groups in the community benefit from or carry the costs of the program or project;
4. identifying and effectively using the many forms of expertise both parties bring to the partnership;
5. clearly defining expectations and mechanisms needed for coordination, facilitation of collaboration, development of an environment of innovation, and definition of rewards and penalties; and
6. establishing the procedures and involving all parties in the development and definition of performance measures.

The end goal of these and other accountability measures is to effectively assess performance, engage staff, and generate the incentives to improve results over the extended life of the partnership.

## Accountability in Collaborative Networks of Community Partners

Even more challenging than ensuring accountability through IGAs, contracts, and partnerships is assuring accountability in networks of collaborative partnerships between numerous community partners. We briefly described these networks in chapter 7 (see especially Exhibit 7.3). Such networks often spring up or are formally established to respond to complex problems where the major organizations have limited and shared authority. For example, to provide a comprehensive package of youth social services, a community might involve and coordinate resources and services from local governments, state government agencies, community foundations, community federated intermediary nonprofits, major service nonprofits, religious organizations, small service nonprofits, and for-profit providers. Each network partner is an independent actor, but the primary governmental partners and major federated intermediary nonprofits are typically held accountable for the performance, policy direction, and ethical values of the entire network (Herranz 2007). Communication and negotiation between network members is critical to network success and durability. Ensuring some degree of accountability in the community provider network is a major oversight challenge and an important element of polity governance.

Herranz (2007) argues that governmental, nonprofit, and for-profit organizations bring different sector-based practices, perspectives, opportunities, and limitations to the collaborative network. Each sector has a set of values and standards that establish a normative framework. This framework defines interorganizational relationships including procedural, financial, and social accountability systems and standards; basic service delivery routines; and flexible service customization. Case studies by Herranz demonstrated sector-driven preferences with different governance attributes: a nonprofit-led network preferred highly interpersonal responses to customers, especially with specialized minority populations; a for-profit-led network exhibited entrepreneurial traits; and a government-led network delivered a more standardized set of services with less emphasis on interpersonal ties. These sector preferences loosely correspond with many of the different corrective traditions in the Democratic Balancewheel (chapter 6). Accountability and performance systems should respond to, and make best use of, sectoral differences as Balancewheel correctives.

Provan and Milward (2001) recognize that, in addition to sector differences, many collaborative networks have three levels on which to focus accountability and performance. Evaluating network performance requires considering performance on all three levels as well as on the interaction between the levels. First, the community level of focus considers the network in its entirety and from an outsider's perspective. This view includes elected officials, funders, constituent advocacy groups, and the general public. The community level evaluates performance success of network outcomes based on a change in community condition and on the general resolution of the community's problem. Routine and special session oversight hearings by county boards, city councils, and nonprofit boards of directors provide a political means of reviewing community-level accountability. Media reports and client feedback to elected officials and administrators provide another form of political feedback on collaborative performance.

The second level of accountability responds to the health and function of the collaborative network itself. This level considers the ebb and flow of network membership, the strength of network bonds, and the costs and benefits of being a network member. Provan and Milward argue that establishment of a network administrative organization (NAO) helps to lower the transaction costs of these types of network maintenance operations. Primary governmental, foundation, or intermediary organizations typically serve as the NAO. These major organizations not only provide substantial financial resources to the organization but also set contract terms, administrative and reporting procedures, performance standards, and preferences for service delivery content and

Exhibit 14.8   **Maintaining Accountability in External Relationships**

| | Types of Controls | | |
| Types of Relationships | Political Controls | Organizational Controls | Legal Controls |
| --- | --- | --- | --- |
| Contracts | Low | Medium | High |
| Intergovernmental agreements | Low | High | Medium high |
| Networks | High | Medium | Low |
| Public-private partnerships | High | Medium | Low |

style. These are organization-based control requirements and procedures established by the NAO but extended to many partners throughout the network. Public meetings convened by the NAO and other major network members provide an opportunity for review of network health, function, and direction. These provide another form of political accountability.

The third network level focuses on the organization, or network participant. This level takes an organizational insider's perspective, looking at the full network, its costs and benefits of membership, the health of the individual member organizations, and their ability to survive and deliver services. Accountability should consider effectiveness and compliance at each of the three levels and in interactions between levels.

Bardach and Lesser (1996) offer a set of content criteria by which to evaluate a collaborative network and its performance. Networks are accountable for: (1) results, deciding what to measure, and accountability to network partners and to overseers; (2) setting wise priorities; (3) targeting through and around confining institutional requirements; and (4) system modification and redesign. These criteria call attention to the importance of using political and organizational negotiation skills to generate collective performance from disparate members while recognizing the need to honor the mission and policies of each independent participant organization.

In Exhibit 14.8, we summarize the four types of external relationships public entities rely upon to get their work done and the degree to which each type of relationship relies on the three types of accountability control mechanisms we have discussed in this chapter: political, organizational, and legal. Contracts fall at one end of the spectrum, where lawyers and accountants provide the expert knowledge needed to develop, implement, and oversee contracts. Public-private partnerships fall at the other end of the spectrum, where elected officials bear the primary burden of negotiating agreements that meet the accountability expectations of the general public. In the middle are intergovernmental agreements and networks, where initiative is usually taken by line administrators within the organization to craft agreements that meet accountability expectations. In all cases, elected officials have ultimate accountability by either delegating authority to administrators to undertake the development of external relationship or by personally approving agreements with external entities. In all cases, administrators have considerable discretion to operate within the guidelines they have been provided and/or by crafting agreements they believe will meet the accountability expectations of the elected officials they serve.

## ADMINISTRATIVE ACCOUNTABILITY: ENDURING ISSUES AND CONFLICTS

The history of American efforts to achieve administrative accountability reflects the age-old tension between democracy and bureaucracy. How is it possible for citizens to enjoy a bureaucracy that is responsive to the will of the people without at the same time undermining the independence

Exhibit 14.9   **Summary of Approaches to Maintain Administrative Accountability**

| Types of Abuse | Accountability Solutions |
| --- | --- |
| 1. Rewarding partisan loyalty | Hatch Act |
| | Civil service reform |
| | Antinepotism rules |
| | Codes of ethics |
| 2. Self-dealing | Conflict of interest legislation |
| | Financial disclosure laws |
| | Audits |
| | Post-employment prohibitions |
| | Contracting requirements |
| | Restrictions on acceptance of gifts, favors, etc. |
| | Codes of ethics |
| 3. Incompetence/inefficiency | Civil service reform |
| | Personnel training and development |
| | Management approaches (Theories X, Y, Z) |
| | Codes of ethics |
| 4. Insensitivity to rights/interests of clients | Right to privacy acts |
| | Freedom of information processes |
| | Codes of ethics |
| | Rulemaking |
| 5. Agency self-aggrandizement | Right to privacy acts |
| | Freedom of information acts |
| | Open government provisions |
| | Legislative oversight |
| | Executive control |
| | Codes of ethics |
| | Rulemaking |

necessary to undertake collective action—action that is informed by a long-term view, guided by the best scientific information and analysis possible, and mindful of the needs of the powerless? This question, like the Friedrich-Finer debate presented in the opening paragraphs of this chapter, surfaces a deep and abiding tension among four competing roles the bureaucracy is expected to play in maintaining our political systems: (1) being responsive to the wishes and preferences of the citizenry at large, (2) supporting managerial and policy goals with efficient and effective administration, (3) ensuring sensitivity to the unique needs of local communities, and (4) protecting the constitutional rights of all citizens. Exhibit 14.9 summarizes the various approaches that Americans have taken to ensure democratic accountability. What may at first appear as a very scattered and confused approach to accountability becomes more intelligible when we see that it reflects the multiple and conflicting purposes that Americans expect their career administrators to serve within the American democratic systems of government. In short, the debate over administrative accountability is, in the final analysis, a debate about what the American system of democratic governance can and should be.

## STUDY QUESTIONS

1.  What is meant by political accountability?
2.  What is the significance of Executive Order 12866 in terms of maintaining administrative accountability?
3.  What are the strengths and weaknesses of executive accountability?
4.  What are the strengths and weaknesses of legislative accountability?

5. What are the essential differences between Carl Friedrich's view and Herman Finer's view of administrative responsibility? Who comes closest to reflecting your own view?

6. What are the strengths and weaknesses of the various forms of organizational accountability?

7. What are the strengths and weaknesses of the various forms of legal accountability?

8. What is meant by rulemaking?

9. What are the purposes of public participation in the rulemaking process? How successfully can the rulemaking process accommodate these purposes? To what extent do hybrid rulemaking and negotiated rulemaking solve the problem of participation in the rulemaking process?

10. What is the difference between "judicial review" and "administrative adjudication"?

11. Who has the burden of proof in an administrative hearing?

12. What is meant by the phrase "substantial evidence on the record when considered as a whole"?

13. What are the differences among "a scintilla of evidence," "clear and convincing evidence," "preponderance of the evidence," "substantial evidence," and "beyond a reasonable doubt"?

14. A small city purchases fire and emergency services from an adjacent large city under a 10-year intergovernmental agreement. What blend of accountability mechanisms would you use to ensure legitimacy and performance by both parties?

15. A large city government uses a sealed-bid defined-service contract to clean and maintain multiple restrooms at their major cultural civic center. What role should negotiation controls play in the selection and administration of this contract? What types of control mechanisms are most appropriate to this contract and situation?

16. A large, suburban county government is a major participant and donor to their community social and youth services provider network. What types of accountability control mechanisms should the county use to get results?

17. What controls should the county use with volunteer nonprofits and religious organizations?

## NOTES

1. For a history of the National Performance Review Initiative, relevant documents, and its accomplishments, see the following: John Kamensky, "A Brief History of Vice President Al Gore's National Partnership for Reinventing Government During the Administration of President Bill Clinton, 1993–2001," January 12, 2001; http://govinfo.library.unt.edu/npr/whoweare/historyofnpr.html (accessed December 9, 2007).

Significant groundwork for the National Performance Review Initiative had been laid in the previous administration of President George H.W. Bush, who established a Council on Competitiveness in 1989. Bush charged his vice president, Dan Quayle, with responsibility for reducing the regulatory burden on the economy. On June 15, 1990, the president expressly directed the council to exercise the same authority over regulatory issues as the former Task Force on Regulatory Relief. Executive Orders 12291 and 12498, issued on February 17, 1981, and January 4, 1985, respectively, set forth the specific procedures for the regulatory review process and served as the legal authority for council activities. Initially, the council considered issues in four different areas: preserving free enterprise, gaining access to capital, bringing science to market, and developing human resources. In President Bush's 1992 State of the Union Address, he announced a 90-day regulatory moratorium followed by a 120-day moratorium extension on agency rulemaking. During this period, federal agencies submitted lists of then-current rulemaking and cost estimates to the council for review and consideration.

2. Some scholars who cast a broad net of responsibility for administrators include J.P. Burke (1988), Elkin and Soltan (1993), Frederickson (1996, 1982), Frederickson and Hart (1985), Green (1997), Morgan (1996, 1990), Rohr (1989, 1986), and Rosenbloom (1983, 1971).

3. See Nalbandian (2000, 1994) and Svara (1989a, 1989b).

4. For those who take this deliberation and citizen-centered view of democratic governance, see Elkin (2004); Cook (1996), especially 177–78; Lowi (1979); Box (1998); Fox and Miller (1996); and King and Stivers (1998).

5. See especially Burke (1986); P.J. Cooper (2007); Rohr (1989, 1986); and Rosenbloom (2003, 1983). Also see note 2 above for a summary of other authors who argue for an active and expansive role of administrators in the policy implementation process.

6. For further explanations and illustrations of the administrative burden of proof in rulemaking, see *Richardson v. Perales*, 402 US 389 (1971); *Citizens of Preserve Overton Park v. Volpe, Secretary of Transportation,* 401 US 402 (1971); and Phillip Cooper (2007), chap. 5–6.

7. *Dolan v. Tigard*, 512 U.S. 687, 697–98 (1994).

8. ORS 183.335(2)(b)(C); see *Fremont Lumber Co. v. Energy Facility Siting Council,* 325 OR 256, 262, 936 P2d 968 (1997).

9. Interview with Amy Verant, Oregon Office of the Attorney General, May 3, 2001.

10. See chapter 6 for a review of the discussion of these issues on the role of ethics in public service.

CHAPTER 15

# THE FUTURE OF AMERICAN PUBLIC ADMINISTRATION

[In the United States, there is a widely held belief that] providence has given to each individual, whoever he may be, the degree of reason necessary for him to be able to direct himself in things that interest him exclusively. . . . Extended to the entirety of the nation, it becomes the dogma of the sovereignty of the people. . . . In democratic countries, the science of association is the mother science; the progress of all the others depends on the progress of that one. Among the laws that rule human societies, there is one that seems more precise and clear than all the others. In order that men remain civilized or become so, the art of associating must be developed and perfected among men in the same ratio as equality of condition increases.

*(Alexis de Tocqueville 1835–1840/2000, 381, 492)*

The battle between bureaucracy and democracy is written into our history. So is the fact that democracy must win. All we have left to debate is the cost.

*(Barry Karl 1987, 34)*

We begin this final chapter by reviewing three central themes of this book. First, public administration has played a significant role in shaping the course of American democratic governance. Especially over the past 100 years, it has contributed to the development and implementation of public policy at all levels of government and operates as a powerful agent of efficiency and effectiveness. We have articulated its broader role as a Democratic Balancewheel—juggling competing values that inform our traditions of governance. This role is especially prominent at local levels, where part-time elected officials rely on career administrators to carry out their electoral responsibilities. We end this book by asking how this Balancewheel role can be effectively carried out in the future.

As we observed in chapter 2, most Americans are satisfied with their encounters with administrative agencies. Yet, Americans are also openly skeptical about the capacity of administrative agencies to meet public expectations. This skepticism is reflected in debates about governmental preparedness and response to the bombings of the Twin Towers on 9/11 and subsequent efforts to protect Americans from terrorist threats; the handling of the aftermath of Hurricanes Katrina

and Sandy; the conduct of the wars in Iraq and Afghanistan; and repeated failures to effectively regulate against a long series of financial scandals and crises occurring since the mid-1980s. In response to these concerns, we have witnessed swift executive action to obtain more centralized control over federal agencies, resulting in significant politicization, retirement of many senior career administrators, and extensive privatization, reorganization, and yet more deregulation. The reforms and retrenchment run deep; they presume that old administrative practices are obsolete and that administrative capacity should be lean and minimal.

With the election of a Democrat-controlled Congress in the fall of 2006, we witnessed efforts by Congress to pare back executive reach and reverse some intrusions on long-standing administrative policies and practices. This dynamic intensified with the advent of the financial crisis of 2007–2008; the election of a Democrat, Barack Obama, to the office of the U.S. presidency; the rise of the Tea Party libertarian movement; and the subsequent election in 2010 of a Republican-controlled House of Representatives. Elections are consequential. The consequences of the 2012 election have yet to unfold, but the tension of the last six years will endure. While these battles continue at the federal level, the state and local governments have suffered from recession-induced retrenchment and strident partisan attacks on the public service. And yet, the demand for public services proceeds steadily despite the attacks, and even as federal and state budgetary portend declines.

The debate over who owns or controls public administration reflects a second major theme of this book. Public administrators operate within a context that establishes sovereignty of the people as the first principle of governance. In operationalizing popular sovereignty, however, the framers tempered this principle with significant institutional protections of individual rights; furthermore, they ensured responsiveness to competing claims and powers emanating from coequal branches and divided structures of federal, state, and local governance. Administrators help maintain the balance of powers among the political principals who populate this complex structure. Their balancing role is critical to the integrity of American governance. It is noteworthy, for instance, that throughout the rapid mobilization for wars in Iraq and Afghanistan, and measures taken to enhance security and defense at home, career administrators voiced concerns about retaining the integrity of administrative standards, judgments, processes, and rights. Many of them expressed doubt about hasty projections and impulsive modifications to practices that were carefully built to accommodate balance among competing values. Subsequent assessments indicate that many of their doubts were well founded. Notable too were the lonely voices of some career public servants who warned of the looming dangers of unmonitored and unregulated financial practices that would eventually bring the American and global economy to its knees (cf. Green 2012).

Events such as these give rise to a third major theme of this book. New generations of public administrators need to understand the enduring conflicts at the heart of American governance in order to fully grasp the nature of their roles and the competencies needed to successfully perform their duties. Across more than 230 years of history, the American people have embraced a variety of models of acceptable administration, ranging from very constrained roles at one end of the spectrum to more expansive roles at the other. The public's ongoing ambivalence about public administration reflects their concern for the exercise of governmental power generally.

Simplistic theories of public administration portray it as a mere instrument of the will of elected officials (see chapters 4, 5, and 6)—or even of the citizens directly—without any reference to the mediating role of duly elected officials. While such portrayals are certainly expedient for elected officials, they hardly capture the logic of diffuse and balanced powers that permeate all of our governments. In actual practice, American public administration resembles a coproduction model that mixes subordination and multiple principals with varying degrees of professional autonomy. The ethical and legal theories that underpin this system (summarized in chapters 6 and 14) give

public administration substantial discretion that is structured through a variety of accountability mechanisms. Legal authority recognizes that administrative agencies serve three separate masters—elected chief executives, legislative bodies, and courts—all of which operate under the supervening authority of a Constitution that also divides power by level of government.

As we move further into the twenty-first century, public administration remains saddled with contradictory roles that require public servants to balance competing values. Responsiveness, competent performance, protection of rights, and sensitivity to community values are vital traditions in American democratic governance. We have argued that the Democratic Balancewheel presented in chapter 6 provides an appropriate anchor for public administrators at all levels of government as they work to preserve a regime of ordered liberty. In this final chapter, we explore the adequacy of this model in dealing with challenges that loom on the horizon. We start by reviewing some major demographic, technologic, economic, and political factors that will drive change, and then, through a real case, illustrate how administrators can use the model to cope with them.

## DRIVERS OF CHANGE IN THE TWENTY-FIRST CENTURY

The forces of change that loom large on the horizon present opportunities as well as challenges. Dealing with the looming forces of change will require leadership at many levels, some of it strategic in the sense of shaping the course of events rather than falling victim to them. Others who lead will help us cope with difficulties that arise suddenly and unexpectedly. In either case, career administrators must attend to the capacities of public institutions (including nonprofit organizations and private firms that serve public functions) to sustain the regime, and to promote calm and deliberate action that steadies our resolve to work through our problems in a civil and respectable manner. This is a noble challenge, one that many public servants already understand and take pride in as they perform their duties. The challenges they face make their work interesting and worthwhile, even under dire circumstances. One should bear this in mind as the next generation of public servants assumes the responsibilities of those who went before them.

### Workforce Changes

Public-sector organizations currently face major issues due to retirements, workforce transition, and succession planning. Rapid turnover will continue as an issue for at least the next decade. The General Accountability Office (GAO) reported that 53 percent of the middle managers in the federal workforces qualified for retirement as of 2004 (GAO 2001). Likewise, retirements and staffing turnovers place critical burdens on state, county, and city governments, whose employees constitute 60 percent of public employment (Ehrenhalt 1999, 19–22). These changes pose obvious problems of preserving institutional memory, sustaining best practices and long-standing relationships among cooperating institutions, and transferring to successors the subtleties of maintaining collaborative operating agreements among multiple powers and jurisdictions. This is especially true in local communities, where most of the work is carried out through partnerships and other collaborative mechanisms among public, nonprofit, and for-profit institutions. Implied promises made to stakeholder groups, expectations of the sequencing of public service projects when funding becomes available, and similar kinds of agreements make it possible for social capital to be built and sustained over time. Without continuity in the workforce and proper leadership, this capital is in danger of being lost.

Succession planning poses additional challenges for identifying and acquiring the kinds of abilities that will be needed in the future. While high levels of technical competence are assumed, they are not going to be sufficient in a decentralized, globalized world of fractured jurisdictions.

The flattening of public organizations, increased emphasis on customer service, and the need to build collaborative partnerships at the lower ranks of the organization place much greater emphasis on recruiting individuals who have the capacity to make sense out of muddles, to deal with ambiguity, and to stay calm in tense, conflict-ridden settings. This has always been the case for those occupying leadership positions in the upper ranks of the public service, but these qualities are now increasingly required at lower ranks of public service. Robert Reich finds these qualities in new kinds of workers that he calls "symbolic analysts."

> Symbolic analysts solve, identify, and broker problems by manipulating symbols. They simplify reality into abstract images that can be rearranged, juggled, experimented with, communicated to other specialists, and then, eventually, transformed back into reality. The manipulations are done with analytic tools, sharpened by experience. The tools may be mathematical algorithms, legal arguments, financial instruments, scientific principles, psychological insights about how to persuade or amuse, systems of induction or deduction, or any other set of techniques for doing conceptual puzzles. (Reich 1992, 178)

It would be a mistake to assume that these symbolic analysts are trained exclusively in some new kind of specialty. They may know how to use a variety of specialized tools, but they also know how to integrate their application, to synthesize them with a broader context of ideas and principles. They become generalists who can integrate a broad view with the details and specific needs of administrative, political, and information systems. Undergraduate liberal arts majors are well suited for this kind of work. They are prized for their ability to think, and for their broad, interdisciplinary knowledge. But the rapidly increasing need for such abilities suggests that career officials trained in highly technical subjects such as nursing, medicine, engineering, social work, natural resource management, or the justice fields should look to graduate and continuing education to generalize their perspectives, build symbolic logic skills, and cultivate a tolerance for ambiguity. This presents a challenge for the academics who design and teach graduate and continuing education programs, as these educators need to rethink and adapt their curricula to this pressing need. Public affairs programs that focus on the development of prudential judgment and leadership are perhaps best situated to address the problem.

The bad news is that public organizations must compete for the same skill set that the private sector increasingly finds necessary to maintain a competitive market edge. As we noted in chapters 8 and 9, governments in the United States are ill prepared to compete for talent in this market. The negative attitudes about government service have taken a huge toll on the ability to attract and hold on to the kind of people who can meet the challenges of the future. But decline in the performance and confidence in the business sector over the last decade could cause the pendulum to swing back in favor of public sector careers.

**Growing Demographic and Ethnic Diversity**

In the years ahead, most local communities will grow in size and be composed of an older and more diverse group of citizens. Between 1990 and 2000, nearly 33 million people were added to the national population. This was the largest 10-year increase in U.S. history. The fastest growing regions were the Sunbelt areas of the West and the South. Projecting to the year 2015, the U.S. Census Bureau suggests that America will remain predominantly "white," but that other groups will continue to increase disproportionately. Perhaps the most dramatic result of these changing population trends during the last few years has been that African Americans were replaced by Hispanics as the nation's largest minority group. This is the result of large numbers of immigrants entering the country from Latin America and high birthrates among first-generation Hispanics.

More recent census research conducted by the Pew Research Center indicates that "Hispanics will account for the vast majority—74 percent—of the 10.5 million workers added to the labor force from 2010 to 2020. That share is higher than in the previous two decades. Hispanics accounted for 36 percent of the total increase in the labor force from 1990 to 2000 and for 54 percent from 2000 to 2010" (Kochhar 2012). Hispanic workforce numbers are increasing at the same time that white labor force numbers are beginning to decline. The percent of women in the workforce appears to have peaked at around 59 percent.

The patterns of diversity are not the same throughout America. Most ethnic and racial minorities are concentrated in major urban centers and in particular states. For instance, Hispanics of Mexican ancestry have their highest populations in California, Arizona, New Mexico, and Texas. While these individuals make up only 12.5 percent of the U.S. population, Hispanics now constitute 32.4 percent of California's population, with 77.1 percent being of Mexican heritage. Greater Los Angeles is, in effect, the second largest Mexican city—only Mexico City has a larger Mexican population. Half of all U.S. Hispanics live in California and Texas; however, the presence of people with Hispanic ancestry is now growing rapidly outside of the Southwest as well. This is particularly true in the urban centers of New York City, Chicago, and Florida, and in major farming regions such as the upper Midwest, the Willamette Valley in Oregon, and the Yakima Valley in Washington State.

The 2010 U.S. Census report indicates that the Hispanic population grew from 35.3 million in 2000 to 50.5 million in 2010, accounting for over half of the overall growth in the U.S. population (Ennis et al. 2011). The impact of this diversity on local communities will vary, but issues of race and ethnicity are becoming a growing priority for public administrators generally. There are two visions that have governed the debate over the relevance of minority group identity in the United States. One vision begins with a normative *assimilation* framework, which assumes that the melting pot model experience of European immigrants is the preferable public policy objective. However, this model is challenged by a *multicultural* alternative, which argues that assimilation is neither possible nor desirable for the kind and character of diversity present in many American communities. First, most European immigrants have been able to assimilate within the first or second generations due to their similarity in physical appearance to the majority population. People with darker skin have not been able to assimilate as readily or at all in some cases. This has been particularly true of African Americans and some Hispanics. As a result, assimilation is now often rejected as a goal by "minorities of color" in favor of gaining respect and acceptance as economically and politically equal but separate ethnic groups.

Second, many point out that the assimilation model works best when the size and concentration of ethnic groups is small. However, when the ethnic group is large and when it insulates its members from the dominant cultural patterns of the national society, the assimilation model does not work so easily, as is borne out by the history of large concentrations of ethnic groups in the larger U.S. cities. This has been the case with many African American communities, Mexican Americans and Central Americans in eastern and southern Los Angeles, and some of the Vietnamese immigrants who arrived in the United States in the 1970s and settled in urban areas rather than in small towns. In situations like these, pressures to assimilate are often ignored (Rodriguez 2003).

Those Americans who favor a society that acknowledges the permanent existence of unassimilated or only partially assimilated ethnic/racial minorities generally advocate for multiculturalism (or pluralism). This is essentially a celebration and encouragement of continued diversity, similar to the policy introduced by Canadian Prime Minister Pierre Elliot Trudeau in 1972 in order to hasten the acceptance of a permanently unassimilated French-speaking society in Quebec Province. Today, multiculturalism in Canada is a deep-rooted policy at every level of government and

has been expanded to cover all ethnic groups. For many, this serves as the model to be emulated in the United States.

There are those like Richard Rodriguez, a leading American essayist and social commentator, who argues that the debate between the multiculturalism and melting pot models is largely irrelevant. Constant close contact between people of different ethnic and racial groups in the United States is progressively resulting in a blurring of the differences between them. Rodriguez suggests that Americans are melting into each other genetically and culturally. More and more children are being born with two or more different ethnic or racial backgrounds.

The 2010 Census provides dramatic evidence in support of Rodriquez's argument. Between 2000 and 2010, the number of mixed-race children in America rose by 50 percent, to a total of 4.2 million. Overall, the total number of Americans who self-identify as mixed-race rose by 134 percent, to 1.8 million (Humes et al. 2011). Since the mixed-race population is "overwhelmingly young," these numbers translate into more mixed-race peers for all children, especially in southern and midwestern states, where increases in numbers of mixed-race Americans have been "far greater than the national average" (Saulny 2011). Rodriquez refers to this phenomena as the "browning of America" and asserts that a distinct national culture is developing—one formed largely by various ethnicities borrowing from each other and thereby creating a new cultural synthesis. Rodriguez points to the recent experience of Hawaii and the southwestern states as examples of this homogenizing of people and their cultures into something distinctively new (2003).

In addition to browning, local communities are also graying. By 2025, the baby boomers born in 1955 will be 70. Just under 20 percent of the U.S. population will be younger than 15, slightly less than today, according to the U.S. Census Bureau. The middle of the age spectrum will hollow out, and the number of those 65 and older will swell from 12.4 percent of the population to 18.2 percent. The nation in 2025 is projected to have 43 Social Security beneficiaries for every 100 workers. The graying of America will result in important changes in the configuration of local communities, as resources in all sectors are shifted toward health care clinics, home health services, hearing aid providers, hospitals and hospital equipment stores, physical therapists, and residential care facilities.

Future public servants will be challenged by the "graying" and "browning" of America to craft and implement policies that take into account the unique age, cultural, and language needs of various subpopulations. This will be especially true in the delivery of social services and public education, where scarcity of resources is already straining the capacity of public service systems to meet existing needs.

## The Growth of Income Inequality

The gap between the rich and the poor in the United States has grown over the past several decades. Since 1967, U.S. household income inequality grew by 18 percent. Nearly half of that growth occurred during the 1980s (U.S. Census 2012a).

Between 1979 and 2000 "the real income of households in the lowest fifth (the bottom 20 percent of earners) grew 6.4 percent, while that of households in the top fifth (the top 20 percent of earners) grew 70 percent, with the top 1 percent achieving real income gains of 184 percent." In contrast, during the 1950s and 1960s real income almost doubled for all groups" (Mishel, Bernstein, and Allegretto 2005, 2). In a report titled *The State of Working America: 2004/2005*, the Economic Policy Institute estimated that the bottom 80 percent of American households control only about 16 percent of the nation's wealth. Meanwhile, wages, benefits, and working conditions for workers at the bottom continue to decrease (Mishel, Bernstein, and Allegretto 2005, 12). The United

States ranks third to last among the Organisation for Economic Co-operation and Development (OECD) nations in terms of income equality.

Since 2000, the number of poor Americans has grown considerably. The official poverty rate hovered at about 15 percent in the four years between 2008 and 2012, up from 12.1 percent in 2002. The 2012 Census indicates that 49.1 million Americans have fallen below official poverty thresholds, up from 42.9 million Americans in 2009 and 34.6 million in 2002 and slightly over 22 million in 1973 (U.S. Census Bureau 2012).[1] The official poverty rate in 2000 (11.3 percent) was about the same as 1973 (11.1 percent) despite the fact that real capital income grew 66 percent over the same period (Mishel, Bernstein, and Allegretto 2005, 12). Any changes in the poverty rate since 1981 are almost entirely the result of market forces, not the result of any changes in the tax system or transfer payments to the poor (Mishel, Bernstein, and Allegretto 2005, 339–40).

While the Census Bureau figures reveal a significant number of Americans living in poverty, many experts argue that the measures used by the federal government drastically underestimate the real scale of poverty in America—primarily because the official poverty thresholds are considered "too low." The Economic Policy Institute believes a more realistic poverty threshold for a family of four would be in the area of $30,000 a year—and that a more accurate estimate of the poverty rate in America would be at least 30 percent of the total population (Mishel, Bernstein, and Allegretto 2005, 12). The 2010 Census provides new supplemental measures of poverty and lower-income levels that rise as high as 146 million, almost half of the population.

There are clear implications for administrators of the growing income gap between the bottom and top of the economic spectrum. Politically it means heightened tension between the haves and the have-nots, and this can easily spawn grassroots movements such as Occupy Wall Street, which appears to have awoken many Americans from a sense of complacency and called their attention to the vast disparities of wealth; the multiple problems of the poor, including jobs, housing, health care, and wages; and the shrinking of the middle class in the United States.

Wide disparities of wealth in democratic societies typically lead to political instability, a condition that most Americans now acknowledge as present and most regrettable. Our political parties are highly polarized and seemingly incapable of finding any common ground other than disenchantment with government. Administratively, in this era of severe recession, high public and private debt, and intense debates over the direction of public policy, the social service needs of the community are competing against other basic services like education, police, fire, water, and prisons. Even when some of these services are provided by a cost-of-service approach, the customers paying these costs do not clearly separate their tax bill from their water, sewer, or other bills for a designated service. This leaves citizens experiencing an undifferentiated increase in the costs of government. Alternatively, the proliferation of fees for service and special tax rates for enumerated services leave citizens wondering what the "general government taxes" actually do cover. These conditions place public servants in the unenviable position of reminding and educating a polarized public of the enduring needs of communities, the importance of investing in infrastructure, and the obligation to take care of the growing number of dispossessed people in our society who require a social service safety net.

### Permanent Fiscal Crisis with Increased Emphasis on Managing for Results

It is likely that U.S. governments will face continued fiscal stress for the foreseeable future (Green 2012; Osborne and Hutchinson 2004). Many officials have been sounding the alarm for decades over rising debt, growing costs of entitlements, and ownership of the U.S. debt by China and Japan. David Walker, a former comptroller general of the United States, estimated that if the

present U.S. rates of spending and taxation continue, the U.S. government will be bankrupt by the year 2040 (Walker 2007). The financial crash of 2007–8 and the ensuing Great Recession have likely accelerated this time frame substantially—and have certainly heightened the controversy about it. The continuing taxpayer revolt, along with the protracted recession, makes significant tax increases an unlikely solution, and the heated politics surrounding public debt has led more to stalemate than progress.

A complicating factor at the local level is the proliferation of government jurisdictions and special districts, which tend to fracture the political will and the economic resources that could be pooled to help cope with the fiscal crisis. All of these jurisdictions depend heavily on property tax revenue, which has been severely restricted by a combination of property tax limitations and a depressed housing market. At the same time, local jurisdictions, like the national government, are facing a growing pension and retirement obligations as the "boomer" generation retires. These conditions will result in increased pressure on local career administrators to coordinate with other jurisdictions for tax levies, for service consolidation, and for educating citizens about what they are getting for the taxes they pay. Pressures will increase to do more with less or to provide the same levels of service while cutting expenditures. At some point, it will no longer be possible to continue operating programs at meaningful levels of service. Elected officials risk their careers when trying to remedy this situation with tax increases. Career administrators will need to take a leadership role in convincing both the public and the elected officials of what to do when public institutions reach the breaking point; clearly, only certain programs will be salvageable with the funds available.

The scarcity of public funding often pushes public administrators to the nonprofit and commercial sectors in the search for alternative funding. On the positive side, moving beyond the public sector opens opportunities for broader public and advocacy group support for public projects. For example, funding for the construction of new buildings and programs on many public university campuses demonstrates a blending of minimal levels of state support with extensive support from private foundations, escalating tuition and fees from students, and enterprise revenues from the private commercial sector.

## The Rising Importance of Native American Indian Tribes and Tribal Governments

Since the early 1960s, there has been a fundamental transformation in the relationship between native American Indian tribes and U.S. state and local governments. Charles Wilkinson argues that the rise of modern Indian Nations, particularly since World War II, is best understood as one of the great civil rights struggles in American history. Scholars of the history of American Indians (Pevar 2002; Wilkinson 2005) describe the relationship of the U.S. federal government and tribes as troubling at best.

Most scholars offer an annotated timeline denoting eras characterized by the policy orientation of the federal government toward tribes. For example, Wilkinson (2004) offers the following eras: preconstitutional (1532–1789), the formative years (1789–1871), allotment and assimilation (1871–1928), Indian reorganization (1928–1945), termination (1945–1961), and "self-determination" (1961–present). The formative era is denoted by the robust engagement of the federal government in treaty making with tribes and early federal court decisions affirming treaty rights, the sovereignty of tribes making such treaties, freedom from state authority, and the process of establishing a federal trust responsibility to tribes. The eras that follow mark a zigzag path of federal policy aimed at diminishing or eliminating tribes, removing Indian people from their lands, or—alternatively—

supporting tribal autonomy, self-governance, and tribal development. The full story is more complex and infinitely more nuanced. Five-hundred and sixty-five tribes control more than 60 million acres nationwide and count some 3 million Native Americans as enrolled members. Each tribe, each portion of each tribe, has its own institutional history with the federal government, other tribes, and other proximate state and local governments. The booming years following World War II gave rise to new pressure by the federal government to gain access to tribal lands and resources. Termination and relocation became the official policy of the federal government toward Indians in 1953, with the passage of House Concurrent Resolution 108. Subsequent laws gave certain states authority to extend jurisdiction over tribal people on tribal lands in specific areas of law. Though not in statute, federal policy in the late 1950s included a massive effort to relocate Indian people from reservations to urban areas. Chicago, Oakland, and Minneapolis, among others cities, were established as targets for relocation efforts with transition offices and programs. Other urban centers—for example, Los Angeles and Portland (Oregon)—saw rapid increases in the population of Native Americans through "voluntary" migration pushed by termination of tribes, sale of homelands, and the crushing poverty in Indian country. The concentration of Indian peoples in urban areas had the unintended consequence of spawning a new identity among Indians based on the commonalities of their histories. It allowed a small but critical number of Indian people to complete higher education, become lawyers, and activate interest in a generation of leaders willing to lead the struggle to assert rights. This "rights-taking period" reversed the termination act, Public Law 280, and reestablished rights to fish, determine tribal membership, and self-govern.

Federal policy for the last forty years officially supports the principle of self-determination and the recovery and enforcement of rights for Native American Indian tribes. However, the rights struggle continues. Tribes continue to seek restoration of tribal recognition; the restoration of homelands; remedies for losses such as the mismanagement of mineral extraction based on trust funds administered by the Bureau of Indian Affairs (BIA); and the achievement of tangible outcomes on the land for rights that have already been secured (i.e., water in the stream and fish in the river).

Every corner of America has tribes with their own stories: Passamaquoddy in Maine, the Quinault in Washington, the Mandan, Hidatsa, and Arikara in North Dakota and the Alaska and Hawaiian natives. Today, some tribes struggle with reestablishing language, culture, and traditional practices. Others grapple with establishing robust governance structures and processes. Still others are building capacity to implement policy of their own design—establishing tribally led programs in health, education, and natural resource management and taking over implementation responsibility from the federal government.

If an earlier generation of tribal leaders emerged to champion the struggle for basic rights, a new generation is emerging to lead governance within tribes, bridge interjurisdictional management among tribes and other governments, and implement the responsibilities implied by the rights they have secured. A generation ago, it was common to find non-Indian professionals working for tribes to implement tribal policy. Today, it is more common that the tribal professionals are Native Americans and increasingly enrolled members of the tribes they serve. These professionals work across policy domains with expertise in fisheries, social work, business management, and health care. Tomorrow will be different, as tribe after tribe builds governance capacity to administer a broadening range of fundamental services such as housing, health, energy, natural resource, economic development, and social programs. Public service leaders at all levels of federal, state, and local government will need to attend to the dynamic changes in the 565 currently recognized tribal governments where the balancing of rights and responsibilities, trustee responsibility and self-determination, and independence and coproduction are added to administrative portfolios.

## Proliferation of Governmental Jurisdictions and Overlapping Structures of Authority

Local jurisdictions have grown dramatically since the 1960s. The willingness to accommodate the desire of citizens to live in enclaves that protect them from the perceived adverse consequences of growth, increased taxes, and undesirable diversity (socioeconomic, ethnic, racial) has resulted in the creation of a complex array of local governing institutions. The pressures that have created these governing entities are not going to dissipate in the foreseeable future. In fact, they will likely continue to increase. As a result, local jurisdictions are preoccupied with issues of taxes and tax bases, annexation, infrastructure provision, land improvement, zoning, and provision of services. These issues place a premium on managing interjurisdictional relationships, and they will grow in importance as jurisdictions are forced to cooperate in managing shrinking resources and accommodating increased demands from citizens for accountability and documented results. Such pressures will likely lead to some efforts at consolidating administrative functions to reduce overhead costs and increase efficiencies in maintenance, information technology, and purchasing. The current push for decentralization will cycle into recentralization. Evidence for this already exists in the consolidation of police and fire services into unified districts, and in nonprofit-sector delivery of social services, where small nonprofits are banding together or are being swallowed by larger entities in order to sustain or improve capacity.

## Confounding the Lines Between Public, Nonprofit, and Private Sectors

The United States was founded on a rule-of-law system that drew a bright-line distinction between the authority of government and the freedom of individuals to pursue their own life course. Civil society and the private market economy are products of individuals freely choosing to associate and organize with others without undue interference from government. This principle is memorialized in the First Amendment right of individuals to worship, to assemble, and to be free from government regulation based on the views and beliefs they hold. Government is free to regulate the time, place, and manner of the exercise of one's liberty, but not the content. This right has been extended to businesses as well as individuals, which has made it legally difficult for government to regulate commercial speech differently than noncommercial speech, or to treat the property rights of corporate entities differently than the property rights of individuals. Corporate entities and associations are composed of individuals whose freedom becomes meaningful through the aegis of organizations.

However, this popularly held belief in a bright line between government and the other sectors is more myth than reality. As we have argued throughout this book, the various sectors are mutually interdependent and have become what they are largely through a codependent and mutually interactive process of development. The faith-based initiatives of the George W. Bush administration (Executive Order 13199 [2001]) intentionally challenged the bright line between government and faith-oriented organizations in the nonprofit sector. The initiatives provide avenues of federal government support to churches and other faith-based groups for the provision of social services, while legal challenges continue to test for a clearer separation between government and the nonprofit sector.

The line between the government, commercial, and nonprofit sectors is also quite porous. For example, the subsidized infrastructure developed by government has made it possible for commerce to thrive. Government uses its contracting authority to enhance the private sector by forbidding public bodies from competing with the private business sector, giving preferences to minority and

small businesses, and imposing other restrictions to enable the private and nonprofit sectors to prosper. But government can also use its authority in ways that undermine both the business and nonprofit sectors and obscure public accountability. These concerns have been at the center of the debate over the decline in legitimacy of the administrative state over the last three decades. As public servants continue to be called upon to rethink the relationship among the sectors, they need to take a leadership role in keeping the right questions at the center of the debate. How do these relationships cultivate healthy growth in each sector? How do they tend to enervate the animating spirit in one sector or another? These issues and concerns are likely to grow rather than decrease in importance in the decades ahead.

The New Public Management and Reinvention of Government movements in the last decades of the twentieth century altered the assumptions about the role of government in organizing and delivering public services. Most governmental entities have accepted the argument that the for-profit and nonprofit sectors can play important roles in coproducing, or even taking over, provision of many government services. Reliance on third-party governance is thus likely to continue growing (Smith and Lipsky 1993, 1–11; Salamon 1999, chap. 5).

One of the less well-known developments in recent years is the deliberate creation of hybrid organizations, what are sometimes called *quasi-governmental organizations* ("quagos") and *quasi-nongovernmental organizations* ("quangos"). The federal government has created 300 of these in the last few decades (Moe and Kosar 2005). While these agencies carry out government-sponsored activities and provide money or mechanisms for funding government activities, they operate outside the legal authority of Title 5 of the *U.S. Code*. This means that they cannot be held accountable through the traditional tools of executive oversight (the budget and general management laws, for instance). The supporters of this trend argue that the goal is "to maximize performance and results"; critics argue that these organizations contribute to a weakened "capacity of government to perform its fundamental constitutional duties, and to an erosion of political and administrative accountability" (Moe and Kosar 2005). Evidence in support of the critics was clearly manifested in the failures of Fannie Mae and Freddie Mac, two government-sponsored enterprises (GSEs) that played a role in exacerbating problems in the mortgage market that led to the financial crisis of 2007–8. These enterprises were first established as government programs, but were spun off as GSEs with more independence so that they could be run almost entirely as businesses. With that independence came a dramatic loss in accountability. These enterprises were promptly taken over by the federal government in the midst of the financial disaster set in motion in December 2007.

Deliberation over the reliance on third parties to provide governmental services has sparked renewed interest in key questions that formed the core of the constitutional debate in 1787: What role should government play in a democratic society? How can that role be assured under a rule-of-law system? For the foreseeable future, public administrators will participate in answering these questions at every level of American democratic government, particularly as they are called upon at the local level to use the nonprofit and private sectors for the delivery of public services.

*Ensuring the Vitality of Nonprofit Organizations*

There are some well-documented adverse consequences for nonprofits that arise from government contracting, many of which we have touched on in our discussion entitled "The Rise and Transformation of the Nonprofit Sector" in chapter 5. In order to comply with government accountability standards, nonprofits may have to fundamentally alter the structure, staffing, and operations of their activities. In the process, they may weaken their capacity to carry out the role we traditionally expect them to perform in civil society. Instead of being composed of passionate volunteers

who devote their energy to the service of a single clientele group, nonprofits get transformed into codependent businesses operated by professionals. This codependency generally moves in one of two directions, neither of which bodes well for the autonomy and independence of either party to the contract. On the one hand, nonprofits may begin to resemble some defense industry subcontractors who manage their business and their relationship to government much as a foster child of a court-supervised parent. On the other, an increasing number of contractees may become so powerful that they effectively coopt public agencies, thus undermining their capacity to serve as potential sources of meaningful social and institutional change (Smith and Lipsky 1993, 5; Berry and Arons 2003, chap. 5). Public accountability and open access are threatened by such arrangements.

*Ensuring Deliberation over the Public Interest*

A less-noticed consequence of relying on the contracting process to deliver public services is that it removes the debate over the social service needs of the community from public view during annual budget deliberations. As we observed in chapter 5, the contracting process transfers issues over the level and quality of needed services to the "business agenda," a technical matter governed by the legal complexities of contracts. Frequently, these items are placed on what is called "the consent agenda," which creates the presumption that they will not be discussed unless a board member takes the initiative to remove the item from the consent agenda. Critics of this approach remind us that the purpose of public deliberations is to engage the community in a debate over the multiple competing and complex political goals of the community. Scholars interested in the functionality of political discourse argue that deliberation is essential to democracy both in policymaking and implementation processes. They suggest that "public space" in which people interact in everyday ways allows people to create meaning and understanding about public values and, through this practice, civil society becomes a reservoir of the habits of good citizenship (Cooke 1996, Elkin 2004; Fox and Miller 1996; Kemmis 1990; King and Stivers 1998). Deliberative processes require balancing competing values that include (1) meeting the needs of the most vulnerable members of society (Smith and Lipsky 1993), (2) maintaining legal accountability to both legislative and executive authorities, (3) balancing the need for individual citizen access and responsiveness with the need for collective action, and (4) facilitating citizen-centered governance that is informed by wisdom and expertise (Box 1998; Moe 1994; Moe and Gilmour 1995). Relying on the contracting process to deliver public services obscures these trade-off issues, removing them from public discussion and locating them in a more private, transactional framework. Perhaps just as important, those served by the contracting process often become an invisible part of the community, out of sight and out of mind. Public service leaders are in a position to remedy constraints on appropriate deliberation in contracting out and ensuring that such contracts carry "democratic content" (Larsen 2008).

*Maintaining Public Accountability*

A final concern that arises from reliance on third parties to provide public services is the lack of public accountability. As the recent contract administration experiences of the wars in Iraq and Afghanistan remind us, when public bodies decide to contract out for services or establish quasi-governmental bodies, oversight is shifted away from elected, deliberative bodies to the contract specialists in accounting and law (cf. Van Buren 2011). This concern for accountability is especially important when the government is giving its power to providers who administer to the needs of the most vulnerable populations: prisoners, juveniles, drug addicts, foster children, and the like. Government control and manipulation of vulnerable populations proceeds properly only when

sanctioned by deliberate democratic processes and safeguards. Contracting gives away responsibility for important authoritative decisions about at-risk segments of society. Program monitoring and auditing are often rudimentary and inadequate for assuring program compliance and maintenance of standards. The policy system interposes courts as institutions that alone can make the most important and life-altering decisions—to deprive people of their liberty or to take children from their homes, for example. In a thousand ways, though, it is our service workers who act at the margin to make fateful decisions about people, or their reports constitute the primary evidence upon which judges rely (Smith and Lipsky 1993, 11–12). In the years ahead, administrative leaders will play a decisive role in determining whether reliance on third-party organizations to deliver public services is carried out in a manner that meets the multiple tests of democratic governance: responsiveness, accountability, effectiveness, efficiency, and equity (Cooper 2002).

## The Increasing Reliance on Technology, and the Promise of E-Government

The rapid growth of the information age has contradictory consequences for the work of government. On the one hand, it arms everyone with access to more information and provides them with the opportunity to share this information more widely with one another. But more information does not mean more knowledge and better-informed decision making. Excessive information can create information overload and pose increased challenges for sorting and ordering the array of data in ways that create relevance and meaning for the common work of the community. It can complicate choices and steer citizens in the wrong directions on which choices to make (cf. Thaler and Sunstein 2009). Data overload can produce confusion, conflict, and indecisiveness.

More information that is widely available can exacerbate the problems of deliberation over the common good in other ways. As groups organize around ever-narrower agendas and mobilize support to make their interests a reality, it can make the work of building a community consensus more difficult to develop and sustain. The challenge is to use the technology in ways that enhance the possibility of creating a shared sense of community, rather than having it used to further divide the community. From a Madisonian viewpoint, which favors a multiplicity of interests, one might argue that the proliferation of information-centered technology ameliorates the adverse effects of faction. As more and more groups organize around ever-narrower interests, the dangers of tyranny of the majority diminish. But the Madisonian vision of interest-group pluralism also assumes that the work of government itself would require the "regulation of these various and interfering interests," which, Madison argued, "forms the principal task of modern legislation and involves the spirit of party and faction in the necessary and ordinary operations of government. . . . It is in vain to say that enlightened statesmen will be able to adjust these clashing interests and render them all subservient to the common good" (Madison 1787, Federalist No. 10, quoted in Rossiter 1961).

An important ingredient to making the regulation of the clash of interests work is "to refine and enlarge the public views by passing them through the medium of a chosen body of citizens whose wisdom may best discern the true interest of the country and whose patriotism and love of justice will be least likely to sacrifice it to temporary or partial considerations" (Madison 1787, Federalist No. 10, quoted in Rossiter 1961). Madison's reliance on the medium of legislative bodies has not met his expectations (see discussion of representation in chapter 6). We believe the career public servant substantially augments this legislative role. This is especially true in local governments, where the part-time status of legislative bodies makes it impossible for them to perform their vital role. Administrative hearings and public processes provide a much underutilized avenue for

creating a shared sense of the public good, or at least for countering what Madison characterized as "partial considerations."

## FRAMING THE FUTURE: PRESERVING THE CONTINUITIES IN CONFLICT

What does the future hold for public service in the face of the many drivers of change discussed in the previous section? We cannot know the answer to this question with any degree of confidence, but one thing is certain: Future public servants will play a major role in helping the American people cope with such changes and in shaping their meaning. It is important that administrators possess the tools necessary to perform this role. In addition to being technically proficient and grounded in the critical values of political society, they must be able to synthesize the factors outlined above into realistic scenarios around which information can be organized, alternatives analyzed, and elected officials and citizens galvanized to undertake creative and collaborative problem solving.

One of the tools we have found useful in assisting administrators in this process is called *scenario thinking*. It was first introduced as *shell-group planning* in the 1970s and now operates under a variety of different names. Scenario thinking assumes that decision making takes place in a fast-changing and highly uncertain environment, where values, behaviors, and social structures are no longer as stable and predictable as they once were. Under these circumstances, traditional planning and forecasting practices on their own are not sufficient for obtaining insights and answers about how to deal with future events.

The goal of scenario thinking is to get participants to think about and cope with an unknown future, without any pretenses that they will be able to predict or control the future. The process begins with identification of the relevant drivers of change. It then asks participants to assess the interplay of these drivers. Assessment is less about obtaining quantitative certainty and more about understanding the "logic" of these forces as they come together to create new waves of change. This process is not unlike what whitewater rafting enthusiasts and fly fishermen do when reading the many currents, eddies, and swirls in a fast-flowing river. They need to be clear about where they want to end up, knowing that they can't alter the forces of change. To accomplish this, they can only read the waters so that the ride of their watercraft or fly is carried as safely and smoothly as possible through the currents to obtain the results they want. The goal of scenario thinking is to encourage participants to think proactively and plan for future developments as they are buffeted by drivers of change (Bonnet and Olson 1993; Ringland 2002; Van der Heijden 2005).

We end this book with an example of scenario thinking in a community "envisioning process." The example illustrates the central theme with which we began: Career public servants help make democracy work. Career administrators occupy unique positions that enable them to maintain continuity over time and provide the institutional support necessary for making democracy meaningful in the daily lives of citizens. With these positions comes an obligation that helps preserve the integrity of America's many governing systems—an obligation to work through changes in the future. This obligation requires the balancing of competing values, which is a challenging but not impossible task, as the story of the Vision Action Network illustrates. This case developed over more than 15 years. It started as a final project for a master's degree in public administration. The authors were senior administrators who carried a dream and gradually transformed it into a reality as they guided the work of a local jurisdiction. It shows how collaborative governance, despite its many difficulties, can still attract and inspire citizens and officials to pursue ambitious goals and, with persistence over time, transform them into reality.

## Doing What Is Right for Juan Gomez

This is an account of the creation of a communitywide collaborative entity. It came about through leadership undertaken by career administrators in one of the richest and fastest-growing counties of the state. What is especially noteworthy about this case is that the community collaboration process was inspired by the plight of Juan Gomez, one of the community's most needy and at-risk residents.

Juan Gomez was a 14-year-old boy who lived his entire life in Cascadia County. He came from a single-parent home headed by his mother, Consuela, who had a history of alcohol abuse and abusive relationships. When Juan was very young, his father returned to El Salvador. Consuela's boyfriend was physically abusive to her, as well as to Juan and his siblings. Consuela's extended family was concerned about Juan's situation and expressed this concern to all who would listen, including social service workers, school officials, housing authority officials where the family lived, members of their Catholic parish, the local health clinic, and a local shelter for runaway teens. Despite the family's best efforts, Consuela said Juan would no longer submit to parental authority without the threat of physical punishment from her boyfriend.

While English was Juan's second language, he always did well in school. But at the age of 13, Juan's grades began to decline and he started developing gang associations. He acknowledged being a member of the "Barrio Riders" and displayed numerous gang tattoos. On several occasions, Juan did not return home in the evening and was reported to the police as a runaway. Each time, the police found Juan and took him to a shelter operated by a local church, where he remained temporarily until he was returned to the custody of his mother.

Juan was diagnosed in 1998 as diabetic and has been treated at the local nonprofit health clinic and twice at the emergency room of two local hospitals. Since Juan and his family do not have health insurance, systematic treatment of Juan's condition has been problematic, especially since it has been unclear what Juan's status is under the state-sponsored health plan.

On April 20, 1999, Juan encountered a boy at school (Javier) who was affiliated with a rival gang and had been seen with Juan's girlfriend. Juan confronted Javier in the school bathroom. A fight ensued, but no weapons were used. Subsequent reports indicate that Juan threw Javier against the wall, then punched and kicked him. Juan then fled the scene, stealing Javier's backpack and pager. Javier suffered abrasions and a badly swollen face. Juan was arrested soon thereafter at a shopping mall. He was taken to the local police station, booked, and given a cursory physical examination in response to complaints of dizziness. At the time, he told officials of his diabetic condition and that he had run out of insulin.

Juan was charged with several counts, including Robbery III (class C felony), Assault IV (class A misdemeanor), Possession of a Controlled Substance II (class C felony), and Carrying a Concealed Weapon (CCW, class B misdemeanor). The drug and CCW charges resulted from the police finding a small amount of marijuana and a 7-inch hunting knife in Juan's backpack.

During the arrest, Juan was hostile and uncooperative with the police, and he made threats to "kick Javier's ass" if the boy cooperated with the prosecution. By the time Juan reached the detention facility, he had calmed down and indicated to the police that he wanted to go home. Juan had limited prior juvenile court contact; he had never been on probation, he had no delinquency court appearances, and he had no prior expulsions from school. As a result of the incident, he had a Theft II (shoplift) and Assault IV charges pending (both class A misdemeanors), and was in warrant status for being unable to be located. The warrant indicated that the judicial officer did not oppose release. This was Juan's first warrant. Consuela and Juan told the judicial officer that they had recently moved and had no idea that the warrant had been issued. In addition to the Theft II and Assault IV charges, Juan was facing expulsion from school.

How can the family, the school, the juvenile justice system, nonprofit social service agencies, churches, and local public officials work together to do what is right for individuals like Juan Gomez? What can be done to prevent further escalation of an already bad situation? More important for our purposes, whose responsibility is it to glue together the pieces of these fragmented systems into a more integrated and community-centered social service system? For the administrators of Cascadia County, the answer was clear: "As administrators, we have leadership responsibility for addressing the needs of Juan Gomez, and the growing number of individuals like Juan." But how can officials take the initiative to do what is right for Juan Gomez when they reside in one of the richest counties in the state, where residents are more concerned about their roads and taxes than they are about the rising social service needs of the community?

**Creation of a Community Planning Process**

For about 15 years, the Cascadia County administrator and his senior deputy had been thinking about how best to harness the array of social services within the county to better meet the needs of residents. As students in an executive MPA program, they had written their master's degree capstone paper on how this might be done. Their thinking was inspired by an article of Charles Levine's that emphasized the important and growing role of career administrators in generating civic capacity through processes of coproduction, and processes that link the public, private, and nonprofit sectors to increase impact beyond what is possible with any single service provider (Levine 1984). But how could they give this kind of idea some legs?

The administrative leaders of the county began in small ways by encouraging collaboration among nonprofit social service providers within the county, and then rewarding them through the budget process when this cooperation and collaboration occurred. They took every opportunity they could to brief elected officials on the changing demographic composition of the county and the potential implications for the delivery of services. But these small steps were not doing much to capture the imagination of the community and its elected officials. Most citizens were concerned about protecting their lifestyle from the adverse impacts of economic development; they were quite oblivious to the needs of those less fortunate and especially to the large increase in the Hispanic population.

The administrative leaders saw a window of opportunity in two triggering forces within the county that might be used to focus greater attention on the growing gap between county resources and community needs. One was the rapid population growth that brought increased demands for levels of service such as police, fire, roads, education, and housing. The second was the growing disparity between the needs of low-income citizens and the county resources that were capped by a series of property tax limitations. These developments persuaded elected officials to convene a countywide community planning process, subsequently called the VisionWest Planning Process.

Once this process was put into place, the administrators employed two strategies to generate interest and community ownership of the process. First, they gathered lots of data and placed it on the VisionWest Planning website. Second, they instigated an "envisioning process" with the community to generate issues of importance to the citizens, along with any suggested solutions they had for ameliorating the problems.

From 1970 to 1995, the population of Cascadia County more than doubled, creating huge pressure on public safety, fire, roads, sewers, and other infrastructure services. The growth was expected to continue. The percentage of people over 55 was projected to grow from approximately 16 percent in 1990 to 26 percent of the total in 2020. During the same period, the percentage of younger adults (ages 20–54) was expected to decrease from 54 percent to 46 percent of the total

population. The relative percentage of Hispanic residents increased significantly from 1990 to 2000, rising from 4.6 percent to 11.2 percent of the total population, and was expected to grow by 200 percent by 2020. One in 15 county residents (and nearly one in 10 children) lived below the poverty line.

This data challenged the accepted stereotype of the county. As the home of the state's high-tech industry, the citizens of the county had enjoyed the benefits of good jobs and high levels of service. The community was viewed as relatively homogeneous, higher end of middle-class, and professional. But other, less visible issues threatened the quality of life: mental illness, home-lessness, hunger, lack of living alternatives for seniors and the disabled, and limited access to affordable health care. The relative affluence of the county obscured the fact that so many residents (one in 15) lived below the poverty line. The envisioning process provided an opportunity to confront the citizens with this demographic information and its social service implications for the community.

Once the elected officials had given their approval to proceed with the community VisionWest Planning Process, the county administrative staff contacted key opinion leaders within the community to obtain their support and participation in a communitywide dialogue. An initial round of discussions was undertaken to identify the key issues of concern to citizens. The following seven topics were identified and served as the template for the rest of the envisioning process: (1) aging and disabilities, (2) basic needs, (3) behavioral health, (4) children and families, (5) education, (6) the environment, (7) housing, and (8) primary health care.

These issues had two things in common: They reflected the growing income disparity within the community, and they affirmed the inability of any single institution to address all of the emerging concerns on its own. Most community planning processes end with the identification of the central issues of concern to the citizens. But the purpose of the VisionWest process was to create communitywide ownership and to identify resources that could be leveraged from the private, public, and nonprofit sectors to address the issues. With that in mind, the county staff emphasized the importance of following up with problem-solving teams organized around each set of issues. These teams held meetings to develop an in-depth survey of the more difficult challenges and most promising opportunities in their respective areas of responsibility. Each team was charged with producing an issue paper that included the following: (1) an overview of the trends and conditions pertaining to that issue, (2) specific issues and strategies identified by the Issue Team, and (3) a short list of key recommendations that participants felt were significant and could be implemented in the next couple of years. The issue papers were made electronically accessible on the VisionWest Planning website. The goal was to have the issue papers serve as a starting point for increasing awareness of these issues, and to use the papers to inform a variety of public, private, and nonprofit plans and initiatives.

A final step in the process involved the faith community. The Cascadia staff knew early on that it was important to involve the religious community in crafting a countywide approach for dealing with the emerging complexity of social needs. The churches provide an untold amount of formal and informal social service to the citizens of the county. They have the loyalty and confidence of the citizens, and they provide connective linkages to the citizenry that are not available through other county, business, or nonprofit service providers.

How was this support and network of trust among religious organizations to be enlisted in the service of the larger needs of the county? The county staff decided to use the same model they had followed in their other outreach efforts: (1) contact the key opinion leaders of the faith community most likely to be supportive of the county efforts; (2) build relationships of personal trust; and (3) then call a more formal meeting to set forth the agenda and ask for the participation of faith-based

organizations. This model produced surprising results. Not only did the faith community respond with great enthusiasm, its members expressed both surprise and gratitude that county officials would expend the effort to do what they had never done on their own. For the first time in the history of Cascadia County, the church leaders began meeting to discuss how they could contribute to the community-building efforts undertaken by the county leaders. What kind of social services were they each providing? Which groups were falling through the cracks? How might they pool and coordinate their efforts? These were the kinds of questions generated in the meetings.

The experience of working together for the first time was so productive and exhilarating that a core group of faith leaders decided to form the Inter-Religious Network, which would operate under the umbrella of the larger VisionWest Planning Process. This new organization is a collection of Christian, Jewish, Muslim, and other faith traditions, brought together to achieve the following goals:

- Provide a forum for ongoing relationship building, information sharing, interreligious dialogue, and community problem solving
- Develop sustainable relationships with other community leaders and participate in efforts to identify, discuss, and mobilize around concerns of mutual interest
- Provide a network of faith leaders that can be accessed easily and efficiently
- Create settings where new and innovative expressions of community leadership by faith-based organizations or individuals may be freely offered
- Provide opportunities for group information-sharing programs and other activities

The creation of the Inter-Religious Network represented the final link in a long chain of events that led to the creation of an entirely new organization to implement and sustain the work of the VisionWest process.

### Transforming Visions into Reality: Institutionalizing Planning Outcomes

Significant changes cannot occur without the efforts and enthusiasm of individual people. However, if the changes are to be truly effective and long lasting, they must be owned by organizations and institutions. A major goal of the VisionWest Planning Process was to create an environment that would sustain change through new policies and new institutional arrangements. Early on, county administrators recognized the need for a vehicle distinct from a governmental body to carry on the work of the VisionWest Planning Process—a forum for the community to talk across jurisdictions, across sectors, across issues, and to discuss, strategize, and mobilize around community priorities. A resonating theme from most of the nearly 2,000 county residents and institutions that participated in VisionWest was that collaborative planning and mobilization should not be a onetime event. Instead, it should be part of a new way of doing business in Cascadia County. In March 2001, a free-standing nonprofit organization called the Vision Action Network was incorporated as an institutional focus of the energy and commitment generated by the VisionWest Planning Process.

Those behind the incorporation effort expected that the network would become the forum for multiple institutions and organizations to contemplate future trends and opportunities, and to build on existing relationships and collaboration. The Vision Action Network serves simultaneously as a gathering place, network, support group, incubator, information sharer, community organizer, and broker. The network's board of directors represent all sectors of the community: small and large businesses, K–12 and higher education, local governments, social service not-for-profits, religious

institutions, and health care organizations. Funding for the organization comes from partners in each of the sectors. The network hired its first executive director in spring 2002. The Vision Action Network established a small number of community councils to engage the recommendations of the issue papers and to work on implementation of the most promising strategies.

## EXERCISING POLITY LEADERSHIP IN THE SERVICE OF DEMOCRATIC GOVERNANCE

The creation of the Vision Action Network touches on a variety of themes central to this book. We begin with the question of the proper role of administrative leadership in the community. How can this role be successfully carried out in partnership with elected officials and the citizens of the community? How can the instrumental role of administrators be reconciled with the constitutive role they perform?

The Vision Action Network came into existence because the administrators believed that public servants have an obligation to be more than passive and instrumental caretakers of policy choices made by elected officials. They took the initiative in creating an agenda to meet the needs of the growing number of weak and powerless members of the community. They did not draw a bright-line distinction between the public, private, and nonprofit sectors. In reaching out across boundaries to create a new third-party institution, they exercised what we described in chapter 12 as polity leadership. Polity leaders undertake risks. First, there was a complex array of stakeholders operating under separate and independent sources of authority; these stakeholders measured their success by different criteria. Second, participants in the process were asked to create a vision for the future based on data that did not correspond to their current experience. It was hard for many to believe that beneath the patina of economic prosperity lay a large and growing core of residents who were poor and in need of a wide variety of social services not currently available. Third, there was the need to create support for the agenda with elected officials and to sustain this support over several election cycles.

After successfully undertaking the risk of launching and managing a civic engagement process that cut across sectoral boundaries and produced a shared vision for the future, the administrators subjected themselves to potential criticism on a variety of fronts. For example, if the Vision Action Network became the functional equivalent of a single supplier—a sort of Walmart for the provision of social services to the community—then the jurisdiction would have given up its authority for balancing the competing needs for efficiency, effectiveness, equity, responsiveness, and due process considerations. The administrative champions of the VisionWest Planning Process spent endless hours pondering how to avoid the worst-case scenario, where a new entity is created that becomes the 800-pound gorilla in the room, has little accountability, and places demands on the political system that result in the breakdown of a working political consensus in the community. To avoid this, the administrators took several precautionary steps to preserve their role as a Democratic Balancewheel:

- They preserved the jurisdiction's authority over the social service agenda and the county budget to support it.
- They resisted using the creation of the Vision Action Network as an excuse to reduce the county's share of funding, and they succeeded in getting this principle memorialized into the county's agreement by elected officials to support the future operations of the Vision Action Network.
- They worked hard to establish the financial independence of the Vision Action Network and set a certain time when the county would no longer provide financial support.

- They made certain that social service groups with special needs could continue to seek funding through the county and would not be tied to any kind of monopolistic role of the Vision Action Network.

The leadership role played by administrators in the Vision Action Network illustrates the Balancewheel role of administrative responsibility. Over a 15-year period, administrative leaders used all of the roles identified with the administrative traditions that have become deeply embedded in the history and practice of public administration. For example, at an instrumental level, the Vision Action Network illustrates the critical importance of the role of administrators in providing the technical competence necessary for participants to obtain trustworthy and reliable information, manage the processes of engagement efficiently and effectively, and produce promised results on time and within budget. But this alone was insufficient. The entire process rested on a foundation of engagement that built trust with critical opinion leaders and stakeholders. To prevent this generation of support from becoming a simple process of coalition-building among elites, administrative leaders expanded the process to obtain ownership by the community at large. In addition to relying on rational planning and civic engagement, administrative leaders were extremely entrepreneurial in the way they went about defining the problem and seeking solutions. They were energetic, creative, and innovative—in short, all of the things we associate with "running government like a business." Finally, they were mindful of their interest-balancing role in bringing interests to the table that would not otherwise have been represented without proactive engagement from county leaders. To accomplish this, administrators reached out to organize and involve stakeholders who previously were not an active part of the political process. In short, the creation of the Vision Action Network required administrators to draw on the legacy of our administrative traditions: balancing competing interests, cultivating civic governance, taking entrepreneurial leadership, maintaining accountability for efficient and effective results, and being responsive to the dominant interests in the community without sacrificing the needs and access of those who have no voice.

Public service leadership requires leaders to size up the constellation of contending forces at play in the community and to assess the range of plausible approaches for engaging citizens and officials in developing institutional responses. This process entails considerable art as well as science. Tacit knowledge and astute judgment of stakeholders, circumstances, and organizational capacity must be linked to systematic analysis. It requires thinking strategically about creating a commonly shared vision; reaching out across public-, private-, and nonprofit-sector boundaries to build support for that vision; and transforming it into institutional forms that can endure after the individual agents of change have left the scene. In the United States, such efforts must be conducted in ways that maintain democratic accountability, preserve the role responsibilities of elected officials, and ensure some measure of responsiveness to citizens of the community. Career public servants work at the center of these efforts and serve as democratic stewards in balancing the tensions among our traditions of governance.

## STUDY QUESTIONS

1. What are the major drivers of change that will most likely affect the future of your organization/department/jurisdiction?
2. Choose two or three of the most important drivers of change and develop the most likely scenarios that you imagine will emerge.
3. The development of a process for collecting and using objective data for decision making played a central role in the successful creation of the Vision Action Network. To what

extent was this useful? Essential? How can objective data and analysis best be used as a leadership tool to foster consensus and collaboration?

4.  What are the lessons that emerge from the Vision Action Network case in terms of creating a commonly shared vision? What do you know about the processes that enable problems to be successfully transformed into issues, and issues transformed into public policy changes? To what extent does the transformational process in this case differ from your own experience? To what extent can the process in this case be replicated?

5.  With term limits and part-time local elected officials, career administrators are playing an increasingly important role in initiating public policy changes. This policy development role stands alongside the traditional roles of career administrators in being good stewards of policy implementation. What leadership lessons emerge from this case about how the role relationship between career public administrators and elected politicians can be successfully managed to achieve lasting change?

6.  To what extent is the polity leadership example in this chapter replicable in your organization setting?

## NOTE

1. The Office of Management and Budget establishes the official measure of poverty used by the U.S. Census Bureau. According to the Census Bureau definition, a family is "in poverty" if the total family income is less than the threshold appropriate for that family. For example, if a family has five members—two children, a mother and father, and a great-aunt—their poverty threshold in 2011 was set at $27,517 (see U.S. Census, "Poverty: Poverty Thresholds," www.census.gov/hhes/www/poverty/data/threshld/index.html). If the mother's income was $10,000 for that year, the father's $7,500, and the great-aunt's $10,000, the total income of $27,500 would mean the family was not "in poverty" according to the official definition. However, government social service programs do not have to use the official poverty measure as eligibility criteria. Low income is defined as being at or below 200 percent of the poverty level.

# CONSTITUTION OF THE UNITED STATES

We the People of the United States, in Order to form a more perfect Union, establish Justice, insure domestic Tranquility, provide for the common defence, promote the general Welfare, and secure the Blessings of Liberty to ourselves and our Posterity, do ordain and establish this Constitution for the United States of America.

**ARTICLE I**

**Section 1**

All legislative Powers herein granted shall be vested in a Congress of the United States, which shall consist of a Senate and House of Representatives.

**Section 2**

The House of Representatives shall be composed of Members chosen every second Year by the People of the several States, and the Electors in each State shall have the Qualifications requisite for Electors of the most numerous Branch of the State Legislature.

No Person shall be a Representative who shall not have attained to the Age of twenty five Years, and been seven Years a Citizen of the United States, and who shall not, when elected, be an Inhabitant of that State in which he shall be chosen.

Representatives and direct Taxes shall be apportioned among the several States which may be included within this Union, according to their respective Numbers, which shall be determined by adding to the whole Number of free Persons, including those bound to Service for a Term of Years, and excluding Indians not taxed, three fifths of all other Persons. The actual Enumeration shall be made within three Years after the first Meeting of the Congress of the United States, and within every subsequent Term of ten Years, in such Manner as they shall by Law direct. The Number of Representatives shall not exceed one for every thirty Thousand, but each State shall have at Least one Representative; and until such enumeration shall be made, the State of New Hampshire shall be entitled to chuse three, Massachusetts eight, Rhode-Island and Providence Plantations one,

Connecticut five, New-York six, New Jersey four, Pennsylvania eight, Delaware one, Maryland six, Virginia ten, North Carolina five, South Carolina five, and Georgia three.

When vacancies happen in the Representation from any State, the Executive Authority thereof shall issue Writs of Election to fill such Vacancies.

The House of Representatives shall chuse their Speaker and other Officers; and shall have the sole Power of Impeachment.

## Section 3

The Senate of the United States shall be composed of two Senators from each State, chosen by the Legislature thereof, for six Years; and each Senator shall have one Vote.

Immediately after they shall be assembled in Consequence of the first Election, they shall be divided as equally as may be into three Classes. The Seats of the Senators of the first Class shall be vacated at the Expiration of the second Year, of the second Class at the Expiration of the fourth Year, and of the third Class at the Expiration of the sixth Year, so that one third may be chosen every second Year; and if Vacancies happen by Resignation, or otherwise, during the Recess of the Legislature of any State, the Executive thereof may make temporary Appointments until the next Meeting of the Legislature, which shall then fill such Vacancies.

No Person shall be a Senator who shall not have attained to the Age of thirty Years, and been nine Years a Citizen of the United States, and who shall not, when elected, be an Inhabitant of that State for which he shall be chosen.

The Vice President of the United States shall be President of the Senate, but shall have no Vote, unless they be equally divided.

The Senate shall chuse their other Officers, and also a President pro tempore, in the Absence of the Vice President, or when he shall exercise the Office of President of the United States.

The Senate shall have the sole Power to try all Impeachments. When sitting for that Purpose, they shall be on Oath or Affirmation. When the President of the United States is tried, the Chief Justice shall preside: And no Person shall be convicted without the Concurrence of two thirds of the Members present.

Judgment in Cases of impeachment shall not extend further than to removal from Office, and disqualification to hold and enjoy any Office of honor, Trust or Profit under the United States: but the Party convicted shall nevertheless be liable and subject to Indictment, Trial, Judgment and Punishment, according to Law.

## Section 4

The Times, Places and Manner of holding Elections for Senators and Representatives, shall be prescribed in each State by the Legislature thereof; but the Congress may at any time by Law make or alter such Regulations, except as to the Places of chusing Senators.

The Congress shall assemble at least once in every Year, and such Meeting shall be on the first Monday in December, unless they shall by Law appoint a different Day.

## Section 5

Each House shall be the Judge of the Elections, Returns and Qualifications of its own Members, and a Majority of each shall constitute a Quorum to do Business; but a smaller Number may adjourn from day to day, and may be authorized to compel the Attendance of absent Members, in such Manner, and under such Penalties as each House may provide.

Each House may determine the Rules of its Proceedings, punish its Members for disorderly Behaviour, and, with the Concurrence of two thirds, expel a Member.

Each House shall keep a Journal of its Proceedings, and from time to time publish the same, excepting such Parts as may in their Judgment require Secrecy; and the Yeas and Nays of the Members of either House on any question shall, at the Desire of one fifth of those Present, be entered on the Journal.

Neither House, during the Session of Congress, shall, without the Consent of the other, adjourn for more than three days, nor to any other Place than that in which the two Houses shall be sitting.

## Section 6

The Senators and Representatives shall receive a Compensation for their Services, to be ascertained by Law, and paid out of the Treasury of the United States. They shall in all Cases, except Treason, Felony and Breach of the Peace, be privileged from Arrest during their Attendance at the Session of their respective Houses, and in going to and returning from the same; and for any Speech or Debate in either House, they shall not be questioned in any other Place.

No Senator or Representative shall, during the Time for which he was elected, be appointed to any civil Office under the Authority of the United States, which shall have been created, or the Emoluments whereof shall have been encreased during such time; and no Person holding any Office under the United States, shall be a Member of either House during his Continuance in Office.

## Section 7

All Bills for raising Revenue shall originate in the House of Representatives; but the Senate may propose or concur with Amendments as on other Bills.

Every Bill which shall have passed the House of Representatives and the Senate, shall, before it become a Law, be presented to the President of the United States; If he approve he shall sign it, but if not he shall return it, with his Objections to that House in which it shall have originated, who shall enter the Objections at large on their Journal, and proceed to reconsider it. If after such Reconsideration two thirds of that House shall agree to pass the Bill, it shall be sent, together with the Objections, to the other House, by which it shall likewise be reconsidered, and if approved by two thirds of that House, it shall become a Law. But in all such Cases the Votes of both Houses

shall be determined by yeas and Nays, and the Names of the Persons voting for and against the Bill shall be entered on the Journal of each House respectively. If any Bill shall not be returned by the President within ten Days (Sundays excepted) after it shall have been presented to him, the Same shall be a Law, in like Manner as if he had signed it, unless the Congress by their Adjournment prevent its Return, in which Case it shall not be a Law.

Every Order, Resolution, or Vote to which the Concurrence of the Senate and House of Representatives may be necessary (except on a question of Adjournment) shall be presented to the President of the United States; and before the Same shall take Effect, shall be approved by him, or being disapproved by him, shall be repassed by two thirds of the Senate and House of Representatives, according to the Rules and Limitations prescribed in the Case of a Bill.

**Section 8**

The Congress shall have Power To lay and collect Taxes, Duties, Imposts and Excises, to pay the Debts and provide for the common Defence and general Welfare of the United States; but all Duties, Imposts and Excises shall be uniform throughout the United States;

To borrow Money on the credit of the United States;

To regulate Commerce with foreign Nations, and among the several States, and with the Indian Tribes;

To establish an uniform Rule of Naturalization, and uniform Laws on the subject of Bankruptcies throughout the United States;

To coin Money, regulate the Value thereof, and of foreign Coin, and fix the Standard of Weights and Measures;

To provide for the Punishment of counterfeiting the Securities and current Coin of the United States;

To establish Post Offices and post Roads;

To promote the Progress of Science and useful Arts, by securing for limited Times to Authors and Inventors the exclusive Right to their respective Writings and Discoveries;

To constitute Tribunals inferior to the supreme Court;

To define and punish Piracies and Felonies committed on the high Seas, and Offences against the Law of Nations;

To declare War, grant Letters of Marque and Reprisal, and make Rules concerning Captures on Land and Water;

To raise and support Armies, but no Appropriation of Money to that Use shall be for a longer Term than two Years;

To provide and maintain a Navy;

To make Rules for the Government and Regulation of the land and naval Forces;

To provide for calling forth the Militia to execute the Laws of the Union, suppress Insurrections and repel Invasions;

To provide for organizing, arming, and disciplining, the Militia, and for governing such Part of them as may be employed in the Service of the United States, reserving to the States respectively, the Appointment of the Officers, and the Authority of training the Militia according to the discipline prescribed by Congress;

To exercise exclusive Legislation in all Cases whatsoever, over such District (not exceeding ten Miles square) as may, by Cession of particular States, and the Acceptance of Congress, become the Seat of the Government of the United States, and to exercise like Authority over all Places purchased by the Consent of the Legislature of the State in which the Same shall be, for the Erection of Forts, Magazines, Arsenals, dock-Yards, and other needful Buildings;—And

To make all Laws which shall be necessary and proper for carrying into Execution the foregoing Powers, and all other Powers vested by this Constitution in the Government of the United States, or in any Department or Officer thereof.

## Section 9

The Migration or Importation of such Persons as any of the States now existing shall think proper to admit, shall not be prohibited by the Congress prior to the Year one thousand eight hundred and eight, but a Tax or duty may be imposed on such Importation, not exceeding ten dollars for each Person.

The Privilege of the Writ of Habeas Corpus shall not be suspended, unless when in Cases of Rebellion or Invasion the public Safety may require it.

No Bill of Attainder or ex post facto Law shall be passed.

No Capitation, or other direct, Tax shall be laid, unless in Proportion to the Census or Enumeration herein before directed to be taken.

No Tax or Duty shall be laid on Articles exported from any State.

No Preference shall be given by any Regulation of Commerce or Revenue to the Ports of one State over those of another: nor shall Vessels bound to, or from, one State, be obliged to enter, clear, or pay Duties in another.

No Money shall be drawn from the Treasury, but in Consequence of Appropriations made by Law; and a regular Statement and Account of the Receipts and Expenditures of all public Money shall be published from time to time.

No Title of Nobility shall be granted by the United States: And no Person holding any Office of Profit or Trust under them, shall, without the Consent of the Congress, accept of any present, Emolument, Office, or Title, of any kind whatever, from any King, Prince, or foreign State.

### Section 10

No State shall enter into any Treaty, Alliance, or Confederation; grant Letters of Marque and Reprisal; coin Money; emit Bills of Credit; make any Thing but gold and silver Coin a Tender in Payment of Debts; pass any Bill of Attainder, ex post facto Law, or Law impairing the Obligation of Contracts, or grant any Title of Nobility.

No State shall, without the Consent of the Congress, lay any Imposts or Duties on Imports or Exports, except what may be absolutely necessary for executing it's inspection Laws: and the net Produce of all Duties and Imposts, laid by any State on Imports or Exports, shall be for the Use of the Treasury of the United States; and all such Laws shall be subject to the Revision and Controul of the Congress.

No State shall, without the Consent of Congress, lay any Duty of Tonnage, keep Troops, or Ships of War in time of Peace, enter into any Agreement or Compact with another State, or with a foreign Power, or engage in War, unless actually invaded, or in such imminent Danger as will not admit of delay.

### ARTICLE II

### Section 1

The executive Power shall be vested in a President of the United States of America. He shall hold his Office during the Term of four Years, and, together with the Vice President, chosen for the same Term, be elected, as follows

Each State shall appoint, in such Manner as the Legislature thereof may direct, a Number of Electors, equal to the whole Number of Senators and Representatives to which the State may be entitled in the Congress: but no Senator or Representative, or Person holding an Office of Trust or Profit under the United States, shall be appointed an Elector.

The Electors shall meet in their respective States, and vote by Ballot for two Persons, of whom one at least shall not be an Inhabitant of the same State with themselves. And they shall make a List of all the Persons voted for, and of the Number of Votes for each; which List they shall sign and certify, and transmit sealed to the Seat of the Government of the United States, directed to the President of the Senate. The President of the Senate shall, in the Presence of the Senate and House of Representatives, open all the Certificates, and the Votes shall then be counted. The Person having the greatest Number of Votes shall be the President, if such Number be a Majority of the whole Number of Electors appointed; and if there be more than one who have such Majority, and have an equal Number of Votes, then the House of Representatives shall immediately chuse by Ballot one of them for President; and if no Person have a Majority, then from the five highest on the List the said House shall in like Manner chuse the President. But in chusing the President, the Votes shall be taken by States, the Representation from each State having one Vote; A quorum for

this Purpose shall consist of a Member or Members from two thirds of the States, and a Majority of all the States shall be necessary to a Choice. In every Case, after the Choice of the President, the Person having the greatest Number of Votes of the Electors shall be the Vice President. But if there should remain two or more who have equal Votes, the Senate shall chuse from them by Ballot the Vice President.

The Congress may determine the Time of chusing the Electors, and the Day on which they shall give their Votes; which Day shall be the same throughout the United States.

No Person except a natural born Citizen, or a Citizen of the United States, at the time of the Adoption of this Constitution, shall be eligible to the Office of President; neither shall any Person be eligible to that Office who shall not have attained to the Age of thirty five Years, and been fourteen Years a Resident within the United States.

In Case of the Removal of the President from Office, or of his Death, Resignation, or Inability to discharge the Powers and Duties of the said Office, the Same shall devolve on the Vice President, and the Congress may by Law provide for the Case of Removal, Death, Resignation or Inability, both of the President and Vice President, declaring what Officer shall then act as President, and such Officer shall act accordingly, until the Disability be removed, or a President shall be elected.

The President shall, at stated Times, receive for his Services, a Compensation, which shall neither be encreased nor diminished during the Period for which he shall have been elected, and he shall not receive within that Period any other Emolument from the United States, or any of them.

Before he enter on the Execution of his Office, he shall take the following Oath or Affirmation:—"I do solemnly swear (or affirm) that I will faithfully execute the Office of President of the United States, and will to the best of my Ability, preserve, protect and defend the Constitution of the United States."

## Section 2

The President shall be Commander in Chief of the Army and Navy of the United States, and of the Militia of the several States, when called into the actual Service of the United States; he may require the Opinion, in writing, of the principal Officer in each of the executive Departments, upon any Subject relating to the Duties of their respective Offices, and he shall have Power to grant Reprieves and Pardons for Offences against the United States, except in Cases of Impeachment.

He shall have Power, by and with the Advice and Consent of the Senate, to make Treaties, provided two thirds of the Senators present concur; and he shall nominate, and by and with the Advice and Consent of the Senate, shall appoint Ambassadors, other public Ministers and Consuls, Judges of the supreme Court, and all other Officers of the United States, whose Appointments are not herein otherwise provided for, and which shall be established by Law: but the Congress may by Law vest the Appointment of such inferior Officers, as they think proper, in the President alone, in the Courts of Law, or in the Heads of Departments.

The President shall have Power to fill up all Vacancies that may happen during the Recess of the Senate, by granting Commissions which shall expire at the End of their next Session.

## Section 3

He shall from time to time give to the Congress Information of the State of the Union, and recommend to their Consideration such Measures as he shall judge necessary and expedient; he may, on extraordinary Occasions, convene both Houses, or either of them, and in Case of Disagreement between them, with Respect to the Time of Adjournment, he may adjourn them to such Time as he shall think proper; he shall receive Ambassadors and other public Ministers; he shall take Care that the Laws be faithfully executed, and shall Commission all the Officers of the United States.

## Section 4

The President, Vice President and all civil Officers of the United States, shall be removed from Office on Impeachment for, and Conviction of, Treason, Bribery, or other high Crimes and Misdemeanors.

## ARTICLE III

### Section 1

The judicial Power of the United States, shall be vested in one supreme Court, and in such inferior Courts as the Congress may from time to time ordain and establish. The Judges, both of the supreme and inferior Courts, shall hold their Offices during good Behaviour, and shall, at stated Times, receive for their Services, a Compensation, which shall not be diminished during their Continuance in Office.

### Section 2

The judicial Power shall extend to all Cases, in Law and Equity, arising under this Constitution, the Laws of the United States, and Treaties made, or which shall be made, under their Authority;—to all Cases affecting Ambassadors, other public Ministers and Consuls;—to all Cases of admiralty and maritime Jurisdiction;—to Controversies to which the United States shall be a Party;—to Controversies between two or more States;—between a State and Citizens of another State;—between Citizens of different States,—between Citizens of the same State claiming Lands under Grants of different States, and between a State, or the Citizens thereof, and foreign States, Citizens or Subjects.

In all Cases affecting Ambassadors, other public Ministers and Consuls, and those in which a State shall be Party, the supreme Court shall have original Jurisdiction. In all the other Cases before mentioned, the supreme Court shall have appellate Jurisdiction, both as to Law and Fact, with such Exceptions, and under such Regulations as the Congress shall make.

The Trial of all Crimes, except in Cases of Impeachment, shall be by Jury; and such Trial shall be held in the State where the said Crimes shall have been committed; but when not committed within any State, the Trial shall be at such Place or Places as the Congress may by Law have directed.

## Section 3

Treason against the United States, shall consist only in levying War against them, or in adhering to their Enemies, giving them Aid and Comfort. No Person shall be convicted of Treason unless on the Testimony of two Witnesses to the same overt Act, or on Confession in open Court.

The Congress shall have Power to declare the Punishment of Treason, but no Attainder of Treason shall work Corruption of Blood, or Forfeiture except during the Life of the Person attainted.

## ARTICLE IV

### Section 1

Full Faith and Credit shall be given in each State to the public Acts, Records, and judicial Proceedings of every other State. And the Congress may by general Laws prescribe the Manner in which such Acts, Records and Proceedings shall be proved, and the Effect thereof.

### Section 2

The Citizens of each State shall be entitled to all Privileges and Immunities of Citizens in the several States.

A Person charged in any State with Treason, Felony, or other Crime, who shall flee from Justice, and be found in another State, shall on Demand of the executive Authority of the State from which he fled, be delivered up, to be removed to the State having Jurisdiction of the Crime.

No Person held to Service or Labour in one State, under the Laws thereof, escaping into another, shall, in Consequence of any Law or Regulation therein, be discharged from such Service or Labour, but shall be delivered up on Claim of the Party to whom such Service or Labour may be due.

### Section 3

New States may be admitted by the Congress into this Union; but no new State shall be formed or erected within the Jurisdiction of any other State; nor any State be formed by the Junction of two or more States, or Parts of States, without the Consent of the Legislatures of the States concerned as well as of the Congress.

The Congress shall have Power to dispose of and make all needful Rules and Regulations respecting the Territory or other Property belonging to the United States; and nothing in this Constitution shall be so construed as to Prejudice any Claims of the United States, or of any particular State.

### Section 4

The United States shall guarantee to every State in this Union a Republican Form of Government, and shall protect each of them against Invasion; and on Application of the Legislature, or of the Executive (when the Legislature cannot be convened) against domestic Violence.

**ARTICLE V**

The Congress, whenever two thirds of both Houses shall deem it necessary, shall propose Amendments to this Constitution, or, on the Application of the Legislatures of two thirds of the several States, shall call a Convention for proposing Amendments, which, in either Case, shall be valid to all Intents and Purposes, as Part of this Constitution, when ratified by the Legislatures of three fourths of the several States, or by Conventions in three fourths thereof, as the one or the other Mode of Ratification may be proposed by the Congress; Provided that no Amendment which may be made prior to the Year One thousand eight hundred and eight shall in any Manner affect the first and fourth Clauses in the Ninth Section of the first Article; and that no State, without its Consent, shall be deprived of its equal Suffrage in the Senate.

**Article VI**

All Debts contracted and Engagements entered into, before the Adoption of this Constitution, shall be as valid against the United States under this Constitution, as under the Confederation.

This Constitution, and the Laws of the United States which shall be made in Pursuance thereof; and all Treaties made, or which shall be made, under the Authority of the United States, shall be the supreme Law of the Land; and the Judges in every State shall be bound thereby, any Thing in the Constitution or Laws of any State to the Contrary notwithstanding.

The Senators and Representatives before mentioned, and the Members of the several State Legislatures, and all executive and judicial Officers, both of the United States and of the several States, shall be bound by Oath or Affirmation, to support this Constitution; but no religious Test shall ever be required as a Qualification to any Office or public Trust under the United States.

**Article VII**

The Ratification of the Conventions of nine States, shall be sufficient for the Establishment of this Constitution between the States so ratifying the Same.

The Word "the," being interlined between the seventh and eight Lines of the first Page, The Word "Thirty" being partly written on an Erazure in the fifteenth Line of the first Page. The Words "is tried" being interlined between the thirty second and thirty third Lines of the first Page and the Word "the" being interlined between the forty third and forty fourth Lines of the second Page.

Attest William Jackson Secretary

done in Convention by the Unanimous Consent of the States present the Seventeenth Day of September in the Year of our Lord one thousand seven hundred and Eighty seven and of the Independence of the United States of America the Twelfth In witness whereof We have hereunto subscribed our Names,

Go Washington
*Presidt. and deputy from Virginia*

Delaware
Geo: Read
Gunning Bedford jun
John Dickinson
Richard Bassett
Jaco: Broom

Maryland
James McHenry
Dan of St Thos. Jenifer
Danl Carroll.

Virginia
John Blair
James Madison Jr.

North Carolina
Wm Blount
Richd. Dobbs Spaight.
Hu Williamson

South Carolina
J. Rutledge
Charles Cotesworth Pinckney
Charles Pinckney
Pierce Butler.

Georgia
William Few
Abr Baldwin

New Hampshire
John Langdon
Nicholas Gilman

Massachusetts
Nathaniel Gorham
Rufus King

Connecticut
Wm. Saml. Johnson
Roger Sherman

New York
Alexander Hamilton

New Jersey
Wil. Livingston
David Brearley.
Wm. Paterson.
Jona: Dayton

Pennsylvania
B Franklin
Thomas Mifflin
Robt Morris
Geo. Clymer
Thos. FitzSimons
Jared Ingersoll
James Wilson
Gouv Morris

# THE BILL OF RIGHTS

## THE PREAMBLE TO THE BILL OF RIGHTS

Congress of the United States
begun and held at the City of New-York, on
Wednesday the fourth of March, one thousand seven hundred and eighty nine.

THE Conventions of a number of the States, having at the time of their adopting the Constitution, expressed a desire, in order to prevent misconstruction or abuse of its powers, that further declaratory and restrictive clauses should be added: And as extending the ground of public confidence in the Government, will best ensure the beneficent ends of its institution.

RESOLVED by the Senate and House of Representatives of the United States of America, in Congress assembled, two thirds of both Houses concurring, that the following Articles be proposed to the Legislatures of the several States, as amendments to the Constitution of the United States, all, or any of which Articles, when ratified by three fourths of the said Legislatures, to be valid to all intents and purposes, as part of the said Constitution; viz.

ARTICLES in addition to, and Amendment of the Constitution of the United States of America, proposed by Congress, and ratified by the Legislatures of the several States, pursuant to the fifth Article of the original Constitution.

## AMENDMENT I

Congress shall make no law respecting an establishment of religion, or prohibiting the free exercise thereof; or abridging the freedom of speech, or of the press; or the right of the people peaceably to assemble, and to petition the Government for a redress of grievances.

## Amendment II

A well regulated Militia, being necessary to the security of a free State, the right of the people to keep and bear Arms, shall not be infringed.

## Amendment III

No Soldier shall, in time of peace be quartered in any house, without the consent of the Owner, nor in time of war, but in a manner to be prescribed by law.

## Amendment IV

The right of the people to be secure in their persons, houses, papers, and effects, against unreasonable searches and seizures, shall not be violated, and no Warrants shall issue, but upon probable cause, supported by Oath or affirmation, and particularly describing the place to be searched, and the persons or things to be seized.

## Amendment V

No person shall be held to answer for a capital, or otherwise infamous crime, unless on a presentment or indictment of a Grand Jury, except in cases arising in the land or naval forces, or in the Militia, when in actual service in time of War or public danger; nor shall any person be subject for the same offence to be twice put in jeopardy of life or limb; nor shall be compelled in any criminal case to be a witness against himself, nor be deprived of life, liberty, or property, without due process of law; nor shall private property be taken for public use, without just compensation.

## Amendment VI

In all criminal prosecutions, the accused shall enjoy the right to a speedy and public trial, by an impartial jury of the State and district wherein the crime shall have been committed, which district shall have been previously ascertained by law, and to be informed of the nature and cause of the accusation; to be confronted with the witnesses against him; to have compulsory process for obtaining witnesses in his favor, and to have the Assistance of Counsel for his defence.

## Amendment VII

In Suits at common law, where the value in controversy shall exceed twenty dollars, the right of trial by jury shall be preserved, and no fact tried by a jury, shall be otherwise re-examined in any Court of the United States, than according to the rules of the common law.

## Amendment VIII

Excessive bail shall not be required, nor excessive fines imposed, nor cruel and unusual punishments inflicted.

## Amendment IX

The enumeration in the Constitution, of certain rights, shall not be construed to deny or disparage others retained by the people.

## Amendment X

The powers not delegated to the United States by the Constitution, nor prohibited by it to the States, are reserved to the States respectively, or to the people.

# BIBLIOGRAPHY

Abbott, Carl, Sy Adler, and Margery P. Abbott. 1997. *Planning a New West: The Columbia River Gorge National Scenic Area.* Corvallis: Oregon State University Press.

Acton, Lord. 1887. "Letter to Bishop Mandell Creighton," April 3. Acton Institute, A. Lord Acton quote archive. www.acton.org/research/lord-acton-quote-archive (accessed January 2, 2011).

Adair, Douglas. 1974. *Fame and the Founding Fathers*, ed. Trevor Colbourn. New York: Norton.

Adams, Guy, and Balfour, Danny. 2009. *Unmasking Administrative Evil.* 3d ed. Armonk, NY: M.E. Sharpe.

Adler, Matthew D., and Eric A. Posner, eds. 2001. *Cost-Benefit Analysis: Legal, Economic, and Philosophical Perspectives.* Chicago, IL: University of Chicago Press.

Administrative Procedures Act of 1946 (APA), P.L. 79-404, codified by P.L. 89-554 (1966), 80 Stat. 378, 5 U.S.C. 551–557.

Alba, Richard, and Victor Nee. 2003. *Remaking the American Mainstream: Assimilation and Contemporary Immigration.* Cambridge, MA: Harvard University Press.

*Alden v. Maine*, 527 U.S. 706 (1999).

Alexander, Ernest R. 1992. "A Transaction Cost Theory of Planning." *Journal of the American Planning Association* 58(2), 190–200.

Alexander, Jennifer, Renee Nank, and Camilla Stivers. 2001. "Implications of Welfare Reform: Do Nonprofit Survival Strategies Threaten Civil Society?" In *Understanding Nonprofit Organizations: Governance, Leadership, and Management,* ed. J. Steven Ott, 276–282. Boulder, CO: Westview Press.

Alford, John. 2002. "Defining the Client in the Public Sector: A Social Exchange Perspective." *Public Administration Review* 62(3), 337–346.

Allison, Graham T. 1971. *The Essence of Decision: Explaining the Cuban Missile Crisis.* New York: HarperCollins.

American Recovery and Reinvestment Act (ARRA). 2009. P.L. 111–5.

*American Tradition Partnership, Inc. v. Steve Bullock,* No. 11–1179 (2012).

*American Trucking Association v. EPA,* 175 f.3d 1027 (DC cir. 1999).

Ammons, David N., and W.C. Rivenbark. 2008. "Factors Influencing the Use of Performance Data to Improve Municipal Services: Evidence from the North Carolina Benchmarking Project." *Public Administration Review* 68(2), 304–318.

Anderson, Dave, Joel Dunn, Megan Fotheringham, Eva Gao, Tim Greeff, and Sandra Johnson. 2003. "The Status of Nonprofit Property Tax Exemption in the State of North Carolina." Terry Sanford Institute of Public Policy, Duke University. Final Report, May. http://sanford.duke.edu/research/students/spring2003-01.pdf (accessed May 26, 2012).

Anderson, James E. 2003. *Public Policymaking: An Introduction.* 5th ed. New York: Houghton Mifflin.

Appleby, Paul H. 1952. *Morality and Administration in Democratic Government.* Baton Rouge: Louisiana State University Press.

———. 1949. *Policy and Administration.* Tuscaloosa: University of Alabama Press.

———. 1945. *Big Democracy*. New York: Knopf.

Arendt, Hannah. 2006. *Eichmann in Jerusalem: A Report on the Banality of Evil*. New York: Penguin.

———. 1963. *On Revolution*. New York: Viking.

———. 1958. *The Human Condition*. Chicago, IL: University of Chicago Press.

Argyris, Chris. 1964. *Integrating the Individual and the Organization*. New York: Wiley.

———. 1957. *Personality and Organization*. New York: Harper and Row.

Argyris, Chris, and Donald A. Schon. 1996. *Organization Learning II: Theory, Method, and Practice*. Reading, MA: Addison-Wesley.

———. 1974. *Theory in Practice: Increasing Professional Effectiveness*. San Francisco, CA: Jossey-Bass.

*Arizona v. United States*, No. 11–182 (2012).

Arnsberger, Paul, Melissa Ludlum, Margaret Riley, and Mark Stanton. 2008. "A History of the Tax-Exempt Sector: An SOI Perspective." *Statistics of Income Bulletin*, Internal Revenue Service (Winter), 105–135. www.irs.gov/pub/irs-soi/tehistory.pdf (accessed May 26, 2012).

Arrow, Kenneth. 1963. *Social Choice and Individual Values*. 2d ed. New York: Wiley.

ASPA National. 2011. "ASPA Code of Ethics: To Revise or Replace . . . The Debate Goes On." American Society for Public Administration National Weblog, September 15. http://aspanational.wordpress.com/2011/09/15/aspa-code-of-ethics-to-revise-or-replace%e2%80%a6the-debate-goes-on (accessed May 3, 2012).

Babbie, Earl R. 1990. *Survey Research Methods*. 2d ed. Belmont, CA: Wadsworth.

*Babbit v. Sweet Home*, 515 U.S. 687 (1995).

Bardach, Eugene and Cara Lesser. 1996. "Accountability in Human Services Collaboratives: For What? And to Whom?" *Journal of Public Administration Research and Theory* 6(2) (April), 197–224.

*Bakke v. Board of Regents of California*, 438 US 265 (1978).

Balfour, Danny. 1992. "Impact of Agency Investment in the Implementation of Performance Appraisal." *Public Personnel Management* 21 (Spring), 1–15.

Bao, Guoxian, Xuejun Wang, Gary L., Larsen, Douglas F. Morgan. 2012. "Beyond New Public Governance: A Value-Based Global Framework for Performance Management, Governance, and Leadership," *Administration & Society*. http://aas.sagepub.com/content/early/recent (accessed December 31, 2012).

Bardach, Eugene, and Cara Lesser. 1996. "Accountability in Human Services Collaboratives: For What? And to Whom?" *Journal of Public Administration Research and Theory* 6(2), 197–224.

Barden, Drew. 2000. *Analytic Methods: Some Notes on Multi-year Revenue Forecasting*. Portland, OR: City of Portland Economist.

Barnard, Chester I. 1938. *Functions of the Executive*. Cambridge, MA: Harvard University Press.

Barone, Michael. 1996. "The Road Back to Tocqueville; At Last, 19th Century Values Stage a Revival." *Washington Post*, January 15, 21–23.

Barrett, Katherine, and Richard Greene. 2008. "Grading the States: The Mandate to Measure." *Governing* (March), 24–95. www.pewstates.org/uploadedFiles/PCS_Assets/2008/Grading-the-States-2008.pdf (accessed June 19, 2012).

Bartle, John R. 2003. "Trends in Local Government Taxation in the 21st Century." *Spectrum: The Journal of State Government* 76(1), 26–29.

Barzelay, Michael, and Armajani Babak. 1992. *Breaking Through Bureaucracy: A New Vision for Managing in Government*. Berkeley: University of California Press.

Baumgartner, Frank R., and Bryan D. Jones. 1993. *Agendas and Instability in American Politics*. Chicago, IL: University of Chicago Press.

Bay, Austin. 2011. *Ataturk: Lessons in Leadership from the Greatest General of the Ottoman Empire*. New York: Palgrave Macmillan.

Bearden, David M. 2003. *The Natural Resources and Environment Function in the FY2003 Federal Budget: An Overview of Programs and Funding*. CRS Report for Congress, January 13.

Becker, Howard S., Blanche Geer, Everett Hughes, and Anselm L. Strauss. 1961. *The Boys in White: Student Culture in Medical School*. Chicago, IL: University of Chicago Press.

Beer, Samuel H. 1978. "Federalism, Nationalism, and Democracy in America." *American Political Science Review* 72 (March), 9–21.

Behn, Robert D., and J.W. Vaupel. 1982. *Quick Analysis for Busy Decision Makers*. New York: Basic Books.

Behson, Scott J., Erik R. Eddy, and Steven J. Lorenzet. 2000. "The Importance of the Critical Psychological States in the Job Characteristics Model." *Current Research in Social Psychology* 5(12), 170–189.

Bell, Daniel. 1973. *The Coming of Post-Industrial Society: A Venture in Social Forecasting.* New York: Basic Books.

Bellah, Robert N., Richard Madsen, William M. Sullivan, Ann Swindler, and Steven M. Tipton. 1985. *Habits of the Heart: Individualism and Commitment in American Life.* New York: Harper and Row.

Benjamin, Martin. 1990. *Splitting the Difference: Compromise and Integrity in Ethics and Politics.* Lawrence: University Press of Kansas.

Bentley, Arthur F. 1935. *The Process of Government: A Study of Social Pressures.* Evanston, IL: Principia.

Berger, Peter L., and Thomas Luckmann. 1967. *The Social Construction of Reality.* Garden City, NY: Doubleday Anchor.

Berlin, Isaiah. 1969. *Four Essays on Liberty.* London, UK: Oxford University Press.

Berman, Evan M., James S. Bowman, Jonathan P. West, and Montgomery R. Van Wart. 2012. *Human Resource Management in Public Service: Paradoxes, Processes, and Problems.* 4th ed. Thousand Oaks, CA: Sage.

Berry, Jeffrey M., and David F. Arons. 2003. *A Voice for Nonprofits.* Washington, DC: Brookings Institution Press.

Birkland, Thomas. 1997. *After Disaster: Agenda Setting, Public Policy, and Focusing Events.* Washington, DC: Georgetown University Press.

Blake, Robert R., and Jane S. Mouton. 1964. *The Managerial Grid.* Houston, TX: Gulf.

Blanchard, Kenneth L., Alan Randolph, and Peter Grazier. 2005. *Go Team! Taking Your Team to the Next Level.* San Francisco, CA: Berrett-Koehler.

Blau, Peter. 1956. *Bureaucracy in Modern Society.* New York: Random House.

———. 1955. *The Dynamics of Bureaucracy.* Chicago, IL: University of Chicago Press.

Blumenthal, Richard. 1969. "The Bureaucracy: Antipoverty and the Community Action Program." In *American Political Institutions and Public Policy*, ed. Allan P. Sindler, 120–179. Boston, MA: Little, Brown.

Boardman, Anthony, David Greenberg, Aidan Vining, and David Weimer. 2004. *Cost-Benefit Analysis: Concepts and Practices.* 3d ed. Upper Saddle River, NJ: Prentice Hall.

Bolman, Lee G., and Terrence E. Deal. 1997. *Reframing Organizations: Artistry, Choice, and Leadership.* 2d ed. San Francisco, CA: Jossey-Bass.

Bonnett, Thomas W., and Robert L. Olson. 1993. *Scenarios of State Government in the Year 2010: Thinking About the Future.* Washington, DC: National Council of State Policy and Planning Agencies.

Bordia, Amit, and T. Cheeseborough. 2002. *Insights on the Federal Government's Human Capital Crisis: Reflections of Generation X, Winning the War for Talent.* Cambridge, MA: Harvard University John F. Kennedy School of Government and Partnership for Public Service.

Bowman, James S., and West, Jonathon P. 2007. *American Public Service: Radical Reform and the Merit System.* Boca Raton, FL: CRC Press, Taylor & Francis Group.

Bowman, James S. 2002. "At-Will Employment in Florida Government: A Naked Formula to Corrupt Public Service." *WorkingUSA* 6(2), 90–102.

Box, Richard C. 1998. *Citizen Governance: Leading American Communities into the 21st Century.* Newbury Park, CA: Sage.

Boyatzis, Richard E. 1982. *The Competent Manager: A Model of Effective Performance.* New York: Wiley.

Boyte, Harry C. 1989. *Community Is Possible.* New York: Harper and Row.

Bozeman, Barry. 1987. *All Organizations Are Public.* San Francisco, CA: Jossey-Bass.

Braithwaite, Valerie. 1998. "Communal and Exchange Trust Norms: Their Value Base and Relevance to Institutional Trust." In *Trust and Governance*, ed. V.A. Braithwaite and M. Levi. Vol. 1. New York: Russell Sage Foundation.

*Brass v. North Dakota ex rel. Stoesser,* 153 U.S. 391 (1894).

Brewer, Gary, and Peter deLeon. 1983. *The Foundations of Policy Analysis.* Monterey, CA: Brooks/Cole.

Bright, Leonard. 2003. "An Empirical Investigation of the Intrinsic Reward Preferences of Washington County Oregon Employees." PhD diss., Portland State University.

Brinkley, Alan, Nelson Polsby, and Kathleen M. Kathleen. 1997. *New Federalist Papers: Essays in Defense of the Constitution.* New York: W.W. Norton.

Broder, David S. 2000. *Democracy Derailed: Initiative Campaigns and the Power of Money.* New York: Harcourt.

Brookes, Stephen. 2008. "Responding to the New Public Leadership Challenge." Paper presented at the Herbert Simon 2nd Annual Conference, April 2008. Manchester, England.

Brookes, Stephen, and Keith Grint, eds. 2010. *The New Public Leadership Challenge*. New York: Palgrave Macmillan.

The Brownlow Committee Report. 1937/1992. In *Classics of Public Administration*, ed. Jay A Shafritz and Albert Hyde, 90–93. 3d ed. Pacific Grove, CA: Brooks/Cole.

Bruce, Donald, and William F. Fox. 2004. *State and Local Sales Tax Revenue Losses from E-Commerce: Estimates as of July 2004*. Knoxville: Center for Business and Economic Research, University of Tennessee. www.ncsl.org/print/press/Ecommerceupdates.pdf.

Bruce, Donald, William F. Fox, William B. Stokely, and LeAnn Luna. 2009. *State and Local Government Sales Tax Revenue Losses from Electronic Commerce*. Report, April 13. Knoxville: University of Tennessee. http://cber.utk.edu/ecomm/ecom0409.pdf (accessed April 22, 2011).

Bryner, Gary. 1995. *Blue Skies, Green Politics: The Clean Air Act of 1990 and Its Implementation*. Washington, DC: Congressional Quarterly.

Bryson, John M., and Barbara C. Crosby. 1992. *Leadership for the Common Good: Tackling Public Problems in a Shared-Power World*. San Francisco, CA: Jossey-Bass.

Buber. Martin. 1958. *I and Thou*. New York: Scribner.

Buchanan, James M. 1991. *Constitutional Economics*. Cambridge, MA: Blackwell.

———. 1986. *Liberty, Market, and State: Political Economy in the 1980s*. New York: New York University Press.

Buchanan, James M., and Robert D. Tollison, eds. 1972. *Theory of Public Choice: Political Applications of Economics*. Ann Arbor: University of Michigan Press.

*Budd v. New York,* 143 U.S. 517 (1894).

Burke, John P. 1988. *Bureaucratic Responsibility*. Baltimore, MD: Johns Hopkins University Press.

Burns, James MacGregor. 1978. *Leadership*. New York: Harper and Row.

Burns, Nancy. 1994. *The Formation of American Local Government: Private Values in Public Institutions*. New York: Oxford University Press.

Burns, Tom, and G.M. Stalker. 1961. *The Management of Innovation*. Rev. ed. Oxford, UK: Oxford University Press.

Caiden, Naomi. 1981. "Public Budgeting Amidst Uncertainty and Instability." *Public Budgeting and Finance* 1(1), 6–19.

Caldwell, Lynton K. 1964. *The Administrative Theories of Hamilton and Jefferson: Their Contributions to Thought on Public Administration*. New York: Russell and Russell.

Calista, Donald J. 1987. "Employing Transaction Costs Analysis as a Theory of Public Sector Implementation." *Policy Studies Journal* 15(3), 461–480.

Campbell, Donald T., and Julian C. Stanley. 2005. *Experimental and Quasi-Experimental Designs for Research*. Boston, MA: Houghton Mifflin.

Carnegie, Andrew. 1889/1962. "Wealth." In *The Gospel of Wealth and Other Timely Essays*, ed. Edward C. Kirkland, 15–49. Cambridge, MA: Harvard University Press.

Carnevale, David G. 1995. "Human Capital and High Performance in Public Organizations." In *Public Personnel Administration: Problems and Prospects*, ed. Steven W. Hays and Richard C. Kearney. 3d ed. Englewood Cliffs, NJ: Prentice Hall.

Carter, Stephen L. 1997. *Integrity*. New York: Perennial.

Carver, John. 2001. "Setting Limits: Standards of Ethics and Prudence." In *Understanding Nonprofit Organizations: Governance, Leadership, and Management*, ed. J. Steven Ott, 25–37. Boulder, CO: Westview Press.

———. 1990. *Boards That Make a Difference: A New Design for Leadership in Nonprofit and Public Organizations*. 2d ed. San Francisco, CA: Jossey-Bass.

Chandler, Alfred D. 1993. *The Visible Hand: The Managerial Revolution in American Business*. New ed. Cambridge, MA: Belknap.

*Chisholm v. Georgia*, 2 U.S. 419 (1793).

*Citizens United v. Federal Election Commission*, 558 U.S. 50 (2010).

City of Chandler, Arizona. 2010. "2010–11 Budget Process Detail." *Adopted Budget, Budget Policies, Process and Decisions,* 48–49. www.chandleraz.gov/Content/2010_11Section3_BudgetPoliciesProcess.pdf (accessed April 3, 2012).

City of Sammamish, Washington. 2012a. "Interlocal Agreements." http://www.ci.sammamish.wa.us/about/InterLocal.aspx (accessed December 11, 2012).

Clark County, Washington. 2011a. *Executive Summary: 2011/2012 Budget Message*. www.co.clark.wa.us/budget/2011-2012/2%20-%20Exec%20Summary/11-12%20Budget%20message.pdf (accessed May 7, 2012).

———. 2011b. "2011–2012 Biennum Financial Plan." In *2011/2012 Biennal Budget.* www.clark.wa.gov/
budget/2011-2012/5%20-%20Financial/11-12%20Financial.pdf#page=1 (accessed May 7, 2012).

*Cleveland Board of Education v. Loudermill,* 470 U.S. 532 (1985).

Clinton, William J. 1993. "Remarks Announcing the National Performance Review," March 3, 1993. Online
by Gerhard Peters and John T. Woolley, *The American Presidency Project.* http://www.presidency.ucsb.
edu/ws/?pid=46291 (accessed December 31, 2012).

Clotfelter, Charles T., and Philip J. Cook. 1990. "Redefining 'Success' in the State Lottery Business." *Journal
of Policy Analysis and Management* 9(1), 99–104.

Clotfelter, Charles T., Philip J. Cook, Julie A. Edell, and Marian Moore. 1999. *State Lotteries at the Turn of
the Century.* Report to the National Gambling Impact Study Commission, April 23. http://govinfo.library.
unt.edu/ngisc/reports/lotfinal.pdf (accessed December 1, 2007).

Cochran, Clark. 1982. *Character, Community, and Politics.* Tuscaloosa: University of Alabama Press.

Cohen, Fay. 1986. *Treaties on Trial.* Seattle: University of Washington Press.

Cohen, Jean L., and Andrew Arato. 1992. *Civil Society and Political Theory.* Cambridge: MIT Press.

Cohen, M.D., James G. March, and Johan P. Olsen. 1972. "A Garbage Can Model of Organizational Choice."
*Administrative Science Quarterly* 17, 1–25.

Cohen, Richard E. 1994. *Washington at Work: Back Rooms and Clean Air.* 2d ed. New York: Longman.

Coleman, James S. 1990. *Foundations of Social Theory.* Cambridge, MA: Belknap.

Collins, Courtney and Rettenmaier, Andrew J. 2010. "Unfunded Liabilities of State and Local Government
Employee Retirement Benefit Plans." National Center for Policy Analysis, Study No. 329, July 29,
2010. http://www.ncpa.org/pub/st329 (accessed December 31, 2012)

Commission on Economy and Efficiency, U.S. House of Representatives. 1912. *Report of the Taft Commission
on Economy and Efficiency: The Need for a National Budget.* 62nd Cong., 2nd sess., H.R. 854.

Committee for Economic Development. 2005. *The Emerging Budget Crisis: Urgent Fiscal Choices.* Wash-
ington, DC: Committee for Economic Development.

Condrey, Stephen E. 2002. "Reinventing State Civil Service Systems: The Georgia Experience." *Review of
Public Personnel Administration* 22(2), 114–124.

Condrey, Stephen E., and Robert Maranto, eds. 2001. *Radical Reform of the Civil Service.* New York: Lex-
ington Books.

Cook, Brian J. 1996. *Bureaucracy and Self-Government: Reconsidering the Role of Public Administration
in American Politics.* Baltimore, MD: Johns Hopkins University Press.

Cook, Thomas D., and Donald T. Campbell. 1979. *Quasi-Experimentation: Design and Analysis Issues for
Field Settings.* Boston, MA: Houghton Mifflin.

Cooper, Phillip J. 2009. *The War Against Regulation.* Lawrence: University Press of Kansas.

———. 2007. *Public Law and Public Administration.* 4th ed. Belmont, CA: Thomson Wadsworth.

———. 2005a. *Cases on Public Law and Public Administration.* Belmont, CA: Thomson/Wadsworth.

———. 2005b. "George Bush, Edgar Allan Poe, and the Use and Abuse of Presidential Signing Statements."
*Presidential Studies Quarterly* 35(3), 515–532.

———. 2003. *Governing by Contract: Challenges and Opportunities for Public Managers.* Washington,
DC: Congressional Quarterly.

———. 2002. *By Order of the President: The Use and Abuse of Executive Direct Action.* Lawrence: Uni-
versity Press of Kansas.

———. 2000. *Public Law and Public Administration.* 3d ed. Palo Alto, CA: Mayfield.

———. 1988. *Hard Judicial Choices: Federal District Court Judges and State and Local Officials.* New
York: Oxford University Press.

Cooper, Phillip J., and Claudia María Vargas. 2008. *Sustainable Development in Crisis Conditions: Chal-
lenges of War, Terrorism, and Civil Disorder.* Lanham, MD: Rowman & Littlefield.

———. 2004. *Implementing Sustainable Development: From Global Policy to Local Action.* Lanham, MD:
Rowman & Littlefield.

Cooper, Terry L. 2004. "Big Questions in Administrative Ethics: A Need for Focused, Collaborative Effort."
*Public Administration Review* 64(4), 395–407.

———. 1991. *An Ethic of Citizenship for Public Administration.* Englewood Cliffs, NJ: Prentice Hall.

———. 1987. "Hierarchy, Virtue, and the Practice of Public Administration: A Perspective for Normative
Ethics." *Public Administration Review* 47(4), 320–328.

———. 1982. *The Responsible Administrator: An Approach to Ethics for the Administrative Role.* Port
Washington, NY: Kennikat.

Cozzetto, Don A., Mary G. Kweit, and Robert W. Kweit. 1995. *Public Budgeting: Politics, Institutions, and Processes.* White Plains, NY: Longman.

Crenson, Matthew A. 1975. *The Federal Machine: Beginnings of Bureaucracy in Jacksonian America.* Baltimore, MD: Johns Hopkins University Press.

Crenson, Matthew A., and Benjamin Ginsberg. 2002. *Downsizing Democracy: How America Sidelined Its Citizens and Privatized Its Public.* Baltimore, MD: Johns Hopkins University Press.

Crewson, Phillip E. 1997. "Public-Service Motivation: Building Empirical Evidence of Incidence and Effect." *Journal of Public Administration Theory and Research* 7(4), 499–518.

Croley, Steven P. 2008. *Regulation and Public Interests: The Possibility of GOOD Regulatory Government.* Princeton, NJ: Princeton University Press.

Croly, Herbert. 1964. *The Promise of American Life.* New York: Capricorn.

Crosby, Barbara C., and John M. Bryson. 2005. *Leadership for the Common Good: Tackling Public Problems in a Shared-Power World.* San Francisco, CA: Jossey-Bass.

Crumpton, Charles David. 2008. "Organizational Complexity in American Local Governance: Deploying an Organizational Perspective in Concept and Analytic Framework Development." DPhil diss., Portland State University, Portland, Oregon.

Crusto, Mitchell. 2000. "The Supreme Court's 'New' Federalism: An Anti-Rights Agenda?" *Georgia State University Law Review* 16(3), 517–532.

Cummings, Thomas G., and Christopher G. Worley. 2005. *Organization Development and Change.* 8th ed. Mason, OH: Thomson/South-Western.

Cyert, Richard M., and James G. March. 1963. *A Behavioral Theory of the Firm.* Englewood Cliffs, NJ: Prentice Hall.

———. 1959. "A Behavioral Theory of Organization." In *Modern Organization Theory*, ed. Mason Haire, 76–90. New York: Wiley.

Daft, Richard. 1992. *Organization Theory and Design.* 4th ed. New York: West.

———. 1984. "Toward a Model of Organizations as Interpretation Systems." *Academy of Management Review* 9(2), 284–295.

Dahl, Robert. A. 1989. *Democracy and Its Critics.* New Haven, CT: Yale University Press.

———. 1964. *Who Governs? Democracy and Power in an American City.* New Haven, CT: Yale University Press.

Dahl, Robert A., and Charles E. Lindblom. 1953. *Politics, Economics, and Welfare: Planning and Political-Economic Systems Resolved into Basic Social Processes.* New York: Harper.

Daley, Dennis. 1988. "Performance Appraisal and Organizational Success: Public Employee Perceptions in an MBO-Based Appraisal System." *Review of Public Personnel Administration* 9(1), 17–21.

*Dartmouth College v. Woodward,* 17 U.S. (4 Wheat.) 518 (1819).

Darwin, Charles. 1859. *On the Origin of Species by Means of Natural Selection, or the Preservation of Favoured Races in the Struggle for Life.* London, UK: John Murray.

Daschle, Tom, and Michael D'Orso. 2003. *Like No Other Time: The 107th Congress and the Two Years That Changed America Forever.* New York: Crown Publishers.

Davis, Kenneth Culp. 1971. *Discretionary Justice: A Preliminary Inquiry.* Urbana: University of Illinois Press, 1971.

Deal, Terrence E., and Allan A. Kennedy. 1982. *Corporate Cultures: The Rites and Rituals of Corporate Life.* Reading, MA: Addison-Wesley.

Dearing, James W., and Everett M. Rodgers. 1996. *Agenda Setting.* Thousand Oaks, CA: Sage.

*Delaware v. Prouse,* 440 US 648 (1979).

deLeon, Peter. 1999. "The Stages Approach to the Policy Process." In *Theories of the Policy Process,* ed. P.A. Sabatier, 19–34. Boulder, CO: Westview Press.

Deming, W. Edwards. 1982. *Out of the Crisis.* Cambridge: MIT Press.

de Tocqueville, Alexis. 1935. *Democracy in America,* trans. and ed. Harvey Mansfield and Della Winthrop. Chicago, IL: University of Chicago Press, 2000.

Dewey, John. 1927. *The Public and Its Problems.* Denver, CO: Swallow.

Diamond, Martin. 1979. "Ethics and Politics: The American Way." In *The Moral Foundations of the American Republic*, ed. Robert Goldwin. 2d ed. Charlottesville: University of Virginia Press.

Diamond, Martin, Winston Mills Fisk, and Herbert Garfinkel. 1966. *The Democratic Republic: An Introduction to American National Government.* Chicago, IL: Rand McNally.

Diesing, Paul. 1982. *Reason in Society.* Urbana: University of Illinois Press.

Dobel, J. Patrick. 1999. *Public Integrity*. Baltimore, MD: Johns Hopkins University Press.

———. 1990. *Compromise and Political Action: Political Morality in Liberal and Democratic Life*. Totowa, NJ: Rowman & Littlefield.

*Dolan v. Tigard*, 512 U.S. 687 (1994).

Dolan, Julia, and David H. Rosenbloom, eds. 2003. *Representative Bureaucracy: Classic Readings and Continuing Controversies*. Armonk, NY: M.E. Sharpe.

Douglas, Mary. 1986. *How Institutions Think*. Syracuse, NY: Syracuse University Press.

Downs, Anthony. 1967. *Inside Bureaucracy*. Boston, MA: Little, Brown.

———. 1960. "Why the Government Budget Is Too Small in a Democracy." *World Politics* July, 76–95.

Dreier, Alexander E. 2005. "Sarbanes-Oxley and College Accountability." *Chronicle of Higher Education* 51(44) (July), B10 . http://chronicle.com (accessed July 5, 2007).

Dresang, Dennis L. 2002. *Public Personnel Management and Public Policy*. 4th ed. New York: Longman.

Drew, Elizabeth. 1979. *The Senator*. New York: Simon and Schuster.

Dropkin, Murray, Jim Halpin, and Bill La Touche. 2007. *The Budget-Building Book for Nonprofits*. 2d ed. San Francisco, CA: Jossey-Bass.

Dunn, William N. 2004. *Public Policy Analysis*. 3d ed. Upper Saddle River, NJ: Prentice Hall.

Dunsire, Andrew. 1979. *Control in a Bureaucracy*. New York: St. Martin's Press.

Dye, Thomas R. 2000. *Politics in States and Communities*. 10th ed. Englewood Cliffs, NJ: Prentice Hall.

Easton, David J. 1965. *A Framework for Political Analysis*. Englewood Cliffs, NJ: Prentice Hall.

Eberg, Jan. 1997. *Waste Policy and Learning: Policy Dynamics of Waste Management and Waste Incineration in the Netherlands and Bavaria*. Delft, Netherlands: Uitgeverij Eburon.

Edelman, Murray. 1964. *The Symbolic Uses of Politics*. Urbana: University of Illinois Press.

Eden, Robert. 1963. *Political Leadership and Nihilism: A Study of Weber and Nietzsche*. Tampa: University Press of Florida.

Edwards, Mary. 2006. *State and Local Revenues Beyond the Property Tax*. Lincoln Institute of Land Policy Working Paper WP06ME1. Cambridge, MA: Lincoln Institute of Land Policy. www.lincolninst.edu/subcenters/teaching-fiscal-dimensions-of-planning/materials/edwards-revenue.pdf (accessed April 11, 2011).

Edwards, Michael. 2009. *Civil Society*. Cambridge, UK: Polity Press.

Ehrenhalt, Samuel M. 1999. *Government Employment Report 6*. Washington, DC: U.S. Government Printing Office.

Elazar, Daniel J. 1987. *Exploring Federalism*. Tuscaloosa: University of Alabama Press.

Elkin, Stephen. 2006. *Reconstructing the Commercial Republic: Constitutional Design After Madison*. Chicago, IL: University of Chicago Press.

———. 2004. "Thinking Constitutionally: The Problem of Deliberative Democracy." *Social Philosophy and Policy* 21(1), 39–75.

Elkin, Stephen, and Karol E. Soltan. 1999. *Citizen Competence and Democratic Institutions*. University Park: Pennsylvania State University Press.

———. 1993. *A New Constitutionalism: Designing Political Institutions for a Good Society*. Chicago, IL: University of Chicago.

Emery, Fred. 1959. *Characteristics of Socio-Technical Systems*. Travistock Document 527. London, UK: Travistock.

Emery, Fred, and Eric Trist. 1965. "The Causal Texture of Organizational Environments." *Human Relations* 18, 21–32.

Ennis, Sharon R., Merarys Ríos-Vargas, and Nora G. Albert. 2011. "The Hispanic Population: 2010." 2010 Census Briefs, May. www.census.gov/prod/cen2010/briefs/c2010br-04.pdf.

Epstein, David. 1984. *The Political Theory of the Federalist*. Chicago, IL: University of Chicago Press.

Ervin, David, Gary Larsen, and Craig Shinn. 2012. "Simple Ecosystem Valuation Can Impact National Forest Management." *Association of Environmental and Resource Economics* 23(1), 17–22.

Etzioni, Amitai. 1983. *An Immodest Agenda: Rebuilding America Before the Twenty-First Century*. New York: New Press.

———. 1961. *A Comparative Analysis of Complex Organizations*. New York: Free Press. Rev. and enl. ed. published as *A Comparative Analysis of Complex Organizations: On Power, Involvement, and Their Correlates*. New York: Free Press, 1975.

Etzioni-Halevy, Eva. 1983. *Bureaucracy and Democracy: A Political Dilemma*. Boston, MA: Routledge and Kegan Paul.

Executive Order 8587. "Amending Certain Provisions of the Civil Service Rules." 5 *Federal Register* (November 7, 1940), 4445.

Executive Order 8802. "Reaffirming Policy of Full Participation in the Defense Program by All Persons, Regardless of Race, Creed, Color, or National Origin, and Directing Certain Action in Furtherance of Said Policy." 6 *Federal Register* (June 25, 1941), 3109.

Executive Order 9980. "Regulations Governing Fair Employment Practices Within the Federal Establishment." 13 *Federal Register* (July 26, 1941), 4311.Executive Order 10987. "Agency Systems for Appeals from Adverse Actions." 27 *Federal Register* (January 17, 1962), 550.

Executive Order 10988. "Employee-Management Cooperation in the Federal Service." 27 *Federal Register* (January 17, 1962), 551.

Executive Order 11246. "Equal Employment Opportunity." 30 *Federal Register* (September 24, 1965), 12319.

Executive Order 11478. "Equal Employment Opportunity in the Federal Government." 34 *Federal Register* (August 8, 1969), 12985.

Executive Order 12866. "Regulatory Planning and Review." 58 *Federal Register* (September 30, 1993), 51735.

Executive Order 13199. "Establishment of White House Office of Faith-Based and Community Initiatives." 66 *Federal Register* (January 29, 2001), 8499.

Farrel, Pam. 1996. *Woman of Influence: Ten Traits of Those Who Want to Make a Difference.* Downers Grove, IL: Intervarsity.

Fayol, Henri. 1949. *General and Industrial Management.* London, UK: Pitman.

*FDA v. Brown and Williamson Tobacco Corp.,* 529 U.S. 120 (2000).

*Field v. Clark,* 143 U.S. 649, 692 (1892).

Fiedler, Fred E. 1967. *A Theory of Leadership Effectiveness.* New York: McGraw-Hill.

Fiedler, Fred E., and Joseph E. Garcia. 1987. *New Approaches to Effective Leadership: Cognitive Resources and Organizational Performance.* New York: Wiley.

Financial Crisis Inquiry Commission (FCIC). 2011. *The Financial Crisis Inquiry Report: Final Report of the National Commission on the Causes of the Financial and Economic Crisis in the United States.* (January). http://www.gpo.gov/fdsys/pkg/GPO-FCIC/pdf/GPO-FCIC.pdf.

Finer, Herman. 1941. "Administrative Responsibility in Democratic Government." *Public Administration Review* 1 (Summer), 340–350.

Fink, Stephen C., Alan C. Marco, and Jonathan C. Rork. 2004. "Lotto Nothing? The Budgetary Impact of State Lotteries." *Applied Economics* 36(21), 2357–2367.

Finkler, Steven A. 2010. *Financial Management for Public Health, and Not-for-Profit Organizations.* 3d ed. Upper Saddle River, NJ: Prentice-Hall.

Fisher, Helen E. 1999. *The First Sex: The Natural Talents of Women and How They Are Changing the World.* New York: Random House.

Fisher, Louis. 1975. *Presidential Spending Power.* Princeton, NJ: Princeton University Press.

Fisher, Roger, Bruce M. Patton, and William L. Ury. 2011. *Getting to Yes: Negotiating Agreement Without Giving In.* 2d ed. Boston, MA: Houghton Mifflin.

Flexner, James T., ed. 1969. *George Washington: Anguish and Farewell, 1793–1799.* Boston, MA: Little, Brown.

*Florida Prepaid Post-Secondary Education Expense Board et al. v. College Savings Bank,* 527 U.S. 666 (1999).

Follett, Mary Parker. 1949. "The Basis of Authority." In Mary Parker Follett, *Freedom and Co-ordination: Lectures in Business Organisation,* ed. L. Urwick. London, UK: Management Publications Trust.

———. 1926. "The Giving of Orders." In *Scientific Foundations of Business Administration,* ed. Henry C. Metcalf. Baltimore, MD: Williams and Wilkins.

Ford, Andra. 2012. "The State of State Taxes." *Time,* April 16, 21.

Forester, John. 1999. *The Deliberative Practitioner.* Cambridge: MIT Press.

Forrer, John, James Edwin Kee, Kathryn E. Newcomer, and Eric Boyer. 2010. "Public-Private Partnerships and the Public Accountability Question." *Public Administration Review* 70(3), 475–484.

Forster, Michael, and Mark Osborne. 2002. *Income Distribution and Poverty in the OECD Area: Trends and Driving Forces.* Economic Studies Report No. 34, 2002/I. Paris, France: Organisation for Economic Co-operation and Development.

Fowler, F. 2001. *Survey Research Methods.* 3d ed. Thousand Oaks, CA: Sage.

Fox, Charles J., and Hugh T. Miller. 1996. *Postmodern Public Administration: Toward Discourse*. Newbury Park, CA: Sage.

Fox, Charles J., and Kurt A. Shirkey. 1997. "Employee Performance Appraisal: The Keystone Made of Clay." In *Public Personnel Management: Current Concerns, Future Challenges*, ed. Carolyn Ban and Norma M. Riccucci. 2d ed. New York: Longman.

Franzen, Robin, and James Mayer. 2008. "Fees Soar Under Property Tax Cap." *Oregonian*, February 3, Sec. F Metro NW, B1, B4.

Frederickson, H. George. 1996. *The Spirit of Public Administration*. San Francisco, CA: Jossey-Bass.

———. 1982. "The Recovery of Civism in Public Administration." *Public Administration Review* 42(6), 501–508.

Frederickson, H. George, and David K. Hart. 1985. "The Public Service and the Patriotism of Benevolence." *Public Administration Review* 45(5), 547–553.

*Fremont Lumber Co. v. Energy Facility Siting Council*, 325 OR 256 (1997).

Friedman, Milton A. 1962. *Capitalism and Freedom*. Chicago, IL: University of Chicago Press.

Friedman, Thomas L. 2005. *The World Is Flat: A Brief History of the Twenty-first Century*. New York: Farrar, Straus and Giroux.

Friedrich, Carl J. 1940. "Public Policy and the Nature of Administrative Responsibility." *Public Policy*, 3–24. Cambridge, MA: Harvard University Press.

Fritschler, A. Lee, and James M. Hoefler. 1996. *Smoking and Politics: Policymaking and the Federal Bureaucracy*. 5th ed. Upper Saddle River, NJ: Prentice Hall.

Frumkin, Peter. 2010. *The Essence of Strategic Giving: A Practical Guide for Donors and Fundraisers*. Chicago, IL: University of Chicago Press.

Fukuyama, Francis. 1992. *The End of History and the Last Man*. New York: Avon.

Full Employment Act. 1946. 15 U.S.C. 1021.

Full Employment and Balanced Growth Act. 1978. 15 U.S.C. 3101–3152.

Furse, Elizabeth. 2000. *Indian Tribes, Their Rights and Responsibilities*. Institute for Tribal Government, Mark O. Hatfield School of Government, Portland State University: Portland, Oregon.

Gabris, Gerald T., and Kenneth Mitchell. 1988. "The Impact of Merit Raise Scores on Employee Attitudes: The Matthew Effect of Performance Appraisals." *Public Personnel Management* 17(4), 369–386.

Gaebler, Ted, John Blackman, Linda Blessing, Raymon Bruce, Wallace Keene, and Paul Smith. 1999. *Positive Outcomes: Raising the Bar on Government Reinvention*. Burke, VA: Chatelaine.

Gaines, Brian J. 2002. "Where's the Rally? Approval and Trust of the President, Congress, and Government Since September 11th." *PS: Political Science and Politics* 35(3), 531–536.

Gaustad, Edwin, and Leigh Schmidt. 2002. *The Religious History of America*. Rev ed. New York: Harper-SanFrancisco.

Gawthrop, Louis C. 1969. *Bureaucratic Behavior in the Executive Branch*. New York: Free Press.

Gelles, Erna. 2001. "Fund-Raising." In *Understanding Nonprofit Organizations: Governance, Leadership, and Management*, ed. J. Steven Ott, 175–181. Boulder, CO: Westview Press.

General Accounting Office (GAO). 2012. *Summary of GAO's Performance and Accountability Report Fiscal Year 2011*. Report GAO-12-5SP, January 26. www.gao.gov/products/GAO-12-5SP (accessed December 31, 2102).

———. 2001. *Federal Employee Retirements: Expected Increase over the Next 5 Years Illustrates Need for Workforce Planning*. Report No. GAO-01-509, April. Washington, DC: U.S. Government Printing Office.

Ghere, Richard K. 2001. "Probing the Strategic Intricacies of Public-Private Partnership: The Patent as a Comparative Reference." *Public Administration Review* 61(4), 441–451.

———. 1996. "Aligning the Ethics of Public-Private Partnership: The Issue of Local Economic Development." *Journal of Public Administration Research and Theory* 6(4), 599–621.

*Gibbons v. Ogden*, 22 U.S. 1 (1824).

Gibson, F., C. Shinn, and J. Locklear. 1990. *The Influence of Social Information: The Case of the Job Characteristics Model*. Salt Lake City, UT: Western Academy of Management.

Gilder, George. 1981. *Wealth and Poverty*. New York: Basic Books.

Gilligan, Carol. 1993. *In a Different Voice: Psychological Theory and Women's Development*. Cambridge, MA: Harvard University Press.

Goggin, M., A. Bowman, J. Lester, and L. O'Toole. 1990. *Implementation Theory and Practice: Toward a Third Generation*. Glenville, IL: Scott Foresman.

Goldwin, Robert, and William A. Schambra, eds. 1980. *How Democratic Is the Constitution?* Washington, DC: American Enterprise Institute.

Goodnow, Frank J. 1900. *Politics and Administration: A Study in Government.* New York: Russell and Russell.

Goodsell, Charles T. 2004. *The Case for Bureaucracy: A Public Administration Polemic.* 4th ed. Washington, DC: CQ Press.

———. 1983. *The Case for Bureaucracy: A Public Administration Polemic.* Chatham, NJ: Chatham House.

Gore, Al. 1995. *Common Sense Government: Works Better and Costs Less.* New York: Random House.

———. 1993. *Creating a Government That Works Better and Costs Less: The Report of the National Performance Review.* East Rutherford, NJ: Plume.

Gouldner, Alvin. 1954. *Patterns of Industrial Bureaucracy.* Glencoe, IL: Free Press.

Government Performance and Results Modernization Act (GPRA). 2010. U.S. Public Law 111–352.

Gramlich, Edward M. 1997. *A Guide to Benefit-Cost Analysis.* 2d ed. Long Grove, IL: Waveland.

Green, Richard. 2012. "The Centrality of Public Morality in John Rohr's Work," *Administrative Theory & Praxis.* December 2008, 34(4), 631–636.

———. "Plutocracy, Bureaucracy, and the End of Public Trust." *Administration & Society* 44(1), 109–143.

———. 2002a. "Alexander Hamilton: Founder of the American Public Administration." *Administration & Society* 34(5), 541–562.

———. 2002b. "Common Law, Equity, and American Public Administration." *American Review of Public Administration* 32(3), 263–294.

———. 1998. "Impartiality and Administrative Statesmanship." In *Active Duty: Public Administration as Democratic Statesmanship,* ed. Peter Lawler, Robert Schaefer, and David Schaefer, 547–553. Lanham, MD: Rowman & Littlefield.

———. 1996. "Statecraft and Institutions in the Age of Iconoclasm." *Administrative Theory & Praxis* 18(2), 74–83.

———. 1993. "Prudent Constitutionalism: Hamiltonian Lessons for a Responsible Public Administration." *International Journal of Public Administration* 16(2), 165–186.

———. 1992. "Constitutional Jurisprudence: Reviving Praxis in Public Administration." *Administration & Society* 24(1), 3–21.

———. 1987. "Oracle at Weehawken: Alexander Hamilton and Development of the Administrative State." PhD diss., Virginia Polytechnic Institute and State University.

Green, Richard T., Robert Forbis, Anne Golden, Jennifer Robinson, and Stephen Nelson. 2006. "On the Ethics of At-Will Employment in the Public Sector." *Public Integrity* 8(4), 305–327.

Green, Richard T., L.F. Keller, and G.L. Wamsley. 1993. "Reconstituting a Profession for American Public Administration." *Public Administration Review* 53(6), 516–524.

Green, Richard T., and Robert Zinke. 1993. "The Rhetorical Way of Knowing and Public Administration." *Administration & Society* 25(3), 317–334.

Greenberg, Gary. 1984. "Revolt at Justice." In *Ethics and Politics: Cases and Commentary,* ed. Amy Gutman and Dennis Thompson. Chicago, IL: Nelson.

Greenstone, Michael, and Adam Looney. 2012. "A Record Decline in Government Jobs: Implications for the Economy and America's Workforce." The Hamilton Project, Brookings Institution (August). http://www.brookings.edu/blogs/jobs/posts/2012/08/03-jobs-greenstone-looney (accessed December 11, 2012).

Greider, William. 1981. "The Education of David Stockman." Atlantic Monthly 247 (December), 27.

Grodzins, Morton. 1960. "The Federal System." In *Goals for Americans: Programs for Action in the Sixties.* Report for the U.S. President's Commission on National Goals. Englewood Cliffs, NJ: Prentice Hall.

Gross, Edward, and Amitai Etzioni. 1985. *Organizations in Society.* Upper Saddle River, NJ: Prentice Hall.

Gulick, Luther. 1946. "Assaying the Record." *The United States at War: Development and Administration of the War Program by the Federal Government.* Historical Reports on War Administration, No. 1. Prepared under the Auspices of the Committee of Records of War Administration by the War Records Section, Bureau of the Budget, U.S. Government Printing Office. Also reprinted with introduction by Paul Van Riper in *Administrative Theory & Praxis* 20(1) (1998), 78–90.

Gulick, Luther, and Lyndall Urwick, eds. 1937. *Papers on the Science of Administration.* New York: Institute of Public Administration.

Gunn, John A.W. 1969. *Politics and the Public Interest in the Seventeenth Century.* Toronto, Ontario, Canada: University of Toronto Press.

Haas, Glenn. 2003. "Restoring Dignity to Sound Professional Judgment." *Journal of Forestry* 101 (September), 38–43.

Habermas, Jürgen. 1985. *The Theory of Communicative Action.* Boston, MA: Beacon.

Hackman, J. Richard, and G.R. Oldham. 1980. *Work Redesign.* Reading, MA: Addison-Wesley.

Halachmi, Arie. 2011. "Imagined Promises versus Real Challenges to Public Performance Management." *International Journal of Productivity and Performance Management* 60(1), 24–40.

———. 1995. "The Practice of Performance Appraisal." In *Handbook of Public Personnel Administration,* ed. J. Rabin, T. Vocino, W. Hildreth, and G. Miller, 321–355. New York: Marcel Dekker.

———. 1993. "From Performance Appraisal to Performance Targeting." *Public Personnel Management* 22(2), 323–344.

Hall, Peter Dobkin. 1992. *Inventing the Nonprofit Sector.* Baltimore, MD: Johns Hopkins University Press.

Hall, Thad E., and Laurence J. O'Toole Jr. 2004. "Structures for Policy Implementation: An Analysis of National Legislation, 1965–1966 and 1993–1994." *Administration & Society* 31(6), 667–686.

Hamel, J., with S. Dufour and D. Fortin. 1993. *Case Study Methods.* Thousand Oaks, CA: Sage.

Hamilton, Alexander, under pseudonym Lucius Crassus. 1802/1977. "The Examination of the President's Message, at the Opening of Congress, December 7, 1802." *New York Evening Post.* Quoted in *The Papers of Alexander Hamilton,* ed. Harold C. Syrett and Jacob E. Cooke, 570–571. Vol. 25. *July 1800–April 1802.* New York: Columbia University Press, 1961–1987.

Hamilton, Alexander. 1799/1975. "To Marquis de Lafayette." In *The Papers of Alexander Hamilton,* ed. Harold C. Syrett and Jacob E. Cooke. Vol. 22, *July 1798–March 1799.* New York: Columbia University Press.

———. 1795/1973. "The Defence of the Funding System." In *The Papers of Alexander Hamilton,* ed. Harold C. Syrett and Jacob E. Cooke. Vol. 19. *July–December 1795.* New York: Columbia University Press.

———. 1791/1966. "Report on Manufactures." In *The Papers of Alexander Hamilton,* ed. Harold C. Syrett and Jacob E. Cooke, Vol. 10. *December 1791–January 1792.* New York: Columbia University Press.

———. 1790/1963. "Report on a National Bank." In *The Papers of Alexander Hamilton,* ed. Harold C. Syrett and Jacob E. Cooke, Vol. 7. *September 1790–January 1791.* New York: Columbia University Press.

Hamilton, Alexander, James Madison, and John Jay, under pseudonym Publius. 1787–1789/1961. *The Federalist Papers,* ed. Clinton Rossiter. New York: New American Library.

Hammack, David C., ed. 1998. *Making the Nonprofit Sector in the United States: A Reader.* Bloomington: Indiana University Press.

Hammill, G. 2005. "Mixing and Managing Four Generations of Employees." *FDU Magazine Online* (Winter/Spring). www.fdu.edu/newspubs/magazine/05ws/generations.htm.

Hardin, Garrett. 1968. "Tragedy of the Commons." *Science* 62, 1243–1248.

Hargrove, Erwin C., and John C. Glidewell, eds. 1990. *Impossible Jobs in Public Management.* Lawrence: University Press of Kansas.

Harrison, Michael I. 1994. *Diagnosing Organizations.* 2d ed. Thousand Oaks, CA: Sage.

Hasenfeld, Yaheskel, Jane A. Rafferty, and Mayer N. Zald. 1987. "The Welfare State, Citizenship, and Bureaucratic Encounters." *Annual Review of Sociology* 13(1), 387–415.

Haskell, Thomas L. 1977. *The Emergence of Professional Social Science: The American Social Science Association and the Nineteenth-Century Crisis of Authority.* Urbana: University of Illinois Press.

Hatry, Harry. P. 2010. "Looking into the Crystal Ball: Performance Management over the Next Decade." *Public Administration Review* 70 (Issue Supplement 1), s208–s211.

———. 2002. "Performance Measurement: Fashions and Fallacies." *Public Performance and Management Review* 25(4), 352–358.

Hayek, Friedrich A. 1948. *Individualism and the Economic Order.* Chicago, IL: University of Chicago Press.

———. 1944. *The Road to Serfdom.* Chicago, IL: University of Chicago Press.

Heclo, Hugh. 2000. "The Future of Merit." In *The Future of Merit: Twenty Years After the Civil Service Reform Act,* ed. James P. Pfiffner and Douglas A. Brook. Baltimore, MD: Johns Hopkins University Press.

———. 1978. "Issue Networks and the Executive Establishment." In *The New American Political System,* ed. Anthony King. Washington, DC: American Enterprise Institute.

Hefetz, Amir, and M. Warner. 2004. "Privatization and Its Reverse: Explaining the Dynamics of the Government Contracting Process." *Journal of Public Administration Research and Theory* 14(2), 171–190.

Held, Virginia. 1984. *Rights and Goods.* New York: Free Press.

Helgesen, Sally. 1990. *The Female Advantage: Women's Ways of Leadership.* New York and Toronto: Doubleday Currency.

Herman, Robert, and Associates. 2005. *The Jossey-Bass Handbook of Nonprofit Leadership and Management.* 2d ed. San Francisco, CA: Jossey-Bass.

Herranz, Joaquin, Jr. 2007. "The Multisectoral Trilemma of Network Management." *Journal of Public Administration Research and Theory* 18(1), 1–31.

Herring, E. Pendleton. 1936. *Public Administration and the Public Interest.* New York: McGraw-Hill.

Hersey, Paul, and Kenneth H. Blanchard. 1981. "So You Want to Know Your Leadership Style?" *Training and Development Journal* 35(6), 34–54.

———. 1977a. *Organizational Change Through Effective Leadership.* Englewood Cliffs, NJ: Prentice Hall.

———. 1977b. *The Management of Organizational Behavior.* 3d ed. Upper Saddle River, NJ: Prentice Hall.

Hersey, Paul, Kenneth H. Blanchard, and Dewey E. Johnson. 2001. *Management of Organizational Behavior.* 8th ed. Englewood Cliffs, NJ: Prentice Hall.

Herzberg, Frederick, Bernard Mausner, and Barbara B. Snyderman. 1959. *The Motivation to Work.* New York: Wiley.

Hirschman, A.O. 1981. *Essays in Trespassing: Economics to Politics and Beyond.* Cambridge, UK: Cambridge University Press.

———. 1977. *The Passions and the Interests: Political Arguments for Capitalism Before Its Triumph.* Princeton, NJ: Princeton University Press.

———. 1970. *Exit Voice and Loyalty: Responses to Decline in Firms, Organizations, and States.* Cambridge, MA: Harvard University Press.

Hooper, David. 2005. *The Oregon State Lottery: Its Background and Approach to Responsible Gambling.* Salem: Oregon State Lottery. http://www.problemgambling.com/oregon.html.

Horowitz, Donald. 1977. *The Courts and Social Policy.* Washington, DC: Brookings Institution Press.

Horrigan, John B. 2004. "How Americans Get in Touch with Government." Washington, DC: Pew Internet and American Life Project. May 24.

House, Robert J. 1996. "Path-Goal Theory of Leadership: Lessons, Legacy, and a Reformulated Theory." *Leadership Quarterly* 7(3), 323–352.

———. 1971. "A Path-Goal Theory of Leader Effectiveness." *Administrative Science Quarterly* 16(3), 321–328.

House, Robert J., and R.N. Aditya. 1997. "The Social Scientific Study of Leadership: Quo Vadis?" *Journal of Management* 23(3), 409–465.

House, Robert J., and T.R. Mitchell. 1974. "Path-Goal Theory of Leadership." *Journal of Contemporary Business* 3 (Autumn), 81–97.

Hult, Karen M. 1987. *Agency Merger and Bureaucratic Redesign.* Pittsburgh, PA: University of Pittsburgh Press.

Hult, Karen M., and Charles Walcott. 1990. *Governing Public Organizations: Politics, Structures, and Institutional Design.* Pacific Grove, CA: Brooks/Cole.

Humes, Karen R., Nicholas A. Jones, and Roberto R. Ramirez. 2011. "Overview of Race and Hispanic Origin: 2010." 2010 Census Brief, March. Washington, DC: U.S. Census Bureau. www.census.gov/prod/cen2010/briefs/c2010br-02.pdf (accessed June 4, 2012).

Hummel, Ralph. 2007. *The Bureaucratic Experience: The Post-Modern Challenge.* 5th ed. Armonk, NY: M.E. Sharpe.

Huntington, Samuel P. 1975. "The United States." In *The Crisis of Democracy,* ed. Michael Crozier, 74–75. New York: New York University Press.

Ilgen, Daniel R., and Janet Favero. 1985. "Limits in Generalization from Psychological Research to Performance Appraisal Processes." *Academy of Management Review* 10(2), 311–321.

Ingraham, Patricia W. 1995. *The Foundation of Merit: Public Service in American Democracy.* Baltimore, MD: Johns Hopkins University Press.

———. 1993a. "Of Pigs in Pokes and Policy Diffusion: Another Look at Pay-for-Performance." *Public Administration Review* 53, (4) (July–August), 348–356.

———. 1993b. "Pay for Performance in the States." *American Review of Public Administration* 23(3), 189–200.

Ingraham, Patricia W., and David H. Rosenbloom, eds. 1992. *The Promise and Paradox of Civil Service Reform.* Pittsburgh, PA: University of Pittsburgh Press.

Ingram, Helen, and Anne Schneider. 1993. "Constructing Citizenship: Subtle Messages of Policy Design." In *Public Policy for Democracy*, ed. Helen Ingram and Steven Rathgeb Smith. Washington, DC: Brookings Institution Press.

Ingram, Helen, and Steven Rathgeb Smith, eds. 1993. *Public Policy for Democracy*. Washington, DC: Brookings Institution Press.

Jeavons, Thomas H. 2001. "Ethics in Nonprofit Management: Creating a Culture of Integrity." In *Understanding Nonprofit Organizations: Governance, Leadership, and Management*, ed. J. Steven Ott, 108–119. Boulder, CO: Westview Press.

Jenkins-Smith, Hank, and Paul Sabatier. 1994. "Evaluating the Advocacy Coalition Framework." *Journal of Public Policy* 14(2), 175–203.

Jennings, Eugene Emerson. 1961. "The Anatomy of Leadership." *Management of Personnel Quarterly* 1(1), 2–10.

John, Richard R. 1995. *Spreading the News: The American Postal System from Franklin to Morse*. Cambridge, MA: Harvard University Press.

Johnson, Donald Bruce, and Kirk H. Porter. 1973. *National Party Platforms, 1840–1972*. Urbana: University of Illinois Press.

Johnson, Robert. 1991. *The Birth of the Modern: World Society, 1815–1830*. New York: HarperCollins.

Johnson, Ronald N., and Gary D. Libecap. 1994. *The Federal Civil Service System and the Problem of Bureaucracy: The Economics and Politics of Institutional Change*. Chicago, IL: University of Chicago Press.

Johnson, Steven. 2002. "The Transformation of Civic Institutions and Practices in Portland, Oregon, 1960–1990." PhD diss., Portland State University.

Johnston, Kenneth B. 1993. *Beyond Bureaucracy: A Blueprint and Vision for Government That Works*. Homewood, IL: Business One Irwin.

Jonsen, Albert R., and Stephen Toulmin. 1988. *The Abuse of Casuistry: A History of Moral Reasoning*. Berkeley: University of California Press.

Jordon, Grant, and William A. Maloney. 1997. *The Protest Business: Mobilizing Campaign Groups*. New York: Manchester University Press.

Jorgensen, Miriam, ed. 2007. *Rebuilding Native Nations: Strategies for Governance and Development*. Tucson: University of Arizona Press.

Jørgensen, T. Beck, and Barry Bozeman. 2007. "Public Values: An Inventory." *Administration & Society* 39(3), 354–381.

Jowell, Jeffrey. 1975. *Law and Bureaucracy: Administrative Discretion and the Limits of Legal Action*. Port Washington, NY: Denellen.

Joyce, Philip G. 2005. "Federal Budgeting After September 11th: A Whole New Ballgame, or Is It Déjà Vu All Over Again?" *Public Budgeting and Finance* 25(1), 15–31.

Judge, Timothy A., Joyce E. Bono, Remus Ilies, and Megan W. Gerhardt. 2002. "Personality and Leadership: A Qualitative and Quantitative Review." *Journal of Applied Psychology* 87(5), 765–780.

Kamensky, John M. 2012. "A Federal Performance Framework: Are We There Yet?" *PA Times* 35(4) (October): 9. American Society for Public Administration. PATIMES.org.

———. 2011. "The Obama Performance Approach: A Midterm Snapshot." *Public Performance & Management Review* 35(1) (September),133–148.

Kamensky, John. 2001. "A Brief History of Vice President Al Gore's National Partnership for Reinventing Government During the Administration of President Bill Clinton, 1993–2001." January 12. http://govinfo.library.unt.edu/npr/whoweare/historyofnpr.html (accessed December 9, 2007).

Kanter, Rosabeth Moss. 2004. "The Middle Manager as Innovator." *Harvard Business Review* 82(7/8), 150–161.

———. 1983. *The Change Masters*. New York: Simon and Schuster.

———. 1977. *Men and Women of the Corporation*. New York: Basic Books.

Karl, Barry. 1987. "The American Bureaucrat: A History of Sheep in Wolves' Clothing." *Public Administration Review* 47(1), 26–34.

———. 1963. *Executive Reorganization and Reform in the New Deal: The Genesis of Administrative Management: 1900–1939*. Cambridge, MA: Harvard University Press.

Kass, H.D., and B.L. Catron. 1990. *Images and Identities in Public Administration*. Newbury Park, CA: Sage.

Katz, Daniel. 1975. *Bureaucratic Encounters: A Pilot Study in the Evaluation of Government Services*. Ann Arbor: Survey Research Center, Institute for Social Research, University of Michigan.

Kaufman, Herbert. 1960. *The Forest Ranger*. Baltimore, MD: Johns Hopkins University Press.

Kearney, Richard C. 1995. "Unions in Government: Where Do They Go from Here?" In *Public Personnel Administration: Problems and Prospects*, ed. Steven W. Hays and Richard C. Kearney, 177–189. 3d ed. Englewood Cliffs, NJ: Prentice Hall.

Kelly, Rita M. 1998. "An Inclusive Democratic Polity, Representative Bureaucracies, and the New Public Management." *Public Administration Review* 58(8), 201–208.

Kelman, Steven. 1987. *Making Public Policy: A Hopeful View of American Government*. New York: Basic Books.

Kemmis, Daniel. 1990. *Community and the Politics of Place*. Norman: University of Oklahoma Press.

*Kendall v. U.S., ex rel. Stokes,* 12 Peters 522 (1838).

Kennedy, John F. 1956. *Profiles in Courage*. New York: HarperCollins.

Kerr, John, Dinesh K. Marothia, Katar Singh, C. Ramasamy, and William R. Bentley. 1997. *Natural Resource Economics: Theory and Application in India*. New Delhi: Oxford and IBH Publishing.

Kettl, Donald F. 1993. *Sharing Power: Public Governance and Private Markets*. Washington, DC: Brookings Institution Press.

———. 1988. *Government by Proxy: Managing Federal Programs*. Washington, DC: CQ Press.

Kettl, Donald F., Patricia W. Ingraham, Ronald P. Sanders, and Constance Horner. 1996. *Civil Service Reform: Building a Government That Works*. Washington, DC: Brookings Institution Press.

King, Cheryl Simrell, and Camilla Stivers. 1998. *Government Is Us: Public Administration in an Anti-Government Era*. Newbury Park, CA: Sage.

King, Martin Luther, Jr. 1963. "Letter from Birmingham Jail." The Martin Luther King, Jr., Research and Education Institute. http://mlk-kpp01.stanford.edu/index.php/resources/article/annotated_letter_from_birmingham (accessed December 31, 2012).

Kingdon, John W. 1995. *Agendas, Alternatives, and Public Policy*. 2d ed. New York: HarperCollins.

Kingsley, J. Donald. 1944. *Representative Bureaucracy*. Yellow Springs, OH: Antioch University Press.

Kirkpatrick, Shelley A., and Edwin A. Locke. 1991. "Leadership: Do Traits Matter?" *Academy of Management Executive* 5(2), 48–60.

Kochhar, Rakesh. 2012. "Labor Force Growth Slows, Hispanic Share Grows." Pew Social and Demographic Trends. Pew Research Center. February 13. www.pewsocialtrends.org/2012/02/13/labor-force-growth-slows-hispanic-share-grows-2/#more-10778.

Koliba, Christopher, Jack Meek and Asim Zia. 2011. *Governance Networks in Public Administration and Public Policy*. CRC Press/ Taylor Francis Group.

Krislov, Samuel, and David H. Rosenbloom. 1981. *Representative Bureaucracy and the American Political System*. New York: Praeger.

Krugman, Paul. 2012. "Prisons, Privatization, Patronage." *New York Times,* June 21. http://www.nytimes.com/2012/06/22/opinion/krugman-prisons-privatization-patronage.html?_r=1&ref=paulkrugman (accessed June 26, 2012).

Lane, Larry M. 1992. "The Office of Personnel Management: Values, Policies, and Consequences." In *The Promise and Paradox of Civil Service Reform*, ed. Patricia W. Ingraham and David H. Rosenbloom. Pittsburgh, PA: University of Pittsburgh Press.

Lane, Larry M., and James F. Wolf. 1990. *The Human Resource Crisis in the Public Sector: Rebuilding the Capacity to Govern*. New York: Quorum Books.

Larsen, Gary L. 2008. "Emerging Governance at the Edge of Constrained Federalism: Public Administrators at the Frontier of Democracy." PhD diss., Portland State University.

Lasswell, Harold. 1936. *Who Gets What, When, and How?* New York: McGraw-Hill.

Lauria, Mickey, ed. 1997. *Reconstructing Urban Regime Theory: Regulating Local Government in a Global Economy*. Thousand Oaks, CA: Sage.

Lawler, Edward. 1999. *Doing Research That Is Useful for Theory and Practice*. Lanham, MD: Lexington Books.

Layard, Richard, and Stephen Glaister, eds. 1994. *Cost-Benefit Analysis*. 2d ed. Cambridge, UK: Cambridge University Press.

Lazenby, Scott. 2009. "City Management Theory and Practice: A Foundation for Educating the Next Generation of Local Government Administrators." PhD diss., Portland State University.

Leach, William D., and Paul A. Sabatier. 2005. "To Trust an Adversary: Integrating Rational and Psychological Models of Collaborative Policymaking." *American Political Science Review* 99(4), 491–503.

Leazes, Francis J., Jr., and Mark T. Motte. 2004. *Providence: The Renaissance City*. Boston, MA: Northeastern University Press.

Lee, Robert D., Ronald W. Johnson, and Philip G. Joyce. 2004. *Public Budgeting Systems*. 7th ed. Sudbury, MA: Jones and Bartlett.

Leo, Christopher. 1998. "Regional Growth Management Regime: The Case of Portland, Oregon." *Journal of Urban Affairs* 20, no. 4 (1998): 363–394.

———. 1997. "City Politics in an Era of Globalization." In *Reconstructing Urban Regime Theory: Regulating Urban Politics in a Global Economy*, ed. Mickey Lauria, 77–98. Thousand Oaks, CA: Sage.

LeRoux, Kelly. 2007. *Service Contracting: A Local Government Guide*. 2d ed. Washington, DC: ICMA Press.

LeRoux, Kelly, Paul W. Brandenburger and Sanjay K. Pandey. 2010. "Interlocal Service Cooperation in U.S. Cities: A Social Network Explanation." *Public Administration Review* 70(2) (March–April), 268–278.

LeRoux, Kelly, and Jered B. Carr. 2007. "Explaining Local Government Cooperation on Public Works: Evidence from Michigan." Working Group on Interlocal Services Cooperation, Paper 26, January. http://digitalcommons.wayne.edu/interlocal_coop/26 (accessed April 1, 2012).

Lertzman, Ken, Jeremy Rayner, and Jeremy Wilson. 1996. "Learning and Change in the British Columbia Forest Policy Sector: A Consideration of Sabatier's Advocacy Coalition Framework." *Canadian Journal of Political Science* 29 (March), 111–133.

Levi, Edward. 1949. *An Introduction to Legal Reasoning*. Chicago, IL: University of Chicago Press.

Levine, Charles. 1984. "Citizenship and Service Delivery: The Promise of Coproduction." *Public Administration Review* 44 (March): 178–187.

Levy, Edward H. 1964. *An Introduction to Legal Reasoning*. Chicago, IL: University of Chicago Press.

Levy, Leonard. 1969. *Essays on the Making of the Constitution*. New York: Oxford University Press.

Lewis, Gregory. 1992. "Men and Women Toward the Top: Backgrounds, Careers, and Potential of Federal Middle Managers." *Public Personnel Management* 21(4), 473–492.

———. 1990. "In Search of the Machiavellian Milquetoasts: Comparing Attitudes of Bureaucrats and Ordinary People." *Public Administration Review* 50(2), 220–227.

Leys, Wayne. 1952. *Ethics for Policy Decisions: The Art of Asking Deliberative Questions*. Englewood Cliffs, NJ: Prentice Hall.

———. 1943. "Ethics and Administrative Discretion." *Public Administration Review* 3(1), 10–23.

Light, Paul C. 2010. "The Real Crisis in Government." *Washington Post*, January 12. www.washingtonpost.com/wp-dyn/content/article/2010/01/11/AR2010011103255.html.

———. 2004. *Sustaining Nonprofit Performance: The Case for Capacity Building and the Evidence to Support It*. Washington, DC: Brookings Institution Press.

———. 1999a. *The New Public Service*. Washington, DC: Brookings Institution Press.

———. 1999b. *The True Size of Government*. Washington, DC: Brookings Institution Press.

———. 1997. *The Tides of Reform: Making Government Work, 1945–1995*. New Haven, CT: Yale University Press.

Lincoln, Abraham. 1857. "Speech at Springfield, Illinois." In the *Collected Works of Abraham Lincoln*. Vol. II, ed. Roy Basler, 8 vols., 398–410. New Brunswick, NJ: Rutgers University Press.

Lindblom, Charles. 1965. *The Intelligence of Democracy: Decision-Making Through Mutual Adjustment*. New York: Free Press.

———. 1959. "The Science of Muddling Through." *Public Administration Review* 19(2), 79–85.

Lindgren, Mats, and Hans Bandhold. 2003. *Scenario Planning: The Link Between Future and Strategy*. New York: Palgrave Macmillan.

Lipsky, Michael. 1980. *Street-Level Bureaucracy: The Dilemmas of the Individual in Public Services*. New York: Russell Sage Foundation.

Litfin, Karen. 2000. "Advocacy Coalitions Along the Domestic-Foreign Frontier: Globalization and Canadian Climate Change Policy." *Policy Studies Journal* 28(1), 236–253.

Long, Norton. 1962. *The Polity*. Chicago, IL: Rand McNally.

Lowi, Theodore J. 1993. "Two Roads to Serfdom: Liberalism, Conservatism, and Administrative Power." In *A New Constitutionalism: Designing Political Institutions for a Good Society,* ed. Stephen Elkins and Karol Edward Soltan. Chicago, IL: University of Chicago Press.

———. 1979. *The End of Liberalism: The Second Republic of the United States*. 2d ed. New York: Norton.

———. 1972. "Four Systems of Policy, Politics, and Choice." *Public Administration Review* 32(4), 298–310.

———. 1969. *The End of Liberalism: Ideology, Policy, and the Crisis of Public Authority.* New York: Norton.

———. 1967. "The Public Philosophy: Interest-Group Liberalism." *American Political Science Review* 61(1), 5–24.

Lowi, Theodore J., and Benjamin Ginsberg. 2000. *American Government: Freedom and Power.* 6th ed. New York: Norton.

Luke, Jeffrey S. 1998. *Catalytic Leadership: Strategies for an Interconnected World.* San Francisco, CA: Jossey-Bass.

Lukes, Steven. 2005. *Power: A Radical View.* 2d ed. New York: Palgrave Macmillan.

Lynn, Laurence E. Jr. 2010. "What Endures? Public Governance and the Cycle of Reform." In *The New Public Governance? Emerging Perspectives on the Theory and Practice of Public Governance,* ed. Stephen P. Osborne, 105–123. London: Routledge.

———. 1998. "The New Public Management: How to Transform a Theme into a Legacy." *Public Administration Review* 58(3), 231–238.

MacIntyre, Alasdair. 1984. *After Virtue.* 2d ed. Notre Dame, IN: Notre Dame University Press.

Madison, James. 1787/1987. *Notes of Debates in the Federal Convention of 1787 Reported by James Madison,* ed. Adrienne Koch. New York: Norton.

Magis, Kristen. 2010. "Community Resilience: An Indicator of Social Sustainability." *Society & Natural Resources* 23(5), 401–416.

Magis, Kristen, and Craig Shinn. 2009. "Emergent Principles of Social Sustainability." In *Understanding the Social Dimension of Sustainability,* ed. Jesse Dillard, Veronica Dujon, and Mary C. King. New York: Routledge.

Mainzer, Lewis. 1964. "Honor in Bureaucratic Life." *Review of Politics* 26 (January), 70–90.

Malek, Frederic V. 1974. "Malek Manual." Executive Hearings Before the Select Committee on Presidential Campaign Activities of the United States Senate, Watergate, and Related Activities, Book 19. Washington, DC: U.S. Government Printing Office.

Mango, Andrew. 2000. *Ataturk: The Autobiography of the Founder of Modern Turkey.* New York: Overlook Press.

Mansfield, Harvey. 1969. "Federal Executive Reorganization: Thirty Years of Experience." *Public Administration Review* 29(4), 332–345.

Mansfield, Harvey, and Della Winthrop, eds. 2000. *Democracy in America.* Chicago, IL: University of Chicago Press.

ManyWorlds. 2001. *Grasping the Future: Comparing Scenario Planning to Other Forecasting Techniques.* Houston, TX: ManyWorlds.

*Marbury v. Madison,* 5 U.S. (1 Cranch) 137 (1803).

March, James G., and Johan P. Olsen. 1990. *Rediscovering Institutions: The Organizational Basis of Politics.* New York: Free Press.

March, James G., and Herbert A. Simon. 1958. *Organizations.* New York: Wiley.

Marini, Frank. 1971. *Toward a New Public Administration: The Minnowbrook Perspective.* Scranton, PA: Chandler.

Maritain, Jacques. 1951. *Man and the State.* Chicago, IL: University of Chicago Press.

Marsh, Langdon, and Craig W. Shinn with Jackie Dingfelder, Jeanna Knobloch, Michael Weisdorf, Derrick Claypool, David Fortney, and Hank Patton. 2012. *Redeveloping Regional Economies for Present and Future Generations.* Draft Report. Institute for Sustainable Solutions, Portland State University.

Martin, Joan. 1996. *Is Leadership Male?* Milton Keynes, UK: Nelson Word Pub.

Mashaw, Jerry L. 1981. "Conflict and Compromise Among Models of Administrative Justice." *Duke Law Review* (2), 181–213.

Maslow, Abraham H. 1943. "A Theory of Human Motivation." *Psychological Review* 50, 370–396.

Mathews, Joe, and Mark Paul. 2010. *California Crackup: How Reform Broke the Golden State and How We Can Fix It.* Berkeley: California University Press.

Mawhinney, Hanne. 1933/2003. "An Advocacy Coalition Approach to Change in Canadian Education." In *The Human Problems of an Industrial Civilization,* ed. Elton Mayo. New York: Macmillan.

Mayer, James. 2005. "Distaste for Tax Increases Feeds State's Growing Reliance on Fees." *Oregonian,* January 30, A1, A8.

Mayo, Elton. 1933. *The Human Problems of an Industrial Civilization.* New York: Macmillan.

Mazmanian, Daniel, and Paul Sabatier. 1989. *Implementation and Public Policy*. Lanham, MD: University Press of America.

McCaffery, Jerry, and John H. Bowman. 1978. "Participatory Democracy and Budgeting: The Effects of Proposition 13." *Public Administration Review* 38(6), 530–538.

McConnell, Grant. 1966. *Private Power and American Democracy*. New York: Knopf.

McCraw, Thomas K. 1984. *Prophets of Regulation*. Cambridge, MA: Belknap Press of Harvard University Press.

McCrone, David. 2007. "Recovering Civil Society: Does Sociology Need It?" Paper presented to the European Sociological Association Conference in Glasgow, Scotland. September 2007.

*McCulloch v. Maryland,* 17 U.S. 316 (1819).

McCullough, Thomas E. 1991. *The Moral Imagination and Public Life*. Chatham, NJ: Chatham House.

McDonald, Forrest. 1985. *Novus Ordo Seclorum: The Intellectual Origins of the Constitution.* Lawrence: University Press of Kansas.

———. 1979. *Alexander Hamilton: A Biography*. New York: Norton.

McDonald, Forrest, and Ellen Shapiro McDonald. 1988. *Requiem: Variations on Eighteenth-Century Themes.* Lawrence: University Press of Kansas.

McGregor, Douglas. 1960. *The Human Side of Enterprise*. New York: McGraw-Hill.

———. 1957. "An Uneasy Look at Performance Appraisal." *Harvard Business Review* 35(3), 89–94.

McSwite, O.C. 1997. *Legitimacy in Public Administration: A Discourse Analysis.* Thousand Oaks, CA: Sage.

Meier, Kenneth J. 2006. *Bureaucracy in a Democratic State: A Governance Perspective.* Baltimore, MD: Johns Hopkins University Press.

Meltsner, Arnold J. 1976. *Policy Analysts in the Bureaucracy*. Berkeley: University of California Press.

Merton, Robert K. 1957. *Social Theory and Social Structure*. New York: Free Press.

———. 1940. "Bureaucratic Structure and Personality." *Social Forces* 18, 560–568.

Michels, Robert, and Seymor M. Lipset. 1968. *Political Parties: A Sociology Study of the Oligarchical Tendencies of Modern Democracy.* New York: Free Press.

Milkis, Sidney. 1993. *The President and the Parties: The Transformation of the American Party System Since the New Deal.* New York: Oxford University Press.

Miller, Sandra, C. Shinn, and W. Bentley. 1994. *Rural Resource Management: Problem Solving for the Long Run.* Ames: Iowa State University Press.

Milward, H. Brinton, and Keith G. Provan. 1998. "Principles for Controlling Agents: The Political Economy of Network Structure." *Journal of Public Administration Research and Theory* 8(2), 203–221.

———. 1995. "A Preliminary Theory of Network Effectiveness: A Comparative Study of Four Mental Health Systems." *Administrative Science Quarterly* 40, 1–33.

Mintzberg, Henry. 1983. *Structure in Fives: Designing Effective Organizations.* Upper Saddle River, NJ: Prentice Hall.

———. 1979. *The Structure of Organizations*. Englewood Cliffs, NJ: Prentice Hall.

Mishel, Lawrence, Jared Bernstein, and Sylvia Allegretto. 2005. *The State of Working America, 2004–2005.* Ithaca, NY: Cornell University Press.

Mitchell, Broadus. 1957. *Alexander Hamilton: Youth to Maturity, 1755–1788.* New York: Macmillan.

Moe, Ronald. 1994. "The 'Reinventing Government' Exercise: Misinterpreting the Problem, Misjudging the Consequences." *Public Administration Review* 54(2), 111–122.

Moe, Ronald, and R.C. Gilmour. 1995. "Rediscovering Principles of Public Administration: The Neglected Foundation of Public Law." *Public Administration Review* 55(2), 135–146.

Moe, Ronald, and Kevin Kosar. 2005. *The Quasi-Government: Hybrid Organizations with Both Government and Private Sector Legal Characteristics.* Washington, DC: Congressional Research Service.

Moe, Terry. 1984. "The New Economics of Organizations." *American Journal of Political Science* 28(4), 739–777.

Mogren, Eric T. 2011. "Governance in the United States Columbia River Basin: An Historical Analysis." PhD diss., Portland State University, Portland, Oregon.

Moore, Mark. 1995. *Creating Public Value: Strategic Management in Government.* Cambridge, MA: Harvard University Press.

———. 1994. "Public Value as the Focus of Strategy." *Australian Journal of Public Administration* 53(3), 296–303.

Morgan, Douglas F. 2005. "The Oregon Bureaucracy." In *Oregon Politics and Government: Progressives*

*Versus Conservative Populists,* ed. Richard Clucas, Mark Henkels, and Brent Steel. Lincoln: University of Nebraska Press.

———. 2001. "Ethics and the Public Interest." In *Handbook of Administrative Ethics,* ed. Terry L. Cooper, 151–175. 2d ed. New York: Marcel Dekker.

———. 1998. "Stewardship." In *International Encyclopedia of Public Policy and Administration,* ed. Jay M. Shafritz. 4 vols. Boulder, CO: Westview Press.

———. 1996. "Institutional Survival in the Postmodern Age: Administrative Practice and the American Constitutional Legacy." *Administrative Theory and Praxis* 18(2), 42–56.

———. 1990. "Administrative Phronesis: Discretion and the Problem of Administrative Legitimacy in Our Constitutional System." In *Images and Identities in Public Administration,* ed. Henry D. Kass and Bayard L. Catron. Newbury Park, CA: Sage.

Morgan, Douglas, Kelly G. Bacon, Ron Bunch, Charles D. Cameron, and Robert Deis. 1996. "What Middle Managers Do in Local Government: Stewardship of the Public Trust and Limits of Reinventing Government." *Public Administration Review* 56(4), 259–266.

Morgan, Douglas F., Richard Green, Craig W. Shinn, and Kent S. Robinson. 2008. *Foundations of Public Service.* Armonk, NY: M.E. Sharpe.

Morgan, Douglas F., and Henry D. Kass. 1993. "The American Odyssey of the Career Public Service: The Ethical Crises of Role Reversal." In *Ethics and Public Administration,* ed. H. George Frederickson. Armonk, NY: M.E. Sharpe.

———. 1991 "Legitimizing Administrative Discretion Through Constitutional Stewardship." In *Ethical Frontiers in Public Management,* ed. James S. Bowman. San Francisco, CA: Jossey-Bass.

———. 1989. "Constitutional Stewardship, Phronesis, and the American Administrative Ethos." *Dialogue* 12(1), 17–60.

Morgan, Douglas F., Kent A. Kirwan, John A. Rohr, David H. Rosenbloom, and David Lewis Schaefer. 2010. "Recovering, Restoring, and Renewing the Foundations of American Public Administration: The Contributions of Herbert J. Storing." *Public Administration Review* 70(4), 621–633.

Morgan, Douglas F., and Kent Robinson. 2000. *Public Budgeting Handbook and Data Sets.* Prepared for Oregon State Fiscal Officers Association. State of Oregon Edition.

Morgan, Douglas, and John Rohr. 1986. "Traditional Responses to American Administrative Discretion." In *Administrative Discretion and Public Policy Implementation,* ed. Douglas H. Shumavon and H. Kenneth Hibbeln. Westport, CT: Praeger.

Morgan, Douglas F., and Dan Vizinni. 1999. "Transforming Customers into Citizens: Some Preliminary Lessons from the Field." *Administrative Theory & Praxis* 21(1), 51–61.

Morgan, Gareth. 2006. *Images of Organization.* Updated ed. Thousand Oaks, CA: Sage.

Mosher, Frederick. 1982. *Democracy and the Public Service.* 2d ed. New York: Oxford University Press.

Mosher, Frederick, and Richard J. Stillman II, eds. 1978. *Professions in Government.* New Brunswick, NJ: Transaction Books.

Moss, David A. 2002. *When All Else Fails: Government as the Ultimate Risk Manager.* Cambridge, MA: Harvard University Press.

Moynihan, D.P., and S.K. Pandey. 2005. "Testing How Management Matters in an Era of Government by Performance Management." *Journal of Public Administration Research and Theory* 15(3), 421–439.

Mullen, Patrick R. 2006. "Performance-Based Budgeting: The Contribution of the Program Assessment Rating Tool." *Public Budgeting & Finance* 26(4), 79–88.

Mullins, Daniel R., and Michael A. Pagano. 2005. "Local Budgeting and Finance: 25 Years of Developments." *Public Budgeting & Finance* 25(4s), 3–45.

Municipal Research and Services Center of Washington (MRSC). 2010. *Performance Audits—Initiative 900.* Report, November. http://www.mrsc.org/subjects/management/performanceaudits.aspx (accessed June 18, 2012).

*Munn v. Illinois,* 94 U.S. 113 (1877).

Murray, Charles. 1994. *Losing Ground: American Social Policy, 1950–1980.* New York: Basic Books.

*NAACP v. Alabama,* 357 U.S. 449 (1958).

Nadler, David, and Michael Tushman. 1988. *Strategic Organization Design.* Glenview, IL: Scott, Foresman.

Nalbandian, John. 2000. "The Manager as Political Leader: A Challenge to Professionalism?" *Public Management (PM)* 82(3), 7–13.

———. 1994. "Reflections of a 'Pracademic' on the Logic of Politics and Administration." *Public Administration Review* 54(6), 531–536.

Nash, George H. 1976. *The Conservative Intellectual Movement in America Since 1945*. New York: Basic Books.

Natchez, Peter B., and Irvin C. Bupp. 1973. "Policy and Priority in the Budgetary Process." *American Political Science Review* 67(3), 951–963.

Nathan, Richard. 1976. "The Administrative Presidency." *Public Interest* 44 (Summer), 40–54.

National Academy of Public Administration (NAPA). 1983. *Revitalizing Federal Management: Managers and Their Overburdened Systems*. Washington, DC: National Academy of Public Administration.

National Association of Counties (NACo). 2011. "2011–2012 FIGA Platform + Resolutions." Finance and Intergovernmental Affairs Steering Committee, National Association of Counties, Washington, DC. www.naco.org/legislation/policies/Documents/Finance%20and%20Intergovernment%20Affairs/FIG%2011-12.pdf.

———. 2004. *The American County Platform and Resolutions 04–05: Statements and Resolutions on Environment, Energy and Land Use, Finance and Intergovernmental Affairs, and Justice and Public Safety*. Washington, DC: National Association of Counties.

National Association of State and Provincial Lotteries (NASPL). 2012a. "Lottery Sales and Profits." NASPL: Resources. www.naspl.org/index.cfm?fuseaction=content&menuid=17&pageid=1025 (accessed May 29, 2012).

———. 2012b. "Member Lotteries." NASPL: About NASPL. http://naspl.org/Contacts/index.cfm (accessed May 29, 2012).

*National Bellas Hess, Inc. v. Department of Revenue,* 386 U.S. 753 (1967).

National Bureau of Economic Research. 2010. "US Business Cycle Expansions and Contractions." September 20. http://www.nber.org/cycles/cyclesmain.html (accessed December 10, 2012).

National Commission on Fiscal Responsibility and Reform (NCFRR). 2010. *The Moment of Truth*. Report of the National Commission on Fiscal Responsibility and Reform, December. Washington, DC: Executive Office of the President. www.fiscalcommission.gov/sites/fiscalcommission.gov/files/documents/The-MomentofTruth12_1_2010.pdf (accessed February 16, 2011).

National Commission on Public Service. 2002. *Leadership for America: Rebuilding the Public Service*. Washington, DC: National Commission on the Public Service.

National Conference of State Legislatures (NCSL). 2010a. "Mandate Monitor Overview." State-Federal Relations and Standing Committees. www.ncsl.org/default.aspx?TabID=773&tabs=854,14,1067#854 (accessed August 8, 2011).

———. 2010b. "2010–2011 Policies for the Jurisdiction of the Budgets and Revenue Committee." State-Federal Relations and Standing Committees, Budget and Revenue Standing Committee. www.ncsl.org/default.aspx?TabID=773&tabs=855,20,632#855 (accessed August 8, 2011).

———. 2007a. "NCSL Supports and Urges Enactment of Sales Tax Simplification and Fairness Act (S.34/HR3396) Action Resolution." www.ncsl.org/statefed/fedbud.htm (accessed November 27, 2007).

———. 2007b. "Standing Committee on Budgets and Review: Mandate Monitor." www.ncsl.org/standcomm/scbudg/manmon.htm (accessed November 26, 2007).

———. 2005. "The Executive Committee Task Force on State and Local Taxation of Telecommunications and Electronic Commerce." Updated September 2007. www.ncsl.org/programs/fiscal/tctelcom.htm.

National Federation of Independent Businesses, et al. v. Sebelius, Secretary of Health and Human Services, et al., No. 11–393 (2012).

National Institute of Justice. 1997. "Key Legislative Issues in Criminal Justice: Mandatory Sentencing." *Research in Action*, January. Washington, DC: National Institute of Justice Research in Action.

Neustadt, Richard E., and Ernest R. May. 1988. *Thinking in Time: The Uses of History for Decision Makers*. New York: Free Press.

Newbold, Stephanie P. 2010. "Toward a Constitutional School for American Public Administration." *Public Administration Review* 70(4), 538–546.

———. 2008. "Teaching Organization Theory from a Constitutional Perspective: A New Twist on an Old Flame." *Journal of Public Affairs Education* 14(3), 335–351.

———. 2006. "All but Forgotten: Thomas Jefferson's Contribution to the Development of Public Administration in the United States." PhD diss., Center for Public Administration and Policy at Virginia Polytechnic Institute and State University.

Nisar, Tahir M. 2006. "Risk Management in Public–Private Partnership Contracts." *Public Organization Review* 7(1), 1–19.

Nishishiba, Masami, Margaret Banyan, and Douglas F. Morgan. 2012. "Looking Back on the Founding: Civic Engagement Traditions in the United States." In *The State of Citizen Participation in America,* ed. Hindy Lauer Schacter and Kaifeng Yang, 21–52. Charlotte, NC: Information Age Publishing.

Niskanen, William. 1994. *Bureaucracy and Public Economics.* Aldershot, UK: Edward Elgar.

Noddings, Nel. 1984. *Caring: A Feminine Approach to Ethics and Moral Education.* Berkeley: University of California Press.

Nord, Mark, Margaret Andrews, and Steven Carlson. 2003. *Household Food Security in the United States, 2002.* Food Assistance and Nutrition Research Report No. FANRR35, October. Washington, DC: U.S. Department of Agriculture, Food and Rural Economics Division, Economic Research Service.

O'Connell, Brian. 1999. *Civil Society: The Underpinnings of American Democracy.* Hanover, NH: University Press of New England.

O'Flynn, Janine. 2007. "From New Public Management to Public Value: Paradigm Change and Managerial Implications." *Australian Journal of Public Administration* 66(3), 353–356.

Ogden, Daniel M., Jr. 1989. *How National Policy Is Made.* Self-published.

———. 1971. "How National Policy Is Made." In *Increasing Understanding of Public Problems and Policies.* Oak Brook, IL: Farm Foundation.

Okun, Arthur. 1975. *Equality and Efficiency: The Big Tradeoff.* Washington, DC: Brookings Institution Press.

O'Leary, Rosemary. 2006. *The Ethics of Dissent: Managing Guerrilla Government.* Washington, DC: CQ Press.

Olsen, Johan P. 2001. "Garbage Cans, New Institutionalism and the Study of Politics." *American Political Science Review* 1(95), 191–198.

Organisation for Economic Co-operation and Development (OECD). 2009. *OECD in Figures 2009.* September 10. www.oecd-ilibrary.org/economics/oecd-in-figures-2009_oif-2009-en.

Osborne, David, and Ted Gaebler. 1993 *Reinventing Government.* New York: Plume.

Osborne, David, and Peter Hutchinson. 2004. *The Price of Government: Getting the Results We Need in an Age of Permanent Fiscal Crisis.* New York: Basic Books.

Osborne, Stephen, ed. 2010. *The New Public Governance? Emerging Perspectives on the Theory and Practice of Public Governance.* London, UK: Routledge.

———. 2008. *The Third Sector in Europe: Prospects and Challenges.* London, UK: Routledge.

Ospina, Sonia. 1992. "Expediency Management in Public Service: A Dead-End Search for Managerial Discretion." *Public Productivity and Management Review* 15(2), 405–421.

Ostrom, Elinor. 1990. *Governing the Commons: The Evolution of Institutions for Collective Action.* Cambridge, UK: Cambridge University Press.

Ostrom, Elinor, Roy Gardner, and James Walker. 1994. *Rules, Games, and Common-Pool Resources.* Ann Arbor: University of Michigan Press.

Ostrom, Vincent. 1989. *The Intellectual Crisis in American Public Administration.* Tuscaloosa: University of Alabama Press.

Ostrower, Francie, and Marla J. Bobwick. 2006. "Nonprofit Governance and the Sarbanes-Oxley Act." *Urban Institute National Survey of Nonprofit Governance Preliminary Findings.* Washington DC: Urban Institute.

O'Toole, Laurence J. 1997. "The Implications for Democracy in a Networked Bureaucratic World." *Journal of Public Administration Research and Theory* 7(3), 443–459.

Ott, J. Steven, ed. 2001. *Understanding Nonprofit Organizations: Governance, Leadership, and Management.* Boulder, CO: Westview Press.

———. 1989. *The Organizational Culture Perspective.* Chicago, IL: Dorsey.

Ouchi, William G. 1982. *Theory Z: How American Business Can Meet the Japanese Challenge.* Reading, MA: Addison-Wesley.

———. 1980. "Markets, Bureaucracies and Clans." *Administrative Science Quarterly* 25(1), 129–141.

Owens, Jeffrey. 2005. *Fundamental Tax Reform: The Experience of OECD Countries.* Background Paper Number 47, February. Washington, DC: Tax Foundation. http://taxfoundation.org/sites/taxfoundation.org/files/docs/fc748ce251c36b57b78dad5654d2898b.pdf.

Oxholm, Carl III. 2005. "Sarbanes-Oxley in Higher Education: Bringing Corporate America's Best Practices to Academia." *Journal of College and University Law* 33(2), 351–376. http://www.drexel.edu/papadakis/sarbanes/sarbanes-oxley_in_hi224C06.pdf (accessed December 31, 2012).

Ozawa, Connie, ed. 2005. *The Portland Edge: Challenges and Successes in Growing Communities.* Washington, DC: Island Press.

*Panama R. Co. v. Ryan,* 293 U.S. 388 (1935).

Parker, Dorothy. 1999. *Health, Civilization, and the State: A History of Public Health from Ancient to Modern Times.* New York: Routledge.

Patton, W. David, Stephanie L. Witt, Nicholas P. Lovrich, and Patricia J. Fredericksen. 2002. *Human Resource Management: The Public Service Perspective.* New York: Houghton Mifflin.

Pearce, Jone L., and Lyman W. Porter. 1986. "Employee Responses to Formal Performance Appraisal Feedback." *Journal of Applied Psychology* 71(2), 211–218.

Perrow, Charles. 1986. *Complex Organizations: A Critical Essay.* New York: McGraw-Hill.

———. 1970. *Organizational Analysis: A Sociological View.* Belmont, CA: Wadsworth.

———. 1967. "A Framework for Comparative Organizational Analysis." *American Sociological Review* 32(2), 194–208.

Perry, James L. 1996. "Measuring Public Service Motivation: An Assessment of Construct Reliability and Validity." *Journal of Public Administration Research and Theory* 6(1), 5–22.

———. 1991. "Linking Pay to Performance: The Controversy Continues." In *Public Personnel Management: Current Concerns, Future Challenges,* ed. Carolyn Ban and Norma M. Riccucci. New York: Longman.

———. 1986. "Merit Pay in the Public Sector: The Case for a Failure of Theory." *Review of Public Personnel Administration* 17(1), 211–218.

Perry, James L., Annie Hondeghem, Lois Recascino Wise. 2010. "Revisiting the Motivational Bases of Public Service: Twenty Years of Research and an Agenda for the Future." *Public Administration Review* 70(5) (September/October), 681–690.

Perry, James L., Trent Engbers, So Yun Jun. 2009. "Back to the Future? Performance-Related Pay, Empirical Research, and the Perils of Persistence." *Public Administration Review* 69(1), 1–31.

Perry, James, and L. Wise. 1990. "The Motivational Basis of Public Service." *Public Administration Review* 50(3), 367–373.

Peters, Guy B. 2001. *The Future of Governing.* 2d ed. Lawrence: University Press of Kansas.

Peters, Guy B., and Donald Savoie, eds. 2000. *Governance in the Twenty-first Century: Revitalizing the Public Service.* Montreal, Canada: McGill-Queen's University Press.

———. 1995. *Governance in a Changing Environment.* Montreal, Canada: McGill-Queen's University Press.

Peters, Thomas, and Robert H. Waterman. 1982. *In Search of Excellence: Lessons from America's Best-Run Companies.* New York: Harper and Row.

Peterson, Paul. 1995. *The Price of Federalism.* Washington, DC: Brookings Institution Press.

Pevar, Stephen L. 2002. *The Rights of Indians and Tribes.* 3d ed. Carbondale: Southern Illinois University Press.

Pfiffner, James P., and Douglas A. Brook. 2000. *The Future of Merit: Twenty Years After the Civil Service Reform Act.* Baltimore, MD: Johns Hopkins University Press.

Powell, Walter W., and Paul J. DiMaggio. 1991. *The New Institutionalism in Organizational Analysis.* Chicago, IL: University of Chicago Press.

President's Committee on Administrative Management. 1937. *Administrative Management in the Government of the United States, January 8, 1937.* Washington, DC: U.S. Government Printing Office. (Also known as the Brownlow Committee Report.)

Pritchett, C. Herman. 1968. *The American Constitution.* 2d ed. New York: McGraw-Hill.

PR Newswire. 2012. "The U.S. Conference of Mayors Reacts to Supreme Court's Arizona Immigration Decision." June 25. http://www.prnewswire.com/news-releases/the-us-conference-of-mayors-reacts-to-supreme-courts-arizona-immigration-decision-160272805.html (accessed October 23, 2012).

Provan, Keith G., and H. Brinton Milward. 2001. "Do Networks Really Work? A Framework for Evaluating Public-Sector Organizational Networks." *Public Administration Review* 61(4), 414–423.

Punch, Keith F. 2003. *Survey Research: The Basics.* Thousand Oaks, CA: Sage.

Putnam, Robert D. 2000. *Bowling Alone: The Collapse and Revival of American Community.* New York: Simon and Schuster.

Putnam, Robert D., and Lewis M. Feldstein, with Don Cohen. 2003. *Better Together: Restoring the American Community.* New York: Simon and Schuster.

Pyhrr, Peter. 1974. *Zero-Base Budgeting.* New York: Wiley.

*Quill Corp. v. North Dakota,* 504 U.S. 298 (1992).

Ragin, Charles C. 1987. *The Comparative Method: Moving Beyond Qualitative and Quantitative Strategies.* Berkeley: University of California Press.

Ragin, Charles C., and Howard S. Becker, eds. 1992. *What Is a Case? Exploring the Foundations of Social Inquiry.* Cambridge, UK: Cambridge University Press.

Randolph, Toni. 2007. "Non-Profits May Lose Property Tax Exemption." MPR News, December 20. http://minnesota.publicradio.org/display/web/2007/12/19/tax/ (accessed May 26, 2012).

Reddin, William. 1970. *Managerial Effectiveness.* New York: McGraw-Hill.

Redford, Emmette. 1969. *Democracy in the Administrative State.* New York: Oxford University Press.

Regan, Helen B., and Gwen H. Brooks. 1995. *Out of Women's Experience: Creating Relational Leadership.* Thousand Oaks, CA: Corwin.

Reich, Robert B. 1992. *The Work of Nations: Preparing Ourselves for 21st-Century Capitalism.* New York: Random House.

Rhodes, R.A.W. 1994. "The Hollowing Out of the State." *Political Quarterly* 65(2), 138–151.

*Richardson v. Perales*, 402 US 389 (1971).

Richardson, James D., ed. 1899. *A Compilation of the Messages and Papers of the Presidents.* Vol. 2. Washington, DC: U.S. Government Printing Office.

Richardson, William D. 1997. *Democracy, Bureaucracy, and Character: Founding Thought.* Lawrence: University Press of Kansas.

Riis, Jacob. 1890. *How the Other Half Lives.* New York: Charles Scribner and Sons.

Ringland. Gill. 2002. *Scenarios in Public Policy.* Essex, England: Wiley.

Riordon, William L. 1963. *Plunkitt of Tammany Hall.* New York: E.P. Dutton.

Ripley, Randall B., and Grace A. Franklin. 1991. *Congress, the Bureaucracy, and Public Policy.* 6th ed. Pacific Grove, CA: Brooks/Cole.

Rittel, Horst, and Melvin Webber. 1973. "Dilemmas in a General Theory of Planning." *Policy Sciences* 4, 155–169.

Ritti, R. Richard, and G.R. Funkhouser. 1977. *The Ropes to Skip and the Ropes to Know.* New York: Wiley.

Robinson, Kent. 2004. "The Contribution of Social Trust and Reliance to Administrative Process." PhD diss., February. Source DAI/A 65-10, Publication No. 3150620. http://gradworks.umi.com/31/50/3150620.html.

Robinson-Hickman, Gill. 2000. *Managing Human Resources in the Public Sector.* New York: Wadsworth.

Rockwell, Theodore. 1995. *The Rickover Effect: The Inside Story of How Adm. Hyman Rickover Built the Nuclear Navy.* New York: Wiley.

Rodriguez, Richard. 2003. *Brown: The Last Discovery of America.* East Rutherford, NJ: Penguin.

Roelofs, Mark. 1991. *The Poverty of American Politics.* Boston, MA: Temple University Press.

Roethlisberger, Frank J., and W.J. Dickson. 1939. *Management and the Worker.* Cambridge, MA: Harvard University Press.

Rohr, John A. 2002. *Civil Servants and Their Constitutions.* Lawrence: University Press of Kansas.

———. 1998. *Public Service, Ethics, and Constitutional Practice.* Lawrence: University Press of Kansas.

———. 1995. *Founding Republics in France and America: A Study in Constitutional Governance.* Lawrence: University Press of Kansas.

———. 1989. *Ethics for Bureaucrats: An Essay on Law and Values.* 2d ed. New York: Marcel-Dekker.

———. 1986. *To Run a Constitution: The Legitimacy of the Administrative State.* Lawrence: University Press of Kansas.

———. 1984. "Civil Servants and Second-Class Citizens." *Public Administration Review* 44 (Special Issue), 135–140.

———. 1981. "Financial Disclosures: Power in Search of Policy." *Public Personnel Management* 10, 29–40.

———. 1978. *Ethics for Bureaucrats: An Essay on Law and Values.* New York: Marcel-Dekker.

Rosen, George. 1993. *The History of Public Health.* Baltimore, MD: Johns Hopkins University Press.

Rosenbloom, David H. 2003. *Administrative Law for Public Managers.* Boulder, CO: Westview Press.

———. 2000. *Building a Legislative-Centered Public Administration: Congress and the Administrative State, 1946–1999.* Tuscaloosa: University of Alabama Press.

———. 1985. *Public Personnel Policy: The Politics of Civil Service.* Port Washington, NY: Associated Faculty.

———. 1983. "Public Administrative Theory and the Separation of Powers." *Public Administration Review* 43(3), 219–227.

———. 1977. *Federal Equal Employment Opportunity: Politics and Public Personnel Administration.* New York: Praeger.

———. 1971. *Federal Service and the Constitution: The Development of the Public Employment Relationship.* Ithaca, NY: Cornell University Press.

Rosenbloom, David H., James D. Carroll, and Jonathan D. Carroll. 2000. *Constitutional Competence for Public Managers: Cases and Commentary.* Itasca, IL: F.E. Peacock.

Rosenbloom, David H., and Robert S. Kravchuk. 2005. *Public Administration: Understanding Management, Politics, and Law in the Public Sector.* 6th ed. Boston, MA: McGraw-Hill.

———. 2002. *Public Administration: Understanding Management, Politics, and Law in the Public Sector.* 5th ed. Boston, MA: McGraw-Hill.

Rosenthal, Cindy Simon. 1998. *When Women Lead: Integrative Leadership in State Legislatures.* New York: Oxford University Press.

Rossiter, Clinton, ed. 1961. *The Federalist Papers.* New York: New American Library.

Rothkopf, David. 2012. *Power, Inc.: The Epic Rivalry Between Big Business and Government—and the Reckoning That Lies Ahead.* New York: Farrar, Straus and Giroux.

Rourke, Francis E. 1984. *Bureaucracy, Politics, and Public Policy.* 3d ed. New York: HarperCollins.

Rozwenc, Edwin C., ed. 1963. *The Meaning of Jacksonian Democracy.* Lexington, MA: D.C. Heath.

Rung, Margaret C. 2002. *Servants of the State: Managing Diversity and Democracy in the Federal Workforce, 1933–1953.* Athens: University of Georgia Press.

*Rutan v. Republican Party of Illinois,* 497 US 62 (1990).

Sabatier, Paul. 1998. "The Advocacy Coalition Framework: Revisions and Relevance for Europe." *Journal of European Public Policy* 5(1), 98–130.

Sabatier, Paul, and H. Jenkins-Smith, eds. 1993. *Policy Change and Learning.* Boulder, CO: Westview Press.

Salamon, Lester M., ed. 2002. *The Tools of Government: A Guide to the New Governance.* New York: Oxford University Press.

———. 1999. *America's Nonprofit Sector: A Primer.* 2d ed. New York: The Foundation Center.

Salisbury, Robert, and John Heinz. 1970. "A Theory of Policy Analysis and Some Preliminary Applications." In *Policy Analysis in Political Science,* ed. Ira Sharkansky, 39–50. Chicago, IL: Markham.

Sanger, Mary B. 2008. "From Measurement to Management: Breaking through the Barriers to State and Local Performance." *Public Administration Review* 68 (S1), s70–s85.

Santini, Jacob. 2004. "Homeless Campus Plans Are Shelved." *Salt Lake Tribune,* October 27.

Sarbanes-Oxley Act. 2002. P.L. 107–204, 116 Stat. 745.

Sathe, Vijay. 1985. *Culture and Related Corporate Realities.* Homewood, IL: Richard D. Irwin.

Saulny, Susan. 2011. "Census Data Presents Rise in Multiracial Population of Youths." *New York Times,* March 24, A3.

Savas, Emanuel S. 1982. *Privatizing the Public Sector: How to Shrink Government.* Chatham, NJ: Chatham House.

———, ed. 1977. *Alternative for Delivering Public Services: Toward Improved Service.* Boulder, CO: Westview Press.

Sayre, Wallace. 1948. "The Triumph of Technique over Purpose." *Public Administration Review* 8(2), 134–139.

Schaar, John. 1973. "The Case for Patriotism." *American Review* 17 (May), 58–99.

———. 1967. "Equality of Opportunity and Beyond." In *Equality,* ed. Roland Pennock and John W. Chapman, 228–249. Vol. 9. New York: Atherton.

———. 1964. "Some Ways of Thinking About Equality." *Journal of Politics* 26 (November), 884–892.

Schachter, Hindy Lauer. 1989. *Frederick Taylor and the Public Administration Community: A Reevaluation.* Albany: State University of New York Press.

Schaefer, Martin, Lawler, Peter Augustine, and Schaefer, David Lewis. 1998. *Active Duty: Public Administration as Democratic Statesmanship.* Lanham, MD: Rowman and Littlefield.

Schattschneider, Elmer E. 1970. *The Semisovereign People.* Hinsdale, IL: Dryden.

Scheberle, Denise. 2004. *Federalism and Environmental Policy: Trust and the Politics of Implementation.* 2d ed. Washington, DC: Georgetown University Press.

———. 1997. *Federalism and Environmental Policy: Trust and the Politics of Implementation.* Washington, DC: Georgetown University Press.

*Schechter P. Corp. v. U.S.,* 295 U.S. 495 (1935).

Schein, Edgar H. 1993. *Organizational Culture and Leadership.* 2d ed. San Francisco, CA: Jossey-Bass.

———. 1985. *Organizational Culture and Leadership.* San Francisco, CA: Jossey-Bass.

Schellhardt, Timothy D. 1996. "Annual Agony: It's Time to Evaluate Your Work and All Involved Are Groaning." *Wall Street Journal*, November 19, A1, A5.

Schick, Alan. 1980. "Budgeting as an Administrative Process." In *Perspectives on Budgeting*, ed. Alan Schick, 1–16. Washington, DC: American Society for Public Administration.

Schiesl, Martin J. 1977. *The Politics of Efficiency: Municipal Administration and Reform in America, 1800–1920*. Berkeley: University of California Press.

Schmidt, Mary. 1993. "Grout: Alternative Kinds of Knowledge and Why They Are Ignored." *Public Administration Review* 53(6), 525–530.

Schon, Donald, 1983. *The Reflective Practitioner, How Professionals Think In Action*. Basic Books: New York.

Schwartz, Peter. 2003. *Inevitable Surprises: Thinking Ahead in a Time of Turbulence*. East Rutherford, NJ: Penguin Gotham.

———. 1996. *The Art of the Long View: Planning for the Future in an Uncertain World*. Redfern, Australia: Currency.

Scott, Richard. 1995. *Institutions and Organizations*. Thousand Oaks, CA: Sage.

Scott, William G. 1992. *Chester I. Barnard and the Guardians of the Managerial State*. Lawrence: University Press of Kansas.

Scott, William G., and David K. Hart. 1989. *Organizational Values in America*. New Brunswick, NJ: Transaction.

Seligman, Adam B. 1992. *The Idea of Civil Society*. Princeton, NJ: Princeton University Press.

Selznick, Philip. 1992. *The Moral Commonwealth: Social Theory and the Promise of Community*. Berkeley: University of California Press.

———. 1957. *Leadership in Administration: A Sociological Interpretation*. Evanston, IL: Row, Peterson.

———. 1949. *TVA and the Grass Roots*. Berkeley: University of California Press.

Sergiovanni, Thomas A., and John E. Corbally, eds. 1984. *Leadership and Organizational Culture*. Urbana: University of Illinois Press.

Shafritz, Jay M. 1973. *Position Classification: A Behavioral Analysis for the Public Service*. New York: Praeger.

Shafritz, Jay M., and Albert C. Hyde. 1992. *Classics of Public Administration*. 3d ed. Belmont, CA: Brooks/Cole.

Shaw, Donald L., and M.E. McCombs. 1977. *The Emergence of American Political Issues*. St. Paul, MN: West.

Shepsle, Kenneth A. 1989. "Studying Institutions: Some Lessons from the Rational Choice Approach." *Journal of Theoretical Politics* 1(2), 131–148.

Shinn, Craig W. 1999. "Civic Capacity: Theory, Research, and Practice." *Administrative Theory & Praxis* 21(1), 103–119.

———. 1993a. *British Columbia Log Export Policy: Historical Review and Analysis*. USDA-Forest Service: Pacific Northwest Research Paper PNW-RP-457.

———. 1993b. "Structures of Northwest Sawmills." PhD diss., College of Forest Resources, University of Washington, Seattle.

Shinn, Craig, Elaine Hallmark, and Laurel Singer. 2012. "Introduction to Collaborative Governance: Participant Workbook." Mark O. Hatfield School of Government, Portland State University, Portland, Oregon.

Simon, Herbert A. 1960. *The New Science of Management Decisions*. New York: Harper and Row.

———. 1957. *Administrative Behavior: A Study of Decision-Making Processes in Administrative Organization*. 2d ed. New York: Free Press.

———. 1947. *Administrative Behavior: A Study of Decision-Making Processes in Administrative Organization*. New York: Free Press.

———. 1945. Sinclair, Upton. 1906. *The Jungle*. New York: Doubleday, Page and Co.

Sirianni, Carmen. 2009. *Investing in Democracy: Engaging Citizens in Collaborative Governance*. Washington, DC: Brookings Institution Press.

Skocpol, Theda 1997. "The Tocqueville Problem: Civic Engagement in American Democracy. *Social Science History* 21(4), 455–479.

Skocpol, Theda, and Morris P. Fiorina, eds. 1999. *Civic Engagement in American Democracy*. Washington, DC: Brookings Institution Press.

*Slaughter-House Cases,* 83 U.S. 36, (1873).

Smith, Adam. 1776/2003. *The Wealth of Nations*. London, UK: Stratton and Cadell. Bantam Classic ed. New York: Bantam.

Smith, Frank E. 1966. *The Politics of Conservation*. New York: Pantheon Random.

Smith, Gerald E., and Carole A. Huntsman. 1997. "Reframing the Metaphor of the Citizen-Government Relationship: A Value-Centered Perspective." *Public Administration Review* 57(4), 309–318.

Smith, Steven R., and Michael Lipsky. 1993. *Nonprofits for Hire: The Welfare State in the Age of Contracting*. Cambridge, MA: Harvard University Press.

Smith, Steven R., and Judith Smyth. 2010. "The Governance of Contracting Relationships: 'Killing the Golden Goose.' A Third-Sector Perspective." In *The New Public Governance? Emerging Perspectives on the Theory and Practice of Public Governance*, ed. S.P. Osborne, 270–300. London, UK: Routledge.

Snowden, David J., and Mary E. Boone. 2007. "A Leader's Framework for Decision Making." *Harvard Business Review* 85(11), 68–76.

Sorauf, Frank J. 1960. "The Silent Revolution in Patronage." *Public Administration Review* 20(1), 28–34.

Spencer, Herbert. 1994. *Spencer: Political Writings*, ed. John Offer. Cambridge, UK: Cambridge University Press.

Spicer, Michael W. 2010. *In Defense of Politics in Public Administration: A Value Pluralist Perspective*. Tuscaloosa: University of Alabama Press.

———. 1995. *The Founders, the Constitution, and Public Administration: A Conflict in Worldviews*. Washington, DC: Georgetown University Press.

Spicer, Michael W., and Larry D. Terry. 1996. "Administrative Interpretation of Statutes: A Constitutional View on the 'New World Order' of Public Administration." *Public Administration Review* 56(1), 38–47.

Starr, Paul. 1982. *Social Transformation of American Medicine*. New York: Basic Books.

State of Arizona. 2012a. *The Executive Budget: Fiscal Year 2013—Appendix*. Office of Strategic Planning and Budgeting, January. www.azospb.gov/documents/2012/FY2013-ExecutiveBudget-Appendix.pdf (accessed June 7, 2012).

———. 2012b. *The Executive Budget: Fiscal Year 2013—Summary*. Office of Strategic Planning and Budgeting, January. http://media.azpm.org/master/document/2012/1/13/pdf/Brewer.bjt.2012-13.pdf (accessed June 7, 2012).

———. 2011. "Summary of Federal Revenue by Area of Government, FY 2010 Through FY 2012." In *Statement of Federal Funds: Fiscal Years 2010–2012*, 3. Report, July. www.ospb.state.az.us/documents/2011/FederalFunds2010-2012.pdf (accessed June 7, 2012).

State of Oregon, Department of Revenue. 2010a. "Introduction." *State of Oregon 2011–2013 Tax Expenditure Report*, 1–4. Salem: Oregon Department of Administrative Services, Budget and Management Division.

———. 2010b. "Summary." *State of Oregon 2011–2013 Tax Expenditure Report*, 5–7. Salem: Oregon Department of Administrative Services, Budget and Management Division.

———. 2004. *State of Oregon 2005–2007 Tax Expenditure Report*. Salem: Oregon Department of Administrative Services, Budget and Management Division.

State of Washington. 2006. "GMAP Accountability and Performance." www.accountability.wa.gov/ (accessed June 19, 2012).

Stefaniak, Angie, and C. Vetter. 2007. "Black Hole or Window of Opportunity? Understanding the Generation Gap in Today's Workplace." Policy Briefs. Salt Lake City: University of Utah Center for Public Policy and Administration.

Steffens, Lincoln. 1904. *The Shame of Cities*. New York: McClure, Philips and Co.

Stever, James A. 1990. "The Dual Image of the Administrator in Progressive Administrative Theory." *Administration & Society* 22(1), 39–57.

———. 1988. *The End of Public Administration: Problems of the Profession in the Post-Progressive Era*. Dobbs Ferry, NY: Transnational Publishers.

Stiglitz, Joseph E. 2010. *Freefall: America, Free Markets, and the Sinking of the World Economy*. New York: W.W. Norton.

———. 2000. *Economics of the Public Sector*. 3d ed. New York: W.W. Norton.

Stillman, Richard J., II. 1984. "The Changing Patterns of Public Administration Theory in America." In *Public Administration: Concepts and Cases*, ed. Richard J. Stillman II. 3d ed. Boston, MA: Houghton Mifflin.

Stivers, Camilla. 2002a. *Gender Images in Public Administration: Legitimacy and the Administrative State*. 2d ed. Thousand Oaks, CA: Sage.

————. 2002b. *Bureau Men, Settlement Women: Constructing Public Administration in the Progressive Era.* Lawrence: University Press of Kansas .

Stoker, Gerry. 2006. "Public Value Management: A New Narrative for Networked Governance?" *American Review of Public Administration* 36(1), 41–57.

Stone, Clarence N. 1993. "Urban Regimes and the Capacity to Govern: A Political Economy Approach." *Journal of Urban Affairs* 15(1), 1–28.

————. 1989. *Regime Politics: Governing Atlanta.* Lawrence: University Press of Kansas.

Stone, Deborah A. 1997. *Policy Paradox: The Art of Political Decision Making.* New York: Norton.

————. 1988. *Policy Paradox and Political Reason.* Glenview, IL: Scott, Foresman.

Stone, Wendy. 2001. *Measuring Social Capital: Towards a Theoretically Informed Measurement Framework for Researching Social Capital in Family and Community Life.* Research Paper No. 24. Melbourne: Australian Institute of Family Studies.

Storing, Herbert J. 1981a. *The Complete Anti-Federalist.* 7 vols. Chicago, IL: University of Chicago Press.

————. 1981b. *What the Anti-Federalists Were For: The Political Thought of the Opponents of the Constitution.* Chicago, IL: University of Chicago Press.

————. 1980. "American Statesmanship: Old and New." In *Bureaucrats, Policy Analysts, Statesmen: Who Leads?* ed. Robert A. Goldwin. Washington, DC: American Enterprise Institute.

————. 1965. "Leonard D. White and the Study of Public Administration." *Public Administration Review* 25(1), 38–51.

Streamlined Sales Tax Project. 2011. "Frequently Asked Questions." www.streamlinedsalestax.org/index.php?page=faqs (accessed April 22, 2011).

————. 2005. "Executive Summary." www.streamlinedsalestax.org (accessed November 26, 2007).

Sullivan, William M. 2004. *Work and Integrity: The Crisis and Promise of Professionalism in America.* San Francisco, CA: Jossey-Bass.

*Sunshine A. Co. v. Adkins*, 310 U.S. 381, 397 (1940).

Svara, James H. 1989a. "Dichotomy and Duality: Reconceptualizing the Relationship Between Policy and Administration in Council-Manager Cities." In *Ideal and Practice in Council-Manager Government,* ed. H. George Frederickson, 53–69. Washington, DC: ICMA.

————. 1989b. "Policy and Administration: City Managers as Comprehensive Professional Leaders." In *Ideal and Practice in Council-Manager Government,* ed. H. George Frederickson, 70–92. Washington, DC: ICMA.

Svedin, Lina. 2012. *Accountability in Crises and Public Trust in Governing Institutions.* New York: Routledge.

Swanson, Guy E. 1970. "Toward Corporate Action: A Reconstruction of Elementary Collective Processes." In *Human Nature and Collective Behavior: Papers in Honor of Herbert Blumer,* ed. T. Shubtani. Englewood Cliffs, NJ: Prentice Hall.

Swindler, William. 1969. *Court and Constitution in the 20th Century: The Old Legality, 1889–1932.* New York: Bobbs-Merrill.

Syrett, Harold C., and Jacob E. Cooke, eds. 1961–1987. *The Papers of Alexander Hamilton.* 27 vols. New York: Columbia University Press.

Szakmary, Andrew C., and Carol Matheny Szakmary. 1995. "State Lotteries as a Source of Revenue: A Re-Examination." *Southern Economic Journal* 61(4), 1167–1181.

Taylor, Fredrick. 1911/2006. *The Principles of Scientific Management.* London, UK: Harper. Repr., New York: Cosimo Books.

Temin, Peter. 1969. *The Jacksonian Economy.* New York: Norton.

Terry, Larry D. 1995. *Leadership of Public Bureaucracies: The Administrator as Conservator.* Thousand Oaks, CA: Sage.

Thach, Charles. 1969. *The Creation of the Presidency: 1775–1789.* Baltimore, MD: Johns Hopkins University Press.

Thaler, Richard H., and Cass R. Sunstein. 2009. *Nudge: Improving Decisions About Health, Wealth, and Happiness.* Rev. and exp. ed. New York: Penguin Books.

Thompson, Dennis. 1985. "The Possibility of Administrative Ethics." *Public Administration Review* 45(5), 555–561.

Thompson, Frank J. 1975. *Personnel Policy in the City: The Politics of Jobs in Oakland.* Berkeley: University of California Press.

Thompson, James D. 1967. *Organizations in Action.* New York: McGraw-Hill.

Tocqueville, Alexis de. 1835–1840/2000. *Democracy in America,* trans. and ed. Harvey Mansfield and Delba Winthrop. Chicago, IL: University of Chicago Press.

Toonen, Theo. A. J. 1998. "Networks, Management and Institutions: Public Administration as 'Normal Science." *Public Administration* 76(2), 229–252.

Trist, Eric L. 1981. "The Evolution of Sociotechnical Systems as a Conceptual Framework for Action Research." In *Perspectives in Organizational Design and Behavior*, ed. A.H. Van de Ven and W.F. Joyce. New York: Wiley.

Trist, Eric, and K.W. Bamforth. 1951. "Social and Psychological Consequences of the Longworth Method of Coal Getting." *Human Relations* 4, 3–28.

Tullock, Gordon. 1965. *The Politics of Bureaucracy*. Washington, DC: Public Affairs.

Ury, William, Jeanne Bret, and Stephen Goldberg. 1988. *Getting Disputes Resolved: Designing Systems to Cut the Costs of Conflict*. London: Jossey-Bass.

*U.S. v. Chicago, St. P. and P.R. Co.,* 282 U.S. 311, 324 (1931).

U.S. Census Bureau. 2012a. *Household Income Inequality Within U.S. Counties: 2006–2010*. American Community Survey Brief. http://www.census.gov/prod/2012pubs/acsbr10-18.pdf (accessed December 31, 2012).

———. 2012b. *Income, Poverty, and Health Insurance Coverage in the United States: 2011*. http://www.census.gov/prod/2012pubs/p60-243.pdf (accessed December 31, 2012).

———. 2011a. "Intercensal Estimates of the Resident Population for the United States, Regions, States, and Puerto Rico: April 1, 2000 to July 1, 2010." Excel table ST-EST00INT-01.xls, Population Estimates: Intercensal Estimates, September. www.census.gov/popest/data/intercensal/state/state2010.html (accessed November 15, 2011).

———. 2011b. "Missouri–Wyoming." Excel table 09sslstab1b.xls, State and Local Government Finance, 2009 State and Local Government. October 24. www.census.gov/govs/estimate (accessed July 18, 2012).

———. 2011c. "U.S. Summary and Alabama–Mississippi." Excel table 08sslstab1a.xls, State and Local Government Finance, 2008 State and Local Government. October 14. www.census.gov//govs/estimate/historical_data_2008.html (accessed July 18, 2012).

———. 2011d. "U.S. Summary and Alabama–Mississippi." Excel table 09sslstab1a.xls, State and Local Government Finance, 2009 State and Local Government. October 24. www.census.gov/govs/estimate/ (accessed July 18, 2012).

———. 2003a. *Statistical Abstract of the United States*. Washington, DC: U.S. Government Printing Office.

———. 2003b. "Income, Poverty, and Health Insurance Coverage in the United States: 2003." *Current Population Reports* (August).

———. 2003c. *Dynamics of Economic Well-Being: Poverty, 1996–1999*. Washington, DC: U.S. Government Printing Office.

———. 1989. *Statistical Abstract of the United States*. Washington, DC: U.S. Government Printing Office.

U.S. Department of Education, National Center for Education Statistics. 2005. "Chapter 1: All Levels of Education." In *Digest of Education Statistics, 2004*. Report NCES 2006-005, October.

———. 2005. "Section I. Elementary and Secondary Enrolment." In *Projections of Education Statistics to 2014*. 33d ed. Report NCES 2005-074, September.

U.S. Office of Management and Budget. 2012. "Historical Tables: Table 15.3—Total Government Expenditures as Percentages of GDP: 1948–2011." http://www.whitehouse.gov/omb/budget/Historicals (accessed June 16, 2012).

Van Buren, Peter. 2011. *We Meant Well: How I Helped Lose the Battle for the Hearts and Minds of the Iraqi People*. New York: Metropolitan Books/Henry Holt.

Van der Heijden, Kees. 2005. *Scenarios: The Art of Strategic Conversations*. Essex, UK: Wiley.

Van der Heijden, Kees, Ron Bradfield, George Burt, George Cairns, and George Wright. 2002. *The Sixth Sense: Accelerating Organizational Learning with Scenarios*. Hoboken, NJ: Wiley.

Van Maanen, John. 1976. "Breaking In: Socialization to Work." In *Handbook of Work, Organization, and Society,* ed. R. Dubin, 67–130. Chicago, IL: Rand McNally.

Van Riper, Paul P. 1983. "The American Administrative State: Wilson and the Founders—An Unorthodox View." *Public Administration Review* 43(6), 477–490.

———. 1958. *History of the United States Civil Service*. Evanston, IL: Row, Peterson.

Van Wart, Montgomery. 2001. *Human Resource Management in Public Service*. Thousand Oaks, CA: Sage.

Verant, Amy. 2001. Interview with Doug Morgan. Oregon Office of the Attorney General, Salem, Oregon, May 3.

Vickers, Geoffrey. 1965. *The Art of Judgment: A Study of Policymaking*. London, UK: Chapman and Hall.

Vinzant, Janet Coble, and Lane Crothers. 1998. *Street-Level Leadership: Discretion and Legitimacy in Frontline Public Service*. Washington, DC: George Washington University Press.

Vo, Lam Thuy 2012. "50 Years of Government Spending in 1 Graph." National Public Radio. http://www.npr.org/blogs/money/2012/05/14/152671813/50-years-of-government-spending-in-1-graph (accessed December 31,2012).

Volcker, Paul A. 2003. *Urgent Business for America: Revitalizing the Federal Government for the 21st Century*. Report of the National Commission on the Public Service. Washington, DC: Brookings Institution Press.

———. 1989. *Leadership for America: Rebuilding the Public Service*. Report of the National Commission on the Public Service. Washington, DC: Brookings Institution and American Enterprise Institute.

Vollmer, Howard M., and Donald L. Mills. 1966. *Professionalization*. Englewood Cliffs, NJ: Prentice Hall.

Vroom, Victor H., and P.W. Yetton. 1973. *Leadership and Decision Making*. Pittsburgh, PA: University of Pittsburgh Press.

Waldo, Dwight. 1948. *The Administrative State: A Study of the Political Theory of American Public Administration*. New York: Holmes and Meier.

Walker, David. 2007. *Saving Our Future Requires Tough Choices Today*. Fiscal Wake-Up Tour, University of Maryland, Baltimore County, October 29. Report No. GAO-08-241CG.

Walker, David Bradstreet. 1999. *The Rebirth of Federalism: Slouching Toward Washington*. 2d ed. New York: Seven Bridges.

———. 1981. *Toward a Functioning Federalism*. Cambridge, MA: Winthrop.

Walzer, Michael. 1992. "Political Action: The Problem of Dirty Hands." *Philosophy and Public Affair* 1(2), 118–228.

Wamsley, Barbara S. 1997. "Are Current Programs Working? Views from the Trenches." In *New Strategies for Public Pay: Rethinking Government Compensation Programs,* ed. Howard Risher and Charles H. Fay. San Francisco, CA: Jossey-Bass.

Wamsley, Gary L. 1985. "Policy Subsystems as a Unit of Analysis in Implementation Studies: A Struggle for Theoretical Synthesis." In *Policy Implementation in Federal and Unitary Systems: Questions for Analysis and Design*, ed. K. Hanf and T.A.J. Toonen, 71–96. Boston, MA: Martinus Nijhoff.

Wamsley, Gary L., Robert N. Bacher, Charles T. Goodsell, Phillip Kronenberg, John A. Rohr, Camilla M. Stivers, Orion F. White, and James F. Wolf. 1990. *Refounding Public Administration*. Newbury Park, CA: Sage.

Wamsley, Gary L., and Mayer N. Zald. 1973. *The Political Economy of Public Organizations*. Lexington, MA: D.C. Heath.

Wanat, John A. 1978. *Introduction to Budgeting*. Scituate, MA: Duxbury Press.

*Ware v. Hylton,* 3 U.S. 199 (1796).

Warshaw, Shirley Anne. 1996. *The Domestic Presidency: Policymaking in the White House*. Essex, UK: Longman.

Weatherford, James M. 2004. *Genghis Khan and the Making of the Modern World*. New York: Crown.

Weber, Max. 1924/1968. *Economy and Society*, ed. Guenther Roth and Claus Wittich. New York: Bedminster.

———. 1924/1947a. *The Theory of Social and Economic Organization*, trans. A.M. Henderson and Talcott Parsons, ed. Talcott Parsons. Glencoe, IL: Free Press.

———. 1904–1905/1947b. *The Protestant Ethics and the Spirit of Capitalism*, ed. Talcott Parsons. New York: Scribner's.

———. 1906–1924/1946. *From Max Weber: Essays in Sociology,* ed. H.H. Gerth and C. Wright Mills. New York: Oxford University Press.

Weick, Karl. 1979. *The Social Psychology of Organizing*. 2d ed. Reading, MA: Addison-Wesley.

Weimer, David, and Aidan R. Vining. 2004. *Policy Analysis: Concepts and Practices*. 4th ed. Englewood Cliffs, NJ: Prentice Hall.

*West Coast Hotel v. Parrish*, 300 U.S. 379 (1937).

Wheelan, Susan A., ed. 2005. *Handbook of Group Research and Practice*. Thousand Oaks, CA: Sage.

White, Leonard D. 1958. *The Republican Era: A Study in Administrative History, 1869–1901*. New York: Macmillan.

———. 1954. *The Jacksonians: A Study in Administrative History, 1801–1829.* New York: Macmillan.

———. 1951. *The Jeffersonians: A Study in Administrative History, 1801–1829.* New York: Macmillan.

———. 1948. *The Federalists: A Study in Administrative History, 1789–1801.* New York: Macmillan.

———. 1926. *Introduction to the Study of Public Administration.* New York: Macmillan.

White, William Allen. 1938. *A Puritan in Babylon.* New York: Macmillan.

Wholey, Joseph S., and Harry P. Hatry. 1992. "The Case for Performance Monitoring." *Public Administration Review* 52(6), 604–610.

Whyte, William H., Jr. 1956. *The Organization Man.* Garden City, NY: Doubleday.

Wildavsky, Aaron. 1993. *Speaking Truth to Power: The Art and Craft of Policy Analysis.* 2d ed. New Brunswick, NJ: Transaction.

———. 1988. "Ubiquitous Anomie: Public Service in an Era of Ideological Dissensus." *Public Administration Review* 48(4), 753–755.

———. 1984. *The Politics of the Budgetary Process.* 4th ed. Boston, MA: Little, Brown.

———. 1979. *Speaking Truth to Power: The Art and Craft of Policy Analysis.* Boston, MA: Little, Brown.

———. 1978. "A Budget for All Seasons." *Public Administration Review* 38(6), 501–509.

———. 1966. "The Political Economy of Efficiency: Cost-Benefit Analysis, Systems Analysis, and Program Budgeting." *Public Administration Review* 26(3), 292–310.

———. 1964. *The Politics of the Budgetary Process.* Boston, MA: Little, Brown.

Wilkins, Alan, and William G. Ouchi. 1983. "Efficient Cultures: Exploring the Relationship Between Culture and Organizational Performance." *Administrative Science Quarterly* 28(3), 468–481.

Wilkinson, Charles. 2005. *Blood Struggle: The Rise of Modern Indian Nations.* New York: Norton.

———. 2004. *Indian Tribes as Sovereign Governments.* 2d ed. Oakland, CA: American Indian Resource Institute.

Williams, Trefor P. 2003. "Moving to Public-Private Partnerships: Learning from Experience Around the World." In *The Procurement Revolution,* ed. Mark A. Abramson and Roland S. Harris III, 217–248. Lanham, MD: Rowman & Littlefield.

Williamson, Oliver E. 1981. "The Economics of Organization: The Transaction Cost Approach." *American Journal of Sociology* 87(3), 548–577.

Wilson, Gerald L. 2002. *Groups in Context: Leadership and Participation in Small Groups.* 6th ed. New York: McGraw-Hill.

Wilson, James Q. 1989. *Bureaucracy: What Government Agencies Do and Why They Do It.* New York: Basic Books.

Wilson, Woodrow. 1887/1996. "The Study of Public Administration." In *Classics of Public Administration,* ed. Jay Shafritz and Albert C. Hyde. 3d ed. Belmont, CA: Brooks/Cole, 1996. Originally published in *Political Science Quarterly* 2 (June 1887), 197–222.

Winter Commission. 1993. *Hard Truths/Tough Choices: An Agenda for State and Local Reform.* Albany, NY: National Commission on the State and Local Public Service and the Nelson A. Rockefeller Institute of Government.

Wisdom, Harold W., and David J. Brooks. 2001. "International Forest Resources Agreements: A Primer." *Journal of Forestry* 99(10), 29–33.

Wolin, Sheldon S. 1989. *The Presence of the Past: Essays on the State and the Constitution.* Baltimore, MD: Johns Hopkins University Press.

———. 1960. *Politics and Vision: Continuity and Innovation in Western Thought.* Boston, MA: Little, Brown.

Wood, Gordon S. 1973. *The Confederation and the Constitution: The Critical Issues.* Boston, MA: Little, Brown.

———. 1969. *The Creation of the American Republic, 1776–1787.* Chapel Hill: University of North Carolina Press.

Woodward, Joan. 1965. *Industrial Organization: Theory and Practice.* London, UK: Oxford.

Wright, Deil S. 1988. *Understanding Intergovernmental Relations.* 3d ed. Pacific Grove, CA: Brooks/Cole.

*Wyeth v. Levine,* 555 U.S. 555 (2009).

Yaffee, Steven Lewis. 1994. *The Wisdom of the Spotted Owl: Policy Lessons for a New Century.* Washington, DC: Island.

Yang, Kaifeng, and Mark Holzer. 2006. "The Performance-Trust Link: Implications for Performance Measurement." *Public Administration Review* 66(1), 114–126.

Yin, Robert K. 2003. *Applications of Case Study Research.* 2d ed. Thousand Oaks, CA: Sage.
———. 1984. *Case Study Research: Design and Methods.* Beverly Hills, CA: Sage.
Yin, Robert K., and Donald T. Campbell. 2002. *Case Study Research: Design and Methods.* Thousand Oaks, CA: Sage.
Young, Mary B. 2005. *Building the Leadership Pipeline in Local, State, and Federal Government.* Washington, DC: CPS Human Resource Services. www.cps.ca.gov/documents/resources/CPS_Pipeline_8.23.05.pdf (accessed January 15, 2012).
———. 2003. *The Aging-and-Retiring Government Workforce: How Serious Is the Challenge? What Are Jurisdictions Doing About It?* Lexington, MA: The Center for Organizational Research.
Yukl, Gary A. 2012. *Leadership in Organizations.* 8th ed. Englewood Cliffs, NJ: Prentice Hall.
———. 1981. *Leadership in Organizations.* Englewood Cliffs, NJ: Prentice Hall.

# INDEX

*Italic* page references indicate charts, graphs, or boxed text.

ABA, 62
Ability to pay principle, 286
Accountability. *See also* Legal accountability; Political
    accountability
  advisory committees, 436–437
  conflict, 448–449
  democratic, 448, *449*
  ethics and, 437–438
  executive-centered approach to, 416–417, 420–421
  Executive Order 12866 and, 416–417, *419–420*
  in external relationships, maintaining
    background information, 438–441
    collaborative networks of community partners,
      447–448
    grants and negotiated contracts, 443–445
    intergovernmental agreements, 441–442
    issues, enduring, 448–449
    public-private partnerships, 445–446
    sealed-bid defined-service contracts, 442–443
  financial, 320–321
  internalized standards of conduct and, 438
  legislative-centered approach to, 421–425
  maintaining, 463–464
  managerial, 321
  mechanisms, 105, 131
  negotiated rules and, 436–437
  open government and, 153
  open records laws and, 437
  organizational, *415*, 425–427
  overview, 413–415, *415*
  principle, 114, 131
ACLU, 68
Action planning, 409
Actor-based policy process model, 393–395, *394*
Adair, Douglas, 204
Adjudication, administrative, 436
Administrative accountability. *See* Accountability
Administrative change, understanding, 43–44

Administrative discretion
  abuses of, 67–68, *69*
  bureaucratic sensibility and, 68–70
  historical perspective of, 51
  leadership and, 65–66
  in nonprofit organizations, 51–52, 65–66
  organizational culture and, 68–70
  types of, 60–65
  ubiquity of, 52–60
Administrative efficiency, 107–108, 112–113
Administrative law, 10, 12–13
Administrative practice
  institutional perspective of, 42–49, *45*
  legitimacy of, 37–40
  reflective, 49–50
  tacit knowledge in, 41–42
  understanding, 41
Administrative Procedure Act (1947), 429, 434
Administrative responsibility
  accountability principle and, 131
  bureaucratic politics and, 154, 159–161
  constitutional-legal responsibility, 137–141
  Democratic Balancewheel model of, 131, 145–148, *147*
  democratic citizenship, 141–145
  ethical values and, 131
  ethics and, 131, 437–438
  formal-legal responsibility, 136–137
  matters covered under, 130
  ministerial versus discretionary responsibility under
    law, 135–136
  overview, 130–131, 162
  personal ethics and, *155–159*
  public ethics and, 131
  public morality and, 131
  rule by law, 135
  theories, 132–134
Administrative state
  beginning of, 104
  decline of, 118–122
  rise of, 109–118, *111*

Administrative theory, 5
Advisory committees, 436–437
Advocacy, 395, *396*, 400–402
Advocacy coalition policy process model, 395, *396*
AEC, 421
Affirmative action, 219–220, 235
AFSCME, 214, 251
Agency competencies, 228
Agenda setting, 390, *391*
Agricultural policy, 387, 392–393
Allison, Graham, 190
AMA, 62
Ambiguity and budget actors, 329
American Bar Association (ABA), 62
American Civil Liberties Union (ACLU), 68
American Federation of State, County, and Municipal
    Employees (AFSCME), 214, 251
American Medical Association (AMA), 62
American Recovery and Reinvestment Act (ARRA)
    (2009), 274, 296
American Revolution, 8, 76, 90
American Society of Public Administration (ASPA), 438
*American Tradition Partnership, Inc. v. Steve Bullock*
    (2012), 15
Anti-Federalists, 77, 77–83, 109, 139–140, 142, 230, 386
Appraisal, employee, 248–250
Arendt, Hannah, 17
Argyris, Chris, 49–50
Aristotle, 5, 141, 386
Arizona, 338
ARRA (2009), 274, 296
Articles of Confederation, 76–77, 84, 146, 380
ASPA, 438
Assets, revenue from, 280
Assimilation, 456
At-will employment status, 224, 237
Atomic Energy Commission (AEC), 421
Austrian School of economists, 221
Autonomy, 151–152
Available fund balance, 276–278, 281

*Bakke v. Board of Regents of California* (1978), 226
Balance carried forward, 281
Balancing test between agency interests and employee
    rights, 239
Banking industry, 385
Bardach, Eugene, 448
Barnard, Chester, 181, 234
Base budget, 325–326
Bay of Pigs fiasco, 219
Beginning balance, 281
Benefits, employee, 243–244, 246–247
Benefits received principle, 286
Best practice requirements in public policy, 398
BIA, 460
Bill of Rights, 12, 14, 485–486
Blake and Mouton grid, 360, *361*
Blake, Robert, 360, *361*
Bonds, 299–300
Born, Brooksley, 369–370
Bottom-up perspective, 67

Boundary-spanning leadership, 184, 352
Bowling Alone (Engaged Citizen) problem, 84–85, 93,
    130, 146
"Browning" of America, 457
Brownlow Committee Report (1937), 111–113, 120, 132,
    134, 214–215
Brownlow, Louis, 111
Bryson, John M., 351–352, 363–364
Budgets
    actors, 327–329, *330*
    base, 325–326
    centralized control of, 425–426
    consequences of multiple, 322–323
    cycle, 323–326, *324*
    Democratic Balancewheel model and, 313
    effectiveness measures and, 355
    efficiency measures and, 335
    executive-centered, 324–325
    formats
        comparing, *340–341*
        line-item (object code), 331–332, *332*, 342
        overview, 314, 330–331, 342
        performance budgeting, 334–337, *336*
        planning-programming-budgeting system, 333–334,
            *334*
        program budgeting, 333–334, *334*
        zero-base budgeting, 316, 337–338, *338*, *339*
    future of democratic governance and, 342–343
    government, 305–307, 323–326
    historical perspective of, 314–317
    influence on economy, 321–322
    nonprofit sector, 277, 306–307, 317–318
    overview, 312–314
    process, 323–326, *324*
    purposes of, 317–321, *330*
    rules of public, 325
Burden of proof, required, 431–434, *432*
Bureau of Indian Affairs (BIA), 460
Bureau of Reclamation, 107
Bureaucracy
    competing roles of, 448–449
    distrust of, 34
    evaluation of, 53, *53*
    features of, 178
    sensibility, varieties of, 68–70
    street-level bureaucrats, 52–54
Bureaucratic model of justice, 69–70, *70*
Bureaucratic theory, 177–178
Burke, John, 136–137, 145, 154
Burns, James McGregor, 362
Burr, Aaron, 204
Bush, George H.W., 416
Bush, George W., 99, 258, 336, 394, 417, 461
Business agenda, 463
Business and occupation (B&O) taxes, 288–289
Business model, 179

CAFE standards, 392
Cafeteria plan of benefits, 246–247
Caiden, Naomi, 342
Caldwell, Lynton, 204

California, 290, 320
California Integrity Act (2004), 320
Canada, 456–457
Capacity building, 184
Capital project funds, 306
"Capricious advice" sin of public policy, 410
Career administrators, 37
Career public servants, 3–4, 21, 343
Career systems, 253–254
Carnegie, Andrew, 103, 359
Carter, Jimmy, 214, 221–222, 316
Carver, John, 363
Case analysis, 406
Case law, 13
Case studies
  Department of Environmental Quality, 427–429
  Eagle Rock, 347–349, 372–373
  Gomez, Juan, 466–467
  Medler School District system, 265–269, 272, 275, 288, 321, 343
  Prairie County, 167–172, 175, 183–184, 187, 189, 192–196, 236, 247, 256–257
  public library, 27–32, 37, 148–149, 372
  Vision Action Network, 465, 470–471
Cash flows, smoothing out, 299
Catalytic leadership, 363
CBO, 316
CBP, 67–68
Centralized budget control, 425–426
Centralized organizational control, 426–427
Centralized personnel control, 426
Centralized policy control, 425
CFTC, 369
Challenges of public service
  continuities in conflict, 49–50
  institutional perspective, 42–49, 45
  irony of American democratic governance, 34–36
  leadership, 352–362
  legitimacy of administrative practice, 37–40
  overview, 34, 36
  reflective administrative practice, 49–50
  scenarios, 33–34
  tacit knowledge in administrative practice, 41–42
  understanding administrative practice, 41
Chandler (Arizona), 338
Character, appropriate, 201, 202–203, 204, 206–207, 209–210, 213, 220, 224, 229–230
Charitable giving, 46, 273–274, 300–301
Charles I (English king), 75
Chicago School of economists, 221
Chisolm v. Georgia (1793), 96
Cities, expansion of, 116, 118
Citizens United v. Federal Elections Commission (2010), 15
Citizenship, democratic, 141–145
Civic capacity, 48–49
Civic engagement, 142, 152
Civic governance tradition, 146
"Civic-mindedness," 80
Civic republic tradition, 77–83
Civil Rights Act (1964), 217–218

Civil rights movement, 216–221
Civil Service Commission (CSC), 218–219, 222
Civil Service Reform Act (CSRA) (1978), 132, 214, 221–222, 225, 237
Civil service status, 236
Civil society, 47–49, 48
Civil War, 101
Clayton Act (1914), 107
Clean Water Act, 395
Cleveland Board of Education v. Loudermill (1985), 239
Client perspective, 67
Clientele politics, 392, 393
Clinton, Bill, 118–119, 226, 416–417
Coalition for a Livable Future, 188
Code of Ethics, 438
Cold war era, 217
Collaborative agreements, 439
Collaborative networks, 447–448
Collective bargaining, 250–251
Collective preference approach, 121
Collective system, 255
Collins, Courtney, 35
Commercial banks, 385
Commercial republic
  constructing, 380–382
  excesses of, 386–387
Commission on Economy and Efficiency (Taft Commission), 315
Commission system, 420
Commissions, civil service status and, 236
Commodity Futures Trading Commission (CFTC), 369
Common good, 74
Common law, 10, 13
Common-pool goods, 382
Common school funds, 307
Community Action Program, 64
Community capacity, 47–49, 48
Community, fostering, 142–143
Community partners, collaborative networks of, 447–448
Community perspective, 67
Community planning process, 467–469
Compensation, employee, 243–245
Competencies of generalists, 160
Competition, 103
Comprehensive planning, 408–409
Compromise, 161
Conception of rights, 109–110
Conciliatory practice, 364–366
Conflict
  accountability, 448–449
  budget actors and, 329
  continuities in, 49–50, 52, 126–127, 465–470
  organizational, 187–188
Conflicting values, managing, 375–376, 376
Congressional Budget and Impoundment Control Act (1974), 316
Congressional Budget Office (CBO), 316
Consent agenda, 463
Constituency-based policy, 393, 393
Constituent service perspective, 335

Constitutional approach to public administration
  career public servants and, focus on, 3–4
  in democratic republic, 4–6
  doctrinal and formalistic, 17, *19*
  equality and, 7–9
  functionalist, 17, *19*
  Hamilton and, 3
  historical, *20*, 21
  law and
      administrative, 10, 12–13
      common, 12
      constitutional, 10–12
      functions of, in public life, 13–16
      ordered liberty and, 9
      public institutions and, 9–10
      statutory, 10, 12
  meaning of, 16–17, 21
  methodological, *20*, 21
  ordered liberty and, 6–9
  overview, 3
  process-centered, 17, *19*
  regime-centered, 17, *18*
  structuralist, 17, *19*
  typology, 17, *18–20*
  value-centered, 17, *18*
"Constitutional everyman," 76
Constitutional law, 10–12
Constitutional-legal perspective, 67
Constitutional-legal responsibility, 137–141
Constitutional sovereignty, 151
Constitutive legitimacy, 40
Contingency theories, 183–187, 360–362, 364
Continuities in conflict, 49–50, 52, 126–127, 465–470
Contract employment status, 238
Contracting process, 463
Contracts, 238, 400, 442–445
Contractual services employment system, 256–257
Cook, Brian, 144–146
Coolidge, Calvin, 211, 226
Cooper, Phillip, 138, 187, 189, 413
Cooper, Terry, 141–143, 145–146, 150, 159
Cooperation, 103
Cooperative system, 234
Corbally, John, 191
Corporate income taxes, 288–289
Cost-benefit analysis, 399, 403–404, *418*
Cost-effectiveness analysis, 399
Cost-of-living adjustments, 245
Council-manager model of local government, 108
County 2012 Plan, 40
Crassus, Lucius (pseudonym for Alexander Hamilton),
  204
Crenson, Matthew, 206–207
Critical Path Method (CPM), 179
Croley, Steven, 385
Croly, Herbert, 108
Crosby, Barbara C., 351–352, 363–364
Crumpton, Charles David, 188
CSC, 218–219, 222
CSRA (1978), 132, 214, 221–222, 228, 237
Cuban Missile Crisis, 190

Culture, organizational, 68–70
Cycle-centered policy process models, 390–392, *391*
Cyert, Richard, 190

Dairy price supports, 392–393
*Dartmouth College v. Woodward* (1819), 14, 95–96
Darwin, Charles, 103
Davis, Kenneth Culp, 51, 65
Debt instruments, 281, 299–300
Debt service funds, 306–307
Decision making
  backroom, 393–394
  indecision and, 159–160
  iron triangle and, 393–394
  law and, 9
  leadership and, 377
  participative, 256
  patterns of decisions and, 190
  programs and, 190
  public policy and, *401*, 403–404, *404*
  rational choice and, 224, 398–399
Decision matrix, 397, *398*
Decision tree, 404, *404*, *405*
Declaration of Independence, 7–8, 272
Dedicated funds/revenue, 279, 281, 306
*Delaware v. Prouse* (1979), 135
Delivering the goods, 318–319
Democratic accountability, 448, *449*
Democratic Balancewheel model
  of administrative responsibility, 131, 145–148, *147*
  application of, 148–149
  basis of, 7
  budgets and, 313
  career public servants and, 21
  future of American public administration and, 452, 454
  government role and, 272
  liberty and, 7
  of public administration, 17, 21, 138–139, 145–149, *147*
  public policy and, 379, 401
Democratic citizenship, 141–145
Democratic republic
  administration and, 72–74, 85, 87
  constitutional approach to public administration in, 4–6
  debates, founding
      Anti-Federalists and civic republic tradition, 79–80
      Federalists and procedural republic tradition, 78–79
      implications of, administrative, 80–83, 100
      overview, 75–78
  direct democracy and, 98–99, 105
  English roots of American, 74–75
  equality in, 7–9
  Founding Beatitudes of American, 85
  in Greece, 77
  irony of American democratic governance, 34–36
  liberty and, 6–9, 83–85, *86*
  ordered liberty in, 6–9
  politics in, 6
  public administration in, 4–6
  representation through rotation of office and, 98–99
  virtues, 80
Demographic diversity, growing, 455–457

Demotivators, 181–182
Department of Environmental Quality (DEQ) case study, 427–429
Department of Labor (DOL), 239
Department of Natural Resources (DNR), 176
Department of Social Service (DSS), 168–172, 182, 191–192
DEQ case study, 427–429
Diesing, Paul, 312
Direct democracy, 98–99, 105
Disability policies, 400
Discretion. *See* Administrative discretion
Discretionary funds, 306
Discretionary powers, 253
Discretionary responsibility, 135–136
Diseconomies of collective action, 45
"Distant advice" sin of public policy, 410
Distributive policy, 62, *62*, *63*, 392, *393*
Diversity, 8–9, 455–457
DNR, 176
Dobel, J. Patrick, 159, 161
DOL, 239
*Dolan v. Tigard* (1994), 15
Donations, 273–274, 300–301
Dot-com boom (late 1990s), 240
"Double security" against tyranny, 148
Downs, Anthony, 312
DSS, 168–172, 182, 191–192
Duane, William, 99
Due process law, 104, 153
Dunsire, Andrew, 186
Durkeheim, Emile, 177

E-government, 464–465
Eagle Rock case study, 347–349, 372–373
Earned income, 277
Ecological level of analysis, 176
Economic opportunity, 8
Economic Opportunity Act (1964), 110
Economic Policy Institute, 458
Economic regulation, 383, *384*, 385, *385*
Economic well-being, 8
EEO policy, 217, 219–220, 235
Effectiveness measures, 355
Efficiency, administrative, 107–108, 112–113
Efficiency measures, 335
Eisenhower, Dwight D., 215–216, 394
Elazar, Daniel J., 395
Elected officials, 16
Electrical power supply maintenance, 353, *355*
Eleventh Amendment, 96
Ellis, Deborah "Debbie," 154, *155–159*
Employees. *See also* Recruitment and selection of employees
    balancing test between agency interests and rights of, 239
    compensation and benefits of, 243–247
    knowledge, skills, and abilities of, 240
    knowledge workers, 223
    performance and appraisal of, 248–250
    rights and restrictions of, 239

Employees *(continued)*
    status of, 235–238
    temporary, 238
    training and development of, 247–248, *248*
Employment Act (1946), 216
Employment contracts, union and individually negotiated, 238
Employment status, 235
Employment systems, 235
Energetic governance tradition, 146
Energy in the executive principle, 91, 98
Engaged Citizen (Bowling Alone) problem, 84–85, 93, 130, 146
English Restoration (1677), 75
Enterprise funds, 306–307
Entitlement programs, 109–110. *See also specific name*
Entrepreneurial politics, 393, *393*
Environmental Protection Agency (EPA), 63
"Envisioning process," 465, 470–471
EPA, 63
Equal Employment Opportunity Act (1972), 218
Equal employment opportunity (EEO) policy, 217, 219–220, 235
Equal Pay Act (1963), 218
Equal protection clause, 12
Equality in democratic republic, 7–9
"Equality problem," 8–9
Equity principle and concept, 114, 244
Espoused theory, 49, 125, *125*, 417, *417*
Ethic of neutrality, 154
Ethic of structure, 154
Ethical responsibility, 162. *See also* Administrative responsibility
Ethical values, 131
Ethics, 131, *155–159*, 437–438
Ethnic diversity, growing, 8–9, 455–457
Etzioni, Amitai, 234
Evidence, preponderance of, 431–434
Excludability, goods and, 382
Executive-centered administration, 110–113
Executive-centered approach to accountability, 416–417, 420–421
Executive-centered budgeting, 324–325
Executive-centered performance systems, 337
Executive dominance, 132
Executive Order 11246 (1965), 218
Executive Order 12866, 416–417, *419–420*, 431
Executive, refortifying, 139
Expectancy theory, 245
Experimentation, 406, *407*, 408
External compliance mechanisms, 186
External equity concept, 244
External relationships, maintaining accountability in
    background information, 438–441
    collaborative networks of community partners, 447–448
    grants and negotiated contracts, 443–445
    intergovernmental agreements, 441–442
    issues, enduring, 448–449
    public-private partnerships, 445–446
    sealed-bid defined-service contracts, 442–443
Externalities of collective action, 45

Fair Labor Standards Act (FLSA), 239
Fair share, 325–326
Fairness, 37–38, 317, 443
Fannie Mae, 462
Fayol, Henri, 179
Federal Highway Trust Fund, 306
Federal Labor Relations Authority (FLRA), 222, 251
*Federal Register*, 429
Federal Reserve Board, 92
Federal Tariff Commission Act (1916), 107
Federalism, 15
*Federalist Papers, The*, 6, 90–91, 96, 137, 200, 422
Federalists, 77–83, 109, 139–140, 380
Fees for services, 279, 293–295, 301
Fiduciary funds, 307
Fifth Amendment, 434
Financial accountability, 320–321
Finer, Herman, 136, 145, 413, 435
First Amendment, 14–15
Fiscal crisis, permanent, 458–459
"Fishbowl" condition, 153
Fisher, Louis, 258
"Fit character" concept, 201, 229. *See also* Character,
    appropriate
Flat tax, 286
Florida, 237
FLRA, 222, 251
FLSA, 239
FOIA, 437
Follett, Mary Parker, 181, 220
For cause employment status, 224, 236–238
For-profit sector, 39, 45, 277. *See also specific*
    *organization*
Forestry Division, 176
Formal-legal responsibility, 136–137
Founding Beatitudes, 50, 85, 367
Founding era (1789-1828), 94–97, 201, 204–206
Fourteenth Amendment, 12, 104, 380
France, 73
Franklin, Grace A., 393
Freddie Mac, 462
Freedom of Information Act (FOIA), 437
Friedrich, Carl J., 136, 413, 423, 435
Friedrich-Finer debate, 413–414, 448
"Front door" issues, 393
Frontline service providers, 52–54
Fukuyama, Francis, 33–34
Full Employment Act (1946), 286
Full Employment and Balanced Growth Act (1978), 286
Fundraising, 275, 300–303
Future of American public administration
    confounding lines among public, nonprofit, and private
        sectors, 461–464
    continuities in conflict and, 464–470
    Democratic Balancewheel model and, 452, 454
    drivers of change
        diversity, growing demographic, 455–457
        fiscal crisis, permanent, 458–459
        governmental jurisdictions, proliferation of, 461
        income inequality, growth of, 457–458
        managing for results, emphasis on, 458–459

Future of American public administration
    drivers of change *(continued)*
        Native American Indian tribes, rising importance
            of, 459–460
        overview, 454
        structures of authority, overlapping, 461
        technology, 464–465
        tribal governments, rising importance of, 459–460
        workforce changes, 454–455
    overview, 452–454
    polity leadership in service of democratic governance,
        470–471

Gainsharing, 245
Gaming revenue, 280, *296*
GAO, 454
Gates, Bill, 359
General Accountability Office (GAO), 454
General civil service systems, 254
General fund revenue, 278, 281, 306
General government services, 279
General obligation bonds, 299
General will principle, 73–74
Generalists, 160
George (English king), 84
George Washington problem, 84, 130, 146, 199
Georgia, 237
"Getting in a rut" sin of public policy, 410
*Gibbons v. Ogden* (1824), 96
Gilded Age (ca. 1870-1900), 102–103, 207–211
Glidewell, John, 167
Goal displacement, 178
Goals, organizational, 189–190
Goggin, M.A., 395
Gomez, Juan, 466–467
"Good citizenship" traditions, 82–83, *83*
Good service and "good service" problems, 39–40, 56,
    59
Goodnow, Frank J., 132–134
Goods
    common-pool, 382
    delivering, 318–319
    excludability and, 382
    private, 382–383
    public, 45, 382–383
    toll, 382
    typology of, 382, *383*
Goodsell, Charles, 33–34, 52–53, 81
Gore, Al, 417
Governance, democratic
    access tradition, 146
    budget actors' role in, 329
    budget task and, 342–343
    budgets and future of, 342–343
    civic tradition, 146
    competencies, 228
    competent tradition, 146
    constitutional, 366–373
    effective, 152
    energetic tradition of, 146
    fairness of, 37

Governance, democratic *(continued)*
  irony of, 34–36
  minority rights tradition, 146
  networks, 187–189, *188*
  polity leadership in, 470–471
  responsive tradition, 146
  structures, 187, *188*
Governing bodies, 420. *See also specific name*
Government. *See also specific agency or state*
  accountability and open, 153
  administrative law and, 10, 12–13
  balance between states and federal, 96, 100
  budget, 305–307, 323–326
  checks and balances in, 313
  common law and, 10, 13
  constitutional law and, 10–12
  Democratic Balancewheel model and role of, 272
  English roots of, 74–75
  espoused theory of, 417, *417*
  evaluation of, 53, *53*
  expansion of federal, 107, 109–110, *117*, 211
  hard power of, 47
  limited, 14–15, 46, 98–99, 226
  local, 108, 115–118, *117*, 133, 148, 289
  military spending and, 315–316
  in New Deal era, 109–110, *117*, 397
  open, 153
  private-sector business principles and, 120
  public administration and, 132
  reinventing, 64–65, 91, 226, 462
  revenue types in budgeting, 278–282, *282*
  scandals, 102, 221
  separation of powers and, 112, 133, 313
  services, general, 279
  soft power of, 47
  state, 288, 337
  statutory law and, 10, 12
  technology and, 464–465
  theory in action and, 421–425, *422*
  tribal, 459–460
  "visible hand" of, 382
Government Performance and Results Modernization Act
    (GPRMA) (2010), 336
Government-sponsored enterprises (GSEs), 462
Governmental jurisdictions, proliferation of, 461
GPRMA (2010), 336
Grant, Ulysses S., 102
Grants, 301, 443–445
"Graying" of America, 457
Great Britain, 73, 121
Great Depression (1930s), 134, 213, 315
Great Recession (2008), 92, 226, 228, 247, 274, 296, 370,
    459
Great Society, 110, 216–221
Greece, democratic republic in, 77
"Green necklace" park plan, 357, *358*
Greenspan, Alan, 369
Gretzky, Wayne, 369
Gross, Edward, 234
Group-centered leadership theory, 359–360, 364
GSEs, 462

Guaranteed debt, 299
Gulick, Luther, 134, 179–180

Haas, Glenn, *432*
Hamilton, Alexander, 3, 5–6, 74, 78, 91–92, 94–96, 104,
    141, 204, 271–272, 312, 378–379, 386
Hamiltonian model of administration, 92–93, 98, 379
Hard power, 47
Hargrove, Erwin, 167
Hart, David K., 196–197, 209
Hatch Act (1939), 239
Hawthorne Effect, 180, 408
Health care benefits, 246
Health care initiative, national, 15
Heinz, John, 61
Herranz, Joaquin, Jr., 447
Herzberg, Frederick, 181–182
Hidden agenda, 424
Hierarchy of needs, 181–182, *182*
Historical analysis, 406
Historical perspective of public administration
  evolution of public administration as field of study and
      practice, 122–124, *123*
  founding era (1789-1828), 94–97
  Jacksonian era (1829-1869), 97–100
  models of
      Hamiltonian, 92–93, 98, 379
      Jeffersonian, 93–95, 98
      Madisonian, 90–91, 379
      overview, 90
      Washingtonian, 91–92
  New Deal era (1933-1976), 109–118
  New Entrepreneurialism era (1976-present),
      118–122
  overview, 89–90, 124–127
  Populist reform era (1869-1910), 100–105
  Progressive reform era (1910-1921), 105–109
  role during national and state building, 122
Homestead steel strike (1892), 104
Hoosier National Forest (Indiana), 368
Hoover Commission Report, 120, 132, 214–215
Hoover, Herbert, 211
Horizontal equity of taxes, 286
Horowitz, Donald, 68
House Concurrent Resolution 108, 460
HRM. *See* Human Resources Management
Hult, Karen, 173, 186–187, 189, 192, 196
Human Capital Development, 235. *See also* Human
    Resources Management (HRM)
Human relations movement, 180–183
Human Resources Management (HRM)
  changes in mission and philosophy of, 233–235
  collective bargaining and, 250–251
  cooperative system, creating, 234
  employee recruitment and selection
      compensation and benefits, 243–247
      job analysis, design, and classification, 242–243
      overview, 240, *241*
      performance and appraisal, 248–250
      position planning, management, and design, 242
      training and development, 247–248, *248*

Human Resources Management (HRM) *(continued)*
    functions of, 233–239
    "gaming" personnel rules and, 234
    new movement to recast, 235
    overview, 233, 259–260
    public service as political community and, 251–259
    unions and, 250–251
Huntsman, Jon, 236–237
Hyperpluralism, 75, 356

ICC, 104
Idealism, organic, 106
IGAs, 438, 441–442
Ignorance of legislature, 424
IGR policy process models, 395, 397
Illumination study, 180
Impulse of popular passions and fads, 367
Income inequality, growth of, 457–458
Incrementalism, 325–326, 331, 399
Indecision, 159–160
Individual-centered leadership theory, 359, 364
Individual liberty, 7
Individualism, 354, 356
Initiative (recall mechanism), 105
Institution-centered leadership theory, 362
Institutional perspective of administrative practice,
    42–49, *45*
Instrumental approach to public administration, 4–5
Interdependence, 185
Interest-based policy process models, 392–393, *393*
Interest-group advocacy, 141–142
Interest-group liberalism, 230
Interest-group politics, 392, *393*
Interest groups, 141–142, 230, 356, 392
Interests
    deliberation over, ensuring, 463
    multiplicity of, 356
    private, 75, 78–79
    public, 74–75, 252, 463
Interfund transfer, 307
Intergovernmental agreements (IGAs), 438, 441–442
Intergovernmental relations (IGR) policy process models,
    395, 397
Intergovernmental transfers and revenue, 280, 295–299,
    *297*
Internal compliance mechanisms, 186
Internal equity concept, 244
Internal service funds, 307
Internalized standards of conduct, 438
Internet, 302–303, 437
Interstate Commerce Commission Act, 104
Interstate Commerce Commission (ICC), 104
Investment banks, 385
Iron triangle, 393–394
Issue framing, 400–402

Jackson, Andrew, 97–99, 109, 132, 206
Jacksonian era (1828-1869), 80, 97–100, 206–207
Jay, John, 74
Jefferson, Thomas, 93, 95, 379
Jeffersonian Community Building Model, 93–94

Jeffersonian model of administration, 93–94, 98
Jenkins-Smith, H., 395
Job Classification Act (1923), 210, 213
"Job-relatedness" criterion, 217
Jobs
    analysis, design, and classification of, 242–243
    position planning, management, and design of, 242
    rank-in-person system, 243
    rank-in-position system, 243
Johnson, Andrew, 208
Johnson, Lyndon B., 109–110, 118, 215, 218
Johnson, Ronald N., 211
Judicial review, 11
Jurisdictions, 356–357, 461
Justice, Mashaw's models of, 69–70, *70*

Karl, Barry, 452
Kendall, Amos, 132
*Kendall v. U.S., ex rel. Stokes* (1838), 132, 135
Kennedy, John F., 118, 190, 214–215, 217, 251, 316,
    397–398
King George problem, 84, 130, 146, 199
Knowledge, skills, and abilities (KSAs) of employees,
    240
Knowledge workers, 223

Labor unions, 250–251, 255–256
"Lack of timely advice" sin of public policy, 410
Lane, Larry M., 228
Larsen, Gary L., 389
Law. *See also* Administrative law; Constitutional
        approach to public administration; *specific name*
    codifying, 10
    decision making and, 9
    due process, 104, 153
    functions of, in public life, 13–16
    ordered liberty and, 9
    public institutions and, 9–10
    public morality and, 15–16
    rule by, 9, 135, 153
    types of
        administrative, 10, 12–13
        case, 13
        common, 10, 13
        constitutional, 10–12
        statutory, 10, 12
Leadership. *See also* Legacy leadership
    administrative discretion and, 65–66
    Blake and Mouton grid of, 360, *361*
    boundary-spanning, 184, 352
    catalytic, 363
    challenges of public service, 352–362
    commitment to process and, 376–377
    conciliatory practice and, 364–366, *366*, 376–377
    conflicting values and, managing, 375–376, *376*
    constitutional governance and, 366–373
    decision making and, 377
    Founding Beatitudes and, 367
    good, 359–360
    group-centered theory of, 359–360, 364
    individual-centered theory of, 359, 364

Leadership *(continued)*
  institution-centered theory of, 362
  organizational-centered theory of, 362
  overview, 351–352, 373
  plebiscitarian executive, 98–99
  polity, 8, 470–471
  of public institutions, 362–364
  public service as moral, 108–109
  results and, achieving
    electrical power supply maintenance, 353, *355*
    "green necklace" park plan, 357, *358*
    individualism, 354, 356
    interests, multiplicity of, 356
    jurisdictions, multiplicity of, 356–357
    leadership theories, 357, 359–362
    "mad cow" phenomenon, 353, *354*
    overview, 352–354, *354*
  shared power and, 352
  stakeholder analysis and, 374–375
  transactional, 362
  transformational, 362–363
  U.S. Constitution and, 353
  vision and, crafting, 364–365
Legacy leadership
  change and, facilitating, 369–370
  educative and advisory role, 370–373
  overview, 366–367
  protecting substantive values and governing design,
    367–369
Legal accountability
  adjudication, administrative, 436
  advisory committees, 436–437
  case demonstrating constraints on administrative work,
    427–429
  ethics and professional accountability, 437–438
  negotiated rules, 436–437
  open records laws, 437
  overview, *415*
  rule by law and, 135
  rulemaking, administrative, 429–436
Legal correctness, 38
Legislative-centered approach to accountability, 421–425
Legislative dominance, 132
Legislative Reorganization Act, 216
Legitimacy of administrative practice, 37–40
Lesser, Cara, 448
Lewis and Clark expedition, 95
Libecap, Gary D., 211
Libertarian interpretation of U.S. Constitution, 76–77
Liberty, 6–9, 83–85, *86*
Library case study, 27–32, 37, 148–149, 372
Licenses, sales of, 279
Light, Paul, 224–225, 229
Limited government movement, 14–15, 46, 98–99, 226
Lincoln, Abraham, 8, 359
Lindblom, Charles, 190, 399
Line-item budgeting (object code), 331–332, *332*, 342
Local government, 108, 115–118, *117*, 133, 148, 289. *See
    also speciific name*
Logrolling votes, 63
Longevity pay systems, 244

Lottery revenue, 280, *296*
Lowi, Theodore J., 61, 215, 392, 422
Luke, Jeffrey, 363
Lynn, Laurence, 226

"Mad cow" phenomenon, 353, *354*
Madison, James, 72, 74, 76, 137, 140–141, 148, 200, 422,
    464
Madisonian model of administration, 90–91, 379
Majoritarian politics, 393, *393*
*Malek Manuay* (1974), 221
Management theory, 108, 133, 177–185
Managerial agents, 414
Managers
  accountability, 321
  boundary spanning and, 184, 352
  capacity building and, 184
  differentiation among levels and types of, 185
  functions of, 184–185, *186*
  middle, 54–56, 184–185, *186*
  performance measurement of, 108
  senior, 56–60
  street-level, 52–54, 185
  Taylor's (Frederick) view of, 179–180, 209
  technical core, 52–54, 185
Managing for results, emphasis on, 458–459
Manufacturing sector, 101
*Marbury v. Madison* (1803), 11, 95
March, James, 190
Market-adjust pay levels, 245
Market economy, dominance and abuses of, 106
Market failures, 45
Market model of political community, 252
Marshall, John, 16, 96
Mashaw, Jerry, 69–70
Maslow, Abraham, 181–182
McCarthy hearings (1950s), 219
*McCulloch v. Maryland* (1819), 16, 96
McCullough, Thomas, 143, 387
McGregor, Douglas, 182–183
McNamara, Robert, 316
Meat Inspection Act (1906), 107
Meat packing industry, 106
Medicaid, 110
Medicare, 110
Medler School District system case study, 265–269, 272,
    275, 288, 321, 343
Meltsner, Arnold, 410
Memorandum of agreement (MOA), 441–442
Memorandum of understanding (MOU), 442
Merit, 201, *202–203*, 206, 208–209, 211–214, 218–219,
    224, 227–229
Merit pay, 244–245
Merit status, 236–237
Merit systems, 236, 244–245
Merit Systems Protection Board (MSPB), 222
Meritocracy, 201, 204
Merton, Robert, 178
Michigan, 288
Microsoft Corporation, 56
Middle managers, 54–56, 184–185, *186*

Military spending, 315–316
Mills (tax), 289
Milward, H. Brinton, 447
Ministerial responsibility, 135–136
Minority rights and access to governance tradition, 146
Mintzberg, Henry, 173, 196
MOA, 441–442
Modified zero-base budgeting, 337
Monopolies, 45
Moore, Mark, 121
Moral judgment model of justice, 69–70, 70
Moral leadership, public service as, 108–109
Morgan, Douglas F., 184–185, 330
Morgan, Gareth, 353
Morrill Acts (1862 and 1890), 209
Morton-Grodzins, 395
Mosher, Frederick, 213, 215, 253, 255, 258
Motivation, 181–182
Motivators, 181–182, 229
MOU, 442
Mouton, Jane, 360, 361
MSPB, 222
Multiculturalism, 456

NAACP v. Alabama (1958), 437
Nader, Ralph, 393
NAO, 447–448
National Bellas Hess case (1967), 291
National Bureau of Economic Research, 272
National Conference of State Legislatures (NCSL), 298
National Consumers' League (NCL), 107
National Federation of Independent Business, et al. v. Sebelius, Secretary of Health and Human Services, et al. (2012), 15
National Forest Service, 107
National Park Service, 107
National Performance Review Initiative, 416–417
Native American Indian tribes, 116, 459–460
NATO, 76
Natural monopolies, 45
NCL, 107
NCSL, 298
Negotiated contracts, 443–445
Negotiated rules, 436–437
Neoliberalism, 316
Network administrative organization (NAO), 447–448
Network analysis, 404
Neutral competence principle, 102, 106
Neutrality, ethic of, 154
New Deal era (1933-1976)
    cities and special districts in, 116, 118
    executive-centered administration and, 110–113
    federal government in, 109–110, 117, 397
    local government in, 115–118, 117
    nonprofit organizations in, 113–115
    overview, 109
    public personnel administration in, 211–216
New Entrepreneuralism era (1976-present)
    New Public Governance in, 119, 121–122
    New Public Management in, 119–121

New Entrepreneuralism era (1976-present) (continued)
    overview, 118–119
    public personnel administration in, 221–226
New institutionalism, 362
New Public Governance (NPG), 119, 121–122, 123, 124
New Public Management (NPM), 92, 119–122, 123, 124, 132, 224, 275, 414, 438, 462
New science of politics, 78
NGOs, 49
Nineteenth Amendment, 107
Nisar, Tahir M., 446
Nixon, Richard M., 64, 217, 421
Nixon-Watergate scandal, 221
No Child Left Behind Act (2001), 395
Nongovernmental organizations (NGOs), 49
Nonguaranteed debt, 299–300
Nonprofit sector. See also specific organization
    administrative discretion in, 51–52, 65–66
    budgets, 277, 306–307, 317–318
    challenges facing, 39
    charitable giving and, 46, 273–274, 300–301
    confounding lines among public and private sectors and, 461–464
    donations and, 273–274, 300–301
    expanding role of, 107, 113–115
    fundraising, 275, 300–303
    importance of, 46–47
    multiple purposes of organizations and, 175
    revenues, 300–302
    rise and transformation of, 107, 113–115
    Sarbanes-Oxley Act and, 321
    service standards and, 39
    vitality of, ensuring, 462–463
North Atlantic Treaty Organization (NATO), 76
NPG, 119, 121–122, 123, 124
NPM, 92, 119–122, 123, 124, 132, 224, 275, 414, 438, 462

Obama, Barack, 15, 226, 336, 453
Object code budgeting, 331–332, 332, 342
Occupational Safety and Health Act (OSHA), 239
"Occupy" demonstrations, 238
Off-road vehicle (ORV) policy, 368
Office of Management and Budget (OMB), 316, 417, 425, 427
Office of Personnel Management (OPM), 222
Office of Special Counsel (OSC), 222
Ogden, Daniel M., Jr., 395
Ohio, 238
Old-Age and Survivors Insurance Trust Fund (OASI). See Social Security
O'Leary, Rosemary, 159, 368–369
Olsen, Johan, 190
OMB, 316, 417, 425, 427
Open government, 153
Open records laws, 437
OPM, 222
Ordered liberty, 6–9
Oregon, 292–293, 338, 434–435
Oregon System, 105
Organic idealism, 106

Organizational-centered leadership theory, 362
Organizations. *See also specific name*
  as abstract units of analysis, 176
  accountability of, *415*, 425–427
  bureaucratic model of, 177–178, 180
  business model and, 179
  conflict and controversy, 187–188
  contingency theory and, 183–187
  control of, centralized, 426–427
  culture of, 68–70
  defining, 174
  goal displacement and, 178
  goals of, 189–190
  governance networks of, 187–189, *188*
  governance structures of, 187, *188*
  Hawthorne Effect and, 180
  human relations movement and, 180–183
  illumination study of, 180
  management theory and, 177–183
  multiple purposes of, 175
  outcomes and, 190
  outputs and, 190
  oversight in bureaucratic, 178
  overview, 173–175, 196–197
  perspective of, 67
  policy of, 187–189
  politics and, 187, 189–191
  Prairie County case and, 175, 183–184, 187, 189,
    192–196
  public administration traditions and, 191–192
  scientific management model of, 179–180
  standard operating procedures in, 178
  study of, 1761–1777
  theory of
    Barnard, 181
    development of formal, 177–180
    Follett, 181
    Gulick and Urwick, 179–180
    Herzberg, 181–182
    Maslow, 181–182
    McGregor, 182–183
    Taylor (Frederick), 179–180
    Weber, 177–178
  trained incapacity and, 178, 185
  uniform, myth of, 175
Orientation and budget actors, professional versus
  political, 328–329
ORV policy, 368
OSC, 222
OSHA, 239
Outcomes, 190
Outputs, 190, *388*, 389
"Overreacting to crises" sin of public policy, 410
Oversight, 178, 420

Pareto, Vilfredo, 177
PART, 417
Partial agency concept, 137–138, 200
Partial blending, 137
Participative decision making (PDM), 256
Partisan disagreement, 424

Patronage, 211–212
Pay broadbanding, 245
PDM, 256
Pendleton Act (1883), 102, 207–211, 223
Penn, William, 75
Perceived need, 434
Perceived theory, 125–126, *126*
Performance budgeting, 334–337, *336*
Performance, employee, 248–250
Performance measurement of managers, 108
Permits, sales of, 279
Personal ethics, *155–159*
Personal income taxes, 179, 288
Personal integrity, *155–156*
Personnel. *See* Public personnel administration
Perspective, organization, 67
Perspective, problem of, 67–68
PERT, 179
Pew Research Center, 456
Philanthropy. *See* Charitable giving; Fundraising
Planning, 408–409
Planning outcomes, institutionalizing, 469–470
Planning process, 467–469
Planning-programming-budgeting systems (PPBS),
  333–334, *334*
Plebiscitarian executive leadership, 98–99
Plunkitt, George Washington, 101–102
Pluralism, 90–91, 214–215, 356
Policy. *See also* Public policy; *specific type*
  agents, 414
  choices, 387–389, *388*
  dynamics, 387–390, *388*
  impacts, *388*, 389–390
  outputs, *388*, 389
  process analysis, 403
Policy implementation. *See* Accountability
Polis model of political community, 252
Political accountability
  to chief executive, 416–417, 420–421
  doctrine, 111–112
  to legislature, 421–425
  overview, 415–416, *415*
Political appointee system, 257–258
Political approach to public administration. *See*
  Constitutional approach to public administration
Political community, 47–49, *48*, 251–259
Political discretion, 63–64
Political ideas, proper, 201, *202–203*, 205, 207, 210,
  213–214, 231
Politics
  bureaucratic, 154, 159–161
  in democratic republic, 6
  interest-group, 392, *393*
  new science of, 78
  organizations and, 187, 189–191
  pluralistic, 214
  technocratic, 213
Polity leadership, 8, 470–471
Polity level perspective on public revenue and
  management, 303–304
Polity-making role of public administration, 44–47, *45*

Pooled interdependence, 185
Pope, Alexander, 330
Populist reform era (1869-1910), 100–105, 207–211
Pork barrel projects and policies, 61–62
POSDCORB, 134, 180
Power industry, 353, *355*
PPBS, 333–334, *334*
Practical judgment, 144
Practice concept, 150
Pragmatism, 106
Prairie County case study, 167–172, 175, 183–184, 187, 189, 192–196, 236, 247, 256–257
Preponderance of evidence, 431–434
President's Committee on Administrative Management, 111
Priority budgeting, 338
Private goods, 382–383
Private interests, 75, 78–79
Private sector, 39, 45, 120, 461–464. *See also specific organization*
Procedural republic tradition, 77–83
Process-centered policy process models, 390–392
Process legitimacy, 37–38
Procurement procedures, 443–444
Products, sales of, 280
Professional career system, 253–254
Professional discretion, 64–65
Professional perspective, 67
Professional treatment model of justice, 69–70, *70*
Program Assessment Rating Tool (PART), 417
Program budgeting, 333–334, *334*
Program Evaluation Review Technique (PERT), 179
Progressive reform era (1910-1921), 105–109, 179, 207–211, 397
Progressive taxes, 286
Project management, 409
Property taxes, 279, 289–290
Proportional taxes, 286
Proposition 13, 290
Proprietary funds, 306–307
Protection of rights, 153–154
Provan, Keith G., 447
Prudence, 144
Public administration. *See also* Constitutional approach to public administration; Future of American public administration; Historical perspective of public administration; *specific issues*
  administrative theory and, 5
  charitable giving, 273–274
  classic, 122, *123*
  constitutional foundations of American, 72–73
  constitutive aspect of, 144–146
  Democratic Balancewheel model of, 7, 21, 138–139, 145–149, *147*
  in democratic republic, 4–6
  donations, 273–274
  "equality problem" and, 8
  espoused theory, 49, 125, *125*
  evolution of as field of study and practice, 122–124, *123*
  government and, 132

Public administration *(continued)*
  instrumental approach to, 4–5
  overview, 21–23
  perceived theory, 125–126, *126*
  philosophies of, distinguishing characteristics of, 94, 122, *123*
  polity-making role of, 44–47, *45*
  practice concept in, 150
  pre-classic nation building, 122, *123*
  public morality and, 149–154
  skepticism toward, American, 452–453
  theory of action, 49–50, 124–125, *125*
  tradition and organizations, 191–192
  U.S. Constitution and, 10–12, 14
Public economies, 45
Public goods, 45, 382–383
Public institutions, 9–10, 362–364. *See also* Public library case study; *specific name*
Public interests, 74–75, 252, 463
Public Law 280, 460
Public library case study, 27–32, 37, 148–149, 372
Public morality, 15–16, 131, 149–154, *156–159*
Public personnel administration
  governance issues
    civil rights movement (1954-1976), 216–221
    Founding era (1789-1828), 201, 204–206
    Gilded era (1869-1921), 207–211
    Great Society (1954-1976), 216–221
    Jacksonian era (1829-1869), 206–207
    New Deal era (1933-1954), 211–216
    New Entrepreneurialism era (1976-present), 221–226
    overview, 200–201, *202–203*
    Populist reform era (1869-1921), 207–211
    Progressive reform era (1869-1921), 207–211
  implications for
    character, appropriate, 229–230
    merit, reframing, 227–229
    overview, 201, *202–203*, 227
    political ideals, proper, 231
    representativeness, 230–231
  overview, 199–200
Public policy. *See also* Accountability; *specific policy*
  advocacy and analysis of, 400–402
  agenda setting and, 390, *391*
  agricultural, 387, 392–393
  best practice requirements in, 398
  character of American, 379–380
  commercial republic and
    constructing, 380–382
    excesses of, 386–387
  constituency-based, 393, *393*
  constitutionalizing differences in, 73
  control of, centralized, 425
  decision making and, *401*, 403–404, *404*
  Democratic Balancewheel model and, 379, 401
  distributive, 62, *62*, *63*, 392, *393*
  dynamics, 387–390, *388*
  economic regulation, 383, *384*, 385, *385*
  evaluation of policy and, 391–392, *391*
  failings of analysis of, 409–410

Public policy *(continued)*
  formulation of policy and, 390–391, *391*
  goods and, public and private, 382–383
  implementation of policy and, 391, *391*
  issue framing and analysis of, 400–402
  legitimation of policy and, 391, *391*
  logic of, 60–61
  market dynamics and, 387
  models of process of
    actor-based, 393–395, *394*
    advocacy coalition, 395, *396*
    cycle-centered, 390–392, *391*
    interest-based, 392–393, *393*
    intergovernmental relations, 395, 397
    overview, 390
    process-centered, 390–392, *391*
  overview, 378–379, 411
  pork barrel, 61–62
  redistributive, *62*, 63–64, *63*, 392, *393*
  regulatory, 62–63, *62*, *63*, 393, *393*, *418*
  rise of analysis of, 397–400, *401*
  self-regulatory, 62, *62*, *63*, 64–65
  "sins" of, 410
  "speaking the truth to power" and, 397–401
  study of modern, 381
  techniques and methods
    case analysis, 406
    cost-benefit analysis, 403–404, *404*
    decision making, *401*, 403–404, *404*
    decision tree, 404, *404*, *405*
    experimentation, 406, *407*, 408
    historical analysis, 406
    network analysis, 404
    overview, 402
    planning, 408–409
    policy process analysis, 403
    quasi-experimentation, 406, *407*, 408
    stakeholder analysis, 402–403, *403*
    survey research, 408
  utilitarianism and, 398–399
  "windows of opportunity" and, 390
Public-private partnerships, accountability in, 445–446
Public revenue and management
  available revenue and spending and, 276–278
  balance carried forward, 281
  borrowing and, 299–300
  cash flows and, smoothing out, 299
  debt instruments, 281, 299–300
  earned income, 277
  Federalism and, 295–299
  fees for services, 279, 293–295
  general fund, 278
  government budget and, 305–307
  grants, 301
  intergovernmental transfers and revenue, 280, 295–299, 297
  lottery and gaming revenues, 295, *296*
  Medler School District system and, 307–310
  miscellaneous revenue, 281
  nonprofits and fundraising, 275, 300–303
  overview, 271–276, 307–310

Public revenue and management *(continued)*
  polity level perspective of, 300–304
  projection of revenue and, art and science perspective of, 304–305
  tax expenditures and, 292–293
  taxation, 279, 282–292
  types of, 278–282, *282*, *283*
  unfunded mandates and, 275, 295–299
  user charges, 279, 293–295
  varying balance of sources of, 281–282
Public space, 463
Public spiritedness, 144
Public value approach, 121
Publius (pseudonym of James Madison), 74, 78–79
Pullman railroad strike (1894), 104
Pure Food and Drug Act (1906), 107
Puritan ideals, 142
Pyhrr, Peter, 316

Quasi-experimentation, 406, *407*, 408
Quasi-government organizations, 462
*Quill* case (1992), 291

Rank-in-person system, 243
Rank-in-position system, 243
Rational choice decision model, 224, 398–399
Rationality, substantive, 144
Reagan Revolution, 14
Reagan, Ronald, 222–223, 225, 316–317, 343
Recall (accountability mechanism), 105
Reciprocal interdependence, 185
Recruitment and selection of employees
  compensation and benefits, 243–247
  job analysis, design, and classification, 242–243
  overview, 240, *241*
  performance and appraisal, 248–250
  position planning, management and design, 242
  training and development, 247–248, *248*
Reddin, William, 360
Redford, Emmette, 214
Redistributive policy, *62*, 63–64, *63*, 392, *393*
Reduced level budget (RLB), 337
Referendum (recall initiative), 105
Reflective administrative practice, 49–50
Regressive taxes, 286
"Regular" players, 371–372
Regulatory commissions, 420
Regulatory policy, 62–63, *62*, *63*, 393, *393*, *418*
Regulatory state. *See also specific law*
  balance among sectors and, 102–104
  expansion of federal government and, 109–110
  rise of, 100–105
Reich, Robert, 455
Reinvention of government movement (1990s), 64–65, 91, 226, 462
Rental revenue, 280
*Report with Special Studies* (1937), 111
Representation, 139–141, 152
Representation through rotation in office, 98–99, 206, 215
Representativeness, 201, *202–203*, 204–205, 207, 210, 214, 220, 225–226, 230–231

Republican virtues, 80
Request for information (RFI), 444–445
Research bureaus, 108
Respect for all persons, 38
Responsibility, 131, 414. *See also* Administrative
    responsibility
Responsive governance tradition, 146
Responsiveness, 38, 152–153
Restricted income, 306
Result-oriented legitimacy, 38–40
Rettenmaier, Andrew J., 35
Revenue. *See* Public revenue and management
Revenue Act (1913), 293
Revenue Act (1917), 293
Revenue bonds, 299
RFI, 444–445
Rickover, Hyman, 421
Right-to-work states, 238
Rights, 109–110, 153–154
Rights of employees, 239
Rights-taking period, 460
Riis, Jacob, 106
Ripley, Randall B., 393
RLB, 337
Robinson, Kent, 330
Rockefeller, John D., 103
Rodriguez, Richard, 457
Rohr, John, 130, 137–138, 140–141, 145–146, 151
Role responsibility and budget actors, 327–328
Roosevelt, Franklin D., 104, 109–112, 116, 134, 211–212,
    359
Roosevelt, Theodore "Teddy," 107, 416
Rosenbloom, David, 138, 216, 227, 230–231
Rotation in office, 98–99, 206, 215
Rough proportionality test, 433–434
Rubin, Robert, 369
Rule by law, 9, 135, 153
Rule, definition of a, 434
Rulemaking, administrative
    burden of proof, required, 431–434, *432*
    definition of a rule, 434–436
    legal sources of authority and, 429, *430*
    overview, 429–431
Rung, Margaret, 231
Rural Resource Management team, 375

Sabatier, Paul, 395
Safe Drinking Act, 395
Salamon, Lester M., 124, 388
Sales of permits and licenses, 279
Sales taxes, 291–292
Salisbury, Robert, 61
Salt Lake City (Utah), 381
Sarbanes-Oxley Act (2002), 320–321
Sayre, Wallace, 199
Scenario thinking, 465
Schein, John, 191
Schon, Donald A., 49–50
School districts, 116. *See also* Medler School District
    system case study
Science of association, 49, 77

Scientific management, 108, 133, 159, 179–180
Scott, William G., 196–197, 209
Sealed-bid defined-service contracts, 442–443
Sectors. *See also specific type*
    balance among, 94–96, 100
    relationship among and characteristics of, 44–47, *45,
        48,* 461–464
Self-interest, 80, 141–142, 252
Self-regulatory public policy, 62, *62, 63,* 64–65
Selznick, Philip, 9–10, 43, 174, 361–362
Senior Executive Service (SES), 222, 225, 258, 426
Senior managers, 56–60
Separation of functions, 133
"Separation of politics from policy" sin of public policy, 410
Separation of powers, 112, 133, 313
Sergiovanni, Thomas, 191
Serial bonds, 299–300
Service delivery, 318–319
SES, 222, 225, 258, 426
Seventeenth Amendment, 12, 139
"Shadow banking industry," 385
Shared power, 352
Shays' Rebellion problem, 84, 130, 141, 146, 199
Shell-group planning, 465
Sherman Antitrust Act (1890), 104
Simon, Herbert, 186, 397
Sinclair, Upton, 106
"Single-shot" players, 371
SIPs, 397
Skill-based pay, 245
"Smell test," 153
Smith, Adam, 176–177, 196
Social contract, 142
Social Darwinism, 103
Social delivery service trends (1977-1996), 113, *114*
Social media, 302–303, 437
Social planning discretion, 62–63
Social Security, 110, 246
Social Security Administration (SSA), 69
Social Security Trust Fund, 307
Soft power, 47
SOPs, 178
Sovereignty, 15, 34, 151
"Speaking the truth to power," 108–109, 397–401
Special districts, expansion of, 116, 118
Special revenue funds, 306
Specialists, 160
Spencer, Herbert, 103
Spillover effects, 110
Spoils system, 97, 102
SSA, 69
SSI, 246
Stakeholder analysis, 374–375, 402–403, *403*
Standard operating procedures (SOPs), 178
Standards of conduct, internalized, 438
State government, 288, 337. *See also specific state*
State Implementation Plans (SIPs), 397
State level tax and spending limitations (TELS), 275
State personal income tax, 279
Status of employees, 235–238
Statutory law, 10, 12

Steffens, Lincoln, 106
Step-and-grade classification systems, 236
Stever, James, 106, 108
Stock market crash (1929), 111–112
Stockman, David, 343
Stoker, Gerry, 121
Stone, Deborah, 160, 233, 252, 378, 400
Storing, Herbert, 5, 141, 159, 411
Strategic level of analysis, 176
Strategic planning, 409
Streamlined Sales Tax Project, 291
Street-level managers, 52–54, 185
Structure, ethic of, 154
Structures of authority, overlapping, 461
Subordination, 151–152
Substantial evidence, 431–434
Substantive rationality, 144
Succession planning, 454–455
Summers, Lawrence, 369
"Superficial and bad advice" sin of public policy, 410
Supplemental Security Income (SSI), 246
Supremacy clause, 11–12
Surrogate mother contracts, 400
Survey research, 408
SurveyMonkey, 408
Survival of the fittest concept, 103
Swanson, Guy, 359
Symbolic legislation, 424

Tacit knowledge, 41–42
Taft Commission, 315
Tammany Hall, 101
Target budgeting, 337
TARP, 272
Tarrif Act (1894), 103
Task analyzability, 185
Tavistock Institute of Human Relations, 183
Tax-bracket creep, 288
Taxes
  ability to pay principle and, 286
  benefits of, 271
  benefits received principle and, 286
  burden for selected state categories, 282, *284–285*
  business and occupation, 288–289
  citizen responsibility in selected nations, *287*
  code, 292
  colonial, 272
  corporate income, 288–289
  cost of, 271
  expenditures, 292–293
  flat, 286
  horizontal equity of, 286
  limitations, 279, 289–290
  personal income, 279, 288
  progressive, 286
  property, 279, 289–290
  proportional, 286
  Proposition 13 and, 290
  regressive, 286
  as revenue source, 279, 282–292
  sales, 291–292

Taxes *(continued)*
  separation of powers and, 313
  state personal income, 279
  system design principles and, 283, *284–285*, 286, *287*
  tax-bracket creep and, 288
  vertical equity of, 286
Taxpayer perspective, 335
Taylor, Frederick, 108, 179–180, 209
Taylor, Jeremy, 75
Technical core managers, 52–54, 185
Technical discretion, 62
Technocratic politics, 213
Technology, 464–465
TELS, 275
Temporary workers, 238
Tennessee Valley Authority (TVA), 362
Tenure Office Act, 208
Term bonds, 299
Terry, Larry D., 351
Theory in action, 49–50, 124, *125*, 421, *422*
Theory X, 182–183
Theory Y, 182–183, 213, 254
Thompson, Dennis, 154, 159
Thompson, James D., 184
Tocqueville, Alexis de, 8, 14, 46, 49, 72–73, 77, 80, 89,
  97–98, 115, 271, 452
Toll goods, 382
"Too big to fail" concept, 385
Top-down perspective, 67
Tragedy of the commons, 45
Trained incapacity, 178, 185
Training and development, employee, 247–248, *248*
Trait-based leadership theory, 359, 364
Transactional leadership, 362
Transformational leadership, 362–363
Treasury Act (1789), 138
Tribal governments, 459–460
Troubled Assets Relief Program (TARP), 272
Trudeau, Pierre Elliot, 456
TVA, 362
Tweed, William Marcy, 101
Twenty-second Amendment, 12

U-2 spy plane incident, 219
UK, 121
Uncertainty, 329, 424
Unfunded mandates, 275, 295–299
Uniform organization structure, myth of, 175
Union employment status, 238
Unions, labor, 250–251, 255–256
United Kingdom (UK), 121
Unrestricted income, 306
Urwick, Lyndall, 134, 179–180
U.S. Army Corps of Engineers, 65, 96, 107
U.S. Border Patrol, 151
U.S. Census Bureau, 115–116, 457
U.S. Census report (2010), 456
*U.S. Code*, 462
U.S. Constitution, 6–7, 10–12, 14, 72–74, 76–77, 94, 138,
  139, 174, 201, 353, 380, 473–483. *See also specific
  amendment*

U.S. Customs and Borders Protection (CBP), 67–68
U.S. Federal Reserve System, 382
U.S. Forest Service, 368, 389
U.S. Justice Department, 69
U.S. Sanitary Commission, 101
U.S. Supreme Court, 11–12, 15, 73, 104, 112, 132, 380, 433. *See also specific casey*
User charges, 279, 293–295
Utah, 242
Utilitarianism, 398–399

Value-based performance governance, *123*, 124
Values, 131, 375–376, *376*
Van Riper, Paul P., 199, 207, 212
Vertical equity of taxes, 286
Veto clause, 138
Vietnam War, 219
"Visible hand" of government, 382
Vision Action Network case study, 465, 470–471
VisionWest Planning Process, 467–469
Vocational excellence, 150
Volcker report (2003), 225
Voluntary Principle, 98
Volunteerism, 93
Voting Rights Act (1965), 220

Wagner Act (1935), 250
Walcott, Charles, 173, 186–187, 189, 192, 196
Waldo, Dwight, 134
Walker, Scott, 238
Wall Street scandals, 92, 226, 320, 369–370, 385
*Ware v. Hylton* (1796), 96

Warren, Earl, 216
Washington, George, 81, 84–85, 91, 201, 204, 359
Washington State, 337
Washington State Parks Department, 372
Washingtonian model of administration, 91–92
Water bureaus, federal requirements for, 63
Watergate scandal, 221
Weber, Max, 177–178, 180
Welfare state, 113–115
Western Electric Company, 180
Wetlands policy, 394
White, Leonard D., 134
Wildavsky, Aaron, 190–191, 331, 342, 378, 386–387
Wilkerson, Charles, 459
Wilson-Gorman Tariff Act (1894), 293
Wilson, James Q., 392
Wilson, Woodrow, 107–108, 132–134
"Windows of opportunity," 390
Wisconsin, 238
Wolf, James F., 228
Wolin, Sheldon, 196, 210
Women's Christian Temperance Union, 107
Women's Trade Union League, 107
Workforce changes, 454–455
Workload measures, 334
World War I, 211
World War II, 134, 213, 221, 315, 362, 397
World Wide Web, 302–303, 437
*Wyeth v. Levine* (2009), 15

Zero-base budgeting (ZBB), 316, 337–338, *338*, *339*

# ABOUT THE AUTHORS

**Douglas F. Morgan** is Professor Emeritus of Public Administration and Director of the Executive MPA Program in the Hatfield School of Government at Portland State University. He has held a variety of public positions, both elected and appointed. His research interests focus on the role career public administrators play in ensuring effective and responsive systems of local democratic governance. His work has appeared in the *Handbook of Administrative Ethics, Oregon Politics and Government, The International Encyclopedia of Public Policy and Administration, Public Administration Review, Administration & Society,* and *Administrative Theory & Practice*. He is currently authoring or coauthoring books on local public budgeting, new public governance and public service leadership.

**Richard T. Green** is Professor of Public Administration in the Political Science Department at the University of Utah. His research interests focus on the connections between constitutionalism, law, and ethics in public administration. His work has appeared in *Public Administration Review, Administration & Society, American Review of Public Administration, Public Integrity, Public Administration Quarterly, Administrative Theory & Practice,* and the *International Journal of Public Administration*.

**Craig W. Shinn** is Associate Director of the Executive Leadership Institute and Associate Professor of Public Administration at Portland State University. His research, training, and technical assistance activities focus on "conciliatory practices" that can improve natural resource policy and administration. He has coauthored *Rural Resource Management: Problem Solving for the Long Term* (with Sandra E. Miller and William R. Bentley; Iowa State University Press, 1994). His articles have appeared in *Administrative Theory & Practice* and *The Journal of Public Affairs Education*.

**Kent S. Robinson** is an Adjunct Assistant Professor in the Public Administration Division at Portland State University. He was formerly Assistant Professor in the Institute of Public Service at Seattle University. His main research focus is on the contribution of social trust and reliance to community governance and administrative practice. Prior to his academic career, he served as a forestry budget, policy, and planning analyst.